Communication Matters

◆

About the Authors

Randall McCutcheon, Director of Forensics, Albuquerque Academy, Albuquerque, New Mexico, has over twenty years of experience teaching speech. He has authored two other books: *Can You Find It?*, a guide to teaching research skills to high school students (It received the Ben Franklin Award for best self-help book of the year in 1990.), and *Get Off My Brain,* a survival guide for students who hate to study. Nationally recognized by the U.S. Dept. of Education for innovation in curriculum, he was selected Nebraska Teacher of the Year in 1985. Other awards include Nebraska's Outstanding Young Speech Teacher of the Year, 1979, and the National Forensic League's Coach of the Year, 1987. He holds membership in the Speech Communication Association, the National Forensic League, and the Catholic Forensic League. He completed his undergraduate work at the University of Nebraska with emphasis in speech and theater. His graduate level work was in the study of rhetoric, persuasion, and interpersonal communication. After nearly a decade of working in radio and television, he has taught in public and private schools in Nebraska, Iowa, Massachusetts, and New Mexico and coached his speech teams to fifteen state and five national championships (NFL and CFL).

James Schaffer, an assistant professor and publications advisor at Nebraska Wesleyan University, earned a Ph.D. in English from the University of Virginia in 1990. He is also a part-time teacher at Lincoln (NE) East High School where he advises the *Muse,* a monthly humor magazine.

His journalism students have won numerous awards including state and national championships in writing, design, and photography. A strong interest in the space program led Schaffer to apply for the Teacher in Space contest. He became a national semi-finalist and was named state aerospace educator of the year. In 1987 he won a Christa McAuliffe Fellowship from the U.S. Department of Education that enabled him to give over 400 programs on space travel to school and community groups.

He and his wife Mary Lynn, also an educator, have three children—Suzanne, Sarah, and Stephen—who all love to speak.

Joseph R. Wycoff has taught English (American literature) and Speech at Chesterton High School in Chesterton, Indiana, for the past twenty-seven years. For twenty years, he was the coach/director of the Chesterton Speech and Debate Program, which won fifteen Indiana state championships and three consecutive national titles ('89, '90, '91). Mr. Wycoff was named National Speech and Debate Coach of the Year three times. He is a member of the Indiana Coaching Hall of Fame, and in June of 1992, he was inducted into the National Forensic League National Hall of Fame. As an educator and as a coach, he has won numerous awards. Over the past few years, he has traveled to nearly thirty states, giving over one hundred instructional/motivational seminars to both students and adults on "burnout," leadership, ethics in competition, and effective communication and has taught summer speech sessions at Bradley University (Illinois), Longwood College (Virginia), and the University of Iowa. He received his Masters of Arts from Valparaiso University (Indiana).

Communication Matters

✦

Randall McCutcheon
Albuquerque Academy
Albuquerque, New Mexico

James Schaffer
Nebraska Wesleyan University
Lincoln, Nebraska

Joseph R. Wycoff
Chesterton High School
Chesterton, Indiana

West Publishing Company

Minneapolis/St. Paul ✦ New York ✦ San Francisco ✦ Los Angeles

Copyeditor: Beverly Peavler
Art: Miyake Illustration
Index: Maggie Jarpey
Composition: The Clarinda Company
Production, Prepress, Printing and Binding: WEST PUBLISHING COMPANY

WEST'S COMMITMENT TO THE ENVIRONMENT
In 1906, West Publishing Company began recycling materials left over from the production of books. This began a tradition of efficient and responsible use of resources. Today, up to 95 percent of our legal books and 70 percent of our texts are printed on recycled, acid-free stock. West also recycles nearly 22 million pounds of scrap paper annually—the equivalent of 181,717 trees. Since the 1960s, West has devised ways to capture and recycle waste inks, solvents, oils, and vapors created in the printing process. We also recycle plastics of all kinds, wood, glass, corrugated cardboard, and batteries, and have eliminated the use of styrofoam book packaging. We at West are proud of the longevity of the scope of our commitment to our environment.

Photo and Cartoon Credits

1 Reprinted by permission: Tribune Media Services; **5** Don Milici; **6 (top)** Reprinted with special permission of King Features Syndicate; **6 (bottom)** Don Milici; **7 (top)** Culver Pictures, Inc.; **7 (middle)** Paul Seligman / Sygma; **7 (bottom)** J. P. Laffont / Sygma; **10** Delta Images / Sygma; **12** Gary Bogdon / Sygma; **13** Don Milici; **18** Tim Schoon / Sygma; **26** DILBERT reprinted by permission of UFS, Inc.; **28** PhotoEdit; **31 (left)** Don Milici; **31 (right)** Don Milici; **34** Don Milici; **36** Don Milici; **40** Don Milici; **41** Tony Freeman / PhotoEdit; **44** Don Milici; **50** THE FAR SIDE © 1984 FarWorks, Inc. Dist. by Universal Press Syndicate. Reprinted with permission. All rights reserved; **53** Don Milici; **54** THE FAR SIDE © FarWorks, Inc. Dist. by Universal Press Syndicate. Reprinted with permission. All rights reserved; **55 (top)** Tony Freeman / PhotoEdit; **55 (bottom)** Tony Freeman / PhotoEdit; **56** Don Milici; **64** Don Milici; **70** Don Milici; **76** Cartoon by Doug Marlette; **79** Rhoda Sidney / PhotoEdit; **82** T. Graham / Sygma; **83** John Neubauer; **86** DILBERT reprinted by permission of UFS, Inc.; **87 (top)** Don Milici; **87 (second from top)** Kashi; **87 (second from bottom)** Kashi; **87 (bottom)** Kashi; **89** Richard Hutchings/ PhotoEdit; **93 (all photos)** Don Milici; **98** Don Milici; **104** Drawing by Lorenz © 1982 The New Yorker Magazine, Inc.; **107** Ira Wyman / Sygma; **111** Erwitt / Sygma; **112** Don Milici; **114 (left)** Don Milici; **114 (right)** Don Milici; **116** Don Milici; **122** Robert Brenner / PhotoEdit; **125** Rhoda Sidney / PhotoEdit; **127** David Hanover; **130** David Hanover; **136** BERRY'S WORLD reprinted by per-

(continued following index)

CONTENTS IN BRIEF

CONTENTS

SPECIAL FEATURES

Communication Works

Communication Breakdown

Communication Breakthrough

PREFACE

✦ As many as nine out of ten students have plagiarized a paper sometime during their college careers, according to a survey conducted by Miami University of Ohio Professor Jerold Hale and two colleagues.

✦ According to Professor Barbara J. Adler of Concordia College, only 28% of speech teachers surveyed actually devoted a class unit to the study of ethics, despite the fact that 90% felt a course should include such a unit.

✦ The Roman teacher Quintilian argued, "The perfect orator is a good man speaking well."

Although Quintilian would have said a "good person" today, the truth in his observation is inescapable. A speaker, a communicator, should be ethical. The authors of *Communication Matters* recognize that it is not enough to bemoan the fact that we are failing to sufficiently discuss ethics and social responsibility in our teaching of communication skills. Therefore, this textbook focuses on developing in each student what Aristotle described as good character, intelligence, and goodwill.

Special features of *Communication Matters* include:

✦ **Communication Works**—These career features spotlight real people who use communication in their occupations.

✦ **Communication Breakthroughs and Communication Breakdowns**—These stories provide meaningful examples for the students to analyze. Discussion questions are asked at the end of each feature.

✦ **Instant Impacts**—These smaller, boxed features contain quotes, anecdotes, and other bits of information that students will find entertaining and informative.

✦ **Taking Charge**—These activities are interspersed throughout the chapters to challenge the students.

✦ **Student Speech**—These examples of student work provide both inspiration and models for discussion.

Each chapter begins with objectives, terms, and a brief preview. The end-of-chapter material includes the following:

1. A Chapter Summary
2. Two Vocabulary Building Exercises

3. Things to Remember
4. Things to Do
5. Things to Talk About
6. Things to Write About
7. Critical Thinking
8. Related Speech Topics

Clearly, students require a textbook that addresses the need for social responsibility today. John F. Kennedy once wrote, "A child miseducated is a child lost." The authors believe that we have already lost far too many children.

Acknowledgments

Randall McCutcheon would like to thank the following individuals for their assistance: Jane Durso—my assistant—for her immeasurable contributions to my creativity and correctness; Tim Averill, Art Chu, Katie Johnson, Sally McAfee—for their invaluable input on chapter rough drafts; David Abaire, Robert Bovinette, Maryagnes Barbieri, Sarah Bynum, Austan Goolsbee, Sue Ann Gunn, Seth Halvorson, Andy Howe, Mark Kutny, Alisa Lasater, James Mallios, Jeremy Mallory, Sharahn McClung, Dr. Michael McElroy, Art Melendres, Bruce Musgrave, Lanny Naegelin, John Nielsen, Vikki Otero, Nancy Van Devender, Coert Voorhees—for their assistance and generosity.

James Schaffer wishes to gratefully acknowledge the generous contributions of Mary Lynn Schaffer who edited the seemingly endless rough drafts, Julie Dickey who did some of the research and many of the interviews, and Jane Holt, Ted Genoways, Jon Ericson, and Charles Fichthorn for their technical expertise. He would also like to thank the people whose stories students may read in the Communication Works features: Scott Young, J. Boman Bastani, Jessie Myles, Twyla Hansen, Steve Gaines, Lindy Mullin, and George Paul.

Joseph Wycoff would like to thank the following individuals for their assistance: Pamela C. Cady, Robert Kelly, Barbara Funke, Robert Funke, Carol Biel, James Cavallo, Jane Anne Wycoff, students from Apple Valley High School (Minnesota) for their class/survey contributions, student speakers from Chesterton High School for their example speeches (or excerpts), the Chesterton High School library staff, and the National Forensic League (Ripon, Wisconsin).

Reviewers

The authors greatly appreciated the efforts of the following reviewers:

Barbara J. Achor	Randall Armstrong	Fran Bogos
Mayo High School	Cass High School	North Albany Intermediate School
Rochester, MN	Cartersville, GA	Pittsburgh, PA
Bette Ambrosio	John A. Birt	Yvette Clark
Highland Park High School	Buena High School	Mayfield High School
Dallas, TX	Sierra Vista, AZ	Las Cruces, NM

Charles Eichler
Glenbard East High School
Lombard, IL

Jed Friedrichsen
Millard South High School
Omaha, NE

Jon L. Fruytier
Southfield High School
Southfield, MI

Connye Griffin
Moore High School
Moore, OK

Gregg Hartney
Charles Page High School
San Springs, OK

Connie McKee
Amarillo High School
Amarillo, TX

Lou Price
Battle Creek Central High School
Battle Creek, MI

Carolyn J. Rhondeau
Fairfield High School
Fairfield, CA

William E. Schuetz
Gregory-Portland High School
Gregory, TX

Michael Setzer
Homestead High School
Mequon, WI

Barbara S. Wilson
Lake Gibson High School
Lakeland, FL

Dedications

to my grandmother

　　　　　—Randall McCutcheon

　To Mary Lynn for her unwavering love and support and to Suzanne, Sarah, and Stephen who make it all worthwhile.

　　　　　　　　　　　—James Schaffer

　I would like to dedicate this book to Bob, Barb, Carol, and Pam for constantly telling me that I was doing something worthwhile and that blue skies were in the future; to my wife, Janie, for working as hard as I did, and for making me learn how to use a computer; and to all teachers, who—even though they are often overworked and underappreciated—still believe that teaching kids is the greatest gift.

　　　　　　　　　　　—Joseph R. Wycoff

CHAPTER 1

Building Responsibility

"Never before has it been so essential to learn to separate the true from the false. We have come to put great emphasis upon education in science and engineering. But speech, rather than science or engineering, may actually hold the key to the future of the world. Science makes George Orwell's *1984* a possibility. Effective speaking may prevent its becoming a reality."

— **Francis Horn, past president of the University of Rhode Island**

Learning Objectives

After completing this chapter, you will be able to do the following.

✦ Understand the communication process.
✦ Recognize your audience as an important element in the communication process.
✦ Realize the importance of both verbal and nonverbal communication.
✦ Understand the duties of an ethical, responsible speaker.

Chapter Outline

Following are the main sections in this chapter.

I   What Is Communication?
II Laying the Proper Foundation
III Building the Proper Motivation

       Student Speech

       Chapter Review

New Speech Terms

In this chapter, you will learn the meanings of the speech terms listed below.

ethics
communication
sender
message
receiver
feedback
written communication
oral (or verbal) communication
nonverbal communication
symbol
intrapersonal communication
interpersonal communication
oratory/orator
rhetoric
logical appeal
emotional appeal
ethical (personal) appeal
dialogue
motivation
stereotyping

General Vocabulary

Expanding your general vocabulary will help you become a more effective communicator. Listed below are some words appearing in this chapter that you should make part of your everyday vocabulary.

epitomize
credibility
mesmerized
navigating
flippant
reciprocal

LOOKING AHEAD

In this chapter, you will learn what communication is and, more specifically, what *speech* communication is. Next, you will learn the role that responsibility plays in the communication process. Finally, you will learn that effective speech communication can be better accomplished when the building of character comes before the building of speech content and skillful delivery.

Part I of this book deals with "The Person: Ethics of Communication" and Chapter 1 with "Building Responsibility." In order to understand how these two titles are connected, let's examine a few of the key words.

Ethics can be a dangerous word to use because it can mean different things to different people. However, few would disagree with the observation that **ethics** refers to a person's sense of right and wrong. If you are an ethical person, you work to do what's right. You have a sense of conscience and a personalized code of conduct that you feel is important in the building of character. An ethical judge strives to be totally impartial when hearing a case in court. An ethical police officer follows the law and values the safety of citizens. Likewise, an ethical communicator puts a high premium on using his or her words constructively and promoting what's right.

Responsibility goes hand in hand with ethics, but what does it mean to be responsible? Parents want their children to be responsible at home, teachers encourage their students to become responsible for class assignments, and employers want responsible workers who will work hard and be on time. Quite simply, being *responsible* means that you will be answerable and accountable for your actions and that you will get done what you say you will. If you are responsible, people can count on you—your word means something. Responsible citizens vote, responsible drivers wear seat belts, and responsible speakers pay attention to the words that they use and the way that they use them.

When you combine *ethical* with *responsible,* you take the first step in building a successful oral communicator.

Before dealing with ethics or responsibility in any more detail, though, let's examine exactly what *communication* means and how the speech communication process works.

I What Is Communication?

When the author Robert Louis Stevenson said, "There can be no fairer ambition than to excel in talk," he was speaking

The participants in a discussion communicate by sending and receiving messages.

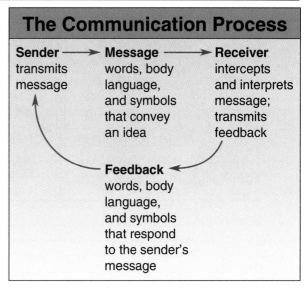

The Communication Process

Sender	Message	Receiver
transmits message	words, body language, and symbols that convey an idea	intercepts and interprets message; transmits feedback

Feedback words, body language, and symbols that respond to the sender's message

In the communication process, the sender transmits a message to the receiver who responds with feedback.

about the art of effective oral communication. **Communication** is the process of sending and receiving messages, and it occurs whenever we express ourselves in a manner that is clearly understood.

The Communication Process

Sam and Lynette are having a discussion about basketball. Sam believes that David Robinson of the San Antonio Spurs is a better basketball player than Isiah Thomas of the Detroit Pistons. Lynette favors Shaquille O'Neil of the Orlando Magic. Both are communicating a message, listening to what the other has to say, and then responding. Consequently, they are actively involved in the communication process, which consists of the sender, the receiver, the message, and feedback.

The **sender** is the one who transmits the **message,** that which is sent or said. The sender starts the communication process by using words. Words are the symbols you use to convey your ideas. Your words must clearly communicate to your listener the exact message you are trying to convey. The **receiver** is the person who intercepts the message and then decodes, or interprets, it. **Feedback** includes the reactions that the receiver gives to the message offered by the sender.

Every day, when you talk on the telephone, write letters, or watch television, you are either sending messages or receiving them. Teachers communicate with students when they give clear directions for taking an exam. Students communicate when they accurately explain the assignment to a classmate who has been absent. Parents communicate when they leave specific instructions for the baby-sitter. When words are clearly put together, they build a solid communication system in-

tended to communicate a specific message.

Any communication that must be read is called **written communication.** When the communication is spoken, it is often called **oral** or **verbal communication.** Your ability to put words together effectively, either in written or verbal form, will help determine your impact as a communicator. In this book, you will be learning specifically how to become a more effective oral communicator, a more persuasive speaker.

Two other ways in which people send messages should be noted: nonverbal communication and symbols. Both are important elements in communication and are further discussed in later chapters, where they can be seen in action.

Nonverbal Communication

While the verbal message involves the actual words being spoken, the nonverbal message might be relayed through facial expressions or body movements. Thus, **nonverbal communication** expresses your attitudes or moods about a person, situation, or idea. The person who is cheerful and sitting up straight communicates through "body language" one sort of message. The person who frowns and slouches communicates another sort.

Nonverbal signals may mean different things to different people. For instance, giving someone the thumbs up sign is a compliment in America but is considered rude and offensive in Australia. In the United States, nodding the head means "yes," but in Greece it means "no." The

Facial expressions and body movements communicate nonverbal messages.

book *Do's and Taboos around the World* goes on to add that waving the entire hand means "goodbye" in America, but in Europe, where only the fingers are used to say farewell, it means "no." The book's editor, Roger Axtell, suggests that we all need to realize the impact that nonverbal communication can have on the receiver.

Symbols

Another way people communicate is through symbols. A **symbol** is anything that stands for an idea and is used for communication. Since symbols represent something else by association, they include both nonverbal and verbal communication.

In a nonverbal manner, the "peace" sign calls for nonviolence. Tangible objects such as the flag can stand for freedom, and the eagle can stand for America. A letter jacket can represent your school. In the award-winning play *A Raisin in the Sun* by Lorraine Hansberry, the small plant signifies the hopes and determination of the family. Nonverbal symbols are powerful, for they speak in pictures and appeal to people's imaginations and emotions.

Words—verbal symbols—can also be powerful. Advertisers often use key words that symbolize desirable qualities, hoping that you will associate the word with their product. Words such as *trust, honesty, heritage, family,* and *America* might be spoken to arouse your sense of community. Words can even *epitomize* the spirit of an entire nation. When Martin Luther King, Jr., said, "I have a dream," his dream eloquently stood for the hope that someday all Americans would stand together with dignity.

The "V" Sign in History

In the 1940s, British Prime Minister Winston Churchill used the "V" sign to rally the British against German aggression.

In the 1960s, the "V" sign stood for peace and nonviolence.

In the 1970s, the "V" sign symbolized victory for President Richard M. Nixon.

Symbols are important in your own life. For instance, taking the time to be well groomed might be worth it. A university study showed that 55 percent of what people think of you is determined in the first thirty seconds! Consequently, even though it is true that "clothes don't make the person," you must realize that what you wear or how you look could be symbolizing something important about you. Is a T-shirt with a vulgar or rude saying worth the price of sacrificing your *credibility?* As a sender of messages to receivers, you must pay attention to the nonverbal communication and the symbols that you use if you wish to be taken seriously as a conscientious communicator.

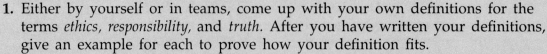

TAKING CHARGE

1. Either by yourself or in teams, come up with your own definitions for the terms *ethics, responsibility,* and *truth.* After you have written your definitions, give an example for each to prove how your definition fits.
2. Nonverbal communication often refers to the attitude you give off to others. What are five positive nonverbal characteristics? What are five negative non-verbal characteristics? Write out your lists. (Example: alert eye contact versus a "Get real!" look while someone is talking.) For each of your ten total items, be ready to say what each communicates. What nonverbal characteristics might help you in school? List them.
3. Bring an item from home, school, or the community that symbolizes something special. Be prepared to share with the class what your symbol means and what it should communicate to others who see it. Could it send different messages to different people? Explain.

II Laying the Proper Foundation

People building a house don't begin by putting up the walls. They begin by establishing a solid foundation that will anchor the rest of the structure. Similarly, you build the ethics of communication and responsibility when you anchor your oral communication to a solid value structure. Command of language, posture, eye contact, gestures, and other speech basics are certainly important and will be covered later in the book, but the "pouring" of your "value structure foundation" must come first. It consists of three essential elements: (1) working to be a good person, (2) communicating constructively, and (3) caring about your audience. Let's look at each separately.

Working to Be a Good Person

The nineteenth-century statesman and orator Daniel Webster said that if all of his talents and abilities except one were taken away, he would ask to keep his ability to speak. "With the ability to speak," he added, "I could regain all that I had lost." Here Webster is telling people of the vital role that speaking can play in their lives. However, he would also say that being a polished speaker isn't enough. Daniel Webster would promote the idea that those who speak should work to make the world a better place.

Some prominent speakers have worked to advance humankind. Some have worked to harm humankind. All of us would agree that Adolf Hitler was a powerful speaker, yet his words led to the deaths of millions of people during World

COMMUNICATION WORKS

Les Mapes, Chairman of the Board for Waffles of California, Inc.

Les Mapes of Buena Park, California, has had a number of occupations throughout his illustrious life, which has spanned nearly seventy years. He has been a singer, business executive, salesman, and part-time bartender. However, it wasn't until he, in his own words, took a chance and acquired a territory from the F. S. Carbon Co. of Buchanan, MI, and became the exclusive distributor of the F. S. Carbon Co. Malted Waffle Flour in California and Nevada that his life took shape. The result? You have probably tasted these delicious Malted Waffles because most of the major restaurant and hotel chains in fifty states (and even in Europe) use this product exclusively.

Les Mapes believes that the key to success is "knowing who you are" and "being honest with both yourself and other people." A firm believer in communication, he was responsible in the beginning days of his company for packing his own truck and then driving for days to various businesses. He notes: "The face to face method of dealing with people can't be stressed enough; people need to see that your word is good and that you will deliver what you promise." Currently, Waffles of California is a multimillion-dollar corporation.

What role did oral communication play in Les Mapes' success? Speaking, he believes, provided him with the outlet he needed to show people that "the positive was possible." Les Mapes and his wife, Peggy (the current president of the company) have shown through a strong work ethic, a sense of responsibility, and the desire to distribute a high-quality product that the "American Dream" is still alive and well.

A special note: No one who calls Waffles of California, Inc., will ever hear a machine. For twenty-four hours a day, Les Mapes has a person answering the phones. Why? There is no substitute for the human voice. According to Les and Peggy Mapes, people will always be communicating with people.

War II. The minister and cult figure Jim Jones *mesmerized* his followers in Guyana, South America, in the late 1970s; hundreds died when he commanded them to commit suicide by drinking cyanide-laced Kool-Aid. Unfortunately, we don't have to look far to see what's wrong in the world. The news is full of people who use their power of speech to dupe the public and take advantage of unsuspecting victims. However, the authors of this text believe that while it would be foolish to ignore people whose words have exhibited a value structure less than desirable,

Polish freedom fighter Lech Walesa, pictured here, has devoted his life to fighting hatred and injustice.

it would be educationally negligent not to be optimistic and promote positive examples and role models.

For instance, contrast the previous two examples with the words of the Polish freedom fighter Lech Walesa, who said to Congress in 1989:

> The world remembers the wonderful principle of the American democracy: "government of the people, by the people, for the people." I too remember these words; I, a shipyard worker from Gdansk, who has devoted his entire life . . . to the service of this idea: "government of the people, by the people, for the people." Against privilege and monopoly, against contempt and injustice . . . I do what I must do.

Here, Lech Walesa is telling the world that he is driven by his sense of conscience, his sense of right and wrong.

Sometimes the most important speaking you do is the speaking you do with yourself. This ability to conduct an inner dialogue with yourself and to assess your

thoughts, feelings, and reactions is known as **intrapersonal communication.** Many of our actions begin with these silent conver-

INSTANT IMPACT

America's Funniest?

The producers of "America's Funniest Home Videos" are finding out what some parents will do to get $10,000. For instance, one video showed a Florida teenager who, while posing for family pictures in her new prom dress, fell off a dock and ended up looking like a drowned rat. The girl's parents later admitted they had staged the fall. Since the TV show's rating moved to number one, producers estimate that there have been at least ten bogus videos made by parents "setting up" their own kids. Producers wonder what these parents probably communicated to their children.

Source: Associated Press.

sations. You must be honest and positive in your self-communication. For instance, when you have done something right, compliment yourself; when there is room for improvement, note to yourself what you can do better the next time. Negative intrapersonal communication occurs when you cloud your thoughts with self-doubt. Saying to yourself, "I can't do this. I'm too stupid!" or "I'm not popular enough for anyone to listen to me!" is counterproductive and doesn't give your talents a chance to work. Be honest but be positive and give yourself the benefit of the doubt. Michael Jordan, the basketball star, says that he loves to be a positive role model for children because "it's the right thing to do." Perhaps his belief is a result of intrapersonal communication. Because intrapersonal communication affects the kind of person you are, what you communicate to yourself should exhibit a solid work ethic, a sense of integrity, compassion for others, and personal honesty. Most would agree that these are some of the qualities that make up a good person.

You should give priority to being a good person, then; but the second element of our value structure foundation is also important.

Communicating Constructively

Besides being able to talk to yourself (intrapersonal communication), you need to be able to talk effectively to others. This form of one-on-one communication is called **interpersonal communication.** Interpersonal communication, which will also be illustrated in other chapters, takes place any time messages are transmitted between two or more people. Interpersonal

INSTANT IMPACT

Speaking Out for Hispanics

According to the U.S. Bureau of Labor Statistics, during the next decade 58 percent of the incoming labor force will consist of minorities. With this in mind, several companies around the nation have taken a leadership role in working with many of these minorities. HISPANIC Magazine recently compiled a list called the HISPANIC 100 that named the top one hundred companies that are providing job opportunities and educational training for Hispanics. Among the companies listed were Ford, General Motors, Chrysler, Hughes Aircraft, Rockwell International, Apple Computer, American Airlines, Coca-Cola, and Dow Chemical. Special note was given to Anheuser-Busch which, since 1982, has given over $4.5 million to the National Hispanic Scholarship Fund.

The companies in the HISPANIC 100 contribute not only jobs and training programs, but also their voices. As their corporate officials travel around the nation (and the globe), many of them speak to audiences on the positive contributions the Hispanic community can make to the corporate world. The HISPANIC 100 are not only training the work force for the twenty-first century, they are also building the reputation and esteem of an important segment of America's population.

communication is not limited to formal speaking situations. Your conversations in the hallway with other students, after class with teachers, at the dinner table with your family, or on the street corner with community members are all examples of interpersonal communication. You have an opportunity to build good feelings and trust between and among people. Your job in communicating in this way is to realize that the spoken word should build, inspire, and motivate others, never belittle or deceive them. Thus, when comedians use words to insult, when politicians use words to distort, when teachers use words to condemn, when businesspeople use words to justify ruining the environment, or when students spread rumors about other students, they are doing an injustice to what speech should do.

Oratory, or **rhetoric,** is the art or study of public speaking. An **orator** is a person who delivers oratory and uses words effectively. The Roman teacher Quintilian called the perfect orator "a good person speaking well." The young AIDS victim Ryan White was certainly a Quintilian-type orator when he spent the last years of his life speaking at schools to educate others about facts and myths regarding AIDS. Ryan White's example should remind every person that people have special talents and knowledge that need to be voiced.

Vicky Wyatt and Jo Ann Burke, two single mothers from Bloomington, Indiana, are also using words constructively. After *navigating* from welfare to a successful life and working their way through college, they formed an all-volunteer support group. The group offers free advice and tries to motivate the jobless to go back to school. These women's words and their lives serve as inspiration to scores of people.

How do you use your words? You must be willing to build up others if you wish to become the effective communicator that this book promotes. This idea carries through to the third and final element that makes up the foundation of your

Ryan White, pictured here, died of AIDS at the age of eighteen. He spent the last years of his life speaking at schools to educate others about AIDS.

value structure, a genuine concern for the audience.

Caring About Your Audience

The noted actor and director Sir Laurence Olivier once said that performers can bring creative life to a play only if they respect the audience enough to think that the audience will understand it. This lesson can also be applied to speaking. The speaker must respect the members of an audience and show a genuine concern for their thoughts and feelings.

The story is told of two hunters who are surprised by a large, vicious bear. Terrified, the first man begins to run but then sees that his friend is slowly lacing up a pair of tennis shoes.

"Are you crazy?" cries the first man. "Those shoes won't help you outrun that bear!"

"I don't have to outrun the bear," the second man replies. "I simply have to outrun *you*."

You must not sacrifice your audience as the second hunter was about to sacrifice his friend. People must be able to expect more from each other. For instance, take into account factors such as age, gender, background, education, and socioeconomic standing before preparing your speech. Before speaking, consider questions such as these:

- ◆ Is this material appropriate for this group?
- ◆ How would I feel if I were asked that question?
- ◆ Am I giving my audience new information?
- ◆ Is my material too difficult or too easy for my audience?

Also, pay attention to audience feedback and then adapt. You might be doing something wrong. Keep in mind that if you are *flippant* in your presentation, you might nonverbally convey the attitude that your audience isn't very important to you. If you are speaking in a dull monotone, you might convey the attitude that you are bored with your audience.

As Olivier implied, the most effective communication occurs when there is *reciprocal* respect between the performer and the audience—or the sender and the receiver.

One way that you can show the audience you care about them is by paying attention to the ideas of the Greek scientist and philosopher Aristotle. Aristotle said that there are three major methods for appealing to an audience: logical, emotional, and ethical. (These methods will also be discussed in Chapter 13, "Speeches to Persuade.")

When preparing a speech, a speaker must consider various aspects of the audience, including age, gender, level of education, and socioeconomic background.

◆ You offer a **logical appeal** when you provide your audience with sequence and analysis in your organization and factual evidence to prove your point.

◆ You offer **emotional appeal** when you "strike a chord" in your audience and appeal to their sense of patriotism, family, justice, or the like.

◆ You offer **ethical** (or **personal**) **appeal** when you show your audience that you have a natural honesty about you, a strong constitution regarding right and wrong, and a no-compromise approach to values.

Remember, **dialogue**, or conversation, that doesn't begin with each person respecting the other often ends in hurt feelings and fractured communication. Taking the time to lay the proper foundation should help alleviate this problem.

TAKING CHARGE

◼

1. List people in your school and community who communicate effectively. What makes them good? Why do you believe them when they talk? Write your responses and be ready to speak to the class.
2. Who in television, movies, and other media communicate (or communicated) the wrong way? What is the harm in how they are/were communicating? Name at least two people and then list the specific harm each causes.
3. Where in school can we all be better listeners and audience members? Why is this important? How can an audience make a speaker feel more at ease? Make a chart with headings for *school*, *home*, and *friends* at the top. For each heading, list how and where you can become a better listener or audience member.
4. Tell of a time when you were in an audience that didn't listen well. Describe the results.

III Building the Proper Motivation

To this point, we have examined what communication is and how a solid value structure is the speaker's foundation. Now we need to take a look at what should be the driving force behind the speaker's words—the motivation.

Motivation is something, such as a need or a desire, that causes a person to act. Two internal forces should be responsible for motivating words: (1) the

COMMUNICATION BREAKTHROUGH

A Worthwhile Conversation

Caleb Ray Lopes, nineteen, of Rohnert Park, California, shares the following story. It shows how effective communication can lead to real understanding.

I wish I could have talked to my teachers about what their lives are like. I went through my senior year always bad-mouthing and playing games with this one English teacher. I only thought about myself and how I felt. I knew nothing about this woman and her private life. The very last day of school, I went to ask this teacher for my final grade and she dropped everything just to talk to me for an hour and a half about our differences throughout the year and to answer some of the ques-tions I had always had about her. I still think about this moment and wonder why she concerned herself with a student who had given her so much trouble. She taught me more in that conversation that day than I had learned all year. I wish I could have learned it before.

Reprinted with permission from Parade. *Copyright © 1991.*

Questions
1. How do you think that both Caleb and the teacher learned a valuable lesson?
2. What roles did both intrapersonal and interpersonal communication play in this story?

---

desire to treat both people and situations fairly and to avoid stereotyping others and (2) the desire to set a good example for others.

Stereotypes

Stereotyping means labeling every person in a group based on a preconceived idea as to what that group represents. To believe that all football players lack intelligence or that all straight A students are "uncool" is unfair. Study after study has shown that people are often uncertain about their futures and lack confidence in those responsible for leading and representing them. However, don't fall into the "stereotype trap" and say, for example, that all politicians or lawyers are dishonest or only out for themselves.

It is possible to form very broad stereotypes—not only about people but about situations. For example, the ideas that all people are dishonest and that nothing is right are stereotypes. You must realize that forming an awareness of your world means seeing more than "doom and gloom." Don't be trapped into thinking that everyone is dishonest or that nothing is right. This attitude makes cynics of us all, and stereotyping makes losers of everyone involved. Keep in mind that every individual must be evaluated on his or her own merit and that every instance must be evaluated for its own impact.

What Symbols Can Say

"Senseless" by Rick Telonder. Symbols can often communicate the same as words. Michael B. Green, twenty-two, a former member of the Crips, one of the nation's most notorious youth gangs, provided this street's-eye view of gangs and what sports apparel can symbolize.

I used to wear British Knights tennis shoes. To us the BK on the side of the shoe stood for Blood Killer. I heard somebody might come out with a new shoe called Christian Knights, so the Bloods (the Crips' rival) will wear them. The CK would stand for Crip Killer. If kids had these shoes, went into the wrong neighborhood and were seen by a rival gang, they could get killed. In Los Angeles, if you wore a Dallas Cowboy jacket, you were a Crip. If you wore a Washington Redskin jacket, you were a Blood. It was the same with hats. Kids got killed over them. Now I'm seeing it's stupid, but back then, I didn't care. It was recreation. . . .

The shoes, the jackets and the hats are just symbols; everybody's got a symbol. I can drive down the street and point out a gang member just by the way he or she dresses. Say we go somewhere. We see a guy in some dress slacks, a nice sweater, loafers. You couldn't convince me that he's a gang member. But then you show me a guy, say, in Levi's jeans, or, say, a Cowboy jacket or a Raider hat, or shoes, he's a gang member. You can tell, just by a dress code.

I've been locked up 2 1/2 years, and I've already lost five friends out on the street. Five. One died because he was in a shopping center and he had on all black. Bloods are red; Crips are either blue or black. Some Bloods came

through there and just shot him, right there on the spot, no questions asked.

I'm going to try to get out of here and do the right thing. I'm learning how to weld, and I'm kind of getting my mind together as to what I want in life. I want to get married, have kids and show them the right way. . . .

The answers? Well, if the parents can't avoid being separated, they should spend time with their kids individually and teach them things. What does your daughter like? Ballet? Put her on those programs. Does your son like baseball? Spend time teaching him. The only way [the gangs] will stop is if parents take their five, six, seven-year-old kids under their wings.

This environment [prison] will make you realize that you were doing wrong out there. One of my best friends in here is a Blood. I knew him on the street. Five years ago I would have killed him. It was like brainwashing. It's programmed into your brain that the Bloods are the enemy. Every time you see a red rag, you shoot.

Michael Green is serving a 63-month sentence in prison.

The above article is reprinted courtesy of SPORTS ILLUSTRATED from the May 14, 1990 issue. Copyright © 1990, Time Inc.

Questions
1. What is the real tragedy of this story?
2. How can symbols destroy the possibility of effective communication? How can they also be used for good?
3. What has Michael realized? What do his words prove?

There's a problem with all this—avoiding negative stereotyping can be difficult. Because so many leaders and heroes have been disappointing and so many con artists and angle players have lied to the public, many people have become skeptical about trusting anyone. We read things like the following on an all-too-regular basis:

◆ A U.S.–CNN poll revealed that one in four Americans believes that the president of the United States often does not tell the truth.

◆ Spiritual leaders have been caught more than once "fleecing their flocks."

◆ Entertainers promise a live performance and then lip-synch their hits.

It is difficult to become motivated to communicate effectively when we hear how often words can work to tear down. Too often, words are empty and promises broken. So where do you go? Where is the answer? Where is your motivation? The answer to all of these questions can be found in you. Much of your motivation to use the spoken word correctly must come from a desire to provide solutions that will make the world a better place. You can do this by working to set a positive example for others.

Setting an Example

Every day you may communicate with your parents, with your brothers and sisters, with the bus driver, with your friends and neighbors, with your teachers and community.

You are making an impression.

You have the opportunity to prove that speaking is power and that your words can work to promote what is good in both ideas and people. Set a positive example for others to follow. *Walk* what you *talk.*

In her 1977 award-winning oration, "The Last American Hero," Indiana student Diane Matesic stated that if society doesn't have people who will use their words to create great and noble things, few great or noble things will ever be created. She added that it is the job of the "common person" to undertake this task. In this view, your motivation to be an effective oral communicator should be based on your drive to create opportunities for today and for the future. People need to be able to count on each other. The following story teaches a key lesson:

UPI—The official Vietnam News Agency says a group of nine American veterans of the Vietnam War is building a clinic in a village pounded by American warplanes in the "Christmas bombings" of 1972. The agency says the American veterans were working with Vietnamese villagers to build the 10-room clinic six miles east of Hanoi. Joe Burns of Hawaii said he came back to Vietnam for two reasons. He said one "was to find some peace of mind." The other was to learn and share the truth about Vietnam and help the victims.

These nine American veterans could easily have stereotyped Vietnam, its people, and its children as the enemy. What did they do, instead? These veterans realized that they had a responsibility to do something much larger. In the truest sense of Quintilian's quote, they were "good persons speaking well."

Recording their last studio album in 1979, the rock group Led Zeppelin produced the famed album *In Through the Out Door.* It had six different covers. The albums were wrapped in brown paper so buyers wouldn't know which cover they were getting until they bought the album, took it home, and unwrapped it. For Led Zeppelin, this marketing tactic was okay.

However, as an effective oral communicator, you should do better than this. You must work to be a "known quantity," a speaker and a person worthy of respect, a role model for others to follow.

The job isn't easy, but the teacher and astronaut Christa McAuliffe was such a person. Even though she died in the tragic explosion of the spacecraft *Challenger,* a poem she took with her on that final flight should serve as inspiration to everyone. It said: "Move over sun and give me some sky. / I've got some wings and I'm ready to fly. / World, / You're going to hear from me!"

Isn't it time that the rest of the world hears from you? Remember: When people

In life, teacher and astronaut Christa McAuliffe, pictured here, set a postive example for others. She died when the spacecraft *Challenger* exploded in 1986.

believe in you, they will believe what you have to say.

TAKING CHARGE

1. Stereotyping is a problem that affects all of society. Make a poster and through both words and pictures, indicate how people can unfairly stereotype others. What is the answer to the problem of stereotyping? Include the answer on your poster.

2. Think of one person in your life who sets a positive example and "walks what he or she talks." Interview the person and find out about his or her (1) personal motivation, (2) personal heroes, and (3) goals in life. Write your findings and be ready to share them with the class. Be sure to include a biographical sketch containing pertinent background information.

STUDENT SPEECH

Catharine Dommer, a high-school student, presented the following award-winning oration in local and state competition and at the 1991 National Forensic League National Speech and Debate Tournament in Glenbrook, Illinois.

Phantom

Breathing lies;
Leering satyrs,
Peering eyes.

So

Run and hide but a face
  will still pursue;
Look around—there's another
  mask behind you!

The Phantom of the Opera! Even sounds mysterious, doesn't it? Andrew Lloyd Webber's hit musical based on the novel features these bizarre lyrics that illustrate the chaotic art of deception. I think that Michael Walsh described the plot well in *Time* magazine: "Ugly guy who hangs out in basement of Paris Opera gets crush on cute chorister . . . goes berserk when boyfriend comes on scene . . . gets ditched by the girl and crawls into a hole to die." Not exactly your typical tale of boy meets girl, boy gets girl, boy loses girl! The Phantom lived in isolation and hid behind a mask to hide his profoundly disfigured face. He *needed* his mask to woo the woman he loved and protect her from the harsh reality.

Unfortunately, the masks that we wear aren't nearly as noble. We've become the land of the Great American Masquerade. And the two most prominent masks in this ballroom of deception are the masks of friendship and leadership.

Now, we're all familiar with that classic tale of back-stabbing romance that tells of how Miles Standish lost the love of his fair Priscilla. He trusted his not-so-faithful friend John Alden to "fix them up." Well, when Alden tried, Priscilla said, "Speak for yourself, Johnny" and in the end it was John who got the girl. But, as Shakespeare once said, "Most friendship is feigning; most loving mere folly." Miles should have studied up on his Shakespeare and done the job himself—because his buddy butchered him!

The *mask* of friendship is all around us, as some phantoms want to win our trust and then betray the friendship. The deceptive masks they wear can victimize those under its spell by victimizing their bodies, taking their money, and destroying their trust.

Take, for instance, Jane Fonda. She makes her exercise videos to prove to women in their fifties that they can still be beautiful. Thus, she has emerged as "a friend of the common woman's body." Columnist Barbara Drakis said that she's made seven million dollars from selling her videos to loyal fans who are willing to *pay* for a body like Jane's with their own sweat, blood, and tears! These Fonda disciples probably wouldn't be as faithful if they knew that "Robo-Fonda" has had facial surgery, a breast lift, tummy tuck, and liposuction. Granted, I'm sure that exercise is a great asset to the beautiful bodies over fifty, but the only thing that Fonda has *proven* is that it's a lot easier to be beautiful when you can afford reconstructive surgery. Yet she still got her seven million.

Many of today's swindlers are comparable to the old-time quack doctors who sold phony remedies. Only today's "quacks" don't need to travel by horse and buggy—they can use today's technology to simply "reach out and touch someone." The National Consumers League said that "small investors lose an estimated $40 billion a year to con men and swindlers," and "much of it over the phone." The most popular scams involve familiar offers like credit repair, penny stocks, travel deals, and precious metals. Once again, the legendary friendly salesman is there to assure you that you're making a wise and worthy investment. Beware of those who wear the mask of "the friend of the consumer," and remember that when an offer sounds too good to be true, it probably is.

So now we have people wearing the mask of friendship on exercise videos and on the telephone. This may sound like nothing to sweat over, but what if I were to tell you that this same masquerade is also being played at hospitals?

The article "Profiting from Pain" from a recent *Time* magazine told of a South Carolina drug ring that got its goods in a macabre way: from cancer victims who were terminal. Ring leaders posed as good Samaritans who stole pain pills and morphine while visiting patients, and later sold them on the streets. Meanwhile, the cancer patients had only aspirin to ease their pain.

The masquerade as "friends of the suffering" enabled the drug dealers to appear unsuspicious. It seems as if we always have to be on our guard for the twentieth century Phantom who tells you to "close your eyes . . . open your mind . . . and trust me." And note that one thing that all of these masqueraders have in common is that they wore the mask of friendship for the money. Benjamin Franklin once wrote, "He that is of the opinion that money will do everything may well be suspected of doing everything for money."

While the financial benefits of deception are tempting to some, others are lured to the masquerade by the desire for power or authority so that they can get what they want. Some need the mask of leadership to disguise their ulterior motives.

Take, for example, optometrist Gary Fisher. He recently claimed that he had medically sound reasons for making women shed their shirts during exams! He said that he was "simply checking for spine curvatures related to eye problems." But one medical expert said that spine curvatures have nothing to do with eye problems. So what *was* Fisher checking for? Or was he just checking? Maybe he needed his "mask of authority" as a medical professional to guise the "peeping Tom."

This peeping peeper practitioner may have been bad, but at least his patients could see him. That's more than Reverend Fluffy can say—he never saw more than a mail-order catalog. This newly ordained minister is actually the puppy of police detective Bruce Walstad. Fluffy was ordained by a mail-order church for a price, and has the papers and title to prove it. So now this "preacher pooch" is officially a spiritual *leader*, even though he can only christen fire hydrants!

It's a small wonder that we have such a problem with deception when credentials can be bought and sold. We can get the reward without the work, the position without the knowledge, the honor without the merit. Granted, few people would ever revere a dog as a reverend. But near my hometown live two women who are filing lawsuits against a reverend who sexually abused them as children. Both became pregnant. How can anyone deceive the faith of a child? They trusted the mask of the leader; then they discovered the madman.

On a larger scale, more than the mind of a doctor and sins of a preacher being dirty—our surroundings are, too. The article, "Pollution Control and Indulgences" by Eugene J. McCarthy elaborated on the government's Clean Air Act. This act attempts to combat pollution by giving industries the freedom to pollute a limited amount. However, if an industry does not pollute as much as its quota permits, it can then *sell* the excess pollution rights. We can now buy the right to pollute! Maybe we're seeing the mask of the environmental protector . . . or are we simply the victims of environmental fraud?

Song lyrics from *Phantom of the Opera* proclaim, "A nation waits, and how it hates to be cheated!" But it seems as if *this* nation has adopted cheating as a survival tactic. We're taught that we have to be tough to be successful, even if toughness isn't in our personality. Now "who is who?" really becomes a complicated game—how can we tell when everyone is busy trying to be someone else?

But the game becomes serious when the children see their role models freely mixing fact with fiction. They watch *The Wizard of Oz* and learn that "the man behind the curtain" is really not a wizard at all—just an ordinary man that used machines to be

powerful—and he was the good guy! Children need to be able to figure out what is real and what is not. If they're confused children, they may become confused adults who never know what they want from life. The book *Married Without Masks* by Nancy Groom says, "Many couples go for years feeling unfulfilled in marriage" because "Being *that close* to another person means vulnerability, and most of us deal with vulnerability by hiding behind self-protective masks."

Remember that "Many people spend their lives climbing the ladder of success only to find, when they get to the top, the ladder is leaning against the wrong building!" *Power of Myth* by Joseph Campbell states, "People say that what we're seeking is a meaning for life . . . I think that what we're seeking is an experience of *being* alive . . . So that we actually feel the *rapture* of *being alive* . . . !" I don't know about you, but when I'm old and grey I want to be able to remember the *better* experiences of life, like sunsets on the lake and roasting marshmallows over a campfire, Christmases with family, Fourth of July fireworks, old friends and new babies. Next to all of that, a life of illusions and disguises sounds very cold—and very lonely.

Whether masks are worn for money, power, or security, we need to be able to find the *real* people behind them. Even the Phantom asked his love to "find the man behind the monster," behind the mask. It's kind of like excavating for the personality somewhere inside a person. In order to convince people that the best things in life may be free, we need to care enough to get that close to someone.

We also need to set our own priorities and reaffirm our beliefs in the power of love and friendship—for *that's* the stuff that life is made of. Once we overcome the fear of being ourselves, we can then be *ourselves* with *each other*.

We might feel as assured as the Phantom of the Opera when he heard, "God give me strength to show you that you are not alone!"

Then, as if at a New Year's masquerade when the clock strikes midnight, we will *all* take off the masks, and see each other as we *really* are.

REVIEW AND ENRICHMENT

LOOKING BACK

Listed below are the major ideas discussed in this chapter.

◆ A good speaker is aware that he or she has an ethical obligation to use the spoken word responsibly.
◆ The four parts of the communication process are the sender, the receiver, the message, and feedback.
◆ Effective communication can be built through writing (written communication) or the spoken word (oral, or verbal, communication).
◆ A key component in communication is nonverbal communication, which includes facial expressions and body language.
◆ Symbols can project a meaningful message.
◆ The foundation for effective oral communication must be firmly laid before any content or delivery work is done.

✦ The foundation for effective oral communication consists of working to be a good person, using communication constructively, and valuing the audience.
✦ Aristotle said that a speaker could use logical, emotional, and ethical appeals.
✦ Intrapersonal communication involves the talking that you do to yourself.
✦ Interpersonal communication is one-to-one or one-to-many communication.
✦ You should work to avoid stereotypes and to set a good example for others.
✦ People must believe in you before they will believe what you have to say.

SPEECH VOCABULARY

For each speech vocabulary word, state the definition as given in the text. Also, copy the sentence in which the word appears. Underline the word. Make sure that you can spell it.

ethics
communication
sender
message
receiver
feedback
written communication
oral (or verbal) communication
nonverbal communication
symbol

intrapersonal communication
interpersonal communication
oratory/orator
rhetoric
logical appeal
emotional appeal
ethical (personal) appeal
dialogue
motivation
stereotyping

GENERAL VOCABULARY

Define each general vocabulary word by using the dictionary. Include the part of speech, the definition as used in the chapter, and an original sentence of your own. Make sure that you can spell each word.

epitomize
credibility
mesmerized

navigating
flippant
reciprocal

THINGS TO REMEMBER

1. Who said, "Speech, rather than science or engineering, may actually hold the key to the future of the world"?
2. What type of communication is involved when you talk with yourself?
3. What historical figure originated the three methods of appealing to your audience?
4. What is one-to-one communication called?
5. The communication process has four components: the sender, the receiver, the message, and _____.
6. When people base judgments of individuals on their preconceived notion of an entire group, they unfairly _____ others.
7. The Michael B. Green story emphasizes how some objects, or _____, can be significant.
8. What did the Roman teacher Quintilian call the perfect orator?

THINGS TO DO

1. Interview a teacher or community member and find out why communication is important to this person. What qualities does he or she try to promote when speaking?

2. Find an article in the newspaper that exhibits "a good person speaking well." Now find an article that shows the opposite. Be ready to share your thoughts with the class.

THINGS TO TALK ABOUT

1. It has been said that "nice guys finish last." What evidence can you find to prove or disprove this statement? What conclusions can you draw? Why do we need ethical and responsible people in society?
2. The professional football player Lyle Alzedo died from an inoperable brain tumor. He attributed his problems to steroids. He said that steroids enhanced his football performance but rendered his immune system helpless. People often sacrifice the long term for instant success. How might this be true in facets of your life (i.e., grades in school, your health)? Where else in society do you see this to be true? Can you find any instances of people who *refuse* to opt for short-term gain? What about historical figures? Explain.

THINGS TO WRITE ABOUT

1. Write a brief biography of one or more of the people discussed in this chapter. What contribution to speaking or society did each make? Was the contribution for good or not? Explain.
2. A popular movie of the late 1980s was titled *Do the Right Thing.* Why is doing the right thing sometimes so difficult? Give at least two reasons, and provide a documented or personal example for each.
3. Certain people in your school are leaders. What makes people follow others? A poll taken in the Midwest in 1990 stated that the trait students valued most in a friend was honesty. Why would you believe this to be true?

CRITICAL THINKING

1. A number of customers from around the country have bought car phones that don't hook up to anything. They are just purchased as "show." Also, at a busy street corner in Chicago, people can rent briefcases by the day for that special "power" look. Do you see any societal problem with these examples, or are they harmless? Explain.
2. Without using the dictionary, define the words *hero* and *leader.*
3. In your opinion, who is the nation's number-1 hero and the nation's number-1 leader? Could this be the same person? Give your reasoning.

RELATED SPEECH TOPICS

Find research to prove that people are taking positive stands regarding the following issues: (Note: You may also include other information about each topic.)

The environment
Education (local and national)
The homeless
Child abuse
Equal rights
Farmers/agriculture

Consumer protection
Entertainment/the media
Politics
The family
Sports

CHAPTER 2

Building Confidence

"Robert Klein, in his comedy routine about the Lamaze method of natural childbirth, points out that the husband's principal role seems to be to remind the wife to breathe. That's funny because it seems absurd that anybody would have to be reminded to breathe. But under stress we sometimes forget how to breathe right. Public speaking is no more difficult than breathing, using chopsticks, or tying a bow tie. The mysterious becomes simple . . . once you know how to do it."

— Charles Osgood,
news commentator and author,
in his article "Speaking Easy"

I'M REALLY NERVOUS ABOUT THIS PRESENTATION FOR THE BIG BOSS. GOT ANY TIPS FOR ME?

REMEMBER TO BRING A BUNCH OF COINS TO JANGLE SELF-CONSCIOUSLY IN YOUR POCKETS.

...AVOID EYE CONTACT AND DON'T PAUSE TO EXPLAIN YOUR ACRONYMS.

I WISH I COULD TELL WHEN YOU'RE KIDDING.

LEARNING OBJECTIVES

After completing this chapter, you will be able to do the following.

✦ Discuss what confidence means and how it is a vital element in effective speaking.
  Recognize the realities of stage fright nd how you can appropriately deal with the problem.
✦ Realize the value of perception as it applies to confidence in your speaking.
✦ Implement the planks of confidence in your speaking.

CHAPTER OUTLINE

Following are the main sections in this chapter.

I What Is Confidence?
II Understanding Stage Fright
III Establishing an Accurate Perception
IV Examining the Planks of Confidence
      Chapter Review

NEW SPEECH TERMS

In this chapter, you will learn the meanings of the speech terms listed below.

confidence	organization
phobia	notes
social phobia	friendliness
performance anxiety	impression
	dedication
stage fright	empathy
topophobia	common ground
phonophobia	newness
perception	conviction
self-esteem	enthusiasm
content	

GENERAL VOCABULARY

Expanding your general vocabulary will help you become a more effective communicator. Listed below are some words appearing in this chapter that you should make part of your everyday vocabulary.

impede	innovation
listlessness	allegory
ruse	assertions
charade	prioritizing
cumulative	mannequin
synonymous	

LOOKING AHEAD

In this chapter, you will learn about confidence and about how you can become a more confident speaker. You will then analyze the different parts of stage fright. Finally, you will see how perception plus the components of confidence can help you become a more believable, self-assured oral communicator.

I What Is Confidence?

Confidence is tough to describe. You can't touch it, taste it, smell it, or feel it, though you know when either you or someone else has it. It can't be bought at department stores such as Wal-Mart or found in cereal boxes. Yogi Berra, former New York Yankee catcher and member of the Baseball Hall of Fame, once said that every time the Yankees took the field, he was very confident that they would win— or they wouldn't. Although humorous, Yogi's remark seems to show that he, like many people, was uncertain exactly what confidence means.

What does confidence mean? Simply put, **confidence** is the feeling you have when you believe in yourself and believe that you have control over a specific situation. In other words, you have confidence when you believe that you can get the job done.

President John F. Kennedy was a confident speaker. Stage fright, however, prevents many people from speaking with confidence.

You may be asking, "How does this apply to oral communication?" and "How do I build confidence?" To answer these questions, let's return to the example started in Chapter 1 about constructing a house. Chapter 1 stated that the construction of a house begins with the pouring of a solid foundation and that a solid value structure is the foundation that anchors the spoken word.

Now, what's the next step?

Carpenters next build the shell of the house by bolting the outside framework to the foundation. This is what gives the house its form or shape. Although it is eventually covered, this skeletal framework is essential. It provides stability against such things as strong winds and powerful rains. Similarly, confidence is the internal skeletal framework of effective oral communication. Anchored to a solid value system, it gives stability to the speaker and makes his or her message believable. Thus, confidence is the attitude of assurance that causes an audience to take a speaker seriously.

But not everyone can speak with confidence, even if they understand its importance. What's the problem? The problem is that confidence in speaking is easy to write about in a book but much more difficult to actually feel in preparing for and giving a speech. Why? Because of stage fright.

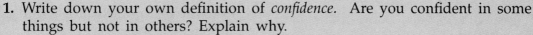

TAKING CHARGE

1. Write down your own definition of *confidence.* Are you confident in some things but not in others? Explain why.
2. Take a class inventory (of at least ten other students) and find out what they consider the most outstanding traits of a confident person (intelligence, outgoing personality, etc.). Why is being confident important if you want others to listen to you? Be ready to discuss your answers with the class.

II Understanding Stage Fright

What is stage fright?

Many of us are petrified at the thought of having to speak in front of other people. Some even suffer from a **phobia,** or a persistent, irrational fear that causes us to avoid specific situations. Of course, everyone suffers fears—it is natural to be afraid in tense situations. But when these fears get out of hand, they are referred to as phobias.

Social phobias involve the fear of being evaluated by others. We may be afraid that we will be embarrassed or that we will look stupid. If so, we may suffer from **performance anxiety,** or **stage fright.** Stage fright is also known as **topophobia,** while **phonophobia** is the overall fear of speaking aloud. People who suffer from phonophobia are often afraid of hearing their own voices or of having poor voice quality.

Stage fright is most evident right before we speak and during the first thirty seconds or so after we have actually opened our mouths. Heart rates can increase to nearly 200 beats per minute at the height of stage fright, nearly double the normal heart rate. Why? Because too often a speaker allows his fears to convince him that the worst is about to happen: Everyone in the audience will finally see and know for sure that he is the most boring, ignorant person alive. He might say to himself, "Who cares about what I have to say?" or "I hate the way I look in front of other people. They'll think I'm ugly."

One thing is true: Stage fright is real and affects countless numbers of people.

Who Gets Stage Fright?

Studies show that many people fear the thought of giving a speech more than they do the thought of dying. Think about that for a minute and you will realize that stage fright is a serious problem.

Many musical performers, used to practicing in quiet, isolated rooms, never adjust to playing before an audience. Such performers may have their careers cut short. The singer Carly Simon had millions of people listen to her records and tapes during the 1970s and 1980s, but later she virtually disappeared from the music scene because of her paralyzing fear of performing in front of live audiences. She suffered from a severe case of stage fright. Carly Simon's case, of course, is extreme, but a speaker who tells you that he or she has never had stage fright or a serious case of "butterflies" is probably lying or trying to impress you.

INSTANT IMPACT

The "Deer" Theory of Stage Fright

Charles Osgood, who offered the quotation that we used to begin Chapter 2, has an interesting theory on stage fright. He says, "Have you ever been driving at night and come upon a deer frozen in the beam of your headlights? Here's my theory. The deer thinks the lights are spotlights, and what has it paralyzed is stage fright. It imagines the worst: It has to give a speech."

Furthermore, anyone who believes that stage fright can't seriously *impede* the development of self-confidence might also believe that a polka band will be the opening act for the Rolling Stones.

It doesn't matter whether you are

◆ introducing yourself to a group of strangers,

◆ calling a girlfriend or boyfriend on the phone for the first time,

◆ answering a question in class,

◆ interviewing for a job,

◆ giving a campaign speech,

◆ explaining your ideas for the prom or for your class float at a committee meeting, or

◆ asking someone to dance.

If a receiver to your message is present, you may suffer varying degrees of stage fright.

What Are the Symptoms?

After being told of a speaking assignment, have you ever had any of these

People can experience stage fright in many situtations, including meeting a new person or answering a question in class.

feelings: headache, upset stomach, dry mouth, cold hands and feet, sweaty palms, squeaky voice, dizziness, fast heartbeat, an urge to hide, a need to use the bathroom, shortness of breath, hot face, or wobbly legs? If you have, you have experienced some of the symptoms of stage fright.

They are normal feelings. Most people do not like to be evaluated or judged. They also do not like the thought of "opening up" to an audience or of having others examine them too closely. Mainly, many speakers lack the confidence to believe that they have something worth-

while to say, that they can say it well, and that people will like them while they are saying it.

The Greek philosopher Socrates said that before we can move the world, we first have to move ourselves. But where do we get the confidence to start moving? How can we make our "internal skeletal frameworks" solid enough to withstand the "strong winds" and "powerful rains" of stage fright? We do these things by making sure that we have an accurate perception of our audience, of the purpose of our speech, and of ourselves.

TAKING CHARGE

1. List three physical symptoms that you experience when you are about to perform before an audience. Rank them from the most predominant to the least predominant.
2. Many speakers find that they lose much of their stage fright as their speech progresses. Why do you think that might happen? Give at least two reasons and offer your reasoning for each. Write your answers.

COMMUNICATION   BREAKDOWN

A Case of Deception

A New York woman, jilted by her fiancé, sought sympathy by faking breast cancer for two years. She said that her condition was terminal. To be convincing, she shaved her head and dieted away 20 pounds. She also feigned *listlessness* and loss of appetite. Even her cancer support group was fooled.

The woman did these things to build up a network of close friends. Dr. Marc Feldman, a psychiatrist in Birmingham, Alabama, said the woman evidently felt that the process of rebuilding a social life for herself after the broken engagement was overwhelming. She wanted a shortcut, lacking the confidence to start over from scratch. Feldman treated the woman after her *ruse* was discovered, while he was director of psychosocial programming at Duke University Medical Center's cancer center in Durham, North Carolina.

The woman, then thirty-five, began the *charade* while working as a corporate secretary. She told coworkers that the cancer already had spread and that her outlook was grim. She modeled her symptoms on the symptoms that a friend of hers had actually had.

After experiencing a gratifying outpouring of warmth from coworkers, she joined a support group because it gave her a ready-made social network, Feldman said in a telephone interview.

"The groups there really work to be unconditionally supportive, very nurturing and warm," he added.

He also said that at times she confronted other cancer patients, saying that they needed "to face their illness head on and that they needed to be more direct in dealing with the issue of cancer."

She was found out when a routine check of medical records showed that she had never seen the cancer specialist she claimed was treating her.

The doctor went on to add that the woman's words were so convincing and she sounded so believable and confident to the others that they never doubted her.

Source: Associated Press.

Questions

1. How did this woman's supposed "confidence" prove to be a negative factor?
2. In the end, who was victimized by her deception? Explain.
3. Even though it is not specifically stated, how did she exhibit her own form of stage fright?

III   Establishing an Accurate Perception

As we will use it here, **perception** refers to how you see things. To perceive means to gain an awareness and understanding of a person, an idea, or a situation. Obviously, an accurate perception is a tool that helps us learn more about ourselves, our objectives, and other people. In contrast, an inaccurate perception can cause us to blow things out of proportion, make a problem greater than it really is, and become our own worst enemies.

For instance, a student from Texas told

| COMMUNICATION | | BREAKTHROUGH |

A Teacher Brings Out the Best in His Students

To the community of Robert W. Coleman Elementary School, 30 year-old teacher Carter Bayton was a miracle. When he arrived at the all-black school in Baltimore, Maryland, there were obvious problems. Many of the elementary students were diagnosed as being learning disabled. They were known as problem students and many were labeled simply "throwaway kids."

The school neighborhood was bad. Drugs and violence were commonplace to the area. Having grown up in the inner city himself, Bayton saw the plight of the children and vowed to change things. He had seen kids like this drop out of school because they saw no future in education. Bayton wanted to reach out and give those kids "a fighting chance."

He was given an all-boy class. Many of the boys lived without a father at home, raised primarily by their mothers. However, Carter Bayton provided a positive role model for the boys. He worked to build their self-esteem. He promised that they would all be reading at grade level within one year. But he also did much more than this.

He stressed the value of hard work and dedication to excellence.

He taught the importance of manners.

He taught them the value of praising something done well.

Carter Bayton made a communication breakthrough. Now, instead of being on the road to ruin, his youngsters are on the road to possible success, both academically and socially.

Carter Bayton of Baltimore, Maryland, has confidently used his spoken words to bring out the best in his class. He promised each student that he would always be there for him.

So far, he has been.

Source: Adapted from Life, "Bayton's Boys Do the Right Thing," *September 1991.*

Questions
1. The article stated that Carter Bayton never raised his voice to his class and that his tone was always warm and friendly. Why do you think this would be an advantage for him in teaching his class?
2. Why are role models important for all of us?
3. Do you think what Carter Bayton was teaching his students could influence their lives at home?

of the time that she had to give a short talk to a local community group. She was well prepared, and her confidence level was high—until she saw a man in the group lean back in his chair and shake his head when her name was announced. She thought that the man was in some way angry or disappointed that she was going to be the speaker. Needless to say, her short speech was less than brilliant. After the speech, the same man approached her and thanked her for sharing her words. He went on to explain that right before she began, he had put eye drops into his eyes because of an allergy—and he hoped that he hadn't been a distraction to her. She learned a valuable lesson: Don't allow your imagination to run wild. Stay calm and give people in your audience the benefit of the doubt.

In constructing a house, carpenters often use a main support beam. This beam runs from one side of a room to another and works to make the internal structure stable. Establishing an accurate, realistic perception is the "main support beam" in building speaking confidence. It is this internal mind-set that allows you to say with a confident attitude, "I see things as they are, not as my fears might lead me to see them."

Your Perception of the Audience

People too often think that giving a speech is a life-or-death situation. They can visualize passing out or throwing up on their audience. They might think, "I know the audience sees my legs shaking" or "Everyone in the room is staring at the bead of sweat that is on the end of my nose."

Unfortunately, since fears are *cumulative*, they may mount and multiply as the speech progresses. Each fear seems to build on the one that preceded it. A speaker may end up with the perception that the audience is much smarter than she, sees everything that she does wrong, and notes each minor flub or stutter. However, research proves that many speaking fears are simply unwarranted. Michael T. Motley, writing for *Psychology Today*, stated:

> Studies on how well an audience perceives anxiety should comfort nervous speakers. Researchers have found that most report noticing little or no anxiety in a speaker. Even when individuals are trained to detect anxiety cues and instructed to look for them, there is little correlation between their evaluations and how anxious speakers actually felt.

A speaker can suffer from fears that multiply during the course of a speech. Studies show, however, that audiences often cannot perceive nervousness in speakers.

This encouraging quote shows that audiences are often unaware of a speaker's nervousness. Remember, your audience will ignore or forgive any type of mistake or awkwardness if they feel that you are genuinely interested in them and that you are genuinely trying to share with them.

Your Perception of the Speech

American author Charles Dudley Warner once said that there is but one pleasure in life equal to that of being called on to make an after-dinner speech, and that is *not* being called on to make one. Part of the problem with giving a speech is the perception of what exactly the word *speech* should mean.

You should see speaking as an opportunity to share something you consider valuable—your message—with your audience. Thus, the word *speech* should not be viewed as being *synonymous* with *performance*. Instead, a speech should be viewed as a chance that you've been given to say something meaningful to others.

Speaking is not putting on a show. Too many times people seem to think of a speaking assignment as a Hollywood screen test. When this happens, they make the assignment more difficult than it needs to be. All of a sudden, they believe that their words and actions have to be extraordinary. Don't fall into this trap!

If you remember that a speech should be seen as a tremendous opportunity to share, an opportunity to enjoy a meaningful moment, an opportunity to communicate verbally with people you care about (your audience), then you can reduce your feelings of stage fright.

The speech is an extension of you. It is an extension of your personality and of your feelings, likes, and dislikes. Have confidence, and see your speech as a potential beacon to guide others, not as a performance that your audience will judge by holding up score cards as judges do in the Olympics.

Steve Bair proves this point nicely. He was competing at Tulsa, Oklahoma, in the final round of the original oratory category of the National Forensic League championship. Only 6 contestants remained out of the over 180 contestants that had started in his category. Thousands of people in the audience had come to see the most talented high school speakers in the United States. Three microphones were on the stage, and there were television cameras and spotlights visible.

Suddenly, it was Steve Bair's turn to speak. Even though he had spoken hundreds of times before, his legs began to shake. He became warm, and his mouth felt like cotton.

He was suffering stage fright.

Steve started talking to himself (remember the discussion of intrapersonal communication). He said, "Hey, I'm not performing for these people. I'm sharing. I'm just a person who cares about people, and I also care about this speech. I care what it has to say. I'm happy that I now have the chance to say it in front of so many people!"

Steve Bair went on to win the national championship.

This true account ought to teach you something: Your speech is not some alien creature to be feared or an enemy that you should run from. Your perception of the speech should include an awareness of how powerful words can be and a vision of how your words can make that power a reality.

Your Perception of Yourself

It is sometimes difficult for people to accept who they are. The media have created so many "beautiful people" that, in comparison, the rest of us may feel we stand little chance. The rock singer Madonna urges people to "strike a pose," and a popular tennis star reveals that "image is everything."

Consequently, it is easy for us to perceive ourselves as not being pretty enough, handsome enough, intelligent enough, or witty enough. The book *One Hundred Percent American* by Daniel E. Weiss states that 99 percent of all women in the nation would change at least one thing about their looks. If you lack confidence in yourself, doesn't it stand to reason that you will also lack confidence in your spoken words?

Of course, in speaking, you should strive for excellence; but you should not think that you always have to be perfect. Don't equate making a mistake with being a total failure. If you do, you might want to give up and not even allow your oral communication the opportunity to succeed. How do you change this sort of negative perception of yourself?

First of all, recognize your own individual worth and like who you are. Fred Mitchell, director of wellness for a midwestern high school, reports the following story:

Once upon a time, an unhappy horse wished for longer, thinner legs, a neck like a swan, and a saddle that would grow on his back as part of his body. He thought all of these things would bring him great happiness, because they would make him more beautiful. Well, it so happened that the horse's wishes were granted and he was given all the things he wished for. But when the horse went to a reflecting pond to admire his improved image, he was horrified. The things that had seemed so desirable individually had become totally undesirable collectively—he had been changed into a camel!

Moral of the story: It is better to improve what you have than to wish for the things you don't have.

This moral also applies to perception and confidence in speaking. If you see yourself as individual and unique rather than different or inadequate, then you can start to build a confidence that stresses your

No one is born with confidence. A speaker can build confidence, however, by recognizing personal worth and not fearing failure.

uniqueness and emphasizes your own personal potential.

Second, don't be afraid to be human. Don't be afraid to acknowledge the fact that you don't do everything perfectly. Politicians, company executives, movie stars—everyone makes mistakes. While it is true that you can make errors and sometimes fail, set out to learn from those failures.

Did you know that a professor at the University of Houston developed a course that became known as "Failure 101"? The object of the course was to convince students that failure should be seen as an opportunity for *innovation* instead of immediate defeat. His students loved the class. It showed them that not always being right the first time can, ironically, lead to discovery. For example, the inventor Thomas Edison faced many failures before he discovered the electric light.

The psychologist John Rosemond adds that confidence, or **self-esteem,** is often the result of this discovery process. He says that no one is born with confidence. On the contrary, confidence is built. When you can face your fears, your frustrations, and even your failures—and still come out standing on your own two feet—then confidence is being nurtured. Remember, you gain confidence every time that you face adversity and come out on top.

How does this apply to speaking?

Very simply, it means you need not be afraid to fail. Don't worry that you are going to "mess up" in your speech. Suppose you make a mistake and realize:

- ◆ that you are using too many note-cards,
- ◆ that you just dropped your note-cards,

- ◆ that your notes are shaking uncontrollably in your hands,
- ◆ that your introduction lacks impact,
- ◆ that your eye contact is only with the back wall,
- ◆ that your knees are shaking,
- ◆ that you are stuttering,
- ◆ that you are opening your mouth but no words are coming out, or
- ◆ that you are sweating.

Don't panic! Remember that you are human. Smile, take a deep breath, and think about how you are going to correct these problems when you speak the next time. And there will be a next time.

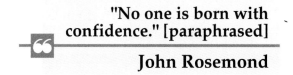

"No one is born with confidence." [paraphrased]

John Rosemond

Sometimes the greatest therapy for stage fright is to laugh at your own mistakes in your speech. Your audience will probably laugh with you because they, like you, are simply human.

What Have You Learned about Perception?

One of the main points that you have learned about perception is that it is a key element in building confidence in speaking. Why? Because an accurate perception of things can help you to overcome stage fright. It will allow you to deal with what is real as opposed to what you might imagine to be real.

To illustrate, let's examine a story from the philosophical past. In *The Republic,* written in the fifth century B.C., Plato offers the famous allegory of the cave. This *allegory* describes people as prisoners in a cave, facing away from the opening of the cave and thus away from the light. Unable to see themselves or anyone else because they are shackled, they see only the shadows on the wall in front of them. Since they are never allowed to turn around and see the light, their perception is that the shadows are what is real.

What's the connection of this allegory to speaking? The answer is this: If you believe that:

◆ your audience is aware of everything you do wrong in your speech,

◆ your speech is a performance rather than sharing, or

◆ you have little to offer as either a person or a speaker,

then you are being victimized by the "shadows" of stage fright and fear. Isn't it time that you "see the light"? The truth is that:

◆ your audience doesn't see everything you do wrong,

◆ your speech is a worthwhile sharing of good ideas and information, and

◆ you have a lot to offer.

Let your perception work for you. Firmly implant the "main support beam"—an accurate perception—that is essential in the overall construction of building confidence.

Next we examine some of the specific planks that make up the confidence framework.

TAKING CHARGE

1. Make a list of your own stage fright symptoms. List what happens to you physically. What thoughts are going through your head when you have stage fright?
2. Interview someone you know who is involved in public speaking or in some form of competition at your school. Write down the ideas that he or she has about how to deal with stage fright. What does this person do specifically to build confidence?
3. There are times when having a perception different from others' perceptions is acceptable (for example, a perception about a painting, a rock artist, or a political issue). List specific things about which perceptions could vary. Be ready to defend your choices either verbally or in writing. In what areas should our perceptions be about the same? Explain your answers.

IV Examining the Planks of Confidence

Once again, think of a house. When you see the shell of a house being put up, you can't help but notice the individual pieces of wood, usually two-by-fours of varying lengths, that make up the walls and the roof. These individual pieces of wood might be referred to as planks.

Let's now take the word *confidence* and use each letter in the word as a figurative "plank." In the process, you will "nail down" some of the major ingredients of confidence:

Content	Dedication
Organization	Empathy
Notes	Newness
Friendliness	Conviction
Impression	Enthusiasm

As you read about each plank, keep in mind that your confidence level will grow with each one you develop.

Content. *Have something worthwhile to say.* You can't be confident as a speaker if you are not confident of your content. It is a good feeling to know that you have researched your topic and have done your homework.

High school students are often unfairly portrayed as having little academic promise or real-world awareness, caught up in MTV and skateboards. Don't allow this stereotype to stand. Show that intellectually you have credibility and deserve to be paid attention to. Audiences respect a person who shares a message that contains facts and pertinent evidence. Build a relevant message with solid content by going to the library, reading newspapers or current magazines, interviewing someone who knows something related to your topic, or watching the news or educational television.

Remember, don't base your speaking on *assertions* or emotional appeals only. Spend time building an evidence file that shows appropriate documentation and obvious "legwork" on your part.

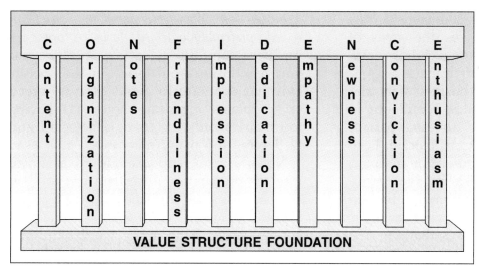

Content, organization, notes, friendliness, impression, dedication, empathy, newness, conviction, and enthusiasm form the "planks" that support the "beam" of confidence.

Referring to key words or phrases on notecards can help a speaker stay confidently on track.

Organization. *Have some type of an outline that is easy for both you and your audience to follow.* It is a reassuring feeling to know that you are operating from a format that is logical. Every speech must have a main idea or main point being addressed, clear areas of analysis, and supporting evidence that fits. An introduction that leads to the thesis statement and a conclusion that summarizes the areas of analysis and provides some ending emotional appeal are also important.

Mark McCormack, a businessman and author, states that he gains confidence in his business dealings by dividing part of his day into five one-hour blocks. Each block has a specific purpose. For instance, one of his one-hour blocks involves *prioritizing* his phone calls and determining exactly how much time, on the average, he can spend on each. He says that this approach gives sequence to his business day and makes the day make sense.

This message can also apply to confidence in speaking. Don't be scatterbrained—don't always rely on "the spontaneity of the moment." Offer clarity and sequence to your audience. Your audience will appreciate your guiding them, and you will feel more confident that your audience is getting your point.

Notes. *Jot down your ideas in a brief, directed (preferably outlined) form.* A notecard can be a comforting "security net" in case you fear losing your place in the speech. However, be sure to avoid the two greatest problems regarding notes: (1) having too many words on a single notecard and (2) having too many notecards.

Notes are not supposed to be a substitute for preparation. They are not for you to read to your audience. Instead, notes should provide you with a memory springboard. Seeing a key word or phrase should remind you where you are and where you should be going in your

A speaker who practices a speech out loud, planning eye contact, gestures, and body movements, will feel more confident when delivering the actual speech.

speech. Used correctly, notes can be your friend. They can be the training wheels of oral communication, keeping you confidently on course and, most importantly, on topic.

Friendliness. *Be congenial.* You can gain confidence if you see that your audience is giving you positive feedback. This positive feedback is often the result of your conveying a warm, friendly attitude. Writing for *Management Digest*, Roger Ailes, a noted author and communication consultant, says that being likable is the "magic bullet" in speaking. He writes, "With [friendliness], your audience will forgive just about everything else you do wrong. Without it, you can hit every bull's-eye in the room and no one will be impressed."

So don't be afraid to smile and to talk to individuals in the room. Don't view your audience as a collective mass of faceless people. Let both your words and your nonverbal communication work for you. Remember, an audience that likes you is more likely to be receptive to your message.

Impression. *Getting off to a good start is essential in building confidence.* How your audience perceives you right from the beginning is very important. Do you, for instance, convey a positive attitude on your way to the front of the room? This text has already referred to the study that showed that 55 percent of what others think of you is determined before you ever open your mouth. If this is true, you should be able to telegraph to your audience the feeling "I'm really glad to be here today" before you begin to speak. This, in turn, should raise your confidence level.

Impression also refers to the way you are dressed and groomed. The issue here isn't money. The issue involves common sense and appropriate judgment. If it is your objective to be taken seriously as a speaker, then never allow your clothing, hair, makeup, or jewelry to get in the way of your message. These things should not draw attention away from your main purpose: effective communication. While it is true that "clothes don't make the person," it is certainly also true that they can help. Showing the audience that you took the time to look good for them means that you respect them. Isn't respect what all of us are after? Build confidence by setting a good example and offering a solid first impression.

Dedication. *Practice. Practice. Practice.* Too many times a student adequately researches a speech and prepares a catchy introduction and a dynamic conclusion, only to forget a basic part of speech presentation—orally practicing the actual delivery of the speech. Confidence does not come about as a result of going over the material mentally in the corner of your room while listening to music through your headphones. You must get used to the sound of your own voice and speak as often as you can. You must try as much as possible to simulate the real thing.

Professionals in both sports and entertainment speak of the countless number of hours that they spend on basics: a simple exercise on the piano, covering first base on a bunt, a simple tennis stroke, or a routine dance step. These professional men and women know the value of practice.

Speaking is no different. Take the time to actually say the words you've worked so hard to create on paper. Practice looking at people while speaking. Practice your gestures. Practice moving to see how your body feels while taking a step. Be dedicated so that when the time comes to speak before an audience, you won't be caught helpless. Instead, you will feel more confident because you will already have been there!

Empathy. *Know how it feels to feel that way.* The term *empathy* means a sincere understanding of the feelings, thoughts, and motives of others. You shouldn't assume that you are the only person with problems during your day. Other people face these same difficulties.

In the novel *To Kill a Mockingbird,* by Harper Lee, one of the characters, Atticus Finch, tells his daughter, Scout, that you never truly understand a man until you "climb into his skin and walk around in it."

As speakers, learn from this advice. You can feel much more at ease if you will take a few minutes to get to know how your audience is feeling. What are they thinking? What's on their minds? Have you made an attempt to "climb into their skins?" Could it be that they are facing problems at home? With their boyfriends or girlfriends? Once you empathize, you will not only understand your audience better, you will understand feedback better. For instance, keep in mind that when an audience is looking out the window, slouching in their seats, or not paying attention, it might simply mean that they are having a bad day.

Have you ever had a bad day? If so, then you will understand and refuse to take things personally. Keep speaking and working for **common ground.** When you establish common ground with your audience, you are saying with both verbal and nonverbal communication, "We're *all* in this together, and together we will work to solve what might be on our minds." The consequence might be that you will become a more confident speaker.

Newness. *Apply some originality.* We often feel confident if we have something new and original to say. This could mean taking a different slant, approaching your topic in your own unique way. A clever anecdote that you've read might make an original way to start your speech. A meaningful quotation that you've discovered could add an original punch to your conclusion. What about charts, graphs, or artwork to accompany your words? If appropriate and well done, they can offer an innovative means of uniquely reinforcing your point.

One of the best ways to put some originality in your speech is to tell a personal story. In his article "We Must Rediscover Our Stories," Richard Louv says that Americans have lost sight of the impact that their personal stories can have. Somehow people assume that if a story isn't at the video store or on a television soap opera, it must be worthless. However, Louv notes that personal stories—family stories—are "real gold." He writes:

> There seems to be a growing hunger out there. The reaction to the Civil War series that aired earlier this year [1991] on PBS [Public Broadcasting Service] is an example of how starved people are for powerful, authentic stories about real people, about ourselves. . . . The new popularity of salons—where people get together to do that most radical of acts, *talk* face-to-face—suggests the hunger.

So tell your story! No one has one quite like yours. Your originality can show your audience that you are a creative, intelligent speaker. It can also help to establish the necessary common ground spoken of earlier and, in the process, add to your confidence in speaking.

Conviction. *Believe in what you say.* Mahatma Gandhi, the Hindu spiritual leader, once said, "One needs to be slow to form convictions, but once formed they must be defended against the heaviest of odds." Even though most of our lives are not as dramatic as this quotation, the message is clear: Know what your principles are, and have the courage to stand up and voice those principles. Confidence can be greatly magnified when you have a strong belief in what your spoken words are conveying.

Some speech topics can be boring unless you add your own special dimension of personal conviction. For example, giving a speech on "My Summer Vacation" can come across as lifeless and monotonous. But what if on your summer vacation, you saw a work by Michelangelo, the sixteenth-century painter and sculptor, that made you realize something about people or art that you passionately wish to share?

Similarly, talking about "My Job" or "My Friends" can be tedious. But what if your job promotes hard work, and you believe that hard work and a strong work ethic are important for success? And what if your friends are the elderly couple down the street, and you have seen firsthand the value of kindness, touch, a smile, and compassion?

Suddenly, each of these "ordinary" topics takes on a new, more vital meaning that you can relate directly to your audience. Your conviction will tell your audience that you take your topic seriously. Your audience will, in turn, take you and your speech more seriously.

Conviction can also allow you to take your mind off of your fears, gestures, and facial expressions and let you focus on your speech content.

Through intellectual and physical enthusiasm, a speaker can excite an audience as well as release nervous energy.

The main point about conviction is this: If you are confident about the importance of your message, then your audience is more likely to be persuaded.

Enthusiasm. *Get fired up!* The character Spock of the science fiction television and movie series *Star Trek* is well known for relying on logic and reason and for exhibiting little emotional involvement. This might work with the audience of science fiction, but it probably won't work with your audience. No one wants to listen to an unemotional *mannequin,* standing lifelessly at the front of the room. You need energy. You need enthusiasm. You need to inspire your audience by showing them that you are "fired up" in two ways that work hand in hand: intellectually, so that your mind is sharp and alert, and also physically, so that your body is actively involved.

The most ordinary speech can become entertaining and delightful if you share your enthusiasm with your audience. Enthusiasm is directed energy. So if you feel "energized," others in the room will feel that same electricity.

Enthusiasm is also often a convenient outlet for much of the nervous energy that stage fright might bring. However, nervous energy must be controlled. When you are about to make a speech, take a few deep breaths. Let yourself relax. Have your body release some of the nervous tension that might develop right before you speak.

Many of the great thinkers have given us advice on the value of enthusiasm. Ralph Waldo Emerson, American essayist and poet of the mid-nineteenth century, said that nothing great was ever achieved without it. One of the best pieces of advice came from the motivational speaker and businessman William McFee, who declared that the world belongs to the enthusiast who can "keep his cool." As a speaker, if you can "keep your cool," yet show your audience that you are excited about being with them and sharing your message, then you are sure to become a more confident communicator.

So where does this bring us?

Abraham Lincoln was once asked how he would cut down a tree if he were given eight hours to complete the job. He responded by saying that he would sharpen the blade on his axe for seven hours—so that he could easily cut down the tree in one hour. In other words, he would spend most of his time preparing so that his job would be easier.

Chapter 2 (as well as Chapter 1) has worked to teach you the same type of lesson regarding directed preparation, a lesson that will be extended in later chapters. Remember, a speech is built in much the same way a house is built—from the foundation up. You are ensuring success with your spoken words when you build a solid confidence framework that exhibits a responsible, ethical approach to communication.

TAKING CHARGE

1. Ten planks of confidence were listed. Can you think of at least two others? What is your reasoning behind each choice? Write your responses.
2. Why is practice essential for success at any undertaking? What problems might develop without it? How can failing to practice your speech hurt your confidence? Be ready to give your answers out loud.
3. Conviction is certainly an important plank of confidence. Name two issues that you feel very strongly about. They may be personal, school, community, national, or world issues. What points would you stress about each if you had to give a speech? Share your views in small groups.

REVIEW AND ENRICHMENT

LOOKING BACK

Listed below are the major ideas discussed in this chapter.

✦ Confidence is the feeling that you have when you know that you can accomplish a certain task.

✦ Confidence in speaking is the internal skeletal framework that is anchored to the solid value foundation described in Chapter 1.

✦ Confidence is the motivating factor behind the power and believability of your words and is an essential element in your being taken seriously by an audience.

✦ Stage fright often threatens a speaker's confidence. We can think of it as a strong wind that works to blow down a confidence structure.

✦ People are often victimized by phobias, or fears that get out of hand.

✦ Everyone is potentially susceptible to stage fright, even professionals, and the symptoms range from a rapid heartbeat to sweaty palms to an upset stomach.

✦ One way to overcome stage fright is to establish an accurate perception of your audience, your speech, and yourself.

✦ Perception is the main support beam of confidence. It challenges you to see things as they really are, not as your fears might lead you to believe they are.

✦ A second way to deal with stage fright and build your speaking confidence is by examining the ten planks of confidence: content, organization, notes, friendliness, impression, dedication, empathy, newness, conviction, and enthusiasm.

✦ Confidence is a consequence of preparation and hard work and is the driving force behind speaking effectiveness.

SPEECH VOCABULARY

1. For each speech vocabulary word, give the definition as it appears in the text. Underline the word. Make sure that you can spell each word.

confidence	perception
phobia	self-esteem
social phobia	content
performance anxiety	organization
stage fright	notes
topophobia	friendliness
phonophobia	impression

dedication
empathy
common ground

newness
conviction
enthusiasm

2. For each of the ten planks of confidence, copy the phrase or sentence from the chapter discussion that best describes what the plank is promoting. Do this in addition to writing down the short descriptive phrase that is given immediately beside each plank.

GENERAL VOCABULARY

1. Define each general vocabulary term by using a dictionary. Include the part of speech, the definition of the word as it is used in the chapter, and an original sentence of your own. Make sure that you can spell each word.

impede
listlessness
ruse
charade
cumulative
synonymous

innovation
allegory
assertions
prioritizing
mannequin

2. Write an original story about "The Day I Overcame My Fear" or "The Day It Was My Turn to Perform!" Use at least twelve words from the combined speech and general vocabulary lists. Underline and number each word.

3. Are there any other words in Chapter 2 that you aren't familiar with? That you don't know how to spell? Find at least three, and add them to your lists.

THINGS TO REMEMBER

Answer the following questions based on your reading of the chapter.

1. Confidence is the feeling you have when you know that you can get the job done. Confidence is the _____ of effective oral communication.
2. A persistent, irrational fear can be referred to as a _____.
3. Another name for performance anxiety is _____.
4. If you specifically suffer from _____, you are often afraid of hearing your own voice.
5. Perception refers to how we see things. Perception is the _____ in building speaking confidence.
6. What percentage of American women would change at least one thing about their looks?
7. A university course known as _____ works to prove the value of effort. The course shows people that they can learn from their mistakes.
8. What famous work by Plato featured the allegory of the cave?

9. What teacher in Maryland is helping young children to build their confidence and their future?
10. Roger Ailes calls what word the "magic bullet" in speaking?
11. Richard Louv states that our real impact in speaking can come from our personal _____, which he refers to as "real gold."

THINGS TO DO

1. Wilma Rudolph was a world-class runner who captured three gold medals for America at the 1960 Olympics. However, it is a wonder she could even walk. A series of childhood illnesses had so crippled her that she was unable to walk until she was eight years old. It was through sheer determination and commitment that she overcame the odds. Research a figure from history who also had the confidence to overcome the odds. Show how something great was accomplished by this person. Also, interview someone in your family or in your community who has exhibited the confidence to do something admirable in the face of adversity. Share your words with the class.

2. Compile a self-improvement chart. On it, list the things about you that you can't change. In another column, list the things about you that you *can* change and that you would like to improve. For each item that you can change, jot down how you are going to improve. Be sure to include areas of speaking in which you know that you can improve.

THINGS TO TALK ABOUT

1. The science fiction writer Ray Bradbury recently said in a speech that Americans, particularly young people, should never watch the evening news. He believes that the news too often erodes our sense of confidence in the future. Is he right? What problems might arise if we don't watch the news? How does what we see on the news affect our personal confidence?
2. It has been said that some people "die with potential." This means that some people never work hard enough to actualize all of their talents or abilities. Why is this such a catastrophe? How can each of us prevent this from happening in our lives?
3. Why are teachers sometimes difficult to talk to, causing students to get stage fright? What role might perception play here?

THINGS TO WRITE ABOUT

1. The things that might give us stage fright as a child are different from the things we could be frightened by later. Explain the stage fright that a child could feel. What about a teenager? What about a parent? A teacher? An elderly person? How can you, as a listener, help others when you know that they are experiencing stage fright?
2. Denice Barsich, whose good-Samaritan

action resulted in the loss of her right leg, hasn't lost her zest for life. She was hit by a car while helping a fellow motorist out of a snow-filled ditch. She says that one of her goals is to "dance at my husband's Christmas party." Denice Barsich has one other objective: not to be bitter and to teach her children about the sanctity of life. (*Source:* Gary Post-Tribune.) What does she teach us by her words? Do we often take things for granted?

3. Organization is always an important element in clear communication. Make a list titled "Three Things I Must Get Done in School." Describe not only what your three objectives are but also how, where, and when you plan to accomplish each. Make another list titled "Three Things I Must Accomplish at Home." Do the same with these. Be sure to be specific.

CRITICAL THINKING

1. Fear in speaking can be a negative factor; however, fear can also sometimes work to your advantage. In what areas besides speaking can fear be a positive element? How can fear work for you in those areas? How can fear work for you in your speaking? Survey others in your class and find out who has had an experience where fear played a positive role. What lesson have we learned about the word *fear?*
2. This chapter has dealt with confidence. Is it ever possible to have too much confidence? What do you see as being the difference between a confident attitude and a "cocky" attitude? How can we keep from having the latter? If you had to select three media figures (from television, film, etc.) who exhibit confidence, who would they be? Why? What media figure is too cocky? Why might this "turn people off?" What lesson have we learned about the word *confidence?*
3. This chapter has discussed how impression is very important for people speaking before an audience. When is forming a quick impression the wrong thing to do? When is it important for you to care what other people think? Should you ever *not* care what others think? Defend your responses with specifics.

RELATED SPEECH TOPICS

How do the following topics relate to points made in Chapter 2? For some, you will need to do some research.

MADD (Mothers against Drunk Driving)
Apartheid
Sexual harassment
Censorship
Left brain/right brain research
Phobias
Cooperative learning in education

Cheating in America
Fire fighters
Peer pressure
Creativity
Work ethic
Interviewing
Law enforcement

Can you think of any other topics?

CHAPTER 3

Listening

 "Conversation in the United States is a competitive exercise in which the first person to draw a breath is declared the listener."

— **Nathan Miller**

"So when Farmer Bob comes through the door, three of us circle around and . . . 'Muriel! Are you chewing your cud while I'm talking?'"

LEARNING OBJECTIVES

After completing this chapter, you will be able to do the following.

✦ Explain the difference between hearing and listening.

✦ Describe five different listening styles.

✦ Explain why good listening habits are important.

✦ Describe the seven deadly habits of bad listening.

✦ Demonstrate how a listener can encourage a speaker to be clear and precise.

CHAPTER OUTLINE

Following are the main sections in this chapter.

I Listening Is More Than Hearing

II Roadblocks to Good Listening

III Effective Listening Strategies

IV The Contributions Listeners Make

Chapter Review

NEW SPEECH TERMS

In this chapter, you will learn the meanings of the speech terms listed below.

passive listening
active listening
hearing
noise
appreciative listening
discriminative listening
comprehensive listening
therapeutic listening

critical listening
testimonials
false comparisons
jump on the bandwagon
listening spare time
stack the deck
name calling
hidden meanings
door openers

GENERAL VOCABULARY

Expanding your general vocabulary will help you become a more effective communicator. Listed below are some words appearing in this chapter that you should make part of your everyday vocabulary.

vulnerable
paraphrase
peripheral
biases
rapport
propaganda

rhetorical
excursions
disintegration
retention
acronym
clarify

Looking Ahead

In one of Shakespeare's most famous plays, *Julius Caesar*, Mark Antony calls on his fellow Romans to "lend me your ears." In this chapter, we will ask you to lend us your ears for some retooling.

Most of us, it seems, are poor listeners, an unfortunate situation that can often lead to mistakes, misunderstandings, and even disaster.

Yet listening is a skill that you can master if you are willing to adopt the right attitude and practice a few simple techniques. If we succeed as good listeners, we not only help ourselves in the quest for knowledge and success, but we also help the speaker, who is heartened by our attention and stirred by our encouragement.

I Listening Is More Than Hearing

You don't know how it happened. You know you were paying attention when your friend started to tell you about an argument she had with her father. But somewhere along the way, your eyes glazed over, and her voice became a dull hum in the background of your mind. When you finally shook yourself out of your trance, she was asking, "So what should I do?" Once again, poor listening has you in hot water.

In a sense, the message of this chapter is, "What you get out of listening depends on what you put into it." As listeners, we tend to think that the responsibility for successful communication lies with the person doing the talking. This attitude causes us to become **passive** listeners. We tolerate distractions—putting up with a noise in the hall, for instance, instead of getting up to shut the door. We pay more attention to how someone talks than to what he or she has to say. And we generally fail to respond to the speaker's message by asking questions or to remember anything that was said. Effective listeners, on the other hand, play an **active** role by guiding the speaker toward common interests. Passive listeners are the sponges in the communications sea; active listeners are the sharks.

Good listening is a valuable skill. *Fortune* magazine rates listening as the top management skill needed for success in business. Listening is also critical to success in family life and among friends. Good listeners do well in school—they follow directions better and don't waste time wondering what the assignment was. Becoming an active listener will help you in your relationships, with your schoolwork, and on the job. Good listening also helps you keep things in perspective: "Nature has given us one tongue, but two ears," wrote the Greek philosopher Epictetus, "that we may hear twice as much as we speak."

Studies indicate that students spend up to 60 percent of their school time listening.

Basically, listening is the process of understanding what was meant, not simply sensing what was said. When you listen, according to Webster's *New World Dictionary*, you "make a conscious effort to hear." Clearly, listening takes effort. By contrast, **hearing** is simply an automatic reaction of the senses and nervous system. I can hear you talking (I can't help it if you speak loud enough), but if I don't like or trust you, I may not *listen* to what you say. Listening is a voluntary act in which we use our higher mental processes. Have you ever noticed how suddenly your ears perk up if you hear the hint of some juicy gossip? Hearing is easy for most of us; listening is hard for all of us. You have to want to listen.

Listening Takes Most of Our Time

Listening is one of the first things we learn to do and one of the things we do most. The average person spends 9 percent of his daily communication time writing, 16 percent reading, 30 percent speaking, and a whopping 45 percent listening. Students spend most of their school time listening—up to 60 percent, according to some studies. Yet despite its importance, we usually take our ability to listen for granted. As we have already said, though, listening isn't easy.

In the first place, we are surrounded by **noise**—the sound of traffic, the roar of jets overhead, even the static on the telephone line—which makes any listening job a challenge. In the second place, we often don't seem to remember even when we do listen. By the time a speaker has finished a ten-minute speech, the average person has already forgotten half of what was said. Within forty-eight hours, another 50 percent has been forgotten. In other words, we quickly forget nearly all of what we hear.

"Wait a minute! Say that again, Doris! . . . you know, the part about, 'If only we had some means of climbing down.'"

The Ship That Couldn't Be Sunk

One of the greatest tragedies in the history of sea travel occurred on the night of April 14, 1912, when the crew of the *Titanic* refused to listen to repeated warnings of icebergs. The crew had been led to believe that this brand-new passenger liner was "unsinkable." Even after the ship struck an iceberg and was slowly sinking, some of the passengers ignored the captain's orders to get into the lifeboats.

When the ship finally began tilting dangerously, it was too late. There weren't enough lifeboats for all the passengers and worse still, the *Californian*, the only other ship in the area (about 10 miles away) made no attempt to reach the wreck. Her radio operator had gone off duty. He, too, wasn't listening. As a result, more than a thousand people needlessly lost their lives.

Unfortunately, the cost of poor listening is high. Poor listening may keep you from doing well on an exam, but it can cost all of us much more. One researcher put it this way: "If each of America's more than 100 million workers prevented just one $10 mistake by better listening, their organizations would save $1 billion." Do workers make many $10 mistakes? You bet. A $10 mistake is as simple as missing a meeting (you weren't listening when the boss mentioned the time), putting an item of stock in the wrong place, or having to retype a letter.

Five Ways to Listen

The radio operator straining to decipher an SOS call isn't listening the way you are when your Aunt Bessie calls from Des Moines to chat. We listen most carefully to what we feel is important to us. We say we're "all ears" when the coach announces the starting lineup or the music teacher names soloists for the big performance, but somehow our ears jam up when mom or dad wants to talk about household chores. The fact is, we have

Enjoying music is considered appreciative listening.

different listening styles for different occasions. How successful we are as listeners may depend in part on choosing the right listening style for the situation.

Perhaps the most basic listening style is **appreciative listening.** We listen appreciatively when we enjoy music, a bird's song, or the murmur of a brook. We need a different style, one called **discriminative listening,** when we want to single out one particular sound from a noisy environment. You discriminate, for example, when you listen for a friend's voice in a crowded room. We use a third style of listening, **comprehensive listening,** when we want to understand. When we listen to directions or instructions, we are using this style.

The fourth learning style is more complex. **Therapeutic listening,** the style practiced by counselors, psychiatrists, and good friends, encourages people to talk freely without fear of embarrassment. Friends

A therapeutic listener accepts, tries to understand, and does not judge what a troubled friend says.

act as our sounding boards when we just want someone to listen. "If I can listen to what he tells me," wrote Dr. Carl Rogers, a well-known psychologist, "if I can understand how it seems to him, then I will be releasing potent forces of change within him." The therapeutic listener in conversation with a troubled friend accepts what is said, tries hard to understand, and above all, makes no judgments.

The fifth style, **critical listening,** is the one we will examine most closely. Critical listeners are the most active of all listeners because they are working hard to decide whether what someone else says makes sense. Critical listeners evaluate what they hear and decide if another person's message is logical, worthwhile, or has value. We need to be critical listeners when someone wants us to buy something, vote a certain way, or support a particular idea. We also need to be critical listeners in school, where *listening* and *thinking* are almost synonymous.

A critical thinker evaluates the logic and merit of what someone else says.

Why Listening Matters

The good listener is popular everywhere. You will make more friends by listening than by speaking. And after awhile, good listeners actually get to know something. Fortunately, active listening is both an attitude we can learn and a set of techniques we can master with practice.

The benefits of good listening are plentiful, and they go beyond just acquiring information. Good listeners encourage speakers to do their best. Good listeners also enhance their own ability to speak by improving their concentration. Best of all, they learn to think better. Listening is, in the final analysis, a thinking skill. It requires us to be selective with our attention, to classify and categorize information, and to sort out important concepts from a stream of facts, jokes, and stories.

Good listening skills are especially important in a society that grants freedom of speech to all people, whatever their views or causes. Listening will rarely get you in trouble. "Silent Cal" Coolidge, perhaps our quietest president, once said, "Nobody ever listened himself out of a job." In the remainder of this chapter, we will focus on how to get rid of bad listening habits and how to acquire some good ones.

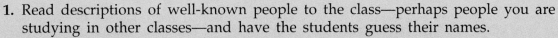

TAKING CHARGE

1. Read descriptions of well-known people to the class—perhaps people you are studying in other classes—and have the students guess their names.
2. Record a portion of a radio talk show or call-in program. Play back what you have recorded several times so that you know it well, and make a list of specific questions about the information presented. Then play the segment for your classmates and ask your list of questions to check for comprehension. Next ask them what feelings they remember being expressed in the segment. Have they listened better for facts or feelings?
3. Stage a class discussion on some controversial topic to test everyone's listening skills. Each speaker must restate the previous speaker's point (to that speaker's satisfaction) before giving his or her own.

II Roadblocks to Good Listening

Even Shakespeare, whose words have been heard by millions all over the globe, regretted poor listening: "It is the disease of not listening, the malady of not marking, that I am troubled withal." Part of the reason listening is difficult is that we spend so little time working on it. Most of the communication instruction we get in school is geared toward reading, despite the fact that we listen about three times as much as we read. Consciously, we seem to pay more attention to what reaches our eyes than to what reaches our ears.

A Small Price to Pay

One reason we may not be good listeners is that it costs us something. To really listen we must *pay* attention. Small wonder that we use the word *pay*, which im-

plies exchanging one thing for another. In listening, we pay out our most personal assets—our awareness, interest, and effort—to receive something in return: information, understanding, and entertainment. Listening is hard work, which is why we do not give our attention easily.

But while we are paying attention, we must also exercise judgment; as listeners, we are especially susceptible to being hoodwinked. The spoken word (probably because the speaker is physically present) affects us much more powerfully than the written word. Researchers say that many of our most deeply held convictions come from things we hear, and not from things we read. A committee of the National Council on the Teaching of English concluded that students' "political ideals and ethical standards are influenced, if not largely determined, by their listening." Unfortunately, however, professional persuaders such as politicians, advertisers, and con artists of every kind know this

COMMUNICATION WORKS

Dr. J. Boman Bastani, Psychiatrist

Dr. J. Boman Bastani is a professional listener. As a psychiatrist, he has helped thousands of patients deal with mental illnesses.

"Sometimes it isn't easy to listen to patients," he says. "You have to want to listen to them; you have to have compassion."

Bastani said that he became interested in psychiatry while he was a hospital intern.

"Many mental illnesses used to be mistaken for a physical condition. I once saw a schizophrenic in the hospital, and his condition was mistaken for something else. It made me see that these people need to be diagnosed and helped in a new way."

By listening to people, Bastani is able to make a clinical evaluation. Occasionally, Bastani evaluates heart transplant candidates. In many cases, he has to make the final decision about who will get a new heart and who will not. Not all of Bastani's cases are that stressful, but many carry great responsibility. For example, he is frequently asked to judge whether someone is competent enough to stand trial.

Most of Bastani's clients just need someone to help them through tough times. He counsels families that have difficulties getting along, couples that are splitting up, and teens who have been considering suicide. These people have one thing in common: They need someone to listen.

"I can't make them do things," Bastani explains. "They have to want to do it for themselves. But I can listen."

---

too. They have learned that people are most *vulnerable* when they are listening. Good listeners must remember that while they should be willing to listen to almost anything, they must never give up their right to think for themselves.

Why Is Listening Difficult?

Among the biggest hurdles to good listening is the very human desire to speak. Why aren't we better listeners? Because most of the time when someone is speaking to us, we're thinking of what we want to say next, not listening at all. We prefer speaking to listening. Good listeners must learn to let go of their egos. Train yourself not to worry about what you want to say until the other person has finished talking.

Our very busy lives (and MTV) have also caused us to develop extremely short attention spans. "We have time to hear," says William Fadie, chairman of the speech department at California State University at Northridge, "but not to listen." Our short attention spans and impatience sometimes lead us to try to guess

COMMUNICATION BREAKDOWN

The College Lecture

College students may look like they're listening to the day's lecture, but their minds may be elsewhere, says Paul Cameron, an assistant professor of psychology at Wayne State University. To prove his point, Cameron fired a gun from time to time during a lecture and then asked students what they were thinking when they heard the shot. He found that:

◆ About 20 percent of the students were thinking about someone of the opposite sex.

◆ Another 20 percent were thinking of a memory.

◆ Only 20 percent were actually paying attention to the lecturer (just 12 percent described themselves as active listeners).

◆ Of the rest, some were worrying, some daydreaming, some thinking about lunch, and 8 percent were thinking about religion.

Cameron obtained these results in a nine-week course in introductory psychology for eighty-five college sophomores. The gun was fired twenty-one times at random intervals, usually when Cameron, who was himself the lecturer, was in the middle of a sentence. We would guess no one speaks out of turn in his class!

Questions
1. How well do you listen to classroom instructions or lectures?
2. What other things do you think about while you're listening?
3. What could you do to help focus your listening skills during class time?

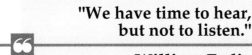

"We have time to hear, but not to listen."

William Fadie

what we think someone will say next. This is a poor habit—first, because guessing ahead will distract you from what the person really says, and second, because you're likely to shape what you do hear to fit what you expect. You will only hear, in other words, what you want to hear.

Bad Habits Make for Bad Company

During the Middle Ages, people worried about committing the seven deadly sins—gluttony, anger, greed, lechery, envy, avarice, and sloth. Today we should worry about falling into the seven deadly habits of bad listening. Any one of them will keep you from becoming an effective listener.

1. *Tuning out dull topics.* Many listeners decide early on that a topic is simply not interesting. This decision rapidly leads to the MEGO syndrome ("My Eyes Glaze Over"). The writer G. K. Chesterton once said that there is no such thing as an uninteresting subject; there are only uninterested people.

   Don't let yourself become a lazy listener. If what you are listening to doesn't seem immediately appealing, listen for something you want or need—an idea, a quote, a story, or even a joke. An energetic listener can nearly always find something of value in what another person is saying.

2. *Faking attention.* It's no sin to be courteous, but sometimes we take good manners to an unfortunate extreme. When we find someone's conversation boring but are too polite (or too afraid) to risk offending the person, we pretend to pay attention, though all the while our minds are a thousand miles away. Don't assume that all a speaker really wants from us is that we *look* like we're listening.

   The listener who is faking attention usually looks as if he were made of cement. When the speaker finishes, the faker awakes with a jerk of the head and a dazed look. Meanwhile, good listeners lean forward with interest, maintain good eye contact, and react in a natural way with smiles, nods, or questioning looks.

To help yourself stay on track, create a mental *paraphrase* of what the speaker is saying—that is, translate the speaker's thoughts into your own words. And repeat key points to yourself periodically throughout the conversation. Both steps will help you maintain an attitude of genuine interest.

3. *Yielding to distractions. Peripheral* noises or movements often affect our concentration. A window drops shut, someone sneezes, a book falls to the floor. All too often, we give our attention to the hubbub of activity around us instead of the speaker in front of us. How often have you let your parents' words fall on deaf ears while you were busy watching television?

   If possible, choose a suitable environment for your communication—someplace relatively free of noise and commotion (it's easy to pull someone aside, even at school, for a relatively private conversation). But if that's not possible, do what you can to change the environment—shut the door, close the window, or ask your neighbors to quiet down.

4. *Criticizing delivery or physical appearance.* Many people abandon their good listening habits when they become overly critical of the speaker's physical appearance or delivery. Regardless of who the speaker is, the content of his message is always far more important than the form of his delivery. Don't use poor physical appearance or speaking style as an alibi for not listen-

1. **Tune out dull topics.**
2. **Fake attention.**
3. **Yield to distractions.**
4. **Criticize delivery or physical appearance.**
5. **Jump to conclusions.**
6. **Overreact to emotional words.**
7. **Interrupt.**

ing. Don't let yourself be put off by someone's manner, accent, or clothing. Be generous enough to overlook lisps, slurs, and mumbles.

You can't expect the speaker always to be coherent. Listen for patterns or key words. Try to find an underlying structure in what the person is saying to help you sort out the important ideas from the details. The fact that a speech is unorganized doesn't mean that it isn't worth something. There may be valuable ideas lurking in the muddle, but you will just have to work that much harder to find them.

5. *Jumping to conclusions.* Be patient. Even if you think you know what the other person is going to say,

---

INSTANT IMPACT

Gender Talk

Do you get irritated when people interrupt? Or are you the one doing most of the interrupting? Studies show that there may be significant differences between the sexes when it comes to stopping a speaker in mid-sentence. Studies show that when a man and a woman are talking, the man makes about 96 percent of the interruptions. But when men talk to men and women talk to women, the number of interruptions are about the same.

Men appear to have a few other gender-specific habits regarding speech. They usually listen to what is being said for about the first ten or fifteen seconds and then begin to think about what they can add to the conversation. Some researchers say that men have been taught since childhood to become problem solvers. As a result, men tend to enter a conversation too quickly. They fail to draw out the speaker with questions or to listen for more information before jumping to a conclusion.

Deborah Tannen, author of a popular book on conversational styles called *You Just Don't Understand,* argues that most women use *"rapport* talk" as a way of establishing relationships. From childhood, she writes, women tend to listen for things they have in common with others. Men, on the other hand, use "report talk" to preserve their independence and maintain status. From childhood, men learn to use talking as a way to get and keep attention. Consequently, they have a harder time learning to be good listeners.

For more information, see Deborah Tannen, You Just Don't Understand, *William Morrow and Co. (New York): 1990.*

restrain yourself. Many listeners are quick to judge before they have carefully heard and understood what is meant. Be sure you understand before you criticize.

Occasionally, personal *biases* against a speaker's background or position ("Does this old man really know anything about a song by Sonic Youth?") interfere with listening. Such biases may cause a listener to ask too many questions, interrupt too often, or try to pick an argument. Again, withhold judgment until you're sure you know the speaker's position.

6. *Overreacting to emotional words.* We all react from time to time to certain words or phrases that push our "hot buttons." If a speaker says, for example, "grade point average," "overdue report," or "parent conference," you might experience a strong emotional reaction, one that blocks out your ability to listen. In such cases, you need to make an extra effort to resist making judgments until the speech is over. Your memory of key facts or arguments may be wiped out by the first rush of hot blood.

Our emotions have a lot to do with our ability to listen. At times, they act as filters to screen out things we don't want to hear. If we hear something that threatens our deepest feelings or convictions, our brains become overstimulated and our ears go temporarily deaf. Instead of listening, we lay plans to trap the speaker or try to think of a question that will embarrass her. Perhaps we simply turn to thoughts that support our own feelings and tune the speaker out. In any event, listening comes to a screeching halt.

When you feel your emotional barriers begin to rise, stay calm. Wait until the talker has finished. Then, and only then, review the speaker's main ideas and make up your mind how to respond.

7. *Interrupting.* "The reason why so few people are agreeable in conversation," wrote the French philosopher La Rochefoucauld, "is that each is thinking more about what he intends to say than about what others are saying, and we never listen when we are eager to speak." Try to find out if you spend most of your listening time thinking about what you want to say. Interrupting someone is an almost certain sign that you don't know or care about what the other person is saying. Check yourself to see if you interrupt people often or try to change the subject frequently. We all risk becoming first-class bores when we interrupt.

TAKING CHARGE

1. Send six students out of the room (we'll call them students A through F). Read a short story to the remaining class members. Call student A back into the room. Ask A to listen carefully as a classmate repeats the story. Then ask Student A to relay the story to Student B as that student enters the room. Following the same procedure, B tells C, C tells D, and so on. Student F finishes the relay by reporting back to the class. After the exercise is complete, reread the original story. How has it changed from student to student? What caused these changes?

2. Try an experiment with distractions. Arrange with your teacher to have several distractions occur sometime during a class presentation—have a student deliver a pass from the office, "plant" a student who will drop a book, or the like. Ask another student to monitor what happens to the class's attention during each distraction. Discuss how these distractions affected students' attentiveness.

3. Ask several students to prepare short talks. Tell them that they may have to speak under very difficult circumstances but that they should continue no matter what happens. Ask the speakers to leave the room and then instruct the class to listen very carefully to what each speaker says until a secret signal is given. At that point the students are to stop paying attention, perhaps by reading books or looking out the window. Call the student speakers back into the room, one at a time, and ask them to give their talks. When they are finished, ask the speakers to discuss how they felt when the class withdrew its attention and what changes they made in their speech as a result.

III Effective Listening Strategies

You can learn to be a good listener. Studies have shown that a little bit of knowledge and a lot of practice can lead to improved listening. To practice well, however, takes the right attitude—the attitude that you will provide the energy and make the effort to become a better listener. To do so, you must stay alert on several fronts at once, working with ears, eyes, and your whole being. Total body listening means, for starters, adopting the right posture for listening: Face the speaker and establish eye contact. Lean forward and nod occasionally. And that's just the beginning. Good listening requires all of our senses and plenty of mental energy.

Knowing When to Listen

Just as there are times to bear down and times to ease up, you should listen more carefully at some times than others. Your attention may lag in driver's education class, for example, as the teacher explains a formula for converting the safe following distance from seconds to feet. When it comes time for your driver's license exam, though, you will summon your most intense concentration.

Listening to speeches works the same way. Knowing how speeches are usually organized, for example, can make us smarter listeners. Then we will be sure to listen most intently when it matters the most. The following discussion illustrates how to listen during each of the three major parts of a speech. (A thorough discussion of how to organize a speech appears in Chapter 8.)

The Beginning

Many people with good intentions try to listen hardest at the beginning of a speech. Actually, this is not the time to be so eager. The beginning may be the most entertaining part of the speech—because the speaker is doing her utmost to gain your attention—but it is usually not the most important. Often, listeners get so caught up in the speaker's jokes, stories, and examples that they forget to be alert for the key idea.

Somewhere shortly after the beginning of a speech, the speaker will state the main idea of her talk. Once you find the main idea, your listening job becomes much easier. Now you will recognize the facts and details in the rest of the speech as they strengthen or reinforce the main idea. If you miss the main idea, these facts and details will send you spinning in all directions. You will keep asking yourself, "Now how does this connect to what was said before?"

Rather than hanging on every word as a speech begins, you should think about the title of the speech and make a few guess-

Good listeners can identify a speaker's main idea, evaluate its accuracy and soundness, and recognize if a speaker is trying to mislead them with rhetorical tricks.

es about what direction the speaker might take. Then, as a good listener, you can pounce on the main idea when it pops up.

The Middle

Be a critical listener during the body of the speech. Your main goal, of course, is to comprehend what the speaker has to say. But this is also the place to test the strength of the speaker's message. Question the support that the speaker uses to defend her assertions. How recent are the speaker's examples? How relevant are the speaker's quotes? What is the source for the speaker's statistics—or has she even given a source? In other words, this is the time to evaluate the accuracy and fairness of what you hear.

The End

During the last part of a speech, the listener must be on guard for emotional appeals and *propaganda*, material designed to distort the truth or deceive the audience. You can tell a speech is nearly over when the speaker repeats the main idea, summarizes her most important support, or says "in conclusion."

Speakers often end their speeches by trying to appeal to the listener's feelings. Your job as a listener is to recognize whether the speaker is misleading you. This is the time to be most alert for *rhetorical* tricks—that is, tricks of language. Such tricks might include **testimonials** ("You should agree with me because many famous celebrities do"), **false comparisons** (comparing unlike things—apples with oranges), or suggestions to **jump on the bandwagon** (everyone is aboard—don't be left out). As a speaker ends her speech, ask yourself whether she has earned whatever she is asking you to give.

Use Your Listening "Spare Time" to Advantage

Although most people speak at a rate of about 125 words per minute, we can listen intelligently to 400 words per minute. That means that we can listen much faster than we can talk. This fact is both a curse and a blessing for listeners.

At the rate a speaker normally talks, you can sandwich many thoughts between his words and still not miss a thing. In other words, most of us find ourselves with a little **listening spare time** on our hands. Stray thoughts may take you away from the speaker briefly, but they don't keep you from grasping his meaning. So you continue jumping back and forth mentally, tuning out and tuning in as you think some of your own thoughts and then turn back to the speaker.

These private *excursions* away from the speaker and into your own thoughts can, however, be dangerous. Let's imagine that you have an especially inviting thought of your own. You follow that thought for a while, longer than you intended, and then suddenly remember the speaker. "Whoops! What was that he just said?"

Unfortunately, you discover you've stayed away too long and missed a critical part of the message. The *disintegration* of your listening has begun. Eventually you give up; it's simply too hard to catch up. You nod your head occasionally for the sake of courtesy, but this is not listening. You've switched over to cruise control.

Fortunately, this extra time can also be a listener's best friend. We can train ourselves to use it to improve our listening skills. Think of yourself as the rabbit in the old story of the tortoise and the hare. The tortoise represents the speaker, who moves down the path at a steady pace. The hare represents you, the listener, who can dash ahead, stop awhile, fall behind, and then catch up again. Listeners can capitalize on their thought-speed to make the most of their listening opportunities.

We can take advantage of our listening spare time in a variety of ways, but the four mental activities described below are probably the most promising.

Explore

One way to use your spare listening time is to anticipate what the speaker will say next. Explore what lies ahead in the speech by asking, "What is this person trying to get at? What does she want me to believe?"

This is a guessing game that pays off, whether your guesses are right or wrong. If you guess correctly, your understanding and *retention* will be strengthened. In effect, you hear the same point twice. If you guess wrong, you instinctively start comparing the point you expected with the one the speaker actually made. You will be more likely to understand the point than if you had never tried to think ahead in the first place.

Analyze

Another way to spend your listening spare time is to analyze the speaker's message. As the speaker makes arguments and defends assertions, ask yourself, "Are these reasons, examples, and facts convincing? Are things exactly as he says they are? Is he leaving anything out?"

Many clever speakers may try to mislead you with deceptive reasoning. They may **stack the deck** against a particular person or idea by giving only one side of the story. They may use **name calling** (giving someone a negative label without any evidence) or many other unbalanced arguments to convince you. But a good listener is a hard sell.

Review

Every so often, you should review what you have heard. Speakers usually allow time for listeners to catch their breath. They may pause, for example, to make a transition: "Now let me talk about . . . " These moments give you a perfect opportunity to review. Mentally run over the points already made, stopping a split second to examine each.

Reviewing helps you understand and remember. Tell yourself that you will have to give a report on this speech sometime, and begin preparing your report while the speech is still going. Planning to share what you have heard with others is a great way to motivate yourself to repeat and rephrase important parts of a speech.

Search for Hidden Meanings

Throughout a speech, you should "listen between the lines" in search of **hidden meanings**. Does the speaker avoid something you think is important? Are there failures or shortcomings the speaker should admit but doesn't? Does the speaker's silence on something indicate it might be a sore point?

A speaker's body language and nonverbal behavior can offer big clues to what she is really thinking. (We will take a close look at body language in Chapter 4.) Often what a person doesn't

INSTANT IMPACT

The Silent Listener

When President Calvin Coolidge was in the White House, he once had a visitor from his home state of Massachusetts. The visitor, Channing Cox, had succeeded Coolidge as governor there and had come to ask Coolidge a question about the business of government. Cox asked Coolidge how he had been able to see so many visitors each day as governor.

"I've heard you always left the office at 5 P.M.," Cox said. "I never leave that early, and often I'm there 'til 9. Why the difference?"

Coolidge thought for a moment and then replied in his usual abrupt manner: "You talk back."

say may be as important as what she does say.

Here is a handy *acronym* that might help you remember these suggestions. Think EARS:

E for explore. Think ahead of the speaker.

A for analyze. Consider carefully what's being said; look at it from several angles.

R for review. Take advantage of your spare listening time to retrace the speaker's steps.

S for search. Be alert for hidden meanings.

TAKING CHARGE

1. Examine magazine ads for examples of propaganda. Look especially for testimonials, false comparisons, deck stacking, and name calling. Which techniques seem to be used most often? Can you find examples of the same techniques in political speeches?
2. Obtain several recorded speeches and play them for the class. Ask your classmates to "listen between the lines" for hidden meanings.
3. Why is the spoken word more persuasive than the written word? Consider the example of Adolf Hitler and other tyrants, as well as positive leaders like Abraham Lincoln and Franklin Roosevelt. Discuss what kinds of leaders are most effective in person.

IV The Contributions Listeners Make

The process of listening involves paying attention, organizing what you hear, and remembering for both the short term and the long term. What we forget, though, is that listeners do more than simply absorb information. They add a vital element to communication: feedback. By listening responsively, you tell the speaker how to behave—whether to continue or back up, speed up or slow down, repeat, explain, or stop. How you show the speaker what you think is one of your most important listening responsibilities.

Providing Encouragement

Sometimes speakers need encouragement to keep going. While silence may be soothing at times among close friends, most speakers interpret it as a sign of boredom. You may intend your silence to be respectful, but a good listener does more than just be still. A good listener is actively involved in what is going on and has contributions to make, sometimes out loud.

We all add a few "uh-huhs" to our conversations. These brief interruptions, called "eloquent and encouraging grunts" by one researcher, are especially important in telephone conversations, where they let the speaker know that you're still on the line; but they work in face-to-face conversations and small group discussions too. They tell the speaker that you're there and still listening.

Short phrases like "Oh?" "How's that?" and "I see" do a little bit more. These so-

A good listener will do the following:

☑ 1. Provide encouragement.
☑ 2. Ask for explanations.
☑ 3. Paraphase the message.
☑ 4. Summarize the message.
☑ 5. Put it down on paper.

called **door openers** are invitations. They indicate to the speaker more acceptance, interest, and understanding than mere silence. Other door openers include "Go on," "Tell me more," "Explain that," and "Really?" Be advised, however, that some phrases can reveal that you're only faking it. If you say, "That's interesting" without any sincerity, the speaker may suspect that you're only trying to be polite.

Asking for Explanations

In many listening situations, you will have an opportunity to ask questions. When you ask a question, you help the speaker make his message more understandable. To get additional information, you might say something like "Would you please *clarify* that?" Other clarifying questions or comments include:

◆ Would you say that again?
◆ I don't understand what you mean.
◆ Excuse me, but could you be more specific?

People are usually delighted to help with a problem, but if you suggest that

COMMUNICATION BREAKTHROUGH

Silence Can Be Golden

In "The Sounds of Silence," one of Paul Simon's most memorable songs, we find people whose conversation has become empty and meaningless:

And in the naked light I saw
Ten thousand people, maybe more.
People talking without speaking,
People hearing without listening,
People writing songs that voices never
  share.

Silence has often been used as a metaphor for the lack of communication. You may give someone the "silent treatment," for example, to tell him or her you have no intention of talking. We honor the memory of someone who has recently died by a moment of silence—in a sense because we can no longer communicate with that person. But silence has an important positive role to play in communication.

Silence is obviously vital when we listen to others, but it also gives us a chance to listen to our own thoughts. Certain religious groups, notably the Quakers, use periods of silence to enhance their spiritual lives. Quakers worship by gathering together in silence. During the long stillness, they patiently wait to hear an inner voice. Anyone who feels he or she has gained a new spiritual insight during the silence can then speak to the group.

Silence, as we have seen in passive listening, also has its drawbacks. Silence robs us of human fellowship if we withdraw from communication because of fear or timidity. It robs us if we sit silently at a meeting when sharing our ideas might help. It robs us when our own nervousness prevents us from talking to friends or making new acquaintances.

Question
Do we need more silence in our lives? Why or why not?

---

they need help, they might get angry. When you are confused, be sure to say something like "Maybe I misunderstood," and not "You aren't being very clear."

Too often we hesitate to ask a question because we're afraid we may look foolish or ask something that everyone else already knows. The truth is that most speakers welcome questions. Questions are a sign of interest, and they also give the speaker valuable clues on whether the message is coming through. Many speakers encourage listeners to talk by saying that "there's no such thing as a dumb question." Make your question a sincere one and fire away.

Paraphrasing the Message

You can also help the speaker by trying to paraphrase her message or repeat in your own words what you think you heard. In this sense, paraphrasing goes a step beyond just asking for an explanation. When we are unclear about what the speaker is saying, we ask a question.

When we think we understand but want to double-check, we should try a paraphrase.

Paraphrases often begin like this:

✦ What I hear you saying is . . .
✦ Correct me if I am wrong, but . . .
✦ In other words, your view is . . .

Summarizing the Message

You can go one more step by summarizing what you see as the main idea in a speech or conversation. When you summarize something, you condense the important points into a brief comment. Some typical summary statements might begin this way:

✦ What you have said so far is . . .
✦ Your key ideas, as I understand it, are . . .
✦ Recapping what you have been saying . . .

Summaries are especially useful with speakers who are long-winded or confusing. Summaries are also valuable when you face a conflict or a complaint. By accurately repeating to other people what you hear them saying, you can show that you understand their position, even if you don't agree with it.

Putting It Down on Paper

The final contribution we can make as listeners is to report back to others on what we have heard. That usually means taking notes—one of the world's best ways to jog the memory. Luckily, just making the effort to take notes almost always improves our listening. Students who take notes understand more and remember more. Taking notes automatically improves our attentiveness. "It helps you focus on the highlights of what is being said," notes Germaine Knapp, a communications consultant.

Taking notes improves attentiveness. Students who take notes understand and remember more.

Note taking also increases the chance that you will review what has been said during the speech. From time to time, a good note taker looks back on his notes to see if they are complete. Such review is crucial to good listening. And, surprisingly, note taking often helps the speaker. Speakers feel flattered when people write down things they say. They usually try to be as accurate as possible if they know someone is keeping track.

TAKING CHARGE

1. The next time you're in a conversation, try an experiment. Discipline yourself not to respond while your partner is speaking. Don't nod, smile, say "uh-huh," or react in any way to anything that is said. Does your partner become irritated or frustrated with you? Ask your partner whether your behavior seemed unusual.

2. Read a short speech aloud to the class. At a point perhaps three-quarters of the way through the speech, stop talking. Ask your classmates to write a short summary of what they have heard and a brief statement of what they expect to hear in the remainder of the speech. When they have finished, read the rest of the speech. Ask the students to check how well they did at predicting what the rest of the speech would be about.

REVIEW AND ENRICHMENT

LOOKING BACK

Listed below are the major ideas discussed in this chapter.

◆ Hearing is an automatic reaction of the senses and nervous system to sound. Listening, on the other hand, is a voluntary act that involves a search for meaning.

◆ Students usually spend about 60 percent of their school day listening.

◆ Poor listening costs us millions of dollars in lost business, mismanaged time, and sheer waste.

◆ Success in listening depends on choosing the right listening style for the situation. Use therapeutic listening, for instance, to help a friend.

◆ The seven deadly habits of poor listening include tuning out dull topics, faking attention, yielding to distractions, criticizing a speaker's delivery or appearance, jumping to conclusions, overreacting to emotional words, and interrupting.

◆ Strong emotions can sometimes prevent us from being good listeners.

◆ Knowledge of how a typical speech is organized can be very helpful to listeners because different sections of a speech call for different kinds of listening.

◆ Because we can listen faster than anyone can speak, we have some "spare time" to use to our advantage. We can use this time to explore, analyze, review, and search for hidden meanings.

◆ Listeners help guide a speaker by supplying encouragement (nods, smiles, and "uh-huhs") or responses that clarify, paraphrase, or summarize.

◆ Note taking can help improve our listening habits.

SPEECH VOCABULARY

Fill in each blank with the correct term from the list below.

passive listening
appreciative listening
therapeutic listening
listening spare time
door opener
jump on the bandwagon
active listening
discriminative listening
critical listening

noise
testimonials
stack the deck
hearing
comprehensive listening
hidden meanings
false comparisons
name calling

REVIEW AND ENRICHMENT
Continued

1. We use _____ when we listen to someone relate her problems, hopes, or dreams, especially when the person doesn't want our approval or advice.
2. A good listener "listens between the lines" by searching for _____.
3. When we recognize sounds, we are _____. If we pay only a little attention to those sounds, we are _____. But if we try energetically to make sense of those sounds, we are _____.
4. If you buy a music album to enjoy, you use _____; but if you intend to write a review of the album for the school newspaper, you use _____.
5. _____ is the kind of listening that will improve your grades, while _____ is the kind of listening that will recognize a friend's voice across a crowded room.
6. We can use our _____ to explore, analyze, and review a speaker's message.
7. Despite the _____ that might distract us from listening to a speaker, we can use a _____ to tell the speaker we want to hear more.
8. Some of the propaganda techniques professional persuaders use are _____ (using the name of a celebrity), _____ (holding up one candidate against a much older one), _____ ("Don't be left out!"), _____ (presenting only favorable evidence), and _____ (mudslinging).

GENERAL VOCABULARY

Use each of the following words in a sentence that helps explain its meaning.

vulnerable
paraphrase
peripheral
biases
rapport
propaganda

rhetorical
excursions
disintegration
retention
acronym
clarify

THINGS TO REMEMBER

1. What is the difference between hearing and listening?
2. What are the five basic listening styles?
3. What are three reasons why listening is difficult?
4. Name the seven deadly habits of bad listening.

5. What should your listening strategy be when you feel strongly moved by what a speaker says?
6. Describe some of the differences between the conversational styles of men and women.
7. What does a good listener look like? In other words, what is the right posture and bearing for a person who wants to listen well?
8. At what point in a formal speech is it important to listen most intently?
9. Of what value are the simple nods and "uh-huhs" that listeners give speakers?
10. When are the best times to review what a speaker has said?

THINGS TO DO

1. To find out how well you listen, try this simple exercise. The next time someone begins a conversation, ask yourself, "Am I really listening or am I just waiting my turn to talk?" Pay attention to your own mental processes. Are you:

   ◆ easily distracted?
   ◆ faking attention?
   ◆ interrupting frequently?
   ◆ daydreaming?
   ◆ jumping to conclusions?
   ◆ finding fault with the speaker?
   ◆ thinking of what you want to say?

   If your answer is yes to any of the items on this list, you have committed at least one of the seven deadly habits of bad listening. What remedies can you suggest?

2. Make a list of listening skills and habits, both good and bad. Then grade yourself on how well you listened during a recent conversation, discussion, or lecture.

3. After a student has given a speech to the class, ask the student to rate the class on its listening skills. What was the typical posture? How attentive were the listeners? What encouragement did they give? What questions did they ask?

THINGS TO TALK ABOUT

1. What role does listening play in our everyday lives?
2. There are certain people who seem naturally to command our attention. Researchers say we listen quite willingly to those who have status (celebrities, for example), those with seniority (parents and teachers, perhaps), those who can do something for us, and members of the opposite sex. Do you agree with this conclusion? Are there other categories of people to whom you pay special attention?
3. How well do we listen in different settings—for instance, at a family meal, in class, at a party, or on the job? Discuss the kinds of differences you notice in listening styles.

REVIEW AND ENRICHMENT
Continued

THINGS TO WRITE ABOUT

1. Compile a list of occupations where listening is vital. Examples might include psychologist, teacher, and minister. Interview someone in your community who works at one of these careers and write a report based on that person's definition of "professional" listening.
2. Examine what topics might cause you to "hear only what you want to hear." Examples might include an issue such as abortion or gun control. What ideas do you have about getting someone to listen to the other side of an issue?
3. Write about the teacher whose lectures you find easiest to understand. Explain what techniques that teacher uses to be successful.

CRITICAL THINKING

1. Poor listening is a failure that most people cheerfully admit. "I can sit and look at a person and never hear a word he says," we say with little or no embarrassment. Why is it that so many of us feel that poor listening is acceptable?
2. Consider the therapeutic role of listening. Why would nonjudgmental listening be so valuable? Why is it that we can sometimes share our feelings freely with a stranger (someone we sit next to on the bus, for instance) but have difficulty being open with close friends or family?
3. To what extent is the old saying "We only hear what we want to hear" accurate?

RELATED SPEECH TOPICS

Silence is (or is not) golden.
Poor listening habits can lead to major problems in business and many other areas of life.
If we spend 60 percent of every school day listening, why aren't we learning more?
We are vulnerable to professional persuaders such as politicians and advertisers because the spoken word is so much more persuasive than the written word.
"Dangling conversations" might describe most of our interactions because we like to talk more than we wish to listen.
Women are better listeners than men (or vice versa).
It's not what we say, but what we don't say that counts.

CHAPTER 4

Nonverbal Communication

> "Watch out for the man whose stomach doesn't move when he laughs."
>
> — Chinese proverb

LEARNING OBJECTIVES

After completing this chapter, you will be able to do the following.

♦ Distinguish between verbal and nonverbal communication.
♦ Explain how the same gesture can have different meanings in different cultures.
♦ Use body language to reinforce your verbal message.
♦ Recognize when someone is not telling the truth.
♦ Interpret nonverbal messages in a conversation.

CHAPTER OUTLINE

Following are the main sections in this chapter.

I Multicultural Messages
II Messages with Two Meanings
III Nonverbal Messages in Conversation

      Chapter Review

NEW SPEECH TERMS

In this chapter, you will learn the meanings of the speech terms listed below.

nonverbal message
body language
gestures
kinesics
personal space
intimate distance
personal distance
social distance
public distance
tone
conversations
timing
eye contact
completion points

GENERAL VOCABULARY

Expanding your general vocabulary will help you become a more effective communicator. Listed below are some words appearing in this chapter that you should make part of your everyday vocabulary.

sympathetic
diverse
anthropologists
comparative
intimacy
stoic
ambiguous
timbre
suppress

LOOKING AHEAD

We speak with our mouths, but we communicate with our entire bodies. In fact, experts say that at least half of all communication is nonverbal. To truly understand other people, then, you must learn how to read their body language as well as interpret their words. You must learn what their facial expressions, hand gestures, and other signals mean. Even people's body temperature can be revealing, as it shows in the color of their faces or the moisture in the palms of their hands. In this chapter, you will learn how to interpret body language, how body language varies from culture to culture, and how to use body language to make your own communication more effective and convincing.

1 Multicultural Messages

You can communicate even when you don't say a word. In 1990, a photographer for *National Geographic Magazine* lined up the members of the U.S. Supreme Court for their official photograph. Justice Sandra Day O'Connor found herself standing directly behind Justice Byron White. According to news reports, Justice O'Connor quietly formed a V with her fingers and held them just above White's head, making the old "rabbit ears" sign.

O'Connor was sending a **nonverbal message** to everyone who saw the picture—a message that said, "We don't take ourselves quite as seriously as it looks." Nonverbal messages play an enormous and often unappreciated role in all our communication.

"You see," said the fictional detective Sherlock Holmes to his somewhat dim-witted assistant Dr. Watson, "but you do not observe." What Holmes meant was that the best way to understand people was to watch them—to notice what they do as well as what they say. The psychologist Albert Mehrabian claims that talking is the least important way we communicate. What counts most, he says, are our nonverbal messages. These messages include the way we sit or stand, how we tilt our heads, our facial expressions, our gestures, and our tone of voice.

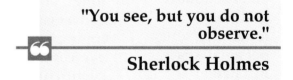

"You see, but you do not observe."

Sherlock Holmes

Understanding nonverbal communication is vital in many ways. It helps us understand, for example, how others react to us and to our ideas. If someone you are speaking to crosses his arms or legs, you may suspect that he feels threatened by what you are saying or disagrees with you. If your listener opens his hands toward you, you may expect agreement or at least a *sympathetic* ear.

People from different cultures often attach different meanings to familiar gestures. One example is the "Hook 'em Horns" sign, made famous by fans of the University of Texas football team. (To make the sign, hold your index and pinky fingers up). In Texas, it signifies support for the team, but beware. In Italy, this sign is an insult; in Brazil, it means good luck; and among Hindus, it means a cow. Being sensitive to the way different people interpret nonverbal messages can help you communicate more effectively wherever you are.

Knowing something about nonverbal communication can also be helpful when you give a speech. Your physical actions can either reinforce or contradict what you say. If you feel nervous about speaking to a group, for instance, you may

avoid looking at your listeners, lean on the podium, or drop your voice to a low mumble. With a little practice, however, you can master a different set of nonverbal habits—mannerisms that will convey confidence and authority. Eventually, by learning to look confident, you may begin to feel confident. In the remainder of this section, we will examine nonverbal customs around the world, paying particular attention to what people mean by how they walk, greet, and touch each other.

Body Language

Body language is remarkably *diverse*. Mario Pei, a communications expert, once estimated that humans produce up to 700,000 different physical signs. The face alone is capable of 250,000 different expressions. Other researchers have identified 5,000 separate hand gestures and 1,000 kinds of postures. Clearly, we send messages by a dizzying array of nonver-

Intense or complicated feelings often express themselves through body language.

bal means. These messages are fun to watch and challenging to interpret.

Body language, or the "silent language," is the way we use our bodies to send messages. A speaker for Toastmasters International once found an effective way to demonstrate to an audience how body language works. He asked his listeners to place their thumbs and forefingers together (as in the OK sign) and then told them to place their hands on their chins. But while he was saying this, he did something different—he placed his own thumb and forefinger on his cheek. Typically, 90 percent of his listeners followed his *actions*, not his words. Despite his instructions, they put their hands on their cheeks, too, just as the speaker did. "In business," notes Susan Bixler, president of Professional Image, "body language always wins out over verbal communication."

> ## "In business, body language always wins out over verbal communication."
>
> ### Susan Bixler

Sometimes you might say, "I am not sure how to express this in words," meaning that your feelings are more intense or more complicated than you can explain. Often, however, these feelings spill out in the form of body language. If a speaker is having difficulty controlling her anger, for example, she might raise her voice or turn away. "No mortal can keep a secret," noted Sigmund Freud. "If his lips are silent, he chatters with his fingertips." Even

though people can control their words and sometimes their facial expressions, there is often a "leakage" of feelings, perhaps in a gesture, a shift of position, or a tone of voice. Any one of these nonverbal signals may help you to interpret the messages you receive.

Try this quick quiz to see how well you can interpret nonverbal messages. Match the action in the left-hand column with the message in the right-hand column:

Action	Message
1. Slapping your forehead with the heel of your hand.	a. "I'm angry."
2. Wrinkling your forehead and frowning.	b. "I forgot something."
3. Tapping your fingers on a desk or table.	c. "I'm getting impatient."
4. Slamming a book down on a desk or table.	d. "I don't understand."
5. Wrinkling your nose.	e. "I don't like that."

For the record, the answers are 1, b; 2, d; 3, c; 4, a; 5, e.

While practiced everywhere, body language is not a universal language, as we have already seen. The familiar "thumbs up" gesture means "everything's OK" when used by a pilot or an astronaut. It has other meanings, however, in other places. North Americans recognize the thumbs up gesture as a sign that you are hitchhiking, but don't use it to get a ride in Nigeria—there, it's a rude insult. Beware, too, of counting with your fingers. When Americans count on their hands, they usually begin with their index finger, but a German starts with the thumb.

Thus, thumbs up in Germany might mean "Please bring me one knackwurst." In Japan, the thumb means five. A German in a Japanese restaurant could accidentally order food for five by holding up one thumb. Knowledge of these varying interpretations might some day save you from a stern look or even a broken nose.

Gestures around the World

If humans can produce 5,000 different **gestures**, why is it that we use some gestures over and over? Probably because they are the ones we need for everyday situations: when we greet each other, when we beckon to one another, and especially when we touch one another. Let's take a closer look at some of these gestures and also examine what similar gestures mean in different cultures.

Signs of Greeting

The most familiar form of greeting in the United States is the ordinary handshake. Some *anthropologists* believe the use of an outstretched hand as a form of greeting goes back far in history. Citizens of the Roman Empire greeted each other with a hand-and-forearm clasp, mainly to show that neither party was carrying a weapon. Some believe the hug or embrace (a form of greeting common in Mediterranean countries) had a similar purpose. The hug gave you physical assurance that no weapons were hiding beneath anyone's robe.

Worldwide, there are many other forms of greeting. In the Middle East, some citizens can still be seen giving the salaam. To give the salaam, you sweep your right hand upward, first touching the heart, then the forehead, and finally up and outward, perhaps with a slight nod of the head. At the same time you say *"salaam alaykum,"* meaning "peace be with you."

Eskimos greet by slapping their hands on each other's head or shoulders. Polynesian men welcome strangers by embracing them and then rubbing their backs. The Maori tribespeople in New Zealand rub noses, and some East Africans spit at each other's feet. Americans traveling to Tibet should especially be on their guard. People there are said to greet one another by sticking out their tongues.

Handshakes. Handshakes seem to come in three styles: gentle, firm, and Texan. Prince Charles of England, who travels widely and must be something of an expert on international greetings, has complained of the finger-crunching grip of Americans, "especially Texans." To make a good impression, your best bet is the firm handshake. Extend your hand and interlock it comfortably with the other person's (that's what the J-shaped curve between your thumb and forefinger is for). Don't pump your arm up and down—just apply even pressure with your whole hand before release.

The French seem to be the "handshakingest" people of all. Peter Mayle, in his book *A Year in Provence*, explains that if a Frenchman's hands are full when he meets another man, he will extend his little finger to shake. If his hands are wet or dirty, he will offer a forearm or elbow. Maybe the French are onto something: Psychologists regard the handshake as one of the most powerful ways of indicating trust or acceptance. The French, however, don't stop with handshakes. Close friendships usually require much warmer greet-

The handshake is regarded by psychologists as one of the most powerful ways of showing trust or acceptance. England's well-traveled Prince Charles, pictured here in Kuwait, is something of an expert on handshakes and other international greetings.

ings. Men kiss, squeeze each other's shoulders, slap backs, punch kidneys, and pinch cheeks. When men greet women or women greet other women, a kiss on each cheek is expected.

Bows. The most polite greeting of all is the bow. In many Asian countries—especially Japan, where style and courteousness are highly valued—a bow from the waist is the preferred way to greet someone. A bow indicates respect and often reflects social status.

Who bows first? In Japanese society, rank is very important. In business, for example, a middle-level manager in a large company outranks a department head from a small company. Therefore, the person of lower rank (in this case, the department head) bows first and lowest. Normally, American travelers are not expected to make a full bow to their Japanese companions, but they might

make a slight bow to indicate that they respect Japanese customs.

You may not be able to learn several foreign languages, but you can master the most important nonverbal signals of other cultures. Since greetings are such an important part of making a good impression, it seems especially important to know how to meet someone from a foreign country. Even being culturally sensitive, however, won't keep you from comical situations. Many Japanese people, especially those who travel abroad, have adopted Western ways. As a result, you may find yourself bowing in a Japanese person's direction just as he reaches out to shake your hand. When cultures collide, we often meet each other somewhere in the middle.

Touching Customs

We live in a world of extremes—some cultures enjoy lots of body contact; others avoid it completely. One psychologist measured this desire to touch by watching how couples behave in busy downtown coffee shops. He found that couples in San Juan, Puerto Rico, touched each other about 180 times per hour, while couples in Paris touched about 110 times per hour. The *comparative* numbers for the United States and Northern Europe were dramatically different. Couples in Gainesville, Florida, for example, touched each other just twice an hour, and couples in London never touched at all.

Here is a rough comparison of how countries around the globe feel about touching:

Enjoy touching	Middle ground	Don't touch
Middle Eastern countries	France	Japan
Latin countries	China	United States
Italy & Greece	Ireland	& Canada
Russia	India	England
		Australia

In a moment of grief, someone's touch can provide comfort and consolation.

Touching is the language of physical *intimacy*. And because it is, the power of touch can be truly remarkable. In May 1985, Brigitte Gerney was trapped for six hours beneath the wreckage of a collapsed construction crane in New York City. Throughout her ordeal, she held the hand of a rescue worker, who stayed by her side as heavy machinery removed the tons of twisted steel from her crushed legs. A stranger's touch gave her hope and the will to live.

Touch appears to affect the sexes differently. Women sometimes react much more favorably to touch than men. In an interesting study, psychologists asked a group of nurses to lightly touch a patient once or twice shortly before the patient underwent surgery. The touching produced a strongly positive reaction—but only among women. It appeared to lower their blood pressure and anxiety levels both before and after surgery. For men, however, the touching proved to be very upsetting. Their blood pressure and anxiety levels both rose. The psychologists suspect that because men are taught to be more *stoic* and to ignore their fears, the touching rattled them by reminding them that life is fragile.

How do you feel about touching and being touched? Salespeople *think* they

| COMMUNICATION | | BREAKTHROUGH |

The Ultimate Gesture

If you feel bewildered by the seemingly infinite number of gestures used around the world, perhaps you would do well to remember the "ultimate gesture." Researchers call it that because it carries more positive characteristics than any other single gesture.

First, this "ultimate gesture" is known everywhere in the world. It is absolutely universal.

Second, it is rarely, if ever, misunderstood. Primitive tribes and world leaders alike know this gesture. They—like you, no doubt—recognize it in others and use it themselves.

Third, scientists believe this particular gesture releases chemicals called endorphins into your system, creating a feeling of mild euphoria.

Fourth, as you travel around the world, this gesture may help you slip out of the prickliest of situations.

What is this singular signal, this miracle, this giant of all gestures? It is quite simply, the smile.

Adapted from Roger E. Axtell, Gestures: The Do's and Taboos of Body Language around the World.

Questions
What other universal gestures or expressions can you suggest?

know—research shows that it is harder to say no to someone who touches you when making a request—but not everyone is happy about being touched by a stranger. Think about your own comfort level when you find yourself in a crowd. Are you relaxed and loose, or does physical contact make you feel awkward and tense?

In some situations, we can't help touching each other. Take a crowded elevator, for instance. Normally, people stand shoulder-to-shoulder and arm-to-arm, accepting such close contact without complaint. The rule seems to be "Touch only from shoulder to elbow, but nowhere else." Even though the Japanese are regarded as a nontouching society, their crowded cities force them to be jammed into subways and trains. Edward T. Hall, an anthropolo-

gist, says the Japanese handle their uneasiness about being packed into public places by avoiding eye contact and drawing within themselves emotionally, thus "touching without feeling."

Touching customs that vary from culture to culture can have unfortunate consequences. Korean merchants in New York have been successful in opening a wide variety of retail shops, but they sometimes give their customers a feeling of coldness. When a customer makes a purchase and receives change, the Korean merchants place the money on the counter to avoid any physical contact. "They won't touch my hand," one customer complained. "They won't even place coins in my hand. It's somewhat cold and insulting. And furthermore, they won't look me in the eyes."

One Korean merchant explained that in his homeland, people are taught to avoid all physical contact with strangers, especially direct eye contact. "We are taught that either gesture could have sexual connotations," he added, "so we carefully avoid them."

The Swedish actress Liv Ullmann once learned that touching is not always welcome. When she toured a famine-stricken area in Bangladesh on behalf of UNICEF, she had an especially warm visit with a woman about her own age. After the conversation was over, Ullmann gave the woman a hug, but she felt her suddenly pull away. Through her interpreter, Ullmann asked why. "In my country," the woman said, "we kiss feet when we say good-bye." Ullmann didn't hesitate—she bent down and kissed the woman's feet. Then they hugged, each woman thus exchanging the ritual of her own world.

Walking Motions

Our every movement is expressive. A scientist who was studying classroom discussions noticed that he could tell whether students agree or disagree with the teacher simply by watching their posture. For example, a student who disagrees might turn sideways in his seat as the teacher talks. A student who agrees might hold a hand under her chin and look right at the teacher. Unlike facial expressions, which can be *ambiguous* (since you can learn to disguise your true feelings through false smiles), body movements are nearly always honest. **Kinesics** is the science of body movements. None of us can exert complete control over every muscle. More often than not, your body movements reveal your true feelings.

INSTANT IMPACT

Riding an Elevator

One of the best places to observe the silent set of body language rules that we all follow is an elevator. Despite its small size, we seem to space ourselves as far from one another as possible.

If there are only two people on an elevator, for instance, they usually lean against the walls. If four people board the elevator, each heads for one of the corners.

When the total reaches five or six people, more complex rules of elevator etiquette come into play. Like dancers in a choreographed musical, they all turn to face the door. "They get taller and thinner," says a psychologist, Layne Longfellow, or at least they try to.

"Hands and purses and briefcases hang down in front of the body—that's called the Fig Leaf Position," he adds. "They must not touch each other in any way unless the elevator is crowded, and then only at the shoulder or lightly against the upper arm."

Riders also have a tendency to look up at the floor indicator; and if anyone speaks, it is usually in a whisper.

Adapted from Roger E. Axtell, Gestures: The Do's and Taboos of Body Language around the World.

One of the most interesting body movements is the walk. Some have called the way we walk a "second signature," because each person's walk is distinctive. Part of the way we walk is due to body structure, of course, but pace and length of stride seem to change with our emotions. If you are happy, you move more quickly and seem lighter on your feet. If you're unhappy, your shoulders droop, and you walk as though your shoes were made of lead. When you want to express confidence, you try to look bigger. You stretch yourself up to your fullest height—head back, chest out, nose up. We call this "walking tall." When you're sad or discouraged, you make yourself look smaller by bending over, tucking your head in, and looking down.

See if you recognize any of these familiar walking styles:

◆ The choppy walk. Imagine the way you walk when you're loaded down with heavy bags. This is a short-paced walk that conveys submissiveness, unfriendliness, or frustration.

◆ The duck walk. Charlie Chaplin, the great comedian of silent movies, walked with his toes pointed out and his body swaying a bit from side to side. The walk became his trademark and signifies an impulsive and independent nature.

◆ The swagger. Swaying hips lead the way for this walk, as the upper body leans back from the pelvis. To some people, this walk shows a lack of self-confidence; to others, it shows too much ego.

Studies show that we tend to like people who have a bounce to their walk, swing their arms, and take long, strong strides. In fact, some psychologists say a long stride is such a positive body movement that you can improve your disposition—and make yourself happier—just by taking longer steps.

Watch My Space

Sometimes we speak of "keeping our distance" from someone we dislike or "getting close" to someone we like. Anthropologists say that we all walk around inside a bubble of **personal space.** The bubble represents our personal territory, and we resent it when someone invades our space.

Americans like to stand about twenty-four to thirty inches apart. This just happens to be an arm's length away. "When two Americans stand facing one another in any normal social or business situa-

tion," says George Renwick, an anthropologist, "one could stretch out his arm and put his thumb in the other person's ear." Asian people stand farther apart. If crowding is impossible to avoid, they ignore body contact by retreating within themselves. Latin Americans and Middle East-erners, on the other hand, stand much closer than Americans, literally toe to toe. They also like to touch their partner's arm or elbow when talking.

The figure below shows one system for measuring how much breathing space people need.

	Type of Space	Measurement of Space	Purpose of Space
	Intimate	under 18 inches	This distance is primarily for confidential exchanges and is almost always reserved for close friends.
	Personal	1½ to 4 feet	This distance is comfortable for conversation between friends.
	Social	4 to 12 feet	This is the ordinary distance people maintain from one another for most social and business exchanges.
	Public	over 12 feet	At this distance, perhaps in a shopping mall or on the street, people barely acknowledge each other's presence. At most they give a nod or a shake of the head.

TAKING CHARGE

1. To observe body language in action, try an experiment the next time you ride a crowded elevator. When you board the elevator, don't turn around and face the door. Instead, stand facing the other people. If you want to create even more tension, grin. Very likely, the other passengers will glare back, surprised and upset. The reason? You have broken the rules. Discuss with your classmates what you discover.

2. To learn more about body language, try a mirroring exercise. Find a partner and stand facing each other. One of you now becomes the mirror image for the other by trying to copy your partner's body movements. Try holding a conversation. After a while reverse roles and repeat the activity. What are each person's characteristic gestures?

3. Pair off with a partner and try to communicate the following feelings nonverbally: frustration, tension, joy, friendliness, anger, hate, and happiness. Think of a few others and see if your partner can guess what emotion you are trying to convey.

II Messages with Two Meanings

Learning to read body language is complicated by the fact that people often express different and even contradictory messages in their verbal and nonverbal behaviors. A common example of this sort of "double message" is the experience we've all had of hearing someone with a red face and bulging veins yell, "Angry? No, *I'm not angry!*" Like this person, you may sometimes try to put on a false front. You try to "keep a straight face," for example, when laughing might hurt someone's feelings or try to act calm when you don't want someone to worry about you.

Many a politician has stood before the voters, chest proudly thrust forward, posture erect, and in a booming voice declared, "If elected, I will be the humble servant of the people." The candidate's appearance, however, and the props behind him all suggest that he is something other than a humble servant. You often face examples of just this kind of inconsistent communication—where one message is expressed in words and quite another is conveyed through facial expressions and tone of voice. The so-called nervous laugh is a good example. The sound indicates amusement but the rest of the person's body shows extreme discomfort. The conflicting body signals show that the laugher is unsure of himself or perhaps frightened by the situation.

We all try to "massage our message" from time to time with body language. In other words, we attempt to use our bodies to disguise our real feelings. For example, we may try to project more confidence than we feel or pretend not to hurt even though our heart is breaking. In this section, we will examine how people use facial expressions and tone of voice to reinforce or, sometimes, to contradict the meaning of the words they speak. We will also discuss how you can detect when someone is not being truthful by observing their body language.

Facial Expressions

Facial expressions are often more convincing than words. Suppose you spill a can of pop or tip over a plant at a friend's house. "Slob!" yells your host, but with a smile and in an amused tone. The verbal message expresses her unhappiness with what you did, but the smile and warm tone reassure you that you are still liked. In fact, according to a study by Albert Mehrabian, facial expressions carry the greatest impact in convincing someone of something.

The head and face are wonderfully expressive and versatile instruments for communicating. Nodding your head up and down means yes—unless, of course, you live in Bulgaria, Turkey, and Iran, where it means just the opposite. Tapping your head with your forefinger can have two meanings. Sometimes it means "that person is very intelligent" and sometimes "that person is crazy." It all depends on the facial expression that goes with the gesture.

Because of their visibility, you pay a great deal of attention to other people's faces, beginning in early infancy. Babies take special interest in the huge faces peering over the crib. Although the face is capable of communicating many emotional states, six emotions seem to be the foundation of

The head and face are highly visible and expressive instruments of communication.

The Eyes Have It

"Look me in the eye" is a command that's been heard by every student at one time or another, but eye contact is not necessarily sought in every culture. In one region of Africa, a U.S. Peace Corps volunteer upset tribal elders because she required students she was teaching to look her in the eye. In the tribal culture, children were not permitted to look adults in the eye. Much the same is true of Native Americans. In many tribes, it is rude to look an older person in the eye. Respect is shown by avoiding eye contact.

most expressions—surprise, fear, anger, disgust, happiness, and sadness. Blends of these primary emotions account for nearly all of our facial expressions.

No one area of the face best reveals emotions, but for any given emotion, certain features are most important. For example, the nose–cheek–mouth area is most important for disgust. For fear, it is the eyes and eyelids. Sadness shows itself best in the brows and forehead, while happiness can be found in the cheeks and mouth.

If you watch a person's face in slow motion (on film or videotape), you discover that people change expressions rapidly. Some expressions last only a few hundredths of a second—in fact, they are so fleeting that they are rarely noticed in everyday conversation. These fleeting expressions reveal a person's true feelings, but they are quickly replaced by deliberate expressions the person feels are more socially appropriate. You can disguise

your face more easily than almost any other part of your body. That means that despite our natural tendency to search faces for meaning, they are not the best place to look.

Tone of Voice

Tone of voice is a more reliable clue to a speaker's feelings. The pitch and *timbre* of a person's voice, his pauses, rhythm, and oddities in pronunciation all have something to say, over and above what is being communicated by the words themselves. Rollo May, a famous psychotherapist, says he asks himself, "What does the voice say when I stop listening to the words and listen only to the tone?" The simple word "oh," for example, says very little as you see it printed here. But in spoken form, "oh" can have many different meanings. According to the way it is spoken, "oh" can mean:

- ◆ "You surprised me."
- ◆ "I made a mistake."
- ◆ "You're a pain in the neck."
- ◆ "You make me so happy."
- ◆ "I'm bored."
- ◆ "I'm fascinated."
- ◆ "I understand."
- ◆ "I don't understand."

The rate of speech also tells us something about the speaker's feelings. People talk fast when they are excited or anxious or when they are speaking about a personal problem. People are also likely to speak faster when they are trying to persuade us or sell something. On the other hand, people tend to talk more slowly when they are depressed, disgusted, grief-stricken, or simply tired.

COMMUNICATION WORKS

Lindy Mullin, Elementary School Coordinator

"You're communicating all the time who you are," says Lindy Mullin, an elementary school coordinator. "The question is, are you communicating the person you believe you are?"

Mullin gives frequent workshops to business and community groups on "Communicating the Best Possible You." She says that for many people, there's a big difference between what they think they're communicating and the message they are actually sending. Much of the time, nonverbal behaviors detract from a more confident-appearing self.

"A first impression is often communicated by the way you carry yourself," she says. "Do you stand in a way that suggests you should be noticed and respected or slighted and ignored?"

Your posture is a habitual behavior that you learn in adolescence. It's a habit no one thinks much about, but it has great importance for your image. If you stand slightly stoop-shouldered, you give the impression that you're carrying the weight of the world. An erect posture suggests you're confident and also enables you to make good eye contact.

In her job as an elementary coordinator, Mullin meets frequently with parents. Many times, these meetings could be negative situations (if the parents have come to school, for instance, to talk about their child's behavior problems). But Mullin feels she can turn them into positives by taking the initiative. She says she always makes sure she is the first to make contact.

"I move toward a person, offer my hand, speak early, and smile. The person who takes the initiative in a conversation is more likely to control the tenor and content," she says.

Be wary, though, of smiling too much. While smiling suggests confidence, it can also be a sign of nervousness.

"Ask yourself if you are smiling too frequently," Mullin says. "Many people smile when they're nervous. If you're in an important or serious conversation, don't smile unless you have a reason to do so."

Mullin also warns about several "power-robbing behaviors." These behaviors can rob you of the authority you need to make an effective point because they suggest you're not really sure of what you're saying. One is smiling too much. Another is touching any part of your body, especially above the shoulders, because it distracts listeners from your real message. Fixing your tie, playing with your jewelry, or fluffing your hair while you speak has the same effect.

Mullin suggests that you assess your own gestures and decide whether they add to your message. "You decide if they're okay or not," she says, "but remember, your nonverbal movements send powerful signals to others about who you are."

How to Tell When Someone Is Lying

According to Desmond Morris, author of *The Naked Ape,* we can control some parts of our bodies better than others. The easiest parts to control are those whose actions we are most aware of. You know the most about your smiles and frowns—you can see them in the mirror. So facial expressions are a poor test of someone's sincerity because they can be controlled easily.

General body postures, on the other hand, can be very revealing because we are not fully conscious of them. We don't usually know, for example, whether we are slumping or standing tall. Legs and feet are of special interest because these are the parts of the body where we are the least aware. Unfortunately, however, the lower portions of the body are frequently obscured from view. That's one reason people giving job interviews are more comfortable sitting behind a desk—their legs can't reveal what they're really thinking.

Besides looking under the desk, what can we do to discover a person's true thoughts? Are there specific body messages we can look for? Morris conducted a series of experiments to provide some answers. He asked a group of nurses to lie about a movie they had seen. He was then able to assemble a set of behaviors that seem to persist during moments of deception. They are as follows.

Decreased Hand Activity

The hand gestures the nurses would normally use to emphasize statements—to drive home a point or to underline something important—were reduced. The reason for this may be that hand actions, which act as "illustrators" of spoken words, are not altogether under our control. You know you wave your hands when you talk, but usually you have no idea what your hands are doing. Unconsciously, when you are not being truthful, you may sense that perhaps your hands will give you away, so you *suppress* them. You hide them, sit on them, stuff them deep into your pockets, or, less obviously, clasp one firmly with the other. The experienced observer, however, is not fooled by this—she knows something is wrong.

Increased Face Touching

We all touch our faces from time to time when we speak, but the frequency of these simple actions rises dramatically during moments of stress, such as lying. Hand-to-face favorites include the Chin Stroke, the Lip Press, the Mouth Cover, the Nose Touch, the Cheek Rub, the Eyebrow Scratch, the Earlobe Pull, and the Hair Groom.

Why these actions indicate lying might be best explained with the Mouth Cover. According to Morris, as false words emerge from the speaker's mouth, one part of his brain becomes uncomfortable and sends a message to his hand to "cover up" what the lips are doing. The other part of his brain, however, cannot permit the cover-up to work. The result is a half-hearted motion, with the hand-to-mouth gesture ending up as nothing more than a slight brush.

You can't be sure, of course, that every case of Mouth Covering, Nose Touching, and so on is evidence of lying. But you should suspect that some kind of basic conflict is taking place. For some reason, the person's thoughts and actions do not

How to Tell if Someone is Lying

Increased face touching can indicate that someone is not telling the truth. Watch for the following behaviors.

Earlobe Pull

Lip Press

Chin Stroke

Mouth Cover

match. The person may not be lying in the strictest sense, but he is certainly hiding something, and his nose touching or other odd behavior reveals that fact to you.

Increased Body Shifting

Most of us can remember squirming as children when we were forced to do something we didn't want to do. Our squirms were symptoms of an almost overpowering desire to escape. As adults, we learn to suppress these actions, but they do not disappear entirely. If you know a person well, you may be able to spot times when he or she seems unusually restless. That body language can indicate that the person is uncomfortable about something. If you notice the restlessness when the person speaks, you might be on the lookout for hidden meanings.

TAKING CHARGE

1. Ask a partner to tell you two stories—one true and one false. Your partner should try to make the false story sound reasonable, so that wild exaggerations don't give the story away. Listen to both stories, carefully observing your partner's body language. Can you guess which story is true? After you have tried to guess, reverse roles and tell two stories to your partner.
2. Watch a film or videotape with the sound off, and try to guess what is being expressed by body language alone. Then play the film or tape again with the volume up. How well did you do with your guesses? Reverse this procedure so that you listen but do not look. How much do you feel you lose by relying only on verbal messages?

III Nonverbal Messages in Conversation

Ordinary day-to-day **conversations,** those small talks you have with friends, acquaintances, clerks, and postal workers, are so common that you usually take them for granted and assume that they require no special skills. Yet conversation is a skill in its own right, and one with great personal value. Conversations enable us to make acquaintances and form friendships. The average teenager, for example, spends two hours on the phone each day (girls a half hour longer than boys) sharing the day's news and gossip. Conversations are genuinely personal speech, and they are also a great place to observe and practice nonverbal communication.

"It is good," said Montaigne, a French philosopher, "to rub and polish our brain against that of others." At its best, conversation is an art, but long before you can become an artist at conversation, you must master the fundamentals. Although the best conversations may seem spontaneous, they all follow certain unspoken rules. When conversation is flowing, you seem to practice these rules with ease. But when conversations become flat or stagnant, you might do well to give the rules special attention. Becoming more conscious of how these rules work should give you more confidence in your conversational ability and help you discover new ways to be interesting.

Starting a Conversation

Almost everyone finds it difficult sometimes to strike up conversations, yet to have friendships, you have to meet people and get to know them. To get to know them, you have to talk to them. At some point, someone has to start, but how do you know what to say and when to say it? Are there techniques to help you break the conversational ice?

Conversations frequently begin with something practical, like the weather—"Great day, isn't it?"—or comments on your partner's health, family, or recent activities. Most of these lines sound like clichés, but don't let that bother you. Conversation openers are rarely original—our nervousness drives away creativity. Most of us rarely do better than, "Hi. What's new?" or "Can you believe we lost that game?" If you're feeling really desperate, you might blurt out, "That's some sweet locker you've got there." Luckily, clichés won't keep a conversation from taking off.

The cleverness of your opening line matters less than the fact that someone recognizes your words (and your presence) as an attempt to start a conversation. Before two people can talk, both must signal that they're paying attention. They must stand reasonably close together, aim their bodies at one another, and exchange glances. Each also needs nonverbal feedback from the other when speaking—a fairly steady gaze, occasional head nods, appropriate facial reactions, and perhaps murmurs of encouragement like "uh-hum" and "yeah." Without these, conversation would soon grind to a halt. The real challenge in beginning a conversation is to establish a relationship of equality and partnership. That depends, to a great extent, on reading nonverbal signals.

Like a good stand-up comic, a conversationalist depends on a good sense of timing. **Timing** frequently determines whether your listener will welcome an opening line or not. Look carefully for nonverbal clues that signal a desire to talk. The psychologist Monica Moore, for example, studied how women indicate that they are willing to be approached. These signs included short glances, head tosses, hair flips, and smiles. (Unfortunately, Moore did not repeat her study for men—you are on your own there.) Such nonverbal signals help a careful observer know when a person might be interested in having a conversation.

Once an opening line has been delivered, however, a reply must follow, or there will be no conversation. If the person who has been addressed wants a conversation, his reply must not be too brief or unenthusiastic. Interest is communicated more by how the voice sounds and by body language than by what is actually said. For example, if you reply in a monotone, even if what you say is clever, you will sound bored—not like someone who wants to talk.

INSTANT IMPACT

Synchronizing Speech

A person who is speaking moves her hands, nods her head, and even blinks in rhythm with what she says. A person who is listening usually nods, blinks, and makes sounds of agreement that mirror the speaker's actions. These nonverbal echoes create an unconscious harmony that helps give people a strong feeling of "being connected." Look for this mirror effect the next time you watch two people conversing.

Striking up a conversation is easiest when it becomes clear that both of you have something in common. At first, conversations touch lightly on many subjects; you exchange questions and answers that help you discover what similarities you may share. Then, after you have selected a topic to focus on, the conversation shifts into high gear.

Helping a Conversation Continue

You encourage or discourage conversation in a thousand different ways through nonverbal behavior—through your posture, eye contact, and gestures.

Posture

How you hold your body can reveal your interest in the subject and how much you like the person to whom you are speaking. If you disagree with what is being said, for example, you will tend to have a "closed" posture. You will hold your head and trunk straight and probably fold your arms. If you are sitting down, you will cross your legs. When you agree with what is being said, you may show an "open" posture. You tilt your head, lean forward, and, if seated, uncross your legs.

Eye Contact

Confident speakers make **eye contact.** They look directly at their listeners when they want to emphasize a point and, especially, when they want to show how strongly they feel about something. A skillful conversationalist learns to look frequently from one face to another in a group, pausing to focus on anyone who is not paying attention. Sometimes, however, a speaker may look away, slowing down or even pausing at the same time. This break in eye contact tells listeners that the speaker is making a special effort to choose the right words and may be searching deep inside for just the right message. Most listeners will be patient with this break for a while but if prolonged, it can become distracting and discourage further conversation.

As a listener, what you do or don't do has a strong impact on your conversational partner. You may choose to look away frequently to lower the level of intimacy (in effect, saying, "This is getting too personal"). You can also look away to express skepticism (as if to say, "I'm not buying this").

Listeners generally give greater eye contact to people who touch their feelings. When your emotions are genuinely aroused, the pupils of your eyes widen. This involuntary reflex acts as a mood signal and usually causes your partner's eyes to widen, too. Use caution here—steady gazing is best reserved for lovers or people who are spoiling for a fight. When the speaker is a stranger, most modest listeners try to look less often and then only briefly.

Because pupil signals are involuntary, you can't learn to control them by practicing in front of a mirror. You can, of course, hide them by wearing dark glasses, a technique favored by the rich and famous. At one time, Italian women used to enlarge their pupils artificially by putting the drug belladonna (Italian for "beautiful woman") into their eyes as a way to look more attractive. But because we speak face-to-face and thus eye-to-eye, you probably won't have much success trying to disguise what your eyes reveal.

You would do better to focus on keeping your verbal message in sync with your personal thoughts and values. That way your eyes won't be saying one thing while your lips say another.

Head Nods and Gestures

You probably like talking to people who give a lot of feedback because they appear to be interested in what you are saying. Feedback can have concrete rewards for the listener, too. Research has shown that applicants who nod during job interviews are hired more often than those who do not.

The anthropologist Ray Birdwhistell discovered that head nodding plays an important role in normal conversation. He found that a listener can encourage a speaker to continue talking simply by making a quick nod every so often during a conversation. Curiously, though, long nods have the opposite effect—they disturb a speaker. Birdwhistell reported that when he used one long nod, the person speaking to him stopped, shifted position, and said, "I was only joking." Double nods seem to cause speakers to speak faster. Triple nods usually stop speakers in their tracks, apparently because they find them so bewildering.

Taking Turns

Have you ever known someone who just didn't know when to stop talking? We usually take it for granted that somehow, effortlessly and efficiently, we will get our turn to speak. "No one would listen to anyone else talk," noted the humorist Ed Howe, "if he didn't know it was his turn next." But taking turns can be a great deal more difficult than it

COMMUNICATION BREAKDOWN

Giving Your Doubles Partner the Cold Shoulder

The score is tied in the last set of the biggest tennis match of your life. Your opponent hits a slicing serve that you return nicely, but then your partner misses an easy shot at the net. You shout, "That's OK," but as you walk away, your body language is saying something else. Your shoulders, eyes, and walk all say that you're upset and irritated.

Gestures and body language are critical to good team chemistry and performance in every sport. Studies show that successful tennis doubles teams consistently have strong, positive patterns of communication. In fact, the better the players, the more communication takes place.

Professional doubles partners communicate after 83 percent of all points played, compared with 69 percent for college teams and just 17 percent for amateur pairs, according to a study by Dr. Jim Loehr for *World Tennis* magazine. The better players tend to communicate longer, too. The pro teams averaged about six and a half seconds of communication between points, as opposed to four seconds for top college teams and only one second for amateur teams.

Successful teams make sure they spend as much time together as possible before the next point begins. Frequent eye contact, shoulder touching, back patting, and high fives are common forms of this nonverbal communication.

What about that big tennis match—the one that opened this feature? If your team is losing, you may fall into negative patterns of nonverbal communication. When this happens—your partner misses a shot, let's say—you may be able to rally your team by practicing positive patterns of communication. As soon as the point is over, meet your partner before moving to your respective positions. When changing sides or moving long distances on the court, turn your body slightly in the direction of your partner as you walk. Give high fives (or some other gesture) to create a feeling of closeness and team unity. Learn to smile or throw a funny look at your partner to break the tension. Say something constructive during difficult times. Your attitude will improve, and so will your tennis game.

Question
How important is communication among players in other sports?

seems at first. In a conversation involving three or more people, for example, you may not get to speak at all if you do not jump in promptly at the right moment. The question here is simply how to tell when it's your turn to talk.

The surest way to take your turn at the right time is to listen for pauses. A pause is the best and most courteous opportunity to enter the conversation, but use caution. Has the speaker finished, or is she just taking a breath? Most of us seem to have a sixth sense about that, because we leap into conversations on remarkably short notice. Research shows that the time lag between when one speaker stops and another begins is just 0.764 seconds. By comparison, pauses during speech (when

Speakers indicate through body language and vocal changes when they are ready to yield their turn in a conversation.

a person pauses without intending to quit speaking) are slightly longer—0.807 seconds. This means that we must have some way of knowing when a speaker is pausing in midstream and when she wishes to turn the conversation over to another speaker.

How can we take turns successfully when there is, literally, just a split second to decide whether to jump in or not? Anticipation is the key. Good listeners look ahead to predict their conversational partner's **completion points.** This is easy when a speaker asks a question, such as "What do you think?" Detecting completion points, however, becomes more complicated when speakers take longer turns and don't ask questions. Fortunately, speakers use body language and vocal changes to show listeners when they are ready to give up their turn.

In one study, psychologists identified five "turn-yielding cues" speakers use to signal that they are ready to become listeners. These cues are (1) a rising or falling tone of voice, (2) drawing out the last few words of a comment, (3) the appearance of words of little meaning (such as "you know"), (4) the grammatical conclusion of a clause, and (5) the completion of a gesture. The more signals you can spot at any one time, the more likely it is that a speaker has finished. If you try to speak when these signals are not present, the result can be a fight for control.

Handling Interruptions

Even though they can be irritating, interruptions are part of almost every conversation. You can easily recognize several kinds of interruptions. First, there are the "simple" interruptions—someone begins to talk before another has finished, effectively shutting the first speaker off. This happens when someone simply can't wait to speak. Then there are "overlaps"—someone tries to interrupt but the speaker continues, creating a situation where two people are talking and no one is listening. Overlaps are common in arguments when neither person wishes to give in to the other. Finally, there are "silent" interruptions—someone takes advantage of a pause, however slight, to interrupt another speaker. In such cases, the first speaker probably resents the intrusion but cannot begin speaking again without seeming rude or insensitive.

People who seek to dominate a conversation tend to use a lot of overlaps. These are subtle interruptions that allow speakers to complete what they are saying before control is snatched away. That way, so the interrupter thinks, the original speaker can hardly complain. Simple interruptions are much clumsier. One person just barges into the middle of another's turn and risks that person's anger. But if you can't avoid being interrupted, are there ways to defend yourself and your right to speak?

The best defense for anyone who is a victim of too much interrupting may be a good offense. Use more authoritative body language. For example, point with two fingers (hold your index and middle fingers together) instead of one. You may look like a flight attendant giving a safety speech, but this is a gesture that plays well. People perceive it as strong and sturdy, while they find a one-finger point more of an accusation. Observe your own speech habits, too, to be sure you aren't giving out unintentional signals of com-

pletion. You may be pausing or making eye contact in a way that suggests you want someone else to speak.

Keeping a Listener's Interest

Perhaps the most important quality of a good conversationalist is the ability to be interesting. If you want to be interesting, start by having a lively curiosity. Stay informed by listening to radio and television programs and by reading newspapers, magazines, and books. Pay special attention to subjects that interest your friends so that you can discuss them intelligently. Since the topics for conversation cover the whole range of human activity, strive to know a little about everything.

Another way to be interesting is simply not to be boring. "Somebody's boring me," said the poet Dylan Thomas, "I think it's me." If you fail to hold people's interest, you are at a distinct disadvantage in conversation. People resent and dislike those who bore them. How can you be sure that what you have to say won't be boring? Let us consider what boring conversationalists do, the better to avoid these habits in the future.

The following list describes the qualities people find most boring in a conversational partner. Check yourself the next time you have a conversation. Are you guilty of any of these behaviors? Are you, for example:

1. Too easily distracted? Do you leap from one thing to the next, avoiding any real substance?

2. Lacking in enthusiasm? Do you use too little eye contact and speak in a monotone?

3. Too eager to please? Do you try too hard to be funny? Are you suffocatingly nice?

4. Too serious? Do you rarely smile? Do you ignore your partner's efforts to be amusing?

5. Too negative? Are you always complaining? Do you only see the depressing side of life?

6. Too passive? Do you fail to hold up your end? Are you too predictable?

7. Too plodding? Do you talk slowly and take too long to make a point?

8. Too preoccupied? Do you show little interest in others and talk mainly about yourself?

9. Too repetitive? Do you tell the same stories and jokes again and again?

Be conscious of your attitudes and habits during your next conversation. If you find that you are guilty of even one of these behaviors, resolve to do better in the future.

Ending Conversations

Few things are more annoying than a conversation that continues long after, as far as you are concerned, it is over. This can especially be a problem in phone conversations, since the person on the other end of the line cannot see your body language. "In face–to–face meetings, it's a nonverbal dance," explains Deirdre Boden, a communications specialist. "You can get intimacy, for instance, simply by leaning your shoulder slightly. On the phone, you have to be more explicit in verbally controlling the conversations."

To avoid continuing a phone conversation beyond either partner's endurance, listen for signals such as sighs, long pauses, and comments like "well. . . ." In a face-to-face encounter, watch for body language such as restlessness (shown by frequent changes of position), less and less eye contact, and a growing spatial distance between the two of you.

When you realize that a conversation is coming to a close, end it quickly but not abruptly. Even if both partners in a conversation know they have finished, a brisk dismissal can hurt someone's feelings. If your partner ignores your signals and still continues to talk, take the initiative and firmly close the conversation by saying something like, "Say, I'm really glad we could have this conversation" or "Let's talk again soon." Be firm, but keep your comments as friendly as possible.

TAKING CHARGE

1. Discuss with your classmates what you consider to be the rules for good conversation.
2. Make a list of verbal and nonverbal signs designed to end a conversation, such as the following:

   "Well, I'd better let you go." (verbal)
   Checking your watch (nonverbal)

REVIEW AND ENRICHMENT

LOOKING BACK

Listed below are the major ideas discussed in this chapter.

✦ Nonverbal messages are a vital part of face-to-face communication.
✦ Nonverbal messages frequently overpower verbal messages.
✦ Although body language is used worldwide, it is not a universal language.
✦ Some cultures are much more comfortable with touching than others.
✦ The distance you keep between yourself and others (your "personal space") helps define the kind of communication that is taking place.
✦ We tend to look for nonverbal messages in other people's faces, but the face is the part of the body that can be most easily controlled and therefore disguised.
✦ We can learn to spot someone who is lying by studying body language. People who are lying tend to use fewer gestures, touch their faces more often, and shift position more frequently.
✦ Nonverbal signals help us understand whether someone is interested in having a conversation with us.

SPEECH VOCABULARY

Match the vocabulary term on the left with the correct definition on the right.

1. nonverbal message
2. body language
3. gesture
4. kinesics
5. personal space
6. intimate distance
7. personal distance
8. social distance
9. public distance
10. tone
11. conversation
12. timing
13. eye contact
14. completion point

a. the distance for a conversation among friends
b. looking directly at your communication partner
c. a verbal and nonverbal exchange
d. the distance we keep between ourselves and strangers
e. style or manner of expression
f. the distance for normal business conversations
g. signal that the speaker is finished
h. sense for when it is appropriate to speak
i. hand or arm movement
j. the distance for personal confessions
k. all our physical movements
l. our "personal territory"
m. the science of body movements
n. any means of communication other than words

GENERAL VOCABULARY

Use each of the following terms in a sentence that illustrates its meaning.

sympathetic   stoic
diverse   ambiguous
anthropologist   timbre
comparative   suppress
intimacy

THINGS TO REMEMBER

1. Approximately how many different gestures can human beings produce?
2. The handshake and other forms of greeting go far back in time. What purpose do anthropologists think these gestures originally served?
3. Name two countries where touching among friends is common and two where it is not.
4. How far apart would two close friends ordinarily stand or sit during a friendly conversation? What about two strangers?
5. What might a tendency to touch his or her face suggest about a speaker?
6. What are some of the best ways to begin and end a conversation?
7. What kind of head nods are most encouraging from a listener to a speaker?
8. How can you handle someone who continually interrupts you?
9. How can you be an interesting conversational partner?

THINGS TO DO

1. Try a game of charades with your friends. Act out movie titles, current events, or fairy tales to see how well you can communicate without words.
2. Watch a film or videotape of the great mime Marcel Marceau. What could a mime teach you about using more expressive body language? Try pantomiming the action of throwing a ball. Have the ball change in weight and size. Have it become sticky, muddy, hot, wet, or cold.
3. Team up with a partner to present a speech. While one person speaks, the other (standing alongside) will use gestures, expressions, and body movements to illustrate the speech. The person who is talking should keep a neutral expression and use no gestures. What conclusions can you draw about the value of nonverbal communication?

```
┌─────────────────────────────────┐
│    REVIEW AND ENRICHMENT         │
│    ─────────────────────         │
│          Continued               │
└─────────────────────────────────┘
```

THINGS TO TALK ABOUT

1. How important is nonverbal communication in everyday life? In school? On the job?
2. How big is your bubble? How much room do you need around yourself to be comfortable? Does that change with different social situations or different people?
3. How do you know when someone is not telling the truth? What clues do you look for?

THINGS TO WRITE ABOUT

1. Keep a log of your personal space for one day. Each time someone initiates a conversation with you, make a note of how close to you that person stood or sat. Observe how the spatial distance between you and others varies according to the following factors: status or authority, sex, age, and social or cultural background of your partner. Compare your log with those of classmates.
2. Write a description of how to do one of these things:

   ◆ Apply makeup.
   ◆ Shoot a free throw.
   ◆ Mix a cake.
   ◆ Wash your dog.

   Remember, this is a written description, not a speech, and it may not include any pictures or drawings. Next, write a speech explaining the same process, and plan to use hand gestures and facial expressions. How many words did body language save you? What parts of the explanation became easier?

CRITICAL THINKING

1. Why do actions speak louder than words?
2. How important is it to be familiar with the body language customs of other countries and other cultures? Would it be better if all cultures had the same body language? Why or why not?

RELATED SPEECH TOPICS

How to speak body language
You're in my space!
The surefire liar detector plan

How to hold an interesting conversation
Read a person like a book
Gestures around the world

CHAPTER 5

Interviewing

"You never get a second chance to make a good first impression."
— **American proverb**

"Senator, you have been described as lazy, humorless, uninformed, unscrupulous, lacking in compassion, and totally unfit for public office. How would you respond to that?"

LEARNING OBJECTIVES

After completing this chapter, you will be able to do the following.

♦ Use interviews to gather material for your speeches.
♦ Schedule an interview at a time and place that will increase its chances for success.
♦ Create open-ended questions to draw out the best possible answers.
♦ Prepare to be interviewed yourself by anticipating questions, rehearsing answers, and dressing appropriately.
♦ Take advantage of opportunities in an interview to emphasize your positive points.

CHAPTER OUTLINE

Following are the main sections in this chapter.

I Using Interviews to Gather Information
II Preparing for an Interview
III Conducting an Ethical Interview
IV Giving Your Best Interview
    Chapter Review

NEW SPEECH TERMS

In this chapter, you will learn the meanings of the speech terms listed below.

interview
interviewer
subject
verbatim
open-ended
 questions
follow-up
 questions

yes–no
 questions
leading
 questions
puff balls
pauses
bridges
sparkler

GENERAL VOCABULARY

Expanding your general vocabulary will help you become a more effective communicator. Listed below are some words appearing in this chapter that you should make part of your everyday vocabulary.

pollsters
proxy
vicariously
grovel
chauffeur
logistical

tedious
fax machines
embalm
unobtrusive
résumé

LOOKING AHEAD

Interviewing plays a vital role in how we communicate with each other. In this chapter, you will learn to use interviews to gather firsthand information. This information will add credibility and authenticity to your speeches. Interviews are also important when you apply for a job or for admission to college. You will learn that this kind of interviewing takes a great deal of mental and physical energy. Careful preparation and sound strategy, however, will help you present yourself as effectively as possible.

I Using Interviews to Gather Information

Interviews are among the best ways to find out something new. Most of the informative reports and speeches you give in school are based either on library research or on firsthand interviews. Talking with an expert can often be more helpful than reading an article or book, and it's almost certain to be more fun. You can spice up any speech with a few well-chosen quotes and stories from a lively interview.

Why Interviews Are Important

An **interview** is a conversation—controlled but not dominated by one person who asks questions of another person. In other words, an interview is a conversation with a special purpose. That purpose might be to learn what people think or to gather information about a new idea or discovery. It might also be to find out more about someone who has applied for a job or admission to college.

Interview comes from a French word, *entrevoir*, which means "to see one another." Interviewing, you might say, is a contact sport—eye contact, that is. A good interview grows out of a personal relationship between people. Don't think of it as Ping-Pong™; think of it as a handshake.

Learning good interviewing skills is one of the smartest investments you can make in your future. People in many different careers do interviews. A book editor interviews prospective authors; an insurance agent interviews clients about their homes, cars, or possessions; a teacher interviews students about their academic problems. A financial advisor, a lawyer, an architect—all these professionals use interviews in their jobs.

We begin this chapter with a discussion of how to be an **interviewer** (the person who asks the questions) because you will frequently use interviews to gather material for your speeches. In the last part of the chapter, we will show you how to be an interview **subject** (*interviewee*, the person who answers). We believe that if you can learn how to conduct a good interview, you will have a better chance of also being a good subject. When your turn comes to be interviewed—for a job, for instance—you will be better prepared by being a good interviewer yourself.

Consider Your Audience

The number of interviews that take place is staggering. Opinion *pollsters* alone conduct an estimated 20 million interviews each year. Add to that the enormous number of job application and college admission interviews, and you have a number that rivals the national debt. We read about interviews every day—when we check the sports page, for example, to see how an Olympic athlete felt about winning a gold medal—and we watch interviews on television. In fact, your ideas about interviewing may have been formed by watching television news shows like "60 Minutes," "20/20," and "48 Hours."

A professional interviewer has one specific purpose: to act as a *proxy* for the audience. We can't all sit down for a chat with Dustin Hoffman, for instance, or Paula Abdul, but we are grateful that someone else can do it for us. Thus, we depend heavily on interviewers to act as our stand-ins. Interviewers head into locker rooms for post-game reports, climb on board Air Force One to interview the president, and travel with troops heading into battle. Popular talk shows like those hosted by Oprah Winfrey and Phil Donahue give audiences the chance to ask questions of celebrities and guest experts. We listen in on these shows hoping that the interviewer asks the questions we'd like to ask, so that we can *vicariously* take part in the interview ourselves.

Popular talk shows allow audiences to address guest experts and famous personalities. Bill Clinton, pictured here, appeared on Phil Donahue's show during the 1992 presidential race.

Your task as an interviewer, then, is to keep the interests of your potential audience in mind. Who will ultimately hear the information you are gathering? The teacher? Your classmates? The general public? Try to ask your subject what those people would like to know. The ability to anticipate what listeners want to know is part of what has made Barbara Walters television's most celebrated interviewer. It's an ability that gives Mike Wallace and his "60 Minutes" crew the courage to leap over barriers and smash down doors in pursuit of a good story.

Be Curious

The quality you need most to become a good interviewer is curiosity. Do you want to know about people's thoughts, words, and deeds? The best interviewers bring a passionate curiosity to the job. They have a burning desire to know. They get the answers people want to hear about fascinating characters and about those caught up in interesting events. Great interviewers are brave enough to ask the natural questions, even at the risk of making themselves seem foolish.

While you may be more eager to interview a star basketball player or a world-class model than to interview your algebra teacher, you must always make an effort to generate some curiosity about whatever person you choose to interview. Everyone has an interesting story to tell, and you can find it if you ask the right questions. Who would suspect, for instance, that your physical education teacher once shot baskets with Michael Jordan or that your math teacher was in a movie as a child?

A lack of curiosity, on the other hand, leads to lazy thinking. If you're not genuinely interested in what your subject has to say, you may find yourself behaving in the following ways:

◆ I make up a list of questions and go through them from beginning to end—no matter what the person I'm interviewing wants to talk about.

◆ I don't listen much to the answer. I just worry about the next question.

◆ If an answer confuses me or the subject mentions something I haven't heard about, I don't like to let on. I just go to the next question on my list.

◆ I'm so edgy about what the person thinks of me that I can never get comfortable. All my energy in the interview goes into playing the role.

Having a great interest in the person you're interviewing helps you overcome self-consciousness. It also drives nervousness away and gives you the courage to interview someone you respect or admire.

Keep in mind that most people like to talk about themselves, their work, and their opinions. The slightest hint that you're interested is often all the invitation they need to start talking. Curiosity might make you seem naive at times, but a true desire to know is the only proven way to bring an interview to life. If you have the right attitude, you may hear yourself making these enthusiastic comments during an interview:

◆ "That's fascinating. Tell me more."

◆ "I had no idea—whatever made them do that?"

◆ "How did you feel when that happened?"

TAKING CHARGE

1. Conduct a "person in the hall" poll. Think of a controversial question that can be answered quickly (yes or no, agree or disagree). The question could relate to school policies or community issues. A possible question, for example, might be "Should we limit all elected officials to two terms?" Ask the question of twenty people in your school. Record their responses and report your findings back to the class. You might even offer your information to the school newspaper as a "roving reporter."

2. Conduct an opinion survey. Work in a small group to develop a questionnaire on some subject of interest. Write or type a list of eight to ten questions on a single sheet of paper and reproduce enough so that you can hand out a hundred copies. Ask if you can pass out the survey in some of your other classes or at lunch. Collect the surveys, tabulate the results, and report the outcome.

3. Watch a televised interview program such as "Larry King Live" or "Nightline." What research do you think was involved in preparing the questions? How did the interviewer react to vague or unsatisfactory answers? Did the interviewer offer any personal information or "open up" to help the subjects talk?

II Preparing for an Interview

"Bend and *grovel* if you must," suggests John Brady, founder of a communications consulting firm, "but get the interview. This may turn you into a wimplike creature, but do it. You ain't got nothing 'til you've got that person sitting down to give you a couple of hours of his or her time." Brady overstates the case, but his point is clear: Without a person to talk to, you have no interview. Carefully choosing a person to interview and arranging a time and place suitable for the interview are problems you must solve before you can ask the first question.

> "Bend and grovel if you must, but get the interview."
>
> **John Brady**

Getting an Interview

John Brady was not above taking his own advice. To get an interview with a famous author, Jessica Mitford, he once volunteered to be a *chauffeur*. Mitford was visiting a college near where Brady lived, but her schedule was packed. College offi-

COMMUNICATION   BREAKTHROUGH

Presidential Announcements

Larry King says that when he walks down the street these days, people stop him and say, "So who are you going to make president this week?"

King, the host of a daily three-hour radio talk program and a nightly television interview program, made history in 1992 when he nudged a reluctant candidate, Ross Perot, into announcing a bid for the presidency. Before the presidential campaign was over, King's program had become a frequent stop for the other major candidates.

Part of King's success lies in his skill as a listener. "I like questions that begin with 'why' and 'how,'" he says, "and I listen to the answers which leads to more questions."

Although King doesn't consider himself a journalist, he says that asking questions comes easily: "My earliest memory is of asking questions. What did you do that for? Why did you do it?"

King grew up in Brooklyn, New York, as the son of Russian Jewish immigrants. At age 22, he took a bus to Miami, changed his name (from Larry Zeiger), and got a job as a deejay on WIOD. Before long he had his own sports show and was soon interviewing local celebrities.

Eventually, after a roller coaster career littered with bankruptcy, six failed marriages, and an arrest for larceny, King found a home in Washington with "The Larry King Show." This program of guest interviews and an open phone line can now be heard on over 300 stations nationwide.

One of King's personal rules is not to prepare too much. "I never drive to work thinking of questions," he says, "but good things follow from what I do.

King says that this method enables him to ask the kind of questions the people in his audience would ask. Rather than try to draw out facts from his guests, King focuses on their feelings, emotions, and motives.

Today, with his trademark slicked-back hair, glasses, and suspenders, King comes as close to being a king-maker as anyone in the media. Over 4 million people tune in each day to find out who and what he's going to listen to next.

Question
What role do talk shows and interview programs play in the American political process?

---

cials had arranged for a student to drive Mitford from campus to the airport when her visit was over, a distance of about seventy-five miles. Brady persuaded the student to let him drive Mitford instead. The student didn't mind ("I really don't know what to talk with her about," he said), so Brady picked Mitford up, turned on his tape recorder, and got a terrific interview.

Most interview situations, of course, aren't that difficult. You will probably find that most of the people you want to talk with are agreeable and cooperative. At times, however, it may take some persistence on your part to get a few of them to agree to speak. And then there are those who are just too busy or stubborn. Let them alone and find someone more willing to talk.

The call-in format of CNN's "Larry King Live" has set the pattern for political interviewing since 1985.

Select a Subject Carefully

No matter how skillful you are, an interview won't work if you haven't chosen the right person. Suppose you decide to do a speech on dreams. You discover a sleep research lab in town by thumbing through the yellow pages of the phone directory. A few calls later, you have scheduled an interview with the lab's director to discuss the current state of research on dreams. By interviewing the sleep lab's director, you are sure to learn more and gain better information than you would have by asking a few friends about their dreams.

Suppose you want to find out about the school dress-code policy. You know that the principal has banned T-shirts with beer logos, but you don't know why. Timidly, you approach a teacher with your questions to avoid speaking directly to the principal—a person you find distant and intimidating. Unfortunately, the teacher doesn't know the background of the policy and is unable to answer your questions. Your only choice is to bite the bullet and set up an interview with the principal. You may then discover that she was only carrying out an order from the school board and that the interview you really need is one with the school board president. You can save time by going to the best source of information first.

By the way, it's probably easier than you think to interview public officials. They know speaking about their job is one of their most important responsibilities. (Most politicians like the attention, too.) Public officials also have access to up-to-date information, and although you may get put on hold, you generally won't be turned down.

The people who are more difficult to reach are sports and entertainment figures, who guard their privacy jealously. But even with celebrities, you should be alert for opportunities. Famous people visit

The prestige and exposure of an article in a high school newspaper might persuade a reluctant subject to grant an interview.

even the smallest towns, and if you don't mind a long-distance phone charge, you can contact almost anyone. Before you call Tom Cruise for a soul-searching interview, however, you should realize that a casual fan doesn't have much pull in Hollywood. Large organizations with enormous numbers of readers, like *USA Today,* can get interviews where you cannot. But don't be discouraged—even a high school paper carries some weight. If you are having trouble setting up an interview, volunteer to write a story about your subject for the school paper. The added prestige (and ex-

posure) may persuade your subject to grant you an interview after all.

Respect Your Subject's Feelings

You should give careful thought to how you approach the person you wish to interview. Assuming that you have wisely chosen a good subject, your challenge is to persuade that person to give you something more than just the time of day. A personal contact—either in person or by phone—is the best way to arrange an interview, but a letter beforehand can pave the way. When you contact your subject, be sure that you have already done the following things:

- ◆ Chosen a day and time for the interview (plus two or three backups).
- ◆ Selected a place (be open; your subject may have a preference).
- ◆ Prepared an explanation of what the interview will cover.

Busy people greatly value their time. They will want to know the scope of your questions and approximately how much of their time you require. Being courteous and specific about these *logistical* details (when, where, and why) shows good manners and will help your subject form a favorable impression of you.

Choose When and Where

The best setting for an interview is a place where you won't be disturbed. You want to have your subject's undivided attention. Many people like to be interviewed where they work—in their offices, for example. That may be convenient for them, but it can create problems for you. The telephone is sure to ring, and coworkers will stop by to chat. Any interruptions during the interview will distract your subject, break the rapport—the feeling of trust and cooperation—you have developed, and stretch out the time the whole interview takes. Getting your subject off somewhere private can do your interview a world of good.

Be sure, too, that you don't cheat yourself on the amount of time you request. Beginners often worry that they will take too much of the subject's time. Consequently, they ask for too little and quit too early. Ask for an hour of your subject's time. You can probably get a good interview in less time than that, but you run the risk of not getting the information you need if you ask for less. You can always leave an interview early, but it's rude to take more time than you requested. By asking for an hour, you also tell your subject that you have plenty of questions and that you feel he or she has valuable and worthwhile answers. If your subject is so busy that only a few moments can be spared, consider interviewing someone else.

As an alternative to one long interview, try scheduling two or three mini-interviews. As you meet with someone over a period of time, your conversations often become more relaxed and revealing. So, for instance, you might spend twenty minutes before school with your subject, pop a quick question or two at lunch, and then stop by after school to finish the interview. Even if you're limited to just one formal meeting, see if you can follow up another time in person or by phone.

Doing Your Homework

Having arranged an interview, your next task is to learn all you can about your subject. "You should read every sin-gle thing that you can possibly get on the person you're about to interview," advises Phil Donahue. "It keeps you out of trapdoors and keeps you from looking foolish."

The preparation you do before an interview helps you create good questions. If you wanted to interview a new teacher at your school, for example, you could find out beforehand where the teacher had previously taught, his area of expertise, and where he went to college. Once you have the basic biographical facts taken care of, you will be free to concentrate on more imaginative questions, the kind of questions that produce the most interesting answers.

If your subject happens to be a prominent person in the community, try the local newspaper office for background material. Most daily newspapers have a clipping file where they store articles from each day's paper. If your subject has ever been in the paper, you can find articles about her in the newspaper's library. If you are planning to interview someone at your school, check past issues of the school newspaper or yearbook.

Reading is not the only way to check up on a subject; you can also talk to people who know the person. Alex Haley, the author of *Roots*, said he routinely contacted the friends, relatives, and even former teachers of people he planned to interview. Going to this much trouble won't keep you from asking a silly question, but it will keep you from asking an ignorant one. When the actress Vivien Leigh arrived in Atlanta for a showing of *Gone with the Wind*, a young reporter began an interview by asking her what part she had played in the movie. Scarlett O'Hara walked out on him.

Make a distinction between a simple question and a foolish one. You can ask the principal about open campus policies in a sensible way, but if you ask how long the lunch period is, you are asking the principal to do your legwork for you—that's a question you can answer for yourself. Nothing will irritate a subject more, especially one who has been interviewed many times, than being asked a question whose answer you could easily have found in many other ways. Asking a subject such questions shows you haven't done your homework. They waste that person's time and undermine his or her opinion of you.

Dress for Success

Students often wonder what they should wear to an interview. Even though you may prefer to dress casually, you should wear whatever you think will bring the best response from the person you are interviewing. Good school clothes (avoid T-shirts and the latest fashion statement) should work well, but an interview with the governor or some other VIP (very important person) is going to require more formal clothing. Your credibility is at stake.

If the governor is used to people who wear suits, you must wear an outfit that he or she will take seriously. You don't have to overdo it, of course—especially if you're going to conduct your interview while leaning on a tractor tire—but you want your subjects to know that you're serious and that their comments will be treated with respect. (We'll discuss how to dress when *you're* being interviewed later in the chapter.)

Don't Be on Time—Be Early

Being on time for an interview is smart; being early is even smarter. Phil Dougherty, a *New York Times* columnist, had a habit of arriving half an hour early for every interview. He would make excuses to secretaries and receptionists—"Gee, you wouldn't believe how fast I got through traffic today"—to cover his eagerness for the interview. Then he would wait in the lobby or reception area, soaking up the atmosphere.

Whether you're using a notepad and pen or a tape recorder, be sure to bring the proper equipment to an interview.

Dougherty got to see the people who worked with the person he wanted to interview. He got a taste for the rhythm of the place, how many times the phones rang, and who was making calls. In short, he got to size up his subject's environment. Sometimes he even got in early and, as a result, could squeeze an extra twenty minutes out of a busy person's schedule.

Of course, being early isn't always possible in school situations, but you should never be late. Being late for an interview sends a negative message: "I don't want to be here." If, for some life-threatening reason, you can't be on time for an interview, by all means call ahead and warn your subject. If you don't, you may find that being ten minutes late has caused your subject to cancel the interview altogether.

Bring What You Need

Be sure you bring the right equipment with you to an interview. You should always have a small notebook and pen, even if you plan to use a tape recorder. The notebook shows your subject that you mean business, and it encourages talking.

Many interviewers use tape recorders to help them remember an interview. For one thing, tape recorders are the only way to be absolutely accurate. With a recorder, you can always be sure of getting information **verbatim** (word-for-word). For another, no matter how good you are at taking notes, you may miss something important. With a tape recording, you can go back and find what you left out of your notes. In many situations, a portable cassette recorder is well worth the bother, especially if the interview is likely to be unusually long.

Here are some tips on using a tape recorder during an interview:

1. Make sure the recorder is working properly and that you have enough tape for the interview. Give your equipment a quick test before you begin the interview.
2. Speak clearly and enunciate. Be sure your subject does too. You won't be able to use the tape later if you can't hear what anyone says.
3. Don't wave the microphone in front of your subject. Set it down between the two of you.
4. Don't talk too close to the microphone. This can cause a blurry, distorted sound.
5. Remember that you must ask the subject's permission to tape the interview. This applies to phone interviews as well as those conducted in person.

Given all that a tape recorder can do, you might be surprised to learn that some professional interviewers prefer not to use one. Some interviewers say they carry only a pen and notepad because a tape recorder can make a subject ill at ease. Tape recordings don't protect you against mistakes, either. "You misquoted me," a subject might say. "I know that was what I said, but it wasn't what I meant."

The biggest problem with tape recordings is that they don't make your job any easier. If your objective is to turn your interview into a speech, you still have to make a transcript—a written version—of the recording to see what you have, and that is a *tedious*, time-consuming process. Further, a tape recorder can't pick up the small details of an interview—your sub-

By preparing a list of questions in advance, you can organize an interview and make efficient use of the time allotted for the interview.

ject's gestures and mannerisms, for example. A tape recorder won't write your speech, either. Many students say that taking notes during an interview forces them to think about their speech as they go and begin to organize its major points. That way, they have a head start.

Asking Effective Questions

Once you've contacted a subject, arranged a time and place to talk, and done a background check, you're ready for the last step before the interview itself: preparing a list of questions. Your goal is to guide the conversation where you want it to go. You want your subject to relax and to talk freely, but you also have an agenda with questions that need answering. The way you phrase these questions and the order in which you present them will determine, to a great degree, the success of your interview.

It is absolutely critical to prepare a list of questions in advance. Doing so will force you to think through the entire interview and plan the best order for your questions. Ideally, the answer to one question will lead naturally into the next. "You start a question, and it's like starting a stone," said the writer Robert Louis Stevenson. "You sit quietly on the top of

> "You start a question, and it's like starting a stone."
>
> **Robert Louis Stevenson**

a hill; and away the stone goes, starting others." Preparing questions ahead of time is also the best way to make sure each minute of your interview counts.

Keep Your Questions Brief

Make your questions brief and to the point. Avoid those complicated two- or three-part questions you may have seen television reporters use during press conferences: "Mr. President, can you tell us what you know about plans to export more wheat, and where those shipments will be going, and when they'll start?" Reporters sometimes resort to these tactics because they know they may only get one crack at their subject's attention and they want to make the most of it.

You would be wiser, however, to give the person you're interviewing a chance to answer one manageable question at a time. Keep your questions simple and direct. If the subject has trouble interpreting your question, rephrase it. For example, suppose you ask the question: "Did the school board drop its laundry program for athletics in the interest of economy or was it bowing to community pressure?" If this question is too much for your subject, try this: "Why do athletes have to wash their own towels this year?"

Use a Variety of Questions

Build your most important questions on the famous five Ws and an H (*who, what,*

why, when, where, and *how*). Imagine, for instance, that the parents of one of your classmates have opened a new pet cemetery in your town. You want to give a speech on how people handle the death of a pet and decide to interview the parents. By using the five Ws and the H, you develop this list of questions:

- ◆ WHO brings their pets to your cemetery? Can you tell me about your customers?
- ◆ WHAT kind of burial or funeral arrangements do they request?
- ◆ WHY do you think people spend so much money on their pets?
- ◆ WHEN did you first decide to start a pet cemetery?
- ◆ WHERE are other pet cemeteries in our region located?
- ◆ HOW do you *embalm* a pet? HOW do you restore the appearance of pets who have been killed in car accidents?

Open-Ended Questions. Strive as much as possible to develop open-ended questions. **Open-ended questions** are similar to the essay questions on a written test. Instead of asking for a narrow response (yes–no, true–false), the question allows the subject to decide how best to answer.

Your goal is to use short questions to produce long answers. For example, instead of asking "Did you really fall into a vat of chocolate?" ask "What was it like to fall into a vat of chocolate?" In the following interview, notice how a student interviewer uses open-ended questions to draw out Martha Quinn, one of MTV's original veejays.

COMMUNICATION WORKS

Charles Kuralt, News Correspondent

Charles Kuralt, a correspondent for CBS News, has had a special assignment for several years. This assignment, which resulted in the "On the Road" program, called for Kuralt to travel all over the United States talking to people from all walks of life, looking for the interesting and "real" stories that Americans love to read about and listen to. Through his travels and reports, Kuralt has created a realistic portrait of late twentieth century America.

Kuralt had the usual TV journalism career until he began his "On the Road" series in 1967. With a small crew of technicians, Kuralt drove across the U.S. looking for interesting stories, the kind that would never be found in the headlines of newspapers or news broadcasts, but absorbing stories nonetheless. "In that first year on the road," Kuralt says, "I fell in love with my native land."

Kuralt's work took him to the stills hidden in the mountains of Kentucky, to recreations of Civil War battles in Virginia. He also visited an environmentalist in Nebraska who picked weeds for his dinner salad.

Kuralt has said that a reporter is "a stone skipping on a pond, taking an instant to tell one story and ricocheting to the next, covering a lot of water while only skimming the surface." Kuralt's comment shows that he has a clear, unaffected view of the importance of the work done by himself and his colleagues in TV journalism. His comment does not, however, even hint at the great joy, pleasure, and insight his reporting has given to millions of viewers.

Q: MTV seems now to be a part of American culture. What's it like knowing you were a factor in that?

A: I'm thrilled that I've been a part of it. A factor? I don't know. I feel like a little piece of plankton in a tidal wave. I don't really know that I had that much to do with it, I just got swept along in it. But it was a wonderful time to be around in the music business, you know, when new things are coming out.

Q: MTV's future seems fairly certain, but what about Martha Quinn's future? What does your future hold?

A: You know, more than anything, I wish I was one of those people who has a plan.

"Oh, I know exactly what I'm going to be doing." You know, like Dolly Parton. I once read somewhere that she has her whole career planned. I hope in my best possible life that I'd have some sort of fun TV work, whether it be a sitcom or fun variety show or something like that.

Q: You've been called a lot of things: "perky," "the all-American girl next door." *Time* **called you a "preppie punk."**

A: Wow, you went back into the archives.

Q: How would you describe yourself?

A: Silky and sensuous [laughs]. How about that? See that spunky thing is just an act; I'm really the most alluring, mysterious person.

Open-ended questions leave room for the subject to maneuver. While such questions may cause you to lose some control over the interview, what you gain is worth it. You may hear the subject tell you something that takes your breath away.

Follow-Up Questions. Inexperienced interviewers tend to look for safety in long lists of prepared questions. Of course, as noted, you must plan what to ask. But a long "must ask" list can drain the life from an interview, turning it into a tedious trip from Question A to Question Z. Along the way, you can miss a lot of good conversation in your concern to cover "everything on my list."

What's the solution? Prepare your list of questions, but stay flexible—be ready to react to the twists and turns of conversation. Listen for intriguing statements, and when you hear one, ask a follow-up question. **Follow-up questions** help you pursue topics that pop up unexpectedly. One of the best questions is simply "Why?" Chase good ideas, even if it means letting some of your prepared questions slide.

To use follow-up questions well, you must think on your feet. Recall for a moment the interview with Martha Quinn. By listening attentively, this interviewer was able to recognize that Quinn's first audition with MTV was something special, an experience that deserved to be explored at length:

Q: How did you get on MTV to begin with?

A: I was a college intern at WNBC in New York, and I had gotten myself through college doing television commercials. And when MTV came out, someone said, "Hey, Martha, that'd be perfect for you." Just a casual comment, and next thing I knew, I was kind of moseying down to the studio to audition for this wacky, weird thing.

Q: Were you nervous?

A: It was not a big deal to me, because I was auditioning every day of my life for, you know, Twix or Clearasil or something. And I was like, "Oh, okay, this is kind of weird, but I'll go check it out."

Q: How did you feel after the audition?

A: When I walked out of the audition, I thought, "Wow, that is the perfect job for me."

Q: And how did you feel later?

A: By the time I went to sleep that night, my life was to be changed for the next *ten years*. Can you imagine? I would like to go back and read my horoscope for that day. Seriously.

Sometimes people tell you things that are so interesting, unusual, or meaningful that they deserve your complete attention, regardless of whatever other question you were poised to ask. Follow your instincts. If someone tells you something of exceptional interest or importance, ditch your old questions and follow this new topic for all it's worth.

Questions to Avoid

Some kinds of questions work better in an interview than others. **Yes–no questions,** for example, are usually trouble and should be avoided. For one thing, they allow your subject to answer the question without telling you anything. They also give the subject an excuse to stop talking.

Suppose that during an interview with Barbara Walters, you said: "Several years ago you caused a sensation by signing a

The Donahue Show

Phil Donahue is one of America's best-known and most highly regarded interviewers. His "Donahue" show, which combines interviews of guests with audience participation, is televised on more than two hundred stations nationwide.

Donahue said he spends the greatest part of preparation time determining who the right people are to invite on the show.

"This is perhaps our single most important decision," he says. "Who is it that we choose to seek information from? Is that person entitled to the kind of attention we give him or her? I think it's a privilege to be able to decide what people and what subjects should go on the public airwaves."

Drawing out an interview subject who doesn't want to be open and forthright demands Donahue's greatest tact:

"I will come back at a guest if I feel that he or she is waffling. I will gently call the guest's attention to the fact that the question has not been answered. But I don't want my program to be an hour of banter and jousting between Phil and the guests."

He also says that knowing as much as possible about your subject ahead of time is vital: "I certainly think it's pretty basic to have a biography of the person you are going to interview. I think you should know how old the person is, and know something about his or her personal life."

Source: Adapted from Parade Magazine.

$5 million contract with ABC. Are you worth that much money?" (At the time, many people thought it was scandalous that a network would pay a female journalist so much money.) If Walters answers yes, she has only told you what you know already—she accepted the contract. If she says no, you think she's just being modest. Either way, you won't have learned anything, and you'll have nothing new to tell anybody else.

But what if you had asked the question this way: "Miss Walters, what do you think of the public reaction to your $5 million contract with ABC?" Now, Walters will be free to talk about how she has earned respect in a male-dominated profession. She might tell you about how she studied camera work and editing or about the thousands of letters she sent and phone calls she made to set up interviews.

If your questions are superficial and limited, the answers will be, too. Reword your yes–no questions into open-ended ones. In most cases, your reworded questions will lead to more interesting and quotable replies.

You should also avoid **leading questions,** because they influence the answers you receive. For example, instead of asking "Was the UFO shaped like a saucer or like a cigar?" say "What was the UFO shaped like?" Let your subjects choose their own words.

"I will come back at a guest if I feel that he or she is waffling."

Phil Donahue

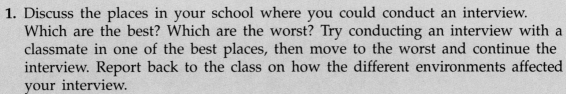

TAKING CHARGE

1. Discuss the places in your school where you could conduct an interview. Which are the best? Which are the worst? Try conducting an interview with a classmate in one of the best places, then move to the worst and continue the interview. Report back to the class on how the different environments affected your interview.
2. Think of a famous person you would like to interview. Write a list of ten questions you would ask that person if you had the chance. (Don't hesitate to do a little research.)
3. Rewrite these yes–no questions to make them open-ended (assume your subject is Bill Cosby):

   ◆ Do you like working on television?
   ◆ Is it important that TV shows have characters who can be good role models for young people?
   ◆ Will you be on television again in the future?

III Conducting an Ethical Interview

The most important thing you can do while conducting an interview may be obvious, but it's still important: Listen well. (See Chapter 3.) Good listening keeps you attentive and encourages your subject to speak. He or she is much more likely to talk openly if it's clear that you are listening carefully. Maintain a polite but professional distance, neither arguing nor agreeing. A head nod from time to time encourages the subject but does not necessarily mean that you agree—it just means you understand.

Try to remember that each time you do an interview, you influence the future. If you treat your subject fairly and honestly, that person is likely to be cooperative the next time someone asks for an interview. On the other hand, if you bungle the job, the subject may swear off interviews forever.

It's not unusual for someone who has had a bad experience to refuse to talk again—several major league baseball players, for example, have taken this position and refuse to talk to reporters. Give your subjects respectful attention no matter what their ideas might be. The people who march to a different drummer often make the best interviews.

Getting Off on the Right Foot

When you arrive for the interview, remind your subject who you are and why you want the interview. You can say, for example, "I'm gathering information for a speech I'm giving to my class." In any

An interviewer should ask sensitive questions in a matter-of-fact way and not appear shocked at the responses.

case, the subject needs to know how you plan to use the information that he or she will provide.

Beginning an Interview

The first part of your interview should include several routine, get-acquainted questions that the subject will have no difficulty answering. These nonthreatening, factual questions get the conversational ball rolling, so to speak. They also give you a chance to show some interest and enthusiasm about the person you're interviewing. Don't be a phony, though; find something that genuinely interests you in what the person is saying.

If possible, use each answer as a springboard for the next question. By carefully drawing upon what the person has just said, you can lead him or her smoothly toward the next question. For example, "You say you enjoy rock con-

certs? Which one was your favorite?" Or, "I'm an oldest child, too, and I always liked being the oldest. How do you feel about it?" Questions like these allow you to "warm up" the subject before you get into the heart of the interview.

Take Quick Notes and Look Up Often

If you're gathering information for a speech, you will certainly want to take notes during the interview. Taking notes gives you a record of what was said and helps you to be a better listener. Note-taking also gives you a convenient and *unobtrusive* way to check off the questions you wanted to ask as you move along.

Most professional interviewers have developed their own brand of speed-writing for taking notes. Some note takers omit vowels and word endings; others use abbreviations. You may already have a few of your own shortcuts. Develop a personal system or study a manual on speed-writing. But whatever route you take, remember that what matters most in an interview is that you can listen, think, and write all at the same time.

Although you do need to take notes, don't let yourself get buried in your notebook. Look up from time to time. It will help your subject to know that you're still holding up your half of the conversation. Many beginners have tried to write down every answer in longhand and then panicked when they forgot a word or didn't hear an important phrase because they were too busy writing. The more effort you spend on preserving the conversation, the less energy you have to keep up with it. Thus, take quick, brief notes and maintain good eye contact.

Handling Sensitive Questions with Care

Some of your questions are bound to hit the subject in a sensitive area. If you sense that the subject is touchy about something, but still think you must ask about that topic, watch for an opening. Wait until your subject happens to mention the sensitive area, then gracefully follow up. Make it seem as if the subject brought it up himself. For instance, you might say, "Really. Now who would accuse you of anything like that? Tell me about it."

If the person doesn't mention the sensitive area on his own, wait until the end of the interview to ask about it. That way you and your subject have had an opportunity to establish some trust. Ask your tough question matter-of-factly, in the same tone of voice as your other questions; don't broadcast that the "bomb" is coming, and try not to react when you

hear something big. The subject will freeze up if he thinks he said something that shocked you.

Beating the Jitters

It can be scary asking tough questions, especially when you need to ask them of adults. When Laurie Lattimore, a reporter for her school paper at Rocky Mountain High School in Fort Collins, Colorado, attended a superintendent's press conference, she found herself wondering whether she had the courage to ask a difficult question.

At issue was a new tax that school officials wanted voters to approve. Without more money, they warned, driver's education and some sports programs might have to be cut. But Laurie wondered if such talk was just a threat. School officials had never explained exactly what they would do if the tax increase did not pass. Surely, she thought, the professional reporters in the room had already thought about that. Would they think she was stupid if she asked such an obvious question?

As time passed, she felt she had to know the answer. Since no one else was asking, Laurie did: "What will you do if the tax increase doesn't pass?"

"I don't know how I got the guts to ask the question," she said later. The other reporters were surprised and a little bit dumbstruck. School officials confessed they didn't know what would happen if the bond issue failed.

"I had mixed feelings," Laurie said. "On one hand I felt like a Woodward or a Bernstein [famous Washington, D.C., reporters]. At the same time, I was scared to death people knew more than I did. I was afraid I'd look stupid. But then I re-

COMMUNICATION   BREAKDOWN

A Bad Day with the Critics

Even when reporters have a chance to talk with a celebrity, things don't always go well. When the Fox TV Network staged a press conference to show off its hit show "Beverly Hills, 90210," Luke Perry (who plays Dylan McKay) was rude and uncooperative.

Many of the TV reporters called Perry "a jerk" for his cocky answers. "Honestly, it didn't go very well today," Perry said later.

At the press conference, Perry refused to answer questions about his age and whether his parents live on a farm. "I am on a TV show," he said. "They are not. They should not have to deal with any of the ramifications of my career."

He also refused to answer a question about whether he is a role model. "Doesn't say role model in my contract. I looked at every page."

Finally, when one critic asked Perry a question about being a teen idol, he said, "I just said I didn't think it was accurate because I'm no longer a teenager. I don't think anybody idolizes me. And yeah, that's what I said, wasn't it? Can we have a show of hands? Is that what I said?"

None of the reporters accused Perry of lying, but afterwards, few had any kind words for his version of "Beat the Press."

Excerpted with permission of the Miami Herald.

Question

How can interviewers best respond to rude behavior from the interview subject?

---

alized the other reporters were scared, too, and I realized I *was* informed."

Being informed and knowing that you have prepared well can give you an extra boost of confidence when you ask tough questions.

Be Persistent

What should you do if someone doesn't answer your question? This happens occasionally to every interviewer. The fact that someone talks in response to your question does not mean that the question has been answered.

Sometimes, a person may misunderstand your question. In that case, restate or rephrase it. Don't be afraid to ask a question twice. Doing so won't make you look dumb or hard of hearing; most people, in fact, are impressed that you know what you want.

Of course, sometimes people will ignore your question and try to answer a different one, one they would prefer answering. Here you need some tact, but you also need some determination. Ask the question again if you aren't satisfied with the answer. If you sense the subject is reluctant to talk about that particular question, try being silent for a moment. Many times, an uncomfortable silence tells the subject that you want to hear more.

In fact, silence is one of the best ways to get another person to talk. Be patient if you think your subject is dredging up some long-lost memory. Remembering can take time. Let your subject break the silence. If you are quiet, the subject realizes that you are waiting for what you hope will be the rest of the answer.

Concluding the Interview

When you have finished all your questions, give your subject one last chance. Say, "Is there something else you would like to tell me?" Usually, there is. After that, thank the person and take your leave. A thank-you note a day or two later adds a classy touch to your interview.

Write up your notes as soon as possible after the interview, while the subject's words are still fresh in your mind. Your notes make much more sense to you then than they will a few hours later. In fact, if you wait several days to read over your notes, you may find that they no longer make sense at all. Don't hesitate to check a fact if you're in doubt. Was the figure she gave you $1 million or $10 billion? A mistake makes both you and your subject look bad.

Conducting Interviews over the Phone

An interview is probably best done face-to-face, but sometimes that just isn't possible. As an alternative, you may wish to interview someone over the telephone. A phone interview forces you to really concentrate on what your subject is saying. Here's a suggestion. When you're conducting a phone interview, close your eyes and just listen. Listen to each answer for fresh and interesting thoughts. You'll hear with an intensity you've never experienced before.

Keep in mind, though, that it's all too easy to let your mind wander when you don't have your subject right in front of you. Eventually, you doodle, thumb

If your mind wanders while you are conducting a telephone interview, you might miss original and interesting thoughts and fail to pursue worthwhile ideas. Therefore, keep distractions to a minimum.

through a paperback, or think about an assignment for another class. When you check your notes later, you notice ideas you should have pursued and ideas that don't make sense. Finally, you find that you don't have what you need. When you do a phone interview, then, keep distractions to a minimum.

TAKING CHARGE

1. Pair off with a classmate and interview one another. Imagine that your classmate is new to the school and you will soon give a short speech introducing him or her to the rest of the class. Prepare a list of at least ten questions and find out something fascinating.
2. Arrange with your teacher to have a public official visit your class for a group interview. Have each member of the class prepare three questions ahead of time. Then, during the conference, notice whether any questions are repeated. Are class members listening well and creating follow-up questions, or are they simply sticking to the questions they have prepared?
3. Conduct a practice interview in front of the class, and then ask the class to critique your effort. For a twist, ask your subject (perhaps a teacher or administrator) to be as uncooperative as possible. How can an interviewer deal with a potentially hostile subject?

IV Giving Your Best Interview

Now let's turn the tables and examine the strategies and techniques you can use when you are being interviewed. As we mentioned earlier, you will surely have many opportunities to be interviewed—for a contest, a job, or admission to college—and all of these occasions can be highly stressful. In fact, an interview may be one of the most nerve-racking experiences you will ever face. Yet even the toughest interview teaches us about ourselves and how to handle certain situations better in the future. Interviews can also lead to fame, fortune, and opportunity. If you can call up the right attitude, you may find an interview to be a pleasant and productive experience.

Interviews are certainly vital to your future success. Increasingly, college admissions officials are relying less on standardized test scores (the ACT and SAT, for instance) and giving greater emphasis to personal interviews. Consequently, how well you do in an interview can determine whether you are accepted by the college of your choice. Sooner or later, too, you will interview for a job. Almost every employee, from cook to corporate president, won the job through a successful interview. How you conduct yourself in interview situations will be a great test of both your speaking and your listening skills.

Have the Right Attitude

Perhaps the most important ingredient in a successful interview is a positive attitude. You should remember that prospective employers are not out to embarrass you or trip you up; they only want to gain an accurate impression of you and your abilities. In particular, they want to know how you get along with other people. Of course they are interested in your qualifications, but they can get that information on paper. When they call you in for a personal interview, they want to find out whether you are a capable and reliable person, someone they would enjoy being around.

No one doubts that interviews are crucial to getting a job. Guyla Armstrong, assistant professor of business at the University of Nebraska-Kearney, says that the interview is the most critical part of the hiring process. "Your personality and how you conduct yourself during the interview have the greatest impact on your chances of landing the job," she says.

Armstrong warns that most people "will blow some questions." Many students, in particular, perform poorly in their first interviews because they don't prepare, don't dress right, and don't know what to expect. You should realize, she says, that the person interviewing you will probably be about twenty years older than you and will expect you to show poise and maturity.

The interview is a social ritual that begins with a cordial welcome, a handshake, and a series of rather standard questions such as "Tell me about yourself" or "How

During a job interview, be alert for opportunities to introduce positive points about yourself.

did you first become interested in our company?" Later in the interview, you will probably have an opportunity to ask questions about the job or about the company doing the hiring.

Don't underestimate the importance of asking questions, says Mike Waddell, a placement counselor. Not asking questions, especially questions that are pertinent to your future, is one of the worst mistakes you can make. Ask, for example, where the person you want to replace has gone. The answer may tell you something about your prospects for job advancement if you should be hired.

Dress to Create the Right Impression

Just as you dress in a certain way when you conduct an interview, you should give careful thought to what you wear when you are being interviewed. Dress for the interview in the clothes you would probably wear on the job. "People take what you wear as information," says Judith Waters, a New Jersey psychology professor. She advises people to avoid carrying clunky bags or briefcases, to be sure never to dress better than the person interviewing them, and to pay special attention to shoes. "Being well-heeled means something," she says.

Here are some all-too-common appearance choices you should avoid:

1. An outfit that doesn't look together (as if the pieces weren't meant to be worn with each other).

2. Clothes that don't fit.

3. Poor grooming (hair out of control, overdone makeup, dirty fingernails).

4. Dressing too casually (blue jeans).

INSTANT IMPACT

Dressing for the Interview

Dressing for an interview is probably easier for young men than young women. Young men know they can't go wrong with a suit and tie. Women, on the other hand, have a more difficult job choosing clothes to create the right impression.

In a study of hiring practices, personnel managers were asked to watch video interviews of women wearing four different styles and then make hiring recommendations. The four styles ranged from "least masculine"—a light beige dress in a soft fabric with a small round collar, gathered skirt, and long sleeves—to "most masculine"—a dark navy suit and a white blouse with an angular collar.

Women wearing the most feminine dress were chosen least often. But women wearing the most masculine dress were not the favorite choice of the personnel managers, either. That title went to the women who wore the next-to-most-masculine dress, a beige suit with a blazer-style jacket and a rust-colored blouse with a bow at the neck. Something middle-of-the-road, then, seems most likely to create the right impression.

Source: Adapted from Peter Marsh, Eye to Eye, *Salem House Publishers, 1988.*

5. Wearing something too revealing (if Madonna would wear it, skip it).

Be Alert and Energetic

During the interview, you should try to show energy and enthusiasm. Sit on the edge of your chair and lean slightly forward. When you make gestures (and it's helpful to do so if they come naturally), get your hands about chest high. Using gestures burns off tension, oils your voice, and looks good—it makes you animated. Maintain good eye contact. If you have trouble looking the interviewer in the eye, try looking at different parts of the person's face for variety.

Pay attention to the interviewer's name and use it occasionally in your answers. That helps the interviewer know that you notice people and remember their names. As much as possible, turn the conversation toward things you know and keep it away from unfamiliar topics. Rehearse comments about your strongest assets ahead of time and look for opportunities to mention them.

Make Positive Points

To some extent, you need to be assertive during an interview. Prepare a short list of positive points you wish to make about yourself. Perhaps you want to be sure your future employer knows about your work experience, how well you're doing in school, or your plans for the future. Whatever the case, prepare a list of points you want to be sure to bring up during the interview, whether the interviewer asks you about them or not.

How can you get your positive points across? Be alert for situations where you can bring them into the conversation. Here are a few possibilities:

1. **Puff balls.** Puff balls are easy questions lobbed in your direction. A typical puff ball might be: "Tell me about yourself." Use a question like this as a springboard to tell the in-

terviewer something you have planned to say. Puff ball questions give you the perfect chance to put your best foot forward. But beware: If you haven't practiced ahead of time, a question like this may leave you at a loss for words. When the interviewer throws the door wide open, be sure you're ready.

2. **Pauses.** Inevitably, you will feel a lull in the conversation. Every interview has some downtime. Perhaps the interviewer has looked down at her notes, scratched her shoulder, or taken a sip of coffee. In any case, a pause gives you another chance to take the offensive. Remember, you're not a witness in a murder trial; you don't have to wait to be cross-examined. While the interviewer is momentarily distracted, jump in and offer to talk about a subject that you know will show your skills and abilities to best advantage.

3. **Bridges.** A bridge means a transition from one answer to another. Suppose the interviewer offers you a question that calls for a brief answer. The interviewer might ask, for example, "Have you ever been late for work before?" Obviously, the interviewer expects a one-word answer—yes or no—but you can do better. You first answer the question—"Yes," you say, "I was late once." Then, by cleverly using a bridge, you turn the original question into something else you wanted to talk about. "I was late once," you say, "but it was because I saved a boy from drowning. It was raining and I saw this kid swept into an

Practice answers to tough questions you think an interviewer might ask. If possible, videotape and later analyze a rehearsal interview.

open culvert. I stopped immediately and called 911." (Be sure, of course, that any story you tell about yourself is true.) This bridge gives you a chance to show how responsible you are—so responsible, in fact, that you realize some things are even more important than being on time.

Once an opportunity for making a positive point presents itself, make the most of it. As well as possible, try to give a focused answer. Make a key point and put it up front. In other words, give a short, pithy answer—"I have experience" or "I love to flip burgers"—and then provide the details. Positive points aren't enough if they sound like propaganda. So add on a **sparkler**—something that makes the point come alive: an analogy, a story, an anecdote, or a quote. Prove it and make it memorable.

Confront Tough Questions

Good planning means that you have anticipated the tough questions already and given some thought to how you might answer them. Practice answering questions that will give you difficulty. The interviewer may want to know, for example, why you've never held a job for more than three days. You should guess that a question like this will be coming and have a reasonable answer in mind—for example, "I've had many responsibilities at home, looking after my younger brothers and sisters, but they're all in school now." No matter how well you prepare, however, you will occasionally run into an extra-tough, surprise question.

In such a potentially dangerous situation, take a moment or two to gather your thoughts. Never let yourself feel pressed to answer a question without thinking. When you pause before answering, you show your poise. Before long, a reasonable answer should come to you. In case it doesn't, however, here are a few stalling techniques to "buy time" while you search your brain for an answer:

1. Say the interviewer's name once slowly while you think.
2. Restate the question.
3. Address the "issue"—that is, use general comments while you ponder the specifics.

It won't hurt, either, to ask the interviewer to give you a moment to think. You wouldn't want to do this very often—the interviewer has other things to do, too—but there's nothing wrong with calling a brief time out.

Once in a while, the best answer to a tough question is simply "I don't know." You can't know everything, and most interviewers appreciate your honesty if you admit that. The worst mistake you can make in an interview is to try to bluff your way along when you really don't know what you're talking about. Don't worry about impressing anyone—be yourself and be the best person you can be.

Interview Checklist

As a final check before you go to a job interview, ask yourself these questions:

1. Do I have a copy of my *résumé?*
2. Have I brought a list of three references with addresses and telephone numbers?
3. Am I going alone? (Don't take anyone else with you.)
4. Am I sure I'll be on time?
5. Have I dressed neatly and appropriately?
6. Even if I feel tired, can I remember to sit up and look alert?
7. Can I remember not to criticize others, especially past employers?
8. Can I make good eye contact with the interviewer?
9. Can I remember the interviewer's name and use it?
10. Can I remember to thank the interviewer?

TAKING CHARGE

1. Invite a local personnel officer to visit your class to discuss interview procedures. Ask your guest to conduct some sample job interviews among your classmates.
2. Develop a list of ten positive points you could make about yourself in an interview. Compare your list with a classmate's, and critique each other's list.
3. Create a set of clothing guidelines for a variety of job interviews. What should you wear when you interview for a job, say, at a fast-food restaurant? A hospital? A department store?

Review and Enrichment

Looking Back

Listed below are the major ideas discussed in this chapter.

✦ Interviews play an important role in our efforts to gather information as well as to apply for admission to college or to gain a job.

✦ The best place for an interview is a location where you can have your subject's complete attention.

✦ Learn as much as possible about the person you wish to interview before speaking with him or her.

✦ Dress appropriately for an interview. Wear whatever you think will bring the best response from the person you are interviewing.

✦ You must be on time for an interview, and bring a pen and notebook. Some interviewers also like to use a tape recorder.

✦ It may be best to begin an interview with several get-acquainted questions, questions that will put your subject at ease.

✦ Questions should be brief and to the point.

✦ Open-ended questions allow the subject great flexibility in answering. Such questions can sometimes lead to new and surprising pieces of information.

✦ Follow-up questions help you pursue statements that need clarifying.

✦ Yes–no questions and questions that require a one-word answer should be avoided for the most part.

✦ Keep eye contact with your subject. Don't become so wrapped up in note taking that you forget to hold up your end of the conversation.

✦ Prepare thoroughly when you are the subject of an interview. Find out as much as you can about the company or college you are interviewing with, and be sure to remember the name of your interviewer.

✦ Gestures are useful during an interview to burn off tension, oil your voice, and help you seem animated and energetic.

✦ Stress a few positive points about yourself when opportunity permits.

✦ Take your time during an interview, and don't feel pressured into answering quickly. Nothing will hurt your chances more than giving an answer without thinking it through.

Speech Vocabulary

Match the speech vocabulary term on the left with the correct definition on the right.

1. interview
2. interviewer

    a. a "soft" question

    b. a transition from a question to a positive point

3. subject
4. verbatim
5. open-ended
   question
6. follow-up
   question
7. yes–no question
8. leading question
9. puff ball
10. pause
11. bridge
12. sparkler

c. word-for-word
d. a purposeful conversation
e. a question that follows a train of thought
f. supporting material—a story or quote, for example
g. the person who asks the questions
h. a lull in the conversation
i. the person you wish to interview
j. a question that requires a one-word answer
k. a question that leaves room for answers
l. a question that hints at the answer

GENERAL VOCABULARY

Use each of the following terms in a sentence that illustrates its meaning.

pollster
proxy
vicariously
grovel

chauffeur
logistical
tedious
fax machine

embalm
unobtrusive
résumé

THINGS TO REMEMBER

1. What is the difference between an *interviewer* and an *interview subject?*
2. If, as an interviewer, you find yourself overly concerned with your next question or whether your subject likes you, you may lack an important quality. What is it?
3. Why would the principal be a better source of information than a teacher for some speeches? For what speeches would a teacher or a student be the best source?
4. What are some reasons why a subject's office, although convenient, is not the best place to conduct an interview?
5. Name several sources of information you could use to find out about the person you wish to interview.
6. Under what circumstances, if any, would blue jeans and a T-shirt be appropriate clothing for an interview?
7. What are some of the reasons you might want to use a tape recorder during an interview?
8. What are the advantages of writing out your questions before the interview?
9. Why should you avoid asking yes–no questions?
10. The best strategy for an interviewer to take is to pretend to agree with everything the subject says. True or false? Why?
11. What kind of preparation should you do when you are going to be interviewed?
12. Name three opportunities that may present themselves during an interview, opportunities for you to talk about your own positive points.

THINGS TO DO

1. Attend a local press conference. They are called frequently by state and local officials. Prepare a few questions ahead of time. Ask the officials if you can ask questions; if not, compare your questions with those asked by professional reporters. Evaluate the quality of the questions asked and the responses given.

2. Check up on yourself. Send a follow-up sheet to a person you have recently interviewed. Ask that person about how he or she thought the interview went. Were you, for example, courteous, well prepared, and alert? Were your questions thoughtful and to the point? Use the evaluation to improve future interviews.

3. Have two students interview the same person in front of the class. Have one person stay outside the room while the other interview is going on. Discuss the differences in both questions and responses.

4. Assume you have been assigned to interview the president of your student council. What research should you do to prepare for the interview? What questions would you ask?

THINGS TO TALK ABOUT

1. What problems are caused by the need to take notes at an interview?
2. What are some of the ways you might deal with a situation in which a subject is reluctant to give out any information?
3. Can you think of any situations in which a phone interview might be preferable to a face-to-face interview?
4. Discuss who the best subjects would be for a variety of speeches. Have half the class think of the speeches and the other half think of the best people to interview. For example, who would be the best subject on the history of homecoming at your school? The first basketball team? The growth of women's athletics?

THINGS TO WRITE ABOUT

1. The following list represents some typical kinds of questions you might be asked in a job interview. Think of some job you might like to apply for and answer the questions with that job in mind. You may wish to add additional questions of your own for further practice.

   ◆ In what school activities have you participated? Why? Which did you enjoy the most?

   ◆ What jobs have you held? What experience did you gain and why did you leave?

   ◆ What courses do you like the best? The least? Why?

   ◆ What do you know about our company or business?

   ◆ Why do you think you would like this particular job?

   ◆ Do you prefer working with others or by yourself?

◆ What do you expect to be doing five or ten years from now?

◆ How would you describe yourself?

◆ How do you work under pressure?

◆ What two or three things are most important to you in your job?

2. Oral history has become a popular way to learn about the past. Draft a proposal for an oral history of your school, a local institution in your community, or a major national event.

Examples of such events could include the explosion of the space shuttle *Challenger*, the beginning of the Gulf War, or Hurricane Andrew. Include research subjects, possible interview subjects, and sample question lists.

3. Compare your note taking techniques with those of classmates. Do you use an outline form? If not, do you use some combination of letters, numbers, indentions, underlining, stars, or some other system for separating major points from minor ones? What can you do to improve your system for taking notes?

CRITICAL THINKING

1. What personal qualities and skills does a person need in order to be a successful interviewer?
2. What are some of the ways interviews can be misused? Could a company, for instance, use job interviews to find out what people think of competing companies?
3. At what point does a person's right to privacy limit what interview questions can be asked? Where can the line be drawn between public and private activities?

RELATED SPEECH TOPICS

Barbara Walters
Larry King
Edward R. Murrow
How to get into the college of your choice
How to apply for a job
TV talk shows
The ethics of "sound bite" news reporting

Future employment opportunities
Teen workers and the minimum wage
An individual's right to privacy versus the public's right to know
Dressing for success
How to succeed at a job
The most interesting person I have ever met
How to write a résumé

CHAPTER 6

Group Discussion

 "Nothing is interesting if you're not interested."

— Helen MacInness

"What's this about your refusing to attend another meeting today because you want to *get some work done?*"

LEARNING OBJECTIVES

After completing this chapter, you will be able to do the following.

✦ Explain why cooperative attitudes are necessary for group discussions.
✦ Describe the major kinds of group discussions.
✦ Discuss the factors that determine the success of group discussions.
✦ Identify the steps of the problem-solving process.
✦ Develop a list of questions you could use to direct a group discussion.

CHAPTER OUTLINE

Following are the main sections in this chapter.

Ⅰ Working Together Makes Sense
Ⅱ Group Problem Solving
Ⅲ How to Contribute to a Discussion

Chapter Review

NEW SPEECH TERMS

In this chapter, you will learn the meanings of the speech terms listed below.

discussion
cooperative
competitive
panel
forum
round table
symposium
town hall
  meeting
cohesion
criteria
brainstorming

constructive
  conflict
disruptive
  conflict
moderator
questions of fact
questions of
  interpretation
questions of
  evaluation
consensus
groupthink

GENERAL VOCABULARY

Expanding your general vocabulary will help you become a more effective communicator. Listed below are some words appearing in this chapter that you should make part of your everyday vocabulary.

consultation
team teaching
cooperative
  learning
sequential
scenario

bombard
status quo
polarizing
apathetic
monopolizes
paraphrases

LOOKING AHEAD

We are all born into a group—our families—and spend much of our lives interacting with groups. Groups are important because they have more power than any one person, and their decisions usually carry great weight. In this chapter, you will learn how to help shape group decisions by partici- pating in discussions. A good group discussion is a spirited exchange of lively thoughts, clever remarks, and interesting stories. You will learn here how to make valuable contributions to the discussion as well as how to ap- preciate different points of view.

I Working Together Makes Sense

You know how it goes. Joe gets an idea and sketches it out on a piece of paper with a few doodles. Then along comes Mary, who says, "Hey, wait a minute— that makes me think of something. . . ." Soon Fred comes over and says, "But look, if we change this or add that, we can probably make your idea better." Be- fore long, a group of people working to- gether has surpassed what any one per- son could have accomplished working alone.

We do some things better by our- selves—reading, for example, or riding a unicycle—but we do many things better in groups. Doctors frequently work to- gether, although they call it *consultation.* Teachers work together, and call it *team teaching.* And more and more, students are working together in school. Many schools are moving away from traditional styles, in which students work independently, to- ward a style called *cooperative learning.*

In cooperative learning, students work as a team, each contributing something to- ward a group goal. Group work helps us learn the skills we need to cooperate in an increasingly interdependent society. A strong group goal can help us overcome our reluctance to ask for help or perhaps to offer help to another student. Group work also helps us overcome some of the misunderstandings we have because of our different racial or ethnic backgrounds. When we have a stake in each other's success, we have a strong motivation to cooperate.

The Right Attitude for Group Work

We all think of ourselves as individuals, but we actually gain much of our identity through participation in groups. You may discover how grown-up you are, for ex- ample, in family discussions about who gets to use the car, or how persuasive you can be in a student council meeting on where to hold the prom. Group discus- sions help us learn something different

Students learn important social skills, like cooperation, while working in groups toward a common goal.

about ourselves from what we learn in unplanned and spontaneous conversations. Group discussion has a goal.

We can define **discussion** as a cooperative exchange of information, opinions, and ideas. In practical terms, discussion is one of the best methods we have for solving problems. In a discussion, group members help bring all sides of a problem to the surface for consideration. We tend to talk each other out of biases and preconceived ideas. More importantly, we are usually willing to support solutions if we have played a part in developing them ourselves.

An ideal group member is open-minded, someone who can interact with fellow group members in a **cooperative**—rather than **competitive**—atmosphere. A discussion, for example, is not a debate—you don't have to defend a particular point of view. All discussion is dynamic; people are welcome, even encouraged, to change

their minds as they hear other ideas and gain more information.

Discussion does require patience. Compared with conversation, discussion can seem somewhat slow because every member has a chance to speak, and some people who aren't listening well may repeat what's already been said. Many of us complain, too, that meetings waste time. The people who do most of the talking may seem to have the least to say. You may sometimes feel you must give in to work with a group. You may not agree with the group's decision, for instance, but you don't want to make everyone upset with you by being difficult.

Just because group discussion isn't perfect, however, doesn't mean it isn't valuable. Like everything else, group discussion works when we make it work. The best discussions give each of us a chance to be heard and, more importantly, a chance to make good decisions.

INSTANT IMPACT

Businesses Find Teamwork Productive

Schools are becoming more cooperative, and so are American businesses. Many companies have already discovered that teamwork means higher morale and greater productivity. Jerry Junkins, president of Texas Instruments, says, "No matter what your business, teams are the wave of the future." Consider these success stories:

✦ At a General Mills cereal plant in Lodi, California, teams of workers schedule, operate, and maintain machinery so effectively that the factory runs without any managers during the night shift.

✦ A team of Federal Express clerks spotted and eventually solved a billing problem that was costing the company over $2 million a year.

✦ Teams of workers in Sheboygan, Wisconsin, helped Johnsville Foods decide to go ahead with a major expansion. The workers convinced top executives that they could produce more sausage if allowed to streamline the process. Since 1986, production is up 50 percent.

These teams have proven that groups can be more effective than the old boss–worker arrangement at getting the job done and doing it well.

In many ways, discussion is the basis for our democratic system. We face conflict every day—rubbing shoulders with each other—but we can find ways to re-solve our differences. Through sharing information, ideas, and feelings in discussion, we can find solutions that help all of us become wiser and more understanding people.

If you prefer just to let things happen and go with the flow, you will not do well at discussion. Discussion is purposeful talk by people who are committed to working together. A discussion is truly effective only when each member takes his or her share of the responsibility. Too often, discussions are held back by people who avoid that responsibility. Whenever one group member decides to let others do the work, that person weakens the discussion. All members must be committed to listen, to think, and to reason with one another.

Discussion Formats

Group discussions take many forms. You may be most familiar with classroom discussions that focus on interpreting literature or analyzing historical events. You may also be familiar with group or club meetings that use parliamentary procedure. (See Chapter 18 for a description of those rules.) There are, however, other kinds of discussions, including the panel, the symposium, and the town hall meeting. Let us take a closer look at each.

Panel Discussion

The **panel** is a relatively informal discussion that takes place before an audience. Panel members, often three or four in number, sit facing the audience. Most of the time panelists talk directly to each other, but each may make a short introductory speech. Panel discussions help audiences become better informed on particular issues. A school might set up a panel discussion on teen sexuality, for example, and use a teenage mother, her parents, a school counselor, and a representative from an adoption agency as panel members.

An open **forum** may follow the panel discussion. During the forum, panel members invite questions and comments from the audience. Often a discussion leader will field the questions and restate them if they are unclear or could not be heard by everyone. The leader then directs the questions to specific panel members or to the panel as a whole.

A special kind of panel discussion called a **round table** is commonly used in business and industry. As the name suggests, a small group of participants, usually three to eight, talks about a topic of common concern while sitting around a table or in an open circle. If a number of accidents have occurred in a manufacturing plant, for example, the company supervisors might be asked to discuss their suggestions for new safety procedures. Presidential cabinet meetings are another good example of round table discussions, as are many Sunday morning television news programs.

Symposium

A more formal kind of discussion is the **symposium.** The usual purpose of a symposium is to present opposing points of view. During a symposium, invited experts deliver short speeches on a particular subject. A discussion leader usually introduces each speaker and may give a brief statement at the end of each presentation to link together the entire discussion. Each speaker stands and faces the audience, and after all the speeches have

been heard, the audience may ask questions or make comments.

A school might schedule a symposium, for example, if it is planning to build a new gymnasium. Symposium speakers might include an architect, an athletic director, a city planner, and a concerned taxpayer worried about the potential cost.

Town Hall Meeting

Another kind of discussion is the **town hall meeting,** a form that dates back to the early American colonies. In those days, colonists would assemble in a large hall to discuss their problems. A vote would usually be taken after the discussion to settle the issue. Today, satellite technology enables people all over the country to take part in town hall meetings on television.

Television anchorperson Ted Koppel hosted a famous town hall meeting in which American citizens asked questions of two major foreign leaders—Mikhail Gorbachev and Boris Yeltsin. Ross Perot, who ran for president as an independent candidate in 1992, may have foretold the future when he promised "electronic town hall meetings" where citizens from all over the country could speak their minds to the president via telephone and television hookups.

Factors for Success

Some discussions work better than others. We can improve a discussion's chances for success by paying attention to two physical factors—the size of the group and how group members are seated. We should also consider one psychological factor—group cohesion.

Members of discussion groups seated in circles report more satisfaction with their contributions and more confidence in their ability to solve problems.

Group Size

Face-to-face communication helps make a group a group. Clearly, the size of a group affects how comfortable people are in sharing their ideas. Some researchers say five to seven members is the best size for a group, because people participate better in small, informal settings. Even the least talkative person, research has shown, will talk in a small group. Groups of four or fewer, however, are too small because they lack the diversity needed to give the discussion some spark. Furthermore, in such small groups people can be too busy working on personal relationships to get down to business.

Groups of more than seven people are often too big. In these groups, quiet persons rarely talk and then only to people with high status. (People gain status in a group by virtue of their age, expertise, experience, or personality.) In groups of more than ten, a few people do most of the talking while the rest listen.

As a group gets bigger, of course, each person has fewer opportunities to speak. Consequently, large groups can alienate some members. Thus, many large groups delegate most of the work to small groups called *committees*.

Seating Arrangements

The way people are seated in a discussion can have a good deal to do with its success or failure. If someone in the group takes a central position—at the head of a U-shaped group of chairs, for

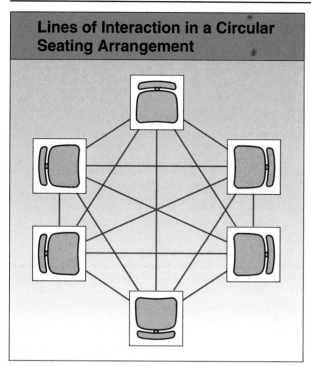

Lines of Interaction in a Circular Seating Arrangement

A circular seating arrangement allows direct communication among all participants in a group discussion.

example, or in front of a row of desks—talk appears to flow through him. That person then dominates the discussion. On the other hand, if the group sits in a circle, all participants can easily look at one another, and talk tends to flow from member to member or from a member to the entire group without being channeled through one person. Class discussions sometimes fail to come to life because of their unfortunate physical arrangements. If the teacher stands at the front of the classroom and all comments are directed toward him or her, there is little student-to-student interaction.

Studies show that people who participate in groups with circular seating feel more satisfied with their contributions, more pleased with the group's work, and more confident that they have done well in solving problems than those who participate in leader-oriented groups. People in groups also need breathing space. Studies of rats, monkeys, and humans show that close confinement produces high levels of stress. Cramped quarters seem to increase conflict and aggression. If the members of your group don't know each other well, have them sit several feet apart. As they get to know each other, they will probably move closer together.

Cohesion

The success of a group discussion also depends on an intangible quality called **cohesion.** When members have respect for each other, share some of the same values, and look to each other for support, they may be called cohesive. Generally, cohesive groups are those in which people are pulling in the same direction. In contrast, members in a noncohesive group seem to care less about what the group does than about their own personal goals.

If belonging to the group is important, members will become more cohesive. Belonging to groups matters to many people because it gives them a chance to socialize and feel a sense of purpose. When a group has a good track record—when it has a history of solving problems, for example—its members will more likely remain loyal. On the other hand, if a group fails to meet its objectives, members may lose interest in belonging and show little enthusiasm for finding new members. Thus, success in group discussions often leads to more success because it helps build cohesion.

TAKING CHARGE

1. Conduct a discussion self-critique by asking yourself these questions: How well do I participate in discussions? How often do I speak? Do I see myself as a regular or occasional contributor? Is there something I can do that isn't being done well by anyone else in the group?
2. Watch a televised discussion (a news program like "Meet the Press" would work well) and analyze the discussion in terms of the size of the group, the seating arrangements, and what the group accomplished or failed to accomplish. How did each individual member's knowledge of the topic influence the discussion?

▥ Group Problem Solving

We form groups to do a variety of tasks. Sometimes the purpose of the group is to gather information (you might join a study group, for example, to help you pass that chemistry exam) and sometimes to make decisions (should our Spirit Week theme be *Wayne's World* or *Batman Returns?*). But groups are never so important as when they are formed to solve problems.

Stick to the Pattern

Unlike conversations, which flow from topic to topic on a whim, discussions generally follow a logical, *sequential* pattern. This allows everyone to know what progress is being made toward solving the problem being discussed. By relying on an established pattern, groups can complete their work quicker and with less wasted effort.

Many discussion groups follow a pattern developed by an American educator and philosopher named John Dewey. Dewey said that discussion members need to cultivate what he called the "vital habits of democracy." Members need to "follow an argument, grasp the point of view of another, expand the boundaries of understanding, and debate the alternative purposes that might be pursued." The following six steps are a modern update of Dewey's system. If you stick to them in problem-solving discussions, you should have a good chance for success.

1. Define the Problem

The first step in solving a problem is to make sure you understand the problem. This may require the group to consider how the problem came about and why it needs to be solved. The group should also establish what problems it does not want to consider. In other words, a group tries to limit its objective so that it can focus on finding a specific solution for a specific problem.

COMMUNICATION   BREAKTHROUGH

Group Therapy Aids Cancer Survival

It may seem hard to believe, but medical researchers are proving that group discussions can actually help you live longer.

David Spiegel of the Stanford University School of Medicine says that group therapy sessions for cancer victims have prolonged their lives. The sessions focused on helping patients improve communication with their families, face their fears about death, and provide emotional support to one another.

Researchers found that breast cancer patients who participated in weekly group therapy sessions lived significantly longer—by an average of eighteen months—than women who received only regular medical care.

Although the exact reasons for the effectiveness of group sessions remain a matter of guesswork, researchers note that patients who share intense emotional bonds seem better able to accept their physical problems. In the process, they chip away at "the social isolation that often divides cancer patients from their well-meaning but anxious family and friends," the investigators concluded.

Women who attended the group sessions for the study may also have lived longer because the sessions helped them adjust to their medical treatments, maintain a healthy diet, and exercise regularly.

Question
In what ways does group participation restrain our worst habits and encourage our best ones?

To see how this step might work in real life, consider the following *scenario.* The story is based on an incident that really happened (the names and places have been changed). A recent pep rally at Centerville High School has everyone upset. The principal interrupted the rally during one of the skits because he found it offensive and in poor taste. He has suspended the nine students who were involved, and he threatened to ban all pep rallies for the rest of the school year.

Now a group of student leaders, including members of the student council, the captains of the athletic teams, the editors of the newspaper and the yearbook, and several cheerleaders, has gotten together to see what can be done. Let's listen in on their discussion.

"I think the principal is completely out of bounds on this one," says Fred Jones, captain of the football team.

"I do, too," replies Nancy Bounds, a cheerleader. "But let's face it. We aren't going to make him change his mind about the suspensions. Those students and their parents are going to have to fight that one."

"Nancy's right," comments Bob Biggs, student council president. "But maybe we can do something about his ban on pep rallies. I think we can make a big enough stink that he'll let us have some more pep rallies, especially if we can prove that responsible people will be in charge."

These students have identified their problem—a possible ban on pep rallies—and have begun to define that problem by limiting it. The students are upset with the principal for suspending nine of their classmates, but they're not going to let that issue sidetrack them from their real goal—namely, to get pep rallies reinstated for the rest of the year.

By the way, this is a good place to warn you that many groups start their business without recording what happens. Later on, when they want to remember what someone said, they discover that nobody was keeping track. Most groups would be wise to select a recorder who will be responsible for writing down important ideas and major decisions.

2. Establish Criteria for a Workable Solution

After defining the problem, the group should decide on **criteria,** or a set of standards, that their solution must meet. By establishing these standards at the beginning of a discussion, much unnecessary arguing can be avoided. It would do no good, for example, if a new club planned a fund-raising dance and then found out the school calendar was already full. If the group had first determined that open dates were available, they could then have discussed the kind of fund-raising project they wished to have.

The students in our pep rally group have agreed, after considerable debate, on the following criteria:

1. Pep rallies should continue to be part of the regular school schedule.
2. The pep rallies will continue to be planned and organized by students,

but the students must have faculty supervision.
3. No students should be suspended or disciplined for participating in pep rallies, provided the faculty sponsor has been involved in planning the skits.
4. The pep rallies will not use vulgar jokes or offensive language, although school officials should recognize that rallies are meant to be fun.

The students have everything they want in this list—a guarantee that rallies will be run and organized by students and a promise that the administration will not punish students who participate in pep rallies. But they also believe that the list contains a few things important to the principal—faculty supervision and a promise to keep the rallies free of the kinds of jokes that caused the problem in the first place.

Once the group has established its criteria for an acceptable solution, it can get more specific about what exactly must be done. In our example, the students know they want at least a minimum number of rallies, with a maximum of student input. They know, in other words, what a possible solution might look like.

3. Analyze the Problem

The next step in a discussion is to analyze the problem. The object is to break the problem down into small pieces for closer inspection. Some groups call this fact-finding. When a doctor analyzes a patient's condition, for example, she begins with a thorough examination. She takes an inventory of the patient's current condition (pulse, blood pressure, temperature, and so on), and she examines the pa-

Modern Update of John Dewey's System for Discussion

1. **Define the problem.**

2. **Establish criteria for a workable solution.**

3. **Analyze the problem.**

4. **Suggest possible solutions.**

5. **Evaluate each solution and select the best one.**

6. **Suggest ways for testing or carrying out the solution.**

tient's medical history, looking for possible clues as to what has caused the patient to become sick. Similarly, groups gather as much information as they can to throw light on a particular problem.

Our pep rally students spent some time talking about other school problems that might have caused the principal to be so sensitive:

> "Say, do you remember that swimsuit issue in the school paper last month?" says Bob.
>
> "I sure do," responds Tammy Swanson, the newspaper editor. "The principal was really upset with us—at least that's what our advisor said."
>
> "And he wasn't too happy about all the publicity we've had lately about teen mothers," comments Renee Larson, another cheerleader. "I know he got quite a few phone calls from angry parents."
>
> "I guess maybe he has good reasons to be a little touchy right now," says Bob.
>
> "That might be right," replies Nancy, "but I still think he overreacted. Maybe we can

change his mind if we can prove to him that we have a responsible plan."

We tend to forget that problems don't happen overnight. Most usually have long histories. Learning the background of a problem can often help us gain insights into why people react to the problem the way they do. It never hurts to see the situation from another person's point of view.

4. Suggest Possible Solutions

The fourth step in the problem-solving process is to propose as many solutions to the problem as possible. One of the best ways to create solutions is called **brainstorming.** In brainstorming, a group tries to *bombard* the problem with fresh ideas. Every idea is welcome; none are laughed at or rejected.

Group members offer their ideas as quickly as possible, not bothering to decide whether the solutions are practical. The process should stir each member's creativity. "Everyone is creative," says James Ferry, president of an idea development company in Boston. "It's just a matter of making them believe it." The theory behind brainstorming is that the more ideas a group can produce, the more likely it will be to find one that works.

Alice Salmon, editor of the school yearbook in our pep rally case, shows her cre-

> **"Everyone is creative. It's just a matter of making them believe it."**
>
> **James Ferry**

ative thinking when she suggests that pep rallies be scheduled at the beginning of each athletic season, rather than once a month as they have been in the past.

> "I think one pep rally for each sports season is enough," she says. "That way we can have a more positive purpose. We can focus on wishing our teams well instead of focusing on the opponent. I hate those rallies where all we do is chant 'Kill the Bulldogs' or 'Throttle the Meadowlarks.'"
>
> Another student, Miguel Fuentes of the cross-country team, reminds everyone that good rallies take lots of effort.
>
> "Alice has a point. It's hard work to make a good skit," he says. "We've got to make sure the principal understands that."
>
> "I have an idea," offers Tina McIntire of the volleyball team. "If the principal won't let us have any more pep rallies, let's boycott all the games. Let's all stay away from the football field this Friday night."

Once the group has generated a large number of ideas (including some like Tina's that will be rejected in the end), it may discover that the obvious solution is not the best. Too often, a group reaches this phase only to have someone say, "Well, it appears pretty obvious what the solution ought to be," or "I guess we're pretty much in agreement." Comments like these undermine discussion because they stop any further thinking. No solution should be accepted until several have been proposed, examined, and compared. Accepting a solution without considering the alternatives is like playing the lottery: It gives the group only one chance, and a feeble one at that, to succeed.

5. Evaluate Each Solution and Select the Best One

The next step is to consider your options. If two or three solutions seem equally good, the group members should turn back to their criteria and make a careful comparison. Does each solution meet the standards they agreed on in the second step of this process? If not, that solution should be changed or eliminated. The best solution is the one that most clearly fits the criteria.

In the case of our pep rally students, they have decided to support Alice's idea about one pep rally per season.

> "I really like Alice's idea," says Renee. "I think it will show the principal that we're acting in good faith if we're willing to give up some of the pep rallies we've had in the past."
>
> "I agree," says Tammy, "but if the principal is going to buy our idea, we've got to convince him our rallies will be in good taste."
>
> "Let's don't go overboard here," comments Bob. "I want to remind him that pep rallies are supposed to be fun. Can't we be outrageous without being offensive? He was a teenager once—where's his sense of humor?"
>
> "How about this," offers Fred. "Let's take Alice's idea, urge the principal to trust the faculty sponsors, and keep Plan B as a backup."
>
> "Plan B? What's Plan B?" says Tammy.
>
> "If the principal won't let us schedule pep rallies during the regular school day, maybe he'll let us have them before or after school."

6. Suggest Ways for Testing or Carrying Out the Solution

Discussing how to carry out a solution is the final step in the problem-solving process. Group members must make sure that their solution is practical. If possible, the group might give their idea a brief test. That's what our pep rally students decided to do.

"How about this?" says Alice. "Let's take our idea to the pep club sponsor and several of the coaches first. They might have some suggestions for us."

"Why not?" says Miguel. "And if they like the idea, they might tell the principal they're supporting us."

"Sounds good to me," responds Tammy. "I'd like to have all the backing I can get when we take this to the principal."

INSTANT IMPACT

Self-Help Groups on the Rise

Self-help groups are booming. An estimated 16 million Americans now belong to about 500,000 self-help groups, and the number is growing each year.

Self-help groups offer their members both moral support and practical information. Research has shown that people who join such groups are frequently better off, emotionally and physically, than those who face their problems alone. When you find someone with the same worry, you tend to feel less isolated and gain more self-esteem.

Self-help groups exist for a great variety of personal problems. Some groups help people cope with a crisis, such as a divorce or death in the family. Other groups are aimed at changing addictive behavior, such as drug abuse, smoking, or overeating. Still others, so-called "one-step-beyond" groups, help friends and relatives of the person with the problem, such as the families of stroke victims or elderly grandparents. Some self-help groups even work toward changing public policies. The Alliance for the Mentally Ill, for example, is working to get more supervised housing for the mentally ill.

Managing Conflict

A good discussion will inevitably cause conflict. "Where all men think alike," said the columnist Walter Lippmann, "no one thinks very much." Differences of opinion—over ideas and issues—are the very heart of discussion. Problems that appear simple at first become more complex as you discover what other group members have to say on the subject.

Discussion can cause disagreements between members over facts, interpretations, and solutions. And such conflict will surely produce stress. We all find it difficult, for instance, not to take attacks on our ideas personally. Yet, only when we entertain conflicting ideas can we understand how complex most problems really are. Conflict, effectively and sensitively managed, can be extremely valuable in our efforts to reach the best solution.

Conflict as a Positive Force

As Mark Twain said, "A difference of opinion is what makes a good horse race." Discussion is not worth the trouble unless a genuine problem is at stake and people have real differences about how it should be solved. Peter Drucker, a well-known management consultant, says that disagreements are valuable because they provide alternative ways of looking at a

> "A difference of opinion is what makes a good horse race."
>
> **Mark Twain**

Differences of opinion among group members can provide alternative ways of looking at a problem.

problem. Alternatives, he says, are necessary if a group is going to do better than simply approve the first idea that comes along.

Constructive conflict develops when members use their differences to discover the best ideas and not to score points against one another. Group members should especially seek out ideas that are contrary to the prevailing opinions. Find a few "off-the-wall" ideas, solutions that seem far-fetched at first. By analyzing these ideas, the group will become less committed to the *status quo* and more willing to try something new.

Disruptive Conflict

Some conflict, however, can be disruptive. **Disruptive conflict** can destroy a group by *polarizing* the members (dividing them into competing sides that refuse to compromise) and by turning the discussion into a debate where personal victory is more important than a successful group decision. If "getting my way" is more important to you than helping the group, you have lost that cooperative attitude so essential to good discussion. If the captain of the football team in the pep rally example, for instance, had insisted on having a rally before each home game, his stubbornness might have made it impossible for the group to go ahead with its plan.

Almost every group has a few people who become nuisances—people who seem to fight the discussion process every step of the way. Often, these people can learn to be productive; they're simply acting like nuisances temporarily because they are bored or distracted. The health of the group, however, depends on dealing with them head-on. Look for the following behaviors in your next meeting and take

COMMUNICATION   BREAKDOWN

Peers Discourage Academic Achievement

Apparently, many girls still consider it a social handicap to be smart. Despite the women's movement and plenty of successful role models, one of the last things many girls want is a reputation as a good student. Girls who get good grades are labeled "brains" and run the risk of becoming social outcasts.

One female student at New York City's Hunter High School put it this way: "I make straight A's, but I never talk about it. . . . It's cool to do really badly. If you are interested in school and you show it, you're a nerd."

The popular culture—through television, movies, magazines, and videos—drums in the message that it is better to be popular, sexy, and cool than to be intelligent, accomplished, and outspoken. Peer pressure seems to reinforce these negative ideas in both boys and girls. Researchers at an all–African American high school in Washington, D.C., found that able students faced strong pressure not to succeed in school. If they did well in their studies, they might be accused of "acting white." Other successful students were called names ("brainiacs"), ignored and excluded, and even fell victim to physical assaults.

Such attitudes certainly discourage academic achievement. If boys and girls who study are ridiculed as "goobs" and "dweebs," then many children are going to avoid studying.

We all need to take a hard look at our own attitudes. If we say or do things that discourage people from seeing themselves as future engineers, doctors, or scientists, we need to change our ways. We must not allow peer pressure to put down academic achievement. Success in school requires the same motivation and effort as achievement in sports or music. Student groups can either support the struggle to achieve in school or reject it as a waste of time. By our participation in groups, we help determine which path our groups will take.

Source: The New Republic, *March 6, 1989.*

Question
What are some negative and positive examples of peer pressure in your school?

---

steps to turn these negatives into positives.

Nitpickers want everything spelled out and will quibble until they get what they want. "If it weren't for me," such people seem to be thinking, "this group would be in trouble." Nitpickers need to have a say, but not get their way. Be sure these group members get opportunities to speak, but insist they keep their comments brief.

Eager beavers want to offer a solution whether they have given it any thought or not. In their eagerness, they may distract the group's attention from ideas that have been more carefully considered. If the group can help funnel their enthusiasm, eager beavers can turn into valuable members, especially if the group asks them to back up their ideas with facts and reasoning.

Fence sitters don't dare take a position until they're sure what the "key people" will say. If the group can make it clear, however, that their opinions really matter, they may slowly gather courage and begin to say what they think, not what they think they should say.

Wisecrackers are the group clowns, people who seek attention in any way possible. Wisecrackers appear more often in groups where members are bored and looking for a diversion. In a more serious group, members quickly become impatient with such antics. If you find a wisecracker or two in your group, pick up the pace of the discussion—your group may have too much time on its hands.

Superior beings look down their noses at the whole business. Perhaps they didn't want to be part of the group in the first place. The group's best course with these members is to make them feel needed. The group must show it values their opinions, regardless of how superior and indifferent these people appear.

Dominators don't know when to quit talking. Once aware that they're preventing others from contributing, however, they can become top members. Making such persons recorders or evaluators (members who must be quiet during the meeting) is one way to help them become more aware of who's talking and who isn't during the group process. Once they know this, they may be more receptive to other people's ideas.

TAKING CHARGE

1. Observe a discussion from start to finish (you might watch a city council, school board, or legislative meeting). Can you state the problem or issue the group attempted to resolve? How many of the members actually took part in the discussion? Did the discussion follow the steps outlined in Dewey's problem-solving process? When the group got off course, did any members make an effort to steer the discussion back to the main point? Speak, if possible, with one of the participants after the discussion and compare your impressions with hers.

2. Learn to deal with annoying group members. Plan a topic of discussion for a group and label six cards ahead of time with the words "nitpicker," "eager beaver," "fence sitter," "wisecracker," "superior being," and "dominator." Secretly give one card to each of six persons in the group. Ask each person with a card to play that role as well as possible (refer back to the chapter text for a description of each role). As the discussion develops, observe how other students react to the six card-holders. Notice what kind of leadership develops and what kinds of frustrations occur. After the discussion, ask the class what they thought each of the six card-holders was doing.

III How to Contribute to a Discussion

Groups need participation from every member because people are more likely to support decisions that they play a role in shaping. On the other hand, group members become *apathetic* or even hostile toward ideas that are handed to them from on high. During World War II, government officials tried to convince people to use less popular meats, such as kidneys and sweetbreads, as a conservation measure. A follow-up study showed that while only 3 percent of those who heard lectures on the subject used these meats, 32 percent (ten times as many) of those who discussed the idea in group meetings were persuaded to do so.

Contributing as a Participant

We can't all be leaders, at least not all of the time. But everyone in a discussion has an important role to play. Indeed, the group can only be as effective as its weakest member. Remember, the objective of a group is to blend the knowledge, information, and reasoning of every member into a decision that represents their best collective thinking.

As a member of a group discussion, you have a number of responsibilities. Some of them involve the way you present what you have to say:

1. Be clear and simple. Reinforce what you say with looks and gestures.

2. Encourage members to react to your ideas. Questions like "Was I clear?" "What do you think about what I just said?" and "Do you have any questions?" indicate that you want feedback.

3. Be interesting. Although most of us dislike performing, it doesn't cost much to speak with vitality and enthusiasm.

When presenting an idea, a group member should be direct, interesting, and open to feedback.

4. Offer reasons for what you say. Make sure you take into account what other people are thinking. "The fool tells me his reasons," Aristotle said, "the wise man persuades me with my own."

5. Think before speaking, but don't think so long about what you want to say that an opportunity slips by. When your comment matters, seize the moment.

Active Listening

Everyone who participates in a discussion must also be an active listener. That means that even if you don't have anything to say at a particular time, you aren't free to loaf. You need to examine ideas as they are presented and figure out whether you understand them. Then, when it's your turn to contribute, you can make a meaningful comment.

As you listen to what others say, try to be impartial. Free yourself from preconceived ideas. Don't be like the person who says, "My mind is made up. Don't confuse me with facts." This sort of person comes to a discussion unwilling to accept any opinions different from his own. If left unchallenged, such a person can wreck the whole discussion.

Most important, be attentive and courteous. If you find yourself asking people to repeat themselves or to go back over ground they have already covered, you are slowing the process down and making the meeting dull for everyone. Avoid making silly or irrelevant comments. Contributions to the discussion are meaningful only when they connect with what has just been said.

Preparing for Discussion

It's a fact of life that you often come to a discussion group with your head full of other thoughts and interests. You probably have not reviewed your notes or even tried to decide what you think about the issues that will come up in the meeting. But taking a little time to prepare can pay big dividends, both for you and for the group. Preparation is largely a matter of looking ahead. By thinking out what questions and objections might be raised about your position ahead of time, you will be better able to cope with the give-and-take of the discussion process.

It's also a good idea to know how you work under pressure. Some people love the hubbub of discussion—and enjoy each conflict that arises. Others find arguments and clashes over ideas very stressful. Understanding who you are will help you define your role in a group. Try experimenting with varying degrees of participation to find your best comfort level.

No matter what, always keep in mind that you have skills and talents to offer the group. You may take good notes or be able to make a joke at a tense moment. Try to find out what the group needs from you. Be aware, though, that if you start out as a silent member, people will expect you to be silent the next time. They may try to encourage you to talk at first, but if you don't respond, they may come to ignore you. So, in short, don't wait for the second meeting to make a contribution; take the plunge right away.

Contributing as a Leader

Although some groups can function well for a time without a leader, there are clearly times when every group needs one. A certain nudge of guidance seems to be necessary for a group to function smoothly. For that reason, it may be unwise for a group to wait for a leader to emerge naturally. Instead, the group should designate a leader, at least for a particular meeting or for a particular goal. With a designated leader, the members of the group know who is responsible for settling disputes and maintaining an atmosphere where everyone's comments are welcome and appreciated. Without such a person, groups can break into cliques, become chaotic, or just waste time.

Leadership may change hands as the attitudes of the group or the areas of discussion change. Members may want the leadership of one person on one topic and turn for leadership to someone else at another time. The group decides not only whom it will follow but also how much authority it will give to the leader and how long it will accept that person's leadership. Fortunately, any interested member can learn to be an effective leader.

What a Leader Should Know

Any member should be willing and prepared to become a leader if asked. We can summarize a discussion leader's responsibilities this way:

1. A good leader should know how to run a meeting.
2. A good leader should know the people in the group.
3. A good leader should know the issues the group will discuss.

A discussion leader should pay her greatest attention to matters of procedure. She knows how to run a meeting, partly by virtue of experience and partly by a solid understanding of parliamentary procedure (see Chapter 18). This allows her to remain impartial. She becomes a neutral mediator to whom the participants in a discussion can turn when disagreements threaten to get out of control.

A shrewd leader should know the people in her group. That way she can plan to calm down those who talk too much and encourage those who talk too little. She should know who can be relied on to speak and who needs to be prodded.

A leader should also have a full grasp of the issues the group will discuss. This does not mean that the leader has to know more than anyone else. In fact, a competent leader may know very little about specific details. She must, nonetheless, understand the nature of the problem and the most productive way to analyze it.

Getting a Meeting Started

The leader of a group is first and foremost a **moderator.** A moderator must get the discussion started, keep the discussion moving, and bring the discussion to a close. Getting a discussion started can be a major challenge, especially for an inexperienced leader. Most groups need to be led into useful discussion. Imagine a situation where your leader, after finishing his introduction (which might be a brief welcome and a reminder of why the meeting has been called), simply says, "Well, who wants to begin?" This tactic is almost certain to fail. Groups need greater direction, especially in the beginning.

A useful method for starting a discussion is to pose a question. This opening question should be directed to the group as a whole and not to any one individual. It would be unwise to put someone on the spot this early in the discussion.

COMMUNICATION WORKS

Twyla Hansen, Grounds Manager

The football team can't play without her, the neighbors don't understand her, and she seems to have a knack for raising money without really trying. She is Twyla Hansen, grounds manager for Nebraska Wesleyan University.

When Hansen isn't planting trees and shrubs, she spends her time communicating with staff, administrators, alumni, and the public.

Her most important communication, she says, comes during weekly staff meetings with the people who mow the grass, trim the shrubs, and prune the trees. It wasn't easy for her to be accepted into what had been exclusively a man's world, let alone to be the leader of the group.

"You have to be careful not to crush a person's spirit," she says. "Even when I'm not happy with something someone did, I'll start with a compliment. I'll say I'm really happy with how you mowed here, but not so happy with what you did over there."

Most important, Hansen says, "you have to mean what you say."

Hansen also meets frequently with campus administrators to coordinate outdoor events and activities (she helped construct a frisbee golf course around the dormitories). She also meets regularly with alumni groups. On one occasion, she happened to mention a secret wish she had for a lilac garden on campus. Before the meeting was over, the alumni members had raised $1,500 among themselves for Hansen's garden.

When Hansen got in trouble with her neighbors, however, a group meeting might have avoided a confrontation. Several of her neighbors, it seems, didn't appreciate her lawn—a swath of four-foot-high prairie grass and wildflowers—which presents a stark contrast to their Kentucky blue grass. Blue grass lawns, however, take lots of water and fertilizer.

When the city weed inspector asked Hansen to cut her lawn, citing the neighbors' complaints and a city ordinance, she refused. She showed the inspector how each plant in her yard was listed in a book of state wildflowers. When she explained that she was saving natural resources by not mowing and watering, he decided to leave her property alone. Next time, Hansen vows, she'll let the neighbors in on what she's doing.

Moreover, the question should be general rather than specific.

Most discussion questions can be grouped into three categories: fact, interpretation, and evaluation. **Questions of fact** ask group members to recall information that touches on the business at hand. **Questions of interpretation** ask them to give their opinions on what the information means. **Questions of evaluation** ask

A group's leader is responsible for getting the discussion started, keeping it moving, and bringing it to a close.

members to agree or disagree with possible solutions and to make value judgments.

A leader should use interpretive questions at the beginning of a discussion and, if possible, write them out ahead of time. Suppose you are preparing to lead a group discussion. Pick a question you are wondering about. The best interpretive questions are those that you have no ready answers for but that you believe can be answered. Prepare a question for the group and then ask yourself whether the group has enough information to deal effectively with the question. If it does not, throw that question out and find another.

Good interpretive questions are questions you care about, questions that really matter. You can never be sure, of course, that everyone in the group will share your enthusiasm for a particular question, but if you are eager to get an answer, chances are in your favor that others will be, too. If you don't care, why should anyone else?

We can summarize the qualities of good interpretive questions like this:

1. They contain doubt.
2. They can be answered.
3. They are likely to interest the group.

Think back for a moment to the students who were worried about their pep rallies being canceled. During their discussion, they asked several interpretive questions: "What will students think about having fewer pep rallies?" "How will the principal react to our idea about faculty supervision?" "How important are pep rallies, anyway?" They also asked at least one question of fact: "Have we ever had problems with pep rallies before?" and one evaluative question: "Is this plan good for our school?"

Keeping the Discussion Going

Once underway, a well-informed group will usually move along without much prodding from the leader. Good leaders strive for balanced participation. More often than not, groups have at least one person who talks too much and one who talks too little. Leaders should work to see that everyone participates and that no one *monopolizes* the group's time. If several speakers try to speak at once, preference should be given to the one who has spoken less. Sometimes real diplomacy is needed to keep the discussion from becoming one-sided. Leaders must rely on tact and good humor to see that everyone talks but that no one talks too much.

Leaders must be especially careful with members who are reluctant to speak. For example, leaders should resist the temptation to ask a timid person a direct question. This tactic can backfire because if the person is taken by surprise, he will be even less likely to speak thereafter. It may be safe, however, to ask for a comment on an idea already being considered, as in "Sean, what do you think of Samantha's idea?"

Leaders should provide occasional *paraphrases* of what someone has said. They may sometimes need to repeat in their own words what a member has said, especially if the person has been talking for a long time. Leaders should also provide occasional summaries of what the group has accomplished so far. Summaries help the group avoid repetition and spotlight areas of agreement or disagreement. Both paraphrases and summaries help everyone know where the group is in the discussion.

Setting an Example

A leader can increase the members' desire to participate by recognizing and praising (when appropriate) their contributions. Leaders give such recognition with statements like "That's an important point. Thank you for bringing it to our attention," as well as nonverbal support like good eye contact and head nodding. Carefully timed praise also encourages group loyalty. Finally, leaders should avoid sending negative nonverbal signals. For example, the leader shouldn't yawn when someone else is talking. Nothing will turn a group off quicker than an inattentive leader.

Closing the Discussion

At some point, the leader will move to end the discussion. A leader should be alert for signs that the group is ready to quit, or at least ready to be done with the question at hand. The group may begin to repeat itself, to take up minor points, or

INSTANT   IMPACT

American Political Conventions

The political conventions of America's Democratic and Republican parties are as much circus as serious debate, but they come close to serving as national discussions. Every four years the parties get together to name their presidential nominees and draft their platforms—their "wish lists" for the country.

Sometimes, however, there are too many voices and too many opinions. This chaotic situation is especially bothersome if a party is trying to make a great show of unity. During the 1992 Democratic convention in New York City, staff members of Bill Clinton, the party's presidential nominee, took unusual steps to make sure that all delegates sounded as if they were in agreement.

In an impressive example of groupthink, Clinton staffers distributed sets of "talking points" each night during the convention. These points included suggested answers to reporters' questions. When delegates were interviewed on television or for their hometown newspapers, they just said about the same things every other delegate said. In essence, they stuck to the "script."

Was this brainwashing? Probably not. Clinton staffers said they were simply managing the news. They said it was a useful skill to master—especially if they found themselves in the White House someday.

Adapted from U.S. News & World Report, *July 27, 1992.*

to wander away from the question. When this happens, the group members have probably gone as far as they can with the issue. The leader must also be aware of any time limits (the bell is about to ring, for instance) that mean the discussion must stop. In either case, it is time to settle the question.

The ideal conclusion of a group discussion is for the group to reach a **consensus.** Consensus means a *nearly* unanimous agreement among the group's members about a particular solution. It happens most often when members unselfishly seek common ground. But it doesn't happen all the time, and it never happens without a great deal of effort.

As desirable as consensus is, you should be on guard against giving up an argument or a position too easily just to go along with the group. In its most extreme form, this desire to go along with the group causes people to abandon their own personal beliefs. People sometimes call this very human desire to get along **groupthink** because we let a group do our thinking for us. If you let your friends talk you into doing something, you have become a victim of groupthink. Thinking for yourself within a group can be tough, but no group can profit when its members give up their own individuality.

TAKING CHARGE

1. Make a list of interpretive questions for a discussion on one of the following topics:

   ◆ What qualities should a good presidential candidate possess?
   ◆ Are college entrance requirements too easy (or hard)?
   ◆ Is year-round school a good idea?
   ◆ Should term limits be imposed on all elected officials?

   Once you have selected a topic and written a list of interpretive questions, write five factual questions and three evaluation questions for the discussion.

2. Find an article in the newspaper that explains how two groups disagree on an issue. Analyze how each group would respond to these questions:

   ◆ How does our side see the problem?
   ◆ What solution can we suggest?
   ◆ What are the advantages of our solution?
   ◆ What are the disadvantages of our solution?

   Can you suggest a way these two groups could resolve their differences and settle on a compromise solution? Must one group give in, or can both groups find a middle ground?

REVIEW AND ENRICHMENT

LOOKING BACK

Listed below are the major ideas discussed in this chapter.

◆ Group discussion is a cooperative process in which participants exchange information, discuss ideas, and solve problems.

◆ Group discussion is especially valuable because people are more likely to support decisions they have had a share in making.

◆ Among the more public forms of discussion are the panel, the symposium, and the town hall meeting.

◆ The ideal group size is five to seven people. Groups with fewer members tend to lack diversity, and larger groups do not have enough opportunities for everyone to participate.

◆ Many groups use a standard problem-solving process based on John Dewey's steps of reflective thinking.

◆ Differences of opinion within a group should be encouraged as a way of exploring alternatives.

◆ Disruptive conflict can occur when individual members put greater importance on getting their way than on supporting a group decision.

◆ Good participants use active listening skills and watch for the right moment to speak when their comment will have the most impact.

◆ Although some groups can function without a leader, most groups profit from having one because the leader can make the group function more smoothly and effectively.

◆ A leader can begin a discussion by asking an interpretive question, which requires members to provide evidence and reasoning to support their opinions.

◆ The leader can also help the group by providing occasional summaries of what has gone on and paraphrases of what members have said.

◆ Groups must strive for consensus, but they must also be on alert for groupthink, where their personal beliefs are overcome by the pressure to conform.

SPEECH VOCABULARY

Match the speech term on the left with the definition on the right.

1. discussion
2. cooperative
3. competitive
4. panel
5. forum

a. difference of opinion that leads to creative alternatives

b. set of standards for evaluation

c. creative process for coming up with ideas

d. discussion format typical of cabinet meetings

6. round table
7. symposium
8. town hall meeting
9. cohesion
10. criteria
11. brainstorming
12. constructive conflict
13. disruptive conflict
14. moderator
15. question of fact
16. question of interpretation
17. question of evaluation
18. consensus
19. groupthink

e. helpful and unselfish
f. informal discussion before an audience
g. independent and self-oriented
h. discussion format in which a few experts give short speeches
i. nearly unanimous agreement
j. social "glue" that holds a group together
k. exchange of information and ideas among a group
l. tendency to conform to group opinion
m. opportunity for audience members to ask questions
n. discussion format involving an entire community
o. disagreement that prevents a group from making a decision
p. a question about opinions
q. a question about value judgments
r. a question about information
s. impartial person who organizes a discussion

GENERAL VOCABULARY

Match the content term on the left with the correct definition on the right.

1. consultation
2. team teaching
3. cooperative learning
4. sequential
5. scenario
6. bombard
7. status quo
8. polarizing
9. apathetic
10. monopolize
11. paraphrase

a. express or interpret something in other words
b. dominate to the exclusion of others
c. to attack vigorously or persistently
d. showing little feeling or interest
e. educational style in which teachers work together
f. dividing into two opposing sides
g. situation in which two or more colleagues, such as doctors, confer on a case
h. educational style in which students work in teams
i. plot outline
j. having a logical, step-by-step pattern
k. the existing state of affairs

THINGS TO REMEMBER

1. Give three reasons why discussion is one of the best methods for solving problems.
2. Why is a group of five more likely to have a successful discussion than a group of three or a group of twelve?
3. What are the six steps of the problem-solving process?
4. What is brainstorming?
5. What are the major duties of a group discussion leader?
6. Explain the difference between questions of fact, questions of interpretation, and questions of evaluation.
7. Why should a leader occasionally summarize what the group has done?
8. What is a consensus?
9. How can you prepare for a discussion?

THINGS TO DO

1. Make a participation diagram of the next discussion you attend to chart how many times each person speaks and to whom. On a sheet of paper, arrange a group of circles to represent the group members and where they are seated. Put each person's initials in his or her circle. Next, draw lines to connect each circle with every other circle.

    Each time someone says something to someone else, put a slash mark through the line connecting the two people's circles. If an individual makes a comment to the entire group and not to anyone in particular, place a mark inside that person's circle. At the end of the discussion, you can analyze the group's interaction. Who spoke the most? The least? Where were most of the comments directed?

2. Ask your teacher to choose two groups of five students each. The remainder of the class will form one large group. Ask each group to discuss the same question, perhaps "Should school lunches be catered by fast-food chains like McDonald's or Burger King?" Have an observer in each group report back to the class on how many people participated and how much they said. Are there noticeable differences between the participation levels in larger and smaller groups? Were the decisions the same in each group?

THINGS TO TALK ABOUT

1. What would you do if the following occurred in a group discussion?

   ✦ One person who obviously has not done any research on the topic criticizes many valid remarks made by other members.

   ✦ Two members sit and whisper to one another while other members talk about the topic.

   ✦ One member insists on dominating the discussion. The fact that this person has many notes shows that he or she has done plenty of research.

   ✦ The discussion leader shows signs of being hopelessly disorganized. The group is drifting and beginning to repeat itself.

   ✦ One member is so busy taking notes on the discussion that he or she is not saying anything.

2. How does discussion differ from conversation?
3. Why is equal participation from all members a good goal for group discussion?

THINGS TO WRITE ABOUT

1. Write a letter to a leader in your school or community. Ask that person for a definition of leadership and a few examples of how good leadership has made a difference. Share the reply with your classmates.
2. Suppose your class wanted to plan a school assembly to better inform students on the dangers of driving while intoxicated. Would it be better to have a panel discussion, symposium, round table, or town hall meeting? Why? Explain your answer in a one-page paper.

CRITICAL THINKING

1. How important is it to achieve consensus in a group discussion?
2. How can you tell whether conflict in a group discussion is creative and constructive or self-centered and disruptive?

RELATED SPEECH TOPICS

Groups make better decisions than individuals

Commercials insult our intelligence

A friend is someone you can talk to

The value of the movie ratings system

Things my parents taught me

Things I wish my parents had taught me

Leadership styles of famous people

CHAPTER 7

Researching Your Speech

"If truth is beauty, then why don't more people get their hair done at the library?"

— Lily Tomlin

LEARNING OBJECTIVES

After completing this chapter, you will be able to do the following.

- ✦ Discuss the impact of the Information Age on your future.
- ✦ Develop a plan that will help you focus your research efforts.
- ✦ Identify four shortcuts that will reduce the time you spend researching.
- ✦ Use the card catalog to find resource material for your speeches.
- ✦ Distinguish between plagiarism and intellectual honesty.

CHAPTER OUTLINE

Following are the main sections in this chapter.

I The Information Age
II Your Research Plan
III Using the Library
IV Using What You've Found

      Student Speech

      Chapter Review

NEW SPEECH TERMS

In this chapter, you will learn the meanings of the speech terms listed below.

audience analysis
interlibrary loan
database
on-line
card catalog
author card
title card

subject card
serendipity
table of contents
index
plagiarism
paraphrasing
ghostwriters

GENERAL VOCABULARY

Expanding your general vocabulary will help you become a more effective communicator. Listed below are some words appearing in this chapter that you should make part of your everyday vocabulary.

prerequisite
entrepreneur
alienate
microcosm
havens
nuclear family

crooned
compendium
malice
attribution
egregious
discourse

Looking Ahead

How can you find your way out of the library bewilderness? Shortcuts can help you better use your research time effectively as you acquire the necessary information to prepare a successful speech. Note taking is essential to any research effort—but how do you decide what to write down? What is plagiarism, and how can you avoid intellectual dishonesty? These questions and others arise as you research any topic for an upcoming speech. Developing the ability to find the answers to such questions is a necessary *prerequisite* for anyone who wants to survive in this Information Age.

I The Information Age

We live in the Information Age. More than 50,000 books are published each year in the United States. Our store of knowledge and information is doubling every five years. The author Richard Saul Wurman points out that "a weekday edition of the *New York Times* contains more information than the average person was likely to come across in a lifetime in seventeenth-century England." It is not surprising, then, that the enormous amount of available information can be overwhelming to the student researcher in need of evidence for an upcoming speech.

At the same time, students are becoming increasingly aware that information skills are essential to survival in the world today. Whether you're a college student studying the latest advances in organ transplants or a young *entrepreneur* starting an auto repair shop, you need to know how to find the right answers. This crucial concern was addressed by the members of the U.S. National Commission on Libraries and Information Science. They asserted that "a basic objective of education is for each student to learn how to identify needed information, locate and organize it, and present it in a clear and persuasive manner."

This chapter is a step in your journey toward this goal. Clearly, the process of researching supporting materials for each of your assigned speeches challenges you to become a more effective problem solver. As a problem solver, you will soon experience the thrill of the hunt, the joy of finding that juicy—but effectively hidden, until now—bit of information. The trick, of course, is to have a plan.

II Your Research Plan

Let's assume you have just chosen a speech topic. Chances are that you know something about the topic. Fortunately, one of the best ways to begin organizing your thoughts is to assess what you al-

INSTANT IMPACT

Knowing It All

Dr. Michael B. McElroy, Chair of the Department of Earth and Planetary Sciences at Harvard University, has concluded the following.

The libraries of Harvard University alone contain eleven million volumes. Assuming that each volume has about 150 pages, with about 400 words per page, we may calculate the store of wisdom at Harvard to run to approximately 660 billion words. If we assume that the accomplished reader can process about 50 words per minute, it is easy, for a skilled arithmetician at least, to estimate how long it would take to survey the material at Harvard. The answer is a staggering 25,000 years, and that does not allow time for sleep or other distraction.

Source: Randall McCutcheon, Can You Find It?, *Free Spirit Publishing (Minneapolis, MN): 1989, p. 1.*

ready know. You will soon realize, though, that with most topics you need assistance. Successful speeches require supporting information. Supporting information requires specific research. Specific research provides sources to quote—people who know more about a given topic than you. The Greeks referred to this process of accumulating information as building a "storehouse of knowledge."

Before you start accumulating information, you should have a carefully thought-out plan. If you are like most beginning researchers, though, you don't yet know how to plan—how to play the research game. Although you can gather supporting materials from such methods as interviewing or surveying, most of the re-

TAKING CHARGE

Using Dr. McElroy's formula (described in the Instant Impact "Knowing It All"), calculate how long it would take to read all of the books in your school library.

Most speech topics can be researched in a library.

search game is played in the library. Entering a library, though, you may feel as if you are trapped inside some gigantic alien pinball machine—the flippers frozen, the tilt beyond your control. Thus, the time you spend "playing library" is largely wasted.

So how do you avoid wasting time? Speakers disagree as to the best method. Some begin with a rough outline of the speech and then find evidence to support the subpoints. Others do some preliminary research and then create an outline that incorporates the facts that they have gathered. In choosing one of these approaches perhaps the most important factor is how much you know about the topic before you begin. If you are speaking on the topic "We must reduce unemployment" and you are not well informed about economic theory, then you should probably do some preliminary reading before making any decisions about how to organize your speech. If, on the other hand, you are speaking on the topic "The student council should play a more active role in the school," you might want to start by jotting down a rough outline of your views on the topic.

To save more time, consider finding an expert to give focus to your research. A phone call to a government official, a college professor, or an author can save you hours of wading through books and articles that are not relevant to your search. Experts can suggest the best sources on a particular topic, and they often can provide quotable statements to incorporate in your speeches. You can even become your own expert by undertaking opinion polls on controversial topics or by conducting a series of interviews with representatives on both sides of a specific issue.

As you gather information for your speech, remember to adapt to the audience that will hear your presentation. For example, a speech before your classmates during second period may require less formality than a commencement address before members of the community. In any speaking situation, keep in mind that the audience may not have the same interests as you do. Skateboarding, for example, may occupy your every waking thought but be of little consequence to most members of your audience. Therefore, you have to plan your speech—no matter what the topic—by first considering the needs and expectations of those people who will be listening to you. This process, **audience analysis,** involves asking yourself the following questions:

✦ What do the listeners already know about my topic?

✦ How do I capture their interest?

✦ How formal should my language be?

✦ What should I avoid saying that might *alienate* some audience members?

✦ What can I say to change the minds of people who might disagree with my positions?

You should make it clear that you care about your audience and that you want to share the information in your speech with them. Audience analysis is treated further in Chapter 13.

TAKING CHARGE

Now it's your turn. Choose a potential topic for a speech and call up a local expert. (If you are seeking information about a problem facing the nation, toll-free numbers are sometimes useful. For example, you can phone the Environmental Protection Agency for guidance on a speech about harmful pesticides.) Make certain that you first identify yourself and the nature of your inquiry. Then ask the expert for possible ways to find the best information on the topic you have selected. Finally, be certain to thank your expert.

Some ideas:

✦ Contact a political science professor from a nearby college about sources to use in speaking about the many changes in Eastern Europe.

✦ Contact a local author for a speech on the difficulty of pursuing writing as a career.

✦ Contact a town official for information to include in a speech on the growing need for social services in society today.

✦ Contact the state attorney general's office to gather information for a speech on mail-order fraud.

✦ Contact a senior citizen in your community to get information about the history of the community in which you live.

COMMUNICATION BREAKTHROUGH

Library Business Booms in Hard Times

Libraries become *havens* for the unemployed during hard economic times. Patricia Glass Schuman, past president of the Chicago-based American Library Association, says that people use libraries not only to look for jobs but also for entertainment. They turn to the library for a video or a book when they can't afford to go to the movies.

Jobless patrons, according to the Associated Press, "empty shelves of career-guide books and raid newspaper bins for help-wanted ads." Some libraries expand their services to meet the needs of the unemployed by offering a job-listing telephone service.

The Skokie Public Library in suburban Chicago has turned one room into an Employment Resource Center. Once a week, the library places job listings and other career information there. People who need résumés can get help from the reference librarian. To guide people in planning job-information searches, the reference librarian conducts thirty-minute interviews.

Clearly, the 15,500 libraries in this country are an immense resource, providing not only volumes and volumes of books but also the expert skills of professional librarians who care.

Question
What other services do you think libraries could provide for the unemployed?

III Using the Library

"You know what scares me," the author Stephen King once said, "are people who don't use the library." King was suggesting that a trip to the library is a crucial step in preparing any piece of writing—your next speech, for example. You can significantly increase your credibility as a speaker (what the Greek rhetorician Aristotle called your *ethos*) by quoting authoritative sources. A medical doctor, for instance, is likely to know more about the causes of sports injuries than you.

Therefore, you need to supplement your personal knowledge with solid research. Unfortunately, as we suggested earlier, the

> "What scares me are people who don't use the library."
> **Stephen King**

mushrooming store of information makes it difficult to know where to begin and how to conduct a successful search for supporting material for your speeches. Most students feel lost in the beginning, "deskperadoes" fenced in by inexperience. But hang in there. Do not be intimidated by the library. Your frustration, your ini-

A reference librarian can offer valuable research assistance, either in person or over the telephone.

tial wild goose chases, will soon end as you become more efficient, more productive.

How do you get the most out of a library? To help you use the library, this section describes some useful shortcuts and then tells you how to find books and periodicals. It also discusses other sources of information found in the library.

Four Shortcuts

Four shortcuts will help you use your research time effectively:

1. Whether you use your school library or another nearby library, make certain to take advantage of the reference librarian's knowledge. Reference librarians are trained to answer your questions and to give you guidance in your research efforts. They can save you hours of disappointment. They know things that many teenagers do not (that Socrates was not an Indian chief, for example). And they actually enjoy helping you find the right information, so don't be afraid to ask.

2. A public library's reference department will usually give you assistance over the phone. These librarians will find facts for you—for free. If you need to know, for example, the Supreme Court's most recent ruling on capital punishment, or how to get financial aid for college, then "reach out and touch" the "someone" with answers: the reference librarian.

3. If your library does not have the book you want and you can wait for a few weeks, try interlibrary loan. **Interlibrary loan** is a cooperative system by which libraries lend specific books to one another on order. In other words, a library in Boise, Idaho, may mail to your library that hard-to-find work on the finer points of fly fishing for the mere cost of postage and an insurance fee.

4. Although the computer has no intelligence of its own, it offers certain advantages over traditional approaches to finding information. The

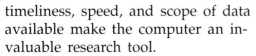

Using key words that describe a speech topic, a library computer can search on-line databases for possible sources of information. A card catalog, whether traditional or computerized, tells which books are in the library and where they are located.

timeliness, speed, and scope of data available make the computer an invaluable research tool.

To find information by computer, you must search on-line databases. A **database** is simply a collection of related information. **On-line** services provide rapid access to many computer databases containing information on many topics. More and more libraries are subscribing to one or more specialized on-line database services. Often, there is a charge for requesting a database search. Check with your librarian about costs before you are forced to write a check.

Note that a search through databases is limited by what a particular database includes and by how well you choose "key words," those words that best describe the desired information. For example, in researching a speech on the disintegration of the *nuclear family*, you might begin a subject search by typing the key word *divorce* into the computer. Some other key words you might try include *single parents* and *child care.*

Finding Books with the Card Catalog

When Kermit the Frog *crooned*, "It's not easy being green," he might well have been describing the challenge awaiting you in the **card catalog.** The inexperienced, or "green," researcher, though, soon discovers the value of understanding this library resource. The card catalog tells you what books the library has and where you can find them. The catalog in-

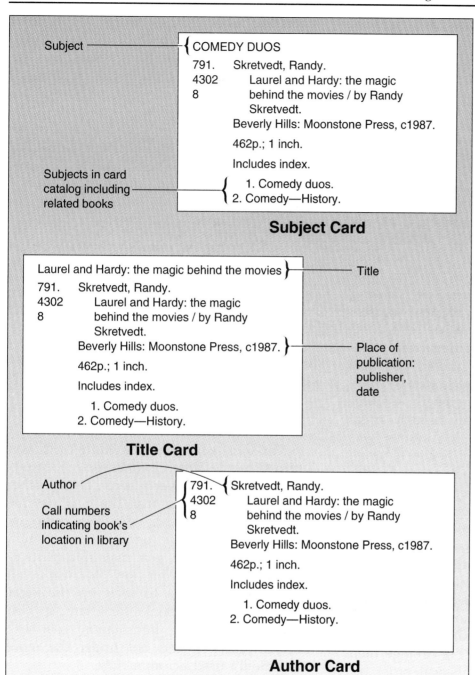

Subject

COMEDY DUOS

791.   Skretvedt, Randy.
4302   Laurel and Hardy: the magic
8   behind the movies / by Randy
           Skretvedt.
       Beverly Hills: Moonstone Press, c1987.

       462p.; 1 inch.

       Includes index.

Subjects in card
catalog including
related books
           1. Comedy duos.
           2. Comedy—History.

Subject Card

Laurel and Hardy: the magic behind the movies ————— Title

791.   Skretvedt, Randy.
4302   Laurel and Hardy: the magic
8   behind the movies / by Randy
           Skretvedt.
       Beverly Hills: Moonstone Press, c1987. ————— Place of
                                                    publication:
       462p.; 1 inch.   publisher,
                                                    date
       Includes index.

           1. Comedy duos.
           2. Comedy—History.

Title Card

Author

Call numbers
indicating book's
location in library

791.   Skretvedt, Randy.
4302   Laurel and Hardy: the magic
8   behind the movies / by Randy
           Skretvedt.
       Beverly Hills: Moonstone Press, c1987.

       462p.; 1 inch.

       Includes index.

           1. Comedy duos.
           2. Comedy—History.

Author Card

Each library book is represented in the card catalog
by an author card, a title
card, and a subject card.

cludes three kinds of cards: The **author card,** the **title card,** and the **subject card.** When you don't have specific books in mind, then you should examine the sub- ject cards available on your topic choice. If you know the author or title of a par- ticular work you need, you can begin your search by examining one of those cards. Today, many libraries have computerized their catalogs. You can do title, author, and subject searches with the computerized catalog, too. If you've used one card catalog, you know how to use them all.

When you find a card on a book you want, record the call number printed in the upper-left-hand corner of the card so that you can locate the book on the library shelves. (A tip: When you find the book you are seeking, examine the nearby books for related information. Books are grouped by subject matter, and you might accidentally discover other material that you can use in your speech. Making pleasant discoveries by accident in this way is known as **serendipity**.)

Whether you use a traditional card catalog or a computerized catalog, you will find it necessary to locate books by their call numbers. Two call number classification systems are commonly used to organize library works. The first system was created in the 1870s by an acting librarian at Amherst College named Melvil Dewey. The Dewey Decimal System identifies categories of books by three-digit numbers, as shown in the accompanying table. The second system, the Library of Congress system, offers many more categories. As shown in the table, it uses twenty-one letters of the alphabet instead of the ten numerical digits. Some school libraries use one of these two classification systems for their works of nonfiction but arrange their books of fiction in alphabetical order according to the author's last name.

Finding Things in Books

Now that you've found that book, you should become familiar with two sections that are found in most works: the table of contents and the index.

The **table of contents** outlines for you the general plan of the work. A table of contents may include the page number where a chapter begins, a summary of the content of each chapter, and a breakdown of each chapter into its major sections. For example, in the book *High School: A Report on Secondary Education in America*, the author, Ernest Boyer, provides this information in the table of contents:

Part III: What Every Student Should Learn

5. Something for Everyone   71
6. Literacy: The Essential Tool   85
7. The Curriculum Has a Core   94
8. Transition: To Work and Learning   118
9. Instruction: A Time to Learn   141

If you are preparing a speech on the value of literacy, then the table of contents makes it clear that you should turn to page 85. If, however, you are preparing a speech on the Scholastic Aptitude Test (SAT), then you might be stumped if you turned to the table of contents.

The index to Boyer's book, on the other hand, informs you that the SAT is discussed on pages 132–134. The **index** (a Latin word meaning "one who points out") tells exactly where you may find particular information. The key to using an index effectively is to look up the right term. In Boyer's book, for example, you must look up the information you seek under *Scholastic* and not under the more commonly used acronym *SAT*.

Finding Periodicals

The card catalog is not the best place to look for articles in journals, magazines, newspapers, or other periodical publica-

The Dewey Decimal System	The Library of Congress System	
000 General Works	**A** General Works	**M** Music
100 Philosophy & Psychology	**B** Philosophy & Religion	**N** Visual Arts
200 Religion	**C** Auxiliary Sciences of History	**O** *omitted to avoid confusion with the numeral zero*
300 Social Sciences	**D** History (General)	
400 Languages	**E** History (U.S.)	**P** Language & Literature
500 Pure Sciences	**F** History (U.S., Canada, Latin & South America)	**Q** Science
600 Technology & Applied Sciences		**R** Medicine
	G Geography, Anthropology, & Recreation	**S** Agriculture
700 The Arts & Recreation	**H** Social Sciences	**T** Technology
800 Literature	**I** *omitted to avoid confusion with the numeral 1*	**U** Military Science
900 History & Geography		**V** Naval Science
	J Political Science	**WXY** *omitted*
	K Law	**Z** Bibliography & Library Science
	L Education	

tions. For these articles, you will need to look in various indexes.

You might, for instance, try the Newsbank Electronic Index, a computer service that accesses 2 million newspaper articles. This reference resource contains information on virtually every newsworthy issue in the United States. In addition, newspapers like the *New York Times* have their own indexes.

For journals and magazines, you should use a periodical index. The listings in a periodical index are usually arranged by subject and author. Perhaps the best-known general index of this type is the *Reader's Guide to Periodical Literature*. The *Reader's Guide* is an index to the articles in three hundred familiar and generally popular magazines. Some libraries also subscribe to the ProQuest computer system, which holds information on articles from more than seven hundred different popular and scholarly publications. ProQuest searches a CD periodical index for references to any word or word combination you use to activate the system. Unlike the *Reader's Guide*, ProQuest includes abstracts, or summaries, of the articles so you can tell whether they are pertinent to your topic.

Other Sources of Information

Other sources of information that can be found in the library include almanacs, at-

COMMUNICATION WORKS

Andy Howe, Librarian

"It makes everything better," says Andy Howe, "not only during their years in school but for the rest of their lives." Howe, a librarian, is committed to helping students learn the process of research as a lifetime skill. She jokes that it is much easier to teach students than adults, because adults would rather have the sought-after materials "handed to them."

Howe, a librarian at Albuquerque Academy in New Mexico, did her undergraduate work at the University of Colorado. She received her Master of Library Science degree from Southern Connecticut State College while working in a nearby public library. This experience taught Howe that passive book tending was not as important as becoming a leader in the educational process.

Stressing the importance of communication skills in this process, Howe notes that a librarian needs to know how to ask the right questions. In order to help someone, the librarian must first determine what information is desired, what information is necessary. Howe explains, "If a pizza-loving student asks how many anchovies were imported into the United States last year, for example, then I must be prepared to recommend possible reference works that might deliver in just a few minutes."

Howe reminds us that the library has an answer for everyone, whether the question is what the *zip* in *zip code* means, who the patron saint of hairdressers is, or how to join the Christopher Morley Knothole Association. Maybe you're checking out the inside information on buying a used car. Or you're planning a family vacation to the Big Apple. Or you're preparing your next speech for class. Howe says, "No matter what it is that is most important to a student, information about it can be found in the library."

lases, biographies, encyclopedias, and collections of quotations.

Almanacs

Almanacs are annual publications that provide you with a storehouse of statistics and general facts. The *World Almanac and Book of Facts,* one of the most popular almanacs, describes itself as a *"compendium* of universal knowledge." This knowledge includes everything from off-beat stories about the world's dumbest robbers to the sports records of your favorite college and professional teams. You will find an almanac useful for learning the order in which the events of a particular year happened, as well as discovering facts about countries and their governments. The *Facts on File Yearbook* and the *Information*

Please Almanac are also available in most libraries.

Atlases

Atlases are collections of maps—in essence, graphic illustrations of many of the facts found in almanacs. *Rand McNally Goode's World Atlas,* for example, may give you geographical information for your speeches. It contains maps, tables, and indexes concerning "water resources, minorities, income, education, life expectancy, population change, labor structure, and westward expansion," in addition to maps of climate, rainfall, and time zones. A special feature is the pronunciation index. The *Times Atlas of the World,* too, is noted for its coverage and accuracy.

Biographies

If your speech topic includes discussing a well-known individual, you should consult a biographical reference work. *Biography Index,* published since 1949, is a quarterly, cumulative index to biographical material in both books and magazines.

You should know in researching biographical material that few biographical collections bother to verify facts. Generally, the people who are written about fill out questionnaires. Sometimes they lie. Consider the case of one hoaxer who managed to get a fictitious biography of his dog into *Who's Who in America.*

Unlike *Who's Who, Current Biography* details both positive and negative information about the biographees. *Current Biography,* issued monthly and then published annually as a combined volume, contains "brief, objective, accurate, and well-documented biographical articles about living leaders in all fields of human accomplishment the world over."

The multivolume *Dictionary of American Biography* (DAB) is known for its scholarly articles and objectivity. The prose in the DAB is a bit more stuffy than that in *Current Biography,* but its thoroughness and reliability make it worth checking.

Encyclopedias

The American Library Association hails the *Academic American Encyclopedia* (AAE) as "the most current and up-to-date encyclopedia in the English language for high school, college, and adult readers." The AAE has entered the computer age—it is available in three electronic formats as well as the printed version. In coverage and style, though, the new *Encyclopedia Britannica* is reputed to be the most scholarly. No matter which encyclopedia you choose, make certain that you read the introductory material in the first volume. The editors will clue you in on how to find the out-of-the-ordinary material in that particular reference work.

Specialized encyclopedias can help you research some speech topics. For a speech on genetic engineering, for example, you might want to use the *McGraw-Hill Encyclopedia of Science and Technology.* The *International Encyclopedia of Social Sciences* covers topics in fields such as anthropology, history, political science, and sociology.

Quotation Collections

Books of quotations are important tools for speakers. You can add spice—a colorful phrase, a clear example, a humorous insight—to almost any speech with a well-chosen quotation. *Bartlett's Familiar Quotations* is probably the most familiar collection and the most widely available. You may want to turn to *Peter's Quotations,* though, for the thoughts of more current individuals. If you were preparing a speech on the topic of perfectionism, you might use the following quotations from the *Penguin Dictionary of Modern Quotations* to suggest that we all make mistakes.

"As soon as I stepped out of my mother's womb on to dry land, I realized that I had made a mistake—that I shouldn't have come, but the trouble with children is that they are not returnable." (Quentin Crisp)

"The working of great institutions is mainly the result of a vast mass of routine, petty *malice*, self-interest, carelessness, and sheer mistake." (George Santayana)

"You've always made the mistake of being yourself." (Eugene Ionesco)

TAKING CHARGE

Choosing key words is vital in conducting computer searches. If you wanted to write a speech on the subject of crime, you would first need to narrow the topic. For example, you might narrow it to computer crimes. You can choose key words to create other possible approaches to the general subject of crime. To keep the topic of your speech from being too broad, you might consider typing into the computer some of these key words:

Alcoholism and crime	Hate crimes	Rural crime
Crimes without victims	Juvenile delinquency	Violent crime
Education and crime	Organized crime	

For other key words on the topic of crime, consult *Subject Headings*, a reference work published by the Library of Congress.

Now it's your turn. Try to think of key words that you might use for a subject search on the following topics: drug use, football, the environment, nutrition, military spending, or some other topic that you intend to use for a speech.

IV Using What You've Found

Once you've located books or articles on your speech topic, how do you use them effectively? Which information do you include? What about quotations from your sources? This section discusses taking notes and quoting material. Finally, it describes how one student successfully carried out a research plan.

Taking Notes

Whenever you investigate a written source of information or interview an expert, you should take notes. A rule of thumb is to record more notes than you think you will ever need because a return trip to the library is inefficient and calling an expert for a second interview is impolite. On the other hand, don't record everything. Select information that makes you think "Wow, that's important" or

A researcher should take notes whenever investigating a written source of information or conducting an expert interview.

"Gee whiz, that sure would sound great to my audience." Your notes should be organized so that you can easily incorporate them into your speeches. You may find it useful to write your notes on three-by-five or four-by-six cards. If you place only one item of information on each card, then it is a simple matter to shuffle the cards until you're satisfied that you have the subtopics arranged in a logical order.

Each notecard should have a general heading at the top and a complete source citation at the bottom. Use quotation marks if you are copying the text verbatim.

> *Commitment to Liberty:*
>
> *"Let every nation know, whether it wishes us well or ill, that we shall pay any price, bear any burden, meet any hardship, support any friend, oppose any foe, in order to assure the survival and success of liberty."*
>
> *John F. Kennedy from his inaugural address, delivered Friday, January 20, 1961.*

Important information from source materials can be recorded on notecards. Each notecard should contain one item of information, with a general heading at the top and a complete source citation at the bottom.

Quoting Material: Avoid Heavy Lifting

Plagiarism is copying or imitating the language, ideas, or thoughts of another and passing them off as your original work. In discussing plagiarism, it is important to draw some distinctions. Material considered "common knowledge" is traditionally (by agreement among those in the scholarly community) handled differently than material protected by copyright. That means you do not need to quote a source if you are reciting a fact that is available from many sources (for example, that George Washington had wooden dentures). The general rule is this: If you're in doubt, name your source. As Mark Twain advised, "When in doubt, tell the truth." If you give credit, of course, then you are not plagiarizing. This brief excerpt from a student speech on the need for more heroes shows one way to name the quoted source: "A 1989 *Time* maga-

> **"When in doubt, tell the truth."**
>
> **Mark Twain**

zine/CNN poll revealed that over 40 percent of Americans had no heroes."

Paraphrasing another's unique ideas is not an acceptable way of avoiding *attribution*. **Paraphrasing**, or simply rewording the original passage, is still taking someone else's ideas. Excessive paraphrasing made Senator Joseph Biden of Delaware the most famous political plagiarist of our time. On September 12, 1987, the *New York Times* reported that Biden, then a presidential candidate, had "borrowed" crucial passages of a campaign speech he gave in Iowa from a speech Neil Kinnock, a La-

Senator Joseph Biden, pictured here, withdrew from the 1988 presidential race after it was discovered that he had plagiarized crucial passages of a campaign speech.

bour party leader, had delivered during his election campaign in Britain.

> "Why am I the first Kinnock in a thousand generations to be able to get to university? . . . Was it because our predecessors were thick? . . . Was it because they were weak, those people who could work eight hours underground and then come up and play football, weak? It was because there was no platform upon which they could stand." (Kinnock)

> "Why is it that Joe Biden is the first in his family ever to go to a university? . . . Is it because our fathers and mothers were not bright? . . . Is it because they didn't work hard, my ancestors who worked in the coal mines of Northeast Pennsylvania and would come up after twelve hours and play football for four hours? . . . It's because they didn't have a platform on which to stand." (Biden)

More revelations about Biden soon surfaced. According to Thomas Mallon, in his book *Stolen Words*, Biden took words from Robert Kennedy and "from Kennedy's onetime rival Hubert Humphrey . . . borrowings from John F. Kennedy were revealed, too. Most damaging of all came the report that at Syracuse University Law School, in 1965, Biden had been accused of plagiarizing a paper. Biden withdrew from the presidential race."

Mallon highlights the irony in this case: "Nearly all 'original' political speeches are, after all, plagiarized—composed by paid **ghostwriters** before delivery in the first person by the candidate himself: a universally accepted form of mutual back-scratching."

Students find themselves tempted to plagiarize for many reasons: The pressure to get good grades and low self-esteem are often cited as causes. If you feel that you must have that A or that your own ideas are of little worth, plagiarism is not the answer. The consequences of stealing another's work are high. Some students have failed courses, and others have been expelled from school. People have lost their jobs.

For example, in July of 1991, H. Joachim Maitre, dean of the College of Communication at Boston University, resigned after having been accused of plagiarism. In Maitre's commencement speech, several passages were identical or nearly identical to an article written by Michael Medved, a PBS film critic. Following the accusation, Maitre said he "must have slipped into a black hole." You can avoid that same black hole by simply doing your own work.

Putting Your Research Together

Ideas for your speeches can come from almost anywhere, but your research should follow a plan. The student speech at the end of this chapter was inspired by a conversation among some high school friends driving to a restaurant for dinner. The students were complaining that imagination was seldom rewarded in life. One of the students decided to research the importance of imagination for an upcoming speech. His research plan followed the ten steps listed below:

1. Discussed the idea with his most "imaginative" friend. The friend contributed the story that eventually became the conclusion—the four-year-old child, who, after seeing a production of *Peter Pan*, screamed at the top of her lungs as the curtain was descending, "Don't bring the curtain down yet. We're not ready."

COMMUNICATION BREAKDOWN

Putting Words in Their Mouths

"Washington is a ghost town. Practically everybody here who's somebody hires somebody else who's a ghostwriter to craft the words that get spoken or published. It's a distinguished Washington tradition. Thomas Jefferson penned George Washington's Farewell Address. Walter Lippmann drafted Woodrow Wilson's 'Fourteen Points.' Theodore Sorensen wrote John F. Kennedy's Pulitzer Prize–winning book, *Profiles in Courage.*

Hardly anyone expects the most *egregious* offenders, presidents and presidential candidates, to bother writing all their own words. Hubert Humphrey elicited little more than amusement when he finished a campaign speech in 1972 by crisply folding his address into his pocket, then adding, 'And now for a few words of my own.' . . . The last presidential candidate to insist publicly that he wrote every one of his speeches was Adlai Stevenson in 1952, and he was lying.

From politicians to business leaders, judges to sports figures, our public *discourse* is carried forward on the backs of a battalion of anonymous scribes. Leaders in nearly every profession depend on helpers to put words in their mouths. Even journalists are getting into the act and hiring assistants to write their columns. If college or high school students relied on ghosts the way most public figures do, they'd be expelled on charges of plagiarism. The fact that they bought the words rather than stole them would not be considered a defense."

Source: Ari Posner, "The Culture of Plagiarism," The New Republic, April 18, 1988, p. 19.

Question

It is not uncommon for politicians, sports figures, movie stars, and others (often reciting the words of a ghostwriter) to receive $10,000 or more for a speaking engagement. What do you think of this practice?

---

2. Visited the library. Checked card catalog for books on imagination. Looked up both *imagination* and *creativity* in the *Reader's Guide.* Read several articles and scanned two books for supporting materials. Took careful notes.

3. Found definition of *imagination* in the dictionary.

4. Talked to mother about the subject and was reminded that at three, he had often sung the opening lines

from the musical *Peter Pan.* Chose the structure of the Peter Pan story as an organizational approach for the speech.

5. Asked speech teacher for additional materials and was given three more books. Took more notes.

6. Went to a local mall. Spent two hours observing and recording examples that illustrated a lack of imagination.

7. Interviewed an astronomy teacher about Albert Einstein.

8. Called the University of Nebraska psychology department. Interviewed three professors about their views on imagination.

9. Studied the newspaper each day for relevant information. Found the quotation from former hostage Terry Anderson.

10. Attended the movie *Hook* to get more ideas for the Peter Pan approach.

With the information gathered from these ten steps, the student put pen to paper. Several revisions later, he delivered the finished speech to his classmates. Because the student had carefully researched and thoroughly prepared his speech, his performance was well received by the other students.

TAKING CHARGE

Study the research plan of the student who wrote the speech on the importance of imagination. Choose a topic for a speech that you would like to present. After coming up with at least five steps you would take in researching this topic, share your ideas with the rest of the class.

STUDENT SPEECH

Coert Voorhees, a high school senior, presented this speech in his effective speaking class. The speech discusses the importance of imagination.

We're Not Ready

I know a place where dreams are born,
and time is never planned.
It's not on any chart,
you must find it in your heart.
Never Never Land.

My mother tells me that when I was three years old, I often sang these opening lines to the musical *Peter Pan.* The story of Peter Pan, a boy who never grew up, and the three children who had the imagination to believe in him, has always appealed to me. So, curious, I went to see the movie *Hook.* In the movie, Peter Pan has grown up to become Peter Banning, a Captain Hook of industry. And he is not able to fly again—to save his children—until he believes, until he uses his imagination. And it's because I also believe that I ask you to find it in your hearts to nurture the imagination in our children. For, as Jane Conoley, chair of the Education Psychology Department at the University of Nebraska, argues, "The future depends on developing this internal power of imagination."

But in order to ensure that dreams are born, we must first visit a place where the imagination is not nurtured, Always Always Land, if you will, and secondly, we must nurture the imagination by showing our children how they too can fly to Never Never Land.

But where is Always Always Land? That's right, the American shopping mall. Let's visit the malling of America with J. M. Barrie's three children, Wendy, Michael, and John. As they walk through the main entrance, they are immediately confronted by a six-foot inflatable Gumby, a decadent display of Santa Fe style, and a sign that reads simply, "SEARS LAWNMOWERS ON SALE NOW."

Not in the market for a lawnmower, they enter Waldenbooks instead, where a shelf of the latest video releases catches Wendy's eye. Prominently displayed next to the shelf is a list from the magazine *Entertainment Weekly* of the top-ten-selling videos in the country. Four of them are Teenage Mutant Ninja Turtles releases, including the number one seller, "Pizza by the Shred." Next to it is a list from *Harpers Weekly* of the top twenty best-selling children's paperback books of 1990. Eight of the top ten are about the Mutant Ninja Turtles. Now, it might be too much to expect for our parents to deny their children these popular action figures and donate the money instead to Headstart programs that would give every disadvantaged child in this country a chance. But is it too much to ask for our Education President to stick his neck out, or do something . . . anything? According to "CBS News," when President Bush vacations in Kennebunkport, Maine, the cost for providing security for a single fishing trip would be enough funding to enable mobile libraries, for a year, to place books in the hands of every child who does not have access to a public library. If President Bush were willing to give up fishing for just one day, no child in this country would be without a book. Is it any wonder that no one has ever attempted to describe him as the Imagination President? Meanwhile, John and Michael are busying themselves at the magazine rack. John is holding a copy of *Time* magazine and reading Dr. Seuss's obituary. He learns that the single accomplishment of which Dr. Seuss was most proud was getting rid of Dick and Jane. Michael tugs at John's sleeve. He says he wants to go to Radio Shack.

When the children enter Radio Shack, they are mesmerized by the soft glow emanating from an entire wall of television screens. Patricia Marks Greenfield, professor of psychology at UCLA, conducted a study which showed that childrens' storytelling abilities dramatically decreased after watching only one episode of the Smurfs.

Shaking their heads, the children leave Radio Shack. They see a shop across the hall that they have never seen before. It doesn't seem to belong in Always Always Land. The name of the shop is Ye Olde Maps. The children study the mall directory carefully, but the shop is not listed, yet they have always known how to get there. Second to the right and straight on till morning. Inside the shop, the children are greeted by a mapmaker who points them to a map of the ancient world. On the lower left-hand corner of the map lurks a dragon. The mapmaker explains that on ancient maps, the dragon symbolized unknown territory. When people would look at the map, they would see the dragon as a symbol for danger; they would therefore associate danger with the unknown. Yet the explorers with courage and imagination saw the dragon as a symbol for opportunity to conquer the unknown. The mapmaker reminds the children that they should slay their own dragons every day.

Suddenly, the children realize that there are other people in the shop, other people with the imagination to dwell in Never Never Land. In the back, Albert Einstein and Maya Angelou are conversing. When Wendy asks them what they are doing, Einstein replies that they are trading stories, and would the children like to hear one of his? He reminds them that imagination is more important than knowledge and proceeds to tell them how he invented the theory of relativity. He locked himself in a closet for hours on end and closed his eyes. He says he did this because every time he opened his eyes to the outside world, he saw Newtonian physics. In that dark closet, Albert Einstein slayed his dragon. Out of the corner of her eye, Wendy sees something. It's Dr. Seuss. He is frolicking in his singsong world of ziffs and zuffs, of nerckles and nerds, of cats in hats, and of a grinch who stole Christmas. John is overjoyed at the sight of Dr. Seuss and realizes that the imagination of this great man lives on in the characters he created.

The sight of John's happy face reminds the poet Maya Angelou of her visit to her childhood home of Stamps, Arkansas. She tells Wendy and her brothers the same thing she told the children of that small town: "When I look at you, I see who I was. When you look at me, I hope you see who you can become."

Maya Angelou is right. Wendy, Michael, and John, as well as the children in Stamps, Arkansas, can become whomever they want. Perhaps the next Albert Einstein, the next Theodor Seuss Geisel, and even the next Maya Angelou, but only if we as a society make that dream possible. By now some of you might be saying to yourselves, so what if our children spend most of their time shopping for values in a mall, instead of learning about the value of imagination in the library? So what if we leave them at the mercy of the Captain Hooks of industry, the people more interested in profits than possibilities? So what if we fail to nurture the imagination in our children? On December 4, 1991, Terry Anderson, the last of thirteen U.S. hostages, was released by captors in Lebanon. At his welcome-home press conference, the question that reporters asked him again and again was this: How did he manage to survive during 2,455 days in captivity, most of those days shackled in chains? He said that the one thing that kept him alive was his ability to imagine. The threat of death compelled him to create a place to escape, an eerie oasis of imagination. This oasis that Mr. Anderson described was his own Never Never Land.

Four years ago, a touring company of *Peter Pan* had just finished its performance and the actors were on stage for the curtain call. As the curtain was descending on Never Never Land, a four-year-old child stood on her chair and screamed at the actors, "Don't bring down the curtain yet. We're not ready."

REVIEW AND ENRICHMENT

LOOKING BACK

Listed below are the major ideas discussed in this chapter.

✦ More than 50,000 books are published in the United States each year. Our store of information and knowledge doubles every five years.
✦ Before you start accumulating information, you should have a research plan.
✦ To save time, consider finding an expert to give focus to your research.
✦ The successful speaker is effective in adapting to the audience.
✦ Thorough research will increase your credibility as a speaker.
✦ Consulting with a reference librarian can save you valuable time.
✦ A database is a collection of related information.
✦ The card catalog or computerized catalog is your way to know what books the library has and where to find them.
✦ The Dewey Decimal System and the Library of Congress system are two important call number classification systems.
✦ The table of contents outlines the general plan of a book.
✦ The index helps you locate particular information in a book.
✦ The best known periodical index is the *Reader's Guide to Periodical Literature*.
✦ Notes should be organized so that you can easily incorporate them into your speeches.
✦ When taking notes, you should place only one item of information on each notecard.
✦ Plagiarism is intellectually dishonest.

SPEECH VOCABULARY

Match the speech term on the left with the definition on the right.

1. database
2. on-line
3. card catalog
4. author card
5. index
6. table of contents
7. interlibrary loan
8. paraphrasing
9. plagiarism
10. ghostwriter

a. a cooperative system among libraries
b. a system providing rapid access to many databases
c. a collection of related information
d. restating in your own words
e. using another person's ideas as your own
f. a place to find out where books are in the library
g. a source of information in the card catalog
h. someone who writes for another person
i. the general plan of a work
j. from the Latin for "one who points out"

GENERAL VOCABULARY

Define the following terms and use each in a sentence.

prerequisite
entrepreneur
alienate
microcosm
havens
nuclear family

crooned
compendium
malice
attribution
discourse
egregious

THINGS TO REMEMBER

1. The Greeks referred to the process of accumulating information as building a
_____.
2. A weekday edition of _____ contains more information than the average person was likely to come across in a lifetime in seventeenth-century England.
3. Libraries in cities frequently double as informal _____.
4. _____ is a cooperative system by which libraries lend specific books to one another on order.
5. An _____ system provides rapid access to computer data bases.
6. The card catalog includes three kinds of cards: _____, _____, and _____.
7. The _____ is an index to the articles in over three hundred popular magazines.
8. _____ is a Latin word meaning "one who points out."
9. _____ is copying or imitating the language, ideas, or thoughts of another and passing them off as your own.
10. _____ penned George Washington's Farewell Address.

THINGS TO DO

1. With the help of a reference librarian, find articles that discuss plagiarism. Take note of the consequences suffered by those plagiarists used as examples.

2. Create a card catalog entry (an author card) for a book that you might write someday.
3. Ask a librarian to help you devise a scavenger hunt in the reference section. The hunt should acquaint you with some of the most important reference works. For example, you might be asked to find the origin of the word *nerd*. Your search would lead you to a dictionary of word and phrase origins.

THINGS TO TALK ABOUT

1. What is wrong with excessive paraphrasing if you give credit to the original source?
2. To support their positions on controversial issues, politicians often quote opinion polls. What issues in your school would lend themselves to opinion polling?
3. Many libraries across America have closed their doors or have significantly cut back their services. What do you think can be done to increase financial support for them?

THINGS TO WRITE ABOUT

1. Write an essay about plagiarism. A possible topic: Why intellectual honesty matters.
2. *The Catcher in the Rye* ranks first among books that have been censored. Write an essay in which you examine censorship as it affects what books are on the shelves of a school library.
3. According to the author Richard Saul Wurman, "Information anxiety is produced by the ever-widening gap between what we understand and what we think we should understand. It is the black hole between data and knowledge." Write a creative essay or a play describing a typical day in the life of someone terrified by the information explosion.

CRITICAL THINKING

1. Most politicians have ghostwriters. Imagine a future in which politicians were required to offer sound ideas instead of sound bites. Would different candidates be elected to office? Why or why not?

2. Budget cutbacks force your school district to place the books in your library up for auction. Administrators decide, though, to let the students keep three reference works. Which works would you save as the most valuable? Why?

3. Matt Fraser, a senior in Bethel, Washington, shocked the administration at his high school by using sexual innuendos in a nominating speech before an all-school assembly. As punishment, administrators attempted to deny Fraser the right to give a graduation speech that had previously been scheduled. Fraser contacted the American Civil Liberties Union, and the subsequent lawsuit went all the way to the Supreme Court. Should limits be placed on a student's freedom of speech? What, if any, guidelines should be adopted? How would you research information to be able to discuss this important issue?

RELATED SPEECH TOPICS

Celebrity speakers: have tongue, will travel

Ghostwriting: the invisible touch

To quote or not to quote, that is the question

Information skills: a survival course

Facts are useless in emergencies (with apologies to David Byrne)

The school librarian: a friend in deed

Censorship of student speeches: how far is too far?

Information anxiety

The forgotten skill: thinking about thinking

Computer databases: something gained, something lost

Interesting information about a reference book I just discovered

CHAPTER 8

Organizing Your Speech

"Every great man exhibits the talent of organization . . . whether it be in a poem, a philosophical system, a policy, or a strategy."

— **Baron Lytton, nineteenth-century British dramatist and novelist**

"To me, things are organized when all of the piles of clothes in my room are stacked to the same height!"

— **Lucille Ball, American comedienne, star of "I Love Lucy"**

You're not messy. You're organizationally impaired.

LEARNING OBJECTIVES

After completing this chapter, you will be able to do the following.

◆ Apply effective organization to aspects of your daily life.

◆ Outline your ideas so that they are easy to follow.

◆ Create appropriate introductions and conclusions for your speeches that will give positive first and final impressions.

◆ Develop a meaningful body for your speech that shows clarity and logical progression.

◆ Recognize and use the various patterns of organization for speeches.

CHAPTER OUTLINE

Following are the main sections in this chapter.

I What Is Organization?

II The Introduction

III The Body

IV The Conclusion

Student Speech

Chapter Review

NEW SPEECH TERMS

In this chapter, you will learn the meanings of the speech terms listed below.

introduction
quotation
narrative
link
thesis statement
preview
  statement
body
outline
purpose
  statement
subordination

main headings
supporting
  materials
transitions
chronological
  pattern
climactic pattern
spatial pattern
cause–effect
  pattern
problem–
  solution pattern

GENERAL VOCABULARY

Expanding your general vocabulary will help you become a more effective communicator. Listed below are some words appearing in this chapter that you should make part of your everyday vocabulary.

vested
equilibrium
gigantic
fiasco
jeopardy

enhanced
haphazardly
intensification
indented
inhibitions

LOOKING AHEAD

In this chapter, you will learn about organization and about how directed planning can often be beneficial in both your personal life and your speaking. In addition, you will work with the three parts of the speech— the introduction, the body, and the conclusion—and examine the individual parts that make up each. You will learn about outlining and then examine five types of organizational patterns that can help you develop your thoughts. You will also recognize how important it is for the introduction, the body, and the conclusion to work together for maximum speaking effectiveness.

I   What Is Organization?

In the ancient Babylonian culture (2700–538 B.C.), a home builder had to "bet his life"—literally—that his house would hold up. According to the Babylonians' Code of Hammurabi, if a builder made a house that collapsed and caused the death of the house's owner, the builder was also put to death. Needless to say, the builder had a profoundly *vested* interest in constructing a house that was guaranteed to be strong and reliable.

The consequences of a poorly presented speech aren't nearly so dramatic or life-

Effective organization is the blueprint for a well-presented speech.

COMMUNICATION WORKS

Robert J. L. Funke, Certified Dental Technician

Robert J. L. Funke is a real American success story. Feeling that college was not for him, he tried a variety of jobs before discovering that he had a real love for the dental field—specifically, the technical side of dentistry. After a number of years of on-the-job training, he is now a successful dental technician with his own lab. While it is the dentist's job to work on teeth, it is the dental technician's job to make teeth. A dental technician creates crowns and bridges, or substitute teeth, for patients who have lost all or part of a tooth. The dentist tells the technician exactly what is needed, and then the technician sculpts the perfect tooth. Teeth created by a dental technician must look natural and be visually appealing, but more importantly, they must fit perfectly so that the patient can chew properly. Funke talks about the role that organization plays both in his twenty-five years of practice and in his personal life.

To begin with, organization means planning. Funke maps out most of his workday the night before. He establishes priorities and determines which tasks are the most urgent and which can wait. To him, knowing the "big picture" is extremely important because it offers direction and purpose to his workday. At the lab, Funke has to keep a close eye on what he is doing, whether it is waxing (a type of "tooth sculpting"), casting gold (which becomes the tooth), or working with porcelain (which provides the color of the tooth). In order to keep organized and use his time correctly, he actually has a one-hour timer that he sets the same way that you would set a timer in your kitchen. The reason? He says, "I often get absorbed in my work and lose track of time. The timer 'jogs' my mind and reminds me that I have something else that *now* has to be done." This is just one of the many self-reminders that he uses to stay organized.

Funke also realizes that the dentists for whom he works should see that he is organized. He makes sure that he is prepared before he goes to speak to a dentist about a specific case. This, he believes, not only makes him a more credible professional, it also allows the discussion to be relaxed and comfortable. His advice: Don't be in a rush, don't be afraid to smile, say what you have to say in a way that is to the point yet friendly, and leave when it's time!

Also a certified flight instructor and accomplished pilot, Funke knows the value of planning and the order in which things are supposed to work. As he says, "When you are in the air, your life—not your livelihood—is on the line." However, he likes the challenge that flying presents. He likes the self-confidence that organization gives his life—plus the sense of personal stability.

Robert J. L. Funke is a dental technician, family man, and pilot, and his advice to you is simple: "The great thing about organization is that it is an investment in your own possibilities."

threatening. The "death of an idea," however, might be the result when a speech fails to communicate because it hasn't been built with care. One way that you as an effective speaker can provide this care is to present your message with clear organization.

Do the following statements sound familiar?

◆ How could I forget to do that!
◆ We should have done this step first!
◆ I have no idea how I'm going to get this job done!

If so, there is a good chance that you need a lesson in effective organization. Before you read the definition of *organization*, let's look at a study that actually shows organization at work.

An informal study conducted in 1992 tried to measure whether student test scores would improve if teachers focused on organizational skills. The teachers, all of whom taught in middle-class, blue-collar communities in the Midwest, gave a test over approximately ten pages of textbook material. The students who did poorly on the exam were told to copy all of the bold-print headings that appeared in the ten pages. Next, each student was to write down at least two ideas that he or she thought were important that were listed under each heading. Finally, each student was to list at least one fact—a specific name, date, or happening—under each of the ideas that he or she had listed. Students were then told to study what they had constructed for a retake of the test material. The results? Records showed that students scored over *fifteen points higher* on the retake than on the first test. Why? The students were now studying with a direction in mind, with a logical sequencing of

material. No longer were they simply randomly memorizing. Now they were working from an individualized system that they had had a hand in constructing.

Effective organization is a systematic plan that makes sense and helps you to get things done. Generally speaking, organization is the logical grouping and ordering of "like" parts. This systematic grouping and logical arrangement allow you to keep a handle on what is happening.

You don't have to read reams of paper to realize what it means not to be organized. Homework doesn't get finished, phone calls don't get made, jobs don't get accomplished, invitations don't get sent out, the car doesn't get washed, and the alarm clock doesn't go off in the morning. Whether at the library or at your locker, without proper organization you waste much time and energy in your frantic rush to find what you are after or to meet deadlines.

In addition to sacrificing time and energy, you might also lose out educationally if you lack organizational skills. A study done at UCLA's Higher Education Research Institute in 1988 found that over 30 percent of all students who entered a four-year college or university in 1984 had to take special courses designed to strengthen their study and organizational skills.

Organization offers you a sense of balance and personal *equilibrium*. Organization helps you take the loose ends of your life, put them in order, and, in the process, keep sane! When eighteenth-century English statesman and orator Edmund Burke said, "Good order is the foundation of all good things," he was implying that through structure and organization, both individuals and societies have the potential to progress.

TAKING CHARGE

1. Organize *tomorrow*. Begin with the hour that you get out of bed. Keep a running record of at least two or three objectives that you would like to accomplish during each hour up to the time that you go to bed. For school, you can list what you would like to accomplish in each class. For leisure time at home, be specific in exactly how you want that time to be spent. Give honest, constructive answers that might actually improve your overall sense of personal organization.

2. Organization is not only time-saving, it can also be life-saving. For instance, what organizational plan does your school (or classroom) have for a fire drill or a tornado alert? List exactly how the drills are organized. What happens first, second, and so on? What about at home? Do you have a family plan of escape in case of fire or emergency? Explain it. If not, design one. Be complete in your explanations.

3. By referring to the newspaper or a current periodical, write about how a specific current situation occurred or was made worse because of a lack of organization. Explain what could have been done instead that might have alleviated the problem. Be sure to include specific names, places, dates, and so on. You may be asked to speak on your findings.

II   The Introduction

Thomas Boyden, an executive for Shell Oil, says that when he was interviewing top collegiate applicants for prospective management positions, he would give each applicant approximately fifteen minutes. During that fifteen-minute evaluation, he would observe three different things: (1) the confidence and congeniality that the applicant showed at first, (2) the sense of logic, organization, and self-discipline that the applicant could exhibit "under fire" during the interview, and (3) the poise that the applicant showed when leaving the interview. In other words, the interview would be divided into three distinct parts, and each part was important in making the whole interview a success.

What is true in the business world is also true in the oral communication world. Just like Boyden's interview, your speech should be organized into three distinct parts that, when presented effectively, can make a positive impression. We now examine these three parts, starting here with the introduction.

A secondary teacher once said that he was confident that his students would always give speeches that had an introduction, a body, and a conclusion—but not necessarily in that order! It is your job to make sure that your speeches are orga-

COMMUNICATION   BREAKDOWN

The Battle of the Crater

One of the most famous battles of the Civil War took place at Petersburg, Virginia, in 1864. Under the leadership of General Ambrose Everett Burnside, federal forces had undertaken the monumental engineering task of burrowing below the enemy and forming a shaft 500 feet in length that stretched under the Confederate lines. The shaft was then filled with four tons of dynamite. When the dynamite was ignited, the explosion blew more than 250 rebel soldiers high into the air and created a *gigantic* hole that measured over 150 feet long, 50 feet wide, and 30 feet deep! The blast was so powerful that both sides stood in awe at its effect, but it didn't take long for the Southern troops, shocked and stunned, to hurry for cover.

The problem for the North was that no clear plan had been developed for a follow-through. General Burnside, as historians tell it, was so shaken by the sight of the blast that he stood at the back of his troops and drank rum. He gave no verbal command. As a result, the Battle of the Crater turned into a *fiasco*.

Acting mainly on instinct, Northern soldiers charged *into* the crater, not to the left or the right of it. No ladders were taken in the unorganized attack, and the men reached the end of the crater only to find that they were trapped. Realizing the plight of the North, the Southern troops regrouped and picked off the federal soldiers like "fish in a barrel."

Civil War experts agree that the absence of effective organization and leadership by the North not only prevented a glorious victory at Petersburg but also cost hundreds of Northern soldiers their lives! To this day, the crater remains in Petersburg, Virginia, as a monument to the soldiers who fought and died there.

Question
What should Northern leaders have done prior to setting off the explosion? Who do you feel is specifically at fault for this tragedy?

---

nized so that you put things in the correct order. That means you should begin with a well-thought-out **introduction.**

Whatever you are doing, isn't it important to get off to a good start? Getting off to a good start often supplies you with the momentum and confidence that you need to complete your task. Many speakers say that, psychologically, the toughest part of a speech is the beginning, or the

introduction. It is during your introduction that you find out whether your audience accepts you. Consequently, a good introduction can "make or break" you because it sets the tone—at least in your head—for the remainder of the speech.

What is an introduction, and what is it supposed to do? See if you can determine the function of an introduction by reading this example. (Remember this introduc-

INSTANT IMPACT

Organizing Your Speech—and Your Life!

Mary Sue Alley Crommelin is the president of the Virginia Association of Speech Coaches. In the summer of 1992, she offered these words regarding her interpretation of the word *organization:*

The organization of a speech begins with an abundance of examples. It is then our job to analyze, to evaluate, and then to put them in a logical sequence. How do they relate? How do they apply? What conclusions can we draw? How does each advance the purpose of the thesis?

The writing of a speech is much like life. Each involves choices. Each involves "evidence" that has to be sorted. We have to sift through all that comes our way, and, in short, throw some choices away as quickly as we would toss aside some pieces of evidence for a speech. Why? Because some choices simply don't fit!

The choices that we make in life—as in a speech—will logically and predictably lead to certain results. We'd better know how to organize and sequence life's events into something meaningful . . . both for ourselves and for humanity.

Like a runner, a speaker must get off to a good start that provides momentum and confidence.

tion. It will be referred to later in the chapter.)

#1 Have you ever heard the saying "Let a smile be your umbrella"? What about the observation "Laugh and the world laughs with you"? Both of these statements deal with how a positive attitude and a sense of humor can make a bad situation a little bit better for both you and the people around you. **#2** However, did you know that your ability to laugh can mean a great deal more than a pleasant smile or momentary delight? As a matter of fact, laughter can be very beneficial in many ways. **#3** Consequently, I would like to discuss the various areas in your lives where laughter can play a significantly positive role. **#4** Let's take a look at how laughter can help you on the job, with your friends and family, and with your health.

Do you see how the interesting information in the beginning (indicated by #1) might encourage an audience to listen? Next, do you see how there is a clear connection made between the introductory material and the speech topic (indicated by #2)? Also, do you see exactly what the speech will be about (indicated by #3)? Finally, do you see a clear statement of the areas that will be discussed in the speech (indicated by #4)?

Basically, an introduction does four things:

1. It gets the attention of the audience.
2. It provides a clear link from your attention-getter to your speech topic, or thesis statement.
3. It gives your specific thesis statement.
4. It presents a preview of the major areas that will be discussed.

Attention-Getters

The first words that you say to an audience must make them want to listen to you. You must "grab" your audience's attention. You have probably heard that telling a joke is a good way to start your speech. No one will deny that humor is refreshing and that everyone likes to laugh. You must ask yourself, however, what type of humor works for you. Is a humorous opening appropriate for your speech topic? What happens if nobody laughs? A humorous approach can backfire.

While it is true that a light, funny attention-getter can be a tremendous boost to your confidence, you do not have to use humor or a funny story to get off to a solid start. Examine your personality and then realistically answer the following questions: "What works for me, and what do I feel comfortable presenting?" With this in mind, let's examine five types of attention-getters that can help you to get your speech off to a smooth start.

1. Asking Questions

One of the best methods of gaining an audience's attention is to get them directly

While a humorous opening can gain an audience's attention, the same effect can be achieved through the use of questions, references, startling statements, quotations, or stories.

involved in what you are saying. Immediately asking your audience a question or a series of questions not only fires up their curiosity about your topic, it also makes them active participants in your speech.

If you were doing a speech called "The Power of Word Building," you might begin by asking your audience this:

> How many of you know the meaning of the word *verisimilitude*? Do you know what *veracity* means? What about the word *verity*? Well, all three of these words have something to do with the word *truth*, and I wouldn't be telling you the truth if I didn't confess that I had to look these words up in a dictionary. However, building vocabulary is a challenge that each of us should accept if . . .

How about these questions for a speech on shifting blame:

> Have you ever heard someone say, "The devil made me do it"? Have you ever heard the expression, "Don't blame me. It's not my fault"? If you answered yes to one or both of these questions, then you would probably agree with me that many people in today's society find it easy to make excuses and blame someone or something else for their problems. I would like to talk about . . .

Do you see how questions can provide the attention-getting spark you want to begin your speech? Sometimes you might ask your audience to respond to your questions by actually raising their hands or speaking out loud. But beware! While this technique can sometimes promote spirited audience involvement, it can also lead to chaos and loss of concentration if the responses to your questions don't turn out as you expected. Are you prepared to handle such a situation? Is it worth the risk?

Often, it is best to use rhetorical questions. Rhetorical questions, like the ones given in the examples, don't really demand a verbal response. Instead, they ask the members of your audience to answer silently in their heads. Rhetorical questions are also "safe" questions because they often answer themselves: "Do any of you like to get your feelings hurt?" "Do any of us in this room want our friends or family to join the thousands who die each year because of people who drink and drive?" Such questions don't demand a response, but they do challenge your audience to think. This type of mental stimulation offers you the potential for immediate attention-getting success.

2. Making References

Like asking questions, making references can allow you to work well with your audience. You might refer to people in the audience, your physical surroundings, other speakers who are on the program, or the significance of the occasion. This approach allows you to be comfortable, congenial, and conversational with your audience by including them in your opening remarks. Audiences like to be included, and including them provides a type of speaker–audience unity that says, "You and I are in this speech together!" For instance, you might say this:

> I see that John and Ina are in the audience. When we first started this class project over two months ago, they were the ones who provided the leadership and enthusiasm that the rest of us needed at that time. The word *leadership* is exactly what I wish to talk about tonight because . . .

Or you might say this:

> For some reason, every time that we are in this auditorium, the air-conditioning is

out. Maybe we should all bring our own fans next time. However, the temperature might not be the only thing that is "sticky" tonight. My topic, "Why AIDS Needs to Be Talked about in Schools," could also make some people warm and uncomfortable. I have confidence, nevertheless, that if we work together . . .

As usual, of course, you must use good taste and common sense. For example, it might be risky to make a casual reference to someone in the audience whom you barely know. Making references should get you off to a positive start with your listeners, not put your speech in *jeopardy*. In general, though, audiences appreciate a speaker who shows that he or she is aware of and in tune with what is happening.

3. Making a Startling Statement

Sometimes your best attention-getter is one that jolts your audience into paying attention. You might be familiar with the story about the speaker who, before her speech, noticed that certain members of her audience were half-asleep, daydreaming, or involved in idle conversations. One thing was certain: They were definitely *not* ready to listen. The speaker calmly walked to the front of the room and suddenly shouted, "SEX!" An immediate hush fell over the audience, and every head turned in her direction. When she saw that the audience was focused on her, she smiled politely and said, "Thank you. Now that I have your attention . . ." Luckily, everyone laughed, and she was able to deliver her speech to attentive listeners. She had figuratively reached out and grabbed them.

Another story has it that a noted football player spoke to a high school about the problems associated with violence in society. While he spoke, he comfortably moved his right hand as if he were "keeping the beat" to a song that only he heard. His first words were these:

> I love music. I love dancing. I love how men and women, young and old, rich or poor, can move and smile and laugh and keep the rhythm to their favorite songs. However, today I'm not here to talk about music—because, ironically, every time that my hand comes down to "keep the beat," a young child is physically or sexually abused in this country. And the violence is real . . .

Picture yourself in this audience. Wouldn't you be immediately drawn in by the speaker and to the tremendous power of his message?

As impressive as this technique might appear, it has its drawbacks. Too many speakers have tried to startle their audiences, only to find that their attention-getters offended people instead. Don't be foolish. An audience will forgive an honest mistake, but it will rarely forgive bad taste! Yes, the startling statement can work for you, but you must use sound judgment and take the time to know your audience.

4. Giving a Quotation

You deliver a **quotation** each time you repeat the exact words that someone else has said. Giving a quotation is a popular attention-getter. For one thing, quotations can add a degree of style and sophistication to speech presentations. For another, quotations are abundant and fairly easy to find, so you can surely find one that fits your needs.

Choose quotations that are clear and appropriate for your speech topic and au-

Introductory Attention-Getters	
❓❓❓❓	**Questions**
👉 👈	**References**
❗❗❗❗	**Startling statements**
" " " " " " " "	**Quotations**
📖	**Stories**

thors who are reliable and can be trusted. Although some famous people need no introduction, it is a good practice while delivering your attention-getter to give your audience some idea of who your author is and what he or she has done that is noteworthy. Why is this the case? Generally speaking, audiences are likely to be impressed if the sources that you are quoting are impressive.

Here's how one student started her speech on "What Has Happened to Friendship?"

> "First in war—first in peace—and first in the hearts of his countrymen." These are the words that began Revolutionary War General Henry Lee's famous funeral oration for George Washington. The quotation shows us a man of conscience and a man who cared for his fellow man. However, do we care for our fellow man today the same as Washington did in his day? I would like to take a look at . . .

The quotation immediately gives the speech an academic and historical flavor. Henry Lee's words say to the audience, "Take this speech seriously and give it your attention, please!" Another student, speaking on "Americans—Why Are We So Gullible?" began with a similar historical quotation:

> "You can fool all of the people some of the time and you can fool some of the people all of the time, but you can't fool *all* of the people *all* of the time." Abraham Lincoln, the author of this quotation, might have added the words *"except* in America," because Americans are often easy prey for those wishing to make a fast buck. Let's examine why Americans are so gullible and take a look . . .

Don't think that your quotation must be serious or must have been delivered by someone who lived centuries ago. On the contrary, some of the most effective quotations are lighter and have been given by people who are alive right now. Take the time to search through your resources so that you can find the quotation that will be the perfect attention-getter for your speech.

5. Telling a Story

One of the most popular attention-getters is the **narrative**—the telling of a story. Everyone loves a story, especially one that is told well. Illustrations and personal accounts can quickly give you an "in" with your audience because these stories give your personality a chance to work and are so much in demand. Americans are storytellers (and story *listeners*) at heart.

Keep in mind that your story should be short and to the point. Don't get so caught up in your account that you lose sight of the purpose of your speech. The best stories are the ones that hold the interest of the audience yet lead clearly into your speech topic.

Have you had an experience that you would call special? Have you gone through some heart-stopping ordeal that you would like to share? Such experiences can make good stories. Here is an example:

A few weeks ago, my mom and dad had gone out for the evening and I was alone at home. About 2 A.M. I heard a noise by the downstairs window. Even though I hoped that the sounds would go away, they didn't. As a matter of fact, they got louder. It sounded as if someone were struggling to reach the latch of the window. I was petrified, but somehow I managed to go downstairs. Slowly, I moved the curtain to see what was outside. You can imagine my fear when I saw two eyes looking right back at me! It was a *raccoon*. The good news is that, in this instance, I was able to deal with my fear. The bad news is that I almost collapsed in the process. What does *fear* mean and how can we . . .

Stories can be insightful, and they can also be fun for you to deliver and your audience to hear. And stories don't have to be personal. They can be interesting accounts about other people, places, events, and so on. Any story can be an effective attention-getter if it sets the mood that you are after and creates an effective picture in the minds of your listeners that relates to your speech thesis.

Let's move on to the next aspect of the introduction, the link.

The Link

Probably the section of the introduction that students most often overlook when preparing their speeches is the **link**. The link is the statement that comes between the attention-getter and the thesis statement and logically connects the two. It

does you little good to have a clever attention-getter if the audience sees no relation between it and the focus of your speech.

Read the following introduction, which was prepared and delivered by a high school student, Carmella Hise. Pay particular attention to the role of the link sentence (italicized):

"I'm going to let you in on a secret that will change your lives. Girls, for just $10, you can learn what makes a guy fall in love and how to make him want you! The right way to flirt! If you act now, we'll rush you our best seller, *Secrets of Kissing*. You see, it's all part of the 'Get Him System,' G.H.—a no-fail love guide that tells you the truth. No more old-fashioned advice that you already know."

Believe it or not, this is more than a mere attention-getter for my speech. This is taken from an actual ad found in the February edition of *Young Miss* magazine.

A speaker must provide a link between the attention-getter and the thesis statement; otherwise, the audience will see no relation between the opening of the speech and its main focus.

My speech for today will deal with one of the words in the last sentence of the ad, old-fashioned; *for it is my opinion that, contrary to what is stated in the* Get Him *ad, maybe a sense of old-fashioned tradition is exactly what we need in today's society.* Therefore, I would specifically like to examine some traditional American values . . .

In addition to clearly explaining her attention-getter, Carmella logically linked the ad in the magazine, and specifically the word *old-fashioned*, to her speech thesis. Suppose you were going to present an informative speech on the responsibilities of your high school stage crew. You could say this:

> Shakespeare said, "All the world's a stage." *Even though I don't want to take a look at the "world's stage," I would like for us to examine our school's stage,* and specifically the role that a stage crew member plays in our drama productions.

Do you see how your link took you where you wanted to be—ready to state your speech thesis? Even though the link can be more than one sentence long, usually one sentence can do the job. The effectiveness and impact of both your attention-getter and your speech thesis are *enhanced* when your link statement connects as it should. In addition, you stand a better chance of "connecting" with your audience.

The Thesis Statement

The third part of the introduction is the sentence that will tell your audience exactly what you will be speaking about. This sentence, which will be discussed further in Chapter 12, "Speeches to Inform," is called the **thesis statement.**

If you have a catchy attention-getter and a smooth link to a thesis statement that is vague, your speech may be unclear. The reason that you wanted to get the audience's attention is that you had something worthwhile to say. That something is your thesis statement, or the focus of what your speech is going to address. Your audience must never wonder, "What exactly is this speech about?" A brief, to-the-point thesis statement can help you avoid such a problem.

One way to make sure that your audience knows that you are introducing your thesis is to tell them. Don't permit your audience to take an organizational "detour." Saying something like "This leads me to my thesis, which is . . . " can be a smart way to make sure that you and your audience are both following the same communication roadmap.

You must also keep your thesis focused. Here is an example of a thesis statement:

> I would like to talk with you about the advantages of community service and why we should all plan to get involved.

The speech is going to be about community service, but it is specifically going to deal with the *advantages* of community service.

The Preview Statement

If you have gone to the movies or watched television, you have no doubt seen previews of upcoming films or television episodes. These brief "snapshots" usually focus on the high points of what you will be seeing later. Similarly, speeches include previews in the form of preview statements.

The **preview statement** is usually one sentence at the end of the introduction that gives the audience an overview of the major areas that will be discussed in the body of the speech. For instance, if you were giving a speech on the negative effects of alcohol, your preview might mention alcohol's physical effects, mental effects, and societal effects. A speech on success stories in the Olympics could include a preview statement on physical preparation and mental preparation.

Of course, the major areas mentioned in your preview statement will be repeated later in the body of your speech with specific examples added for support. Often, the examples and evidence you have collected will determine what your areas of discussion will be and, thus, what your preview statement should include. Although not all speeches have a preview statement, it is often wise to provide one for your audience. Audiences can't catch everything the first time. They might miss your main points when said within the body of your speech. A preview statement tells your audience where your speech will be heading and, as a result, makes the body of your speech easier for your listeners to follow.

TAKING CHARGE

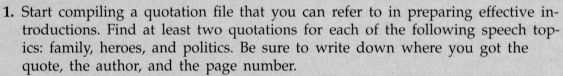

1. Start compiling a quotation file that you can refer to in preparing effective introductions. Find at least two quotations for each of the following speech topics: family, heroes, and politics. Be sure to write down where you got the quote, the author, and the page number.
2. Select one of the attention-getting devices from the chapter and use it as a means of introducing a person in your class to the rest of the class. Be sure to explain your attention-getter, link it to the fact that you are introducing someone, introduce the person, and then mention two areas in which the person is interested. Have some fun, but stay focused on your objective—providing an introduction that will make your friend glad that you are the one doing the introduction. Write out what you are going to say before you do the introducing.
3. Provide preview statements with at least two parts for the following thesis statements.

   Selecting a college involves careful research.
   Adopting a child has genuine rewards.
   The single parent faces many challenges.

Example: For the thesis statement "Winning an Election Involves Careful Organization," preview statements might deal with organizing workers, organizing speeches, and organizing the candidate's image.

III The Body

The **body** of the speech is the heart, the brain, the nerve center of the entire presentation. It is the place where you exhibit in an organized manner your powers of persuasion and reasoning. Audiences need to be convinced. They need to be informed. They need to be shown. After your audience hears your introduction and knows your speech thesis, you need to show or prove your point. You do this in the body of the speech.

Let's take a look at two important ways to make the body of your speech clear and convincing: outlining and using organizational patterns.

Outlining Your Speech

Have you ever taken a trip that involved driving a long distance? If so, someone in your family probably used a map to study various routes and then mark the selected route for the drive.

An **outline** is the speaker's map. It is the way that you give form and direction to your organization. An outline allows you to know not only where you are going but also where you are and where you have been. An outline keeps you on track.

The author Victor Hugo is credited with the quote, "No army can withstand the strength of an idea whose time has come." However, few will support an idea that they can't understand. Similarly, few people can follow a speech that appears to be *haphazardly* thrown together or that is difficult to comprehend because of poor organization.

INSTANT IMPACT

Must Followers Have Focus?

We live in a world where it is desirable to be in charge. Many people who wish to be in charge realize the value of effective organization and seek out what the experts say. They don't have to look far. The bookshelves are loaded with books and pamphlets on such topics as *Management and the Mind* and *Organization and the Power Person*. However, a valuable bit of information was recently released from the Carnegie Mellon Graduate School of Industrial Administration about followers.

According to the Carnegie Mellon report, two of the most important traits of a good follower are self-management and a sense of focus. The report stated that in order for any group to function cohesively and efficiently, followers must have a sense of organization regarding how they manage their time, how they prioritize issues, and how they zero in on what matters and what doesn't. Without skilled followers, the study said, society can become filled with robots—people who are easily manipulated. The study concluded that great leaders are often the result of great followers who see, adhere to, and carry out a definite plan of action.

What's the point? Whether you are in the spotlight or on the sidelines, it takes everyone to make a solution work.

You have probably heard the story about the driver who is miserably lost. Miles off the main highway, he stops to ask a farmer for directions, only to be told, "Sorry, I know where you're goin', but you can't get there from here." It should be comforting for you to know that by following your outline, you can always "get there from here" because you have stayed on your planned speaking course.

How do you actually make an outline? Even though you outline your entire speech, most of your outlining will deal with the body. Therefore, let's use the body of the speech to examine outlining. First, look below at the components of a speaking outline and how they look on the page:

Purpose Statement

I. Main heading (Roman numeral)
   A. Supporting material (capital letter)
      1. Detail (number)

Now let's examine in simple language exactly how a speaking outline works. You will usually begin by establishing the central idea of your speech, or the **purpose statement.**

Purpose Statement

The purpose statement is closely associated with the thesis given at the end of your introduction. It is placed near the top of your paper (without Roman numerals, letters, or numbers) and states both your selected speech topic and your specific purpose in speaking. Here are some examples:

The purpose of this speech is to inform the audience about the pros and cons of midyear high school graduation for seniors.

The purpose of this speech is to explain to the audience the steps that a person must go through in order to become certified in lifesaving.

The purpose of this speech is to persuade the group that immediate action must be

taken if we wish to save our local environment.

In your actual speech, you might not *say* your purpose statement exactly as you have written it. You will probably reword your ideas when you formulate your thesis. However, the purpose statement needs to be written out at the top of your outline to serve as a primary reminder of what your speech is going to be about.

Outlining follows the process of **subordination,** or ranking in terms of importance. Your purpose statement, written at the top of the page, is the most important part of your speech. Everything else spoken—whether in the introduction, the body, or the conclusion—will fall under its direction.

Main Headings

After you have determined your purpose statement, you need to decide what your main headings will be. **Main headings** are the major divisions, areas, or arguments of your purpose statement. They represent the main ideas that you wish to analyze. Main headings are indicated by the use of Roman numerals. For instance, suppose your purpose statement is this:

The purpose of this speech is to show my audience the serious harms related to smoking.

The main headings in the body of your speech might read as follows:

I. Smoking can lead to significant *health problems for the smoker.*

II. Smoking can even affect the *health of others* innocently in the vicinity of the smoker.

III. Smoking can contribute to *economic problems.*

Notice by what is italicized that each main heading is a clear division of exactly what is going to be addressed in the speech.

Supporting Material

Supporting materials provide *intensification* and reinforcement for the main headings. They are listed under the main headings; each main heading has its own supporting statements. Supporting materials make up the "Now I would like to get more specific" sections of the speech. It is in these sections that you present the examples, personal stories, and pertinent observations that all audiences need to hear if they are going to believe you.

It is important to remember that your supporting material must be logically narrower and more specific than your main headings. Furthermore, if your organization is accurate, your supporting materials will not only support each main head but will also link back to support the purpose statement. Keep in mind that while the main headings logically divide and prove the purpose statement, the supporting material extends what has been suggested by the main headings.

Supporting materials are identified in your outline by capital letters. They don't have to be written out in great detail. Most of the time, a key word or phrase should be enough to jog your memory and allow your speaking talents and your preparation to take over. An outline is not supposed to be a substitute for memory. Ultimately, it is up to you, based on your familiarity with your material, to remember what you want to say.

Here are some examples of supporting materials you might use in the previously mentioned speech on the harms of smoking:

> The purpose of this speech is to show my audience the serious harms related to smoking.
>
>   I.   Smoking can lead to significant health problems for the smoker.
>   A.   Lung disease often results.
>   B.   Thousands die each year.
>   C.   Members of my family are among the victims.

Details

Many speakers go one step deeper into the outline and give details. Details narrow the outline even further, providing information that breaks down the supporting material to pinpoint accuracy. When you get to the detail part of your outline, you will almost always be able to include exact names, dates, events, numbers, or personal accounts that will impress your listeners and solidify your point. Note how details, which are indicated by numbers in the outline, can give real impact to the working outline on the harms of smoking.

> The purpose of this speech is to show my audience the serious harms related to smoking.
>
>   I.   Smoking can lead to significant health problems for the smoker.
>   A.   Lung disease often results.
>   1.   Men are at 40 percent greater risk than women.
>   2.   Smoking causes over 60% of all lung problems.
>   B.   Thousands die each year.
>   1.   390,000 die annually.
>   2.   Over 100,000 are under the age of fifty.
>   3.   20 percent are teenagers.

C. Members of my family are among the victims.
1. My grandfather died from lung disease caused by smoking.
2. My father has to take oxygen twice a week.

Details can give life to your speech. They can add dimensions of personality, humanness, and intellectual stimulation to the coldest of topics. As a result, they will help draw your audience members in and make them feel a part of your speech, which is one of your goals.

It is possible to go still further and subdivide the details of your outline, but this isn't generally a good idea. Remember, not only do *you* have to keep track of where you are in your speech, but so does your audience.

And your audience doesn't have a script of your speech handy. Keep things meaningful, but keep your organization simple and easy to follow. You'll be happier with the results.

Proper Outlining Form

As you write your speech outline, you'll want to follow some standard guidelines. For example, notice how the various parts of the outline (the purpose statement, the main headings, the supporting material, and the details) are *indented* differently. The indentions indicate the subordination of ideas. Also notice the use of periods after each Roman numeral, letter, and number.

It is important to remember that each part of an outline should contain at least two items. First, you must have at least two main headings. You can have more than two, and usually you will, but you *must* have at least two. After that, you aren't required to have further subordinate parts, but in each case, if you have one, you must have at least one more. Thus, if you have an A, you should at least have a B. If you have a 1, you should have a 2, and so on. The reason

A speaker should provide details—names, dates, events, numbers, personal accounts—that support the main point of the speech.

for this is that you can't divide anything into one part.

A few students might sometimes perceive the indenting, Roman numerals, letters, and numbers as "busy work." Keep in mind, however, that outlining means order, that order means effective organization, and that effective organization means that you'll be in charge. What the bones are to the body, the outline is to the speech. If you take the time to think of a significant purpose statement, group your ideas logically into main headings, and create valid supporting materials and details, you will be on your way to building a speech that will be ordered, structurally sound, and—unlike some homes in ancient Babylon—certain not to crumble.

Do you remember the example introduction given earlier in the chapter? The thesis was "I would like to discuss the various areas in your lives where laughter can play a significantly positive role." The first main heading might deal with how laughter can help on the job. Let's hear how this main idea might sound if it were used to start out the body of the speech. This speech in its entirety will be outlined at the end of the chapter.

First of all, laughter can help you on the job. Did you know that a sense of humor can help make you a more productive worker? For instance, the pamphlet *Smart Management Skills* states that employees and bosses who will take the time to laugh at their shortcomings are more likely to turn out more work of higher quality. The reason? The pamphlet explains that giving in to your "funny bone" relieves stress and allows you to see the occupational "big picture" better. The consequence, says author John C. Smith, is that "you actually work faster and more accurately if you will laugh and 'not take yourself too seriously.'" Next, laughter can help you cut down on absenteeism from work. A study done at Walker University showed that workers who frequently told jokes and laughed with fellow workers missed 20 percent fewer days a year than workers who were serious most of the time. One worker even added, "The laughing and having a good time makes me want to come to work. I don't like to miss."

INSTANT IMPACT

Advice from a Former First Lady

Barbara Bush, wife of former President George Bush, spoke to the graduates of Pepperdine University in 1992 and told them that family life and contributing to one's community are important measures of success. Speaking to more than five hundred graduates, Mrs. Bush said, "If you had invited the CEO of General Electric, he would have discussed business. If you had invited the head of the American Red Cross, she would have discussed how to help others in distress. But you invited a mother of five to speak, so I'm going to talk to you about your own families."

She went on to add that the graduates would probably never regret missing a certain test or a specific meeting. She noted, however, that they would most certainly miss the times in their lives that they hadn't spent with their husbands, wives, children, or community. The answer, she suggested, was for them to organize their lives so that the important things came first.

Source: Associated Press.

Do you see the main heading? Can you pick out the supporting materials? What about the details? Next, look for the words and phrases that signal where the discussion is going. These expressions—such as *first of all*, *for instance,* and *next*—are termed **transitions.** They will appear throughout your speech, but they are especially helpful in the body of the speech. Transitions allow both you and your audience to know exactly where you are in your speech and how all of the parts of your outline fit together.

See the figure below for some transitions that you might use.

Organizational Patterns

Let's now take a look at some of the ways that you can organize the body of

Transitions are words and phrases that signal how the parts of a speech fit together.

Relationship Intended Between Parts of Your Speech	Possible Transitional Words and Phrases
To add ideas	beyond that, in addition, besides, likewise, moreover, also, futhermore, next, finally
To illustrate or demonstrate	for example, in other words, even though, for instance, that is, to illustrate, specifically, as proof, a case in point
To yield a point	granted, of course, since this is so, although true
To show contrast	conversely, however, nevertheless, on the contrary, on the other hand, while this may be true
To emphasize a point	above all, indeed, more important, in fact, surely, without a doubt
To compare	at the same time, in the same way, likewise, similarly
To show order	first, second, in the second place, finally, in conclusion, last, next
To repeat or restate	in other words, that is to say, in short, in any case
To summarize	for these reasons, in conclusion, all in all, overall
To show relationships in space	close by, nearby, next to, in front of, behind
To show relationships in time	before, afterward, formerly, later, meanwhile, next, presently, previously, subsequently, ultimately, soon after

your speech. Think once again of the trip that you might take in the family car. You could probably use a number of routes to reach your destination. After looking at the various options, you would probably choose the one that best satisfied your needs in terms of time, scenery, road conditions, traffic, or the like. You need to make this same type of study when deciding how to organize the body of your speech.

Just as there are often several roads that lead to a specific location, there are several organizational patterns from which you can choose. Let's take a look at the five patterns of organization that speech teachers from across the country say they find most appropriate for student speeches. As you are reading, keep in mind that these organizational patterns can sometimes be combined for greater effect.

1. Chronological Pattern

The **chronological pattern** of organization puts things in a time sequence, or in the order in which they happened. Chronological order is an excellent choice if you want your audience to see the parts of your speech building into a complete picture from beginning to end. Here are some examples:

The Role of the Political Cartoon in Shaping Public Views

    I.   Colonial times
   II.   Revolutionary days
  III.   Current happenings

The Evolution of Batman as an Heroic Figure

    I.   Initial comic book portrayal
   II.   1950s and 1960s TV show portrayal
  III.   1990s movie portrayal

2. Climactic Pattern

You will often want to save your most important point for last. In the **climactic pattern** of organization, you organize your main headings in order of importance. This type of organization can give your speech dramatic impact because it allows the speech to build in significance.

The Price of Crime in America
    I.   Crime and the economy
   II.   Crime and the schools
  III.   Crime and you and your family

It is also possible to have a chronological pattern of organization that advances in a climactic manner.

The Impact of the Rodney King Beating
    I.   Tape released
   II.   Verdict announced
  III.   Chaos erupted

3. Spatial Pattern

When you use the **spatial pattern** of organization, you are dividing up your topic on the basis of space relationships. The advantage of this arrangement is that your audience can see how the body of your speech fits together by the spatial layout picture that you create for them.

Introducing the Modern School

    I.   Library is the central hub.
   II.   Classrooms radiate from library.
  III.   Offices are extensions.

The World of Drugs

    I.   North American involvement
   II.   South American involvement
  III.   Asian involvement

4. Cause–Effect Pattern

In the **cause–effect pattern** of organization, you are saying to your listeners, "because of *that, this* happened." In other words, the one area (the cause) leads directly to the other area (the effect). Often, the main headings in a cause–effect outline will be the words *cause* and *effect*, and the supporting material will supply an analysis. Here are examples:

Anorexia
    I. Causes
        A. Media influences
        B. Low self-esteem
   II. Effects
        A. Physical problems
        B. Emotional problems

Skin Hunger (people unwilling to touch or hug)
    I. Causes
        A. Age barriers
        B. Stereotype barriers
   II. Effects
        A. Physical problems
        B. Psychological problems
        C. Emotional problems

5. Problem–Solution Pattern

The **problem–solution pattern** of organization does exactly what it says: It presents a problem and then provides ideas about how the problem can be solved. Much like the cause–effect pattern, this method is very logical and gives you an opportunity to show some insightful analysis in areas that are easy for your audience to follow.

There Is a Need to Recycle
    I. Problems
        A. Lack of knowledge
        B. Economics
        C. Lack of incentive
   II. Solutions
        A. Education in schools and the media
        B. Government encouragement
        C. Personal commitment

As mentioned earlier, it is possible to combine organizational patterns. For instance, you could easily combine aspects of the problem–solution pattern with the cause–effect pattern.

Beverly Hubbs, a guidance counselor and spokesperson for the Positive Life Program at a large Midwestern high school, tells both students and parents that many different roads lead to feelings of personal success. Everyone should chart his or her own course on the basis of what works. She says, "All people aren't the same. There is usually a *right answer* out there for all of us if we will take the time to hunt."

This is also good advice for you to follow as you organize your speech. Just as all people aren't the same, all speeches aren't the same. Different topics call for different organizations. You have been presented with five organizational patterns that are tried and true. Combine your content with your originality and choose wisely. Remember, the body of your speech is the majority of your speaking "trip." Organize your speech so that your audience enjoys the journey. Let's now move to the final part of the speech, the conclusion.

> "There is usually a right answer out there for all of us if we will take the time to hunt."
>
> **Beverly Hubbs**

TAKING CHARGE

1. You have seen how outlining and subordination work, moving from general to specific. Using this knowledge, arrange each of the following in the correct outline sequence. Your outline should take the following form (be sure to make indentions):

Topic
   I.
      A.
         1.

   ◆ Baseball, sports, Chicago Cubs, recreation
   ◆ Female authors, literature, Harper Lee, fiction
   ◆ George Bush, politics, executive branch, president of the United States
   ◆ Corvette, transportation, Chevrolet, automobile
   ◆ High school, English, education, American literature

2. Outline the body of an article from a periodical or newspaper. Use an article that contains a clear analysis of a topic. Be sure to write out a purpose statement so that you know exactly what you are proving, and include at least two main headings, two supporting-material areas for each main heading, and two details for each supporting-material area. When you have finished, share your outline with a friend by speaking it so that it makes sense.

3. You have been shown five different types of organizational patterns. Take the following topics and prepare an outline for each. Each outline should use a different organizational pattern. Be sure to use at least two main headings for completeness.

   ◆ Students Are Getting Involved with the Environment.
   ◆ Adults Are Doing Good Things for Kids.
   ◆ The Sports World Is Facing Problems.

4. Using the general topic "Music," try to construct three outlines, using three different organizational patterns. Feel free to narrow the topic so that it fits what you are stressing. Here's an example:

Music and the Orchestra (spatial pattern)
   I.   The conductor
   II. The strings
   III. The horns

COMMUNICATION BREAKTHROUGH

How to Win Friends and Influence People

It has been called "calculatedly corny and cunningly folksy," but the Dale Carnegie course on public speaking and public relations has influenced millions of graduates from all walks of life. The main word that the Carnegie course stresses is *positivism*—looking at what can go right rather than what can go wrong in a person's life and career. Author of the book *How to Win Friends and Influence People*, Dale Carnegie started to advise individuals and businesses on public speaking in 1912. Since that time, more than seventy countries have adopted the principles of the course. Currently, in the United States, more than 150,000 students enroll each year.

Much of the Carnegie success is gained through businesses that pay for their employees to take the fourteen-session course, which costs around $1,000. Even though times are tough economically, Carnegie administrators say that 400 of the Fortune 500 companies, the most prestigious companies in the nation, still send people to take the course.

The course tries to stamp out the *inhibitions* and insecurities that people have about themselves. It is organized around the following principles:

1. Become genuinely interested in other people.
2. Smile!
3. Remember that people want to be called by name.
4. Be a good listener.
5. Talk in terms of the other person's interest.
6. Make the other person feel important— and do it sincerely.

With converts from around the globe, including former Chrysler Chairman Lee Iacocca, the Dale Carnegie approach to feeling good about yourself, about your future, and about other people is a speech communication breakthrough. It allows people to work with real issues and come up with real answers. Millions of people can't be wrong.

Questions
1. Why do you think that the Dale Carnegie course on public speaking is still popular after all these years?
2. How could the six listed principles (above) help you to "win friends and influence people"?
3. Which of the six to you is the most important?

IV The Conclusion

It has been said that if you want to deliver a good speech to your audience, you should "tell 'em what you are gonna tell 'em, tell 'em, and then tell 'em what you told 'em." This statement is not only amusing but also contains a great deal of truth. What is the lesson? First of all, your speech needs an introduction that previews for your audience your specific purpose in speaking. Next, your speech needs a body that proves your point. Fi-

The conclusion summarizes the major points covered in the speech and offers a final appeal or final impression.

nally, your speech needs a conclusion in which you wrap up what you have to say in a neat communication package.

Read the following conclusion for the speech on the positive role that laughter can play. Parts of the speech were used as examples earlier in the chapter. As in the introduction, pay attention to the numbers.

#1 In conclusion, you have seen how laughter can make you a more productive and effective worker, a more sensitive friend and family member, and even a healthier person. I think that, after hearing that laughter can actually help us overcome serious illness and can help terminally ill patients live two to four years longer, we should all start to smile. **#2** The great thing about laughter is that it takes no special talent except a willingness to see the humor in both situations and ourselves. Let's establish and maintain a "laughing attitude." We can all do it—and it costs nothing. **#3** Therefore, the words that you heard at the beginning of this speech, "Let a smile be your umbrella," might be sound

advice. So go ahead and laugh. Hopefully, the world will laugh with you!

The conclusion effectively summarizes the major points of the speech (indicated by #1), presents a solution or an "action step" (indicated by #2), and offers a final appeal or a solid final impression (indicated by #3).

The Summary

The first part of your conclusion is usually the summary. (You might go back and see how the word *summarize* was used in Chapter 3, "Listening.") The summary should remind your audience of the main headings, or major areas of analysis, that you covered in your speech. Sometimes your summary might even include a particularly memorable or hard-hitting detail. (However, the summary should *not* become so repetitive that your audience is left saying, "Wait a minute! Didn't you tell me all of that already?") In addition, you might choose to repeat your speech topic or thesis in the summary. This approach is sound because it guarantees that your audience will see how the remainder of the conclusion fits your thesis. Remember that a summary is a quick wrap-up. Get to the point and then move on.

The Solution or Action Step

The next section of your conclusion is the solution or the "call for action." Here, you can suggest some possible answers to problems that you have identified in your speech. Keep in mind that not all speeches must include profound solutions. Sometimes the best solutions are those that are simple, practical, and easy to understand. And sometimes, no solution at all need be offered. "Do some reading on this subject" and "Try this procedure out" are a few "action steps" that can be offered to an audience that has heard a speech to inform. Overall, solutions and action steps usually fall into three categories: policy, attitudinal, and awareness.

Policy Solutions

A *policy solution* asks your audience to write the president or a congressperson, to start a petition drive for signatures in favor of a local candidate, or to rally as a group for a local march to the capital. Policy solutions usually demand some form of physical action on your audience's part. In addition, policy solutions actively challenge an existing institution or problem.

Attitudinal Solutions

An *attitudinal solution* deals more with attitudes, opinions, and moods. It asks your audience to change or strengthen their mental state regarding an issue. For example, an attitudinal solution could ask your listeners to become more open-minded about people or to change their perspective about what the word *success* really means.

Awareness Solutions

The *awareness solution* reminds your audience to be conscious of what they have heard and possibly implement it in their own lives. The awareness solution is especially appropriate for informative speeches or demonstration speeches, in which the speaker is not offering the solution to a problem. The awareness solution can remind the audience that a wealth of information has been shared—that, for instance, "cross-country skiing can be fun if you will just try to apply the steps that we've looked at today."

Of course, the type of solution you use depends on the type of speech that you are delivering. You do have some choices, though. For example, if your speech deals with the economic problems of the inner city, you can suggest that audience members write to their state representatives to find out what financial assistance plans for the inner city are in the works—a policy solution. Or you can challenge audience members to examine their sense of justice and fair play and urge them to open their hearts to the less fortunate—an attitudinal solution.

You can even offer more than one type of solution. However, be careful. Like your summary, your solution—although very important—should not be too long. Be brief, be direct, and offer a solution or action step that is realistic. Audiences

Sample Outline

Purpose statement: The purpose of this speech is to inform the audience of the positive role that laughter can play in their lives.

INTRODUCTION

I.   Have you ever heard the sayings "Let a smile be your umbrella" and "Laugh and the world laughs with you?"
    A.   Both of these sayings show how a positive attitude and laughter can work to your advantage.
    B.   Laughter can do more than provide a pleasant smile.

II. I would like to discuss the various areas in your lives where laughter can play a significantly positive role.
    A.   Laughter can help you on the job.
    B.   Laughter can help you with family and friends.
    C.   Laughter can help your health.

BODY

I.   Laughter can help you on the job.
    A.   Laughter can make you a more productive worker.
        1.   Mention pamphlet on employees and bosses.
        2.   Giving in to your "funny bone" relieves stress and lets you see the occupational "big picture."
    B.   Laughter helps you cut down on absenteeism.
        1.   Walker University study gives the 20 percent fewer days missed statistic.
        2.   Worker who laughs *wants* to come to work.

II. Laughter can help you with family and friends.
    A.   Family problems can be handled better.
        1.   Northwestern University reports that most family disputes can be "defused" by a well-timed joke or a laugh that the family is involved in together.
        2.   Trust often results from taking the time to laugh with one another.
    B.   People are often drawn to laughter and a sense of humor.
        1.   Friends believe that your ability to laugh with them is a sign that you accept them.
        2.   Psychological study: people are attracted to those who laugh heartily because they see those people as potential leaders.

III. Laughter can also benefit your health.
    A.   Laughter can help people with serious illnesses.
        1.   My aunt who had cancer found that watching cartoons and laughing gave her a positive attitude about her condition.
        2.   Terminally ill patients in Chicago lived two to four years longer.
    B.   Laughter can help with common ailments.
        1.   Doctors state that the energy that it takes to laugh is actually a form of exercise that helps the body fight aches and pains.
        2.   They add that laughing keeps the throat and vocal cords loose and active and helps ward off serious sore throats and colds.

CONCLUSION

I.   Thus, laughter can make you a better worker, a more sensitive family member and friend, and a healthier person.
    A.   It takes no special talent.
    B.   It costs nothing.

II. So "Let a smile be your umbrella" is certainly good advice.

want to hear something that is within the realm of possibility, something that they can actually carry out.

The Final Appeal or Final Impression

Just as it is important to make a good first impression, it is important to make a solid final impression. Your final appeal ends your speech and challenges, inspires, or motivates your audience to consider the significance of your topic. While some speakers may hold to the idea that you should always "leave 'em laughin'," this isn't necessarily true. The tone and nature of your speech should determine your final appeal or final impression.

If you go back to the types of attention-getters discussed earlier, you will see some methods that can be effective for your final lines as well. For instance, asking a question, making a startling state-

ment, giving a quotation, telling a story, or making references can work for you at the end of your speech as well as at the beginning. You might also consider ending the speech the same way that you started it. In other words, if you begin your speech with a quiz, you might end your speech by answering those questions for your audience in a creative, insightful manner. Did you begin with a quotation? Why not end with a quotation that makes a similar point or one that accentuates what your speech has promoted? Just keep this in mind about the words that you choose to end your speech:

◆ They must fit the mood of your speech.
◆ They must make sense.
◆ They should bring some finality to your speech so that your audience realizes that you have finished.

TAKING CHARGE

1. Pretend that you are being given one opportunity to convince your teacher that you deserve an A in the class. Give your reasons, supply evidence, and then end with an effective final appeal or final impression. To evaluate your effectiveness, try recording yourself (on audio or video) and playing it back for the class or a friend to analyze.
2. For each of the problems stated below, offer a different type of solution—policy, attitudinal, or awareness. Write down each solution and be ready to give your solutions out loud.

   ◆ Students are not showing school spirit.
   ◆ The speed limit around our elementary schools needs to be lowered for the safety of the children.
   ◆ Lack of exercise is a national problem.

STUDENT SPEECH

The following speech received special recognition in the 1987 National Forensic League district competition. It was written by Michael Gotch, who went on to become the National Forensic League national champion in original oratory in 1989. (Note: *All* of the words below, even the parts of the outline, were given out loud to the audience.)

A Boring Outline

Introduction

    I. *Attention-getter* definition: dramatic example, pertinent quote, or startling statement to gain the attention of the audience.
       A. All of you are going to die!
       B. I'm going to die, too!
       C. We are not happy about this, are we!
    II. Link to thesis
    III. Thesis statement: Style over substance

Now, even though this is certainly not the best beginning of a speech that you have probably heard, you have to admit that it is generic. And although what I described may sound like something off a black and white box at the local supermarket, it was simply oratory brought down to its most basic form—*the outline*. Now, if I were to give my entire speech like this, totally void of all entertainment, glamour, or gimmick, about half of you would probably be asleep within a short while. Why? Because in a world like ours, if you are not entertaining, pack it up! The way to the top these days lies with the "glitz." However, lately, in our quest for ultimate entertainment, we have forgotten to look beyond the gimmick to see if what lies behind is truly worth supporting. As we examine the situation, three major areas seem apparent. So

let's really go out on a limb and call these areas Roman numerals I, II, and III, and look at each a little more closely.

Body of the Speech

Roman numeral I. The entertainment industry. What better place to start than with our world of film and television. The "movers and shakers." But what has happened to the creativity? Which television shows are the most popular today? The answer: "The Cosby Show," "Family Ties," and "Growing Pains." Bill Moyers seems to have the answer to their success. He stated in a recent interview with *Newsweek*, "These shows are light, enjoyable, and easy to watch," and although a few do work to strengthen some basic family values, most, according to Moyers, "demand nothing more than our attention." They must not demand much from their creators, either, seeing that the "family sitcom" makes up one-third of the programming on television today. Each one seems molded from its predecessor with only minor differences. A night of fun and relaxation isn't bad, but do we ever judge a show on its intellectual value? Now, I'm not saying that we should all go home and watch *Gandhi* and a PBS special on mating flies. However, we do need to think before we decide because lately, entertainment has influenced the way that we make important decisions—decisions about people. This leads me to my second point.

Roman numeral II. Leaders. The simple truth is that today we are no longer looking beyond the "glitz" to examine the person. We are beginning to choose our leaders, political or otherwise, on the basis of their entertainment value. Their style. Before Roy Romer became governor of Colorado, he was a short, pasty-faced man with horn-rimmed glasses. Today, little (if anything) remains the same, thanks to Jo Farell of J. F. Images Modeling Agency. He's now handsomer, thanks to the "gorgeous gray" found by Farell's hairstylist; he also looks healthier due to Elonzo skin care treatments. And he seems friendlier, thanks to a new suit from Brooks Brothers. The reason for this change is not difficult to understand. To win, Romer needed a sharper image. Robert Feeter, president of Marketing Opinion Research of Detroit, states, "If you have the visual right, you have the communication right. It almost doesn't matter what you say." In other words, the *image*, not the *intellect*, controls. This brings me to my final point.

Roman numeral III. Education. Today, we don't want to learn about people or things unless they are fun, exciting, and once again, entertaining. In 1968, "Sesame Street" was hailed as a breakthrough. Learning would be fun. However, studies by Dr. Neil Postman now show that "Sesame Street" doesn't teach children to love school. It teaches them to love school *only* if school is like "Sesame Street." What's so surprising is that many schools today try to be! On October 30, 1986, it was a day like any other at Dominguez High School in Southern California. Classes began at 8 A.M. But along with the usual stream of morning announcements came one *not* so usual. It was an announcement that the United States and the Soviet Union had begun World War III. A state of shock and utter disbelief settled over the school, causing students and teachers alike to flee the classrooms. Of course, this was just a prank—set up by the *principal* of the school. According to one spokesman for the school district, this was just another one of the many ways that the principal tried to "jazz up" the school day.

You see, the harm in focusing on style instead of substance goes much deeper and is much more significant than merely choosing the wrong movie or reading the wrong book. One harm is that we no longer tell the truth—unless the truth sells. Television news programs once thought of as informative and engaging are now becoming little more than video versions of *People* magazine. As a result, we paint ourselves a distorted picture of society, sadly leaving out some important factors, simply because they aren't entertaining. We begin to hear only what we want to hear and flatter our world instead of examine it.

Conclusion

Have we really become such a cold, cruel, unfeeling society? Fortunately, there is a solution, and that brings me to my conclusion. Every good speech has a conclusion, doesn't it? Maybe the answer lies in the word *boredom*. When you ask most people why they constantly need entertainment, a popular response is, "Well, I certainly don't want to be bored!" Did you ever stop to think that when we are *alone*, we can create our own entertainment because we can now exercise our brains and allow *our own imaginations* to work! We can think freely without interruption. There's also a simplicity in boredom which gives us time to organize our priorities responsibly without being swayed or conned. Boredom gives us time to examine and review the day objectively and intelligently—time to give importance to events that deserve it, and time to forget the ones that don't. When you and I can learn to treasure our quiet moments alone as much as we do "At the Movies" or Judge Wapner on "The People's Court," and when we can learn to love simplicity as much as we do hype, then *we will have beaten the system!*

How's that for an outline with a final impression?

REVIEW AND ENRICHMENT

LOOKING BACK

Listed below are the major ideas discussed in this chapter.

+ Organization is the plan that you develop to get things done. Whether for a speech, for your job, or for school, organization brings order and direction to the task at hand.
+ The introduction is the beginning of your speech and usually consists of four parts: the attention-getter, the link, the thesis statement, and the preview statement.
+ The body of your speech is the "meat" of your presentation and must be organized so that the audience can clearly follow what you are saying.
+ Subordinating ideas—ordering them by importance—allows you to effectively outline your speech.
+ The purpose statement is the most critical sentence in your speech because everything else in the speech revolves around it.
+ Main headings (indicated by Roman numerals) are the major subdivisions of your purpose statement or thesis.
+ Supporting materials (indicated by capital letters) divide the main headings into more specific categories and present more detailed information.
+ Details (indicated by numbers) are subdivisions of the supporting materials and often are specific names, dates, statistics, and the like.
+ Transitions are the links that take you from area to area throughout your presentation and keep the audience informed as to where you are in your speech.
+ Different patterns can be used to organize the body of a speech; the pattern to use is the one that will work best with the thesis.
+ The conclusion is the final part of the speech and consists of the summary, the solution or action step, and the final appeal or final impression.

SPEECH VOCABULARY

introduction
quotation
narrative
link
thesis statement
preview statement
body

outline
purpose statement
subordination
main heading
supporting material
detail
transition

chronological pattern   cause–effect pattern
climactic pattern   problem–solution pattern
spatial pattern

1. For each new speech term, find and then write down the definition given in the text. List
   the number of the page on which each word appears. Now write an original sentence
   showing each vocabulary word "in action."
2. Make flash cards. On one side of each card, print a new speech term. On the other side,
   write the definition. Keep track of the words that give you problems and eliminate the
   words that you can handle. This will prepare you for a vocabulary exam.

GENERAL VOCABULARY

vested   enhanced
equilibrium   haphazardly
gigantic   intensification
fiasco   indented
jeopardy   inhibitions

1. Use the dictionary to define the general vocabulary terms. Dictate each of the words to a
   classmate in order to work on the spelling. Next, read the definitions out loud, and have
   the classmate tell you the word that matches each definition. Try mixing up the order of
   the words.
2. Write an original sentence using each general vocabulary word. After you are finished, try
   to write a short essay, titled "What Might Happen If I Don't Organize My Life," using at
   least five of the words. Make your story make sense!

THINGS TO REMEMBER

1. What type of questions don't really ask for a response from the audience?
2. The part of the introduction that combines your introduction with your speech topic is
   called the _____.
3. The _____ states exactly what your speech is going to do and reminds you what
   you must accomplish with your audience.
4. The organizational pattern that uses time as a factor is called the _____
   pattern.
5. Who said, "No army can withstand the strength of an idea whose time has come"?

6. The outline consists of the main headings, plus supporting material, followed by
   _____ .

7. The words or short phrases that link ideas together are called _____ .

8. Name the three types of solutions: _____ , _____ , and _____ .

9. Quotations, stories, and questions are all types of _____ that can be used in the introduction.

10. The organizational pattern that uses space as a factor is called what?

11. Subordinating your ideas means ranking them in terms of_____ .

12. Mentioning people in your audience, mentioning other speakers, and mentioning the room are all types of _____ that you can use to gain an audience's attention.

THINGS TO DO

1. Using as topics the school extra-curricular activities "Sports," "Music," "Academics," and "Other," find all the information that you can and outline your findings. For "Sports," what are the teams? What are their records? Who are the key players? The coaches? An outline for "Sports" might begin like this:

   I. Baseball
      A. 1992 record, 18–3
      B. Strengths
         1. Hitting
         2. Bench strength
   II. Basketball

2. Draw a design layout of your house or your room. Using a spatial organizational approach, make your drawing as accurate and neat as possible. If possible, try to turn in a product that is in color.

3. Make a list of the ten people in the world whom you admire most. What category does each fall under (for example, entertainment, family, politics)? Try to find all of the different ways that your ten choices can be grouped. Be sure to be logical in your groupings.

THINGS TO TALK ABOUT

1. A person speaking about stress management said to her audience: "In this life, where grabbing for the gusto may mean one more demand on an already overflowing life calendar, it's important to decide what's really important." She was referring to the ability to prioritize. How do you think that prioritizing could help cut down on stress in your life?

2. Why is it important to use details when you are trying to defend a particular position? Why isn't your opinion enough? What would be the value of organization if you were trying to convince someone to do something?

3. Which types of introductions and final appeal techniques do you find most impressive? Give your reasoning. Which do you find least desirable? Why?

4. Do some problem–solution brainstorming. What are some school problems? What are a few possible solutions? What are some societal problems? Solutions? Be practical! Also, for each of the following, discuss how a cause–effect relationship could exist: drugs and crime, alcohol and suicide, preparation and success, trust and friendship.

THINGS TO WRITE ABOUT

1. The report "Voices from the Classroom" is based on a survey of nearly 1,500 eleventh and twelfth graders from twenty different high schools around the country. Believe it or not, nine out of ten students said that it is important for parents to help students with homework and to set definite study rules and guidelines! The students said that parents need to start this procedure when children are young. Write an organized paper giving reasons why you agree or disagree with this finding.

2. The same survey, which was conducted by Sylvan Learning Centers, concluded that government should spend more money on education. If you were in charge of how money for education could be spent, what would be—in order—your top three areas? Write an outline, and then construct a paper answering this question. Be sure to offer solid reasoning for your areas.

3. Write a one-page paper detailing the plan that you would have if you could map out your future. Before you write, make an outline. Be sure to include main headings, supporting materials, and details. What about transitions? Think through your reasoning and create a credible plan.

CRITICAL THINKING

1. Did you know that during the Persian Gulf War, the Allied forces had tremendously sophisticated technical equipment—that didn't always work as intended? For instance, orbiting satellites code-named Keyhole provided close-up pictures of jeeps and even license plates, but the commanders often couldn't get a broad view of the battle area and

REVIEW AND ENRICHMENT
Continued

consequently didn't have the "big picture." Why is knowing the big picture important not only in speaking but also in everyday decision making? Explain.

2. Read this statement: "There is a direct correlation between organization and personal discipline. If your speeches are out of order, there is a good chance that your life is, too." Is the quote partly correct? Totally correct? Not correct at all? Defend your responses.

RELATED SPEECH TOPICS

This chapter has dealt with organization and the value of planning in both speaking and life. It has also discussed some patterns that you can use to organize speeches. Give an organized speech dealing with one or more of the following topics (feel free to take an opposing position):

There should be equal pay for equal
  work.
The school day should be shorter.
Cars are complicated machines but can
  be easily explained.
Only juniors and seniors should be able
  to attend the school prom.
Volunteer work should be mandatory for
  high school graduation.
Students should have to pay if they wish
  to be involved in extracurricular
  activities.

Competition has serious drawbacks.
When considering nature, the needs of
  people should always be considered
  before the needs of animals.
A politician convicted of a crime should
  be immediately removed from office.
A student's discipline in class should be
  a significant factor in the student's
  grade in that class.

Note: Outline first!

Now, here's the next step. For the speech topics that you have selected, add an introduction and a conclusion. Do you remember what each is supposed to do?

CHAPTER 9

Logic and Reasoning

> "'I know what you're thinking about,' said Tweedledum, 'but it isn't so, nohow.'
> 'Contrariwise,' continued Tweedledee, 'if it was so, it might be; and if it were so, it would be; but as it isn't, it ain't. That's logic.'"
>
> — **Lewis Carroll**, *Alice in Wonderland*

LEARNING OBJECTIVES

After completing this chapter, you will be able to do the following.

✦ Distinguish among several different types of reasoning and recognize faulty or misleading types.
✦ Better adapt your use of logic to a specific audience.
✦ Analyze your own logic to determine if your conclusions are valid.

CHAPTER OUTLINE

Following are the main sections in this chapter.

I Evaluating Ideas: Methods of Reasoning
II Fallacies
III The Ethics of Audience Adaptation
   Chapter Review

NEW SPEECH TERMS

In this chapter, you will learn the meanings of the speech terms listed below.

evidence
reasoning
logic
induction
case study
sign
analogy
deduction
premises
syllogism
fallacies
hasty
  generalization

false premise
circumstantial
  evidence
causality
correlation
false analogy
ignoring the
  question
begging the
  question

GENERAL VOCABULARY

Expanding your general vocabulary will help you become a more effective communicator. Listed below are some words appearing in this chapter that you should make part of your everyday vocabulary.

integrate
systematic
phenomenon
internship
segregation
degraded
incorrigible

perception
manipulate
distortion
rigorous
rebuffed
rife
expedient

LOOKING AHEAD

If you want to be an effective speaker, you should support your ideas with sufficient evidence and valid reasoning. **Evidence** is anything that establishes a fact or gives us reason to believe something. **Reasoning** is the process of thinking and drawing conclusions about that evidence. You apply the process of reasoning in choosing and developing arguments. **Logic,** the science of reasoning, uses a system of rules to help you think correctly during the process.

Although sound reasoning is an essential component of communication, speakers often spew forth illogical statements that show little understanding of a speaker's responsibility to the audience and to the truth. In this chapter, you will learn the fundamental rules of logical reasoning and how to apply these rules effectively in your speaking. You will also explore how to *integrate* evidence into a speech and how to recognize the faulty logic that often arises. In short, you will take an important step toward becoming more logical and therefore more effective as a communicator.

As you construct arguments, remember that an argument is not the same thing as a fully developed persuasive speech. You should use several arguments to make a complete presentation. Think of writing your speech as if you were building a bridge. Each argument becomes a girder that holds up your bridge. One weak or misplaced girder and the entire bridge may come crashing down.

Your teacher may give you a student speech that uses the different types of reasoning discussed in this chapter to argue that the medicine Prozac should not be banned. To learn how one student built his bridge—his span of arguments—you should carefully study the structure of this persuasive speech.

I Evaluating Ideas: Methods of Reasoning

To become more logical, you must learn about the types of reasoning. Understanding the types of reasoning can make your thinking clearer and more *systematic.*

Inductive Reasoning

In mathematics, there is a technique for proving theorems in which the mathematician uses certain specific cases to help prove a general truth. This process is called inductive reasoning, or **induction.** Induction, though, isn't used only by mathematicians. Anyone who argues from specific

Wayne's World, as a "Saturday Night Live" sketch and then a movie, popularized the use of an affirmative statement followed by the word *not* to express a negative.

instances to a generalization is using inductive reasoning.

Suppose, for example, that you are preparing a speech about the importance of learning to read. You want to determine whether students who begin reading at a younger age earn better grades in school. You find five studies that link early reading with better performance in history but poorer performance in science. Based on inductive reasoning, you can conclude that starting to read at a younger age does not necessarily mean earning better grades.

As another example, think about the local politician who argues in favor of

INSTANT IMPACT

Wayne's World. NOT.

Following the success of the film *Wayne's World*, everyone from the rock star Madonna to the syndicated columnist George Will was tossing out NOTs as if they were *bon mots*. Franklin L. Noel, a federal magistrate in Minneapolis, describes the *phenomenon:* "Rather than using the ordinary syntax, the speaker will express a negative by making an affirmative statement, followed by a brief pause punctuated by the word *not*." For example, *Wayne's World* is the greatest film of all time. NOT.

Laurence Horn, a Yale University professor, became intrigued by his nine-year-old son's use of NOT. His research reveals that the expression may date back to teens growing up in the Midwest in the 1960s. Pamela Munro, author of *Slang U.*, attributes the phrase to the West Coast surfers of the 1980s. Fans of "Saturday Night Live" remember Steve Martin uttering NOT in a 1978 episode in which he played Chaz the Spaz. According to Linda Shrieves of the *Orlando Sentinel*, Martin said to Gilda Radner's character Lisa Lupner, "That's a fabulous science fair project." He paused, then sneered. "NOT!"

Regardless of its origin, the structure of the now-famous phrase is of much interest to logicians. They often use a construction in which a positive statement is followed by *not* when they set out to disprove a statement. So if you want to learn more about logic, rent the video of *Wayne's World* and watch it again. NOT.

year-round school because students in countries that have such a system score better on international math, science, and geography tests than students in American schools. This politician is reasoning inductively.

A special type of inductive reasoning with which you should be familiar is the **case study.** A case study allows you to analyze a "typical" example in great detail so that you can draw general conclusions. For example, to learn more about the life of a journalist, you might undertake a month-long *internship* with the local newspaper and then apply your observations in a speech on the field of journalism as a whole.

Suppose you want to argue in your speech that journalists work long hours. You could record the daily schedules of four different journalists that you meet during your internship. If you find that these four journalists work long shifts, you might argue that it is likely that *all* journalists work long hours. In making this argument, you are using inductive reasoning.

Reasoning by Sign

A special type of inductive reasoning is reasoning by **sign,** in which we draw conclusions about a given situation based on physical evidence. Perhaps the most familiar example of reasoning by sign is the work of Sherlock Holmes, the fictional sleuth. Holmes seemingly could solve the most complicated mysteries by simply studying the dust balls under the sofa. Reasoning by sign can be persuasive. For example, in Sir Arthur Conan Doyle's novel *The Hound of the Baskervilles*, Holmes

Sir Arthur Conan Doyle's fictional detective Sherlock Holmes uses reasoning by sign to solve complicated mysteries.

explains to his associate Watson that it is "elementary" to determine the breed of a dog by observing the dog's teeth marks on a stick.

"Being a heavy stick, the dog held it tightly by the middle, and the marks of his teeth are plainly visible. The dog's jaw, as shown in the space between these marks, is too broad in my opinion for a terrier and not broad enough for a mastiff. It may have been—yes, by Jove, it is a curly-haired spaniel."

He had risen and paced the room as he spoke. Now he halted in the recess of the window. There was such a ring of conviction in his voice that I glanced up in surprise.

"My dear fellow, how can you be so sure of that?"

"For the very simple reason that I see the dog himself on our very door-step, and there is the ring of its owner."

COMMUNICATION BREAKTHROUGH

Separate but Unequal

In 1951, Oliver Brown, an African-American railroad worker from Topeka, Kansas, sued the city of Topeka for preventing his daughter from attending a local all-white school. Eight-year-old Linda Brown was forced to ride a bus for five miles when there was a school only four blocks from her home. The case, which went all the way to the Supreme Court *(Brown v. Board of Education)*, challenged the constitutionality of an 1896 ruling, *Plessy v. Ferguson*. In *Plessy*, the court had decided that *segregation* was permissible as long as blacks and whites had access to "separate but equal" facilities. Thurgood Marshall and his team of lawyers, though, presented evidence demonstrating that "separate but equal" was a logical impossibility. There could be no such thing as "separate but equal" facilities when society was arranged unequally.

In a 9–0 landmark decision, the Supreme Court ruled that segregated facilities *degraded* minorities and prevented them from having equal educational opportunities. As Chief Justice Earl Warren wrote, "separate educational facilities are inherently unequal." *Plessy* was overturned. Although the *Brown* decision applied only to education, it inspired minorities to seek rights in other fields, and it became a turning point in the civil rights movement.

Questions

1. Do you believe that minorities have equal educational opportunities today? Why?
2. What can be done to improve educational opportunities for everyone?

Reasoning by Analogy

Another common method of inductive reasoning is the use of analogy. An **analogy** is an illustration in which the characteristics of a familiar object or event are used to explain or describe the characteristics of a less familiar object or event. Analogies are used by the creators of standardized tests to measure intelligence. For example, "Hand is to person as (a) tree is to sky, (b) dirty is to laundry, (c) foot is to powder, (d) paw is to dog." The point of those tests is not to make you blind from filling in thousands of tiny bubbles with number-two pencils but to see if you can pick out similarities.

When you reason by analogy, you demonstrate similarities as you develop an argument. Suppose that a particular food is found to cause cancer in white rats. You might then reason by analogy that there is some risk to humans as well. Because no two sets of conditions are exactly alike, though, the perfect analogy doesn't exist. (White rats rarely guzzle beer as they gorge themselves on potato chips.) Therefore, you should not rely entirely on an analogy to prove your position in any speech and should always supplement your arguments with other forms of proof.

INSTANT IMPACT

A Sign of the Times

To reach a verdict, juries often depend on witnesses who reason by sign. This method of reasoning, though, is not fool-proof. Take the case of Meir Kahane, who was shot to death in a crowded hall in a Manhattan hotel on November 5, 1990. The prosecution called 51 witnesses to support its charge of murder.

"Many witnesses," reported the *Washington Post*, "testified that they were standing only a few feet away when they heard the shots and turned to see El Sayyid Nosair cradling a .357 revolver and crouching near Kahane." According to one columnist, Charles Krauthammer, Nosair was seen pointing the gun at Kahane by one witness. Furthermore, as Nosair attempted to escape, he shot two people.

The jury returned its verdict on December 21, 1991: not guilty. The judge denounced the verdict as "devoid of common sense and logic" and "against the overwhelming weight of evidence."

Only four months later, the Rodney King jury, too, seemed to go against the weight of evidence in that highly publicized trial. Millions of citizens had witnessed the beating of King on videotape. Most of these citizens—reasoning by sign—believed that the four policemen should be found guilty. The jury disagreed. For three days, the world watched on television as Los Angeles experienced the worst urban violence in the United States in this century.

Millions who witnessed Rodney King's beating on videotape reasoned by sign that the four police officers should be found guilty. When they were acquitted, Los Angeles suffered the most devastating urban violence in the United States in this century.

Deductive Reasoning

A counterpart to inductive reasoning is deductive reasoning, or **deduction.** Inductive reasoning moves from specific instances to a generalization; deductive reasoning moves from generalizations, or **premises,** to a specific instance. Premises are the statements on which reasoning is based.

Consider this simple example of deductive reasoning. It consists of two premises and a conclusion, and it is called a **syllogism:**

1. All students go to school.
2. You are a student.
3. Therefore, you go to school.

Deductive reasoning is not always this straightforward. For example, let's look at the role of judges on the Supreme Court. Their task is to try to apply a set of widely accepted principles (premises)—the Constitution—to specific cases. However, it's often difficult to tell whether the principles actually apply. Therefore, judges must reason from the general principles to the specific cases to decide if the cases are valid.

Suppose that you are preparing a speech in which you plan to argue that flag burning should be allowed. By using deductive reasoning, you can develop an argument based on the First Amendment. The First Amendment is a general principle that is supposed to protect free expression, but does burning the flag count as "expression"? If it does, then you could invoke the First Amendment and, by deduction, conclude that flag burning is legal.

1. The First Amendment says to allow all types of expression.
2. Flag burning is a type of expression.
3. Therefore, flag burning should be allowed.

Of course, the premise that states that flag burning is a form of expression must be true if listeners are to accept the argument in your speech.

TAKING CHARGE

Now it's your turn. Using three of the forms of reasoning discussed in this chapter, develop three arguments for a topic of your choosing. For example, if you were trying to persuade the members of your audience that they should all attend college, you might offer these arguments:

Inductive reasoning—You interviewed ten people who graduated from college, and they all agreed that a college education was a good idea for them.

Deductive reasoning—College-educated people get the better-paying jobs. You want a better-paying job. Therefore, you should get a college education.

Reasoning by sign—The last time you visited a college campus, you saw a group of students having fun at a dormitory party. If you attend college, you will have fun at parties, too.

II Fallacies

The arguments just presented to support college attendance for everyone are not without their flaws. In this section, we examine common forms of flawed arguments, or fallacies. Fallacies are errors in reasoning or mistaken beliefs. They are the do-not's of logic. Because fallacies weaken your credibility as a speaker, it is important to learn to understand, recognize, and avoid them. Some of the more common fallacies include hasty generalizations, false premises, circumstantial evidence, mistaken causality, misuse of numbers, false analogy, ignoring the question, and begging the question.

Hasty Generalization

A **hasty generalization** is a faulty argument that occurs because the sample chosen is too small or is in some way not representative. Therefore, the conclusion drawn based on this information is flawed. For example, you flip through three television channels on your remote control, and all you see are commercials. Your conclusion that the only thing on television is commercials is a hasty generalization—wrong but, unfortunately, not by much. Or suppose that you are an alien from another planet who saw Antarctica on your first visit to Earth. You might conclude that the only inhabitants of this planet were fish and penguins and the only landscapes were glaciers. Your sample size is large—there are plenty of glaciers, fish, and penguins in Antarctica —but your conclusion is still wrong because the sample is not representative of the whole.

False Premise

The **false premise** is an error in deduction. For example, parents like to tell their children, "All teenagers are irresponsible. You are a teenager. Therefore, you are not responsible enough to leave the house tonight." Now study the example to find the premise based on a hasty generalization.

COMMUNICATION WORKS

Art Melendres, Attorney

A witness is on the stand testifying about the time of an accident. Does it make a difference if that witness describes the time of day as "getting dark" or if he says instead that it was "near the end of day?"

"Yes," explains Art Melendres, an attorney, "shades of meaning can affect the jurors' *perception* of the truth. Both responses are right, but they create different images. An ethical lawyer insists that a client tell the truth but helps that client present the truth in the best possible light."

Melendres knew that he wanted to become a lawyer while still in sixth grade. His father invited Melendres to accompany him on a visit to the family attorney—"a very big occasion because I had to dress up as though it were Sunday." The special attention paid to him by the family attorney captured his young imagination. Later, for his debating skill in high school, Melendres won scholarships, which he used to attend the University of New Mexico and the University of New Mexico Law School.

Melendres recalls a law school experience that made it clear to him how difficult it is to reason by sign. "A common practice in the classroom to make that point is a simulated assault on a professor. The professor will be standing in the front of the room—teaching as usual—when a stranger will rush into the room, yell something, and fire blanks from a pistol at the teacher. The teacher collapses to the floor as the stranger hurries from the classroom. A split-second later, the professor rises and begins quizzing the students about what they saw. Without fail, the students will be unable to agree on a physical description of the assailant, what was said, or even how many shots were fired."

Melendres knows that there will be honest disagreements in any system that depends on human judgment, but he worries about the choices made by some attorneys. The choices that mean logic and reasoning are sacrificed simply to get clients off. Celebrity cases, like the William Kennedy Smith rape trial and the Supreme Court confirmation hearing of Clarence Thomas, trouble him. Melendres says, "Although we all have a duty to give someone the best defense because everyone is presumed innocent, there is more of a tendency among lawyers today to think short-term."

Ethical communication matters to Melendres. He says, "I think each person has a responsibility and, in fact, an obligation in a democratic society to premise what they're doing on the truth. The ends do not justify the means."

Although it may be true that you are an *incorrigible* ne'er-do-well, the premise that all teenagers are irresponsible is false. Of course, if you choose to argue the fine points of logic with your parents, they might choose to restrict your opportunity to watch all of those commercials on television.

Circumstantial Evidence

People like to draw conclusions based on **circumstantial evidence**—the evidence at hand. If they rely too much on circumstantial evidence, though, they commit an error in reasoning by sign. For example, it might seem perfectly "logical" to assume that the person holding the smoking gun at the scene of the murder was the one who committed the crime—but is it? What if it turned out that the person holding the smoking gun was trying to defend the person who got murdered, while the actual murderer ran away? The point is that circumstantial evidence only suggests a conclusion; it does not prove it.

Mistaken Causality

To say two events are **causally** related is to claim that one event brings about the other. For example, one billiard ball strikes another and causes the second ball to bounce off the cushion at an angle. There is a causal relationship because the first ball caused the action of the second ball. To say that two events are **correlated,** however, is to claim only that the two events are related in some way. The relationship may not be causal. For example, a bus passes a church every day at twelve o'clock, and the clock in the church tower rings twelve times. The bus doesn't make the bell ring; the two events just happen at the same time.

One of the most common errors in causal reasoning involves assuming that one event causes another simply because it happens before the other. This error usually goes by a Latin name: *post hoc, ergo propter hoc* ("after this, therefore, because of this"). Suppose you pass a major

math test after going out to the movies the night before. If you then count on the cinema instead of careful preparation each time you face an exam, you are guilty of a *post hoc* fallacy.

Playing with Numbers

Many speakers *manipulate* statistics to misrepresent facts. They numb you with numbers in an attempt to persuade you to agree with their cause. Statistics, however, are subject to built-in biases, insufficient samples, and other forms of *distortion*. A classic example of playing with numbers comes from Mark Twain. In *Life on the Mississippi*, Twain, writing in 1874, observed that the lower part of the Mississippi River had been shortened 242 miles during the past 176 years—a little more than a mile and a third each year. Twain concluded, "any calm person who is not blind or idiotic can see that in the Old Oolitic Silurian Period, just a million years ago next November, the Lower Mississippi River was upward of one million three hundred thousand miles long. . . . And by the same token any person can see that seven hundred and forty-two years from now the Lower Mississippi will be only a mile and three-quarters long."

Source: M. Hirsh Goldberg, The Book of Lies.

Although Twain admitted he couldn't afford to tell the whole truth because he had a family to support, not everyone is so honest. You should watch out for speakers who spout statistics to sound impressive. Be especially wary of politicians who use statistics to predict the future. Darrell Huff, in his book *How to Lie with Statistics*, points out that "the future trend represents no more than an educated guess."

False Analogy

As mentioned, no two sets of conditions are exactly alike, so no analogies are perfect. A **false analogy** compares two things that are not really the same.

Analogies are often misapplied. Suppose that you are arguing that students ought to be able to use notes and textbooks during examinations. After all, lawyers don't have to memorize every law, and physicians don't have to remember entire medical journal articles by heart. Rather, in a courtroom or a hospital, they are allowed to look up facts as needed. Similarly, students should be able to use their textbooks during an examination. At first, this argument seems plausible. Isn't the purpose of education to prepare students for the "real world"?

The analogy is flawed, however, because the situations are not really the same. The purpose of a trial or an operation is not to test whether the doctor or lawyer has learned medicine or law, whereas the purpose of a test in school is to see how much students have learned. The situations are fundamentally different.

Ignoring the Question

Speakers often attempt to divert the attention of the audience from the matter at hand. When they do so, they are **ignoring the question.** They may focus on personal attacks or appeal to popular prejudice. Political speeches by politicians from both major parties are *rife* with this strategy. In the 1988 presidential campaign, some campaigners linked Michael Dukakis with

Good Miles per Galleon

"Columbus' calculations were illogical," says Samuel Eliot Morison, "but his mind never followed rules of logic. He knew he could make it, and had to put the mileage low in order to attract support." To the everlasting glory of Spain, Ferdinand and Isabella had perhaps less *rigorous* mathematicians than those of the princes who had *rebuffed* Columbus. The strength of his convictions aside, it is still a lucky thing that in the midst of his 10,000-mile journey, America got in the way.

Sources: Samuel Eliot Morison, Admiral of the Ocean Sea, *Little, Brown, 1943, and* The European Discovery of America, *Oxford, 1974, from Tad Tuleja,* Fabulous Fallacies, *Harmony Books (New York): 1982.*

the early parole of a convicted murderer, Willie Horton. The perception that Dukakis was "soft" on crime—a conclusion not supported by the facts—could not be shaken.

The success of mudslinging (as personal attacks are sometimes called in politics) in recent campaigns makes this strategy a significant threat to the democratic process. As a speaker, you have the responsibility not to mislead. Emotional appeals that resort to the passion of the moment rather than reinforcing the truth should be avoided. As Adlai Stevenson once said, "He who slings mud generally loses ground."

Begging the Question

Begging the question occurs when your argument assumes that whatever you are trying to prove is true. Circular reasoning is a common form of this fallacy. A circular argument assumes that a premise is true, draws a conclusion from the unsupported premise, and then uses this conclusion to prove the premise: "Students will devote more time to studying if they have more study halls. We should decrease the number of classes a student takes and increase the number of study halls if we want students to study more."

A word or phrase may beg the question, as when your grandmother asks, "How do you like my delicious apple pie?"

TAKING CHARGE

To assure that you recognize the fallacies discussed in this chapter, create three of your own. For example, if you were writing a speech as a candidate for president of the student council, you might include these fallacious statements:

◆ In a recent survey, 100 percent of those students polled preferred me for the presidency (playing with numbers—you asked only three friends).
◆ Whenever my opponent speaks at a pep rally, we lose the next game. Therefore, if we want to win, he should be forbidden from speaking (causality—an example of the *post hoc* fallacy).
◆ Furthermore, my opponent shouldn't be allowed to run for office because he, himself, is a loser, a zero, a nothing (ignoring the question—this strategy involves attacking your opponent before he has had a chance to speak).

Now it's your turn. Create three fallacies for one of the following situations:

1. trying to persuade a teacher that you should only have to attend class when you want.
2. discussing with your parents the need for you to have a car of your own.
3. asking your boss for a raise.

III The Ethics of Audience Adaptation

Logic and reasoning are often sacrificed when the speaker says to the audience only what it wants to hear. To vary your convictions and beliefs simply to please the audience may be *expedient,* but it is unethical. Take the politician who promises no new taxes and then, after being elected, raises taxes by calling those increases "revenue enhancements."

Former President Reagan pledged during his 1980 campaign that any tax increase would have to come over his dead body. Later, Reagan approved House Bill 4961, the "Tax Equality and Fiscal Responsibility Act of 1982." This bill generated $99 billion in tax revenues, and somehow the president survived. Republican leaders referred to the legislation not as a tax bill but as a reform bill because they knew what the voters wanted to hear.

Of course, members of both political parties are guilty of expedience. Author Paul K. Conkin reports that Lyndon Baines Johnson was assigned to a desk job during World War II but desperately wanted to see combat so he could build for himself a reputation as a war hero. After extensive personal lobbying in Washington, Johnson got his first and only shot at a low-level reconnaissance mission. Upon boarding the plane, nervousness overtook him, and he left the aircraft in search of a bathroom. Before Johnson returned, he was replaced by another soldier. Through an odd twist of fate, the plane was shot down, and only one man survived. The survivor and the future president both were awarded Silver Stars. Johnson never mentioned that he

During his 1980 presidential campaign, Ronald Reagan promised he would not increase taxes if elected. Two years later, however, he approved a new tax bill, which he euphemistically called a "reform bill."

wasn't on that plane, and from that day on, he often wore in public the ribbon that signifies a war hero.

As a citizen in a democracy, you have an obligation to be highly skilled in the use of logical reasoning. You must recognize half-truths and untruths so that those who misuse the power of speech cannot turn it against you. Furthermore, you have the responsibility to communicate what you know to be the truth.

An ethical speaker should try to give the audience the information that it most needs. If audience members are prejudiced, the ethical speaker should be the objective voice of reason. The Ku Klux Klan, for example, may not want to hear such a voice at

COMMUNICATION   BREAKDOWN

Love Is a Fallacy

In his humorous short story "Love Is a Fallacy," Max Shulman describes the blossoming relationship between Dobie Gillis, a law student, and Polly Espy, the young woman of his dreams. Dobie, somewhat of a sexist, feels that he must teach Polly to think so that she might be a suitable wife for a successful young attorney. (The story was written in 1951. Fortunately, attitudes have changed since then.)

As the story opens, Polly is dating Dobie's roommate, Petey Bellows. "Cool . . . and logical" Dobie comes up with a plan. Petey has "nothing upstairs" and wants a raccoon coat; Dobie has a raccoon coat and wants Polly. A deal is struck.

On their first date, Polly responds to dinner with "Gee, that was a delish dinner!" and to a movie with "Gee, that was a marvy movie!" On the drive home, she says "Gee, I had a sensaysh time!" Dobie determines that she must learn the rules of logic as soon as possible. Polly finds the lessons difficult at first but more fun than "dancing." After five grueling nights of study, Dobie tires of logic and decides to turn to matters more romantic.

"Polly, tonight we will not discuss fallacies."

"Aw, gee."

"My dear, we have now spent five evenings together. We have gotten along splendidly. It is clear that we are well matched."

"Hasty generalization," says Polly. "How can you say that we are well matched on the basis of only five dates?"

"My dear, five dates is plenty. After all, you don't have to eat a whole cake to know it's good."

"False analogy. I'm not a cake. I'm a girl."

Dobie has taught Polly well—for when he finally asks her to go steady, she replies that she has already promised herself to Petey Bellows. Outraged, Dobie asks, "Can you give me one logical reason why you should go steady with Petey Bellows?" Replies Polly, "I certainly can. He's got a raccoon coat."

Questions

1. How important is it to be "cool" today?
2. How important is it to be "logical"? Why?

TAKING CHARGE

Now it's your turn. Reread the excerpt from Shulman's short story "Love Is a Fallacy." Incorporating your knowledge of contemporary attitudes, write your version of what would happen between Dobie and Polly if they were dating today.

one of its rallies, but a speaker who believes in equal rights for everyone must challenge any practice that is discriminatory.

Furthermore, you should never present false evidence. Never appeal to the emotions of your listeners at the expense of logical reasoning. Never pretend to be an authority on a subject if you are not. In short, the responsible speaker must always be ethical. The Roman historian Sallust made the role of the responsible speaker clear: "Prefer to *be* rather than to *seem* good."

> "**Prefer to *be* rather than to *seem* good.**"
>
> **Sallust**

REVIEW AND ENRICHMENT

LOOKING BACK

Listed below are the major ideas discussed in this chapter.

◆ Speakers should support their ideas with valid evidence and correct reasoning.
◆ Reasoning is the process of thinking and drawing conclusions about evidence.
◆ Inductive reasoning uses specific cases to prove a general truth.
◆ Reasoning by sign is drawing conclusions about a given situation based on physical evidence.
◆ An analogy attempts to describe a fact or set of data in terms of its similarity to another fact or set of data.
◆ Deductive reasoning moves from generalizations, or premises, to a specific instance.
◆ Common fallacies include the hasty generalization, the false premise, circumstantial evidence, confusing correlation with causality, playing with numbers, the false analogy, ignoring the question, and begging the question.
◆ Logic and reasoning are often sacrificed when the speaker says to the audience only what it wants to hear.

SPEECH VOCABULARY

Using the speech terms listed below, fill in the blanks of the sentences in this exercise.

induction   circumstantial evidence
deduction   begging the question
case study   hasty generalization
sign   false analogy
causality   ignoring the question
correlation

1. The federal government has recently declared that it wants to learn more about how states spend their budgets. It is planning to conduct a _____ of Arkansas's budget plans over the past five years.
2. You study drunk driving laws in twenty states and conclude that harsher driving penalties could benefit every state in the nation. This process is an example of reasoning by _____ . However, twenty states might not be a large enough sample to justify changing the laws in all states. The conclusion, if false, might turn out to be a _____ .
3. "The fact that my client was present at the scene of the crime does not mean that she is guilty," argued the attorney. "Her presence is merely _____ ."

4. "Ninety-five percent of serial killers have milk in their refrigerators. Therefore, milk has a 95-percent chance of causing one to become a serial killer." This flawed reasoning is an example of two things that have _____ but not _____ .

5. If a highway patrol officer observes a car weaving from lane to lane and deduces that the driver of the swerving car may be drunk, he is reasoning by _____ .

6. When you reason from general premises to specific cases, you are using the process of _____ .

7. By labeling an opponent in an election as a liar and a thief, you are _____ (unless, of course, you are telling the truth).

8. If the authors of this book asked you, "How do you like this great quiz so far?" they would be _____ .

GENERAL VOCABULARY

Define the following terms and use each in a sentence.

integrate	perception
systematic	manipulate
phenomenon	distortion
internship	rigorous
segregation	rebuffed
degraded	rife
incorrigible	expedient

THINGS TO REMEMBER

1. What is the difference between inductive and deductive reasoning?

2. A case study allows you to examine a _____ example in great detail in order to draw more general conclusions.

3. Sherlock Holmes was known for his ability to examine physical evidence and reason by _____ .

4. Because no two sets of conditions are alike, the perfect _____ doesn't exist.

5. The fallacy of _____ often occurs when you rely on a sample that is too small or is not representative of the whole.

6. Assuming that one event causes another because it happens before the other is committing an error in reasoning known as the _____ fallacy.

7. When Mark Twain predicted that the Mississippi River would someday be only a mile and three-quarters long, he was guilty of _____.

8. Circular reasoning is a common form of the fallacy known as _____.

9. When Dobie Gillis informs Polly Espy that you don't have to eat a whole cake to know it's good, she replies that his assumption is a _____.

10. Speakers who attempt to divert the attention of the audience from the matter at hand are guilty of _____.

THINGS TO DO

1. Attend a public discussion or political speech on a current "hot" issue (or watch a speech on television). List the fallacies you hear. Try to decide whether the speaker is advancing the truth or a personal cause.

2. Pick a topic that a friend and you disagree about. Construct arguments for both sides that are free from fallacious reasoning.

3. Research the use of logic and reasoning in television advertising. Discuss with your classmates how advertising claims violate the principles of logic.

THINGS TO TALK ABOUT

1. You learned earlier that we live in an information age. Do you think that this abundance of information has helped us become more logical, or do you think that all of the facts and figures allow us to more easily "play with numbers"?

2. Why is it important for a citizen in a democracy to understand the process of reasoning?

3. Is logic or evidence more important in a speech?

4. What careers rely heavily on the use of logic and reasoning?

THINGS TO WRITE ABOUT

1. Create a fictional character that is the "evil twin" of Star Trek's Mr. Spock. Every statement made by this character is illogical. Write a brief monologue in which this flawed reasoning is evident.

2. Write an essay about a school rule that you believe is wrong. Try to provide a logical alternative to this rule.
3. Construct an imaginary conversation between a man and a woman in which one person is always logical and the other is not (reread the Max Shulman story for inspiration).

CRITICAL THINKING

1. In *Abrams v. United States* (1919), Justice Oliver Wendell Holmes wrote, "When men have realized that time has upset many fighting faiths, they may come to believe even more than they believe the very foundations of their own conduct that the ultimate good desired is better reached by free trade in ideas—that the best test of truth is the power of the thought to get itself accepted in the competition of the market."

   As members of a democratic society, we continually evaluate the validity of the "marketplace theory." For example, can the truth survive competition? Do minorities have the same coinage of exchange in the marketplace? How should we test the "truth"?
2. The phone book has been described as the ultimate example of unbiased writing—no opinions involved, just a list. Often, our biases interfere with our ability to present logical speeches. How can we balance the need for truth with our desire to persuade people to agree with our opinions?
3. In attempting to give her client the best possible defense, how far should an attorney go in persuading the jury? Can she justify omitting facts that might damage her client's case, even though that information might better serve the truth?

RELATED SPEECH TOPICS

Aristotle and logos
Mudslinging in politics
Sound bites: Does logic bite the dust?

Father does not always know best
Doublespeak
The assassination of JFK: Conspiracy?
Advertising claims

CHAPTER 10

Effective Language

"I know that you believe that you understand what you think I said, but I'm not sure that you realize that what you heard is not what I meant."

— **Richard Milhous Nixon,
thirty-seventh president of the United States,
1969–1974 (resigned)**

"Words are like leaves; and where they most abound,
Much fruit of sense beneath is rarely found."

— **Alexander Pope,
eighteenth-century English poet**

LEARNING OBJECTIVES

After completing this chapter, you will be able to do the following.

- ◆ Know why the language you select must be exact.
- ◆ Show how the spoken word differs from the written word.
- ◆ Know the value of using language that creates word pictures.
- ◆ Understand the musical language created through the use of sound devices.
- ◆ Recognize language that can prevent effective communication.

CHAPTER OUTLINE

Following are the main sections in this chapter.

I Language Exactness

II The Spoken Word versus the Written Word

III Creating Word Pictures: Figures of Speech

IV Making Music with Words: Sound Devices

V Language to Avoid

       Student Speech

       Chapter Review

NEW SPEECH TERMS

In this chapter, you will learn the meanings of the speech terms listed below.

concrete words	hyperbole
abstract words	understatement
denotation	personification
connotation	euphemisms
imagery	repetition
metaphor	alliteration
simile	assonance
analogy	consonance
allusion	parallel structure,
antithesis	or parallelism
oxymoron	jargon
irony	slang

GENERAL VOCABULARY

Expanding your general vocabulary will help you become a more effective communicator. Listed below are some words appearing in this chapter that you should make part of your everyday vocabulary.

tangible	compression
conscience	pervasiveness
picturesque	cadence
radicalism	emancipation
crystallize	demeaning
anonymous	braille

LOOKING AHEAD

In this chapter, you will learn that effective oral communication depends in part on accuracy and economy of language. You will examine the figures of speech used to create the language of effective imagery. In addition, you will be introduced to the sound devices that help to produce the "music" heard in language. Finally, you will be warned about specific types of language that should be avoided because they can create communication barriers between you and your audience.

1 Language Exactness

Imagine that you are in the circus. You are an acrobat performing high above the ground without a net, and the path you must follow from point A to point B is merely a tightrope. Your steps must be measured and exact. One false step and your career, as well as your life, could be over. You know that your movement must be absolutely precise. Simply being "close" to the tightrope would likely result in your becoming a memory in the circus world.

What do you do? You touch, you feel, and you don't move until you know that the next step is exactly right.

This chapter isn't about the circus world, but it is about exactness—the exactness of language. Like the tightrope walker, you must painstakingly search for exactly the right next step, only now it doesn't involve the high wire. Now, it involves searching for the most effective words and phrases to communicate your ideas. The correct words can make a sensational impression on your audience. The wrong words can cause you to fall, creating a hushed silence in your unresponsive audience.

Mark Twain told us that the difference between the right word and the *almost*-right word is the difference between lightning and the lightning bug. Indeed, there is a world of difference between the word or phrase that will say exactly what you mean and the word or phrase that is simply "in the ballpark." For example, here are a few automobile accident reports that have been filed by people insured by the Omaha Property and Casualty Insurance Company and State Farm Insurance, Bloomington, Illinois:

- ◆ I pulled away from the side of the road, glanced at my mother-in-law, and headed over the embankment.

- ◆ An invisible car came out of nowhere, struck my vehicle, and vanished.

- ◆ I was on my way to the doctor with rear end trouble when my universal joint gave way, causing me to have an accident.

Excerpted from Richard Lederer's Anguished English.

Even though you might laugh at these reports, they prove a significant point: Selecting the wrong word or using unclear phrasing can lead to communication that is not only confusing but embarrassing.

No one is exempt. Even as brilliant an orator as John F. Kennedy, former president of the United States, can make an error. A popular story involves the conclusion of Kennedy's powerful speech at the Berlin Wall in 1963. Kennedy wished to say, "Ich bin Berliner!"—meaning, "I am a Berliner!" However, what he said was, "Ich bin *ein* Berliner!" In German, words for nationalities are not preceded by articles (*ein* is an article meaning "a" or "an"). It happens, though, that *Berliner* is also the name of a pastry. Thus, what Kennedy really told the German people was, "I am a jelly doughnut!" Even the best communicators can make mistakes if they are not careful.

In earlier chapters, the building of a successful speech was compared to the building of a well-constructed house. We can extend that comparison here by saying that the successful builder of a speech knows that effective language is what covers the planks of confidence (discussed in Chapter 2). It is true that your words can't be *seen*, as the outside of a house can be, but they certainly can be *heard* by your audience. When effective language covers your internal skeletal structure of confidence, and both are anchored by your solid value system foundation (discussed in Chapter 1), you are on your way to establishing a communication "open house" that is sure to draw an audience. We now examine several aspects of effective language: the spoken word versus the written word, figures of speech, sound devices, and language to avoid.

II The Spoken Word versus the Written Word

You probably have a favorite author. If you don't have a favorite yet, you will someday. Perhaps there is a good book that you like to read over again, an editorial that says exactly what you believe, or a poem that contains words that you never grow tired of reexamining. One of the fantastic things about the written word is that you can *see* it—as often as you like.

Language that is written down allows you the luxury of digesting and understanding the content at your own speed. It may take you several attempts to totally comprehend the written word, but that's all right. You don't have to "get it" the first time. You can always go back and reread.

In other words, the written word has a distinct advantage over the spoken word: It offers language that you are given time to consider, and with time often comes understanding. Think about how often you didn't understand a reading assignment in school until you had gone over the assignment a second, a third, or even a fourth time.

Studies show, however, that over 90 percent of all communication is not written but spoken. Indeed, the word *language* comes from the Latin word *lingua*, which means "tongue." The language of speech must be different from written language if it is to communicate effectively. The audience must "get it" the first time. With the spoken word, you rarely have a second chance to make an impact on your audience.

What must the good speaker keep in mind regarding language if he or she

The written word can be digested and understood at the reader's own pace.

wants to make the right impression? The good speaker knows the value of two key words: *accuracy* and *economy.*

Accuracy of Language

The average person has a vocabulary of approximately 10,000 words. You might use a certain part of your vocabulary only with your friends, and another, rather different part only with your parents or other adults. Why? Because you realize that certain language is appropriate in some situations but not in others. Even with this realization, however, we may use words that are confusing to those listening because those words don't accurately communicate what we *think* that we are saying. We may be speaking about one thing while our audience is hearing something totally different.

If you want to be an effective speaker, regardless of the situation—with your friends at the mall, with your teachers, with people you've just met—you need to understand the importance of language accuracy. *Accuracy* means using words that say exactly what you mean. How can you develop accuracy in your verbal expression? Let's start by taking a look at concrete words as opposed to abstract words.

Concrete and Abstract Words

Concrete words name things that we can perceive through sight, hearing, touch, taste, or smell. **Abstract words,** on the other hand, don't deal with the senses but are names for qualities, attributes, concepts, and the like. For example, words such as *baseball, car,* and *radio* are concrete words. They name things we can see and hear and touch. Compare this list with the words *relaxation, transportation, enjoyment,* and *recreation.* These words are much more general. As a result, they are open to personalized interpretation.

COMMUNICATION WORKS

Julie Ann Trella, Certified Shorthand and Registered Professional Reporter

Julie Trella had always been fascinated by law, and even though she ruled out being a lawyer at an early age, she decided to be part of the courtroom scene. Unable to attend a four-year college because of financial problems, she chose to put her many high school business courses to work. She decided to live at home and attend an area college. The Chicago College of Commerce offered a 2½ year associate degree in business, and Julie's specific area of interest was becoming a court stenographer.

What does a court stenographer do? Trella says, "Anyone who has ever watched a courtroom drama surely has noticed the person near the front of the courtroom taking down on a little machine everything that is being said. I'm the person who operates that 'little machine.'" Using a specially designed phonetics typewriter, Trella must eventually produce through computer translation a written copy of what was said. It is her job to be exact with language. She adds, "I like my job because it offers a nice income, variety, and a solid job market. If you can do what I do, there is work out there for you. However, with the job comes responsibility. The lawyers and the judge must be precise with language—but if I don't record the words correctly, then the whole case might be misinterpreted. The wrong word can leave the wrong impression!"

Trella has also realized the value of language in her interpersonal communication skills. She says that "you talk with attorneys in the pretrial. The words that you use—your vocabulary, your grammar—all add up to how seriously they take you. In a sense, your language is your credibility." She has also learned one other thing: "I have learned that the most effective communication is accomplished by using a few well-chosen words, but using them well. The legal profession has introduced me to a new world of vocabulary, and I learn something new every day."

Currently a successful court stenographer, Trella also has a word of advice for students still in high school. "When I was in high school, I never paid attention to language. Words and the way that I used them didn't matter. I want to tell you that effective language leads to understanding, understanding leads to knowledge, and knowledge leads to success. Words are now my life!"

And now, due to hard work and the drive to succeed, life for Julie Ann Trella is very good.

Look at a few lines of a song that you've probably heard several times:

Take me out to the ball game
Take me out with the crowd
Buy me some peanuts and Crackerjack
I don't care if we never get back

Can you identify the concrete words that are used to help create the atmosphere of a baseball game? Can you almost "taste" the peanuts and Crackerjack? These *tangible* objects are being used to communicate a message. As here, it is often highly effective to use concrete words that say clearly what we want our audience to hear. In contrast, using abstract words without clearly defining them means taking the risk of not communicating accurately with the audience. When this happens, your language is not working for you. It might even be undermining your intent. Sometimes the most effective language is created when the speaker uses concrete and abstract words together, clearly and accurately.

Denotation and Connotation

Closely associated with the terms *concrete* and *abstract* are the terms *denotation* and *connotation*. **Denotation** refers to the basic meaning of a word, which can easily be found in the dictionary. **Connotation** refers to the meaning of a word that goes *beyond* the dictionary definition; it is the meaning we associate with the word.

What about the word *mother*? *Mother* can be defined as "a woman who bears a child," but many of us would also associate *mother* with ideas such as love, friendship, and family. Suppose you were going to speak on the idea that women ought to have the same opportunities as men in the job market. It would probably be unwise to say, "I think that women can make excellent contributions to any job and should be paid the same as men. Women shouldn't be limited to *simply being mothers!*" Because of connotations associated with the word *mother*, this statement might imply to some people in your audience that you see mothers as next to worthless, that you are anti-family, or that raising children is easy.

It is desirable to use words that clearly denote a certain meaning. You must think through the different connotations that a word might have before you use it in your speech. For example, the words *rebel, loner, eccentric,* and *mediocre* might mean one thing to you but something entirely different to your audience.

In 1983, a talented high school speaker was competing at Park Hill High School in Kansas City, Missouri. His topic dealt with women and the positive role that they were playing in society. He wished to stress that women were self-sacrificing, practical, vital for family stability, and important parts of our societal makeup. To communicate this message, he said proudly, "In today's world, the woman has become the most important *commodity* that man possesses." In his mind, he was showing how valuable women were because of their usefulness to society. However, in the minds of some others, women were being compared to pork bellies on the Chicago Stock Exchange! Needless to say, there was a difference of opinion as to what the word *commodity* actually meant.

Luckily for the speaker, the majority of the audience laughed (most of them were women) because they knew what he was trying to say. The story shows, though, that using inaccurate language can lead to disaster.

Abstract words, in particular, may have many different connotations. For example, consider the words *success, failure, family, patriotism,* and *justice.* How might these words be interpreted differently by different people? For example, is "success" in your eyes the same as it might be in someone else's?

Don't think that you must always avoid abstract words because of this difficulty. Abstract words can be powerful. They can inspire us and appeal to our emotions. We must, however, use them with care.

Economy of Language

Just as you must be accurate in the words that you select for your speech, you must also be economical in the number of words that you use. Keep in mind that your audience, contrary to what they must do when reading the written word, must remember all that you say. Economy means "careful or thrifty use." Thus, *economy of language* suggests carefully managing the *quantity of words* you use to communicate verbally.

The famous essay "Civil Disobedience" by Henry David Thoreau was originally delivered as a lecture in 1848 under the title "Resistance to Civil Government." It dealt with the role of individual *conscience* versus the role of state authority. Here is a portion of that speech:

> Must the citizen ever for a moment, or in the least degree, resign his conscience to the legislator? Why has every man a conscience, then? I think that we should be men first, and subjects afterward. If I devote myself to other pursuits and contemplations, I must first see, at least, that I do

"Civil Disobedience" by Henry David Thoreau, pictured above, is a masterpiece as an essay but was a failure as a speech because its dense language could not be absorbed all at once.

> not pursue them sitting upon another man's shoulders. I must get off him first, that he may pursue his contemplations too. . . . There will never be a really free and enlightened State, until the State comes to recognize the individual as a higher power.

This material given as a speech had little impact. It wasn't until later, as an essay, that it gained prominence. Can you see why it would be difficult to digest as a speech?

This speech offers a great deal of intellectual content to absorb at one time. In addition, notice the number of words that it takes for Thoreau to say what he thinks. As an essay, "Civil Disobedience" is a masterpiece because readers can take the time to study the words and ideas in print. As a speech, it would probably be difficult to listen to. Why? If spoken language becomes long and involved, the listener can get lost.

How can we prevent this? It is Thoreau himself who offers us sound advice when he states in his masterpiece *Walden*, "Simplify, simplify." Apply his advice to both your spoken words and the organization of your ideas if you wish the audience to "march to your drum beat."

How? First of all, pay attention to the number of words that it takes for you to say something. For instance, look how each of these statements might be shortened.

Original Statement: At the beginning of the day before I have my breakfast, I always work to keep my blood circulating and my body fit.

Shortened Statement: I like to exercise first thing in the morning.

Original Statement: Because of the way you look and because we have always had so much fun together, you and I might not find it a bad thing to talk and do stuff together.

Shortened Statement: I'd like to spend some time with you.

Original Statement: The recession and financial difficulties are leading low-, middle-, and upper-class Americans to tighten their belts and take their pocketbooks seriously.

Shortened Statement: Money problems are affecting most Americans.

Original Statement: The way that my math teacher evaluates me in school shows that there are areas in which I can do a lot better.

Shortened Statement: I'm failing algebra.

INSTANT IMPACT

I Didn't Mean to Say *That!*

Earlier in the chapter, you read how John F. Kennedy meant to say one thing but said something else to the German people. Translation problems are quite common. Someone at the United Nations once entered a common English saying into a translating computer. The machine was asked to translate into Russian and then back into English the saying, "The spirit is willing, but the flesh is weak." The result was, "The wine is good, but the meat is spoiled." When Pepsi-Cola invaded the Chinese market, the product's slogan, "Come alive with the Pepsi generation," was translated as "Pepsi brings back your dead ancestors!" Language "details" like these can make the difference between saying exactly what you mean and missing the mark.
Source: Richard Lederer, Anguished English.

Notice how words can get in the way and clutter up your message. This "clutter" can sometimes confuse your audience. Remember to avoid unnecessary prepositional phrases ("In the beginning of the story at the top of the page"). Avoid using too many clauses run together in one sentence ("The main character, who is in his mid-twenties, knows that the sister who is hiding in the closet is innocent because she wasn't at the scene of the crime that had taken place earlier"). Avoid repeating the same idea with different wording ("The main character was an excellent student, had received A's on her report card, and had always done very well in school").

One effective way to be simple and direct is by using rhetorical questions. Rhetorical questions are the questions that you ask the audience but that you don't really intend the audience to answer out loud. For example, "What do all of these statistics mean?" and "Where is the solution to this problem?" are rhetorical questions. Each could allow you to say with one question what it might have taken you two or three sentences to explain otherwise.

The term *economy* also applies to your speaking organization. Don't allow your organization to become too complicated. As we said in Chapter 8, "Organizing Your Speech," it is important that you provide your audience with a simple, easy-to-follow outline. The audience should know exactly when you are moving from your introduction to your speech thesis statement and what your major areas of analysis are going to be.

In speaking, as in writing, simple, straightforward transitions are also helpful. ("This brings us to our second point" and "In conclusion, let's look at where we've been" are examples. A list of transitions appears in Chapter 8.) You must inform your audience where you are, where you have been, and where you are going so that their speech journey with you is a simple and meaningful one.

Remember, you know where you are going. Your audience doesn't. As mentioned, the audience members for a speech don't have the option of going back and rereading what they missed the first time. It is your job to take their hands and lead

TAKING CHARGE

1. This section discussed abstract words and gave some specific examples. Write out your own personalized definitions (don't use the dictionary) for the abstract words *honesty*, *patriotism*, and *friendship*. Talk with a classmate to see what your definitions have in common. What are the differences? Be ready to discuss your findings in class.
2. There are literal definitions (denotations) for the words *politician*, *gang*, and *home*. However, each of these words also has different connotations. Discuss as a class what meanings might be associated with these words beyond the dictionary definitions.
3. Make a list of three words that you believe have different connotations that might cause problems in a speech if not carefully explained. What meanings might each word have? Be ready to give examples to explain your reasoning.
4. Find material from the newspaper, a book, or a magazine that is difficult to understand because too many words are being used or the wording is unclear. Rewrite the paragraph to make an effective speech. First, read the material to the class as it sounds in print. Next, deliver your newly created words as they would sound in a speech.

them. Lead them with economy of words and a simple organization that makes sense.

The twentieth-century Irish poet and playwright William Butler Yeats once said, "Think like a wise man, but communicate in the language of the people." If you will give priority to accuracy and economy when choosing your language, then you might achieve with your spoken words the spirit of what Yeats is saying. Let's now take a look at how figures of speech can make your language memorable to your audience.

III Creating Word Pictures: Figures of Speech

You have probably heard stories about how ancient royalty, without the advantages of the printing press or modern postal service, used messengers to communicate from kingdom to kingdom. (You have probably also heard that some of these messengers were put to death for being "bearers of ill tidings.") The messengers, similar to the deliverers of our twentieth-century "singing telegrams," would often sing the words of the messages using rhyme and colorful, descriptive language. The use of *picturesque* language, presented in a musical manner, undoubtedly made the message easier to remember. It also made a pleasing sound to the ears of those listening. Spoken language is most effective when it creates music for the ear and pictures for the imagination.

Language that creates pictures in our minds and excites our senses is called **imagery.** *Figures of speech* are specific types

of imagery. Here, we classify and describe figures of speech in terms of three working categories: comparison, contrast, and exaggeration. Understanding figures of speech and then using them effectively will make your speeches more descriptive.

Comparison Imagery

From each pair of statements which one has more impact?

Education is important.
Education is the key that unlocks many of life's opportunities.

You have to work hard to make a marriage work.
Marriage is like a plant: If you care for it and give it time and attention, it will grow and prosper.

You are not always nice to me.
Why must you always play *Napoleon* whenever we're together!

The second example in each pair is more dynamic and presents a more exact picture. The first example in each pair isn't necessarily wrong; it is simply not as lively.

The second example in each of the pairs uses comparison imagery. *Comparison* involves showing similarities. As mentioned, *imagery* refers to word pictures. Consequently, to use *comparison imagery* means to show similarities through the use of picturesque language. Let's take a look at the three most common forms of comparison imagery: metaphor, simile, and allusion.

Metaphor and Simile

A **metaphor** is a figure of speech, not using the word *like* or *as*, that compares two usually unrelated things. A **simile** is the same as a metaphor, except that it uses *like* or *as* to make the comparison.

For example, if you are speaking about the value of a high school diploma, you could say:

A diploma is very important for your future.

Instead, you could say:

A *diploma* nowadays *is* your potential *ticket* to success.

The second example is a metaphor. It compares a diploma to a ticket, a ticket that can send you on your way toward a successful future. The comparison shows that, even though diplomas and tickets are basically different, they are similar because each is of definite worth. Do you see how a metaphor can help to liven up your language?

If you wanted to stress that our government is spending large amounts of money each day, you could say:

Every day, our government spends exceedingly large quantities of money.

Alternatively, you could say:

Every day, our government *spends money* as fast as McDonald's *sells hamburgers!*

The second sentence is a simile, indicating that Washington is like the fast-food industry when it comes to handing out millions of dollars (rather than millions of hamburgers) each day.

If you used the fast-food image throughout your speech, you would be creating an analogy. An **analogy,** which can also take the form of a story, is the extended use of a metaphor or a simile.

Allusion

Another way to create an effective word picture is through the use of allusion. An **allusion** is a reference to a well-known person, place, thing, or idea.

©1992 Bil Keane, Inc.
Dist. by Cowles Synd., Inc.

"Those are the house's bones."

Earlier, a reference was made to Napoleon, showing how someone was comparing a friend in a relationship to a dictator, implying that the friend was acting very bossy. Obviously not a comparison to be taken literally, the Napoleon allusion made the point that one person was not happy with the other's "I'm in charge" attitude.

What would it mean if you referred to a community member as Scrooge? A classmate as Bart Simpson? A school athlete as Michael Jordan? The pencil drawing on a desk as a Picasso? Your car as the *Enterprise?* Your girlfriend as Marilyn Monroe? Your boyfriend as Bigfoot? Allusions such as these can give the listener an immediate mental "snapshot" of what you are saying.

A Meaningful Metaphor

Robert W. Goodman is the father of Andrew Goodman, one of three civil rights workers who were murdered in 1964 in Mississippi. In response to his son's death, Goodman said, "Our grief, though personal, belongs to the nation. The *values* that our son expressed in his simple action of going to Mississippi are still the *bonds* that bind this nation together—its Constitution, its law, its Bill of Rights."

Contrast Imagery

At the conclusion of John F. Kennedy's 1961 inaugural address are the famous words, "Ask not what *your country can do* for you: Ask what *you can do* for your country."

> **"Ask not what your country can do for you: Ask what you can do for your country."**
>
> **John F. Kennedy**

Be sure, however, that your audience knows what the reference means. Remember, the most effective allusions are commonly recognized by just about everyone. It does little good to use an allusion if it leaves your audience wondering what you are talking about. For example, if you were giving a speech about a hunting trip that you took, and you wanted to compare your rifle to something very special, it would *not* be advisable to use an unexplained allusion to Killdeer. Killdeer was the name of the rifle that the heroic character Natty Bumppo used in James Fenimore Cooper's nineteenth-century classic *The Deerslayer.* Your audience probably wouldn't be impressed because the reference is obscure. On the contrary, they might be confused, think that you didn't articulate some words crisply, or be upset at your talking "over their heads."

Use good judgment. Effective language involves creative comparisons that stick with your audience. If the comparisons don't stick, the language wasn't effective.

In 1916, president-to-be Warren G. Harding said, "We must have a citizenship *less* concerned about what government can do for it and *more* anxious about what it can do for the nation."

The statements by Kennedy and Harding are very similar, and both use the technique of contrast to make their point. Reread what each said. Kennedy contrasts the ideas of *country* and *you*, while Harding exhibits contrast with the words *less* and *more*. *Contrast imagery* is the general term used to describe language that sets up opposition for effect. Contrast imagery often takes the form of antithesis, oxymoron, and irony.

Antithesis

Antithesis is the specific balancing or contrasting of one term against another, which is its opposite. For instance, look at these pairs of words: hot–cold, young–old, dry–wet, up–down, small–large, ignorant–knowledgeable, success–failure, love–hate, literate–illiterate, leader–follower, careful–

careless, temporary–permanent, somebody–nobody. These are a few examples of antithesis. A fair question right now would be, "How can I *use* antithesis in my speech to make the impression I want?"

Suppose you are giving a speech on the "Age of the 1960s." You want to explain how the sixties were often a time of *radicalism* and extremism. How about this for a start?

> It was the *best* of times; it was the *worst* of times.
> It was an age of *wisdom*; it was an age of *foolishness*.
> The Mission? Impossible.
> Martin Luther King had a dream; black was beautiful, but white was supreme.
> It was A Hard Days Night for civil rights.
> You say Yes. I say No.
> You say, Stop, and I say, it's time to go, go, go!
> There was hope and despair; there were good works and sin.
> But the answer, my friend, was Blowin' in the Wind.

> While it is true that in the sixties our nation rejoiced at landing on the moon, our nation also mourned the deaths of President Kennedy and Reverend King. The sixties was a time of hula hoops and hippies, but it was also a time of crisis and confusion. The sixties took on a manic–depressive personality, and as Carol A. Emmens states in her book *An Album of the Sixties*, "The trademark of the sixties was extremism."

Do you see antithesis at work? Do you hear when you read the passage aloud how logically it leads into the speech topic of the sixties and extremism? This is the actual beginning of Michelle Petty's 1989 Indiana State Championship speech. She chose the contrast imagery of antithesis for her introduction because, as she said, she didn't want her audience to sim-

ply *hear* about the extremism of the 1960s. Instead, she wanted her audience to experience the extremism through her spoken words.

The antithesis in the first two sentences is indicated for you. Go through the rest of the introduction and find the other examples of antithesis. Also find the allusions. Why do you think that Michelle used some song references, and what do they add to the introduction?

Whether it be in the early 1600s, when Captain John Smith said about his Jamestown, Virginia, settlement, "Our *comedies* never endured long without a *tragedy*," or in a present-day television commercial talking about cornflakes ("Taste them *again* . . . for the *first time!*"), the use of antithesis is an effective technique.

Oxymoron

Another type of contrast imagery places words that are in opposition directly side by side. This apparent word contradiction is called an **oxymoron**. The oxymoron forms a contrast image that often jolts listeners and demands that they think and pay attention. Note the following examples:

> She is the *momentary love-of-my-life*.
> My parents want me to have such *boring fun*.
> Because I always fall gracefully, friends say I have *athletic clumsiness*.
> Parents of teenagers often exhibit *smiling insecurity*.
> Why must our society have so many instances of *selective equality*?
> An *honest cheater* in school should always tell his friends how he does it.

An oxymoron can create not only a quick, clever image for your audience to envision but also some impressive intellectual pictures that you can proudly display.

In his epic poem the *Iliad* (which was based on stories passed down orally from generation to generation), the ancient Greek poet Homer used an oxymoron in the phrase "the delicate feasting of dogs." The obvious contrasting of the words *delicate* and *feasting* (since dogs do not feast delicately) formed the image Homer wanted. He was able to *crystallize* a scene and a message by carefully selecting two words.

Irony

Irony is a figure of speech using words that imply the opposite of what they seem to say on the surface. When you use irony, you are using contrast because you say one thing but mean something entirely different.

Here is a story that shows how irony can be used in "picture making." You wake up Monday morning to find that your alarm clock hasn't gone off and that you are going to be late for school. Because you are in a hurry, you pour orange juice on your cereal instead of milk. The bowl spills and runs onto your English homework. Your mother lets you off at the front door of the school, and you notice that you have two different-colored socks on. As you rush in the door, a friend in the hallway says hello to you and asks how your morning is going.

Your response: "Fine! Great! I'm having a *tremendous* morning."

What you *really* mean is, "This is a *terrible* morning. I wish I had stayed in bed!" It's obvious here that your words don't say what you really mean.

Here's another example. A television news commentator was giving an account of how a rock music fan filed a lawsuit in 1992 against the rock group Motley Crüe, claiming that the intense volume of the group's music at a sold-out concert he attended damaged his hearing. Said the news commentator, "Yes, you certainly wouldn't go to a rock concert thinking that there was going to be *loud music,* now, would you?"

Did he actually mean those words? Of course not. What he was saying to his television audience was, "How in the world could someone go to a rock concert and not expect loud music? Loud music and rock concerts go together."

Of course, the speaker's delivery helped to show everyone watching and listening that he didn't mean what he was actually saying. The creative power of contrast allowed his *real* message to come through to his audience. Irony is most effective when your words and your delivery work together.

Exaggeration Imagery

Our third and final category of figures of speech is exaggeration imagery. To *exaggerate* means to make something greater than it actually is. Francis Bacon, a seventeenth-century English philosopher, essayist, and statesman, once said that the only people who should be forgiven for exaggeration are those in love. In addition to "those in love," Bacon might have included "those speaking." While exaggeration in some situations—exaggeration of evidence in the courtroom, for example—might not be a wise idea, exaggeration of imagery in front of an audience can do wonders to accentuate the words we speak. Three types of exaggeration imagery are hyperbole, understatement, and personification.

Hyperbole

Mark Twain gave us Tom Sawyer. William Shakespeare gave us Falstaff. Both of these famous authors gave us likable literary characters who exaggerated the truth. Tom Sawyer made too much of adventure, and Falstaff made too much of himself. Both humorously overstated their accomplishments. This overstatement is called **hyperbole,** and for speakers it is a method of saying more than what is true for the sake of emphasis.

Have you ever heard statements like these?

I *called you a million times* last night, and the line was always busy!

I have *worked my fingers to the bone* cleaning this house!

Mom, I *don't have a single thread of clothing* to wear to school!

I *laughed my head off!*

No one actually called a million times, had bare bones for fingers, was totally without clothes, or had his head come off. Hyperbole is a form of imagery that blows a picture out of proportion and stretches audiences' imaginations.

It can also add a refreshing touch of humor. For example, a basketball team had lost seventeen consecutive games when it finally won one. In its next game, it won again on a last-second shot. The student announcer, who was broadcasting from his school radio station, chanted wildly over the air, "The *streak* is still alive! The *streak* is still alive!"

Exaggeration imagery can intensify your message tremendously. You should not, however, exaggerate to the point that no one believes or trusts what you have to say. Use exaggeration to enhance your speech, but be sure to convey your message in unambiguous language.

Figure of Speech	What it Does
Metaphor	Compares two usually unrelated things, without using *like* or *as*.
Simile	Compares two usually unrelated things, using *like* or *as*.
Allusion	Refers to a well-known person, place, thing, or idea.
Antithesis	Balances or contrasts a term against its opposite.
Oxymoron	Places opposite terms side by side.
Irony	Implies the opposite of what seems to be said on the surface.
Hyperbole	Makes more of something.
Understatement	Makes less of something.
Personification	Gives human characteristics to nonhuman things.

The use of any number of the figures of speech listed here can make a speech more descriptive.

COMMUNICATION BREAKDOWN

Dealing with "Doublespeak"

Euphemisms are words we sometimes substitute for words that are harsh or distasteful. Euphemisms often avoid the truth, lack clarity, and are more evasive than helpful.

Pentagon officials won the 1991 Doublespeak Award, which is given yearly to the individuals or groups that have done the most outstanding job of using language meant to "bamboozle, befuddle, and obfuscate." The award was given in November by the National Council of Teachers of English to the Pentagon (U.S. Defense Department) for giving us an "armed situation"—not a war—in the Persian Gulf.

War is tough on words, according to the English teachers. The Gulf War was rich in euphemisms, says William Lutz, a Rutgers University professor and chairman of the organization's Committee on Public Doublespeak.

For instance, bombing attacks against Iraq were "efforts," and warplanes were "weapons systems." When pilots were on missions, they were "visiting a site." Buildings were "hard targets," and people were "soft" ones. Bombs didn't kill. They "degraded, neutralized, cleansed, or sanitized." Killing the enemy was termed "servicing the target."

The allies were also guilty as charged by the teachers. The government of Saudi Arabia, unable to accept U.S. female soldiers, called them "males with female features."

Adapted from the Gary Post-Tribune *1991 wire service report.*

Question

How could euphemisms or "doublespeak" potentially lead to a communication breakdown?

Understatement

Whereas hyperbole makes *more* of something, **understatement** makes *less* of something. Even though understatement doesn't exaggerate, it can logically be included in this section because it is the antonym, or opposite, of hyperbole. Understatement uses language that "draws the listener in" because it cleverly "distorts" in its own way and makes us see an absurdity more clearly. Here are some examples of understatement:

Families out of work and without a paycheck can experience some economic *discomfort.*

The winner of the basketball Slam Dunk competition can jump *a little.*

Clearly, a family without a paycheck could experience major financial problems, not mere *discomfort;* and a Slam Dunk champion would probably soar, not jump *a little.*

Understatement doesn't always have the shock power of hyperbole, but it can work as an effective language tool. For instance, a student who was giving a speech on the problems of modern technology offered as an example the radar gun that police departments often use to catch speeders. Trying to show that the

Pentagon officials won the 1991 Doublespeak Award for their use of euphemisms to describe the "armed situation"—rather than war—in the Persian Gulf.

devices aren't always accurate and that motorists can sometimes be unfairly victimized, he produced evidence showing that a radar gun once mistakenly clocked a *tree* going over thirty miles an hour!

He followed this example by saying, "Now isn't it obvious that the radar gun might show a *slight difference* in what it registers as your speed and the speed that you're actually traveling?" The words *slight difference* were obviously understating what he actually meant (the difference between zero and thirty miles per hour is more than slight). Nevertheless, they created the impact that he was after. The image was powerfully made through "reverse exaggeration," or understatement.

Personification

The final type of exaggeration imagery is personification. **Personification** is giving human characteristics to nonhuman things. Walt Disney, the cartoonist, thrilled millions of people by making animals and other parts of nature act like humans. People are fascinated when trees can talk, when the sun can smile, or when flowers can dance. All of a sudden, these things are like human beings.

Personification communicates a message through language and pictures that people can easily understand. Personification can be as effective in speaking as it is in animation, for it allows the listeners to visualize in human terms. Look at these examples:

The *eyes* of jealousy can be deceiving.
Don't allow dishonesty to *sneak up* on you!
Crime can *dress up* in a number of different disguises.

Jealousy doesn't have eyes, dishonesty can't physically sneak up, and crime can't dress up. Each example takes something abstract (jealousy, dishonesty, and crime) and adds a human dimension for increased emphasis.

If you are still wondering how exaggeration imagery can be an important, colorful part of your speaking, take a look at how a college student in 1990 used powerful imagery to tell a powerful story. She wishes to remain *anonymous*, but she also

COMMUNICATION BREAKTHROUGH

The Gettysburg Address

The Gettysburg Address was delivered by President Abraham Lincoln on November 19, 1863, in Gettysburg, Pennsylvania. It was delivered on the field where four months earlier the Battle of Gettysburg had been fought. Lincoln's speech was to dedicate the site as a graveyard, a memorial for those Civil War soldiers who had died in the battle.

Although it received little attention at the time, the speech is an acknowledged masterpiece of *compression*. Its simplicity (the speech lasted less than three minutes) contrasted greatly with the two-hour speech of the accomplished orator Edward Everett, who had spoken earlier that same day.

The Gettysburg Address was a communication breakthrough because it eloquently put into words the belief that, even for a country torn by civil strife, there was hope for the survival of democracy and of the nation.

> Four score and seven years ago our fathers brought forth on this continent, a new nation, conceived in Liberty, and dedicated to the proposition that all men are created equal.

> Now we are engaged in a great civil war; testing whether that nation, or any nation so conceived and so dedicated, can long endure. We are met on a great battle-field of that war. We have come to dedicate a portion of that field, as a final resting place for those who here gave their lives that that nation might live. It is altogether fitting and proper that we should do this.

> But, in a larger sense, we can not dedicate—we can not consecrate—we can not hallow—this ground. The brave men, living and dead, who struggled here, have consecrated it, far above our poor power to add or detract. The world will little note, nor long remember what we say here, but it can never forget what they did here. It is for us the living, rather, to be dedicated here to the unfinished work which they who fought here have thus far so nobly advanced. It is rather for us to be here dedicated to the great task remaining before us—that from these honored dead we take increased devotion to that cause for which they gave the last full measure of devotion—that we here highly resolve that these dead shall not have died in vain—that this nation, under God, shall have a new birth of freedom—and that government of the people, by the people, and for the people, shall not perish from the earth.

We will examine the Gettysburg Address later in this chapter.

Question
Why is it ironic that Lincoln's message was delivered on a Civil War battlefield?

---

wishes for her story to be heard and her realizations about life to be shared.

Her speech, which was delivered to her introductory college speech class, dealt with her attempt to commit suicide while in high school. She mentioned how, after her mother discovered that she had taken sixty-four prescription pills, it seemed that "every swirling, flashing, red light in the entire city converged on my house" (hyperbole). She described the ride to the hospital, the frantic work of the nurses, and how reality was confused and distorted for her. She said at the end of this terrifying account, "Yes, I had had better mornings in my life!" (understatement).

The audience roared with laughter, and laughter was what she wanted at that point. However, her concluding words deserve our special attention. She said,

> I learned from this experience. I lived through it. I learned that dying means forever. Looking back on the emergency room, the psychiatric ward, and the long months of treatment that followed is like reliving a nightmare. It now seems so long ago, but the reality is still fresh, and the lesson is well learned.

> Life, I now realize, is a wonderful gift. Don't ever abuse it. When life opens up its arms to you, accept its embrace. Have a love affair with life . . . forever!

The personification of *life* near the end, in which life is described as opening its arms, is a beautiful, moving image that depicts not only how she felt but also the inspirational message that she wanted her audience to feel.

In this speech, the speaker was a messenger, similar to the messengers of old. However, she didn't bring "ill tidings." Instead, she brought people a lesson about the sanctity of life. Her honesty and her imagery combined to communicate the best that language has to offer.

TAKING CHARGE

1. Make a list of at least three television or radio advertisements for products or services that use imagery as a sales tactic. Be ready to say what specific figure of speech is being used (simile, antithesis, etc.) for each and why the advertisement is effective.
2. Create your own product to sell on television or radio, and design a figure-of-speech advertising campaign that you believe will sell it. Create at least three advertisements using different types of imagery. Be ready to explain your creations. If you were going to put your advertisements in print, what would you do differently?
3. Choose a specific speech topic (war, education, music, or the like) and write your own examples of oxymoron, antithesis, irony, hyperbole, understatement, and personification that relate to the speech topic you have chosen. Be prepared to give the examples out loud to the class.
4. Create your own metaphor or simile for the following: your report card, music, pizza, and money. (Example—simile: My best friend, John, is like a compass. He always gives me a sense of direction as to where I'm going with my life.)

IV Making Music with Words: Sound Devices

We have discussed the importance of figures of speech and have shown how language can "come alive" when speakers use imagery to excite the imaginations of the audience. Now, what about the *sound* of the language when spoken?

The *music* of words can combine with the *imagery* of words to make communication even more effective. Maybe this is the reason why nearly 20 million greeting cards are sold every day in the United States. Greeting cards, for the most part, are written in language that speaks in pictures and sounds pleasing to the ear. Most of us are attracted to language like this.

The twentieth-century English playwright Christopher Fry once said: "The pleasure and excitement of words is that they are living and generating things." Much of the *living* and *generating* that Fry speaks of is the result of well-chosen sound devices that we can cleverly incorporate into our speaking. Most of the music of language is derived from some form of **repetition,** the act or process of repeating. Here, we look at two ways of using repetition to make music with words: repeating individual sounds and repeating words or groups of words.

> **"The pleasure and excitement of words is that they are living and generating things."**
>
> **Christopher Fry**

Repeating Individual Sounds

We can repeat individual sounds in three ways: through alliteration, assonance, and consonance.

Alliteration

Say each of the following sentences out loud:

*P*arents *p*rovide their children with the *p*ower to succeed.
*C*aring about *c*ourtesy shows *c*onsideration for others.
The *w*ill to *w*in is the combination of a *w*ork ethic plus the *w*illingness to dedicate yourself to a *w*orthwhile cause.

As you can see, in each sentence, a sound is noticeably repeated—in the first sentence, the *p* sound; in the second sentence, the hard *c* sound; and in the third sentence, the *w* sound. All of these sentences exhibit the sound device known as alliteration. **Alliteration** is the repetition of the initial sound of two or more words that are close together.

All you have to do to see the *pervasiveness* of alliteration is to watch television or to read the tabloids at the supermarket checkout counter. Weather forecasters might say, "Yes, folks, the *w*inter *w*inds *w*hipped through the *w*indy city of Chicago today," stressing the first *w* sound in the words *winter, winds, whipped,* and *windy* to make their forecast stand out and make people take notice. Similarly, a tabloid headline could read, "My Mother Married a Martian."

Do you see why alliteration works? It gives special significance to the specific language you choose to speak. In the following passage, the American patriot Benjamin Franklin used alliteration as a key sound ingredient to enhance the impact of his statements regarding the newly formed Constitution of 1787. Read this speech out loud so that you can better hear the language at work.

Mr. President,

I doubt . . . whether any other convention . . . may be able to make a better constitution; for, you assemble a number of men, [with] all their prejudices, their passions, their errors of opinion. . . . From such an assembly can a perfect production be expected? It therefore astonishes me, Sir, to find this system approaching so near to perfection as it does.

He went on to add:

Thus I consent, Sir, to this Constitution, because I expect no better, and because I am not sure that it is not the best.

The repetition of initial *m*, *p*, and *b* sounds in nearby words draws attention to Franklin's statements. Can you hear the musical element that alliteration offers when you say the words aloud?

Assonance

Read Franklin's speech again. What about the words *may*, *able*, and *make* at the beginning of the speech? Notice the long *a* sound in each word. The repetition of vowel sounds is known as **assonance.** The vowel sounds can occur anywhere in the words. Thus, the sentence, "We believe that peace means a chance for all of the oppressed people of the world," plays on the long *e* sound for effect.

Consonance

In the sentence just used above, examine the words *peace*, *oppressed*, and *people*. Notice that the *p* sound is repeated not only at the beginning of *peace* and *people* but also near the middle of *oppressed* and *people*. The sound device used here is known as consonance. Whereas assonance deals with repeated vowel sounds, **consonance** is the repetition of consonant sounds anywhere in words.

Let's look at another example of each way to repeat individual sounds, so that all three will be clear:

◆ I love to leap in the air and land in the lake. (*l* sound, alliteration)

◆ I love to hike high in the mountains and see the sunrise. (long *i* sound, assonance)

◆ In dealing with hardships in life, depend on your friends for support. (*d* sound, consonance)

Rereading Franklin's speech should show you that all three of these devices can be used simultaneously. Go through the speech again and point out places where alliteration, assonance, and consonance work together to form the melodious "beat" or rhythm that gives the message its music and makes the language more memorable.

Repeating Words or Groups of Words: Parallel Structure

A student in a high school speech class was talking about his commitment to automobiles. He said, "If you want to be knowledgeable about a car engine, you have to work, work, work!" He later mentioned that he worked on cars "before school in my garage, during school in automotive class, and after school at a friend's house." He finally said, "Treat your car with respect. Your car will take care of you only when you take care of your car."

Whether he knew it or not, the student was using parallel structure to help convey his message. Using **parallel structure,** also known as **parallelism,** means using the same grammatical form to express ideas that should, logically, be treated equally. Often, parallelism involves repeating words or phrases.

Look at what the student speaker said. Notice how he repeated the word *work* three times for emphasis. He also repeated the word *school* in three successive phrases that are grammatically and logically related. He concluded by stating, *"Your car will take care of you* only when *you take care of your car."* Notice how the two parts of the sentence use the same form and almost the same words. Parallel structure reinforces an idea or a series of ideas. It also creates a musical effect for the audience, which helps a speaker get the message across more convincingly.

Let's go back to the Gettysburg Address (Communication Breakthrough, page 264) and analyze three specific instances in which Abraham Lincoln brilliantly implemented the technique of parallel structure:

1. At the beginning of the third paragraph, Lincoln declares, "But, in a larger sense, *we can not dedicate—we can not consecrate—we can not hallow*—this ground." Music, a driving *cadence,* results from the repetition of the word arrangement introduced by *we can not.*

2. Two sentences later, Lincoln states, *"The world will little note . . . what we say here,* but *it can never forget what they did here."* Even though

only a few of the words are repeated, the structure of the two parts of this sentence is the same.

3. Finally, Lincoln concludes by declaring "that this nation, under God, shall have a new birth of freedom— and that government *of the people, by the people,* and *for the people,* shall not perish from the earth." The parallel structure of the three prepositional phrases offers a climactic ending to one of the most monumental speeches ever delivered in American history. In addition, "this nation . . . shall have a new birth of freedom" and "that government . . . shall not perish from the earth" are strikingly similar in construction.

We conclude this section by examining how another speaker of Lincoln's time, Frederick Douglass, used parallel structure. Frederick Douglass was born a slave in Maryland around 1817 and became a prominent voice in the antislavery movement. A well-educated man, Douglass saw that *emancipation* was a necessary step in the black man's struggle for complete independence. During the Civil War, he helped organize regiments of black soldiers for the Union Army, and later in his life he held numerous government positions. Note that Douglass delivered the following speech in 1865 at the annual meeting of the Massachusetts Anti-Slavery Society, two years after Lincoln's Gettysburg Address. (Be sure to read the speech out loud.)

What the Black Man Wants

Everybody has asked the question . . . "What shall we do with the Negro?" I have had but one answer from the beginning. Do nothing with us! Your doing with us has already played the mischief with us.

Do nothing with us! If the apples will not remain on the tree of their own strength, if they are worm-eaten at the core, if they are early ripe and disposed to fall, let them fall! I am not for tying or fastening them on the tree in any way, except by nature's plan, and if they will not stay there, let them fall. And if the Negro can not stand on his own legs, let him fall also. All I ask is, give him a chance to stand on his own legs! Let him alone! If you see him on his way to school, let him alone,—don't disturb him. If you see him going to the dinner table at a hotel, let him go! If you see him going to the ballot-box, let him alone,—don't disturb him! . . . Let him fall if he can not stand alone! If you will only untie his hands, and give him a chance, I think he will live.

By now, it should be clear that your *speaking* effectiveness is often only as good as your *language* effectiveness. Part of language effectiveness involves avoiding certain language pitfalls that can cause both you and your audience to take a "communication tumble."

Frederick Douglass, pictured here, was born a slave in Maryland around 1817 and became a prominent voice in the antislavery movement.

TAKING CHARGE

1. Reread the speech by Frederick Douglass. Find and be ready to discuss at least two examples of parallel structure as it has been explained in the chapter.
2. Construct three original sentences. In the first sentence, use at least three words that show alliteration. In the second sentence, use at least three words that show assonance. In the third sentence, use at least three words that show consonance. Each sentence should be different.
3. In newspaper and magazine headlines, find two examples of effective sound devices (alliteration, assonance, consonance, or parallel structure). Next, apply what you have learned. Find an ordinary headline and rewrite it, creating your own original headline. You might want to write a serious headline, and then create a more humorous one.

ⅴ Language to Avoid

The quotation spoken by President Nixon on the first page of this chapter is an excellent example of how *not* to communicate. Even though you may be able to figure out what the quotation means eventually, who wants to wait? Besides, audiences don't have time to stop and figure out a confusing statement when a speech is being delivered. The next idea is on its way.

You have already seen one communication problem, euphemisms, in the Communication Breakdown (page 262). Euphemisms cloud clear communication by offering language that is puzzling and distorted. Unfortunately, the losers are usually the listeners.

Here, we take a look at three other language areas that you should avoid in your speaking: jargon, sexist language, and shocking or obscene language.

Avoid Jargon

Jargon usually refers to the specialized vocabulary of those in the same line of work, such as doctors or computer programmers. Because only a small group of people understand what the language means, it is often unintelligible to most of the general public. In this sense, it is similar to **slang,** nonstandard words that may also be associated with certain groups, such as teenagers.

Like euphemisms, jargon is often heard in government circles, but it can pop up in any discussion. A young high school debate coach was speaking to a beginning debate class. He kept using terms such as "first AC" (first affirmative constructive

speech) and "DAs" (disadvantages). He also talked about the value of good "ev" (evidence). The problem was that his class had no idea what his terms stood for. Debate jargon proved to be a barrier to good teaching.

Suppose you are giving an oral presentation about your job as an usher at the movie theater. How effective would the communication be if you said the following?

> My job is working at this *barn*. I started out being on the *spooge patrol*, but later I became a *rip-and-grin*. Part of the fun of my job is watching *Pepsi skaters* and getting food from the *picnickers*. It's disgusting when I see something gross such as a *tongue-knot*, but, overall, I like my job and would recommend it to you.

Let's translate what this means based on a *Newsweek* magazine article from January 1992:

barn—nickname for a large, old-time movie theater

spooge patrol—ushers who have to scrape the slime from under seats

rip-and-grin—usher who takes tickets

Pepsi skaters—people who slip on the soda-soaked floor

picnickers—people who bring their own food

tongue-knot—a couple necking throughout the film

You can see how jargon can be a significant problem in effective communication and why jargon is certainly language to avoid when speaking.

Avoid Sexist Language

Sexist language is language that unfairly groups women, and some would argue men, into stereotyped categories. Such stereotyping can be *demeaning*. Schools, textbooks, speakers, and even dictionaries are now recognizing the importance of fair play regarding the language used for men and women.

Society has traditionally associated girl babies with pink blankets and boy babies with blue blankets, girls with dolls and boys with trucks. Similarly, society often seems inclined to stereotype males as tough, take-charge, dominant leaders and females as weak, passive, subservient followers. Is this fair? Your spoken language must show that you believe that both sexes possess and can demonstrate equal abilities and talents and that gender has no relevance to a person's worth.

A prominent leader was speaking to a large community group about sound financial planning for the town. He presented a well-organized, thought-provoking speech. He concluded by saying: "This is going to take hard work by everyone. So if the little ladies in the audience will help the men of the house by keeping the kids quiet and the food warm, we can use our brain power to work out a plan that I believe will succeed!"

How do you think this conclusion was received?

Even though the speaker, in his own mind, was trying to be "folksy," women in the audience were justifiably offended. The implication was that the men could think but that the women couldn't—so they should cook, dust, and perform "home" duties.

Look at these pairs of words: *man*kind–humankind, *father*land–homeland, spokes*man*–spokesperson, congress*man*–representative, *man*-hours–working hours,

and *man*made–synthetic. Do you see how the second word in each pair avoids the sexist connotation that the first word presents?

Don't think that sexist language applies only to women. How fair is it, for example, to use the term *housewives*, when nowadays it is not uncommon for men to stay at home and contribute to house duties? Why not use the term *homemaker*, instead, in your speech? Remember, avoid any language that unfairly stereotypes men and women. Always keep in mind that the words you speak should promote the idea that all people have dignity.

Avoid Shocking or Obscene Language

Speakers often try to appeal to their audiences by speaking casually or by using "street language." Street language, however, can be shocking to an audience not expecting it. Use good judgment. While shocking language might draw your audience's attention, it can also quickly turn off most people.

Obscene language is any language that offends by going against common standards of decency. Since what is considered obscene may vary from area to area, speakers must avoid any possibility that their words might be construed as indecent. Consider what happened to a Florida football team after it won the 1992 Cotton Bowl. Six members of the team on their return home were kicked off an American Eagle commuter flight because they used obscene language to airline employees. The players' spoken language offended almost everyone around them.

Using an off-color story or a derogatory term will not improve your speech. Making a shocking yet meaningful statement, however, can be effective. In Maryland, there are billboards that proclaim this message to motorists in large letters:

VIRGIN

Teach your kids it's not a dirty word.

This advertisement draws special attention due to the shocking nature of its key word and makes an important statement to the parents who read it and believe in its sentiments.

The word *virgin* is shocking, but the billboard has received a positive response from citizens in Maryland. If your language is shocking for no reason and has a negative effect on your audience, you are in trouble. A student once started his speech by walking to the front and saying, "Hello, morons!" To him, this was clever. Granted, some of the students in the audience laughed, but many were offended by his introduction.

If you find yourself about to include shocking or obscene language in a speech, ask yourself the following questions. Is a curse word worth the price? Is vulgarity ever worth the sacrifice of effective verbal communication? The answer to each question is no. Your audience deserves more.

Let's conclude this chapter with the story of Helen Keller, which attests to the power of language.

Helen Keller was born in Alabama in 1880. She was diagnosed early in life (at eighteen months) as being unable to see, hear, or speak. Doctors early on said that she was mentally retarded and that she would never be able to function as a normal human being. However, when Helen was eight years old, Anne Sullivan, from the Perkins Institution and Massachusetts

Helen Keller, pictured here with her teacher Anne Sullivan, said she would rather be able to hear than to see because an effective speaker could create with words all the images her eyes could not perceive.

School for the Blind, began working with her. The two were to be close companions for nearly half a century.

Helen Keller learned from Anne Sullivan what words meant. Anne Sullivan spelled into the palm of Helen's hand the names of such familiar things as *doll* and *puppy.* At first slowly, but later rapidly, Helen learned the names of objects. Within a few years, Helen was reading and writing *braille* fluently.

When she was ten, Helen pleaded to be taught how to speak. Miss Sullivan discovered that Helen could learn by placing her fingers on the larynx of her teacher's throat and sensing the vibrations.

The story is told of how Helen Keller was once asked which she would choose if she had the choice, seeing or hearing. She said that she would choose hearing. If she could hear the language used effectively, she said, the speaker could create for her all those things that her eyes could not see. In other words, spoken language would allow her to "see" in her imagination, and she would have the best of both worlds.

TAKING CHARGE

1. Interview a friend, a parent or relative, a teacher, or a community member who works at a job that has a specialized vocabulary. Have the person name and then define for you at least five terms that could be categorized as jargon. Finally, ask the person to explain how jargon can sometimes be beneficial at the workplace. Write down the responses and be prepared to offer a short speech to the class.

2. Using jargon or shocking language with a particular audience might be considered appropriate; using that same language with a different audience, however, might be considered inappropriate. Write a one-page paper describing how the same jargon or shocking language might be received by different audiences. Be sure to identify the audiences and explain why you believe that a language adjustment would be wise.

3. You have already been given some examples of sexist language that can easily be changed (*man*kind becomes *human*kind, for example). In student groups of two or three, think of three to five additional terms you have heard or read about that your group could make genderless. Each group should share its findings with the class.

STUDENT SPEECH

Kelly Slater finished fourth in the United States in oratory at the 1990 National Forensic League National Speech and Debate Tournament, held in San Jose, California. Her speech, entitled "The Real Thing," dealt with a contemporary society that often values what appears to be real over what is actually authentic.

The Real Thing

The arena is set.
The multitudes are hushed in antici-
    pation,
crammed into a coliseum filled with
the stench of sweat,
waiting for the combatants to appear.
Suddenly, without warning,
they emerge, cutting through the
dense humidity in
regal attire, robes of rich hues
and majestic style. As the mighty
enemies slowly lumber toward the
    center,
their stage and battlefield, the throng
falls into a rhythmic cadence of cheering,
booming voices proclaiming their
allegiance to either side.
Older generations prepare to shelter
    their young,
for they know
blood will soon be shed.
Achilles and Hector?
No.

Power Women of Wrestling!

Yes, it's Queen Kong and Lady Godiva, folks, known for her "pretzel hold" of death. You know, it's always been my dream to live a day in the life of Lady Godiva. However, for many, this dream can become reality with the help of Larry Sharpe and his New Jersey wrestling academy, "The Monster Factory." For just three thousand dollars and four to six months of training, Sharpe turns out new meat-hungry monsters left and right, instilling in them three basic techniques: (1) make the matches look real, (2) fake the injuries, and (3) mold the outcome, so that the audience buys it. However, the tactics of Sharpe's Monsters and the Power Women of Wrestling have unfortunately worked their way beyond the ropes of the ring and into the arena of the real world. As a result, we've reached the point where if it looks real, we'll take it. Whether it is or not is of little priority because we'd just as soon make it, fake it, or mold it.

It's been said that sometimes truth is stranger than fiction. Ironically, sometimes they're the same thing. Have you ever taken a road trip with your family and just couldn't seem to keep the kids occupied? Well, there's a hot new game out in Nebraska called "Fun with Roadkill." However, with this game you will not only be relieved of thinking of a new game to play, but relieved of taking a vacation at all, because "Fun with Roadkill" is a video-cassette. You can just pop this video-vacation into the VCR at your convenience and not have to worry about stopping for "potty breaks." What could be better?

We can stage vacation; we can stage roadkill; we can even stage war. Did you know that between 1984 and 1987, CBS aired four different accounts of what it claimed to be the war in Afghanistan. However, it was recently revealed that the scenes were not real, but a mixture of recreations—scenes of training camps and not actual combat. It makes you wonder if what you're seeing on the news is real anymore. Perhaps the greatest irony lies in the fact that this particular footage won the most prestigious award in broadcast journalism. Just what are we rewarding? Perhaps this use of deception to get the prepackaged product that is quick, easy, and ready to use is as far as we'll go, but unfortunately it isn't. We'll go past the point of merely making things look real to actually faking it, when we flat out lie. And that's our second area.

Finley Peter Dunne once said, "A lie with a purpose is one of the worst kind, and the most profitable." Artist Mark Kostabi certainly agrees, and he's proud of it. Four years ago, Mr. Kostabi decided that making deals and sustaining an image were more important than his original work. As a result, he now pays other artists between $4.50 and $10.50 an hour to imitate his art and forge his signature. In 1988, he earned over one million dollars doing this. Well, he didn't exactly earn it. Mark Kostabi may be a liar, but at least he admits it. In fact, I'd expect that from someone with those values. However, I was surprised when I read that all of Bill Cosby's books were written by two other men. Do you recognize the name Peggy Noonan? You should, because when we hear the president give a speech, it is sometimes her words that we hear. Now, I'm not indicting the president [Reagan or Bush], but I am wondering what ever happened to the days of the seven Lincoln–Douglas debates, void of teleprompters, speech writers, panels of consultants, and reporters—without the glitz, the glamour, without the blatant deceptions and the fake product. Today, anything can be fake. We have fake food, fake fur, fake jewelry, and fake art. Would you believe that due to recent animal rights protesters, we're now trying to make real fur look like cloth? Ironically, the real product is being made to look like the imitation. Perhaps columnist Marilyn Gardner sums it up when she said, "If life is a true–false test depending on clear distinctions between real and counterfeit, then the

80's may have flunked the final exam." Have we reached the point where we don't know what's real and what's not?

Now, granted, most of us do know that the world of the Power Women of Wrestling is one of orchestrated battles and pseudo-catastrophes. However, when our own world becomes one of "make it" and "fake it," we end up "molding" things that weren't meant to be molded, and we can begin with the entire concept of excellence. Three years ago, my high school adopted a state-wide honors diploma. After its first year, parents complained that not enough kids received it. As a result, the school broadened the standards and lowered the criteria. Now the exclusiveness is gone. When the rules and criteria become putty in our hands, we're molding new standards and broadening our scope to the point of cheating. Just what is excellence anymore? You see, if we don't know what is real, we don't know what or who is good. The result is that the terms *excellence* and *champion* can be neutered, and originality lost in the process. Bill Laimbeer, of the world championship basketball team, the Detroit Pistons, recently received his world championship ring. However, after he learned that over 21,000 replicas were given out to fans, he said, "I felt cheated. I worked nine years for this. There shouldn't be any copies."

You see, some things just weren't meant to be faked or copied—the sound of a baby's first laugh, the first day of school, a first kiss, a real Monet, a live performance of Beethoven's Fifth Symphony, a grandparent holding his grandchild for the first time, the wondrous moment of birth. For, in oneness there is beauty, and in beauty we just might find the truth.

Paul Slansky, in his book *The Clothes Have No Emperor: A Chronicle of the American 80's*, describes America as a "stage set with fake money, fake art on the walls and a clumsy supporting cast that holds no one accountable." However, the eighties are over, and I'm convinced that we can make the nineties more than a mere carbon copy of the past decade. If we (1) hold fast to our standards, and (2) reward and recognize the original, then we just might make it.

The arena awaits once again.
Centered in an amphitheater void of
  sound
the lights are dim
the clothes drab
but the eyes of the enemies—
exploding with the lust for battle.
This time there will be a winner.
This time not the Power Women of
  Wrestling
but the Power of Wisdom
and the Promise of What's Real . . .
The arena is ours.

REVIEW AND ENRICHMENT

LOOKING BACK

Listed below are the major ideas discussed in this chapter.

- ◆ Choosing the correct words is something like walking a tightrope—it must be done with great care.
- ◆ The spoken word must communicate immediately with the audience, while the written word offers the reader the luxury of time to go back and reread.
- ◆ Accuracy of language and economy of language are two qualities that help create a positive speaking impression.
- ◆ Concrete words name things that you can perceive through your senses (touch, taste, etc.), while abstract words deal with concepts or qualities that are more intangible.
- ◆ Denotation refers to the dictionary definition of a word; on the other hand, connotation goes much further and involves all of the possible meanings that a word might suggest.

◆ Using figures of speech, or word pictures, makes your speaking come alive for your audience.
◆ Comparison imagery stresses similarities and includes metaphors, similes, and allusions.
◆ Contrast imagery gets its effect from putting things in opposition and includes antithesis, oxymoron, and irony.
◆ Exaggeration imagery "blows something out of proportion" for effect. Hyperbole, understatement, and personification are included in this category.
◆ In addition to imagery, sound devices—the "music" found in words—are also important for effective speaking.
◆ Most of the "music" of speech is a result of the repetition of sounds (alliteration, assonance, and consonance) and the repetition of the same or similar words or groups of words (parallel structure).
◆ Certain language should be avoided: jargon, which is understood only by a select group; sexist language, which unfairly stereotypes males or females; and shocking language, which might be viewed as obscene or vulgar by your audience.

SPEECH VOCABULARY

concrete words	allusion	repetition
abstract words	antithesis	alliteration
denotation	oxymoron	assonance
connotation	irony	consonance
imagery	hyperbole	parallel structure, or
metaphor	understatement	parallelism
simile	personification	jargon
analogy	euphemisms	slang

1. For each word in the speech vocabulary list, give the definition as found in the chapter. Feel free to use the dictionary or the glossary as well. Next, prepare a quiz by listing any ten vocabulary words and numbering them from 1 to 10. Give these orally to another student in your class to work on the spelling. Mix up the definitions and letter them from a to j. Have the definitions on a sheet of paper, and instruct the student taking the quiz to write the letter of the correct definition beside each of the vocabulary words you dictated. Correct the papers when you are finished.
2. Create ten original sentences using a total of at least ten different vocabulary words (you may use more) from the speech vocabulary list. Your sentences must be divided into the following groups: two sentences with alliteration, two sentences with assonance, two

sentences with consonance, two sentences with personification, and two sentences with hyperbole. Have some fun and make your sentences enjoyable and entertaining. Also, be sure that they make sense. Be prepared to give your sentences out loud to the rest of the class.

GENERAL VOCABULARY

tangible	crystallize	cadence
conscience	anonymous	emancipation
picturesque	compression	demeaning
radicalism	pervasiveness	braille

1. For each general vocabulary word, write the definition as given in the dictionary. In addition, find the page on which each word appears and copy the sentence out of the book so that you can see how the word is used.
2. Write an original sentence for at least five of the general vocabulary words.

THINGS TO REMEMBER

1. The term _____ differs from the term *denotation* in that it refers to the meaning of a word that goes beyond the dictionary definition.
2. A metaphor compares two unrelated things without using *like* or *as*, while a _____ makes a comparison that uses *like* or *as*.
3. Hyperbole exaggerates for effect and says more than what is true, while its opposite, _____, makes less of something to get a desired response.
4. The repetition of the sounds at the beginnings of two or more words that are close together is called _____.
5. A question that really doesn't call for a response from the audience is a _____.
6. Language that unfairly stereotypes males or females is called _____.
7. The famous American humorist who said that the difference between the right word and the almost-right word is the difference between lightning and the lightning bug was _____.
8. Referring to something or someone well known in order to make a creative comparison is called making an _____.

9. Giving human characteristics to nonhuman things is called _____.
10. Homer wrote the famous Greek epic, the _____.

THINGS TO DO

1. Go to your school or public library and find a speech. You can find speeches in books or in periodicals such as *Vital Speeches*. Analyze your speech by listing the concrete words and the abstract words, the various imagery, and the key sound devices used. What is effective to you, and what is unclear or lacks impact? Be specific. In addition, be sure that you can give a complete explanation of your entire speech and what it means.

2. Find someone in your school or community who is familiar with sign language or the world of the deaf. Interview the person and discover how the language works.

3. Think of a pleasant experience that you have had. Using a tape recorder, close your eyes and record your memories. Use vivid imagery and descriptive phrasing. Next, play back the recording. Did your language work for you? If not, go back and repeat the task—this time choosing a different experience.

4. Keep a notebook listing the various jargon that you hear around school, at your job, at home, and so on. Include definitions of the terms. Over time (week to week, month to month), does the language seem to change? Why?

THINGS TO TALK ABOUT

1. In Oregon, a newspaper has said that it will not print or recognize any sports teams that have mascots degrading the American Indian. Thus, team names like the Braves and the Redskins will not be mentioned. What is your opinion about this issue? What about a professional women's basketball team called the Missies or the Babes? What is your reaction? Are such names sexist? Why or why not? Where should we draw the line as to what language is offensive and what language is not? Be logical and give evidence whenever possible.

2. Find a copy of Benjamin Franklin's "The Way to Wealth." Notice how this collection of maxims (sayings) not only teaches a lesson but also communicates through effective language. Give your favorite maxims from the work and explain what image or sound devices they use.

3. Are commercials fair in their language? One television advertisement spoke of the need for romance and the "personal touch" in listeners' lives. For those interested, a phone number was given. When people called, however, a *recording* talked to them. Of course, there was a phone charge. When is the advertiser at fault in such situations? When are we at fault? What language should we especially look out for?

4. Do we speak in hyperbole more than we realize? Discuss the exaggerations that you hear in school, in your extracurricular activities, and at home. Why do we exaggerate? When is it wrong? Is it ever right?

THINGS TO WRITE ABOUT

1. Forming oxymorons can be fun and challenging. (An example is "cold war.") Write five of your own. Also, create some euphemisms for these jobs: dog catcher, window washer, custodian, elementary teacher, chaperone to a dance, and person who cuts lawns. (An example is a short person being called "vertically challenged.") Have fun, but make them make sense.

2. Write an introduction for a friend in class as if you were going to introduce him or her to your club or social group. Fill your introduction with jargon. Now rewrite the introduction and replace all of the jargon with standard language. Be prepared to read your introductions out loud.

3. Write a description of how your day has gone so far. Stress in your language the following: personification, parallel structure, and simile or metaphor. Describe not only what is happening on the outside but also what is happening in your "inside world."

4. Write about a favorite song of yours. Why are the words to the song important to you? What do they mean? What are your favorite images in the song? What pictures does the song bring to mind? Be specific and give examples.

CRITICAL THINKING

1. Currently, in Australia, teenagers have a language of their own. The statement, "She was given *the elbow* by her boyfriend," for example, means that she was "dumped" by her boyfriend. When do you think that it is appropriate to use slang? When is using slang a bad idea? Can slang ever be a problem for your audience? What can you do to make sure that this isn't a problem for *you?*

2. The Hindu leader Jawaharlal Nehru once said, "A language is something infinitely greater than grammar and philology [scholarship]. It is the poetic testament of the genius of a race and culture, and the living embodiment of the thoughts and fancies that have molded them." What does this quotation mean? What does Nehru mean by "poetic testament"? Is language greater when it comes from the head? From the heart? From both? Explain your response.
3. At the beginning of this chapter, you saw a statement by Richard Nixon. Here is a statement by another past president of the United States, Dwight David Eisenhower: "How can we appraise a proposal if the terms hurled at our ears can mean anything or nothing. . . . If our attitudes are muddled, our language is often to blame." What is Eisenhower saying? Eisenhower was speaking specifically about the government in this quote. Can you think of any examples in which the "language of government" seems to take on different meanings? Can you find any instances in which governmental language is muddled and confusing? What about the language of sports? What about the language used in your home?
4. Go back and reread the speeches by Lincoln and Douglass. Both speeches seem to deal with aspects of life, death, and hope. Give specifics to prove this. How does each author handle each concept a little differently?

RELATED SPEECH TOPICS

This chapter has dealt with effective language. The following topics will allow you to use the tools of effective language in your speeches.

What goes on in my first-hour class
A day at the stock car races
The magic of bicycling
The best thing about a school dance
One hour at my job
"Rush hour" at my house before school
Why I enjoy the beach

If I had only twenty-four hours to live, I'd . . .
Why Valentine's Day is special
The excitement of a sports event
My first day driving
The day I had to perform for an audience

Here are a few speech topics that you can use the library to research. Be sure to find out in your research how your topic relates to language and how you can apply your observations to speaking.

Left-brain versus right-brain research (creativity versus cognition)
Speech writers
Sales and public relations
Newscasters

Slang
Euphemisms
Sexism
Racism
The handicapped

CHAPTER 11

Effective Delivery

"As a vessel is known by the sound whether it be cracked or not, so men are proved by their speeches whether they be wise or foolish."

— Demosthenes,
ancient Greek orator and statesman

LEARNING OBJECTIVES

After completing this chapter, you will be able to do the following.

♦ Analyze the different types of delivery.
♦ Understand what delivery means and how it applies to oral communication.
♦ Explain the components of an effective delivery.
♦ Show how you can improve your speaking delivery.

CHAPTER OUTLINE

Following are the main sections in this chapter.

I What Is Delivery?
II Types of Delivery
III Using Your Voice
IV Using Your Body
V Using Your Face
VI Dynamizing Your Overall Delivery

Student Speech
Chapter Review

NEW SPEECH TERMS

In this chapter, you will learn the meanings of the speech terms listed below.

delivery
manuscript method
memorized method
extemporaneous method
impromptu method
vocalized pauses
power source
vocal process
phonation

oral cavity
rate
pitch
monotone
inflection
volume
articulation
pronunciation
platform movement
proxemics
gestures
posture

GENERAL VOCABULARY

Expanding your general vocabulary will help you become a more effective communicator. Listed below are some words appearing in this chapter that you should make part of your everyday vocabulary.

regurgitating
telegraph
morale
methodically

syllables
alienated
superficial

LOOKING AHEAD

In this chapter, you will first learn that your delivery is the actual "selling" of your verbal message. Next, you will look at various methods that you can select to deliver your speech. Finally, you will analyze the specific components of delivery—your voice, your body, and your face—and see how the most effective verbal and nonverbal message is delivered to your audience when these three work in harmony.

I What Is Delivery?

Once, while talking to a group of college students, the jazz musician Miles Davis was asked, "Mr. Davis, what specific musical philosophy do you give credit for making your trumpet style what it is?" Miles Davis looked calmly at the student and said, "The only way that I ever started to get any type of 'style' was when I picked up my trumpet and blew!"

Similarly, you have no real speaking impact until you actually speak. The manner in which you speak is called your **delivery.** Delivery refers to the mode you use to transmit words to your audience. When we discuss delivery, we're talking not about "what you say" but about "how you say it." It might be said that your delivery is your style of presentation, your personalized means of giving life and significance to your words. If we put this in a mathematical format, it might look like this:

Words + Speaker = Delivery.

All good speakers know the value of delivery. Chapters 1 and 2 discussed how the speaker begins to build a good speech by constructing a solid foundation made up of values and the planks of confidence. Regardless of how solid the foundation of a house might be, few people would buy the house if the outside were in poor condition. Appearance, of course, is an important selling point. Delivery is the "outside selling point" of a speech.

Effective delivery added to a substantial value structure and confidence that motivates our words is sure to add up to a winning speech presentation. Well-written words that are poorly delivered will likely have little impact on an audience. Poorly written words delivered with great style will also probably fail to affect the audience. However, well-written words delivered with purpose and conviction will prove to be convincing.

Realtors in the nineties have a term to describe something certain people do when they try to sell their homes. It's called *dynamizing.* This means that the owners will take time and special care to "spruce up" the appearance of their homes to make a dynamic first impression. You need to give this same type of care and effort to dynamizing your speech delivery. Let's start by examining the different types of delivery you might choose. Like Miles Davis, let's now "pick up the trumpet and start to play."

II Types of Delivery

A number of singers can deliver the same piece of music, yet each singer will probably sound different from the others when the notes come out of his or her mouth. The country style of Garth Brooks, for example, doesn't sound the same as the rock style of Paula Abdul or Elton John. Different people have different approaches based on what sound works and what sound doesn't work for them. The same is true for speakers.

What works? What types of delivery can you use to guarantee that the audience receives the message and that the message it receives is the message you wish to send? Here, we take a look at four different types of deliveries: the man-

uscript method, the memorized method, the extemporaneous method, and the impromptu method.

The Manuscript Method

First of all, there is the **manuscript method.** In this type of delivery, you write out your material word for word and then deliver your speech from a lectern, or a stand used to hold your papers. You primarily *read* your material. Presidents of the United States often use the manuscript method of delivery because they want to be absolutely sure of their words and the phrasing of their ideas. Judges and lawyers might use a script when speaking to the press. A sports figure could even use the manuscript method to give a prepared statement about retiring.

A good thing about the manuscript method is that when you use it you are unlikely to make an error in the content of your speech. The words are right on the paper in front of you. Also, most like-

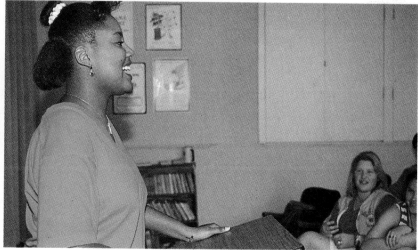

A speaker using the manuscript method of delivery primarily reads a speech from written materials placed on a lectern or other stand. A speaker using the memorized method of delivery commits an entire speech to memory and recites it without the use of notes or papers.

ly, you will have had ample time to plan exactly what you want to say. Often, the manuscript method is an excellent way for new speakers to practice getting up in front of people. The manuscript functions as a "security blanket" and allows speakers to be more comfortable with their audience.

There are, however, potential problems with this method. You might lose touch with your audience because you are concentrating on your papers. While you are looking at your speech, you can't be looking at the people in the room. Remember, if the members of your audience do not feel that you are involved with them, they will very quickly "turn you off," and you will lose credibility as a speaker. People don't believe someone who won't look at them. In short, there are real advantages to the manuscript method, but be sure not to allow the words on your paper to take priority over the eyes of your audience.

The Memorized Method

The second type of delivery is the **memorized method.** In this type of delivery, you commit every word of your speech to memory. You use no notes and have no papers to place on the lectern.

The memorized method has many of the same advantages as the manuscript method. You know each word of your speech by heart. Each idea has been thoroughly examined beforehand and each word carefully put into place. You can even have a good idea of where appropriate gestures, facial expressions, and movement will fit.

Here, too, there are difficulties, however. Even though it might seem that memorizing your speech would make you more relaxed and confident in your delivery, that is not always the case. As a matter of fact, you might become even more tense the second you realize that you have forgotten a word in your speech. Your eyes will glaze. Your body will become rigid. You will appear frightened or unsure of yourself.

How many times have you seen someone responsible for introducing a speaker memorize the material and then forget his or her place? The result is usually embarrassment. Have you ever seen students running for student government, class office, or offices in school clubs who have memorized their speeches, only to go absolutely blank the first time their eyes met the eyes of the audience? Can you think of any other similar examples? Has it ever happened to you?

The main problem with the memorized method is that you usually end up spending so much time thinking of the words in your head that you forget to share your message honestly. Like the manuscript method, the memorized method of delivery puts the *words* in charge! Remember, *you* must be in charge. Audiences don't want to see a robot in front of them simply *regurgitating* words from a memorized speech. Audiences want to listen to people who will talk to them person to person, openly and honestly. As with the manuscript method of delivery, then, be careful. Always give your utmost attention to the eyes of your audience.

The Extemporaneous Method

The third type of delivery, and perhaps the best, is the extemporaneous method. With the **extemporaneous method,** you don't write out your speech word for word, nor do you commit the words to memory. You may use an outline to keep your carefully prepared ideas in order, but you are free to choose on the spot the words that you will use to voice those ideas. You have some verbal latitude.

A three-by-five or four-by-six notecard is often used for the extemporaneous speech. For example, you might want to jot down major transitions (discussed in Chapter 8) or some words or phrases that make your speech flow from one section to another (*in the first place, next, last,* and so on). You could include key words related to major divisions to make sure that your main points are clear ("The *economy* is my next area of concern"). But you are also free to do some thinking "on your feet."

The greatest advantage of the extemporaneous method is that you can be natural; you can be yourself. You can look at your audience and know where you are going in your speech and how your audience is reacting to what you're saying. The extemporaneous form of delivery allows you to pay attention to audience feedback and, if needed, to do some immediate adjusting.

Another good thing about the extemporaneous method of delivery is that your body is allowed to become a part of the communication process. Since you are not confined to your script or to your mental recall, you can let your body *telegraph* some of the attitudes, some of the nonverbal messages that your words are conveying.

It is no secret that the extemporaneous style is the most believable. It is the most believable because it allows *you* to be *you.* It allows you and your audience to connect logically and emotionally. There is some danger that when you use the extemporaneous method you may flub up your fluency or forget something you wanted to say. In the long run, though, this is the type of delivery that can dynamize an audience.

The Impromptu Method

Finally, we'll take a look at the **impromptu method.** *Impromptu* means "not rehearsed." This type of delivery involves speaking "off the cuff," usually for a relatively short time. With the impromptu method, you have no time for preparation. The impromptu method thus calls for a quick mind and instant audience analysis.

The impromptu type of delivery, like the extemporaneous type, allows you to be yourself. You don't have time to be "phony" with your audience or to appear artificial or contrived. Many of the good points that characterize the extemporaneous method of delivery also apply to impromptu speaking.

An effective impromptu speaker can come across as witty and intelligent. The point is that a quick impromptu style of delivery can be impressive if you have the talent, organizational skills, and confidence to pull it off.

As you might expect, there are drawbacks to the impromptu method of delivery. With no notes, you might lose your train of thought and appear disorganized. Also, you might be at a loss for the right word and come across as lacking an adequate vocabulary. Probably the greatest problem with impromptu speaking is the potential for "dead space," those seconds in which you don't know what to say. This is where **vocalized pauses,** such as "and a," "you know," "like," and "uh," are often used as filler. If used too often, vocalized pauses can become extremely dis-

COMMUNICATION WORKS

Susan S. True, High School Director

Susan S. True is the assistant director for the National Federation of State High School Associations, located in Kansas City, Missouri. Her duties include being the editor of all the national rule books relating to field hockey, boys' and girls' gymnastics, swimming and diving, and spirit and volleyball. It is her job to make sure that the different states have a unified approach to and an understanding of the rules. True also represents high school athletics on the board of directors of three Olympic governing bodies: the U.S. Field Hockey Association, the U.S. Gymnastics Federation, and the U.S. Volleyball Association. She has been a university professor, a coach, and a women's athletic director. Currently, she serves on the Board of Trustees of the Women's Sports Foundation.

True stresses the value of communication outside of the regular school curriculum. Even though they take place after school, athletics (and related fields) represent an extension of education, with effective communication playing a vital role.

Here, True speaks on oral communication and her role as a communicator. Her message is one that she shares with adults and students whenever she speaks throughout the year at numerous conferences and clinics.

In the service-oriented, interdependent world of today, it is so important for people to develop effective communication skills. The role of good oral and written communication in personal and/or corporate success is discussed in most books about success— success as a student, a teacher, a spouse, a friend, an employee, or an employer. Good communication skills are the key to satisfactory interpersonal relations, and they are an important part of establishing and maintaining good *morale* within professional or volunteer organizations. Effective communication skills are essential when making a sale, whether it is the selling of a product or the selling of an idea.

Verbal communication is especially important. Verbal communication relies on the fact that you are familiar with the rules of grammar and proper sentence structure. These skills are not limited to composition. Improper use of a word or phrase can lead to misinterpretation of the message being sent. It is important for you to know that the more you know, the wider the audience that you can reach. Give yourself all of the advantages you can to be a good speaker; this includes taking the time to work with words, in general.

On a personal note, I am rarely at a loss for words in informal situations. I am fairly comfortable speaking to a group about a subject about which I know a great deal.

However, I still have a problem speaking to a large group. I do not enjoy it! This is especially true when I am asked to speak on a topic where I'm not myself "the expert." So what do I do?

I don't quit. I prepare. I work hard. I realize that there are going to be people out in the audience who care about what I have to say. I owe it to them to take the time to be a good speaker.

COMMUNICATION WORKS (CONTINUED)

The same is true for you. Work at speaking. It will be a little easier each time the challenge is met. And like any other skill, it will not improve by your merely reading or hearing about it. You must get actively involved. Make an audience understand you; let your words "touch" someone or teach them.

Everyone needs effective oral communication skills. Even a professional athlete who is paid millions has to be able to answer questions from the media and communicate with teammates and coaches. One of the reasons for heavyweight boxing champion Muhammad Ali's popularity during his prime was that he was more articulate than boxers had been before him, or since. One of the reasons that Bart Conner has been more successful than the other two 1984 members of the gold medal men's gymnastics team who have gone into broadcasting is his ability to communicate verbally the technicalities of the sport in an educational, entertaining, and understandable way.

One final thought. I work with coaches and students all year on how to compete in athletics—the rules and the specifics. However, let's not forget that *all of us* communicate in a number of ways. Students need to be reminded, as I remind the people in our programs, that a person's appearance, initial treatment of other people, and nonverbal use of the face and body are powerful communication instruments.

tracting to an audience because they prevent a fluent presentation of your ideas. Usually, when our fluency goes downhill, so does our confidence. It's no wonder that impromptu speaking is the most frightening of all of the delivery options.

In spite of its drawbacks, impromptu speaking is probably the type of speaking you will most often be called on to do in your life. Don't run from it. At home, at school, at community functions, on the job, or with friends, impromptu speaking is a necessity. Think about it. Have you ever been asked to give your reasoning for an answer in class or to state your opinion on an issue? Have you ever been asked to say how you feel emotionally? To explain why you think your idea might work? To describe a problem that you perceive? To solve a community concern?

You can do it! Think in simple terms, prepare a list of organizational words that

you can always go to, be clear, and be brief. Don't forget the value of reading and being informed. You must recognize that the impromptu method of delivery is a real-world necessity. If you practice it, you can master it.

Comparing Delivery Methods

So what does all of this mean? Which type of delivery is best? The answer is that you will often incorporate parts of all four types in your speaking. There will be times when you will want to read a section of your material to your audience, such as when you have a list of facts or a long quotation that you don't want to misquote. Also, you may find that memorizing your introduction and your conclusion will help you feel more confident. In addition, having a working outline that allows you to extemporaneously "speak on your feet" is a good way to gain credibility with your audience. Finally, the impromptu method of delivery makes you believable because you are responding without preparation "on the spot," much as a television reporter does at the scene of a major news happening.

Whichever method of delivery you use, remember that you are showing your audience how you choose to say your words. Say them with thought, say them with feeling, and, most of all, say them well.

Next, we'll take a look at how you can use your voice to make your delivery come alive.

TAKING CHARGE

1. Name two musicians who you think are very similar in their delivery techniques. Name two musicians who are very different in their delivery styles. Explain how each pair is similar and how each pair is different.
2. Practice three of the four methods of delivery using the student speech at the end of this chapter by Joseph M. Wycoff. First, find a paragraph that you enjoy and deliver it to a classmate or to the class by reading from a script. Next, try to commit that same paragraph (or most of it) to memory and deliver it. Finally, using a three-by-five or four-by-six notecard, deliver that same paragraph and look down at your notecard only when you need to be reminded of key words or phrases. Which method is the most effective for you? Why? Be ready to discuss your answers with the class.

III Using Your Voice

It doesn't matter whether you are a weight lifter, a car, or a scientist; you need a power source. A **power source** is the energy that makes things go. The power source for the weight lifter is muscle. The power source for the automobile is the engine. A scientist uses brain power. For speakers, the power source is the entire **vocal process.**

The power source used to produce the voice is also used to help us breathe, chew, and swallow. However, in the vocal process, it is specifically our breathing system that provides the power for voice production, or **phonation.** The breathing system consists of the lungs, the rib cage, and all of the associated muscles. Let's examine how all of this works.

First of all, there are the lungs. From the lungs, we get the air necessary to produce sound. However, the lungs have no muscles; they are just two sacks, like balloons, waiting to be filled with air. We fill them when we breathe in. The muscles of the chest can help in this filling process, but the real power source for breathing is the diaphragm.

The diaphragm is a muscle that separates the chest from the abdominal area. It reaches from the front of the ribs to the spine. Breathing from the diaphragm, not the throat, produces an effective voice and helps produce a resonant voice, or a full, rich voice that is easily heard and pleasant to the ear.

Bette Ambrosio, a speech teacher at Highland Park High School in Dallas, Texas, has a method of teaching diaphragmatic breathing. First, she has her speech students lie down on the floor and put both of their hands on the diaphragm area, fingertips touching. If they are breathing correctly, the fingertips will part at each breath. "If the fingertips don't," she says, "students are chest breathers! Chest breathers are short of breath and weak in volume." Put her exercise to good use and breathe correctly from your diaphragm.

Where does the air go after it leaves the lungs? From each lung, it travels through a tube called a bronchus. The bronchi meet and form the trachea, or windpipe. The windpipe leads upward to the larynx (pronounced *lar inks*), also known as the voice box, which is the voice-producing organ. The vocal cords are located in the larynx. From the larynx, air moves on to the pharynx, which is the cavity in the back of the mouth and nose, otherwise known as the **oral cavity.** The pharynx is connected to the outside air.

This overall power system performs two major functions for the speaker:

1. It delivers the air needed to speak.
2. It regulates the amount of air specifically needed to speak.

While it is true that the product of your power source is only air, it is also only air that goes into a tire. Just as tires without air don't roll, voices without a suffi-

cient amount of air don't communicate well. You must "pump up" your lungs to give your words a smoother ride.

Having covered some basics of voice production, we move next to specific features of voice. These are rate, pitch, volume, articulation, and pronunciation.

Rate

Rate is the speed at which we speak. The average rate of speaking is approximately 120 to 150 words per minute. Sometimes people speak too fast, and sometimes they speak too slowly. Most of the time, if you have a problem with rate, it will be that you are speaking too fast. People often speak more rapidly than they realize. Furthermore, when people are in any way frightened (as when they have stage fright), they tend to speed up.

When speakers talk too rapidly, audiences don't have time to understand fully what is being said. The words are difficult to understand, and the meaning is unclear. Of course, it is possible to speak too slowly, but most of the time, this is better than speaking too fast. Your audience can adjust to a rate that is very deliberate, but it has a very difficult time hurriedly trying to digest a ton of information.

There is another problem with speaking very fast. When you speak too rapidly, you run out of breath. This makes you swallow at awkward times, start to sweat, or think that you are going to pass out. Thus, a fast rate makes everything go wrong.

How can you avoid speaking too fast?

Take a deep breath (as basketball players do at the free throw line), give each word its due, and speak deliberately and with feeling. Your audience will not only understand your message better but will

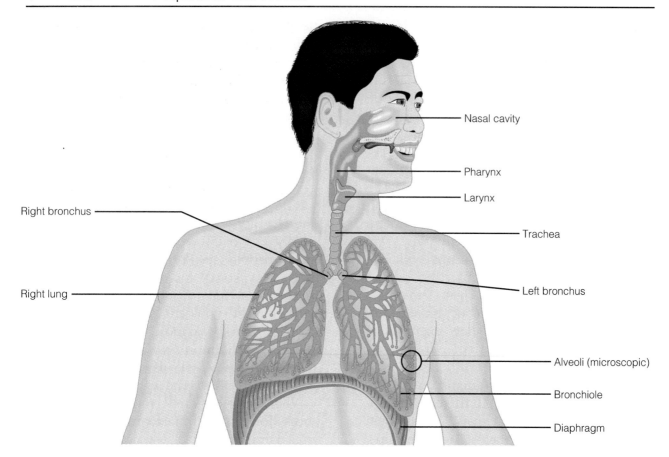

The respiratory system, pictured here, provides the power for phonation (voice production) in the vocal process.

also have the time to actually feel as you do. With a slower rate, you can think on your feet. In addition, you can read audience feedback and tell how you are doing. Think about watching your favorite video cassette while fast-forwarding the entire time. All of the film might be shown, but the video will not be fully enjoyed because the words won't be heard or understood. Don't play your speech at the wrong speed.

History can teach us a lesson. Demosthenes, who gave us the introductory quotation on this chapter's cover page, is credited by scholars as being the greatest of the Greek orators. His teachings represent the highest achievement in Greek rhetoric. As a small child, he apparently stammered or had a speech defect. To overcome this, he placed pebbles in his mouth so that he would be forced to speak slowly and deliberately. Believe it or not, this method made him slow down his rate of speech. This slower rate allowed him to pronounce words accurately and enunciate distinctly. The rest is history.

We have emphasized one important point about rate: Speak slowly enough. It is also important to vary your rate somewhat, as you will see in the next section.

Pitch

Pitch refers to the vocal notes that you hit while speaking—the highs and lows of your voice. Think of a musical scale played on the piano. At one end is a low note, and at the other end is a high note. Of course, there are many notes in between.

You can't easily sell a house whose exterior is dull and lifeless; likewise, you can't "sell" a speech delivered in a very narrow vocal range—you will bore everyone to death. In other words, you must avoid monotone. You speak in a **monotone** when you deliver all of your words *methodically* at almost the same rate and pitch.

Rate and pitch work hand in hand, as illustrated in the following diagram:

P
I
RATE
C
H

If you vary your *speed* of speaking and the *notes* that your voice hits, then you will be on your way to using your voice well for an effective delivery. Imagine a bouncing ball moving all around the two words shown above. As the ball is bouncing, your rate and pitch are showing variety and are working well together. However, if the bouncing ball stops bouncing and just stays in one spot, you are in trouble. You are hitting a very small vocal range at the same speed. You are in "the dead zone," and what is dying is your speech.

How many times have you complained about a teacher who always spoke the same way at the same speed? You probably said, "That teacher just about puts me to sleep every time he lectures! Why can't

he liven things up a little?" The same is true for you.

Of course, you can't liven things up by simply hitting different notes at random. You can, however, use pitch to give the most important word or words in a sentence more emphasis. By giving a particular word more emphasis, you make the audience aware that some of your words are more important than others. Altering your vocal tone or your pitch is called voice **inflection,** and it is often used to help create emphasis.

Repeat the following sentence, each time emphasizing a different word for a different effect.

- ◆ *I* think that you are the best.
- ◆ I *think* that you are the best.
- ◆ I think that *you* are the best.
- ◆ I think that you *are* the best.
- ◆ I think that you are *the* best.
- ◆ I think that you are the *best.*

Analyze how emphasizing a different word each time changes the meaning of the sentence. Now repeat each sentence again and make it a question. Do you see the impact that your voice can have?

In addition to emphasizing your words through the variation of rate and pitch, you can, of course, emphasize words or ideas through volume, which is the next area of analysis.

Volume

It does little good for you to have an outstanding speech if no one can hear you. On the other hand, people don't want to hear your words shouted at them. You must thus learn to control your

INSTANT IMPACT

A Kingly Voice?

Charlemagne (742–814) was an early king of France. He was considered one of the greatest warriors of his time. He stood nearly six feet five inches tall and weighed just short of three hundred pounds. Charlemagne had particularly strong legs and powerful arms. It was said that he was among the finest hunters and riders in his court and that he could kill a man with a single blow of his fist. However, he was often the object of ridicule (behind his back, of course) because he spoke in a voice so high and squeaky. His contemporaries compared his voice to the voice of a twelve-year-old child.

speaking volume. **Volume** is the loudness or softness of your voice.

Picture yourself in these situations:

◆ seated next to a friend at a rock concert

◆ seated next to a friend before the morning announcements at school

◆ seated next to a friend in the library

◆ seated next to a friend at a funeral

How would your volume be different in each situation?

These examples might be obvious, but you will need to vary your volume for other situations as well. For instance, the volume you use at the family dinner table will be quite different from the volume you use to give a speech in English class. The volume for a round-table discussion in science greatly differs from the volume for addressing a crowded room at a community function. Your volume is adequate when everyone in the room can comfortably hear you.

This means that you have to be alert to physical problems that might arise. What do you do if you are speaking in a small room and the air conditioner is blasting? What if the windows are open and the sound of automobiles and machinery outside is loud and distracting?

Of course, you could walk over and turn off the air conditioner or shut the windows. But this might be unwise if the weather is hot and muggy. Your audience might revolt. Thus, it is wise always to be ready to speak over any problem by adjusting your volume level. If the audience is saying to itself while you are speaking, "Turn it up, please!" you will probably soon be "turned off." Don't let this happen. Give your words a chance to be heard.

How can you accomplish this? By practicing taking deep breaths and using the power source described earlier, you can have adequate volume in any speaking situation. Breathe from your diaphragm, open your mouth, and drop your lower jaw. Allow the natural amount of air moving through the oral cavity to create the volume you desire. Take deep breaths in through your nose, or inhale, and slowly release the air through your mouth as you form your words, or exhale.

Articulation and Pronunciation

In the hit musical *My Fair Lady*, Professor Henry Higgins worked to turn the lowly Eliza Doolittle into a lady. He tried

In the musical *My Fair Lady*, Henry Higgins tries to refine lowly Eliza Doolittle's articulation and pronunciation.

to rid her of her accent by having her repeat such classic lines as, "The rain in Spain falls mainly on the plain." She was to speak slowly, clearly, and distinctly, making sure to pronounce the long *a* sound in the words *rain* and *Spain*. Professor Henry Higgins was working with the way Eliza Doolittle used her voice. Specifically, he was working with her articulation and pronunciation.

> "The rain in Spain falls mainly on the plain."
>
> **Eliza Doolittle**

Articulation refers to the crispness, the distinctness, with which we say the *syllables* in a word. The jaw, the lips, and the tongue are known as the main articulators.

Do you say your words clearly, or do you sometimes have the "mushmouth syndrome," in which syllables in words are run together or omitted entirely? Most of us are aware that the word *probably* has three syllables, for example, but we often leave out the middle syllable and say *probly*. Can you think of similar examples?

Middle *t* sounds (water, matter, better, for example) are particularly troublesome. You might have a tendency to articulate a *d* sound instead of the *t*. Another problem is the *ing* sound at the ends of words (coming, going, swimming). Don't drop

COMMUNICATION BREAKDOWN

Meaningful Conversation?

Many experts agree that too often American children are unfairly stereotyped as being rude and uncaring. To hear some people speak, all young people have these faults. Obviously, this type of labeling is unfair. However, few would disagree with the statement that there are too many instances of dishonesty, materialism, and violence.

But who is to blame?

It has been stated that the schools are partly to blame. Vietnam, the sexual revolution, and all forms of civil disobedience have left educators fearful of promoting to students the concepts of right and wrong because "who's to say what's right?" Education is still dealing with this values dilemma.

What about the family? In the last twenty-five years, the divorce rate has quadrupled. Today, half the children in the United States will spend part of their childhoods in single-parent homes. A Rutgers University sociologist believes that children are becoming less and less important in their parents'

lives. He says, "Fading is the fundamental assumption that children are to be loved at the highest level of priority."

What about parent–child communication?

In 1965, the average parent spent roughly thirty waking hours a week with his or her children, according to the Family Research Council in Washington, D.C. Today, it's seventeen hours. Of that time, "meaningful conversation" takes up a grand total of four and one-half minutes, reported Richard Louv in his recent book *Childhood's Future*. Another interesting note: The average child watches twenty hours of television a week.

Source: Carole Carlson, Gary *(Indiana)* Post Tribune, *December, 1991.*

Questions

1. Can you think of reasons why parents and their children are spending less time together now than they did years ago?
2. What problems might result from children watching television so much more than they talk with their parents?

---

the final *g* sound so that the word becomes *swimmin'*.

Poor articulation is most evident in the way people say entire sentences. Have you ever heard these:

"Whataya gonna do d'night?"	(What are you going to do tonight?)
"Didja see'm doot?"	(Did you see him do it?)
"Doya wanna talk ter onaphone?"	(Do you want to talk to her on the phone?)

Articulation problems most often occur when people speak too fast, fail to open their mouths when they speak, or fail to use their tongues adequately to produce specific sounds. To avoid these problems, don't be lazy with your voice. Slurring words might work for the main character in the movie *Rocky*, but it will do little to impress the people listening to you.

The actor James Earl Jones has a deep, booming voice and superb articulation. You can clearly hear every syllable of every word he says in his plays and movies.

Did you know that as a child he stammered so badly that he was forced to write notes to his friends and teachers if he wanted to communicate?

How did he overcome this speaking problem? He went through speech therapy. He also joined his high school speech and debate team. In other words, he was aware of his speaking problems and actively worked to overcome them. Follow this example of James Earl Jones and practice to make your articulation the best that it can be. It will show your audience that you are serious not only about your verbal message but also about your individual words and sentences—their crispness, their clarity, their sharpness.

Pronunciation refers to saying the sounds of a word properly and stressing the correct syllable. Nothing can destroy a good speech more quickly than a mispronounced word. It shows the audience that you haven't done your homework in preparation for your speech. Two excellent ways to improve your pronunciation are to use the dictionary whenever in doubt and to listen to how intelligent people around you are using the word.

There are several areas in which you should be especially careful. Be sure that you have learned how to pronounce a person's name, the name of a country, or the name of a special group before you speak. Be careful in pronouncing foreign names and scientific terms, too.

Speech therapy and participating on his high school speech and debate team helped actor James Earl Jones overcome a severe childhood stammer.

TAKING CHARGE

1. You need to know the range of your vocal rate. Say the sentence, "I can speak at this speed and still be understood." Say it slowly at first. Now pick up speed. Find the slowest rate and the fastest rate at which you can be under-

Taking Charge (Continued)

stood. Also find a medium rate. Your slowest and fastest rates should be the slowest and quickest you would ever speak in normal speaking situations. Do this exercise out loud, or your own voice might frighten you later when you hear it! If possible, use a tape recorder.

2. Make a list of at least two other situations when you might use a slower rate of speech. Create a sentence that you might say at each of these times. What would be your emotional mood at these times? Explain. Now, make a list of several times when your rate would be faster. Again, create a sentence for each. How might the mood be different at these times? Can you think of sentences that could be said either slowly or quickly and still have impact? List these sentences and be ready to give them out loud, showing the differences in rate.

3. What is your pitch? How high and how low can you speak? Say the line, "This is the range that I wish to use in my speaking." Start out near the middle of your vocal range and go down, note by note (as in a musical scale), until you reach the bottom of your pitch range. Now repeat the process to find the top of your range. Remember that your pitch should include notes that you would use in speaking. Never use falsetto, an artificially high voice. What are two or three instances or situations in which you would use your low notes? What emotions would be involved? Create at least two sentences for each situation. Do the same for your high notes.

4. As a class and then in small groups, say the tongue twisters below out loud. With each, start slowly and repeat, trying to pick up speed. If you are slurring, you need to stop and go back to a more controllable rate. You—and your mouth—must be in charge.

   a. Pat's pop shop
   b. Chrysanthemum/geranium
   c. Aluminum/linoleum
   d. Unique New York
   e. Red leather/yellow leather
   f. Toy boat
   g. Sister Susie's sewing shirts for soldiers.

Now, try these tougher ones.

   h. Peter Piper picked a peck of pickled peppers. If Peter Piper picked a peck of pickled peppers, where is the peck of pickled peppers that Peter Piper picked?

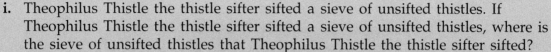

TAKING CHARGE (CONTINUED)

    i. Theophilus Thistle the thistle sifter sifted a sieve of unsifted thistles. If Theophilus Thistle the thistle sifter sifted a sieve of unsifted thistles, where is the sieve of unsifted thistles that Theophilus Thistle the thistle sifter sifted?

    j. Betty Botter bought some butter. "But," she said, "this butter's bitter. If I put it in my batter it will make by batter bitter. But a bit of better butter will but make my batter better." So, she bought a bit of butter, better than the bitter butter, that made her bitter batter better. So, 'twas better that Betty Botter bought a bit of better butter.

5. What common, everyday words can you think of that people often mispronounce? What names of American leaders or foreign leaders are often a problem? What about names of cities or foreign countries? Make a list for each of these categories. Allow the dictionary and key communicators (teachers, reputable broadcasters, or media figures, etc.) help you take charge of any pronunciation problem.

IV Using Your Body

In the novel *The Scarlet Letter,* by Nathaniel Hawthorne, many of the seventeenth-century Puritan characters show one face to the public but are very different on the inside. While this "two-sidedness" might be an excellent literary device for character and thematic analysis, using it in your speaking isn't smart. Your body, like your voice, must be a positive extension of your message. You can't allow your speech to say one thing while your body is saying something entirely different.

Chapter 1 mentioned nonverbal communication, and Chapter 4 discussed it at length. Nonverbal communication doesn't actually deliver your words, but it does deliver your attitude about those words.

You read about body language in Chapter 4. When you deliver a speech, many things you do with your body—standing with one leg bent, tilting your head back, slouching, lowering your chin, keeping your arms in extremely close to your body, leaning toward your audience, standing with your entire body rigid, or standing relaxed with your hands comfortably at your side—convey nonverbal messages to your audience. If you are speaking on the value of leadership in your school, but your body telegraphs to the audience that you are bored or uneasy, who in the world would want to follow you?

Your body language, then, is a key contributor to nonverbal communication. So is your face; we will deal with that later in the chapter. Let's now take a look at two other aspects of using your body: platform

Communicating through Body Language

While delivering a speech, what you do with your body conveys a nonverbal message to the audience.

  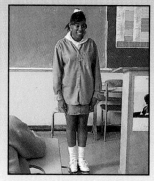 

movement and gestures. Both are important in promoting an effective delivery.

Platform Movement

A good speaker is similar to a good dancer in that both must have a sense of rhythm. In the speaker, all body movement should have a rhythmic flow so that it appears fluid and natural and fits with the words being spoken. This rhythm should be apparent in the speaker's platform movement.

Very simply, **platform movement** means walking or stepping in a directed manner from one spot to another while speaking. Obviously, it need not involve a real platform. While you may at times be on stage (introducing a guest speaker for a class or school convocation, for example), you are usually simply standing at the front of your classroom or some other room when you deliver your speech.

Before discussing what you should do, let's take a look at what you *shouldn't* do regarding platform movement:

◆ Don't pace back and forth as if you were a "duck at a shooting gallery."
◆ Don't "wander," or take strolls from spot to spot with no purpose.
◆ Don't try to sneak a movement, hoping that your audience won't see you move.
◆ Don't avoid movement because you are afraid you will look silly.

Movement should accentuate and reinforce your speaking. It should be logical and make sense to your audience. Platform movement not only shows your audience that you are literally moving from one part of your speech to another but it also gives the audience a break from staring at you in one spot the entire time. It provides a type of "eye relief." This

COMMUNICATION BREAKTHROUGH

Hearing Your Favorite Book

Among people who spend a lot of time behind the wheel of an automobile or on a stationary bicycle, a new form of "reading" has emerged—the audio book. That's right! You can now *hear* your favorite book. Before the mid-1980s, the audio-book business was nonexistent, but in today's market it has annual sales of over a billion dollars. Anyone with an automobile tape deck or a portable cassette player is fair game.

"What we find," says Leslie Nadell of Random House Audio Publishing, "is that once people have listened to one cassette they become instant converts."

Even though many literary purists might be bothered by the abridged versions of the works, the audio cassettes have gained praise from authors themselves. All authors must approve the material before it is put on the market. People who listen to the tapes have been impressed by the excellent voices and the vibrant, exciting delivery that many of the speakers present on tape.

Many of the best readers are the authors themselves. Glowing reports have been turned in for John le Carré and Eudora Welty, as well as E. B. White (*Charlotte's Web*). The worst reader so far: Norman Mailer. Of the actors, John Lithgow sounds as excellent on tape as he does in the theater. By the way, the largest customers for the audio cassettes are public libraries.

Adapted from: Katrine Ames, "The New Oral Tradition," Newsweek, 1991.

Questions
1. Some people might argue that the audio book takes away from the reader's imagination; however, what possible advantages could the audio book offer?
2. Can you think of specific instances where the audio book would be a practical asset?
3. Why do you think that libraries are the largest customers of audio books?

makes you a little more dynamic and exciting if you do it correctly.

"But how do I move, and when are the right times to move?" you may ask. There are three situations that allow for effective platform movement.

First of all, it is logical to move when you are going from one section of your speech to another. For instance, after you have delivered your introduction, you might want to move in order to set up and draw attention to your thesis or topic sentence. In addition, many speakers like

to use movements between their main points and again before their conclusion. These movements add variety and give special importance to specific sections of their speeches. Always begin your speech by "squaring up," or centering yourself with your audience (not with the room). You should also end your speech near the middle of your audience. This adds a touch of cohesion, courtesy, and completeness to your speech.

Second, movement is often effective when you are changing your emotional appeal. Suppose you are describing the problems that teenagers face in society today. You might be speaking at a fairly even rate and emotional level. However, when you start listing the startling statistics related to teenage suicide, your emotional level might rise. You might start speaking more quickly and becoming more emotionally intense. At this point, a platform movement might be logical to show that your body is as involved as your words in what you are communicating. Similarly, if you were speaking on the problems of stereotyping teenagers, and then began to report on the great things that teenagers have done for others, such as donating to charities and to community projects, a change in emotional level and movement might be appropriate. When your emotions are in action, often so are your feet! Allow your movement the chance to help set the speaking mood you want.

Finally, platform movement is often appropriate when it "just feels right" to you. Don't let rules always direct what you do in speaking. Sometimes it is appropriate to simply allow yourself to be yourself. After you have worked and practiced your speech, trust your communication instincts.

You might have an urge to move while delivering an example or while giving your conclusion. Go ahead and give it a try. Your audience (and your teacher) will let you know after you are finished if your movement was distracting or ill timed.

Platform movement should be done so naturally that your audience isn't even aware of it. You shouldn't have to be told how to move or at what speed. You simply move while delivering your speech as you would move anywhere else. When you are walking in the hallway at school, no one has to tell your legs and feet what

to do. You move and walk instinctively. Let your legs and your body work together so that your movement is believable, parallels the tone of your speech, and, most of all, is *you.*

Nevertheless, there are a few specific points to remember about *how* to move.

1. Always move in a comfortable, relaxed manner by leading with the leg in the direction you are moving. If you are walking to the right, for example, move the right leg first. If you are moving to the left, move the left leg first. There are two good reasons to do this. The first is that it keeps your body "open" to the audience. If you are crossing your legs over as you move, you might turn almost sideways and present a profile to your audience. When this happens, your audience members lose part of your face and potentially part of your words. They can't hear what you might be delivering to the walls. The second reason is that it keeps you, believe it or not, from tripping over your own feet. You would be amazed to hear the number of stories about men catching their shoes in the cuffs of their pants or women hitting a heel on the other shoe or foot. How embarrassing!

2. Move toward your audience. When you are moving in your speech, your walking should be directed toward some portion of the audience or even a specific audience member. You should be moving as if to say, "Here is a point that I particularly want you to hear." In other words, you are moving because you are

Platform movement can be effective when going from one section of a speech to another, when changing an emotional appeal, or simply when it feels natural.

sharing your words with your listeners. Vary the direction of your movement. This is a good way to make sure that no portion of your audience feels neglected or ignored.

Of course, you shouldn't make the angle of your movement too extreme, and you shouldn't move so close to an audience member that he or she might feel uncomfortable. Be aware of proxemics, or how much physical space you leave between you and your audience. Use your common sense in determining your distance from the audience. Know the speaking area, and always make sure that you can comfortably move back to the center of the room, leaving an appropriate amount of space between you and your audience.

3. Know exactly the number of steps that you are going to take. You can usually be comfortable with taking one step forward, toward your audience, or using a three-step or a five-step method.

The three-step method is fairly easy to master. You simply take your first step (moving the correct leg, of course), cross over with the second step, and then move the first leg forward so that you are once again standing firmly on both feet. This method is appropriate for moving in smaller areas, but it is recommended in any setting because it is easy to control. Control is what you are after.

The five-step method works exactly the same way as the three-step method except that, obviously, you take two more steps. This method can be used in larger speaking areas. The danger with the five-step method is that you might forget what you are doing and start to roam around the front of the room.

Even though an experienced speaker might not need to plan exactly how many steps to take (i.e., three steps or five steps), a beginner should. The beginning speaker needs to develop a firm sense of discipline. So keep your movement centralized and be sure to avoid situations in which you might lose control of your movements and walk right out the door (as tempting as it might be).

Gestures

Even though they are nonverbal, gestures definitely communicate. **Gestures,** as explained in Chapter 4, are actions in which the body or parts of the body move to express an idea or emotion. We might think of **posture** referring to the position of the body when it is still (as when your teacher tells you, "Stand up straight. Stop slouching. Don't lean on that desk. Get your hands out of your pockets."). Gestures, however, refer to the body in motion.

Let's take a look at how gestures specifically relate to delivery. Like platform movement, gestures should be natural and fit what you are saying. Gestures should not be contrived, or artificial. Body gestures are usually associated with the arms and hands, the shoulders, and the head. Like a good symphony, a good sports team, or a smoothly running engine, gestures work best when all of these parts work together. A good speaker does not allow an individual part of the body to work in isolation.

If you want to know how to gesture effectively, then watch people when they

INSTANT IMPACT

"Delivery" Has Its Day in Court

Creators of a play about the rock legend Janis Joplin won a key court ruling recently. Heirs of the blues/rock-and-roll singer, who died in 1970, had sued the authors of the play, titled *Janis*, claiming that they had exclusive rights to Joplin's performance style. The heirs claimed that they had the rights to her "voice, delivery, mannerisms, appearance, dress, and actions (gestures included) accompanying her performance."

The judge disagreed, saying that even though Janis Joplin's style was indeed unique, people have too many similarities in delivery for one person to claim them exclusively. If the heirs' position were upheld, the judge questioned, how could comedians ever imitate a celebrity without facing a possible lawsuit?

talk. Watch what the shoulders do when the hands are in motion. Notice how the head can accentuate a point.

Probably the single greatest problem that you might have will involve this question: What do I do with my hands?

Eighteenth-century American clergyman John Witherspoon once said, "Never rise to speak till you have something to say; and when you have said it, cease." In other words, he was advising all speakers not to overdo it with their words. This same principle can be applied to gestures.

Make your gestures clear, but don't over-do them. There is nothing wrong with having your arms and hands comfortably at your sides, at your "base." This relays to your audience that you are relaxed and in control.

> "Never rise to speak till you
> have something to say;
> and when you have
> said it, cease."

John Witherspoon

If you are holding notecards in your hands, you may hold them with one hand or with both hands. Either way, your notes should be comfortably held at your waist, and they should not be a distraction.

Even though some instructors permit students not using notes to put their hands behind them or folded in front of them, it is best to start practicing as soon as possible bringing your hands back to your sides.

When you do gesture with your hands, bring your gestures up and out. Remember, again, that these gestures aren't supposed to be the center of attention. They are supposed to supplement your content.

Here are three tips that can help you become more comfortable with your hands.

1. Learn the Gesture Zone

It is important that you develop a sense of control with your hands. Too often, our hands will take off, almost as if they had minds of their own, and do things that

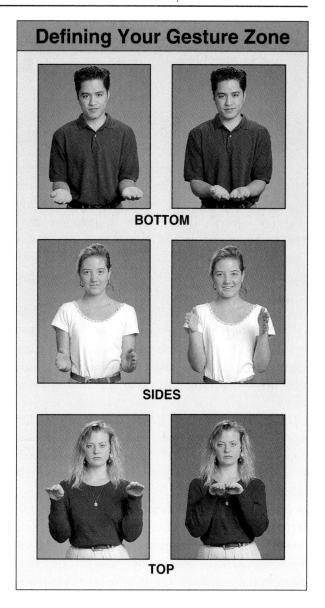

Defining Your Gesture Zone

BOTTOM

SIDES

TOP

we aren't aware of. One method that will help you control your hands is to learn your gesture zone, just as a baseball player learns the strike zone.

The gesture zone is an imaginary box in front of you, similar to a television screen. To find your gesture zone, start by placing your arms in front of you with your palms up and your elbows fairly close to your body. Your arms should be near waist level. Now draw the *bottom* of the gesture zone by moving your hands together. Repeat this to get a feel for how your hands can move near your waist and be effective.

Next, put your hands back in the original position—arms in front of you with both palms facing up (don't get your arms too far apart). Turn your hands so that your palms are at right angles to the floor (parallel to your body). Move your hands up and down, but be sure never to go higher than your shoulder area. (From the audience's point of view, if you gestured higher than the shoulder area, your face would be partially covered by your gestures, and this should never happen.) You are now drawing the *sides* of the gesture zone.

Finally, after you have found the sides of your gesture zone, draw in the *top* by repeating the procedure you used to find the bottom, only now turn your palms down so that they are facing the floor.

Now, draw the entire gesture zone. Do it again. Notice how your box ranges from your waist to just below your shoulders. Practice gesturing inside of this imaginary control zone. Certain gestures will call for you to gesture outside of the zone, but don't get fancy until you know what you are doing. Pay particular attention to gestures that are too sweeping or wide. The idea is to keep the audience focused on your face.

2. Learn to "Lift and Lay" Your Hands

Gestures can be a distraction if you don't work at doing them correctly. Three common errors in gesturing are the following:

◆ The "fly away" gesture, in which your hands simply shoot out from your sides like missiles and appear directionless.

◆ The "judo-chop" gesture, in which you appear to mercilessly and repeatedly hatchet your message into the minds of your audience.

◆ The "penguin-wave" gesture, in which you have your hands down at your side and then attempt to gesture by simply flicking your wrists or fingers as a penguin might flick its wings while walking on land.

In contrast, when you "lift and lay," you lift your arms and hands so that they move comfortably up and out, and then lay your hands at the end of a gesture as if you were laying them on an imaginary ledge or a table. Of course, this takes place in the gesture zone. Even though the distance traveled isn't great, this technique gives a sense of control and finality to your gesture.

3. Practice the "String" Idea

As mentioned, taking the time to watch and analyze people while they are speaking is a good idea. It teaches you about what happens during both verbal and nonverbal communication. It also teaches you what makes sense and what doesn't. For instance, have you ever seen anyone gesture without moving a portion of his or her upper body—the shoulders, the neck, or the head? Unless you are watching a science fiction movie, the answer is no.

When you speak informally yourself, you don't think about your body. However, you should think about it. If you are upset about a test score and throw your hands up in despair, what do you do with your shoulders? Your head? Do they move, also? If you are questioning a group about its position on a controversial issue, and you use your hand and fingers emphatically to make your point, what do you do with your head? Does it move? Of course.

What does all this have to do with the "string" idea?

Imagine that you have a long piece of string. Hold one end with one hand and the other end with the other hand. Now, tie the two ends together. Place the string around your neck. Pretend to place one arm (or both) through the other end of the loop, as if it were a sling. What happens when you extend that arm? Doesn't the string force your head to move, too?

What is the point of this exercise? The "string" idea is simply a good way to re- mind yourself to keep the upper portion of your body actively involved when gesturing.

After a while, you will begin to do some things that are more natural for you. At first, though, paying attention to these three tips—the gesture zone, the "lift and lay," and the "string" idea—will give you a good start on gesturing properly and making your hands believable.

You may feel uncomfortable practicing gestures. Remember, though, that it makes little sense to spend a great deal of time writing out speeches and hardly any time working at the exercises needed to become a good speaker. All good musicians pay their dues by doing drills. The drill work may be monotonous, but in the long run, the basics are invaluable. Performing nonverbal "gesture drills" is a good way to give precision to your body movement.

TAKING CHARGE

■

1. List at least five types of hand and arm gestures that people use and the emotions or attitudes that go along with them. Create a sentence to go with each emotion or attitude and gesture. Be prepared to demonstrate.
2. Identify two common problems that you see people having with their fingers while gesturing. In your opinion, how can these problems be corrected?
3. You move at different times during a speech. Can you think of three important times? You have read about the one-step, the three-step, and the five-step methods of platform movement. When would you use each? How might your attitude or intent be different with each? Why is it wrong to move too much? What is the problem with never moving?

Ⅴ Using Your Face

Probably the most important nonverbal element in an effective delivery is your face. Studies have shown that more than the words spoken or even the body language, the face determines whether someone is believed or not. The expressions on your face while you talk can show your audience how you feel about them, how you feel about your material, and how you feel about yourself as a speaker.

You have already read about the role of nonverbal communication; however, this text can't emphasize enough the importance of your unspoken attitude. Quite frankly, if your face doesn't "sell it," your audience doesn't "buy it." If you are speaking on the importance of fund-raising for a class project, but you convey to class members that they are beneath you in intelligence—not by your words but by your facial gestures—how can you expect them to ardently support your position? You will only have *alienated* them.

If you are speaking on the rights of minorities and how street people are being victimized, but your face gives off an expression that says you are uninterested, bored, or disgusted, what is your audience to think about your attitude toward your subject matter? What if you are discussing this serious topic and a broad smile appears on your face? Why are you smiling? Your face just doesn't match the mood or tone of the speech.

One of the most common errors in speaking is to present a well-thought-out speech, only to have its impact ruined by an absolutely petrified facial expression. If you seem frightened, you lose credibility. If you appear to lack confidence in yourself, your audience will lack confidence in both you and what you are saying.

"A picture is worth a thousand words," and your face while you are speaking *is* that picture. What part of the face is the most important?

The Eyes

"The eyes are the windows to the soul." This famous quotation is vital for the good speaker to understand. It is through your eyes that the people in your audience will primarily judge you: your overall honesty, your conviction about your message, and your genuine concern for them.

An effective delivery depends on your ability to look at the people in your audience and make meaningful eye contact with them. Forget about the myths you might have heard about looking at the tops of heads or imagining your audience sitting in their seats dressed in just their underwear. How silly! These are simply foolish shortcuts intended to make you seem to have eye contact when you are actually avoiding your audience's eyes.

Are you nervous? Are you a little intimidated by the speaking assignment? If the answer is "Yes, I definitely am!" then you do not need the *superficial* "quick fix" of pretending to have good eye contact. You need to face the problem and learn the value of eyes.

Keep these points in mind:

1. Look at each person for a number of seconds before moving on to a different person in the audience. This is referred to as sustained eye contact. Deliver a sentence or two, making sure that you are not mak-

ing the audience member nervous or paranoid. You don't want to have a "stare-down" contest or stand too close. Your intent is to make the people in your audience realize that you are interested in each and every one of them. Remember, you are not looking at each person simply because you think that you're supposed to. You are offering sustained eye contact because you care about what each member of your audience thinks. Think of your speech as a gold mine and share its wealth with your audience through eye contact.

2. Don't forget to make eye contact with people at the far sides of the audience. Some speakers forget about the people at the extremes of the room, the far left and the far right (both in the front and in the back of the room). Beware of having tunnel vision and speaking only to those seated immediately in front of you or those directly in the center of the room. It only makes sense that the more people you look at, the more people you have the potential to influence. Look to the corners.

3. Make eye contact with people, not things. Your goal is to make a positive impression on your audience. Consequently, you shouldn't talk to the back wall or the parking lot outside the window or empty desks.

Of course, you can look up or off once in awhile if you are in thought. For the most part, though, your eyes should go to the eyes of your audience. Remember, if you avoid eye contact, you probably won't be trusted. Don't negate all of your hard work by delivering some of your best material to the floor. Give people priority!

Audience Feedback

One of the best reasons for you to have good eye contact with the members of your audience is that it allows you to see how they are reacting to what you are saying. You can read the feedback. Are people fidgeting in their chairs? Do they appear irritated? Are they smiling and nodding their heads? Are they leaning toward you, or are they leaning away from you and avoiding eye contact? Do they look confused?

You need to pay attention to feedback so that you can make the necessary adjustments. For instance, you might see that some people in the back of the room are straining to hear you. This should direct you to move closer to them or to raise your volume level. You might notice that some people are wrinkling their brows as if they don't totally understand your point. Stop and explain. Audience feedback is your communication effectiveness yardstick. Take the time to look at your audience and see how you are measuring up.

TAKING CHARGE

1. Find a paragraph in print and deliver it in front of a mirror. Keep a list of what your eyes do as you deliver various parts of that paragraph. Next, form groups. Each person should deliver to his or her group the paragraph that he or she has worked on. Other group members are to comment on whether or not the speaker's eyes are doing what he or she has described them as doing on the list made earlier. The group may also make suggestions for improvements. Finally, each person should deliver his or her paragraph to the group again, implementing the suggestions that the group has offered.

2. Make a list of five emotions or attitudes (fear, sadness, joy, or the like) that your face can convey without using words. Form groups of two or three and see if other group members can guess the emotions or attitudes on your list based on your facial expressions. Be sure to give priority to what your *eyes* convey.

3. Read the two selections that follow as if you were a news commentator seated behind a desk. Even though these selections were not delivered as speeches, each allows for a variety of facial expressions. Discover how you would deliver each. Remember the value of variety.

   a. The first selection is from *The American Crisis* by Thomas Paine. Paine's first pamphlet, *Common Sense*, appeared in January of 1776, at a time when most Americans were hoping that the conflict with England could be resolved. However, Paine pointed out the necessity for a break from England and the need for "an open and determined Declaration for Independence." Shortly afterward, this selection was written.

   These are the times that try men's souls; The summer soldier and the sunshine patriot will in this crisis, shrink from the service of his country; but he that stands now, deserves the love and thanks of man and woman. Tyranny, like hell, is not easily conquered; yet we have this consolation with us, that the harder the conflict, the more glorious the triumph. What we obtain too cheap, we esteem too lightly. . . . It would be strange indeed, if so celestial an article as FREEDOM should not be highly rated. Britain, with an army to enforce her tyranny, has declared that she has a right not only to TAX but "to BIND us in ALL CASES WHATSOEVER," and if being bound in that manner is not slavery, then there is not such a thing as slavery upon earth. . . . If there must be trouble, let it be in my day, that my child may have peace!

   b. The next selection shows a very different style of writing with a completely different tone. It is an excerpt from a book by Andy Rooney, of the television program "60 Minutes," called *And More by Andy Rooney*. The chapter is entitled "Memory."

What does AWACS stand for again, do you remember? Advance Warning something. Advance Warning American Command Ship? That's not it. I'll have to ask someone or look it up. And who was Lyndon Johnson's Vice President? You ought to remember a simple thing like that and I ought to myself, but I don't. There are times when I'm overwhelmed by my vast lack of memory. The other day I forgot my home phone number, and we've had it for thirty years.

I remember reading that we all start losing brain cells that make up the memory when we reach about age twenty, but this debilitating influence the years have doesn't seem to have much to do with my problem. I couldn't remember anything when I was eighteen, either.

Being tall and being able to remember things are probably the two most desirable human characteristics I don't have. Because I am neither tall nor able to remember things, I look for ways to diminish the importance of height and memory.

The trouble with people with good memories is that they keep wanting to show it off to you by remembering things you don't want to hear. Everything reminds them of something they've done before. . . . I'd rather wait until I'm all through living and then review my life and times. Right now, I'm busy with today.

If you delivered these two selections with basically the same facial expressions, then you are not using your face properly. What did you notice that your eyes were doing at different points? Your eyebrows? Your mouth? Your neck and shoulders? Be prepared to read one or both of the selections to another student, a group, or the entire class.

VI Dynamizing Your Overall Delivery

You have now read about some of the components that make up an effective delivery. Primarily, you have looked at the importance of your voice, your body, and your face. All must work together if you wish to dynamize your verbal message.

If you pay attention to the best speakers, you will notice that the parts of the body and the voice often go together, creating a satisfying blend of all of the individual elements. Notice that when a good speaker starts to speak, the movement, the gestures, and the words work together harmoniously. Such speakers may make it all look smooth and easy, but it's not. Getting there is a consequence of paying attention to and practicing the parts that make up the whole.

If you are saying, "But I simply can't deliver a speech, and I can't get any better," remember this story: It has been said that you can't make a silk purse out of a sow's ear. In other words, you can't make something beautiful from something supposedly ugly. Did you know that a scientist did! He purchased a sow's ear from

Andy Rooney uses facial expressions to enliven his presentations on the television program "60 Minutes."

the stockyards and ground it down to a gelatinous state. He then devised a method to produce a form of thread from this matter. With the thread, he created two beautiful, elegant purses. One of them is currently on display at the Smithsonian Institute in Washington, D.C. He did it to prove that nothing is impossible if people put their minds to the task.

Apply this lesson to your speech delivery. Don't ever give up. Whether it be in music, athletics, academics—or speaking—the great ones never do.

STUDENT SPEECH

Joseph M. Wycoff, from Chesterton High School in Indiana, is the most successful high school speaker in the history of the National Forensic League's national tournament—a five-time national finalist and two-time national champion. This is an excerpt from a national championship oration Joseph delivered in 1987, when he was a junior in high school. The place is Princeton High School in Cincinnati, Ohio. He is speaking in front of approximately 3,000 people. As you read this speech, try to imagine all of the delivery elements and how they could work together for effect.

Who's Playing the Drum?

You know, there's a real science and precision to speaking, and I've taken it upon myself to analyze some of the specialized components that go into the making of a successful speech. I've noticed that one of the most important factors is that you have to have something different to set yourself apart from the crowd. Now, I'm sure that

STUDENT SPEECH

Continued

the burning question in all of your minds is, "Why is he standing at the far right side of the microphone?" Well, that's simple. [Pointing] Everyone else stood over there in the center. I'm different. Another thing. Everyone likes to come up to the front and establish eye contact, get a good rapport with the audience—face to face. [Considers, and then turns his back to the audience] How's this for memorable? *Now,* I'm an individual!

I would like to apologize for standing at the far right and turning my back on you, but you do have to admit that I did come across as being an individual. I had *style!* No purpose, but a lot of style. Ironically, being an "individual" contradicted the very thing that I was trying to accomplish: to communicate effectively. But if I had done what everyone else does, it might have been seen as unoriginal and weak . . . and that's exactly my point. It seems that in America today, it's no longer noble to follow, to conform, or to be a part of the group.

Let's face it, followers have a bad name. It's not hard to understand why the problem exists. General Custer did not give followers a good name. Jim Jones at Guyana gave followers the appearance of mindless fanatics. Then, of course, there was General John Sedgewick. He, at the Battle of Spotsylvania in 1864, stood proudly before his men and stated, "Men, don't worry. They couldn't hit an elephant at this dist . . . " I think we have all known the feeling of being led by someone who is not totally on the ball. It's frustrating! We could do it better than he or she could. And so, like the Scylla and Charybdis of Homer's *Odyssey,* we find ourselves faced with a similar dilemma. Either (a) we will follow *no one,* or (b) we will follow *anyone.*

I am reminded of a sign on an Indianapolis lawn which seems to proclaim our modern attitude: "Set of encyclopedias for sale. Never been used. Teenage son knows everything!" We "know it all" appears to be our motto. Evidently, Jane Fonda thinks so. Author Ralph Schoenstein states that recently in an interview with Ms. Fonda, when asked to name some of her heroes, she replied that she had none. Her attitude epitomizes a "Me" generation. Schoenstein goes on to state that when he interviewed a group of third graders and asked them to name some of their heroes, one child responded with Michael Jackson, Spider-man, and God, thus naming a new holy trinity. But nearly half responded with "Me." Well, we can hardly blame the children. Maybe they are just a reflection of what they have been taught. In our schools, we now have Gifted and Talented programs and advanced learning courses, all for the purpose of "molding tomorrow's *leaders.*" Who would ever think of teaching them to follow?

We're a society that wants to do it on our own. Why? Maybe it's because of our ambition, lack of trust, or maybe the blow to our egos when we see incompetence and Teflon-tongued con men rise to the top. Nevertheless, Joseph Epstein of Northwestern University points out that the modern individual seeks to rise above the group as opposed to working with it, and, in the process, helps to destroy our sense of community and commitment to others.

Did you ever wonder why our government at times seems to be so confused? Well, it turns out that it is not just the quality of some leaders, but the quantity as well. Veteran military reporter Arthur T. Hadley in his book *The Straw Giant* states that part of the problem, at least with our military, is a case of "too many chiefs and not enough Indians." He comments that there has never been a totally successful operational test of the Minuteman missile. The reason is that we have plenty of people who know how to give the orders, but not enough trained personnel who know how to carry them out.

What's wrong with wanting to lead? Nothing. However, there is something wrong when *so many people* want to direct . . . that few or none are left to actually go in that direction. We end up with a case of "divided we stand," or, as in our second area, "united we fall," when we will follow anyone.

It looks as though we are losing the skill of how to be conscientious conformists. We forget a lesson that my father tried to teach me very early. "Before you march to the beat of a different drummer, look back and see *who's playing the drum!*" It's odd to think that a recent survey tells us that at least one-third of all college students firmly believe in ghosts, Atlantis, flying saucers, and Bigfoot. On a college quiz, answers like these were given for general knowledge questions: The Great Gatsby was a magician in the 1930s; Socrates was an American Indian chieftain; Christ was born in the sixteenth century; and who will ever forget that great Roman emperor, Sid Caesar?

Our lack of knowledge, as well as our decision sometimes not to open our eyes to the obvious, may very well be the reason that so many of us are willing to follow a Jim Jones . . . the reason why a group of conscientious individuals at a soccer game can become a violent mob in Europe and kill 56 people . . . or at home become a mob at a Who concert and kill 11. It seems that oftentimes we lose our sense of personal judgment when we are in a group.

Yet, both Aleksandr Solzhenitsyn and Albert Einstein have pointed out that we must *stop* seeing the group this way and start seeing it as a combining of personal strengths . . . for our own survival.

How many students are really impressed by the classmate who always has to make an extra comment, appropriate or not, while the teacher is talking, or the classmate who just doesn't have the common sense to sit down and shut up? For teachers, how about administrators who come up with brilliant projects and programs, but don't inform anyone how those programs are supposed to work, and are, therefore, faced with ridicule and chaos? When was the last time that you or anyone else you know volunteered for anything?

What it can basically come down to is . . . for whom or what are we willing to sacrifice?

"Feel free if a relationship becomes dull or sluggish to move out, and don't feel guilty because in our generation lasting relationships between any two people are no longer practical." This is a quote from psychiatrist David Viscott in his book *Feel Free*.

Have we gotten to the point where the simple group of two can no longer function together? How sad if he's right.

But that's also where our hope lies. Some people do believe as David Viscott, but I hope that I am not far off in the assumption that most of us do not. We find commitment in relationships important and necessary. There *are* heroes out there for the follower. In 1982, when a 737 crashed into the icy waters of the Potomac River, *one man* kept other passengers afloat and even passed his lifeline, saving many, before he himself drowned—a commitment to humankind.

In the final analysis, we are all followers.

STUDENT SPEECH

Continued

We are students following teachers, employees following bosses, children following parents. We shouldn't have to apologize for those roles. We need to realize that there is no shame in following. First, we are important. The brain may control the heart, but without the heart the brain dies. Second, because we are so important, we have to start becoming conscientious conformists, not

blind . . . just lemmings at the cliff's edge.

To whom are you willing to say with pride, "I will follow you." There are plenty of people out there: at home, at work, at school. People who are willing to show that the conformists, the followers, the team players are noble, humble, and essential . . . if we will all be willing to stop . . . and listen for the drum beat.

REVIEW AND ENRICHMENT

LOOKING BACK

Listed below are the major ideas discussed in this chapter.

- ◆ Your speaking delivery is the way you actually "sell" your words, or the verbal and nonverbal manner in which you actually present your material.
- ◆ There are four types of delivery: manuscript, memorized, extemporaneous, and impromptu.
- ◆ The extemporaneous method is the method most often recommended, although elements of all four types might be used at different times.
- ◆ The voice is the instrument that carries your words, and your diaphragm is the main power source for effective speaking.
- ◆ The air that you need for speaking fills your lungs and advances to your oral cavity. This air then provides you with the power needed for adequate speaking volume, or the loudness or softness of your voice.
- ◆ Simply having the air to speak isn't enough. You must speak at a comfortable rate, or speed, with a pleasant pitch range, or range of notes.
- ◆ Good speakers vary their pitch and rate often to avoid speaking in a monotone and to add life to their words.
- ◆ Good speakers also know when to use emphasis. Emphasis is the stress that you give certain words that you wish to accentuate.

◆ You must also be sure not to slur your words or run them together. You must articulate clearly.

◆ In addition, it is essential that you know how to pronounce all the words that you are going to use.

◆ Another key element in developing an effective delivery is the use of your body. Even though using your body is nonverbal, it definitely communicates a message to your audience.

◆ Platform movement involves actually taking steps while speaking. This movement can range from one step to as many as five steps. The number of steps that you take depends on the size of the room, the size of the audience, and your emotional intent at the time of your movement.

◆ You should always keep in mind the distance between you and your audience. This knowledge can keep you from making audience members feel uncomfortable. It can also keep you from getting yourself in a tight spot involving space.

◆ Hand gestures are probably the gestures that concern speakers most. "What do I do with my hands while speaking?" is a common question.

◆ Hand and arm gestures should be kept, for the most part, in your gesture zone. This is an area the size of a television screen that extends from your waist to your upper chest.

◆ Facial expression may be the most important part of your oral communication. When you nonverbally involve your face in your delivery (and everyone does), the audience can see how you really feel about your material, yourself, and them.

◆ The eyes are crucial for an effective delivery. You must sustain eye contact with each audience member long enough to make him or her feel a part of your speech.

◆ Effective eye contact also makes your audience trust you and what you say.

◆ Overall, the best speakers use the elements of an effective delivery *together*. All aspects of the voice, the body, and the face work as a symphony of components.

SPEECH VOCABULARY

delivery	phonation
manuscript method	oral cavity
memorized method	rate
extemporaneous method	pitch
impromptu method	monotone
vocalized pauses	inflection
power source	volume
vocal process	articulation

> ### REVIEW AND ENRICHMENT
> #### Continued

pronunciation   gestures
platform movement   posture
proxemics

1. The vocabulary list for Chapter 11 is rather extensive. Divide the speech vocabulary list into two fairly even sections. For each word in one list, give the definition as given in the chapter. Feel free to use the dictionary or the glossary for additional information. Also, for each word in this list, write an original sentence using the word correctly.
2. For the second list, provide the definition as given in the chapter. Then, instead of writing individual sentences, write a story or a series of paragraphs using the words. The topic of your story is up to you. Make sure it makes sense.

GENERAL VOCABULARY

regurgitating   syllables
telegraph   alienated
morale   superficial
methodically

For the general vocabulary terms, use the dictionary to find the definitions. Make flash cards. Write the word along with a sentence that you've composed on one side, and write the definition on the other side. When you can spell, define, and use a word, place its card to the side. This way, you can isolate your problem areas. Even though flash cards might sound elementary, they work.

THINGS TO REMEMBER

Supply the answer to each of the following questions based on the information given in the chapter. Be ready to defend your answers by supplying the page number for each answer.

1. The speed at which you speak is known as your speaking _____.
2. The highs and lows, the notes, that your voice hits while you speak is known as your speaking _____.
3. Presidents often use the _____ method of delivery to make sure that they don't make an error in their content.

4. The method of speaking that is referred to as "not rehearsed" is _____.
5. What specific parts of the body are used in the gesture zone?
6. When you look at someone in the audience while you are speaking, it is a good idea to use _____ eye contact.
7. When you actually take steps in a speech presentation, you are using _____ movement.
8. The crispness and distinctness of your words show that you have good _____.
9. Proxemics involves a sense of how much _____ there is between you and your audience.

Matching: Supply the correct letter.

1. Type of delivery that combines the use of notes with the ability to use words and ideas on the spot.
2. Not using emphasis or varying pitch and rate results in this.
3. French king with a high-pitched voice.
4. Wrote *The American Crisis*.
5. Loudness or softness of the voice.

a. Charlemagne
b. extemporaneous
c. impromptu
d. rate
e. monotone
f. articulation
g. volume
h. Paine
i. Rooney
j. pitch

THINGS TO DO

1. When you evaluate someone's speaking, you use a *critique sheet* to identify what the person did correctly and what he or she needs to continue to work on. Construct your own critique sheet. Include all of the specifics discussed in the chapter under the main headings "Using the Voice," "Using the Body," and "Using the Face." List these specifics down the side of a sheet of paper. Now make three columns that read "excellent," "adequate," and "needs improvement." When each person speaks, you can simply place a check in the appropriate column for each specific delivery item. Every item should receive some type of check. This lets the speaker know how he or she did and what to work hardest on for future speeches. Your teacher might give you some other items to include on your critique sheet. Use the critique sheets when evaluating your

REVIEW AND ENRICHMENT

Continued

own speech and when evaluating the speeches of others.

2. Make a voice chart or graph. Write a paragraph on a topic about which you feel strongly. Now give it orally. Plot on a chart or graph where your voice moves. Does your pitch go up? Does it go down? Is there variety? Are you using all of your pitch range? If not, you are not totally delivering your message to your audience. A tape

recorder is an excellent aid for this exercise.

3. Make an educational video of students walking in the hallway, at a dance, or at some other type of gathering. Take note of how their voices and body movements work together as they talk to each other. Pay attention to their nonverbal communication, also. What did you learn? List your top five observations.

THINGS TO TALK ABOUT

1. An effective delivery depends on all of the parts working together. Why is cooperation so important for any success? How can even little things prove vital for success? Give some specific examples. How does this relate to our democratic system of government and the role of the individual citizen?

2. How does the spoken message differ from the written message? What are the advantages and disadvantages of each? What is the advantage that verbal emphasis gives to the speaker? What about eye contact? Is it possible for your words to be saying one thing while your eyes say something else? Talk about instances when this might be the case.

3. You have probably heard the phrase "the thrill of victory and the agony of defeat," popularized on a television sports program. Defeat often occurs because some athlete couldn't "deliver" under pressure. In athletics or any other area, why do some people often allow pressure to get to them and keep them from delivering their best efforts? What might be on their minds? How does this specifically relate to delivering a speech? What's your constructive advice?

4. Why do you think that, with the public, a good speaker with an excellent delivery has an advantage over a brilliant thinker who has trouble speaking? Give examples of this phenomenon from the news, your school, history, or your community. Does this advantage *always* exist?

5. Robert Frost once said, "Half the world is composed of people who have something to say and can't, and the other half who have nothing to say, and keep on saying it." What does this quotation mean? How does it fit politicians? Media figures? Educators? Other students? Parents? You?

THINGS TO WRITE ABOUT

1. It has been said that our words can inform, but it is our body language that will tell the *real* truth. Research has shown that a jury, in deciding how believable someone's testimony is, will value nonverbal communication more than verbal communication. Why might this be true? Give three ways in which your body can show others that you are not telling the whole truth. In what situations might you do these things?

2. When you effectively deliver, you get the job done. Select one character from literature who, despite the odds, delivered and achieved his or her objective. What individual elements helped him or her succeed? (Be sure to have your teacher or parent approve your literature selection before you write.)

3. Why is impromptu speaking so valuable? Describe two situations in which you might be able to use your impromptu ability. How would your voice, your body, and your face have to work with your words? Write at least one paragraph on this topic.

4. When the Dallas Cowboys were playing the Chicago Bears in the 1991 National Football League playoffs, the Cowboys' quarterback, Steve Beuerlein, repeatedly drew the Bears offsides. One of his linemen later stated, "My man, Steve, he's got that voice." This meant that Beuerlein varied his rate, pitch, and emphasis in calling the signals and thus confused the opposition. (The Cowboys won the game, too.) Write a report on a current or historical figure noted for his or her distinct voice or speaking style. Include key biographical information.

5. You often hear people say, "It doesn't matter how I talk. My friends can understand me." Can you think of two key reasons why everyone needs to learn the skills of correct articulation and pronunciation? Explain each reason. What do we sometimes think about people who slur their words and sentences? Give them one piece of advice that they could apply immediately to correct their problem.

CRITICAL THINKING

1. Nineteenth-century Irish politician Daniel O'Connell said, "A good speech is a good thing, but the *verdict* is the thing." This means that the audience has to determine whether

you've delivered or not. Rate three people, famous or not, whom you consider to have delivered in some fashion. They might have developed an idea, performed an amazing feat, or excelled during a time of crisis. Explain what they did, how they did it (the steps involved), and the impact that their delivery had.

2. A national poll conducted in January 1992 asked people to identify the brightest, most intelligent people. The top five vote-getters (in order) were Carl Sagan, astronomer, author, and director of Cornell's Laboratory for Planetary Studies; Norman Schwarzkopf, retired U.S. Army general, who led the Allied forces against Iraq; William F. Buckley, Jr., the host of the television show "Firing Line"; Bill Moyers, writer and television host; and George Bush, former president of the United States. Discuss the backgrounds of these people with your teacher. What has each delivered to American society? What do these five seem to you to have in common? Do you see any major differences? Finally, why are there no entertainers, sports figures, or Nobel prize winners on the list? Be specific.

3. You've read about the value of delivery in oral communication. There is no question that the method of delivering your words is of paramount importance if you wish to influence your audience. Consider the following words: "I know that one is able to win people far more by the spoken than by the written word, and that every great movement on this globe owes its rise to the great speakers." The author of these words was Adolf Hitler. When can a tremendous delivery be misleading? What do we need to guard against?

4. Name the television personality whose delivery you believe is best at selling a *product*. Name the person in your school or community whose delivery you believe is best at selling an *idea*.

5. Which to you is of greater value in a speech, content or delivery? Be specific. Feel free to both compare and contrast.

RELATED SPEECH TOPICS

This chapter has shown how the best speaking occurs when all of the parts work well together. With that in mind, examine these possible speaking topics.

The system of checks and balances used by the three branches of our government: executive, legislative, and judicial

Cooperative education or team teaching

The United Nations

Adoption or foster children

Any championship sports team

A well-known orchestra

The human brain: Networking

The Japanese educational system

The Olympics

The Special Olympics

CHAPTER 12

Speeches to Inform

"Obviously, a man's judgment cannot be better than the information on which he has based it."

— **Arthur Hays Sulzberger, publisher,** *New York Times*

LEARNING OBJECTIVES

After completing this chapter, you will be able to do the following.

♦ Identify the major types of informative speeches.

♦ Find a good subject for an informative speech, narrow that subject to a manageable topic, and compose a sharply focused thesis.

♦ Develop interesting material for your speech, through the use of anecdotes, quotes, and definitions.

♦ Capture a listener's attention with suspense and humor.

♦ Integrate audio and visual aids into your speech.

CHAPTER OUTLINE

Following are the main sections in this chapter.

I Speeches That Instruct, Inform, and Clarify

II Turning a Subject into a Speech

III Audio and Visual Aids

Student Speech

Chapter Review

NEW SPEECH TERMS

In this chapter, you will learn the meanings of the speech terms listed below.

public lecture
status report
briefing
fireside chat
chalk talk
advance
  organizers
cultural literacy
narrowing
thesis
anecdote

quotation
definition
maps
diagrams
graphs
handouts
overhead
  projector
model
cutaway
demonstrations

GENERAL VOCABULARY

Expanding your general vocabulary will help you become a more effective communicator. Listed below are some words appearing in this chapter that you should make part of your everyday vocabulary.

concise
concrete
distinctions
ambiguous
intuition
demographics
trivia

senile
etymology
simultaneously
chunking
infographic
spontaneity

LOOKING AHEAD

Providing information, a task we perform hundreds of times each day, is one of the most common and important forms of communication. Yet the techniques for providing information efficiently, gracefully, and in a way that will interest the listener are not well known.

In this chapter, you will discover how to better understand your audience's wants and needs, how to find a subject listeners will want to learn about, and how to narrow that subject so that you can make meaningful and well-informed comments about it. You will also discover methods for illustrating your information, both verbally (through examples, descriptions, and definitions) and visually (through photographs, slides, maps, and diagrams). While any informative speech you give must be accurate, you never escape the responsibility of being interesting.

I Speeches That Instruct, Inform, and Clarify

A lot of talking goes on in the world, and a large part of it is done to give instructions, provide facts, or clarify ideas. At home, at school, and at work, many of our communication efforts go toward providing information to others. You give someone directions to study hall and you tell classmates what went on when they missed a day of school. You explain how to do something, what something is, how it works, or how it is used. In short, you provide information to others every day in a hundred different ways.

The complexity of this task may range from giving simple directions (Where's the library?) to explaining a complicated process (What is photosynthesis?). It may be as basic as merely announcing facts (the plans for the next school dance) or as complex as giving an oral report based on

research (the causes of the Gulf War). In each instance, however, your emphasis is on statements of fact. Your goal is to make the listener understand.

Deep down, we are all curious. It's this curiosity that makes informative speeches such favorites with audiences. Further, you will discover that telling people something new is great fun. You will also learn that being knowledgeable about a subject gives you confidence when you speak. Many students find that giving informative speeches is closer to real life than any other speech assignment.

Types of Informative Speeches

As mentioned, we frequently give informal informative speeches to strangers needing directions, classmates making up missed assignments, and so on. In addition, we sometimes find ourselves in more formal situations where we must provide information. Before long, your teacher will probably ask you to give an informative speech to the class. The assignment may ask you to describe an object ("give a speech on the brain"), to explain a process ("give a speech on how to use a 35 mm camera"), or clarify a concept ("give a speech examining the idea of nonviolent resistance"). In the world outside your school, speakers find a variety of opportunities for giving informative talks. They include the following.

1. The public lecture. As a result of a person's special interest or expertise, he or she may be invited to give a **public lecture** to a community group or club. If you take a trip to a national student council convention, for example, you may be invited to give an account of your trip to the local Kiwanis Club; and the Garden Club might be interested in your research on the super-tomato.

2. The status report. Every business and social group must keep up-to-date on its various projects. Periodically, the group will ask a knowledgeable person to give a **status report** indicating what has been accomplished so far and what plans exist for the future. Suppose you are a committee chair for a volunteer organization that works with senior citizens. If your committee is planning a senior prom, you may be asked to give a status report on prom plans to the group as a whole.

3. The briefing. The **briefing** is a very common informative speech used to tell members of a group about changes in policy or procedure.

You may need to tell the members of your swim team about how to order team T-shirts, or perhaps you may want to tell the yearbook staff about a new layout plan.

4. The fireside chat. Named for a famous series of radio broadcasts given by President Franklin Roosevelt, **fireside chats** usually feature a group leader addressing the concerns, worries, and issues of the moment. Your principal may schedule fireside chats with parents to review school goals and policies.

5. The chalk talk. The speaker giving a **chalk talk** relies on a visual aid (the chalkboard). We can easily imagine a coach showing the team how to arrange its defense or a director outlining plans to present a stage play by using this technique.

Other familiar kinds of informative speeches include sermons, graduation speeches (often called *valedictories*), funeral speeches, and public addresses (often given on the occasion of some special event, such as the dedication of a new swimming pool or fitness trail). Many informative speeches are followed by a question-and-answer period, which gives the audience a greater chance to participate.

The Six Cs of Informative Speaking

As an informative speaker, your goal is to shed light on a subject by sharing facts that you have learned through experience, observation, listening, and reading. You can explain, for example, how to bake a cake or describe the drugs being used to fight AIDS or discuss how rock musicians rehearse a stage show. As you do so, you

President Franklin D. Roosevelt, pictured here in 1935, delivered a famous series of radio broadcasts known as "fireside chats." During these broadcasts, Roosevelt spoke informally about possible solutions to the nation's problems.

introduce facts that are new, show old facts in a new way, and clear up misunderstandings. Your main responsibility is to be accurate, but you must also strive to be clear. The response you want from your listeners is basically, "I understand what you said."

More specifically, we can break down the goals of informative speaking into six Cs, the better to remember them. Ask yourself the following questions as you prepare a speech:

1. Is my information so *clear* that everyone will understand?
2. Is my information so *concise* that no one's time will be wasted?
3. Is my information *complete?*
4. Am I confident that my information is absolutely *correct?*

5. Have I provided *concrete* examples so that the audience can see my point?
6. Can I *connect* my information with what I know about my audience?

Let's take a closer look at each of these goals to explore just how they can best be accomplished.

1. Be Clear

Surprising as it may seem, being clear is neither easy nor simple (try explaining how to program a VCR to someone). How can you be sure your listeners will understand what you mean?

Many speakers make a special effort at the beginning of a speech to help listeners by defining a few important words and phrases. These definitions can be as short as a single word or, in a few special cases, as long as the entire speech. This might be the case, for example, in a speech entitled "The HIV Virus." The purpose of a definition is to create some common ground between speaker and listener. In particular, plan to explain any technical terms that may be new to your audience. But keep these terms to a minimum—you can baffle listeners with too many terms that make them scratch their heads.

Another part of being clear is making *distinctions*. We make distinctions by saying what something is and, especially, what it is not. Negative definitions clear your listeners' path of obstacles. You could make a distinction, for example, between the space shuttle's liquid fuel engines, which can be turned off, and its solid fuel booster rockets, which can't. Anticipate situations where your listeners might find your remarks *ambiguous*. Ask yourself as you prepare a speech, "Could this point be taken more than one way?"

One sure way to make distinctions is through the technique of compare and contrast. A comparison explains how two things are similar. A contrast explains the differences. If you wrote a speech about the movies based on Stephen King's books, for example, you might compare them with horror films of the past such as *The Phantom of the Opera* and *Dracula*. You might contrast them with science fiction films like *Aliens* or *Star Trek*. Be sure, however, that what you use for a comparison is familiar to your listeners. If you compare Stephen King to Jules Verne, most high school students will probably follow your comparison. But if you compare King to H. P. Lovecraft, a less well known author, your audience may be lost.

In the final analysis, the value of being clear must be balanced with other, competing values—the value of being concise, for example. If you spend too much time and effort striving for clarity, you may lose your listeners' interest. Audiences often find long explanations boring. Further, if you are too obvious, you lose the element of surprise. A good speaker learns to balance a variety of desirable qualities without emphasizing one at the expense of another.

2. Be Concise

Many government officials these days seem to work for the Department of Redundancy Department, or at least they talk as if they did. Too often, official proclamations seem to make fifty words do the work of ten. Expressions like "Please repeat that again" or "These two are both alike" say the same thing twice. Be conscious of your own language use. Notice whether you say things like "These pens are identically the same" or "She arrived at 8 A.M. this morning." We are all guilty of being too wordy from time to time, but it's a habit that can be broken.

The secret of being concise is to make each word count, and the best way to do that is to use precise and specific language (see Chapter 10 for further details). Using precise language means choosing the word that most accurately fits your meaning. For example, don't say *tree* if you mean *oak*, and don't say *temporarily reassigned* if you mean *fired*. To become more precise, you may need to enlarge your vocabulary. The smaller your vocabulary, the less chance you have of communicating effectively. Take advantage whenever possible of lessons designed to increase your word power.

COMMUNICATION BREAKTHROUGH

Surgeon General's Report on Smoking

Few government reports have had the drama or impact of the one that was delivered on January 11, 1964, in the auditorium of the Old State Department Building in Washington, D.C.

On that Saturday morning, a day carefully chosen to make headlines in all the big Sunday newspapers, Surgeon General Luther Terry told the nation that "cigarette smoking is a health hazard of sufficient importance . . . to warrant appropriate remedial action." In other words, it's time to do something about smoking.

Although the basic facts about smoking and health had been known for some time, the federal government kept shying away from the issue. Not until 1962 did President Kennedy decide that the government should study the problem. Kennedy asked Terry, the nation's chief health officer, to select an expert committee that would decide, simply, "Is smoking bad?"

Terry and ten people chosen from leading universities worked like prairie dogs, burrowing into stacks of research five stories underground in the basement of the National Library of Medicine at Bethesda, Maryland. After fourteen months of study,

the committee issued a 150,000 word report that made the following points.

- ✦ Cigarette smoking "contributes substantially to mortality"—that is, smoking can kill you.
- ✦ Cigarette smokers have a death rate almost eleven times higher than nonsmokers. The sharpest risk from smoking is lung cancer.
- ✦ It helps to quit smoking.

As a result of Terry's report, the major TV networks decided to reexamine their advertising policies. Within a few years, smoking ads had disappeared from the nation's television screens. Later, the government required cigarette makers to carry warning messages on their ads and packages. The number of smokers in the United States began to decline. But it would have been very difficult to change attitudes without Luther Terry's dramatic announcement.

Questions
1. How effective have efforts been to educate students on the dangers of smoking?
2. Can public speakers help change people's behavior?

3. Be Complete

No speech can be complete in the sense of covering all the possible material. You can, however, create a sense of completion in the minds of the audience by raising certain expectations and then satisfying them. Tell the audience you have three major points. When you say "first," they

know you are beginning, and when you say "third," they know you've reached the end. They won't expect a fourth or fifth point even though they realize you haven't covered the subject as thoroughly as possible.

Statements that forecast what the audience can expect are called **advance organizers.** If you say to your audience, for

An informative speaker should be clear, concise, complete, correct, and concrete, and should connect with the audience.

example, "I'm now going to present the three reasons local officials have tried to censor rap music," the audience is set to listen for three different chunks of information. If you introduce each reason with a reinforcing statement, such as "Now let's take a look at the first cause," the audience is reminded of the structure of your speech. When an audience perceives that your speech has a plan and can begin to recognize pieces of that plan as a recurring pattern, they will feel more satisfied when you finish speaking.

Working from a plan forces you to put your information in order. Clearly, some information is more important than other information. If you fail to distinguish major points from minor ones, the listener must try to remember everything and hope to sort things out later. Since no one

can do this, a great deal of the information will be forgotten. This is one of the reasons so many students have trouble taking notes. They assume that everything a teacher says is equally important. As a result, their notes look like a hodgepodge of large concepts and tiny details. In contrast, when listeners have a sense of what to expect, that pattern helps them to separate more important ideas from less important ones. As a result, not only do they remember more, but they remember what the speaker believes is most important.

4. Be Correct

There is no substitute for being accurate. Checking and double-checking the accuracy of the information you present goes right to the heart of your credibility. One of the best ways to convince an audience that your information deserves their attention is to tell where you found it. As in any communication, when you use ideas that are not your own, you should indicate the source of your material. Writers can do this with footnotes, but speakers need a more subtle technique.

Normally, you include the identity of your sources in your speech. These brief identifications usually come at the end (but may also come at the beginning) of the information itself. For example, you might say, "The verdict in the subway shooting trial was an outrage to justice, according to an editorial writer in this morning's paper," or "In an article in the February 27 issue of *U.S. News*, we read that cheating on standardized tests is widespread."

You don't need to use all the information that would appear in a bibliographical citation. In fact, it would be a poor idea to do so. Usually, the name of an author or the name of a magazine, newspaper, television show, or movie is sufficient. An inquisitive listener can catch you after the speech to gain a complete rundown of your sources.

5. Be Concrete

Another valuable technique for making an informative speech effective is to be concrete. Focus on the immediate and the actual. Instead of talking in abstractions, talk in terms of people, places, and things. Individual cases are far more interesting than generalities.

Don't talk about candy if you can talk about Reese's Pieces. Plan your speech on the women's movement around a particular person, perhaps Gloria Steinem. Focus your speech on new filmmakers by concentrating on one, like Spike Lee.

A concrete example helps listeners get a mental picture of what you mean. Let's suppose that you have decided to make a general point like this: "Most accidents happen at home." So far, so good, but at this point the audience has only a vague idea of what you mean. The careful speaker immediately supports every general statement with an example: "Kerry Shea, a fourteen-year-old, said she 'just lost control' of her toothbrush and swallowed it. 'I was brushing the back of my tongue,' she added, 'because I saw on TV that it helps to get a lot of sugar that way, when the toothbrush slipped and I swallowed it.'"

Concrete examples contain physical details. If you were doing a speech on teen crime and needed a concrete example, you could use the case of the New York City transit system. Kids there were caught stealing subway tokens by sucking them

out of turnstile slots. According to one official, some kids were making fifty to a hundred dollars a day. This example has great details—subway tokens, turnstiles, and teens performing weird physical stunts.

Sometimes you may find that a series of short examples works best to support your main point. At other times, a long storylike example may be what you need. In any event, you should never let a general statement stand alone without a supporting example.

6. Connect

The last C, connect, requires you to analyze the people who will be in your audience. This may be difficult because most of us tend to see the world from a single point of view—our own. Without ever meaning to, we become prisoners of our own perspective; we have little awareness of what another person is thinking or feeling. With a little extra effort, however, we can learn to imagine how the world looks to someone else. In this case, we can imagine what it would be like to hear our own speech. The more we can predict how an audience will interpret what we say, the better we will be able to communicate.

If you are speaking to classmates, you already have a number of insights into their backgrounds and attitudes. Think how you would react if you heard your speech for the first time—would it strike you as interesting, informative, and up-to-date? Or dull and old hat? Your own *intuition* can help guide you as you prepare a speech for a group of peers.

You can probably make a good guess, for example, about what your classmates know and don't know. Such guesses will help you avoid the mistake of delivering a speech on how to water ski to a classroom full of experts on the subject. If the audience knows quite a bit about your subject, find a new angle to highlight some less well-known aspect of it.

Of course, you sometimes need to prepare a speech for a general audience—an audience of parents, community members, or other adults—an audience you don't know well. You can probably learn some things about the audience by asking the person who invited you to speak. But for the most part, you must depend on educated guesses to predict what kind of people are in the audience and what they have in common.

You can make some assumptions about an audience by studying their *demographics,* that is, their social, economic, and cultural characteristics. Will the members of the audience, for example, tend to come from the same neighborhood, be about the same age, or have similar political opinions? You may wish to consider the following checklist when you think about the audience you will be facing:

1. How many people of what age and what sex will be present?
2. What are their interests, attitudes, and beliefs?
3. What do they know about the subject?
4. What is their attitude toward it?

Generally speaking, you may assume that adult audiences have what is called *cultural literacy.* **Cultural literacy** describes the information that an average American citizen can be expected to know. The average listener should know that Columbus sailed in 1492 and that Columbus is the capital of Ohio, for example, but not that *Goodbye, Columbus* is a book by Philip Roth. You won't need to explain a refer-

INSTANT IMPACT

Being Brief

Brevity, Shakespeare told us, is the soul of wit. Unfortunately, we don't always take his advice to heart. Audiences appreciate speakers who get to the point quickly. Don't be like the speaker who told his listeners, "I've been asked to speak for thirty minutes. I don't have enough material to fill that time so I'll talk for ten minutes and make it seem like thirty."

One of the most popular informative speeches given on a regular basis is the president's inaugural address. On a January day following each election, the nation's leader outlines a vision for the future. The shortest inaugural address in history was the first—George Washington spoke just a few minutes, and his speech was a bare 135 words. The longest address was a fatal one. William Henry Harrison delivered a two-hour 9,000 word speech in 1841, straight into the teeth of a freezing wind. Harrison came down with a cold the following day and died a month later of pneumonia. Take the hint.

ence to the Supreme Court or the Supremes, but you will have to explain the term *supremacist.*

Simply put, sensitivity to the audience is one of the keys to successful communication. While you can't choose your audience, you can choose a speech to fit a particular audience. Knowledge of the audience can help you fine-tune your speech as you make changes, both large and small, to suit a specific group of listeners. For more information on audience analysis, see Chapter 13 on persuasive speeches.

TAKING CHARGE

1. Explain how your approach would change if you were to give a speech on the effects of cigarette smoking to five different audiences: classmates, parents, people between the ages of twenty and twenty-five, retired people, and elementary-school children.
2. Using the same five audiences as above, suggest three topics best suited to each.
3. Develop a survey to measure attitudes toward a variety of possible speech topics (the media, government, the entertainment industry), and give the survey to several classes in your school. Tabulate and analyze the results. Discuss what these results tell you about potential listeners.

II Turning a Subject into a Speech

Almost without exception, students' biggest gripe about giving speeches is "I don't know what to talk about." Finding an interesting and appropriate subject is always a challenge, but never more so than with an informative speech.

Find a Subject

Knowledge is the stuff from which new ideas are made. But knowledge alone won't write your speech. Anyone can compile a list of facts, but it takes an alert mind to connect those facts.

Suppose you decide to do some research for a speech on national holidays. You gather a number of facts, but they seem to have nothing to do with each other. Now think of those facts as dots in a dot-to-dot puzzle. Unfortunately, no one

> "Discovery consists of looking at the same thing as everyone else and thinking something different."
>
> **Albert Szent-Gyorgyi**

has numbered the dots. You have to do that for yourself. "Discovery," noted the Nobel-Prize-winning physician Albert Szent-Gyorgyi, "consists of looking at the same thing as everyone else and thinking something different."

The key to inventing good speech topics is having a creative mind. What matters is not so much what knowledge you have (although that's important, of course) but what you do with what you know. Being creative with knowledge means using crazy, foolish, and impractical ideas as stepping stones toward more realistic ones. It means breaking the rules occasionally and looking for ideas in unusual places. It means changing your point of view to look at the subject in a new way.

Play with metaphors. Metaphors are comparisons between unlike things. You might describe life as an elevator—it has its ups and downs, but what you hate are the jerks. Try making an unusual comparison in your speech. You could compare the breakup of the Soviet Union with the breakup of a relationship, for example, or national elections with family discussions.

Creative thinking frees us from dull routine. When we stay on our old thought paths, we probably won't find fresh ways of looking at something. We tend not to ask new questions about old ideas. But if we take a creative approach, we are much more likely to "think differently." And thinking differently is part of inventing good speech topics.

Where, then, can we look for topics, assuming we have the right attitude?

Personal Experience

You already have a lifetime of experience, and it can be a major source of information. No matter what the topic, firsthand knowledge contributes unique and original information. Even if your own knowledge is incomplete, it provides a good starting point for further research.

You are almost certainly an expert on something—whether it's changing the points and plugs on a car or baking chocolate chip cookies. Think small. Find an area of interest where you have considerable experience—something you collect, for example. Perhaps you have a ferret for a pet, perform as a magician for birthday parties, or volunteer at the local hospital. Anything you do often and do well is a likely topic for an infor-

Personal talents and interests can make good speech topics.

mative speech because you can speak from experience. That gives you instant credibility.

Observations

Another place to look for speech topics is your immediate environment. Everything you read may turn out to be usable information. Whenever you find a scrap of unusual information, file it. You might read, for example, that a newspaper carrier delivering the *Los Angeles Times* heaved a copy of the Sunday paper toward the front lawn of a Hollywood mansion. The paper hit a pet dog, dozing on the porch, and killed it. A subsequent report by the newspaper industry noted that, at an average of 2.3 pounds per day, the *Times* is the heaviest newspaper in the world. Such an item could make a nice lead-in for a speech on the mass media and its ability to overwhelm us.

You might also take the opportunity to be a "participant observer." We all attend meetings, sports events, and public performances. What you see and hear during these events may prove to be just what you need for an interesting speech.

Suppose, for example, that the local auditorium is sponsoring a cat show. Perhaps you could attend and research a speech on strange hobbies. What would possess a person to spend hours every day grooming a cat? A branch bank may hold an open house. What better chance to get the lowdown on checking accounts for teens? You can turn almost anything that happens in your neighborhood into an effective informative speech, given the right frame of mind.

Surveys

Thanks to our consumer-driven economy, we have become survey-happy. Almost everyone, it seems, wants your opinion. Were you happy with the mechanic who changed your oil? Have you tried the new cereal with nuts, raisins, and tree bark? Did the plumber communicate effectively when he fixed the leak in your sink? Surveys—whether by phone or in person—are used increasingly by businesses and political groups. Luckily, all these surveys provide new sources of information and new ideas for speech topics.

Thanks to a poll sponsored by the Corporation for Public Broadcasting, for example, we now have a good idea of what teens have on their minds. America's school-aged kids, we learn, are more worried about getting AIDS than about getting into college. Their single greatest worry (58 percent, according to the poll) is about making money as adults. Other big worries include pollution and the environment (56 percent), getting AIDS (48 percent), not being successful (47 percent), not getting into college (46 percent), and having to fight a war (44 percent). Certainly not every speech needs to push a listener's panic button, but topics related to listeners' interests are likely to be successful.

Thus, another way to find a good speech topic is to consider your listeners' interests and concerns. You can discover those through polls and surveys, of course, but you can also find out by less scientific means. Listen to the subjects that come up again and again in your conversations. Be alert to news events, trends in movies and television, prominent personalities, and interesting ideas that crop up in your classes. Clever speeches grow from the smallest of insights—sometimes a little-known scientific fact or discovery will lead to a fascinating speech.

Narrow Your Subject

Finding a subject is only half the battle in creating an effective informative speech. A subject is a broad area of knowledge, such as romantic literature, astronomy, or soccer. A topic is one particular aspect of a subject. Once you have chosen a general area, you must cut your subject down to size, **narrowing** it to manageable proportions. You can't expect to cover every aspect of your subject in a ten-minute speech, so you have to make some choices about what to include.

Suppose, for example, that you decide to speak about America's westward expansion. You can whittle that enormous

The results of a survey determining listeners' interests and concerns can be a source of possible speech topics.

subject down by confining it within certain boundaries. You could start by limiting your topic geographically, to a certain area of the West, say, California. Then you could limit your subject to a particular time, perhaps 1849, when the gold rush took place.

The following guidelines may help you narrow your subject down to manageable size:

1. Limit your subject in time. A speech on the high cost of presidential elections could be limited to just one month of the 1992 campaign.

2. Limit your subject in space. In a speech on recycling efforts, avoid state or national statistics and concentrate on efforts in your own community.

3. Limit your subject in extent. Instead of describing all the elements

of a well-balanced diet, tackle just one. Speak about how eating fiber affects health, for example.

4. Limit your subject using the principle of divide and conquer. Just when you think you have a manageable topic, try dividing it in half. Let's say you have narrowed your original idea—the world's most famous fictional detectives— to the career of Sherlock Holmes. Now narrow that topic down again: Focus only on Holmes's uncanny sense of smell.

The process of limiting your subject is helpful in several ways. First, it forces you to say more about less; second, it helps you focus your research; and third, it helps you decide what belongs in your speech and what does not. Every speaker can find many tempting pieces of material—funny stories, clever quotes, odd bits of history—but the problem of choosing what to keep is critical, especially when you may be limited to a five-minute speech or less. Sometimes even the most interesting material must be left out to keep your speech focused and on track.

State Your Thesis

Once you have a manageable topic—the California gold rush, for the sake of discussion—you've made great progress, but you're not out of the woods. The next step in turning an idea into a speech requires that you make a positive statement about your topic, a statement often called a **thesis** or sometimes a "statement of purpose."

In your research on the California gold rush, for example, you learn that the employee of a pioneer named John Sutter discovered large nuggets of gold near Sutter's mill. As news of the discovery spread, thousands of adventurers rushed to the area to stake their claims. These "forty-niners" helped boost California's population from about 15,000 to more than 100,000 in less than a year, and their free spending turned San Francisco into a flourishing city.

This research leads you to develop the thesis for your speech: "The California gold rush sparked the development of the city of San Francisco." Now you've got something you can hang your hat on. A thesis should take the form of a declarative sentence with a subject and a verb, and it should convey in clear language the most important message of your speech. Remember that the more you sweat working out a sensible thesis in advance, the less you'll have to sweat once you begin to speak.

Some sample topics and thesis statements might include:

Topics	Thesis
Teenagers and fads	The slang teenagers use often comes from popular movies, such as *Wayne's World*.
Healthy lifestyles	Eating five servings of fruits and vegetables each day can dramatically reduce your chances of getting cancer.
Famous musicians	Beethoven's hearing loss may actually have helped him compose music.

Support Your Thesis

Once you have a topic and a thesis, you can turn to the matter of developing your support. For the sake of argument, we will assume that you have already completed your research. The problem at hand is how to use material that you have uncovered to support your thesis. "I am rather like a mosquito in a nudist camp," said one writer. "I know what I ought to do, but I don't know where to begin." Let's look first at the kinds of material your research has turned up and then at how you can use that material to bring your speech to life.

Facts

"Just the facts, ma'am," says Sergeant Joe Friday, a policeman on the old television show "Dragnet," and that's the attitude many of your listeners may take. Information is built on a network of facts—those small statements about peo-

> ❝ "Just the facts, ma'am."
>
> ## Joe Friday

ple, events, and other phenomena that make games like Trivial Pursuit possible.

William Shakespeare, for example, had been dead seven years before his plays were published. That statement is a fact; you can look it up. At his death, Shakespeare left just one thing to his wife: his second-best bed, a decision that has amused historians ever since. Neither of these statements may throw much light on Shakespeare's life or career, but they are both facts because they can be verified. Their accuracy can be determined by anyone with access to the right documents.

All facts are true; *actual facts, real facts,* and *true facts* are redundant phrases. If a thing is not true, it is not a fact. Facts are the basic building blocks of a speech—they support everything you say. Without them, an informative speech is just a house of cards, ready to topple at the slightest breeze. But some facts are more important than others. The fact that the juice of one lemon, if diluted thinly enough, could cover the state of Oregon is both true and meaningless. The world is full of facts. The challenge is to make facts count for more than mere *trivia*.

Facts should be used to support ideas. Suppose you wish to prepare a speech on the life of Marie Curie, one of the world's greatest scientists. The thesis of your speech is that Curie overcame many dis-

---

INSTANT IMPACT

Library Backlog

You may doubt whether anyone has a bigger mess than you do in your bedroom, but whatever clutter you've got pales in comparison with the world's largest library. At last count, the Library of Congress had 36 million items—maps, manuscripts, motion pictures, photographs, music scores, sound recordings, and books—in storage, waiting for the day sometime in the distant future when they will be made available to the public.

Most of the material is stored in a huge warehouse in Landover, Maryland, a thirty-minute drive from Washington, D.C., and all of it awaits inspection and classification so that the public can find it. Meanwhile, four million new items pour into the library every year.

Library backlogs are "a common condition in the age of the information explosion," says Michael Shelley of the library staff. "We've focused a great deal of attention on this."

Congress has ordered the library to cut the mountain of backlogged material to 8 million items by the turn of the century, but only time will tell if the nation can clean out its attic sooner than you can clean up your room.

---

advantages and achieved success at great personal sacrifice. To convince the audience that your thesis is sound, you present the following facts (among many others):

◆ As a young student at the University of Paris, Curie lived on sixty cents a day.

- She could afford to buy only two sacks of coal for the winter and spent many nights shivering under towels, pillow cases, extra clothing, and any other scraps she could find.

- The science community doubted her discovery of a new element, radium, and challenged her to prove her claim.

- After four years of struggle, she and her husband produced one decigram of radium (about half the size of a small pea) by boiling down and refining eight tons of ore.

- Despite an opportunity to patent a radiation treatment for cancer, Curie refused to accept any money for her discovery. "It would be contrary to the scientific spirit," she said.

Taken together, these facts help convince the audience that you know what you're talking about.

Statistics are a special kind of fact—a fact expressed in numbers—and they can be particularly difficult for listeners to grasp. "It is now proved beyond doubt," noted the author Fletcher Knebel, "that smoking is one of the leading causes of statistics." If you use numbers, round off or approximate wherever possible. Avoid saying "two hundred and ninety-six point five," for example, if you can accomplish your purpose by saying "about three hundred."

Everyone Loves a Story

Although facts are the backbone of an informative speech, they are not the only kind of material you can use. Another form of information, and one of the most appealing, is the **anecdote.** An anecdote is simply a short story that illustrates a point. Although people often think of anecdotes as humorous, they can also be sad or touching.

Anecdotes can be easily located in a variety of resources, including *The Little, Brown Book of Anecdotes* (edited by Clifton Fadiman). In this volume, you will find stories like these:

- Hank Aaron, baseball's greatest home-run hitter, came to the plate in the 1957 World Series. The catcher, Yogi Berra, noticed that Aaron's bat was turned the wrong way. "Turn it around," Yogi said, "so you can see the trademark." Aaron never moved his gaze from the pitcher, but said without a moment's hesitation: "Didn't come up here to read. Came up here to hit."

Anecdotes can be used in an informative speech to prove a point. You can use a personal anecdote or one involving a famous person, like Johnny Carson.

COMMUNICATION		BREAKDOWN

When Information Isn't Enough

Sometimes information isn't enough to solve a problem. When Judge Clarence Thomas was nominated to the Supreme Court by President Bush in 1991, he couldn't have known that his confirmation hearings would cause a national debate over how men and women treat each other in the workplace.

During the hearings, Anita Hill, an Oklahoma University law professor who had once worked for Thomas, came forward to state that Thomas had sexually harassed her. Hill said that Thomas had repeatedly asked her out for dates and had made suggestive remarks.

Thomas denied the allegations and insisted that he was sensitive to how any person, regardless of race or sex, was treated on the job.

The result of this disagreement became a high-stakes tug of war with both Hill and Thomas trying to convince millions of American TV viewers and one hundred U.S. senators that they had been greatly victimized.

One television expert, S. Robert Lichter, said that in the camera's eye, Thomas and Hill were equally believable. "In trials by media, we've gotten used to clear winners and losers," Lichter said. "I'm not seeing that here. I'm seeing both sides doing a good job."

Thomas, who spoke first, was forceful and eloquent, casting himself as the victim of a witch hunt. Hill, whose voice trembled but whose poise never cracked, seemed equally convincing when she gave a detailed account of the offenses she said Thomas had committed.

In the end, the Senate narrowly approved Thomas's nomination to the Supreme Court (a lifetime job), never directly answering the question of who was telling the truth.

Source: Lichter was quoted in the Los Angeles Times.

Question

In case of conflicting stories, how can we determine whether one set of facts is more accurate than another?

✦ Johnny Carson, long-time host of a television talk show, was asked by a reporter once what he would like his epitaph to be. "I'll be right back," was Carson's reply.

✦ Sophocles, the Greek dramatist, was brought before a court of law at the age of 89 by his son. The son, who wanted to have his father declared *senile*, was afraid that Sophocles would leave him out of his will. To prove his soundness of mind, the aging playwright read passages from his new play, which had not yet been performed. The judges dismissed the case.

Anecdotes spice up a speech. The Aaron anecdote could be used to illustrate a speech on concentration, the Carson anecdote to illustrate how television has changed our daily habits, and the Sophocles anecdote to illustrate how we treat senior citizens. People love to hear stories because stories dramatize ideas and situations. Stories are also far more memorable than any other kind of information. Carefully chosen, one or two anecdotes can give your speech the pizzazz it needs, but use caution. Keep in mind that anecdotes can also distract listeners from your main point and entertain more than they inform.

Quotable Quotes

Another form of information that you can use to develop your speech is the **quotation.** Again, resources are relatively easy to find. *Bartlett's Book of Quotations* is undoubtedly the most famous, but there are other, more lighthearted books that might help. One such book is *Morrow's Contemporary Quotations,* where you can find gems like these:

◆ "The first problem for all of us, men and women, is not to learn, but to unlearn."—Gloria Steinem, feminist

◆ "Awopbopaloobopalopbamboom!"—Little Richard, rock star

◆ "I love Mickey Mouse more than any woman I've ever known."—Walt Disney, animator

Quotations can be used more freely than anecdotes because they are much briefer. They also help add credibility to your speech. "Wow," your listeners may think, "Abraham Lincoln agrees with this speaker!" Quotations also have their drawbacks. If you quote someone unfamiliar to your listeners, they may become confused. Quotations can be overused. You may find that the speech is no longer yours, but belongs instead to all those you are quoting. Used wisely, though, quotations tend to make audiences think you are both well read and believable.

Keep in mind that if you use a direct quotation you are obligated to credit the source. Using a quotation without indicating where it comes from is plagiarism.

Defining Your Terms

A fourth kind of information to use in developing your speech is the **definition.** Sometimes simply defining a term is the best way to get an audience headed in the right direction. You may, for example, wish to use a familiar word in a special way. "I am using the word *dude* not in the sense of a would-be cowboy," you might explain, "but in the sense of a 'hip buddy,' the kind of person who says 'totally' for true and 'not even' for false."

You may also wish to trace the history of a word for your listeners. This tactic might help them understand why your choice of a particular word is accurate. Etymological information (*etymology* means the origins of words) can sometimes help correct mistaken ideas. Cinderella's glass slipper, for example, is not glass at all in the original version. In the older, French version of the story, Cinderella wears a *pantoufle en vair* ("a slipper of fur"), but a translator apparently confused *en vair* with *en verre* (meaning "of glass"). Now all English-speaking people think Cinderella wore a glass slipper (rather uncomfortable, don't you think?).

The most complete guide to the history of words and their evolving definitions is the *Oxford English Dictionary* (actually not one book but a twenty-volume set with over 500,000 entries). An enormous resource, this dictionary will test your patience, but the results may be worth the effort. You can discover, for example, that *quarry*, which we would use as a synonym for *prey* (the hunters sought their *quarry*), was first used to describe the parts of a deer that were given to the hounds after a hunt. The history of a word can itself become the topic of an informative speech.

Descriptions

Descriptions, the final form of information we will discuss here, can put a lasting picture in the listener's mind. Suppose you want to tell an audience about the difference between an alligator and a crocodile. You could explain their physical features, of course, but why not try a fresh twist? Consider this "personalized" description:

> Alligators have rounded snouts and crocodiles have pointed ones, though if your leg is caught in either, you probably won't appreciate the difference. If the jaws are completely closed around your leg, you might look on either side of the snout to see whether a lower tooth is jutting outside the upper lip. If it is, the creature is a croc.

Descriptions can help you emphasize certain aspects of your topic. They can bring to life an interesting character or create a vivid impression of a particular place. Practice writing descriptions and then try including them in your speeches.

Begin and End Well

We won't spend much time here discussing how to organize a speech because that topic is covered in Chapter 8. But we will examine a few strategies for beginning and ending an informative speech. Introductions typically take no more than 5 or 10 percent of the speech. Similarly, a conclusion is also brief—usually about 5 percent of the entire speech. Nevertheless, these two parts have an importance out of all proportion to their size.

Starting Out

The introduction helps establish your credibility and sets the stage for your thesis, but first it must gain your listeners' attention. Many speakers gain attention through humor. You have almost certainly heard a speaker begin with a joke or two before getting down to the meat of the speech. You may also have wondered whether the jokes had anything to do with the rest of the speech. Unfortunately, they often don't. For humor to be truly effective in gaining an audience's attention—and more importantly, for preparing listeners to be receptive to your message—it must support or illuminate the rest of what you have to say.

Suppose you plan to give a speech on defensive driving. You might begin by telling the audience some of the more preposterous explanations drivers have given to excuse their behavior:

◆ "My car was legally parked as it backed into the other vehicle."

◆ "The guy was all over the road; I had to swerve a number of times before I hit him."

◆ "A pedestrian hit me, and went under my car."

Source: Files of State Farm Insurance.

The excuses should get you a few laughs, but they also suggest your major point: that most people are unaware of their own bad driving habits.

COMMUNICATION WORKS

Jesse Myles, State Race Equity Director

It's often been said that you should enjoy what you do. Jesse Myles, the race equity director for the Nebraska Department of Education, says that enjoyment is the key to giving speeches. He also feels that "you have to believe in what you're doing."

As an equity officer, Myles helps schools deal with multicultural issues and desegration. He leads many workshops and seminars where he gives speeches on racism. Once in a while, he gets heckled by the audience.

"Sometimes I might say or do something that is offensive to some people," he says. When those people, in turn, act maliciously toward him, Myles says, "You have to know where they're coming from, acknowledge, and debate it."

No one enjoys having to put up with hostility, but Myles has found that heckling can sometimes lead to progress. It can produce "attitudinal changes, getting people to examine themselves."

The audience always has a major impact on what Myles says. "I look at how familiar they are with the subject matter. When I speak to parents and then students on the same subject, I won't say the same thing. When I talk on prejudice and racism, I base it on what I think the audience knows."

Myles adds, however, that you shouldn't pick a topic based on what you think the audience will like. The important thing is to have a valuable message.

"I really want people to understand what I'm saying."

If humor doesn't come naturally to you, don't force yourself to tell a joke. It is far worse to massacre a good joke with a weak delivery or bad timing than to use a different approach. Try, instead, to find some common ground with the audience. Begin by speaking about something that you share with the audience—refer to the game last Friday or an unusual substitute teacher. If you speak to an adult audience outside the school, find subjects of com-mon interest—local sports teams or current events—to use as openers.

A third technique for beginning an informative speech is to use a question. By asking a rhetorical question—one that listeners answer in their heads, not with their voices—you can involve audience members in the problem. "Where do ideas come from?" you might ask, not expecting the audience to respond verbally but hoping that their mental wheels will start turning. Questions appear to work especially well with short speeches where the audience can keep your question in mind throughout your talk.

Other techniques for beginning a speech include using an interesting quotation, describing an unusual personal experience, or making a startling statement. If you suspect that your audience may not be interested in your topic, at least at first, try some suspense. Make them wonder "What is she leading to?" In any event, make sure that the opening you choose is comfortable for your personality and suitable for your topic.

Finishing Up

The conclusion offers you one last chance to hit home with your main message. Too many speakers either end their speeches abruptly or ramble on aimlessly until they exhaust both the topic and the audience. A poor conclusion—or no conclusion at all—can destroy much of the impact of an otherwise effective speech. Even though a conclusion is a relatively short part of the speech, it is worth the time and effort to make it effective.

Your conclusion should almost always include a summary of the main points of the speech. Here, you repeat your major points, but in different words. For example, a speaker who began with the statement "The French don't know how to camp" ended with this: "We Americans should instruct our French cousins in the fine art of camping, for their vacation's sake." Because you want your conclusion to be interesting, however, you may want to add something to give it greater impact—a lively story or an interesting quotation, for example.

You signal the audience that you are reaching the end of your speech by both verbal and nonverbal cues. Many speakers use words like *in conclusion*, *finally*, or *let me leave you with this*. Often a speaker's tone becomes larger, grander, or more sweeping as he launches into his conclusion. These verbal cues should only echo, however, what the listeners already know if they have been following the structure of your speech. Nonverbally, you can signal the listeners that the end is near by subtle changes in your delivery. You can move a few steps, change position, increase your volume, or step up the pace.

One last technique worth mentioning gives listeners a psychological sense that the speech is over. They feel it in their bones, exactly the kind of feeling you get in a theater when you know a movie is over *before* the credits begin to roll. But what is it that gives you that feeling? In many cases, you feel that way because you realize that the speech (or movie) had returned to the place where it began. As the poet T. S. Eliot wrote, "The end of all our exploring will be to arrive where we started and know the place for the first time."

Suppose, for example, that you began a speech on how memory works with a story about your grandmother. You spoke of how she could remember events that happened many years ago much more vividly than those that happened yesterday. In your conclusion, you return to your grandmother's story by showing that for her, time is like a great meadow where people and events spanning eighty years exist *simultaneously* and peacefully together. The listener hears an echo of your beginning and knows that the speech has come full circle.

TAKING CHARGE

1. Narrow the following subjects into speech topics. Then write a reasonable thesis for each:

   ◆ rain forest
   ◆ indoor sports
   ◆ heroes and heroines
   ◆ scientific discoveries
   ◆ household chores

2. Find an anecdote related to a famous person of your choice.
3. Take a technical subject, like how a TV works, and define five terms related to that topic.

III   Audio and Visual Aids

"You can't really appreciate the thrilling beauty of these South American aardvarks unless you can see and hear them in their natural surroundings." Surprisingly, however, the speaker of these words is stuck in a classroom in Billings, Montana, nowhere near the Amazon jungle. Is there a way this speaker can bring his audience nearer the subject? There is, indeed. "Luckily," the speaker continues, "I have brought with me some slides I took in Brazil, and I've also brought some on-the-spot recordings of the noises the aardvarks make."

When you can't bring the real thing to your audience (in other words, nearly all the time), you can arrange the next best thing. In the aardvark example, a speaker brought both pictures and sound to an audience. Such material is referred to as *visual and audio aids.* Visual aids include anything the audience can see—photographs, cartoons, color slides, videotapes, posters, transparencies, or chalk drawings. Audio aids include anything the audience can hear—music, sound effects, or recorded conversations. The use of these devices can sometimes spell the difference between a ho-hum and a humdinger of a speech.

Visual aids, especially, can help a speaker make a point because vision is our most dominant sense. Research tells us that we pay twenty-five times as much attention to visual suggestions as we do to audio suggestions. "One seeing," says an old Japanese proverb, "is better than a hundred times telling." Still, every speaker should remember that no matter how powerful or striking her visual aids may be, they are meant to enhance and not replace a well-constructed speech.

Two-Dimensional Visual Aids

Two-dimensional visual aids are any illustrations that can be represented on a flat surface. They include charts, diagrams, maps, drawings, and photographs. These visuals can be conveniently displayed on a classroom chalkboard (either drawn there or held up with tape) or on a flipchart (a large pad of paper mounted on an easel). They can be projected on a screen or held up by hand for the audience to see. If the speaker can show the visual without having to hold it, he will be free to use a pointer to describe particular features.

Photographs, Drawings, and Cartoons

If a picture is worth a thousand words, then using one in your speech can mean a big savings in time. Furthermore, with a photo you can make people see things that you can't easily explain. Using photographs in a speech, however, can be a tricky business. Make sure that you mount them on heavy construction paper or art boards so that they are easy to handle. The photos themselves should be at least 8 by 10 inches (preferably larger), so that the audience can see them easily. As with other visual aids, you should hide or cover the photos until you are ready to use them and then put them out of sight again when you are done.

Drawings are popular visual aids because they are easy to prepare. If you can use a compass and a straightedge, you can draw well enough for most speeches. If the drawing you need is too complicated for you to draw, find an art student who can help. Cartoons, a special kind of drawing, use humor or satire to make a

---

INSTANT IMPACT

Our Mother Tongue

During the 1992 presidential campaign, doctors sent Governor Bill Clinton into quarantine to rest his sore throat. Clinton, like many others in business, education, and entertainment, depends on his voice every day. When he misuses his voice, he can't work. In times of stress and pressure, we all tend to let tension slip into our throat muscles, which tighten and crowd our vocal cords, causing us to sound shrill, raspy, or harsh.

Luckily, there's a cure, and it involves no gargles, salves, or warm-up exercises. If you find that you are straining during a speech, the cause can often be found in your mouth. Too many of us talk with our throats and not with our tongues. Say the following sentence and hold the *l* sounds for a count of three: "Throw the ball over the wall." If you feel your tongue tense up on the *l*, you're straining your throat. Practice saying that sentence until you can do it with a relaxed tongue.

True speaking fluency results from smooth tongue action. You make thirty-one of the thirty-eight sounds in English with your tongue, the other seven with your lips, and none with your jaw. But if you typically open your mouth wide, you'll probably overuse your jaw, drop it toward your throat, and strain your voice. If you clear your throat a lot, if your voice sounds husky or you have a lot of phlegm, don't accept these symptoms as personality traits. They aren't. They are signs of strain and shouldn't be ignored.

point. The editorial page of a newspaper can be a good place to get ideas for your own cartoons.

Graphic Representations

Maps, diagrams, and **graphs** are among the many other two-dimensional visual aids that speakers, particularly in the business world, use with success. Maps are certainly the best way to show a geographical relationship. If you want to show the route of the Appalachian Trail from Georgia to Maine, a map is a necessity.

Diagrams are useful when you want to explain a process. If you want to show how an internal combustion engine works, for example, a diagram might save you time and help your audience achieve a better understanding. Graphs are useful for showing relationships among statistical data, such as the crime rate or the increasing price of comic books. It's hard to wring emotion out of numbers, but you can sometimes give them appeal by turning them into graphic images.

One of the problems you may face with aids like these is the time-consuming process of making them in the first place. Business speakers often have a design staff that can spend weeks preparing a sales chart. Since you don't have that luxury, you must decide whether the time you need to prepare an exciting visual will take too much of the time you need to construct the speech itself. However effective a visual aid might be, it will not hide a weakly written speech.

Fortunately, modern computer graphic arts programs are now available in most schools. You can use programs like Aldus Freehand, SuperPaint, or Adobe Illustrator (to name just a few) to create imaginative and interesting illustrations. Journalists refer to these as *infographics (information + graphics)*, and examples of them can be found in most newspapers and magazines. All these graphic representations should be displayed in the same way as photographs and drawings.

Chalkboard Aids

One of the easiest visual aids to use is a chalkboard. The chief advantage of using a chalkboard is that you can put information up as you need it and can erase material that is no longer needed. Luckily, no one expects blackboard work to be beautiful, so long as the drawing or writing is large and clear. Chalk gives you more flexibility and *spontaneity* than any other kind of visual aid.

Many teachers discourage the use of chalkboards, however, for one important reason: How can you use a chalkboard without turning your back to the audience? Once a speaker turns her back on the audience, more than eye contact is lost. If ever there were an opportunity for the listener's mind to wander, this is it.

With a little forethought, you can overcome this problem. Write out most of what you think you need ahead of time and cover it. Stick to very short messages. If you do write while talking, stand to the side so the audience will focus its attention on the words as they appear. And consider a handy alternative to the chalkboard—the overhead projector, which we will cover shortly.

Handouts

Handouts include any fliers, brochures, or information sheets that you prepare ahead of time and duplicate so that each member of the audience can have a copy.

On the plus side, handouts look professional, and people can take them home after your speech. On the negative side, they can create distractions. It takes time and trouble to distribute handouts, and your audience may study them instead of making eye contact with you. An experienced speaker usually passes out handouts at the beginning of a speech or at the end so as not to interrupt the speech itself.

Projections

Speakers can use a variety of devices to project a visual aid on a blank wall or screen. These devices include an **overhead projector** (a simple device that projects and magnifies material from a transparent sheet of plastic) and a slide projector. The overhead projector can be effective even if some lights are left on, while a slide projector requires that the room be completely dark. Other projection devices include a videotape playback machine and a motion picture projector. Motion picture films may be available in your school or local library, but libraries are increasingly stocking up on videotapes which are often cheaper and more convenient to use.

Overhead Projector

A variation on the chalkboard approach is the use of an overhead projector. One advantage of using an overhead is that you can prepare transparencies ahead of time and then lay them on the overhead for viewing. Be sure you become familiar with the projector ahead of time, paying special attention to how to straighten and focus the image.

If you wish to keep some of the image covered, use a large index card that is thick enough to cover the image and heavy enough to stay in place. Try to avoid reading the transparency to your audience. Instead, point out the highlights. Above all, stand out of the way so that the image can be easily seen.

Slides

Color slides are a popular way to illustrate an informative speech because they have a size and vividness unmatched by almost any other visual. Great care must be taken, however, to select only slides that really illustrate the point you wish to make. Many speakers make the mistake of using too many slides and risk boring their listeners. Be sure that the slides you use are sharply focused and have good contrast. A slide that is hard to see is not worth showing.

As valuable as they are, slides have been overused and can easily lull an audience to sleep. Because they have to be used in a darkened room, the slides themselves become the focal point of your speech. Listeners turn their attention from you to the slides, and it may be difficult to get their attention back.

Videotape and Film

The rapid development of easy-to-use camcorders means that you can now create your own videotape to illustrate a speech. Most schools have camcorders or some form of television recording equipment that is available to students. A speech on the fundamentals of pole vaulting, for example, could be improved with video clips of someone actually vaulting.

If your school has a video playback machine that enables you to use special techniques like freeze frame and slow motion, so much the better.

You might also wish to use material that you have recorded from national or local television programs. A speech on the problem of racism in America, for example, could be illustrated by a video clip of a current rap song. Pay close attention to copyright laws to be sure that you do not make illegal use of anything. Often, sponsors permit limited educational use of their programs. Copyright laws do change from time to time, and your teacher will have current information to help you.

Videotapes are so popular and easy to use that many speakers ignore film as a possible visual aid. Nevertheless, most school districts and many public libraries have a wealth of informative films available. If you decide to use a film, be sure you familiarize yourself first with how to operate a projector. In the case of both videotape and film, you should remember that your speech, and not the visual aid, is what counts. Don't think an exciting video can save a dull or poorly researched speech.

Three-Dimensional Visual Aids

Sometimes an actual object—something with height, width, and depth—can make a greater impression than a picture or projection. If you were to give a speech on someone who collected porcelain dolls, for example, showing the audience actual dolls would have much greater appeal than simply using pictures or slides. In some cases, especially with smaller groups, it may even be possible to let the audience handle the objects. If you decide, however, to pass an object among the members of the audience, be aware that you will lose the attention of each listener in turn as he or she examines the object.

Models

Occasionally, an object is too large to bring to a speech. You would have a tough time, for example, wheeling in the space shuttle *Discovery* for a talk on space research. But you could use a scale **model.** A plastic model of the space shuttle, scaled down to perhaps one-twentieth of the actual size, would enable you to show the features and functions of the vehicle in an informative way. Similarly, you could make an inexpensive but useful model of a camera with a large box (to represent the body of the camera) and a piece of tin foil over an opening in the box (to show how the lens and shutter work).

Cutaways

A variation of the model idea is an object called a **cutaway,** which is essentially a model sliced in two. Your model of the space shuttle, for example, may have a removable side panel that would allow the audience to look inside, the better to examine the flight deck or the crew's quarters. A rather grisly form of this idea toured a number of state fairs some years ago. It seems a cow with stomach problems had been fitted with a plastic window in its side, enabling fair-goers to watch the cow's digestive system in action.

Both models and cutaways need to follow the same rules we have discussed for

Using a three-dimensional model can give an informative speech greater impact.

other visual aids. They must be large enough to be seen and clearly relevant to the point under discussion. In addition, the speaker must be sure to practice handling the objects so that he won't drop or fumble them at a crucial moment.

Demonstrations and Sound Recordings

Sometimes, simple **demonstrations** can be effective visual aids. The visual aids for a speech on baking chocolate chip cookies might include a spatula, mixing bowls, cookie sheets, and all the ingredients. It's one thing to talk about preparing dough and another to see it happen. Your creativity and imagination will serve you well in determining when a demonstration is appropriate.

Audiotapes and records have something in common with film and videotape, but they can perhaps more conveniently be grouped with demonstrations. You may wish to use an audiotape in a speech on animal communication, for example, to demonstrate the sounds whales make. An audiotape of informal conversation might be helpful in a speech on regional dialects. If you use an audiotape, you must be sure that the recording is clear and is loud enough for all to hear. Practice using the audiotape and make sure, before speaking, that the tape is cued to the correct position.

Guidelines for Using Aids

Now that we have discussed a variety of audio and visual aids, we want to give you a few guidelines for their use. Whatever visual image you use must be large enough for the audience to see. The larger the audience, the larger the visual aid must be. For an audience of classmates, you can probably use images no larger than a sheet of paper. Even with an audience the size of a normal class, however, the larger the image you can provide, the more likely it is to be meaningful.

You should master the mechanics of any equipment you plan to use. Take the time needed to become familiar with devices like overhead and slide projectors. Set up any equipment you need early so that you are not adjusting it or fiddling with it while delivering your speech. Make sure you have chalk available if you're using the chalkboard and markers if you're using an overhead. Have any handouts you need available and have a plan for distributing them quickly and efficiently.

Remember, too, that the visual aid is not the audience. Rookies tend to speak to the aid as if it could hear. Avoid turning your back on the audience. If you need to look at the visual aid, get plenty of practice so that you are thoroughly familiar with the procedure you're going to follow. Television weathercasters appear to be pointing at features on a weather map, but in fact the weathercaster's image has been superimposed over a map located in another part of the studio. These speakers have learned how to point to something without looking at it. You can do the same. Learn to use charts and maps with no more than a sidelong glance.

The following summarizes our advice for the use of audio and visual aids.

◆ Be sure the aid is large enough to be seen or loud enough to be heard.
◆ Be sure the aid contributes to the idea being presented. If you can get along without it, don't use it. It takes time away from the rest of your presentation.
◆ Don't stand in front of the aid.
◆ Talk to your listeners, not to the visual aid.
◆ Keep any visual aid out of sight until you are ready to use it, and then put it away again when you have finished.
◆ Don't overdo a good thing. A long succession of slides or charts can become boring.
◆ Practice, practice, practice.

Finally, remember that visual or audio aids are only a means to an end. If these aids overwhelm the speech or draw undue attention away from you as the speaker, you would be wise not to use them. Don't forget that you yourself are a visual aid. Consider whether the clothing you plan to wear will contribute or detract from your message. Can you give a serious speech in a clown costume or a humorous speech in your best suit?

TAKING CHARGE

1. Create ten imaginary slides you might use to illustrate a speech on your school that you plan to give to foreign exchange students.
2. Outline the steps you would follow in demonstrating your favorite dance.
3. Create a graph or chart comparing the shoe sizes of your classmates.

STUDENT SPEECH

Everyone talks about the weather, but no one does anything about it. At least that's the way it used to be as high school speech champ Lisa Kargo explains in this informative speech on the beneficial effects of cold. Notice how skillfully she blends many facts and theories together. Notice, too, how she gives credit to her sources.

Chill Out

It was the kind of incident that made you say—only in New York City. A man suddenly stops on a busy sidewalk and begins to take off his clothes. In a flash he is stripped all the way down to his . . . shirt and slacks.

I know, you're disappointed that he didn't grin and bare it. But before we accuse our New York friend of wrong undoing, consider that the temperature outside that day was two degrees below zero—the kind of day when even the icicles are frozen stiff. But if the New York weather was cold, why did our friend attempt sudden exposure? You'll have to wait a few major ideas and some subpoints for the answer.

According to scholar Joseph Campbell, myths and legends about the cold abound in Western culture. But lately, scientific research has uncovered new dimensions about the cold and freezing. At the University of Minnesota this past year, a dedicated group of doctors spent a million dollar endowment studying the effects of freezing on humans, animals, food, and even tools.

Most people hate the cold, and with reason. In the Midwest we have four kinds of winter—cold, colder, coldest, and use an icepick to take off your clothes. Cold weather causes illness and thousands of injuries and deaths. But the very same cold that brings misery and death can potentially be one of man's most benevolent friends.

In order to melt our perceptions of the cold, I will discuss the following three areas: initially, cold effects, then icy miracles, and finally, frozen medical wonders.

Dr. Cameron C. Bangs, an expert on cold weather injuries, notes that it doesn't require below-zero temperatures before the body begins to react to the cold. Mild cold causes a process known as *vasoconstriction*. The process begins when the brain senses that inner organs are losing their warmth.

In vasoconstriction, the body's blood vessels narrow to reduce blood flow to the surface of the skin. This process minimizes heat loss and keeps warm blood flowing to the heart, lungs, brain, and spinal cord. For this reason people who are stranded in blizzards can survive with skin temperatures as low as 40 degrees because the significant organs inside the body are still warm.

Some weather is just too cold for the normal body process—you know, the kind of weather that makes Midwesterners go to Alaska for the winter. Exposed to this kind of cold, the body will shut off the bloodflow to the brain and lungs, leaving only warm blood for the spinal cord and heart. People who have been this cold sometimes hallucinate for hours even after warming up.

After the body performs vasoconstriction, it tries to warm itself by an alternative method—shivering. Shivering occurs when all the muscles contract simultaneously—even the muscles in your jaw—which is why your teeth chatter.

Every once in a while, the body will quickly open up and let blood flow all over for a short period of time. According to Shawna Vogel, in the February 1988 edition of *Discover* magazine, this is why the man in New York, and thousands of others like him, feel extreme warmth and strip off their clothes. Some get so carried away they strip down only to their beads of perspiration.

Our bodies have specific, programmed reactions to the effects of cold. And these reactions bring about icy miracles.

On a frozen December day in 1984, four-year-old Jimmy Tontlewicz went outside to play. He wandered too far out on the ice in Lake Michigan and crashed through the thin barrier to the frigid water below. He remained there for twenty minutes yet doctors revived him.

We've all heard of cases like Jimmy's—people who crash through a frozen lake or pond, stay under for long periods of time, and then miraculously recover. These people are alive today because of a genetic response to the cold called the *mammalian dive reflex*.

Seals, another mammal, stop breathing when they dive underwater. Their pulse decreases, which reduces stress on the heart. Vasoconstriction occurs at rapid speed, and blood flows only to the heart and brain.

Seals can control their dive reflex, but for humans, it only works in times of intense cold and shocking, life-threatening trauma. An accident victim's pulse is very faint, and they may even experience some paralysis because blood is shut off to the spinal cord. But rescuers now know that the cold keeps the body alive. In fact, they say that no one is dead until they are WARM and dead.

But don't go out and start skating on thin ice. The older you get, the less likely that the mammalian dive reflex will save you. Another advantage of youth.

The cold brings about icy miracles, and modern medicine is beginning to recognize the potential of the cold in enacting frozen medical wonders. In the future, the cold and freezing may cure many a malady.

For example, what can you do for a headache? Take aspirin? Put on a hot pack? The January 1987 issue of *Health* magazine reports that ice packs can actually cure the common headache. Dr. Seymour Diamond states that a headache is caused by swelling in the brain's blood vessels. The cold will constrict the blood vessels, therefore curing the headache. I wish I had the ice concession at school right before final exams.

Other medical uses for the cold have surfaced in just the past five years.

The July 11, 1987, issue of *Science News* reports that liver tumors can now be frozen as an alternative to surgery. After such procedures, a majority of patients show no evidence of the tumor.

The same issue of *Science News* reports on cryosurgery, or the freezing of cancer cells. Cancer cells contain water, and exposing them to extreme cold freezes the water and thus kills the cells. Cryosurgery also freezes the surrounding blood vessels to prevent any recurrence.

You have to admit that having your dead body frozen and revived years later sounds like science fiction, but Avi Ben Abraham, chairman of the American Cryonics Society, states that "we're fighting the

---

STUDENT SPEECH

Continued

most significant struggle in history, the struggle of life against death."

The Trans Time Company of Oakland, California, is one of several companies around the country practicing cryonics or the freezing of bodies. Many people with inoperative diseases have had their bodies frozen after death, hoping to be revived in an age when their disease can be cured. Others opt for freezing in hope of finding a time when man has cured the most deadly of diseases—death itself. The same cold that makes your nose run may be giving others the gift of the ancient gods—immortality.

The cold may be a source of discomfort, but we are slowly discovering that it can be one of the most benevolent of nature's gifts. People stripping off clothes because of the cold doesn't only happen in New York City. But rumors are circulating that New Yorkers have a sure cure for cold and freezing. They call it July.

REVIEW AND ENRICHMENT

LOOKING BACK

Listed below are the major ideas discussed in this chapter.

◆ Much of our daily communication is designed to give instructions, provide facts, or clarify ideas.

◆ Speakers who hope to inform their audience should be sure to be clear, concise, complete, and correct. They should also use concrete examples and take their listeners' interests and attitudes into account.

◆ One reason we sometimes have difficulty imagining what our listeners are thinking is that most of us are wrapped up in our own points of view.

◆ Asking some basic questions about your listeners can help you prepare an effective speech. Feature what you know about your audience in your introduction.

✦ Finding a subject to speak on is nearly always a problem. Speech ideas can come from surveys, newspaper articles, conversations, and other classes.
✦ Create a manageable topic by limiting the subject in time, space, and scope.
✦ A clearly focused thesis will help you decide what material belongs in your speech and what does not.
✦ Develop your speech through the use of appropriate facts, anecdotes, quotations, definitions, and descriptions.
✦ Audio and visual aids can help your speech by reinforcing your message and enhancing your presentation.
✦ Visual aids must be large enough to be seen easily and significant enough for your topic to make their use worthwhile.
✦ Audio and visual aids are valuable if used confidently and gracefully but can detract from your speech if presented in a clumsy or distracting way.

SPEECH VOCABULARY

Fill in each blank with the correct word from the list below. No word can be used more than once. Not all words will be used.

briefing	diagram
advance organizer	overhead projector
narrowing	demonstration
quotation	status report
handout	chalk talk
cutaway	cultural literacy
public lecture	anecdote
fireside chat	graph
definition	model
thesis	map

1. You would be wise to depend on what you know of history, science, and literature, your _____, when you suspect someone has made a mistake.
2. Three useful visual aids include a _____, which tells you where places are on the earth's surface; a _____, which shows you how something works; and a _____, which shows relationships among numbers.
3. An _____ can show an audience cartoons, drawings, and other materials on a screen without darkening the room. It has a surface that can be written on with a marker.
4. After choosing a subject, you can limit it by _____ and then condense your major point into a _____.
5. To bring appealing material to your speech, you can use a short story—called an _____—or a statement from a famous person—a _____.
6. Some of your teachers may be fond of giving a _____, while the coach standing at the blackboard is more likely to give a _____.

REVIEW AND ENRICHMENT
Continued

7. From time to time, the president's press secretary gives reporters a _____. The president may give a more personal talk on radio or television called a _____.
8. Organizations often hear a _____ from a representative of one of their committees.
9. A statement such as "I will first describe the best breeds for show animals and then look at poodles in particular" helps preview a speech for the audience and is called an _____.
10. A small-scale version of the Globe Theater is called a _____. If part of it can be removed so people can see inside, that portion is referred to as a _____.
11. One kind of visual aid, which includes flyers that can be distributed to the audience, is called a _____. Another kind, which requires the speaker to show the audience something through physical movements, is a _____.

GENERAL VOCABULARY

Use each of the following words in a sentence that illustrates its meaning.

concise	senile
concrete	etymology
distinctions	simultaneously
ambiguous	chunking
intuition	infographic
demographics	spontaneity
trivia	

THINGS TO REMEMBER

1. What are some ways in which we provide information every day to others?
2. Name the five major kinds of informative speeches.
3. What are some of the ways a speaker can support general statements?
4. Define the term *cultural literacy*.
5. What are some of the questions you might use to learn more about your audience?
6. List several good methods for finding a subject for a speech.
7. How can a potential subject be narrowed into a manageable topic?
8. What are the characteristics of a thesis?
9. What can a speaker do if the audience's attention appears to wander?
10. Why is it important to master the mechanics of any visual aid you plan to use before you give the speech?
11. What should you keep in mind if you decide to use a chalkboard during your speech?
12. What effect does the clothing you wear have on the impact of your speech?

THINGS TO DO

1. Attend a school or public meeting on a significant issue. Check the paper to find when and where the meeting will take place. Community organizations that meet regularly include the city council, the school board, clubs, and support groups. As you listen, sort out the comments people make according to what is genuine information and what is simply opinion. Determine a rough ratio of information to opinion and report back to the class.
2. Practice giving directions to classmates. Tell them how to get to your house from school or how to drive to various locations around town.
3. Write to a government agency or your congressperson for information on a subject of interest.

THINGS TO TALK ABOUT

1. Consider whether the explosion of new information over the past few years has been a blessing or a curse. Are high school students, for example, better informed than their peers of ten or twenty years ago?
2. How can a speaker learn more about the audience? Some speakers claim they can "read" an audience and make instant adjustments to their listeners. Is this possible? If so, what kinds of signals is the speaker observing?
3. What techniques might a speaker use to keep audience interest at a high level?

THINGS TO WRITE ABOUT

1. Write a letter to the editor of your local newspaper regarding the public image of high school students. Teenagers perform much of the volunteer work and convenience labor that keep a community going, but often face negative stereotypes. Use facts, quotations, and anecdotes to support your position.
2. Gather a group of five anecdotes and five quotations to use in a speech about the "typical" day of a high school student.
3. Write a set of directions on how to build or make something (for example, how to bake a cake or assemble a toy). Trade your set of directions with another student and give a demonstration speech using that person's directions. (Hint: For fun, don't deviate in any way from the other person's instructions!)

REVIEW AND ENRICHMENT
Continued

CRITICAL THINKING

1. Neil Postman wrote a book about how we all need to develop better "crap detectors." He meant that we need to be alert to what we hear. Some of the information we hear is misleading, based on weak evidence, or just plain wrong. What are some of the ways we can improve our crap detectors so that we can sort out useful and accurate information from all the rest?

2. In what areas do high school students need more information? Consider the area of health education. Do teens know what they need to know about AIDS, drug and alcohol addiction, and birth control? How do teens get their information on these subjects, and what role does public speaking play in presenting such information?

3. How can a high school speaker develop greater credibility when speaking to an adult audience? How can an adult speaker hold the interest of a high school audience?

RELATED SPEECH TOPICS

Contemporary American musicians (or writers, artists, etc.)
The future of cable television
New medical frontiers
The dangers of tanning
Tattoos: A bizarre fashion statement
How safe is bungee jumping?

What is a laser beam?
The causes of smog
Jazz—America's music
What makes a good driver?
The Peace Corps

CHAPTER 13

Speeches to Persuade

"He who wishes to exert a useful influence must be careful to insult nothing. Let him . . . consecrate his energies to the creation of what is good. He must not demolish, but build."

—Johann Wolfgang von Goethe, nineteenth-century poet and dramatist, author of *Faust*

"Well, at least I know that my speech was stimulating!"

LEARNING OBJECTIVES

After completing this chapter, you will be able to do the following.

♦ Recognize the specific features of the persuasive speech.
♦ Apply what you have learned about effective persuasive speaking to both your dealings with others and your own life.
♦ Analyze the type of audience to whom you are speaking.
♦ Adapt your persuasive approach to match the makeup of your audience.
♦ Understand and implement the logical, emotional, and personal appeals.

CHAPTER OUTLINE

Following are the main sections in this chapter.

I What Is Persuasive Speaking?
II Analyzing Your Audience
III Appealing to Your Audience
   Student Speech
   Chapter Review

NEW SPEECH TERMS

In this chapter, you will learn the meanings of the speech terms listed below.

persuasive
  speaking
supportive
  audience
uncommitted
  audience
unbiased
indifferent
  audience
captive audience
opposed
  audience
compromise

disclaimer
logos
proof
pathos
ethos
goodwill
integrity
reputation
sincerity
competency
credentials
composure

GENERAL VOCABULARY

Expanding your general vocabulary will help you become a more effective communicator. Listed below are some words appearing in this chapter that you should make part of your everyday vocabulary.

temperament
cognizant
analytical
palatable

assert
instinctively
liaison

LOOKING AHEAD

In this chapter, you will learn about persuasive speaking. You'll learn effective techniques to enable you to convince others to "buy" what you are "selling," whether it be a product, a belief, an attitude, or an idea. Next, you will analyze the various types of audiences that you might have to persuade and the specific methods of persuasive speaking most likely to be effective for each of these audiences. Finally, you will see how the understanding and implementation of Aristotle's three appeals can add both depth and impact to your persuasive speaking.

I What Is Persuasive Speaking?

Would you like to talk to your parents about having some friends over for a party this weekend? Would you like to have a later curfew? Would you like to convince your science teacher that it would be a good idea to work in groups for the next major project? Would you like to make a little more money per hour when you baby-sit for the neighbors? If you answered yes to any of these questions, then you had better know how to speak persuasively.

From time to time in this book, the building of a good house has been used as a working metaphor to parallel the building of a good speech. Just as there are different designs for houses, there are also different types of speeches. You learned about one type, the informative speech, in the last chapter. An informative speech might be thought of as comfortable yet rather basic and functional in its design, while the persuasive speech—as you will find out in this chapter—could be said to exhibit a more creative and dramatic structural layout. Let's enter the neighborhood of persuasive speaking.

Attempting to teach her students about the persuasive speech and about how it differs from the other types of speeches, a teacher gave the following explanation to her class: "Remember, if you show us how to put a car engine together, that's a demonstration speech. If you explain to us how the car engine works, that's an informative speech. If you then convince us *to buy* the car, that's a persuasive speech!"

A persuasive speech asks your audience to "buy" something that you are selling. It can be a product, but it can also be a belief, an attitude, or an idea. While the informative speech primarily supplies important information in order to increase understanding, the persuasive speech goes one step further and asks the audience to *do* something based on the information presented.

It doesn't matter whether you are speaking in a court of law, influencing some sort of public policy, or simply convincing your friends to see a particular movie, **persuasive speaking** demands that you effectively (1) induce your audience to believe as you do and (2) influence your audience in order to cause some sort of directed action to take place.

Consider the following situations:

◆ You wish to convince your parents that you should be able to attend a local concert.

◆ You want to convince your teacher that more time is needed to complete a class project.

◆ You wish to show your friends that drinking and driving do not add up to an intelligent way to have a good time.

In each of these situations, you would need to be a persuasive speaker. First of all, you would have to awaken a belief on the part of your listeners that what you are proposing is a good idea. Next, you would have to show them that you have a well-thought-out plan of action available. Finally, you should be able to convince your audience that your plan of action is realistic and the right thing to do. People act and react on the basis of what they want, how they think, and how they feel. Consequently, it is your job to "push the right buttons," whether logical or emotional, so that your audience agrees with what you are promoting.

Scholars say that the greatest Roman orator was Marcus Tullius Cicero. In his work *On Oratory*, Cicero said that the skilled speaker is a person of learning and insight. The most important insight that a speaker must have is knowledge of his or her audience. As a skilled persuasive speaker, your first task is to evaluate accurately and perceptively how your audience feels about you and your message. This evaluation, called *audience analysis*, is an invaluable element in the persuasive speaking process. You have to realize that giving a "canned speech," a planned speech that you deliver the same way to every group, is not always going to work. Each audience is unique. You must be ready to make the needed adjustments so that your spoken words are appropriate and get (or keep) the audience on your side. Next, we'll take a look at the different types of audiences that you might have to persuade.

TAKING CHARGE

◼

1. Write a report on the Roman orator Cicero. What contributions did he make to his society? Be specific. Why do you think that "learning and insight" regarding the audience is of value to the persuasive speaker? Give specific examples.

2. Make two lists. In the first, list products that you might have to persuade people to buy. In the second, list ideas that you might have to promote. Before you make your lists, think of specific instances in school, in your community, on the job, or with your friends that would involve a persuasive approach on your part. Be ready to discuss your lists with other students.

Analyzing Your Audience

A sign in a high school locker room says:

Get Ready to Play!

Below the sign is a picture of the next opponent. Key statistics about that team, information on each team member, and a team analysis sheet that projects what the individual players and the team will do in specific game situations are listed beneath the picture. Studying the picture and statistics for several days will help prepare the team for the upcoming game.

Just as good athletes must be aware of the strengths and weaknesses of their opponents, good persuasive speakers must be aware of the attitudes and beliefs of their audiences. These speakers might post a sign that says:

Get Ready to *Speak!*

As Chapter 2 told you, your audience should never be perceived as the enemy. However, your audience deserves to be well scouted, or analyzed. You cannot prepare the most effective, persuasive speech if you have not taken the time to get to know the people who will be listening to you. How old are they? What is their economic status? Will most of them be male or female? What about their political or religious views? How many will be in attendance? How many are in favor of your position? Against it?

Suppose you were speaking to these groups:

◆ A parent group about chaperoning a school dance.

◆ A group of community business owners about sponsoring a school money-making project.
◆ Your neighborhood about an extensive local clean-up campaign.
◆ Your teachers on the need for them to teach an extra class each day.

Wouldn't the mood or *temperament* of your audience be different in each situation? Wouldn't the mood vary depending on what you were asking the group to "buy"? Most likely, the range would be from very positive to very negative. You owe it to your audience to be *cognizant* of the speaking climate and to present your message accordingly.

Authorities generally agree that most audiences can be classified into one of four categories: supportive, uncommitted, indifferent, and opposed. Often, your audience will be a mixture of these four types. Keep in mind that regardless of the type of audience you are addressing, *your main purpose is to gain the most number of supporters possible.* Use all of the tools at your disposal. An effective introduction and conclusion, a sharp appearance, convincing arguments, congeniality, and a sense of humor can help you persuade your audience.

The Supportive Audience

Every speaker would like to have a supportive audience. The **supportive audience** is friendly. Its members like you and what you have to say. This is the easiest audience to address because the members are ready to support and promote your ideas. Laughter, hugs, and handshakes come easily with this group. A political candidate asking his staff for its continued efforts after a big win would be facing a supportive audience. A school team asking the student body at a pep rally for continued support would probably be met with enthusiastic cheers. Your main objective with listeners in this type of audience is to reinforce what they already accept. You want to strengthen your ties with them.

Generally, the supportive audience doesn't need a great deal of information. Sometimes, though, the supportive audience has "bought" you as a person but doesn't know much about what you are "selling." In such a case, you need to take the time to present your material thoroughly. For instance, students might strongly support you for a class office because you are well known, well liked, and well respected. If, however, you propose a new home-room concept as part of your platform, you had better be ready to offer persuasive, well-thought-out details to support your idea. If you don't, your supportive audience might begin looking for another candidate.

The supportive audience is a speaker's dream. Don't take these listeners for granted, though. Your key to persuasive success is to keep them fired up and enthusiastic about you and your objectives.

The Uncommitted Audience

You have a good chance of persuading the **uncommitted audience** because the uncommitted audience is neutral. This type of audience isn't for you or against you; its members simply need information in order to make up their minds. The prevalent attitude among the members of the uncommitted audience is usually, "OK, let's hear what you have to say. Convince me!" It is then your job to be convincing.

When you are interviewing for a job, the employer will usually be impartial. The employer isn't taking sides; she wants the best person for the job, whoever it might be. Similarly, a scholarship committee or a representative from a college you wish to attend will most likely be **unbiased,** or objective. These interviewers want the best applicants to be rewarded and accepted; they have no reason to favor one student over another. With these audiences, you have the task of selling yourself, your talents, and your potential. Specific information such as your past working experience, your current grade point average, your participation in extracurricular activities, and your community involvement might provide the substance needed to bring your listeners over to your side.

Examples of uncommitted audiences can be found every day in courts of law. It's the lawyer's job to persuade the jury that the client is innocent. The jury is, of course, uncommitted until all of the evidence is in and fairly weighed. Only then can a rational, just decision be reached. Similarly, you face a type of jury every time you speak in front of an uncommitted audience. You can often win your case if you present your position clearly and persuasively and support it with solid information.

The Indifferent Audience

With the **indifferent audience,** your job as a persuasive speaker gets a little tougher. This type of audience is difficult to deal with because its members are apathetic toward you. You don't really excite them. They aren't opposed to you, but they can appear openly bored. Part of the

In 1992, attendants at a picnic honoring presidential candidate Bill Clinton constituted a supportive audience. Jury members at the William Kennedy Smith rape trial in December, 1991, on the other hand, represented an uncommitted audience.

problem is that the indifferent audience is often a **captive audience,** an audience that is being forced to be in attendance. Often, the listeners don't believe that what you are saying is relevant to their personal situations.

The indifferent audience often needs a dose of shock therapy to cure its ills. Your job might be to jar the members of this type of audience into paying attention to what you have to say by offering a different approach. It is also your job to show them how your message is applicable to their lives. Information is important, but information alone is not enough.

For instance, a teacher was working with a group of students whose academic performance was less than noteworthy. The students kept telling him that their main objective was to get out of school, get a job, make some money, and buy a car. He couldn't persuade them to im-

prove academically until he tried a new approach. The teacher brought in three business owners from the community who told the students what it took to get hired in the current job market. The teacher also had a car salesman come to the class. The car salesman went through an itemized analysis of how much money per week each student would have to make in order to buy a car and to pay for gas, insurance, and repairs. The students then vividly saw that without basic academic skills, they couldn't get a job that would pay enough for them to buy what they were after. Things now made more sense to them. They saw a *reason* to try.

This particular approach won't work in every situation. You must put forth the effort to find an approach that will get the attention of the apathetic audience. Be dynamic in your approach, and show your listeners that what you are selling is im-

INSTANT IMPACT

Ms. Persuasion

Robin Morgan, current editor of *Ms.* magazine, recently spoke to students at the University of Kansas about the feminist movement and the work yet to be done. She told the audience that two-thirds of the world's nonliterate people are female and that 90 percent of all refugee populations are women and children. The irony, she added, is that even though there isn't a world problem that doesn't impact on women, women are rarely consulted or involved in finding solutions.

Twenty years earlier, Morgan had spoken at the University of Kansas, and her words were so persuasive that the administration was forced to create a Women's Studies Department.

She now urges women to continue to be activists but advises them to seek power through the political system.

portant to them and has a direct bearing on their personal well-being.

The Opposed Audience

Be ready to handle a potential confrontation with the **opposed audience.** The members are hostile to you, to what you are promoting, or to both. Unlike the supportive audience, this type of audience feels no warmth for you and is in no way sympathetic to your feelings or your cause.

With the opposed audience, your objective should simply be to get a fair hear-

ing. Try your best to determine specifically what your audience is hostile about: You? Your cause? A specific statement that you made previously?

When you have reached a conclusion, work with the audience to put out the flame of that specific fire. It is often a wise approach when addressing a hostile audience to show that you are willing to **compromise,** or make some concessions of your own. Let these listeners know that you see merit in some of their arguments and that you aren't perfect.

A student government representative was to address the student body of a rival school. When she was introduced to the assembly, many of the students hooted, hissed, and booed. However, her first words were:

I'm not surprised at your reaction. May I share with you that I am currently scared to death! Even though we might be adversaries on the basketball court, could we be friends at this assembly and meet each other halfway? Could we forget our differences and work together today? I respect so many things about your school. Today, I trust that we can share with each other about how our respective schools operate. I also trust that one of you will catch me if I faint!

The audience laughed. The students were also courteous throughout the remainder of her speech. The speaker had endeared herself to her audience through her personality and her sense of fair play.

Another way to gain favor with the hostile audience is to use a disclaimer. A **disclaimer** tells listeners what you are *not* saying or lets them know that you don't consider yourself the All-Knowing Expert on Everything. This reduces the tendency the audience might have to overgeneralize your views. For example, if you were speaking to a group of school officials about the need for a skateboard area, you could say something like this:

> Now I'm *not* saying that every time students have a concern the school should bow down and passively agree. I'm also *not* saying that I am the person who has all of the answers. However, I would appreciate it if you would listen . . .

You stand your best chance of getting a fair hearing from the members of an opposed audience if you can do the following things:

1. Convince them that you know how they feel and believe that their position has worth.

2. Avoid needless confrontation.
3. Create a situation where there aren't winners and losers.

You have now read about the four types of audiences that you might face in a persuasive speaking situation. You have also been given advice on how to deal with each. However, analyzing your audience is only the first part of your speaking task. What do audiences like? Why are they drawn to some speakers but not to others? Next we'll take a look at how to be an appealing persuasive speaker.

TAKING CHARGE

1. Talk to five different people—another student, a teacher, a parent, an administrator, and a neighbor or community member—and have each give his or her own personal definition of what persuasive speaking means. Ask these people to give you specific examples of how their definitions have worked for them in the past.
2. Interview someone you consider an excellent persuasive speaker. It can be either a student or an adult. Make a list of what this person tries to do in order to sell an idea or a product. What does this person advise you to avoid if you wish to persuade others?
3. Persuasive speaking isn't limited to formal situations and large audiences. You use it in your personal life and in your interpersonal communication every day. Discuss situations in which you have to be persuasive: (1) with your friends, (2) with your teachers, and (3) with your parents. What would be your approach to selling each audience?
4. List one real-life example in which you might have to deal with (1) a supportive audience, (2) an uncommitted audience, (3) an indifferent audience, and (4) an opposed audience. Remember, an audience might be as small as one person.

III Appealing to Your Audience

The saying "Love is blind" means that a couple in love tend to overlook each other's faults or weaknesses. The saying also suggests that people are attracted to others for a variety of reasons. Some of the reasons can be logically explained, and some can't. Often, we are unable to articulate why we are drawn to certain individuals or things—that is, why they appeal to us.

What exactly does the word *appeal* mean? Let's scrutinize the word a little more closely. *Appeal* has two different meanings. It can mean "an urgent request." It can also refer to what is attractive or interesting about someone or something. Everyone finds certain people, books, movies, automobiles, or music personally appealing. What about persuasive speakers? Must they have appeal?

If your job is to convince others, it makes sense that you must present an appealing image and message. A persuasive speaker without appeal is like a race car driver without a car; both lack the vehicle needed to bring about success. How can you develop appeal as a speaker? How can you arouse a favorable response when addressing your audience?

In Chapter 1, you read about Aristotle and the art of persuasion. Aristotle, in his work *Rhetoric,* stated that the persuasive powers of a speaker depend on his reasoning, the emotions that he is able to stir in his listeners, and his character. In other words, a speaker's success is the result of his *logical appeal,* his *emotional appeal,* and his *personal appeal.* Each of these deserves a closer look.

Logical Appeal

Someone once said that each person's mind has its own logic, but that it does not often let others in on that logic. As a persuasive speaker, you must definitely let others in on how your thoughts go together. Nothing can turn off listeners more quickly than a speech that has them scratching their heads in befuddlement.

With a logical appeal, you appeal to the intellect of your audience by offering a clearly defined speech that contains solid reasoning and valid evidence. The logical appeal is also known by the Greek name **logos.** It satisfies the *analytical* side of your audience and says to your listeners, "I want this to make sense to you!" and "Do you see how all of this logically fits together?" You can promote your logical appeal by being organized and by offering proof to your audience.

Be Organized

One way to enhance your logical appeal is by presenting a well-organized speech (the topic of Chapter 8). A student speaker was talking to a woman's club about America's preoccupation with entertainment. She said:

> The way to the top these days lies with "putting on a show." However, in our quest for "ultimate entertainment," we've forgotten to look beyond the sizzle to see if what lies behind is truly worth supporting. As we examine this situation, three major areas seem apparent: (1) the entertainment industry, (2) our political system, and (3) education. Let's look at these areas individually . . .

Not only is the beginning of this speech well organized, but it is also easy to un-

Three Appeals in Persuasive Speech

Logical appeal—The speaker offers an organized, clearly defined speech containing solid reasoning and valid evidence.

Emotional appeal—The speaker's words arouse feelings in the audience like anger, disgust, compassion, etc.

Personal appeal—The speaker wins the audience's trust through honesty, competency, and credibility.

INSTANT IMPACT

Good News about Bad Habits

Do you know anyone who has a bad habit? Maybe it's putting things off, avoiding chores around the house, not being on time, or saying "ya' know" all the time. Now, there is hope for helping people to break bad habits. Researchers have discovered that if you are trying to persuade someone to break a bad habit, you might have to make from *five* to *seven* attempts before the advice sinks in and starts to work. The experts also say to vary your persuasive approach for quicker results. What's the message? Don't give up! Persistent persuasion just might pay off.

---

derstand. It told the audience specifically what the speaker's thesis was and what her three major areas of analysis would be.

An editorialist on a television station was alarmed at the number of young adults who, because of financial hardships, were being forced to return home and live with their parents. The editorialist said that over 50 percent of adults between the ages of eighteen and twenty-four were living with their parents. She then gave three reasons why this might be occurring:

◆ Problems in the availability of jobs.

◆ Problems with job layoffs.

◆ Problems college students had in paying back student loans.

Her reasons were clearly stated and logically *palatable* to the audience. However, you can't merely *assert* that what you are saying is true. Audiences need proof.

Offer Proof

Providing proof is another means of appealing to logic. As you read in Chapter 9, **proof** is specific evidence; proof is that which establishes the truth of something. It is part of the supporting materials and details discussed in Chapter 8.

For instance, suppose you were having a discussion with a group of friends about art. Someone says that too much of what is considered art today is nothing but trash. That person objects to the National Endowment for the Arts giving "all of its money" to art that is considered obscene.

You could object by saying, "Oh, yeah, what do you know?" or "I suppose you could do better!" Neither response would persuade your friend to come over to your way of thinking, though. If, instead, you told him that even though some of what he says might have merit, he should consider that over the past twenty-five years, nearly 100,000 grants have been awarded by the National Endowment for the Arts. Of those 100,000 grants, fewer than 20 have been considered controversial.

Do you see how these facts provide proof? Providing proof shows your listeners that you have intelligence, and intelligence is appealing.

Working to improve your logical appeal is a smart thing to do. However, logic by itself isn't always enough. You can also appeal to others emotionally.

Emotional Appeal

What do the following topics have in common?

- ◆ The homeless
- ◆ Cruelty to animals
- ◆ Nuclear power
- ◆ Abused children
- ◆ The elderly
- ◆ Sex education in schools
- ◆ Abortion
- ◆ Victims of crime

Of course, it would be easy to find volumes of information on each and present tons of facts. However, all these topics cause many people to react *instinctively* in an emotional manner and let their feelings show. As Aristotle reminds us, emotional appeal is a major consideration in persuasive speaking. Indeed, it often has a stronger impact on an audience than logic or reason. People would like to think that they make decisions based on reason. The truth is, however, that most people rely on their feelings as much as—or more than—their reason. An individual knows that the car that gets thirty-five miles per gallon is the smart buy, but he may go with the sportier model with the sun roof and the CD player instead.

If it is true that logical appeal aims for the brain, then emotional appeal aims for the heart. Emotional appeal, or **pathos,** involves striking a chord in people's insides and exciting their feelings of love, anger, disgust, fear, compassion, patriotism, or the like. Notice, for example, the intensity of William Barrett Travis as he tried to "light a fire" under the people of Texas and all Americans while he was defending the Alamo against Mexican forces in 1836:

> Fellow citizens and compatriots: I am besieged by a thousand or more of the Mexicans under Santa Anna. I have sustained a continual bombardment and cannonade for twenty-four hours and have not lost a man. The enemy has demanded a surrender at discretion; otherwise the garrison are to be put to the sword if the fort is taken. I have answered the demand with a cannon shot, and our flag still waves proudly from the walls. *I shall never surrender nor retreat.* I call on you in the name of liberty, or patriotism, and everything dear to the American character, to come to our aid with all dispatch.

His words got the attention of the entire country, and even though the conflict turned into a massacre, the phrase "Remember the Alamo" became a national battle cry. The words hit an "emotional nerve" and inspired people's patriotic spirit. Would logic have worked as well? Probably not.

The late prime minister of England, Sir Winston Churchill, once said that "the human story does not always unfold like a mathematical calculation on the principle that two and two make four. Sometimes in life they make five or minus three." He was saying that life is not always logical. Often, it is the emotional, intangible world of our feelings that charts the real course of life.

All people are full of potential laughter, remorse, hopes, and dreams, and your ability to move people depends on stirring their emotions. Few people enjoy listening to uninterrupted evidence, long lists of facts, and cold, sterile statistics. They may enjoy listening, though, if that evidence is presented in a manner that excites them. Read how a high school student, Kate Eifrig, used evidence, but primarily emotional appeal, to persuade her audience. In regard to the Persian Gulf War, she asks:

> What could be more significant than thousands of human lives? Evidently, fast production was of monumental worth to the military leaders in the Persian Gulf. Did you know that a recent independent Pentagon study announced that many of the military repair parts used in the Persian Gulf War were defective! Some were termed *inoperable*. Some of these parts were bolts for fighter planes' electrical systems and missile compartments.
>
> How could the government buy these parts without checking them first? Is rapid and careless repair worth sacrificing lives?

Do you see her evidence? More importantly, do you *feel* her message? Do you see why her audience would be shocked and alarmed by this portion of her speech? Kate was saying to her audience, "Let's take action and demand that our government value people more than fast production!" She used evidence to help set the emotional tone that she was after.

Your tone refers to your vocal quality, but it also reflects your overall manner of nonverbal expression. Your attitude about your words as you deliver them contributes to your tone. The tone could be angry, considerate, hopeful, or optimistic, for example. The tone with which you deliver your words can have astounding impact. In 1938, Orson Welles's radio production "War of the Worlds" caused a nationwide panic by dramatizing a supposed invasion from Mars and presenting it in the form of a newscast. His tone of urgency was so real that many Americans believed him and thought that space creatures had landed.

Even though the emotional appeal is aimed at stirring the emotions in your audience, keep in mind that your audience's reaction is often based on *your* emotional telegraphing. Telegraphing, which was mentioned in Chapter 11, means leading the way and showing your audience the emotion you wish them to feel by feeling it yourself. How is an audience supposed to feel sympathy or outrage if you aren't supplying an emotional example for them?

Let's examine a real-life story. It involves a woman's fight to have a stoplight constructed at a busy intersection. The town board of her midwestern community was initially opposed to supplying money for the stoplight. At a meeting of the board, town "experts" provided numerous facts and figures to show that the stoplight was not needed. Even though they agreed that cars traveled at high rates of speed through the area and that accidents had occurred, they also argued that few of the accidents were serious and that

In 1938, Orson Welles' radio broadcast dramatizing an invasion from Mars caused a nationwide panic. His urgent tone of voice convinced many that the events he described were true.

there had been only one fatality over a two-year period.

Then the woman spoke. She gave facts about the number of speeding tickets issued at the intersection by the police each month and about the number of people from a nearby subdivision who had to cross the intersection each day to get to a local shopping mall. However, she concluded her presentation by holding up a picture of a small child about eight years old. In a compassionate, caring speech, she told her listeners that the child in the picture was that *one* traffic victim. The woman was not the child's

mother, but a friend of the family. She said that she didn't want the members of the board or any other members of the audience to experience the pain of losing a child. A stoplight, she pleaded, could help prevent that pain from becoming a reality.

The town board voted unanimously to construct the stoplight. Her emotional involvement set the tone for her persuasive message and helped turn the town board around. She turned foes into friends in part by using a logical appeal but even more by establishing a strong emotional bond between her and her audience. She cared about the stoplight, yes, but she also showed others that she cared about them and their welfare. Showing the audience that you have their interests in mind is a key component of Aristotle's final appeal, the personal appeal.

Personal Appeal

A famous Hollywood producer once said that he didn't know exactly what talent was but he knew it when he saw it. Personal appeal is much like talent in that people know when someone has it, and they know when someone doesn't have it. Having personal appeal, or **ethos,** means that your listeners will buy what you are selling because they trust in you and your credibility—your believability. Donald Queener, a nationally recognized speech and debate educator who has coached scores of interpretation and oratory champions, says that of all the appeals, personal appeal is the most desirable and the most effective because it can be *immediate.* It can work with an audience instantaneously.

If you have personal appeal, your listeners trust you. You come across as having their best interests at heart, and your **goodwill** proves that you care about them and about worthwhile issues. Even though being well liked is important for the effective speaker, congeniality is *not* what Aristotle was stressing in his use of the term *personal appeal*. Each day, the news is full of stories about smiling, friendly swindlers who dupe unsuspecting victims. Instead, Aristotle focused on two essential elements, which he believed formed the backbone of personal appeal: honesty and competency.

Honesty

People are attracted to honesty. If you are honest, you tell the truth and exhibit personal **integrity,** or a strong sense of right and wrong. Your audience believes what you have to say because your **reputation**—how you are known by others—proves that you are a person of your word and therefore someone to be taken seriously. Honesty has appeal for two reasons. It shows others that you will be an example of what you say—that you will "practice what you preach." It also reveals that you are a person of **sincerity,** of genuineness, and that you mean what you say and speak from your heart.

Don't think that appealing to an audience through honesty is limited to interpersonal communication or large audiences. Sometimes you can be your own audience. Chapter 1 used the term *intrapersonal communication* for these situations. Intrapersonal communication involves the talks that you have with yourself. Often, you can persuade yourself to take a particular course of action based on your own honesty and your personal character. You might make a crucial decision on the basis of believing that "honesty is the best policy" and feel good about your decision. In other words, honesty can direct your decision making and actually encourage you to appeal to yourself.

There is a group of more than four hundred actors, writers, and agents who want to change the world. Known as Young Artists United and using the motto "It's Cool to Care," they speak at high schools on the dangers of drugs and alcohol. They also spend some of their time painting orphanages and funding teen runaway centers. The actor Michael J. Fox said that he is involved in the group because he wants to give something back to a world that has given him so much. When Fox, the star of *Back to the Future* and several other films, spoke at one Los Angeles school, a student responded this way:

> I really listened to what this guy said today, and it made me think about what I'm doing with my life. I hear that he does this kind of stuff for kids all the time. He acts as if he really cares, you know, really wants the best for us. I paid attention because he was being straight with us, being honest. I believed him.

In the example above, Michael J. Fox, representing many others who feel the same way, used his personal appeal—his reputation and his honesty—in order to appeal to students to do what's right. He told them: "If you don't do drugs, continue to stay away from them," and "if you are involved with drugs, take action and change the course of your life before it is too late!" This is a good example for all of us to follow. Clearly, honesty can do more than make us appealing speakers; it can also help us contribute to changing people's lives.

Competency

We now turn our attention to the second essential element of Aristotle's personal appeal, competency. **Competency** means capability. If you are a competent person, you can get the job done. You probably have a solid work ethic and value being prepared.

People who are known to be competent often have impressive **credentials**, or qualifications. These might include an extensive education, a number of outstanding achievements, or a long list of successes in a particular field. Indeed, most people equate competency with hard work and expertise in some particular field. They are impressed by the person who can offer a clear, focused stance on a topic because of expertise of this kind. Special expertise gives such a person the ability to speak with confidence and composure.

A somewhat different kind of expertise is a knack in dealing with people. Have you ever heard someone called a "people person"—someone who just naturally gets along with everyone? If you are a "people person," you stand an excellent chance of convincing your listeners to agree with you because you, too, present your message with confidence and composure.

Speaking with **composure**—speaking in a calm, controlled manner—telegraphs to your audience that you are in charge of the situation. The competent speaker adheres to the saying, "Never let 'em see you sweat!" After all, few listeners will be willing to count on a person who "rattles" easily or "chokes" when the pressure is on. Remember, if those to whom you are speaking don't believe that they can count on you, then they probably won't be persuaded by you, either.

Providing clear examples for Aristotle's personal appeal is difficult, because much of the persuasive power of this appeal comes from a form of internal energy that doesn't translate well to the printed page. However, one particular example might illustrate this quality. Read out loud the words of Thomas Jefferson, delivered on March 4, 1801, at the first inaugural address in Washington, D.C. Notice the tone that he establishes and how he attempts to persuade the people of a young nation to aid and to support him during his presidency:

> I shall often go wrong through defect of judgment. When right, I shall often be thought wrong by those whose positions will not command a view of the whole ground. I ask your indulgence for my own errors, which will never be intentional. . . . Relying, then, on the patronage of your good will, I advance with obedience to the work.

Jefferson's words exemplify how honesty and competency can work hand in hand to produce a feeling of confidence. "We're all in this together," he seems to say. "We can work as a team to achieve success."

You might be saying, "This isn't the era of Aristotle, and the year 1801 was a *long* time ago. How do I actually apply all of this to my own life and to today's world?" Maybe this example will help.

United Approach

A group of students from Apple Valley High School in Minnesota, under the direction of award-winning speech coach, debate coach, and teacher Pamela Cady,

COMMUNICATION BREAKTHROUGH

The Nixon–Kennedy Debate of 1960

(Note: Presented here is an account of how a communication breakdown and a communication breakthrough occurred simultaneously during one of the most famous debates in American history.)

On September 26, 1960, the genius of technology brought the American public the first of four televised debates between the Republican presidential nominee, Richard M. Nixon, and the Democratic presidential nominee, John F. Kennedy. This was indeed a monumental event, for Nixon and Kennedy would come together, face to face, to be evaluated by more than 70 million viewers. Each candidate was trying to persuade the nation that he was the person to lead the country. Before the first debate, Nixon was the front-runner in the polls; Kennedy was a distant second. However, after the first debate, Kennedy made a significant breakthrough. He did it mainly through an amazing appeal, an almost immediate bond that he formed with television viewers. Nixon, on the other hand, lost ground.

John F. Kennedy came to Chicago, the site of the first debate, organized and prepared. He was aware of pertinent information regarding domestic policy, and his staff had prepared him well. When Kennedy arrived at the studio before the airing of the live debate, he wore a dark gray suit and a white shirt. However, he noticed that the lights from the camera caused a type of glare off the white shirt. Consequently, he had a staff member dash back to his hotel room and get a blue shirt. He changed into the blue shirt minutes before the broadcast, and this is the shirt that millions saw.

Nixon, on the other hand, was alone the entire day of the first debate. He had been ill; thus, his complexion was white and pasty-looking, and he had deep eye shadows. Because he arrived at the studio with just a little time to spare, he wasn't aware of how his light-colored suit and his white shirt meekly faded into the background when hit by the studio lights. To make matters worse, even though Nixon wore makeup to cover his "five o'clock shadow," it didn't prevent the camera from picking up the sweat as it ran down his face.

What was the result? Kennedy came across as having more appeal. Even though Richard M. Nixon was a skilled debater and handled himself admirably in addressing the issues (those who listened to the debate on radio called it a draw), he failed to persuade the voters who watched that he was the more capable presidential candidate. He had lost the "impact of images" battle. When Kennedy spoke, he was calm, controlled, and energetic; he spoke to America as a man with a vision. When Nixon spoke, he appeared tense, almost frightened; and instead of speaking to America, he spoke to Kennedy. Richard M. Nixon was in the midst of a communication breakdown, for psychologically he had exhibited to 70 million viewers that he lacked the power and the imagination of his political counterpart who was standing just a few feet from him.

As one observer said, "Every time that the two men were close together for the nation to see, Kennedy would win a little and Nixon would lose a little." While it might be true that television turned the tide, it was John F. Kennedy who persuasively turned around some skeptical Democrats who saw him in action. He also turned around millions of voters, who now recognized him as a real political force instead of a young, inexperienced upstart.

The outcome: John F. Kennedy defeated Richard M. Nixon for the presidency in one of the closest elections in the history of the country.

Questions
1. Which of the appeals do you think Kennedy used most effectively?
2. Where do you think Nixon made his mistake(s)?
3. How important was image in this debate and why do you think it turned the tide in favor of Kennedy?
4. How could radio broadcast have resulted in a different outcome to the debate?

During the first of four televised debates between presidential candidates Richard M. Nixon and John F. Kennedy in 1960, Kennedy won millions of voters with his calm yet energetic performance, while Nixon lost ground due to his tense, even fearful, delivery.

was asked this question: "If you had just gotten your driver's license, what would you say to your parents to persuade them to allow you to drive the family's brand new car?"

At first, the students responded with short, one-sentence answers, including, "I'd cry, stomp my feet, and scream 'Please!'" However, after they had studied this chapter, they compiled a much more thorough list, utilizing all three of Aristotle's appeals. What do you think of these persuasive ideas?

The following represent logical appeals.

- ◆ "Wouldn't my driving be more convenient than your having to drive me everywhere?"
- ◆ "I could help you with the errands!"
- ◆ "There would be less chaos at home with people rushing to drive everyone everywhere."
- ◆ "I could learn how to follow directions."
- ◆ "I have done well in Driver's Education. The school and state believe that I am a good driver."
- ◆ "I have checked it out, and the insurance would not go up much."
- ◆ "The new car would be less likely to have engine problems."
- ◆ "I'll pay for my own gas and insurance, plus I will keep the car clean."
- ◆ "I'll be sure to call you when I get where I am going."

The following represent emotional appeals.

- ◆ "When you were a kid, didn't you want to be given some responsibility, too?"

- ◆ "Will you consider my driving if I only ask on special occasions? You know how *special* some things can be, don't you?"
- ◆ "If I'm driving, you don't have to worry about my being in a car where the driver has been drinking."
- ◆ "I would feel so proud for others to see me in our new car!"
- ◆ "I would never ask if I thought you didn't trust me."
- ◆ "How would you feel always having to bum a ride with people?"
- ◆ "I would love the responsibility!"
- ◆ "I know that you worry about me, so out of respect for you two, I would be extra careful."
- ◆ "I would love you guys so much!"
- ◆ "This would really enhance my self-esteem."
- ◆ "Think what this could do for our communication. We would talk more and understand each other better!"

The following represent personal appeals.

- ◆ "I promise to always tell you the truth about where I am going."
- ◆ "I don't feel that it is right that my friends always have to drive."
- ◆ "Since my sister was allowed to drive a nice car when she first got her license, I think that this would be the fair thing to do, don't you?"
- ◆ "Please don't judge me before I have had a chance to prove to you that I can handle this."
- ◆ "Have I ever let you down? (I mean when it *really* counts!)"

◆ "I would like to show you that I can be as disciplined with a car as I have been with my life."

◆ "I give you my word that I will be a good and responsible driver."

Some of the statements could fit into more than one category, couldn't they? The sophomore students, after discussing their ideas, decided that using a "united approach"—using two or three of the appeals—would give them a better chance for success than a one-dimensional approach. One student noted that her mother and father would require different approaches. She decided that her mother would need to be approached with logic, while her father would probably relate better to the emotional argument. Does this sound familiar? As you can see, you can persuade more convincingly when you intelligently use Aristotle's three appeals.

Persuasive speaking is not easy to explain. So many human factors go into what makes a person convincing that it is difficult to offer a real-world prescription for success. Often, you will have to devel-op the ability to read your audience and to use in the same persuasive speech all that this chapter has presented. This won't be an easy task.

However, don't believe that good persuasive speakers are simply born with talent or that "you either have it or you don't." There is a step that you can take that will enable you to move closer to being the convincing speaker that you wish to be. What is that step?

The saying goes that the world is made up of three groups: those who watch things happen, those who make things happen, and those who wonder, "What just happened?" Be a person who makes things happen. Join the "movers and shakers" of the oral communication world. Work to understand what persuasive speaking is, who your audience is, and how Aristotle's appeals can work to your advantage. Then you will have an excellent opportunity to convince others to accept your ideas, motivate others to act, and—yes, as the teacher explained at the beginning of the chapter—persuade someone to buy the car!

TAKING CHARGE

1. It has been said that if you try to argue emotion, you will lose every time. This means that if, instead of using logic and analysis to persuade someone, you "fly off of the handle" and let your feelings dominate you, you will rarely persuade others. Write a one-page paper explaining at least two major problems that arguing emotion with someone (even with yourself) can cause. What solutions could you provide for these problems, or what could you do instead of arguing emotion? Could using a personal appeal or logical appeal help? Specify how in your one-page paper.

TAKING CHARGE (CONTINUED)

2. Keep a journal for at least one day. In the journal, write down all of the times that you had to use persuasive speaking. You might, for example, ask someone out on a date. You might plead with your younger brother or sister to do one of your chores at home. Keep close track of when persuasive speaking is a part of your communication life, regardless of how small that part is. Next, note which appeal or appeals seemed to work best for you—logical, emotional, or personal—and explain why you think this was the case.

3. Here is your dilemma: You are running for a class office against a very popular student. You are not the most beautiful (or the most handsome) person in your class, but you are a hard worker, and you care about excellence. One of your biggest obstacles is that you are brand new to the school, having only been in class for one month. At your previous school, you made good grades and were well liked and respected by students and the faculty. Prepare an extensive list, like the sophomores' list of arguments to drive the family car, giving all the logical, emotional, and personal arguments that you could use to appeal to the student body.

STUDENT SPEECH

Two very popular types of persuasive speaking are oratory and extemporaneous speaking. (Each of these will be discussed in more detail in Chapter 14.) In 1987, Austan Goolsbee, a student speaker from Milton Academy, in Milton, Massachusetts, was named the national champion in extemporaneous speaking and the national runner-up in oratory at the National Forensic League National Speech and Debate Tournament. Here is his award-winning oration.

Rite of Passage

To become a man in the ancient African Lesu tribe, a boy had to dodge burning branches hurled at him by his father. To become a woman in the Tlingit culture, a girl had to live for an entire year in a dark room sewing and plucking duck feathers. In New Zealand, a youth had to take a knife, venture into the ocean, and kill a shark. And for the Ubatu, the challenge was slaughtering a wild boar, using a wooden spike.

Today, such rites of passage seem utterly ridiculous. Yet every year two million of America's youth engage in their own barbaric rite. Herded into crowded assembly rooms, huddled behind tiny desks, armed with only two soft lead pencils, these adolescents embark on a perilous mission: to choose the best of 3,600 possible ovals, as they undergo three hours of rigorous torture. That's right, they take the Scholastic Aptitude Test—the S.A.T.

The process, according to Bob Greene in his article "Testing Time," is both intimidating and brutalizing. Therefore, since we can read so much meaning into a single action, we need to consider whether we are more humane than a tribe in Ula Watu, where children become adults by diving head first from a cliff.

In the United States, our dive is into a neatly printed, federally protected test booklet. For entrance into college, it's a must. Status and self-esteem depend on it. In Illinois, one gubernatorial candidate based his entire platform on the S.A.T.—"Scores are down, so vote for me!" Yes, when the scores slide, the country shakes, and everyone looks for an answer—anything from poor schooling to too much television. Researchers Ernest Sternglass and Steven Bell have even attributed the problem to nuclear fallout! But wait a minute, isn't that taking things just a little bit too far?

George Madus, director of the Boston Institute for the Study of Testing, reminds us that the S.A.T. was created in 1919 for the purpose of helping educationally disadvantaged children to show themselves intellectually competent. Unfortunately, the few

hundred students who got to participate in that goal have been dwarfed by today's goal: Do well, prove yourself, and get into college. Should one test loom so important in today's society? Before you answer, join me for a look at some valid concerns, and then at an alternative to our rite of passage.

The first concern is the actual basis for the test. Supposedly, it's a measure of that elusive quality called "learning potential." Sadly, it does little to evaluate the student who does well because of hard work. Consider the case of David. David is a good student who applies himself and earns good grades. But David has one flaw. He doesn't excel on standardized tests of aptitude. The result? The S.A.T. classifies him as a candidate with low potential. How does a test judge your academic potential? Well, if you can define words like *desuetude* and *lascivious*, then you have average potential. To rank at the top, you need to know words like *ouabain*, which is an African poison, or *schistosomiasis*, an endemic disease mentioned in the novel *Lord Jim*. I'll admit, such words may come in handy on a really boring date when you have nothing else to talk about, but do they really demonstrate learning potential?

Another distressing fact is that the distribution of scores seems remarkably similar to the distribution of income. George Owen, in his classic study of the S.A.T., *None of the Above*, points out that whereas students from families with incomes less than $6,000 a year get an average combined score of 771 out of a possible 1600, their counterparts from families with incomes greater than $50,000 a year score 1002. According to Owen, it's because the test reflects a socioeconomic bias because of different levels of concept identification that test-makers inaccurately consider.

A third problem is the ease of cramming. Stanley Kaplan lives a quiet, inauspicious life outside school. Inside, though, Kaplan has become the high schooler's dream. Mr. Kaplan teaches students how to beat the S.A.T. It's like giving an Ubatu youth a submachine gun to go after that boar. Of course, the administrators of the test, the Educational Testing Service, deny that coaching can help. But E.T.S. is ignoring the facts. Quite simply, Kaplan's average student raises his score 125 points—250 points if he's serious about it. A true test of aptitude should not be so vulnerable. You see, the S.A.T. tends to repeat questions from year to year and follow a set pattern. Without any emphasis on course work, some students have simply discovered how to beat the ovals—and all it costs is $200 to $500 to learn test-taking skills.

Coaching doesn't come cheap, and if you can't afford it, you take your chances. Aptitude now has a price. And that price has made the S.A.T. big business, which is the final concern we need to examine. According to *Forbes* magazine, this multi-million-dollar testing service is the "biggest monopoly in the country." New York state senate testimony describes E.T.S. as an "educational country club that pampers overpaid researchers who sit around all day and contemplate their psychometric navals." No wonder they're so obsessed with ovals! Are these the people we want to dictate the direction of American education?

You see, students are supposed to be in high school to learn. Potential and achievement are not the same thing. As a study by *Phi Delta Kappan* magazine concludes, "School is supposed to encourage serious-

ness not sloth, but the present system, which emphasizes the S.A.T., fails miserably." Still, some researchers argue that it has value because it predicts possible success in college. In response to this argument, the dean of admissions at Brown University says that as an accurate predictor, the S.A.T. ranks "just one step above random." True, the S.A.T. does provide some useful information; it is a check on grade inflation, and it does make some national comparisons possible. But isn't there a better way to achieve the same result?

Fortunately there is, and if we are sincerely committed to a valid educational process, it's time to abandon the S.A.T. Instead, we need to replace it with a new test—one that doesn't try to measure elusive aptitude or intangible potential. The answer, according to the Carnegie Foundation for the Advancement of Teaching, is an Advisement and Achievement Test, an S.A.A.T. The difference is that this test will measure what a student has actually learned and point out basic areas of ability. I know, replacing one test with another might seem to some people as crazy as moving Iran to Libya, but, actually, it can eliminate many of the current problems.

First, if a student scores poorly, no longer will we pretend that the fault is his academic potential. Instead, we will be able to see where individual students, and schools, are succeeding and failing, and then make corrections. Rather than testing on nonessential vocabulary, students will be tested on essential mastery of their subject matter. At the same time, it would reduce the possibility of cramming, what Judson Jerome, professor of English, calls "brain jamming to beat the system." Students will be encouraged to develop better

STUDENT SPEECH
Continued

study and retention skills rather than simply try to beat the test. As Dennis Williams, in his article "Is the S.A.T. a Dirty Word?" points out, if a student knows he will be tested on Shakespeare and geometry, then he has a real incentive to *learn* Shakespeare and geometry. The end result will be a reduced emphasis on the whims of test makers and a greater emphasis on the knowledge of test takers. Eventually, we may be able to remove the business influence from testing altogether and get back to the real business of learning. Moreover, because the S.A.A.T. is also geared toward advisement as well as achievement, it can help the 30–40 percent of high school seniors who choose not to go to college by advising them on careers that fit their particular talents.

My request to you today is that you consider the possibilities. No, the S.A.A.T. won't solve all the problems. Yes, it will probably create some new ones. But it will also give a renewed emphasis on the value of learning, and isn't that what education is all about? Today, we have come to the point where our society's ridiculous rite of passage, the Scholastic Aptitude Test, needs to be retired to the anthropology books. What we put in its place should have only one judging criterion: It should be more than a *meaningless rite*, it should be *educationally right!*

REVIEW AND ENRICHMENT

LOOKING BACK

Listed below are the major ideas discussed in this chapter.

◆ Persuasive speaking involves your ability to convince your audience to believe as you do and then to take your recommended course of action.

◆ Persuasive speaking means that you are trying to "sell" a product, an idea, an attitude, or a belief.

◆ To become an effective persuasive speaker, you must keep in mind that people react on the basis of what they want, how they think, and how they feel.

- ✦ The Roman orator Cicero reminds us that the effective persuasive speaker is a person of learning and insight.
- ✦ Audience analysis occurs before you speak and is your estimation of how your audience feels about you and your verbal message.
- ✦ Audiences are often divided into four categories: supportive, uncommitted, indifferent, and opposed.
- ✦ The supportive audience likes you and what you are saying; this audience simply needs persuasive reinforcement to keep it fired up.
- ✦ The uncommitted audience hasn't made up its mind about you or your message; your job is to provide the information needed to win audience members over to your side.
- ✦ The indifferent audience can take you or leave you; you need to persuade this group by showing its members that what you are saying has relevance and practical application to their lives.
- ✦ The opposed audience doesn't like you or what you have to say; with this group, simply try for a fair hearing.
- ✦ Audiences are often combinations of these four categories; consequently, you must make the necessary adjustments in order to deal effectively with each specific audience type.
- ✦ For the persuasive speaker, the word *appeal* refers to what makes someone attractive or interesting to an audience.
- ✦ According to Aristotle, persuasive powers depend on logical appeal, emotional appeal, and personal appeal.
- ✦ Logical appeal (logos) attracts an audience with an analytical, reason-based approach to persuasion.
- ✦ Emotional appeal (pathos) hits the heart of the audience and stirs feelings of love, anger, compassion, patriotism, family, or the like.
- ✦ Personal appeal (ethos) links the speaker with the audience because of the speaker's honesty and competency.
- ✦ The best persuasive speaking is often the result of combining the various appeals as appropriate for the makeup of the audience.

SPEECH VOCABULARY

persuasive speaking
supportive audience
uncommitted audience
unbiased
indifferent audience

captive audience
opposed audience
compromise
disclaimer
logos

REVIEW AND ENRICHMENT
Continued

proof	integrity
pathos	reputation
ethos	sincerity
credibility	competency
good will	composure

1. For each speech vocabulary word, find the definition as given in the text. Write the definition beside the word, along with the number of the page on which you found the information. Next, write an original sentence for each word to show the word in action. Finally, select five speech vocabulary words that are most important to you. Explain why you made these choices and how the speech vocabulary words can assist you as a persuasive speaker.
2. Prepare a quiz. On the left side of your paper, list fifteen of the speech vocabulary words (number them 1–15). However, leave out a few letters from each word. For example, you might write "per---si-e s-eaki-g" for *persuasive speaking*. The person taking your quiz must fill in the missing letters to spell each word in its entirety. Next, on the right side of your paper, list (in mixed order) the definitions for your fifteen words and letter them from *a* through *o*. The person taking the quiz must place the letter of the correct definition beside each speech vocabulary word. Be sure to prepare an answer key for your quiz ahead of time.

GENERAL VOCABULARY

temperament	assert
cognizant	instinctively
analytical	liaison
palatable	

1. Use the dictionary to define each of the general vocabulary words. Dictate each word to a classmate in order to work on the spelling. Next, read the definition of each general vocabulary word out loud, and have your classmate tell you the word that matches the definition. Try mixing up the words.
2. Write an original one-page story titled "The Day I Made My First Sale!" You are to decide what you are selling. Are you going to sell a product? Are you going to try to convince someone that your idea is a good one? Use at least five of the general vocabulary words (underline them) in your story. Your story should make sense.

THINGS TO REMEMBER

Mark the following statements true (A) or false (B). Remember, a statement must be totally
true *in order for you to mark it with the letter A.*

1. Cicero described the most effective speaker as a person of learning and insight; he did
   this in the work *Rhetoric*.
2. Persuasive speaking is the art of convincing others to in some way "buy" what you are
   "selling," whether it be a product, an idea, an attitude, or a belief.
3. The term *speaking climate* refers to the temperature of the room in which you are going
   to be speaking.
4. The first Kennedy–Nixon debate showed that the person who is the most knowledgeable
   will always be the person who convinces the voters.
5. The word that describes a calm and controlled manner of speaking is *composure*.
6. You exhibit a sense of good will when you show audience members that you care about
   them and their well-being.
7. Aristotle's three appeals are logical, emotional, and personal.
8. When you are giving a persuasive speech, it is the job of the audience to make the
   necessary adjustments so that your speech has impact.
9. A captive audience is one that is totally supportive of you and is captivated by what
   you have to say.
10. The uncommitted audience is usually neutral or unbiased toward you and what you
    have to say. This type of audience is like a jury in that it will wait until you have
    provided all of your material before it makes a decision on whether or not to be
    persuaded.

THINGS TO DO

1. Go to the library and find additional
   material about the Kennedy–Nixon
   debates. What are some specific things
   that took place in the first debate? In
   the other three debates? Prepare a
   report detailing your findings. You
   may be able to find recordings of the
   debates. If you can, listen to the
   persuasive techniques of the two
   candidates. List the pros and cons of
   the persuasive speaking of each.
2. People in sales are often experts at
   effective persuasive speaking.
   Interview someone in sales and find
   out how he or she "reads" an
   audience and how he or she deals
   with an opposed audience. Finally,
   find out how the salesperson feels

REVIEW AND ENRICHMENT

Continued

about the three appeals—logical, emotional, and personal. Which works best for the salesperson? Do the three often work together? Get specific, detailed answers and examples, if possible.

3. Make a chart describing the appeals used in at least six commercials that you see on television (you might also include radio advertisements or billboards). In one column, list the name of the product being advertised. In the second column, name the type of appeal (or combination of appeals) being used—logical, emotional, or personal. Finally, give a quote (exact words) from the commercial or advertisement that proves your point. At the bottom of your chart, state which appeal you feel is the most persuasive and why.

THINGS TO TALK ABOUT

1. In the quotation that opens this chapter, Goethe states, "He who wishes to exert a useful influence must be careful to insult nothing." What does this quotation mean? Is Goethe saying that you must *never* take a stand or hold fast to a position? Does this mean that you must always give in to your audience? In what way is this quote good advice for the persuasive speaker? Is it ever possible for an excellent idea to be presented in the wrong way to an audience? Can you think of a specific example?

2. A national survey of more than 270,000 high school students was conducted in 1992. The survey concluded that student boredom is the result of (1) unvarying routine in the school day, (2) uninspiring subject matter, (3) unimaginative teaching, and (4) failure to make a connection between what students are expected to learn and real life. Which of these four would you put first? Explain. Are the teachers the only ones to be blamed? How can the students, the parents, the community, the teachers, and the school administrators *all* use aspects of persuasive speaking to help remedy the negative perceptions that the survey notes? Don't forget to consider intrapersonal communication as well as interpersonal communication skills.

THINGS TO WRITE ABOUT

1. One important ingredient of personal appeal is *reputation*, or how you are known to others and what they think of you. Why do you think that your reputation could be an important factor in whether or not you could

persuade someone? Write a one-page paper detailing how a positive reputation could aid your persuasive effectiveness. Give examples to prove your points.

2. In speaking, you *compromise* by finding a workable middle ground that is acceptable to both you and your audience. Write three reasons why compromising is a wise idea for those trying to persuade others. Next, give specifics to show when compromising could help you to persuade (1) your parents and (2) your friends. Finally, when is compromising the wrong thing to do?

CRITICAL THINKING

1. It has been said that the most difficult audience that you will ever have to persuade is *you*. Why do you think that many people believe this statement to be true? Why are you often your most threatening audience?

2. During the Civil War, a woman named Mrs. Rose O'Neal Greenhow was a famous spy for the Confederate army. She was beautiful and intelligent and traveled in the highest circles of Washington society. Even though she lived in the North, she made no secret of her sympathies for the Southern cause. In her heart, she was doing what she believed was right; however, her ability to acquire and pass on vital information about Union troop movements led to the deaths of hundreds of Northern soldiers. Was she right or wrong for what she did? Give solid reasoning for your position.

3. If you had to rank the three persuasive appeals—logical, emotional, and personal—which would be first, second, and third? (You can have no ties.) Would the type of audience you were persuading ever change your ranking? Give examples.

4. Which do you think is more difficult to sell to an audience, a product or an idea? (Be sure to define what you mean by the word *product*.) Give your reasoning. Are the two ever combined, so that you are persuading your audience to accept both a product and an idea (a belief or an attitude)? Provide evidence.

RELATED SPEECH TOPICS

Here are some topics that you can consider for "instant" classroom speaking. Even though these topics can be fun and are basically impromptu, be sure to remember Aristotle's appeals and to apply a clear organizational pattern.

Persuade your audience that

Dogs are better pets than cats (you can substitute or change the pets).

Year-round school is a bad (or good) idea.

A school dress code is a good (or bad) idea.

Students should have a voice in how their school is run.

Classroom tests are helpful (or not helpful).

Discipline is needed (or not needed) in your life.

The group is more important than the individual in a society (you can reverse these).

Reputation is more important than accomplishments or awards (you can reverse these).

Now go to the library and do some research on one or more of the following topics:

Abortion

Nuclear weapons

Sex education in schools

The homeless

Scientific experimentation on animals

Capital punishment

Diplomatic immunity

The prison system

Smoking

Drunk drivers

Instant replay in sports

Minority hiring

Women's rights

U.S. business competition with Europe and Japan

Censorship

Keeping in mind all that the chapter has said, construct a persuasive speech that will bring your audience over to your way of thinking. Remember, you should attempt to persuade your audience on the basis of what you personally feel is the right position for you to take. Mean what you say!

CHAPTER 14

Speeches for Special Occasions

 "I am the most spontaneous speaker in the world because every word, every gesture, and every retort has been carefully rehearsed."

— **George Bernard Shaw**

"And so, without further ado, here's the author of 'Mind over Matter' . . ."

LEARNING OBJECTIVES

After completing this chapter, you will be able to do the following.

◆ Define the specific purposes of several special occasion speeches.
◆ Discuss the characteristics of many of these speeches.
◆ Describe some of the more popular contest speeches.
◆ Describe the difference between impromptu speaking and the other special occasion speeches.
◆ Deliver an impromptu speech.

CHAPTER OUTLINE

Following are the main sections in this chapter.

I Courtesy Speeches
II Ceremonial Speeches
III Contest Speeches
IV Impromptu Speaking

Chapter Review

NEW SPEECH TERMS

In this chapter, you will learn the meanings of the speech terms listed below.

speech of
  presentation
speech of
  acceptance
after-dinner
  speech
commencement
  address
commemorative
  speech
testimonial
  speech

eulogy
original oratory
extemporaneous
  speaking
dramatic
  interpretation
humorous
  interpretation
impromptu
  speaking

GENERAL VOCABULARY

Expanding your general vocabulary will help you become a more effective communicator. Listed below are some words appearing in this chapter that you should make part of your everyday vocabulary.

reiterate
eloquent
dignitary
transformation
miffed
procession
hoke

embroiled
belie
converse
evoking
combustion
suffice
refrain

LOOKING AHEAD

In accepting an Academy Award, Dustin Hoffman took this special occasion to speak of others: "How many other Oscar-caliber actors are out there, undiscovered?" Although you, too, may remain an undiscovered actor, you will probably be called upon someday to speak at a public gathering. Special occasion speeches are part of our everyday lives. These speeches are special because they focus on particular situations: an address given at a school assembly, a testimonial speech offered at an awards banquet, a eulogy spoken by a friend at a funeral.

To ensure that the speech is indeed special, you will want to make it memorable. How can you do that? When you present a special situation speech, you should pay close attention to language usage and delivery skills. A special occasion—a graduation ceremony or a funeral, for example— often requires much more formality than your classroom presentations. Furthermore, you must always remember the expectations of the audience and meet those needs.

Although the primary purpose of most special occasion speeches is not to inform or persuade, they do require the same fundamentals of public speaking, the same analyzing of purpose. In this chapter, you will learn to present three general types of special occasion speeches: courtesy, ceremonial, and contest speeches. You will also learn about impromptu speaking for special occasions.

▌1▐ Courtesy Speeches

You present a courtesy speech to fulfill certain social customs. If you need to say "thank you," for example, you may find yourself preparing a speech of acceptance. Typical courtesy speeches include introduction, presentation, acceptance, and after-dinner speeches.

Introductions

If you have had the uncomfortable experience of being the new kid in school, then you know the need for successful introductions. Waiting to make friends can be one of the loneliest periods in a person's life. You find yourself wondering if you will be accepted by the other students. You worry about what they think of you, what they might be saying about you.

Although more formal than making friends in a new school, speeches of introduction matter in the same way because they break down the barriers between people. Introductory speeches serve two functions: to make the audience want to hear the speaker and to make the speaker

COMMUNICATION BREAKTHROUGH

Working for Peanuts

Charles Schulz, the creator of Peanuts, was invited to give a speech in 1980 to a group of four hundred exceptional high school students. This special occasion was an opportunity for Schulz to offer advice that might be useful to these young people. He recalls that he had great difficulty in coming up with an appropriate subject. After much soul searching, he decided against discussing the need for dedication and hard work. He chose, instead, to break away from what he considered the trite recommendations he suspected the students had heard so many times before.

In his book *You Don't Look 35, Charlie Brown!*, Schulz shares what he said in this special occasion speech.

"'I am not one to give advice,' I said, 'and always hesitated to do so with my own children, but tonight I am going to give you some advice that is very important. . . .' I then told them to go home and begin asking questions of their parents, to stop saying things to their parents, and instead begin asking things about their parents' pasts that demonstrate a real interest, and pursue the questioning. 'Don't stop until you have learned something about your father's first job or your mother's early dreams. It will take energy, but it will be infinitely worthwhile, and it must be done now. It must be done before it is too late.'"

Source: Charles M. Schultz, You Don't Look 35, Charlie Brown! *Holt, Rinehart, and Winston (New York): 1985, United Feature Syndicate.*

Questions
1. Do you agree with Charles Schulz that his advice is very important?
2. What would you say if you had the opportunity to speak to a group of high school students on a subject of your choosing?

want to address the audience. You need to achieve these goals in only a minute or two.

Because most speeches of introduction are brief, they must be well planned. You should plan to do some or all of the following in your speech:

1. Refer to the occasion that has brought the audience together.
2. Name the speaker (mention the name again at the end of the introduction).
3. Build enthusiasm by relating information about the qualifications of the speaker.
4. Share information about the subject to heighten interest, if the speaker wishes you to do so.
5. Explain why this speaker is to give this talk to this audience at this time.
6. Conclude by welcoming the speaker to the microphone or the podium.

Most successful speech writers of introductions are fans of Mark Twain. Why? Twain understood one factor that contributes to a memorable speech—humor. If you can combine humor with a meaningful message, then your chances for writing an effective introduction are greatly increased. Consider the following excerpt from one of Twain's many humorous speeches of introduction.

> I see I am advertised to introduce the speaker of the evening. . . . As a pure citizen, I respect him; as a personal friend for years, I have the warmest regard for him; as a neighbor whose vegetable garden adjoins mine, why—why, I watch him. That's nothing; we all do that with any neighbor. General Hawley keeps his promises not only in private but in public. . . . He is broad-souled, generous, noble, liberal, alive to his moral and religious responsibilities. Whenever the contribution box was passed, I never knew him to take out a cent. He is a square, true, honest man in politics, and I must say he occupies a mighty lonesome position. . . . He is an American of Americans. Would we had more such men! So broad, so bountiful is his character that he never turned a tramp empty handed from his door, but always gave him a letter of introduction to me. . . .
> Pure, honest, incorruptible, that is Joe Hawley. Such a man in politics is like a bottle of perfumery in a glue factory—it may modify the stench if it doesn't destroy it. And now, in speaking thus highly of the speaker of the evening, I haven't said any more of him than I would say of myself. Ladies and Gentlemen, this is General Hawley.
> Source: Albert Bigelow Paine, Mark Twain: A Biography, Harper and Brothers: 1940, Dora L. Paine.

Twain's introduction takes a few satirical swipes at General Hawley, which is fine, but you must be careful not to embarrass the person you are introducing. Hawley was a public figure and a personal friend; therefore, Twain could take certain liberties in this particular case. Good judgment is always a must.

Here are a few reminders for making a successful introductory speech: Check the pronunciation of all words, including the speaker's name; verify the accuracy of all biographical and other information; analyze the audience's expectations.

In many memorable speeches of introduction, Mark Twain, pictured here, combined humor with a meaningful message.

Speeches of Presentation

When a person receives a gift or award, a **speech of presentation** is needed. The presentation speech is usually brief. Of course, the length depends on the formality of the occasion. Typically, when you give a speech of presentation, you are speaking on behalf of some group, and you should reflect the shared feelings of that group. You can focus those feelings by choosing words that give deeper meaning to the circumstances that surround this special occasion. For example, the audience's expectations at a retirement party vary significantly from those at the annual Motion Picture Academy Awards ceremony. Certain guidelines, however, generally apply.

1. State the person's name early in the presentation (unless building suspense is appropriate).
2. Explain the award's significance as a symbol of the group's esteem.
3. Explain how the person was selected for the award.
4. Highlight what makes this person unique (use anecdotal information and a brief list of achievements).
5. Hand the award to the recipient.

Here is an example of a typical speech of presentation. The speech was given by a student to honor her teammate who was about to receive the Most Valuable Player award on their high school golf team.

No one is more deserving of Most Valuable Player recognition than Alysen. True, she is only a sophomore, but she led the team as if she were our most experienced golfer. If you've ever played a round of golf with her, you know what I mean by "led." In any foursome, she always seemed to be ten paces in front of everyone else, and you felt like you had to run to keep up.

And this year, no one was able to keep up with her or with her success. As a district medalist and a top ten finisher in the state championship, Alysen capped what was a remarkable year in competition. But speaking on behalf of her teammates, we are most proud of Alysen for the character she demonstrated both in victory and defeat. We voted her this honor because of that character. If she made a birdie or if she missed a three-foot putt, there was always a smile for everyone, a joy in the simple playing of the game.

As Will Rogers once observed, "It is great to be great, but it is greater to be human." So this Most Valuable Player award is presented to Alysen—a great human being.

Speeches of Acceptance

Jack Benny, on accepting an award, once ad-libbed, "I don't deserve this, but then, I have arthritis and I don't deserve that either." Even though recipients of awards or gifts usually have some advance notice, a **speech of acceptance** is most often, at least in part, impromptu (impromptu speaking was introduced in Chapter 11 and is discussed again later in this chapter). Even if you are able to prepare your acceptance speech, part of it will need to be impromptu because you will need to tailor your remarks to what was said by the presenter. The remarks that you make serve a double purpose: to thank the people who are presenting the award or gift and to give credit to those people who helped you earn this recognition. The formality of the situation should guide you in preparation, but generally you should consider the following:

1. Be brief, sincere, and direct.
2. Thank the group for the award.
3. Discuss the importance of the award to you.
4. Thank others who helped you win the award—minimize your worth, praise the contributions of your supporters.
5. *Reiterate* your appreciation.

If you have ever been a member of a team that lost the big game, then you can appreciate Adlai Stevenson's famous concession speech—a speech in which he "ac-

> **"I don't deserve this, but then, I have arthritis and I don't deserve that either."**
>
> **Jack Benny**

cepts" not an award but defeat. In that speech, he compares himself to a boy who has stubbed his toe in the dark—"too old to cry, but it hurts too much to laugh."

Stevenson was one of the most *eloquent* politicians of the twentieth century. Consider this excerpt from his speech accepting the nomination as Democratic candidate for president on July 26, 1952.

I accept your nomination—and your program.

I should have preferred to hear those words uttered by a stronger, a wiser, a better man than myself. But after listening to the president's [Harry Truman's] speech, I feel even better about myself.

None of you, my friends, can wholly appreciate what is in my heart. I can only hope that you understand my words. They will be few. . . .

And, my friends, even more important than winning the election is governing the nation. That is the test of a political party—the acid, final test. When the tumult and the shouting die, when the bands are gone and the lights are dimmed, there is the stark reality of responsibility in an hour of history haunted with those gaunt, grim specters of strife, dissension, and ruthless, inscrutable, and hostile power abroad. . . .

Let's face it. Let's talk sense to the American people. Let's tell them the truth, that there are no gains without pains, that we are on the eve of great decisions, not easy decisions, like resistance when you're attacked, but a long, patient, costly struggle

which alone can assure triumph over the great enemies of man—war, poverty, and tyranny—and the assaults upon human dignity which are the most grievous consequences of each.

After-Dinner Speeches

As hard as it may be to swallow at the time, many banquets or meals are followed by someone presenting what is known as an **after-dinner speech.** The traditional after-dinner speech is expected to be entertaining. Remember, though, that you can be entertaining without being "funny."

The key is to enjoy yourself, and then the audience is more likely to enjoy your presentation. On these occasions, most audiences want a message of some sort presented in a lighter, if not humorous, way. Be likable. Share your message in a relaxed and uncritical way, and adapt to the mood of the audience. If the audience is not responding to your "humorous" stories, then you should shift the focus of

INSTANT IMPACT

Robot Redford Reflects

Commencement speakers generally feel a bit nervous but pleased to have been asked. But at Maryland's Anne Arundel Community College later this month, the not-entirely-welcome commencement speaker will feel nothing, because he is an it: a 5 ft. 2 in. tall, 175-lb. mobile machine loaded with a computer named, by its California manufacturer, Robot Redford.

Surprisingly, the invitation originated with the dean, Anthony Pappas, who wanted to dramatize the high-tech *transformation* of the working world. Says Pappas: "This will call attention to the college's new unit in computer sciences and technology." Some among the 551-member class are *miffed.* "I don't like the idea," says Kimberly Roy, the student-government president. "It is not a human being like we are. We deserve more."

Robot Redford, remotely controlled and made of fiberglass and aluminum, will march in the academic *procession*, but will not be dressed in gown and mortarboard. "We don't want to *hoke* it up," says Sara Gilbert, a spokesperson for the college. The address will be delivered from the wings to the robot's speaker by its creator Bill Bakaleinkoff. Says he of his creation: "As soon as he gets ten minutes into his speech, they'll forget that he's a robot. Afterward they'll probably take him to the local malt shop and buy him new batteries."

Source: Time, *May 9, 1983, p. 39.*

your speech away from jokes to avoid "bombing."

The casual style that you need requires careful preparation. You should organize your presentation around a theme. All of your supporting material—illustrations, statistics, examples, narrations, anecdotes—should relate to that theme. The following excerpts are from a Nebraska student's state championship after-dinner speech. Note how all of the supporting material reinforces his theme of "too many intellectuals."

A dim chamber.
Velvety dust creeping across the floor.
The scent of dead books.
Blue haze falls from the pipes as a dreary voice flows from a shadow in the corner. Seven enchanted bibliophiles cluster around a worn, scarred table, performing the ancient rites. These members of the Duluth Directory on Deductive Discussion carry the illness.

Another scene. The depths of a dirty, empty library hold the bodyless mind of one Aristotle P. Chaucer, Jr. Pen choked by white hand, it struggles across the paper, attempting to write that crucial document for which so many wait. The Fred Friendly Fan Club Constitution is in the hand of one afflicted by that same disease.

Still another scene. A hand attached to some distant brain guides a stub of chalk on an enormous gray slate. Chalk dust settles to the floor as the long-sought formula for the chemical composition of armadillo saliva is revealed. The same malaise affects this being.

Yes, a plague creeps through our society. While some euphemistically refer to the illness as knowledge, we now recognize it for what it really is: the cancerous growth of intellectualism.

While the illness receives very little attention—the telethon never made it on the

"It is entirely possible that someone in this room is an intellectual."

Student State Champion

air—millions of Americans are afflicted with this awful disease. It is entirely possible that someone in this room is an intellectual.

I perceive your sudden nervousness as you wonder if the person next to you is a carrier. Don't worry. While it is true that "a little knowledge is a dangerous thing," small doses encountered by most people present an insignificant health hazard—our lack of logical thinking provides natural immunity. . . .

When we realize, however, how firmly entrenched in our society intellectualism is, we begin asking ourselves more and more: "GEE WHIZ, what can we do?" Well, the first step in halting the spread of intellectualism is the realization that you—yes, you—may suffer from some latent form of this syndrome. It is important, then, that you examine yourself weekly for these symptoms of intellectualism.

1. Sitting in the park, staring at pigeons, and thinking of hunchbacks and Dylan Thomas.
2. Talking to yourself and (here's the important part) not understanding a word you say.
3. Knowing that Norman Mailer doesn't work at the Post Office.
4. Taking your phone off the hook to watch "Firing Line."
5. Wearing a corduroy smoking jacket with leather elbow patches.
6. Laughing at the thought of what H. L. Mencken would have said if he met Gertrude Stein.
7. Worrying about being hit by space junk.

TAKING CHARGE

Now it's your turn. Try your hand at preparing a courtesy speech. Write and deliver a brief speech of introduction for one of the following:

1. A friend running for the student council.
2. A teacher recognized for excellence in the classroom.
3. A college financial officer addressing the senior class about scholarship opportunities.
4. A local politician asking students to volunteer their time in community service.
5. A karate expert demonstrating the art of self-defense at an all-school assembly.

Ⅱ Ceremonial Speeches

Ceremonial speeches are usually part of a formal activity. The addresses given on these special occasions often help the audience tie the past, present, and future together. The most common types of cere-monial speeches are commencement addresses and commemorative speeches, which include testimonials and eulogies.

Commencement Addresses

Some high schools select a member or members of each graduating class to pre-

A commencement address should acknowledge the significance of the graduation ceremony as the beginning of a new phase in the graduates' lives.

COMMUNICATION BREAKDOWN

Against All Odds

Special occasion speeches are sometimes *embroiled* in controversy. Carrie Mae Dixon, the top student at Jack Yates Senior High School in Houston, Texas, was allowed to deliver the valedictory address despite being seven months pregnant. Dixon was concerned that school officials would stop her speech because she was pregnant for a second time. Officials stated that there was no policy to prevent her from speaking.

During commencement ceremonies, Dixon shared the stage with other honor students including Mark Nealey, her boyfriend and father of her unborn child. Dixon also was recognized as an honorable mention for the award of outstanding graduating girl. In her speech, she told her 400 classmates, "You and I are special. We made many sacrifices and some of us even went against all odds."

The Associated Press reported that Dixon became a center of controversy when "an article about her for the school paper was killed by Principal Chester Smith." The arti-

cle "detailed Dixon's first pregnancy, and how she was shuffled among relatives after her mother died and her stepfather deserted her and eight siblings."

Smith stated that a U.S. Supreme Court ruling in 1988 gave school authorities the right to censor school newspapers. In Smith's opinion, the article about Dixon was too "personal."

The student who wrote the censored story said Dixon's scholastic achievements *belie* stereotypes that pregnant teenagers can't go far in life.

Questions
1. How many examples of communication breakdown can you find in this story?
2. What are some of the other odds teenagers face today that might keep them from succeeding in life?
3. Do you believe that Carrie Mae Dixon should have been allowed to present the valedictory speech? Why or why not?

sent a valedictory, or farewell speech. Another common practice is to invite a *dignitary* to address the graduating class. In either case, the speaker is giving a **commencement address,** or graduation speech. A commencement address should both acknowledge the importance of the ceremony and honor the graduates. The challenge for the speaker is to keep the attention of restless students and relatives who are already looking past the ceremony and toward the future. Therefore, most commencement addresses pay respect to

the past but focus on the future of the graduates. If you are chosen to speak at a graduation ceremony, you should choose examples and illustrations that celebrate the collective experiences of the audience members. Humor, if appropriate, can ease the tension and make the ceremony more enjoyable for everyone. Successful commencement speakers are positive and uplifting.

The graduation speech excerpts that follow were given by a young woman who wanted to thank her classmates and teachers for trusting her enough to be completely honest and open. The speaker uses a nudity metaphor to describe this baring of souls.

> I am grateful to you for exposing yourself. I am glad you let me see you naked because although I have found small scars and slight discolorations, I am struck mostly by how beautiful you are. . . .
>
> I trust you. With your tolerance and your love and your own nudity, you have stripped me down and relieved me of the stereotype I had built for myself. I am grateful to those people who have helped me look beyond the leather jacket and the big hair; who have helped me recognize what I was hiding underneath all that stuff: I am a young Eurasian woman who is as unique and nutty as each of you, but who is also as ordinary and human as each one of you. I don't know how else to express how grateful I am except by saying, Class of 1990, I will get naked for you anytime. I know that a few of you will do the same for me. . . .
>
> So when you're out there on your own, and you feel overwhelmed and afraid and defenseless, resist the urge to put on your armor. I have never believed in such a large and good-looking collection of naked people before. So, as the old saying goes, when you got it, FLAUNT IT. And Class of 1990, we have definitely got it.

Commemorative Speeches

You have heard the expression, "a picture is worth a thousand words." Some commemorative speakers in our country's history demonstrate that the *converse* is true: the right words are worth a thousand pictures. A **commemorative speech** is an inspiring address that recalls heroic events or people. John F. Kennedy's inaugural address, Douglas MacArthur's "Old

President Bill Clinton delivered a ceremonial speech at his inauguration on January 20, 1993.

Soldiers Never Die," and Ronald Reagan's speech following the *Challenger* disaster are commemorative speeches that succeeded in capturing our collective imagination, in inspiring us to reaffirm ideals, in taking snapshots of history.

Another example is Franklin Roosevelt's first inaugural address, delivered on March 4, 1933. That address contains one of the most memorable lines in speechmaking history: "The only thing we have to fear is fear itself." According to William Safire, that phrase was added at the last moment to avoid the negativity in an earlier draft: "This is no occasion for soft speaking or for the raising of false

> "The only thing we have to fear is fear itself — nameless, unreasoning, unjustified terror which paralyzes needed efforts to convert retreat into advance."

Franklin D. Roosevelt

hopes." The lesson for you is that careful revision can strengthen not only a commemorative speech but any writing that you do. Let's look more closely at Roosevelt's revised draft in the following excerpt.

> This is preeminently the time to speak the truth, the whole truth, frankly and boldly. Nor need we shrink from honestly facing conditions in our country today. This great nation will endure as it has endured, will revive and will prosper.
> So, first of all, let me assert my firm belief, that the only thing we have to fear is fear itself—nameless, unreasoning, unjustified terror which paralyzes needed efforts to convert retreat into advance.

Roosevelt's inaugural address recalls a special event. Other commemorative speeches are given to honor individuals— the testimonial speech and the eulogy.

Testimonials

You have witnessed countless testimonials by simply watching television ads. When Michael Jordan hawks a particular brand of athletic shoes or you are told that "nine out of ten doctors agree," the advertisers are hoping that the prestige of their spokespersons will persuade you to purchase their product.

INSTANT IMPACT

More than Fourscore and Seven Years Ago . . .

On the afternoon of November 19, 1863, Abraham Lincoln delivered his Gettysburg Address. This famous commemorative speech consisted of only ten sentences and lasted less than three minutes. In the years since Lincoln's brief remarks, millions of American students have committed these cherished words to memory. At the time of the speech, though, news coverage of Lincoln's address varied from praise to condemnation.

- ◆ *Chicago Times*—"Mr. Lincoln did most foully traduce [slander] the motives of the men who were slain at Gettysburg."
- ◆ *Chicago Tribune*—"The dedicatory remarks of President Lincoln will live among the annals of man."
- ◆ *London Times*—"The ceremony was rendered ludicrous by some of the sallies [lively remarks] of that poor President Lincoln. . . . Anything more dull and commonplace it would not be easy to produce."

Cashing in on the name and prestige of someone else, though, is not the only form of testimonial. A **testimonial speech** is an address of praise or celebration honoring a living person. The purpose of these presentations is to pay tribute to a special person—to generate appreciation, admiration, or respect. These speeches are often given at celebrity roasts or as toasts at retirement dinners or wedding celebrations. You may hear a testimonial speech at a farewell banquet for a fellow worker. The length of these speeches varies, but generally they last no more than a few minutes.

How can you make your testimonial speech successful? First, research carefully the person honored. If you can offer insights into what makes the person so deserving, your speech will be more successful. Language choice is crucial; the level of formality should fit the occasion. The tone of your speech should be warm and caring. A creative approach with appropriate humor that makes this special event memorable is desirable. Remember, the audience is there to pay tribute as well. Honor their feelings by *evoking* a strong sense of celebration.

In a heartfelt tribute to Earvin "Magic" Johnson delivered on February 16, 1992, at the Forum in Los Angeles, Johnson watched and listened as Kareem Abdul-Jabbar expressed what must have been in the minds of everyone who loves the game of basketball. The special occasion was the retiring of Johnson's team number, 32.

Ladies and gentlemen, here we are again, and it's a whole lot of emotion in this moment. You know it's gonna be awful hard for me to do this, but I'm gonna do the best I can. It was a long time ago when we first welcomed this young man out here on this court. And in the interim, he's taught us a whole lot. He's taught us a lot about him. He's taught us about ourselves. He's taught us about the game of basketball. He's taught us about winning. He's taught us about perseverance. And all of our lives are enriched by him.

I think the most important thing for me was that Earvin made me realize that I was having a good time. It's difficult sometimes, you know? You get caught up in the difficult part of your job, and you don't realize what it is you're doing, and what it is you're sharing with everybody, the whole basketball-loving public in America, and all the great Laker fans we have here.

And I want to say personally . . . I just got back from Boston last week and you wouldn't believe it, I know you wouldn't believe it, but the people there, they miss us. And that came as a big shock to me. But walking down the streets of Boston and hearing people saying how much they wish we were still out there going at it again, so they could have some enjoyment.

Thank you Earvin. Thank you very much. I just want to say in those times when we'd be driving through the outskirts of Detroit on a cold winter's night, and you'd have me smilin', thank you Earvin. We love you. I love you. Good luck.

Eulogies

A **eulogy** is generally thought of as a speech given to praise or honor someone who has died. The speaker, therefore, should try to relate to the audience the significant meaning in that person's life. Because eulogies are usually delivered at funerals or memorial services, the speaker must respect the religious beliefs of members of the family as well as the deceased.

In preparing a eulogy, you should decide whether you want to choose a biographical or a topical approach. As you attempt to chronicle a person's entire life, you will discover that the biographical speech often contains so many details that you lose the significance of the moment. In the topical approach, however, you can focus on personal qualities or specific achievements from which the audience can gain inspiration or understanding.

Although the tone of a eulogy is almost always solemn and the language sincere, you can be creative in your choices. You must, however, select details with great sensitivity and care. The following two examples pay tribute to the deceased in different and unusual ways.

One ninth-grade student eulogized her grandmother in a speech that reminds us that we all have "unfinished business."

> Dear Grandma,
>
> I'm not quite sure why I'm writing this letter. I know you don't have a P.O. box up there. I just want a chance to tell you how much I miss, need, love, and thank you.
>
> Unfinished business. We each have our own unfinished business. My math homework was due Tuesday, and I'm only on problem 3; I can't spend the night at Jenny's because I haven't finished vacuuming the den; and I won't receive my allowance until all the leaves are raked and bagged. Oh, we all have our own incomplete chores, but I'm referring to another kind of unfinished business—the kind between my grandmother and me.
>
> So often loved ones are taken away, and inevitably we grieve, but too many times our lasting sorrow overwhelms us because we fail to tell others how much we love them in the living years. I deeply regret not telling my grandmother her importance in my life. If only, if only I'd said goodbye, eye to eye, heart to heart. If only we all told our loved ones how much we need, love, and thank them before it's too late. If only we finished our business.
>
> Grandma, I need you. I need the crumpled Kleenex always waiting in your pocket to wipe away my tears, and I need your bedtime fairy tales that taught me morals and made me smile. But most of all I need your good advice.
>
> Today, in our independent society, we seldom feel the need to verbally accept others' spiritual gifts. Psychiatrist and author Gerald G. Jampolsky writes, "giving means that all of one's love is extended with no expectations." If only we would accept that gift of extended love and then express our appreciation.
>
> I love your comforting arms that swallow my troubles with every hug. I love your shiny white locks. With every curl lies a bit of wisdom. I love your presence.
>
> Playwright Thornton Wilder states, "There is a land of the living and a land of the dead, and the bridge is love, the only survival, the only meaning." If only we could communicate our love in the land of the living, it could form the bridge to the land of the dead.
>
> Grandma, I thank you for your lessons in life: you taught me to plant pansies and make apple pies, but you also taught me through love that all things are possible.
>
> Thanks that are so often felt but so seldom expressed. It doesn't go without saying. In the book of Job, chapter 1, verse 21, we learn, "The Lord giveth and the Lord taketh away." So before he takes what he's given, let us tell those special individuals what they've given to us. Let us finish our business.

Following the death of the newsman Harry Reasoner, his longtime friend Andy Rooney eulogized him on the television program "60 Minutes."

> His friends here at "60 Minutes" have lived with Harry's death for five days now. It's not a good thing to have to do. People keep asking how we feel. How does anyone feel when one of their best friends dies? Reporters ask a lot of dumb questions. "How do you think he'd like to be remembered?" "What one thing do you remember most about Harry Reasoner?" After twenty-five years of working with him, traveling with him, eating and drinking with him, what one thing do I remember most? Ridiculous.
>
> Harry was an infinitely complex person. It's hard to believe that great brain with everything that was in it is gone. He

wasn't like anyone I ever knew. If you think you know what he was like because you saw him so often here on "60 Minutes," you're wrong. No matter what you thought he was like, I can promise he wasn't like that. [Highlights from Reasoner's illustrious career followed, with voice-overs by Rooney.]

I talked with Harry about death—his and mine—as recently as six weeks ago and I know he had no intention of dying. Harry was the smartest correspondent there has

ever been on television, but he did more dumb things than most of them, too. He would not have died at age sixty-eight if this were not true. How does the smartest man I have ever known lose a lung to cancer and continue smoking two packs of cigarettes a day? I'm sad but I'm angry, too, because Harry was so careless with our affection for him.

Source: CBS, Inc. 1987. All rights reserved. Originally broadcast on August 11, 1991, over the CBS television network as part of 60 Minutes.

TAKING CHARGE

Now it's your turn. Prepare a brief eulogy to honor someone you know, a celebrity, or a historical figure. Refer to the examples that you just read for inspiration and ideas.

III Contest Speeches

Each year, thousands of students participate in interscholastic speech competition. A tournament hosted by a high school or college takes place somewhere in the United States almost every weekend of the school year. If you would like to benefit from this valuable activity, you should discuss with your speech teacher the opportunities available at your school.

The rules that govern speech contests vary from state to state and between the national organizations—the Catholic Forensic League and the National Forensic League—that offer competitive events. With a few exceptions, the speech events generally fall into two categories: public speaking and interpretation. (Two other

types of events, debate and congress, are discussed in Chapters 15, 16, and 17.) Some of the more popular events include original oratory, extemporaneous speaking, and dramatic and humorous interpretation.

Original Oratory

The **original oratory** is a speech contest event in which you write on a topic of your own choosing. Most states require that you memorize your speech and limit it to ten minutes in length. The key to oratory is to remember that it is a persuasive speech. In order to be convincing, therefore, you should pick a topic you feel strongly about. Typical topics include everything from child pornography to ne-

In interscholastic speech contests hosted by high schools and colleges, students generally compete in two categories: public speaking and interpretation.

glect of the elderly. The text of an oration that won the national championship in 1987 is included in Chapter 11.

Oratory demands careful and complete preparation. The successful orator "lives" with her speech over a period of weeks or months. Painstaking revision and updating of the materials are therefore necessary to keep it fresh.

In preparing the speech, use the organizational principles outlined in Chapter 8, and choose language for grace and precision. Keep in mind that the rules often limit the number of quoted words you can have in your speech—the National Forensic League, for example, allows no more than 150. You have the responsibility to cite the sources from which you obtained ideas. A rehash of a *Reader's Digest* article is insufficient and, if extensively paraphrased, unethical. Furthermore, do not expect your speech coach to write

your oration for you. The event is called "original" oratory for a reason.

Extemporaneous Speaking

If you enjoy discussing current events, **extemporaneous speaking** may be for you. "Extemp," as it is known, requires that you analyze a current topic and prepare within thirty minutes a speech on that topic. Generally, you draw three topics from an envelope and choose one for your speech. Typical topics, usually in question form, include such issues as:

◆ Should we increase taxes to reduce the budget deficit?

◆ What is the future of Eastern Europe?

◆ How can we win the war on drugs?

Once you have selected a topic, you refer to files or collected newspaper and

INSTANT IMPACT

The Speech Collector

"Curse of a Malignant Tongue," "Not Just a Farmer," and "Before the Diet of Worms" are just a few of the many "world famous orations and speeches" included in Roberta Sutton's *Speech Index*, an index to collections of speeches. Charity Mitchell's *Supplement 1966–1980* adds more recent works. These references include responses to toasts, responses to speeches of blame, speeches concerning commencement, speeches concerning *combustion*—usually not at the same time—and many others. The date and place of presentations are given, along with the anthology in which they appear.

magazine articles that you have brought to the tournament. During your speech, you quote from those articles to help support your answer to the question. The challenge is to organize your thoughts and present them in a clear and meaningful way in only five to seven minutes. Some tournaments allow you to use one note card; others do not. Judges are instructed to evaluate your performance on how well you answer the question you have chosen.

Dramatic and Humorous Interpretation

The interpretation events allow you to choose the material you want to perform. Do you have a favorite role in a play that your theater department is not going to produce? Have you ever wanted to be more than one of the characters in a play? **Dramatic interpretation** and **humorous interpretation**—sometimes separate categories and sometimes combined—give you the opportunity to share your acting talents. To paraphrase Whoopi Goldberg, you are the show.

The fine line between acting and interpretation is discussed in Chapter 19. *Suffice* it to say that in the memorized interpretation events, the competitors are generally "acting from the waist up." While in the scripted events, the reader is expected to "suggest" rather than "become" a character.

The rules for interpretation events vary greatly from state to state. For example, some states permit extensive movement, and some do not; some permit singing, and some do not. Each judge, too, seems to have a different philosophy about what is preferable, what is acceptable.

How, then, do you know what to do? The skills you need to become an "interper" are treated at length in Chapter 19. In general, study the rules for each tournament carefully, and try to make artistic decisions that honor the integrity of your selection. Do not rewrite Shakespeare because you can't understand *whence* and *whilst* and *woo*. If you perform "The Belle of Amherst," do not give Emily Dickinson a southern accent. Do not scream or cry as a way to win favor from the judge when it is clear that the character you are playing would not.

Give much thought to the kind of material that is suitable for you. Try to choose a selection that fits your personality and stretches you as a performer but is not beyond your grasp. For example, a male

COMMUNICATION WORKS

Lanny Naegelin, Speech Program Coordinator

"My mother wanted me to be a lawyer," admits Lanny Naegelin, coordinator for five high school speech and theater programs in San Antonio, Texas. As one of the most successful coaches in the history of the National Forensic League, Naegelin may not have fulfilled his mother's wish, but he has become an important advocate for communication skills in his school district. Naegelin specializes in helping teachers "bring dynamics" into classroom planning as they develop more effective presentation styles. He also leads workshops at the state level for coaches and students involved in competitive speech.

With over twenty years of teaching and coaching experience behind him, Naegelin has counseled thousands of students. To students new to speech activities, he asks, "Do you realize that during your life, you will present your ideas orally ten times more often than you will write anything?" Naegelin is also quick to point out that the best writers in his English classes have been extemporaneous speakers who used the skills they had learned on the speech team.

In his district, school officials track the students who participate in competitive speech. Sixty-five percent of National Merit Scholars have been members of a speech team. Naegelin states, "Of the top ten to fifteen competitors in each program, all have gone on to college, some receiving Truman Scholarships, Rhodes Scholarships, Marshall Scholarships, Rotary Scholarships—awards that you earn in part by undergoing a severe interview process."

One frustration for most coaches and students, according to Naegelin, is the low visibility of speech programs. Although students in all of the five high schools he represents have won national championships in speech competition, the local newspapers and television stations have provided little coverage. Naegelin says, "If the kid plays football and catches a pass, he's good. That's fine. He gets written up on the sports page weekend after weekend for the ten weeks of the football season, but I can't get one story on a kid who uses his brain."

Naegelin believes that teachers and coaches should sell speech as a step to success. He argues that parents want their children to have better lives, to do well, and that speech is a skill that will help them to do well. His wish: that somebody important would explain on television how speech is essential for success in life. "Anything could happen if we could get someone like Oprah Winfrey, who was a speech competitor herself, or Ted Turner. If it ever caught on, it would grow like gangbusters."

Clearly, Naegelin is a passionate advocate for the teaching of communication skills. He credits his wife for keeping him on track and adds, "I think my mother is happy now because I'm happy." Naegelin explains, "I'm not rich in terms of money, but in terms of the kids I've met, the success I've seen in what they've accomplished, I feel that my being where I am has paid off in far greater ways."

who cannot play female characters should avoid portraying Joan of Arc. Some selections require a number of characters—you should be certain that you can make them all unique and believable. Character differentiation that is mechanical or distracting is undesirable. In tournament competition, your goal is to make the performance so affecting, so real, that the judge forgets it is a contest.

Other Contests

If you are seeking scholarships for higher education, some clubs and organizations sponsor speech contests for cash prizes—in many cases, for thousands of dollars. The contests offered vary from community to community but include the following.

1. The American Legion Oratorical Contest. You must write, memorize, and deliver an eight- to ten-minute oration on some aspect of the United States Constitution. The contest also requires that you speak extemporaneously for three to five minutes on one of six of the constitution's articles or amendments. The extemporaneous topics change each year.

2. The Veterans of Foreign Wars' "Voice of Democracy" Contest. You must write and tape-record on cassette a three- to five-minute speech on a theme that changes yearly. A recent theme: "Meeting America's Challenge." You enter the cassette into the competition, and the recording is evaluated for content and delivery.

3. The Optimist Club Oratorical Contest. You write and deliver a four- to five-minute speech on a yearly theme. A recent theme: "If I Could See Tomorrow." Because the competition is for students under sixteen, it provides an excellent opportunity for younger students who might have limited public speaking experience.

But What If You Don't Win?

Most students who compete in speech soon tire of hearing this familiar *refrain* at every award ceremony: "There are no losers today. You are all winners simply by participating." Since speech contests are competitive, it is only natural that you will want to win. Unfortunately, the ranking of contestants is a subjective undertaking. Judges, no matter how well qualified by experience and intelligence, will disagree. One judge may compliment you on your creative approach to a topic; another may say that same approach is overused.

If you are to find satisfaction in speech competition, then you should set your own standards. Strive for excellence as you define it, and settle for no less. Certainly, you need to adapt to the audience—your judges—but not if that means compromising your integrity. In the final analysis, your success in any competitive activity depends on the goals you have for yourself. Satisfy your own high standards of performance, and the reward will always be there. If the only goal you have is to win, you have already lost.

Taking Charge

A popular speech event at some tournaments is original prose and poetry. In this event, the student competitor writes and performs his or her own literary effort. Now it's your turn. Write a poem or a short piece of prose (two to three minutes long) and perform it for the class. Include a brief introduction to help the audience understand and enjoy your performance.

IV Impromptu Speaking

As you read in Chapter 11, **impromptu speaking** is usually defined as talking "off the cuff" with little or no prior preparation. Although it is true that you may be asked, often to your surprise and dismay, to speak impromptu on almost any occasion, you have been preparing for these situations all of your life. You may not be as prepared as you would like, but you have a lifetime of experiences from which to draw. The effective speaker selects appropriate supporting materials from memory, organizes them into an easy-to-follow pattern, and delivers them confidently.

Since impromptu speeches are generally brief, simplicity is essential. You should establish a single point of view, choose one or two clear examples or illustrations, and conclude with a short summary and restatement of your thesis. If you have more than a few minutes for your impromptu presentation, you should subdivide the body of your speech into two or three issues and develop each one with supporting materials. Like all speeches, your impromptu speech should have a definite beginning, middle, and end.

A typical organizational pattern for a brief impromptu speech might include the following.

1. Statement of the main point of your presentation—the thesis. A short introduction to the thesis can be effective if you have the time (and an idea).

2. Support of the thesis with appropriate reasons, examples, illustrations, statistics, and testimony. Ordinarily, you should rely on your first thoughts because if you struggle to generate more information, you may forget your initial ideas.

3. Conclusion with a summary and a restatement of the thesis. Be brief—needless repetition is boring and reduces your credibility as a speaker.

The worst mistake you can make in an impromptu speech is to panic. Panic usually results in uneasy silence or unnecessary rambling. As a prospective impromptu speaker, you should minimize your concerns by reading widely and by being a good observer and listener. Remember, too, that your audience is aware that you're speaking off the cuff and will adjust its expectations accordingly. Most audience members will respond positively if they sense you're trying to incorporate your knowledge into a clear and meaningful presentation.

To help you with your first impromptu speech, here is a student example on the topic "elephants." Note how the student uses a clear organizational pattern and incorporates a variety of supporting materials.

Types of Special Occasion Speeches	
	Courtesy speeches, including introductions, presentation and acceptance speeches, and after-dinner speeches.
	Ceremonial speeches, including commencement addresses, commemorative speeches, and eulogies.
	Contest speeches, including original oratories, extemporaneous speeches, and dramatic and humorous interpretations.
	Impromptu speeches.

There is a story about six blind men touching an elephant. One man feels the tail and says, "Oh, it's a rope." One comes in contact with a leg and thinks it's a tree. Another man grasps the ear and speculates that it's a fan or a leaf. Still another man walks along the side of the elephant and concludes that it's a mountain. But none of these men realizes that it's an elephant. Although this story illustrates how we must see the whole of anything in order to understand it, it is also true that most of us, in fact, do not recognize the whole importance of the elephant.

I believe that we should not overlook the "mammoth" accomplishments of these pachyderms. Let us consider their contributions in two areas: the elephants, themselves, and what the elephants can teach us about ourselves.

Each elephant makes a significant sacrifice for our benefit. Did you know that every time you munch a peanut butter sandwich, you are grabbing goobers out of the mouths of baby elephants?

On a more serious note, in California, many people are beginning to boycott the use of ivory in products. These people are concerned that elephants are hunted down and destroyed just for their tusks. Furthermore, they express the fear that elephants may become extinct some day as a result of man's greed.

This selfish slaughter is even more depressing when we consider what elephants can teach us about ourselves. In one of Dr. Seuss's best-loved stories, Horton the Elephant promises, "I meant what I said and I said what I meant, an elephant's faithful one-hundred percent." This faith, this commitment, is an important lesson for all of us.

But perhaps the elephant is most familiar to us as the symbol of the Republican party. We learned in history class that the elephant as a symbol for Republicans came from the imagination of nineteenth-century cartoonist Thomas Nast. The teacher told us that the elephant was chosen because it is clever but not easily controlled.

So we should be clever enough to remember the accomplishments of these powerful pachyderms, for, as we all know, an elephant never forgets.

TAKING CHARGE

Now it's your turn. Everyone in class is to write three to five impromptu topics, each on an individual slip of paper. Taking turns, you and your classmates should draw three topics and choose one on which to speak. Give yourself a minute to gather your thoughts, and then deliver your impromptu speech in approximately two minutes.

Some sample topics:

◆ All generalizations are false, including this one.
◆ Teenage marriages should be outlawed.
◆ Television is chewing gum for the eyes.
◆ The world is a stage, but the play is badly cast.
◆ The malling of America.

REVIEW AND ENRICHMENT

LOOKING BACK

Listed below are the major ideas discussed in this chapter.

◆ Introductory speeches serve two functions: to make the audience want to hear the speaker and to make the speaker want to address the audience.
◆ Introductory speeches refer to the occasion, name the speaker, build enthusiasm, share information, and explain why this speaker is giving this talk to this audience at this time.
◆ Presentation speeches should reflect the feelings of the group. These speeches usually state the name of the person receiving the award, explain the award's significance, describe how the recipient was selected, and highlight what makes this person unique.

◆ Speeches of acceptance are usually brief and impromptu but generally thank the group for the recognition, discuss the importance of the award, and thank supporters.

◆ The traditional after-dinner speech is entertaining, with all humor used relating to a specific theme.

◆ Commencement speeches should both acknowledge the importance of the ceremony and honor the graduates.

◆ Commemorative speeches recall special events or pay tribute to individuals.

◆ The testimonial speech honors a living person; a eulogy honors the dead.

◆ The original oration is a persuasive speech the contestant writes on a topic of his or her own choosing.

◆ In extemporaneous contest speaking, the speaker draws a topic on a current event and prepares a speech in thirty minutes.

◆ Dramatic and humorous interpretation are contest events for students who want to perform works of literature.

◆ Speech contests for scholarships include the American Legion Oratorical Contest, the Veterans of Foreign Wars' "Voice of Democracy" Contest, and the Optimist Club Oratorical Contest.

◆ Impromptu speaking is a method by which one speaks "off the cuff." Most impromptu speeches begin by stating the main point of the presentation—the thesis. Support for the thesis usually follows, with a brief summary and a restatement of the thesis at the end.

SPEECH VOCABULARY

speech of presentation
speech of acceptance
after-dinner speech
commencement address
commemorative speech
testimonial speech

eulogy
original oratory
extemporaneous speaking
dramatic interpretation
impromptu speaking

In each of the following sentences, fill in the blanks with the missing terms.

1. _____ of _____ matter because they break down barriers between people.

2. Audiences expect _____ to present a message in a lighter, if not humorous, way.

3. A _____ acknowledges the importance of the ceremony and honors the graduates.

4. Testimonials and eulogies are two types of _____.

5. When Michael Jordan hawks a particular brand of tennis shoe, that is a form of _____.

6. A _____ is generally thought of as a speech given to praise or honor someone who has died.

7. An _____ is a speech you write on a topic of your own choosing.

8. In the memorized _____ event, the competitors are usually "acting from the waist up."

9. A popular misconception is that _____ means speaking without preparation.

10. If you enjoy discussing current events, _____ may be for you.

GENERAL VOCABULARY

Define each of the following words and use it in a sentence.

reiterate	embroiled
eloquent	belie
dignitary	converse
transformation	evoking
miffed	combustion
procession	suffice
hoke	refrain

THINGS TO REMEMBER

1. List five guidelines to follow in a speech of introduction.
2. Speeches of acceptance serve a double purpose: to _____ and to _____.
3. In his concession speech, _____ compared himself to a boy who has stubbed his toe in the dark: "too old to cry, but it hurts too much to laugh."
4. Ronald Reagan's speech following the *Challenger* disaster is an inspiring example of a _____ speech.
5. Kareem Abdul-Jabbar's tribute to Earvin Johnson is a form of the _____ speech.
6. If you wanted to find a particular oration in a collection of speeches, which reference work in the library would you turn to?
7. List five guidelines that you might follow in a speech of presentation.
8. _____ is a contest speech event that requires you to draw a topic and prepare a speech in thirty minutes.
9. In the scripted interpretation events, the reader is expected to _____ rather than "become" the characters.
10. List five guidelines to follow in a speech of acceptance.

THINGS TO DO

1. Take inspiration from Charles Schulz and question your parents about their pasts. Choose one incident from those discussions and prepare a short speech on the topic "A Turning Point."
2. Experienced speakers know that libraries contain reference works that are collections of humorous anecdotes. These anecdotes can be used to "spice up" an occasional speech. To learn how to use these valuable resources, find three humorous anecdotes on a general topic of your choosing—fashion, sports, education, health, or the like.
3. Attend a local speech tournament. After watching a few rounds of competition, be prepared to discuss the differences between what these speech competitors did and what you do in class.

THINGS TO TALK ABOUT

1. Some schools—perhaps yours—select students to speak at the graduation ceremony. How should these speakers be chosen? Grades? Talent? Popularity? Who should select these speakers? Administrators? Teachers? Committees of teachers and students?
2. Your best friend has been invited to be the after-dinner speaker at a banquet honoring a basketball coach whose team had a losing record. What advice might you give your friend?
3. Most audiences expect after-dinner speeches to be entertaining. What are some topics that you would find both worthwhile and enjoyable? Why?

THINGS TO WRITE ABOUT

1. Imagine that you are the speech writer for Robot Redford, the computerized robot that gave a graduation address. Write a paragraph for that speech that reflects the "high-tech transformation of the working world."
2. You are invited to be guest speaker at a banquet honoring students who have volunteered their time to community service. Write a speech of introduction for yourself.
3. Write an introduction for one of your classmates that could be used during the next series of assigned speeches in your class.
4. Imagine you have been asked to come back to speak at your twenty-year high school class reunion. Write a brief speech in which you look back on how the world has changed.

CRITICAL THINKING

1. Should eulogies be given only for persons who are praiseworthy? Does every human being have some essential worth? What about a serial rapist or a mass murderer?
2. Lanny Naegelin, coordinator for five high school speech and theater programs in San Antonio, Texas, suggests that students involved in competitive sports get more public recognition than students involved in speech activities. Is that fair? What, if anything, can be done to educate the community about the value of speech?
3. Judging speech tournaments involves subjective evaluation. For example, you have to choose one humorous interpretation over another. This process is analogous to deciding who is funnier, Eddie Murphy or Bill Cosby. How can we more fairly judge artistic endeavors?

RELATED SPEECH TOPICS

Pay tribute to a personal hero.
Present an award or gift.
Accept an award or gift.
Introduce someone famous to the class.
Celebrity roasts
Toasts that butter up

The "occasional speaking" of (choose one):
Jesse Jackson
Hubert Humphrey
John F. Kennedy
Martin Luther King, Jr.
Mark Twain

CHAPTER 15

What Is Debate?

"You raise your voice when you should reinforce your argument."

— **Samuel Johnson**

"Never argue at the dinner table, for the one who is not hungry always gets the best of the argument."

— **Richard Whately (1787–1863),**
English prelate

LEARNING OBJECTIVES

After completing this chapter, you will be able to do the following.

- ✦ Give examples of the ways in which people participate in informal debate.
- ✦ State several advantages of learning the methods and terminology of debate.
- ✦ List and give examples of the communication skills you learn and perfect as you study debate.
- ✦ Define basic debate terms.
- ✦ Prepare and participate in an informal debate.

CHAPTER OUTLINE

Following are the main sections in this chapter.

I Informal Debate

II The Advantages of Debate

III Debate Terminology

IV The Debate Process

Chapter Review

NEW SPEECH TERMS

In this chapter, you will learn the meanings of the speech terms listed below.

debate	burden of proof
formal debate	argument
informal debate	case
filibustering	brief
proposition	constructive
resolution	refute
affirmative	rebuttal
negative	format
status quo	

GENERAL VOCABULARY

Expanding your general vocabulary will help you become a more effective communicator. Listed below are some words appearing in this chapter that you should make part of your everyday vocabulary.

substantive	maturation
electorate	vouchers
gridlock	deficit
prosecution	assumption

LOOKING AHEAD

We do not live in a perfect world. Life is enjoyable for many people much of the time, but it is still full of problems. All people, even the most successful and happy ones, have problems.

You can probably think of plenty of examples: the bully who won't leave you alone, the parent who won't let you stay out late enough, the radio that doesn't work right, your lack of money, and on and on.

You might say that a problem is something that won't work, needs fixing, or is causing unhappiness. It's a situation in which something is wrong, and you're not sure what the best way is to remedy it. Maybe you can see several possible ways to solve the problem, but you're not sure which one would work best. If you were to study and think more about the definition of *problem*, you would realize that a problem is a question—an uncertainty—about what to do.

Debate is a method used to solve problems. The word *debate* comes from a Latin word meaning "to battle." A debate is a battle with words and ideas instead of missiles and tanks. In this battle, opposing sides (words and ideas) fight against each other to see which is the strongest—which is the best answer. This is how debate helps us solve problems. We set the different alternatives against each other to see which will win. In this way we find the best solution.

In this chapter, you are going to learn about a new kind of communication—debate. You'll learn what debate is, its different forms, and its special terminology. You'll also learn how studying and practicing debate can help you throughout your life. In Chapters 16 and 17, you'll learn much more about two specific kinds of debate—Lincoln–Douglas debate and policy debate.

I Informal Debate

We have defined *debate* as a battle between ideas. That means that when people disagree, and each puts forward an idea in an attempt to show that this idea is superior to another, a debate is going on.

When people hear the word *debate*, they usually think first of formal, dignified contests such as those they've seen on television between presidential candidates. They might also think of the formal student contests they've witnessed or heard about between opposing school debate teams. Most of what you will learn in this text about debate has to do with **formal**

On October 15, 1992, George Bush, Bill Clinton, and Ross Perot engaged in the second of three televised presidential debates. The format of the debate called for members of the audience, which was composed of 209 undecided voters, to address questions and concerns directly to the three candidates; a moderator guided the discussion and asked follow-up questions.

debates, which are highly structured debates that proceed according to specific rules. Other forms of debate, which we call **informal debate,** do exist, however. Informal debate is any debate conducted without specific rules. It's an unstructured, open-ended discussion of opposing ideas.

Before we begin our study of formal debate, let's take a quick look at some different types of informal debate. You may be surprised at how much you already know about debate and how many you have already participated in.

Personal Debate

You could say that people debate themselves. This is the intrapersonal communication discussed in Chapter 1. When you have a personal problem, you consider alternatives as you try to solve the problem. Maybe you can't decide whether to go out for the basketball team or the march-

ing band. You like both, but the schedules conflict. There's no way you can do both. In such a case, you might make a list of the pros and cons for both options. You might sit in your room and think to yourself, "If I went out for basketball, I'd get to hang out with all my basketball buddies, but I'd also have to put in a lot of hours of hard work—all that running every night. But if I joined the band . . ." In cases like these, your mind is a battleground for a clash between opposing ideas. In other words, a debate is going on inside your head. Eventually, one side's ideas will overpower the other's, and there'll be a winner. You probably engage in this kind of internal debate several times a week as you solve life's everyday problems.

Disagreements and Arguments

You probably don't need to be told what an argument is. Very few people go

COMMUNICATION   BREAKTHROUGH

Successful New Format for Presidential Debate

On October 15, 1992, in Richmond, Virginia, the three presidential candidates—President George Bush, Governor Bill Clinton, and Ross Perot—got together in the second of their three televised debates. The format (procedure for the debate) was a new one. It had never been tried in the televised presidential debates, which began with the Nixon–Kennedy debates in 1960.

The format called for members of the audience to ask questions. A moderator guided the discussion, picking questions from the audience and asking follow-up questions as she saw fit. Most media commentators and voters agreed afterward that this debate format raised the level of discussion to a higher plane, thereby giving voters more *substantive* material on which to base their voting decisions on November 3.

The tone was set early in the debate when one of the 209 voters making up the audience spoke of the group's desire to hear the candidates confine their comments to the issues. The voters wanted the candidates to refrain from the personal attacks that had characterized the first debate and the campaign as a whole. President Bush stated his opinion that character was a valid issue in a presidential election, and both he and Governor Clinton did make a few charges about their opponents during the debate. President Bush said, for example, that Governor Clinton had been speaking on both sides of the issues and that he was afraid Clinton would "turn the White House into the 'Waffle House'." Despite President Bush's desire to talk about character, however, the debate was devoted almost entirely to a discussion of the candidates' concerns and plans regarding the major issues of the campaign.

Much of the benefit of the new format resulted from the questions asked by the voters. The voters' questions about what the candidates planned to do if elected tended to be more direct and specific than those of the moderators and panel members who typically ask questions in presidential debates. One person asked how the candidates themselves had been affected personally by the recession. Others asked what the candidates planned to do with regard to gun control and education.

Overall, the debate had the flavor of a small town meeting. Compared with the other debates, this debate was more like a conversation about the issues between the candidates themselves and between the candidates and the members of the audience. This debate seemed to epitomize democracy in action. It also provided a breakthrough in communication that many hope will be continued in presidential campaigns to come.

Questions

1. During a debate, do you think presidential candidates should discuss each other's character, or should they limit their discussions to the issues? Should they discuss character during non-debate situations (speeches and news conferences) during the campaign?

2. As a voter, would you want to ask questions in a debate format such as the one described here, or would you prefer that "experts," more knowledgeable journalists and political scientists, ask the questions? Which type of questioning would produce the most valuable information for voters?

Arguments, whether friendly or serious, are debates in that they are battles between opposing ideas.

through life without getting into at least an occasional argument. Of course, there are all kinds of arguments—friendly ones, heated ones, serious ones, amusing ones. All of these arguments are, in a sense, debates. They are battles between opposing ideas.

Your brother claims it's your turn to mow the yard, but you say it's his turn. You give your reasons and try to show your mother or father why his reasons don't make sense. He does the same. In this case, there is a clash of ideas in which a parent acts as a judge to determine whose reasons are better. Your skills as a debater may determine whether you lounge coolly in front of the television or strain and sweat behind the lawn mower.

Group Discussion

Often, members of a group disagree about a course of action. In these cases,

an informal debate occurs. Here's an example. It's a hot summer day, and you and several friends have decided to go swimming. The problem is that some of your friends want to go to the community pool, but some of them want to go to the lake outside of town.

How do you solve the problem? If only one person has a car and a driver's license and that person is bigger and stronger than everyone else and always likes to get his way, the problem is solved. If, however, everyone has equal say, the group will probably solve the problem by listening to the reasons different people give for going to the lake or the pool.

- ◆ The pool is closer.
- ◆ The lake is prettier.
- ◆ The pool water is cleaner.
- ◆ The lake water doesn't have chlorine in it.

- ◆ There will be more boys (or girls) at the pool.
- ◆ They've got a great water slide at the lake.

This battle of ideas would go on for a while, and during the conversation more people would begin to favor either the pool or the lake. The reasons for picking one solution would tend to outweigh those for picking the other. Some members of the group would argue more persuasively than others. Eventually, several people would swing over to one side, and the problem would be solved. The group as a whole would have acted as the jury in deciding the outcome of this informal debate.

Organizations and Meetings

You probably belong to at least one organization that has meetings from time to time: your school class, Girl Scouts, church committee, athletic letter winner club, Future Farmers of America, or yearbook committee. Your meetings may be very informal, perhaps not much different from a discussion among a group of friends. In a larger organization, your meetings might be conducted according to the rules of parliamentary procedure (discussed in Chapter 18). In either case, informal debate will occur as you and the other organization members discuss ways to solve problems.

Let's say, for example, that your sophomore class needs to raise a great deal of money to finance next year's senior prom. You've got several ongoing projects to raise money, but you're looking for one big project for your sophomore year. One person has suggested an elaborate series of car washes every weekend over a six-month period, while another has recommended selling the members of the class as workers to local businesses. Both ideas would require a lot of volunteer time from class members, so it's not practical to do both. One idea must be chosen. A debate begins. If you have a strong opinion as to which method would be the most fun and interesting—and, of course, would raise the most money—you may participate in the debate by giving reasons for or against one of the alternatives. Even if you don't express an opinion in front of the group, you will probably participate in the debate as a judge, since finally the class will vote. Whether you speak or not, you will be participating in an informal debate.

TAKING CHARGE

1. Make a list of the ideas you've "debated" with yourself over the past several days. Compare your list with your classmates' lists. If any ideas appear on more than one list, discuss whether or not the debates led to the same conclusion.
2. Role-play an argument between siblings. First, brainstorm as a class to generate a list of common topics over which siblings disagree. Then role-play the

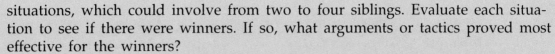

TAKING CHARGE (Continued)

situations, which could involve from two to four siblings. Evaluate each situation to see if there were winners. If so, what arguments or tactics proved most effective for the winners?

3. Assign members of your speech class to observe each of your school's clubs and organizations and each of the classes at your school. Contact the officers of each group to find out when the organization will have its next meeting and whether it would be all right for members of your class to attend as observers. The observers are to report back to the class how much and what types of debate took place in these meetings. Discuss what advantages, if any, would result from the use of more formal debate procedures and skills.

II The Advantages of Debate

There are many ways in which you can benefit from studying and practicing debate. Becoming an accomplished debater will help you immediately and in the future as well. Here are just a few of the advantages of becoming a better debater and a better evaluator of debates.

Career

In many of the careers you might pursue after school, you will encounter situations in which you may or may not be chosen to move up to a position of higher responsibility and pay. In many other careers, your success will depend on your ability to persuade people. Most of the workplace situations in which you'll need to impress and persuade other people will be like debate situations (rather than being like the persuasive speaking situations you learned about in Chapter 13). Managers and coworkers will challenge your opinions the way a debater is challenged. You'll have to think quickly and improvise rather than relying solely on prepared remarks. All of these skills are skills that you can begin developing now as a debater.

Helping Others

We all feel better when we can help other people. Think back to the class meeting example you read about earlier, when the class was deciding how to raise money for the prom. In that situation, the person who understands debate will be able to help everyone in the class. How? By helping the class members focus on the key issues, by presenting the arguments for and against each alternative

COMMUNICATION   BREAKDOWN

Debate Dissolves into Insults and Attacks

Most people would agree that the vice presidential debates held October 13, 1992, in Atlanta, Georgia, did not make a great contribution toward educating the *electorate*. A combination of circumstances and personalities caused a breakdown in communication.

The participants in this debate among vice presidential candidates were:

♦ Vice President Dan Quayle—Republican—running mate of President George Bush.

♦ Senator Al Gore—Democrat—running mate of Governor Bill Clinton.

♦ James Stockdale, professor and retired vice admiral—Independent—running mate of Ross Perot.

The format called for a single moderator to ask questions. The debaters were then allowed to challenge each other's responses. This format made for much more open and direct exchanges between the debaters than was possible in the formats used in the three debates among the presidential candidates. Instead of being a lively clash of ideas, however, the debate disintegrated into a series of insults and attacks between two of the three debaters. The third debater, Mr. Stockdale, was more a bystander than a participant.

Why did this seemingly promising debate fail to reach its potential in helping voters decide which set of candidates to vote for? Let's look at each candidate's performance for clues.

♦ Vice President Quayle spent most of his time criticizing Clinton and Gore. He tried to talk too fast, frequently sputtering and stuttering; and much of the time, he seemed not to be in firm command of the topics and his own strategy.

♦ Senator Gore was extremely well prepared—perhaps to a fault. He seemed stiff, mechanical, and rehearsed. He, too, spent much of his time criticizing his running mate's opponent.

♦ Mr. Stockdale had very little to say compared with the other candidates. Like Quayle, he stuttered and hesitated frequently while searching for the words he wanted. In contrast to Gore, he seemed very unprepared. At one point, he asked to have a question repeated because his hearing aid had been turned down.

Many commentators said that the debate was entertaining. Few, if any, however, said that it helped solve the voters' problem—deciding which candidates deserved their vote on November 3.

Questions:

1. Do you think this breakdown in communication was the result of the debate format chosen or the individual personalities involved? Could this format be effective with different debaters?

2. Do you think it useful to have televised debates with vice presidential candidates, or would you prefer to see an additional debate between the candidates for president?

By learning about debate, a voter can make more informed choices between candidates.

clearly and logically, and by helping the class evaluate those issues fairly.

In debate, you learn to narrow the issues so that they can be examined and analyzed logically, one at a time. You also learn how to present logical, well-supported arguments and how to find and point out errors in other arguments. All of this helps everyone move closer to the truth and to the best solution for the problem. In so doing, you help everyone involved.

As a Voter

As you learn about debate, you will become a more effective evaluator of arguments. You will become a more analytical listener. You'll be better able to pick out the good reasons and spot the faulty ones. If you listen to two candidates debate, you'll be better able to tell which candidate is the best prepared, the most logical, and the quickest thinker—all qualities that would help that person perform her duties successfully if elected. You would also become more knowledgeable and able to make a more informed choice for the candidate you felt had the "right" ideas. Of course, the wiser the choices all citizens make, the more effective the government that results.

As a Citizen

What are some of the "hot topics" at your school or in your community right now? Do you have strong feelings about any of these controversial issues? If so, wouldn't you enjoy standing up at a school board meeting or a city council meeting and clearly and logically pointing out to everyone there why your solution was preferable to the other solutions being offered? If challenged or attacked, wouldn't you gain satisfaction from being able to respond to the challenge with several well-supported counterattacks? Even more important than your personal satisfaction would be the community service that would result from your informal debate efforts. When you feel strongly about an issue, you can help the members of your community by helping them choose the best solution to their problem.

Taking Charge

1. Attend a school debate competition. If your school does not have a team, contact the nearest high school or college team and make arrangements to attend one of its contests. When you return, write two short papers (one to two pages each) entitled "What Excites Me about Debate" and "What Frightens Me about Debate."

2. Pick several different periods in United States history, such as the Revolutionary War, the Civil War, and The Great Depression. Break into groups, with each group taking one of these historical periods. In each group, do some research to identify and learn about an issue that was debated in the U.S. Congress or your state assembly during that period. If possible, obtain transcripts or films of actual debates. Give the class a brief overview of the issue and the circumstances affecting it. Then re-create the debate for the class by either using actual text from the period or creating your own. Have class members vote before the debate as to which side they think they would favor based on your pre-debate overview. Have them vote again after the debate. Did the debate change their minds?

III Debate Terminology

Part of what scares many students as they begin to learn about debate is the terminology. Debate has a language all its own. Many of the terms are not used anywhere except in debate, which means you've never seen most of the terms before, and so you must learn many new words in a hurry. It's like trying to read Shakespeare for the first time or learning chemistry.

Once you learn the meanings of the new terms, though, you can proceed to the more fun and exciting parts of debate. Let's take some time to study the terminology of debate so that we can then move on to actual debating.

Proposition

One of the most important debate terms is **proposition.** A proposition is really just another word for statement. It is the statement of the point to be debated. It states a fact, a belief, or a recommendation to do something. Another way of explaining *proposition* is to say that it's a formal way of stating an opinion. Here are some examples:

◆ The minimum age for drinking alcohol should be raised to twenty-five.

◆ Christopher Columbus discovered America.

◆ Beauty is more important than honesty.

Debaters are very careful about the way they word their propositions. The reason for their concern is that each word in the proposition can have a major influence on what happens during the debate. You will learn more about good and bad wording for propositions later in this chapter.

Resolution

In debate, the word *resolved* added to a proposition means the proposition has been developed and is about to be stated. *Resolved* is a formal word used to introduce a proposition. It doesn't affect the meaning of the proposition; it just introduces it formally. It does imply that some careful thought went into stating the proposition in those exact words.

A proposition that begins with the word *resolved* is often called a **resolution.** Here are some examples of resolutions. Note that these are the same as the

INSTANT IMPACT

Lincoln Slipped but Didn't Fall

Who won the famous Lincoln–Douglas debates (you'll learn more about these debates in Chapter 16)? Stephen Douglas won the election by a vote of 54 to 46 in the Illinois State Legislature, which at that time elected the state's U.S. senators, so you might say that he won the debates. Had Lincoln won the senate seat in 1858, however, he probably wouldn't have run for president in 1860, an election in which he was victorious, to a great extent because of the publicity he received during his debates with Douglas. Thus, Lincoln referred to his "defeat" in 1858 as a "slip and not a fall."

propositions used previously. Nothing has changed in their meaning; they are just more formally stated.

◆ *Resolved:* that the minimum age for drinking alcohol should be raised to twenty-five.

◆ *Resolved:* that Christopher Columbus discovered America.

◆ *Resolved:* that beauty is more important than honesty.

Affirmative and Negative

Affirmative and **negative** are two words that you probably already know. *Affirmative* means yes, or true; *negative* means no, or false.

These terms are very important in formal debate because every proposition is worded so that you must either agree or disagree with it. You either say, "Yes, that is true" or "No, that is false." During a formal debate, one side, called the *affirmative side*, tries to prove that the statement is true. The other side, called the *negative side*, tries to prove that it's false. For example, in a debate of the proposition that the minimum age for drinking should be raised to twenty-five, the affirmative side would argue yes, that it should be raised. The negative side would argue no, that it should not be raised.

Status Quo

Status quo sounds much more complicated than it really is. It simply means the way things are now—the existing conditions. The opposite of status quo is change. If every year for the last ten years your school has had a total enrollment of about 1,200 students, then an enrollment of 1,200 is the status quo. If next year the enrollment suddenly jumped to 2,000, that would be a change from the status quo. In formal debate, the negative side usually defends the status quo, arguing that there's

no need to change—that whatever exists now is what should continue to exist.

Burden of Proof

Burden of proof is a term used in formal debate and in law to refer to the duty or responsibility to prove something. In a criminal trial, for example, the *prosecution* has the burden of proof. It's the prosecuting attorney's job to prove that the accused person is guilty.

There is no burden of proof on the defense attorney. The defense attorney doesn't have to prove that the accused person is innocent. The accused person is "innocent until proven guilty."

In formal debate, the burden of proof is on the debater arguing for the affirmative. He or she must prove that there is a problem with the status quo and that it should change. Just as the jury assumes the accused to be innocent until proven guilty, the debate judge assumes the status quo to be the best solution until proven otherwise.

Argument

You know what an argument is—you've probably had your share. In debate, the word *argument* has a meaning a little different from the one you're used to. Debaters use the word **argument** to refer to a reason for favoring their side of the proposition. The argument also includes the facts that support that reason. Each debater goes into a debate with several arguments that he or she will use to try to win the debate.

Evidence

You also know the word *evidence.* As Chapter 9 pointed out, it refers to information that helps prove something. Fingerprints and eyewitness accounts are evidence in trials. Facts, statements, reports, and quotes from experts are examples of evidence used in debates. Each side tries to find as much evidence as possible to prove its side of the proposition.

Case

If you watch courtroom dramas on television, you've probably heard the lawyers talk about "winning the case" or how they have "a great case." These lawyers are using the word **case** much as formal debaters use it, to mean the total group of arguments. The case is the combination of all the debater's ideas and evidence organized and arranged to be as convincing as possible. Knowing that lawyers carry their written arguments in a brief*case* may help you remember the meaning of this debate term.

Brief

Briefcase may also help you remember another debate term. Again, like lawyers, debaters talk about their briefs. A **brief** is what you might expect—something less than the total—something that's not complete. In debate, a brief is an outline. It's an outline of both the affirmative and the negative cases. Debaters use the brief as a guide and summary before and during the debate. It allows them to see all the relevant issues of the debate at a glance.

Constructive

The word **constructive** has a very special meaning in formal debate. You can see in this unfamiliar word a clue to its meaning. The clue is the familiar word *construct,* which means to build something. In debate, *constructive* describes specific speeches that debaters make during the debate. The constructive speeches are those that put forward an argument—that *build* an argument for one side or the other. When debaters give constructive speeches, they are *building* or presenting their arguments.

Refute

To **refute** something means to show that something is wrong—to prove that something someone said is false. If someone said that your grandmother wears no footwear other than army boots, you could *refute* this by producing a picture of your grandmother in her house slippers. If your teacher said you hadn't handed in your homework, but you then found it in her stack of homework papers, you would be refuting her statement.

An important part of formal debate is refuting your opponent's arguments. You do this by offering evidence to show why your opponent's statements are false. When you refute an argument, you are offering a *refutation.*

Rebuttal

A **rebuttal** is a speech that contradicts an earlier statement. The rebuttal tries to show that the earlier statement is wrong or false. The term probably sounds much like the term you just learned—*refute*—and it should, because their meanings are very similar. In formal debate, there is an important difference, however. Refutation is the act of attacking your opponent's arguments. Rebuttal is the act of countering your opponent's attacks on your arguments so that you can rebuild your argument. It goes something like this:

◆ You present an argument in your *constructive* speech:
"Twenty-five-year-olds are more mature than twenty-one-year-olds, so there would be fewer accidents if we raised the drinking age."

◆ Your opponent *refutes* your argument:
"There is no evidence to support the statement that twenty-five-year-olds are more mature than twenty-one-year-olds."

◆ You *rebut* your opponent's refutation:
"In a study conducted by the psychology department at Harvard, twenty-five-year-olds were shown to score significantly higher on *maturation* scales than twenty-one-year-olds."

TAKING CHARGE

1. Write ten propositions dealing with issues you'd like to see debated. Following each, tell whom you would like to see debate the issue. For example, you might want to see a national high school debate champion and your mother debate the proposition, "Resolved: that adults will no longer be allowed to limit the time their children spend watching television." Be sure to begin each proposition with *resolved.* Make sure that each proposition is a yes–no statement.

TAKING CHARGE (Continued)

2. Write ten sentences in which you describe a status quo situation—for example, "Each state has two U.S. senators." Try to vary the areas covered (sports, politics, religion, education, environment, psychology, economics, and so on) as much as possible. Pick the one status quo you'd most like to change if you could. Tell why you picked that situation in a class discussion.
3. Pick a proposition written by one of your classmates and gather evidence to refute it. Present your evidence to the class.

IV The Debate Process

Let's now look briefly at how a debate works. We'll outline the basic process so that you'll have enough knowledge to conduct a debate in your classroom. In the next two chapters, you'll learn a great deal more about two types of formal debate practiced in high school contests—Lincoln–Douglas debate and policy debate.

Getting Started

Of course, every debate begins with a topic. You need a problem, and you need a proposed solution to that problem (the proposition). While there are countless problems that could be debated, people often pick the more controversial issues. These are the topics about which many people on both sides of the issue feel strongly. Here are some broad issues that could serve as topics for debate:

◆ abortion
◆ sexual education in the schools
◆ *vouchers* for public education

◆ the federal *deficit*
◆ health care legislation
◆ penalties for driving while intoxicated
◆ public employees' right to strike
◆ censorship of rock music
◆ foreign trade agreements
◆ term restrictions for legislators

It's not enough, however, to pick an issue. You can't just pick one of the issues above and say, "Let's debate." To make the issue debatable, you must write a proposition in its proper "yes–no" form. The proposition also needs to focus on one part of the issue, and it must be clearly worded so that there's no confusion about what's being debated.

The careful wording of a proposition is a key difference between debate and the type of heated discussions people sometimes get into. In those discussions, the argument isn't clearly focused on one definite part of the issue. Instead, everybody offers his or her own propositions, and people rarely take the time to define terms. That is why little progress is made in clarifying the issues or solving the problem in such arguments.

Here are some examples of poorly worded propositions:

◆ Resolved: that abortion is bad.

Vague language (what does "bad" mean?); not clear what is being proposed.

◆ Resolved: that the federal deficit should be reduced by raising taxes and cutting military spending.

Two different propositions; can't debate two at once.

◆ Resolved: that the penalties for drunk drivers are not harsh enough.

Doesn't propose a change; must state clearly a proposed change from status quo.

As soon as you have your proposition, you are ready to divide into teams. You need a team for the affirmative, a team for the negative, and a judge. It's up to the affirmative team to prove the proposition. The negative team defends the status quo and tries to discredit the proposition.

Formats

Several different formats are used for formal debate. **Format** refers to the procedure that will be used to conduct a particular debate. The format specifies the order in which the debaters will speak and the amount of time allowed for each speech. The main purpose of establishing a format is to give both sides an equal opportunity to make their cases. Since the affirmative side is proposing change (arguing for the proposition), it goes first and usually speaks last as well. You'll learn more about specific contest formats in the next two chapters. For an informal debate, you can devise whatever format you like, as long as the rules are clear ahead of time and fair to both sides.

INSTANT IMPACT

A Cannon Loaded to the Lips

On January 26 and 27, 1830, Daniel Webster gave what some believe was the most powerful speech ever given in the U.S. Senate in his rebuttal to Senator Robert Hayne's speech five days earlier. They were debating whether the Western Territories should be opened to slavery and whether or not states could overturn laws passed by the U.S. Congress. Hayne favored the states' having this power, arguing for "Liberty first and Union afterwards." Webster ended his speech, which lasted six hours, over the course of two days, by declaring, "Liberty *and* Union, now and forever, one and inseparable." His speech helped convince Americans of the importance of a strong federal government. Perhaps Ralph Waldo Emerson best described Webster's skill as an orator and debater when he called him "a great cannon loaded to the lips."

Strategy

Following are a few general suggestions for preparing and arguing your case. Basically, you want to gather as much evidence as possible to support your case and refute your opponent's case. In the next two chapters, you will learn more specific strategies for winning Lincoln–Douglas and policy debate contests.

◆ Work hard. Many debates are won or lost before they begin. Everyone on the team must work to gather evidence.

◆ Anticipate. In your research, you'll come across evidence that will support your opponent's arguments. Don't overlook this information. Use it to anticipate your opponent's arguments and then plan how you will respond.

◆ Build a sound case. Pick the three or four strongest reasons for your side of the proposition and support those reasons as best you can with strong evidence. Organize your case logically (refer back to Chapter 9).

◆ Listen. Listen closely to what your opponent says. You want to find weaknesses in your opponent's evidence and arguments. There may not be enough evidence, and specific pieces of evidence may be weak. Your opponent might also make an illogical *assumption* based on his or her evidence. For example, the fact that 10,000 seventeen-year-olds were killed in car accidents doesn't prove that the driving age should be raised to eighteen.

◆ Take notes. As the debate goes on, you will need to take careful notes to keep track of both your statements and your opponent's. Formal debaters call their notes a *flow-sheet*, which you'll learn more about in the next chapters.

◆ Speak clearly and logically. Organize your thoughts before you speak so you are sure to make your points. It's important not to get too excited or rushed in your eagerness to refute your opponent's arguments.

TAKING CHARGE

As a class, discuss the various propositions, status quo situations, and refutations that resulted from doing the Taking Charge exercises on pages 428-429. Pick the two or three most interesting, controversial topics and debate those topics.

REVIEW AND ENRICHMENT

LOOKING BACK

Listed below are the major ideas discussed in this chapter.

◆ Debate is a method used to solve problems.
◆ People engage in informal debate with themselves, in disagreements and arguments with others, in group discussions, and in organizational meetings.
◆ Learning about and participating in debate leads to many advantages. You can help your career, help others, and help as a voter and citizen by becoming a better debater and a better evaluator of debates.
◆ Debate has a terminology all its own. It is necessary to learn the meanings of these terms to become a successful debater.
◆ Debatable issues must be stated in proper form to allow for a successful debate. A proposition must be worded so that it can be answered yes or no, it must focus on one part of an issue, it must be clearly worded, and it must not favor one side or the other.
◆ Several different formats are used to structure debates. The affirmative side usually speaks first and last.
◆ To be successful at debate, you must work hard, anticipate your opponent's arguments, build a strong case, listen closely to your opponent's arguments, take notes, and speak clearly and logically.

SPEECH VOCABULARY

Match the speech term on the left with the definition on the right.

1. burden of proof
2. argument
3. status quo
4. evidence
5. case
6. proposition
7. resolution
8. negative
9. informal debate
10. refute
11. brief

a. Information that helps prove something
b. Debate speech that builds an argument
c. Procedures for conducting a debate
d. Existing conditions
e. A formal way to state a proposition
f. A method used to solve problems
g. Yes
h. Statement of a point to be debated
i. Total group of arguments
j. An outline of both the affirmative and the negative cases
k. A debate conducted without specific rules

12. debate
13. constructive
14. formal debate
15. affirmative
16. rebuttal
17. format

l. Reason for favoring a particular side of a proposition
m. Show how something is wrong
n. A speech countering your opponent's attacks on your arguments
o. Structured debate proceeding according to specific rules
p. The responsibility of proving something
q. No

GENERAL VOCABULARY

Write a definition for each of the terms listed below and then use each in a sentence.

substantive
electorate
gridlock
prosecution

maturation
vouchers
deficit
assumption

THINGS TO REMEMBER

1. What is a problem?
2. What is the English translation of the Latin word from which *debate* originated?
3. What is the difference between formal and informal debate?
4. Name four broad areas that can be helped by a person's learning about debate.
5. What word is used to introduce a formal debate's proposition?
6. What are the two sides called in a formal debate?
7. Find a word that means the opposite of *status quo*.
8. Is the negative side in a debate more like the prosecution or the defense in a court trial?
9. Does a debater's case include his or her evidence, or does the evidence include the case?
10. Which comes first, a constructive speech or a rebuttal speech?
11. How many parts of an issue can be included in a properly worded debate proposition?
12. What is the main purpose of establishing a debate format?

THINGS TO DO

1. If your television receives cable broadcasts of either local or national political proceedings (for example, on C-SPAN), tape a debate. Bring the

tape to your class. After watching the tape, analyze the strengths and weaknesses of the debaters involved.

2. Debates usually deal with the most serious, emotionally charged issues. Brainstorm with the class to create a list of the most trivial, unimportant issues possible. Then choose three or four of the least important issues to debate. Divide the class up into two sides for each of those issues and debate the propositions.

3. Survey the school population to find out what issues in your school and community most concern students.

Pick the three or four issues that most concern students and schedule debates for each of those topics periodically throughout the school year. Assign different members of the class to different sides of the various issues, then stage the debates at a scheduled school assembly. Have the student body vote for the winner in each debate. You may want to experiment with various formats. For example, in some debates, members of the student body could ask specific questions of each debate team.

THINGS TO TALK ABOUT

1. Some people seem to enjoy arguments and have a flair for them. Are you one of those people? If so, why do you think you enjoy arguments? If you are not one of those people, why do you dislike arguments?

2. Have you ever held back in an informal debate during a meeting, even though you felt you had something important to say? Why did you hold back? What effect do you think your comments would have had on the course of the discussion and the results?

3. Recall debates you have seen on television or at debate contests. What speeches or qualities of the debaters impressed you the most?

4. When you are engaged in an argument with friends, do you usually get your way? If so, what strategies do you use to convince your friends that your suggestion is the best? If not, what strategies have you observed being used by your friends who usually do win the arguments?

THINGS TO WRITE ABOUT

1. Write a short story of two to four pages. Write it in the third person, with the main character being someone at a school or group meeting.

This character has something to say but is afraid to speak up. What happens?

2. Opportunities for arguments present themselves constantly. As a rule, most of us either respond to the issue and debate it, as long as the other person is willing, or shy away from the confrontation. Write an essay explaining which course of action you believe to be the best. If you think that whether you should debate the issue depends on the issue and its importance, give specific examples as to which issues are worth debating and which aren't.

3. Write a letter to one of your U.S. or state representatives. Ask this person how he or she rates himself or herself as a debater and where and how he or she learned debating skills. Also ask for suggestions on how you could improve your skills.

4. Over the next few days, be aware of debates that you have with yourself. Write out the arguments that each side of you is presenting. Use two different names for yourself, and write the debate as a back-and-forth discussion between the two characters.

CRITICAL THINKING

1. Should meetings of your class and other group meetings make use of formal debate procedures to solve problems? What advantages and disadvantages do you see in using such procedures in those meetings?

2. Why do you think the burden of proof is on the affirmative side rather than the negative side? Why is the status quo considered the best solution until proved otherwise?

3. Identify and evaluate your overall skills as a debater. What are your strongest skills? Your weakest? What are the three to five most important steps you could take to become a more effective debater?

RELATED SPEECH TOPICS

The following list contains several potential topics for debates.

The voting age should be lowered from eighteen to twelve.

Potential voters should be required to pass, with a score of 70 or above, a test covering the prominent issues in a given election year.

Failure to vote in an election should result in a 5 percent increase in a qualified voter's personal income tax for the four years following that election.

Loyalty to parents is more important than loyalty to peers.

The experience gained from a part-time job is more valuable than the money earned in that job.

CHAPTER 16

Lincoln–Douglas Debate

> "Unless philosophers become kings, or those rulers become enlightened, there will be no end to the troubles of states, or, I believe, the troubles of mankind."
>
> — **Plato,** *The Republic*
>
> "Those who deny freedom to others deserve it not themselves."
>
> — **Abraham Lincoln**

LEARNING OBJECTIVES

After completing this chapter, you will be able to do the following.

♦ Discuss what values are, what importance values have, and how questions of value are different from other questions.

♦ Analyze questions in terms of value judgments.

♦ Write cases that argue for and against value propositions.

♦ Debate a complete round in the Lincoln–Douglas format, using your organizational, cross-examination, and rebuttal skills.

CHAPTER OUTLINE

Following are the main sections in this chapter.

I Lincoln-Douglas Debate: A Question of Values

II Preparing for Battle: Writing Cases

III Structuring Your Speeches

Chapter Review

NEW SPEECH TERMS

In this chapter, you will learn the meanings of the speech terms listed below.

Lincoln–Douglas debate

factual proposition

policy proposition

value proposition

value

ought

value premise

first affirmative constructive (1AC)

first negative constructive (1NC)

cross-examination

first affirmative rebuttal (1AR)

negative rebuttal (NR)

second affirmative rebuttal (2AR)

prep time

GENERAL VOCABULARY

Expanding your general vocabulary will help you become a more effective communicator. Listed below are some words appearing in this chapter that you should make part of your everyday vocabulary.

renowned

sanctity

covert

affluent

surrogacy

procreation

commerce

evasive

relentless

gadfly

incisive

dire

LOOKING AHEAD

In this chapter, you are going to learn about one kind of formal debate—Lincoln–Douglas. You will learn how to analyze value propositions, how to write cases, and how to participate in a Lincoln–Douglas debate.

Lincoln–Douglas debate attempts to resolve value conflicts. Resolving value conflicts through debate has always been an important part of our democratic process.

1 Lincoln-Douglas Debate: A Question of Values

Ought police officers be allowed to stop and search your car randomly as a part of the effort to win the war on drugs? Should high school administrators be able to censor student publications? Is it fair for the government to tax the poor to fund new public highways? Although politicians might answer these difficult questions with snappy sound bites—like "Just say no" and "Read my lips"—such questions of public policy still require thorough discussion and much thought.

Indeed, these questions lead to even more difficult underlying questions: Should we value privacy more than we value stopping crime? Should students' rights be different from those of their parents? Does each citizen have special obligations to every other citizen? While these broad questions may sometimes seem to lead to dizzying abstraction and confusing philosophical double-talk, the truth is that such questions are important and can be answered intelligently and understandably.

This chapter will help you learn to persuade others when confronted with issues that involve ethical decision making. You will learn to analyze and to speak about questions of public policy and personal moral choice by attempting to resolve eth-

Abraham Lincoln won the famed Lincoln–Douglas debates with his intellect, strategy, and speaking ability—the same qualities and skills crucial to modern Lincoln–Douglas debaters.

COMMUNICATION BREAKTHROUGH

The Lincoln–Douglas Debates

In 1857, the black slave Dred Scott sued his "master" for his freedom on the basis of his five-year stay in the free territories of Illinois and Wisconsin. The Supreme Court denied Scott a trial. It ruled that Scott was a slave, not a citizen. As a slave, he was less than a person—mere property. Therefore, said the Court, slaves could be taken to any state, free or not, and still could not sue for their freedom. Furthermore, the Court proclaimed that no state could rightly force slaveholders to give up their slaves because to do so would deprive citizens of their property. The *Dred Scott* decision deeply divided the nation and once again thrust the slavery issue into the forefront of political debate.

One year later, Abraham Lincoln, Republican nominee for an Illinois Senate seat, challenged Democratic nominee Stephen Douglas to a series of debates. After Dred Scott, the focus of the debates was fated to be the slavery issue. Lincoln depicted Douglas as pro-slavery and a defender of the *Dred Scott* decision. Although Lincoln opposed slavery, he was forced to adopt the conservative position that he would not force the states to surrender their rights.

Many initially thought that Lincoln, with his unsightly mole, high-pitched voice, lanky stature, baggy clothes, and unshined shoes, had virtually no chance against the polished, confident "Little Giant" Douglas. With his *renowned* oratorical skills, Douglas was considered the foremost debater of his day. Yet Lincoln managed to trap Douglas

in a dilemma: He asked Douglas, what if the people in a state decided to vote to free the slaves? After all, it was Douglas who supported the right of the states to choose.

Douglas was forced to admit that if the people wanted to, they could free the slaves, regardless of the *Dred Scott* decision. In making this admission, Douglas split his party, many of whom were counting on him to defend slavery to the last. Even more importantly, Lincoln captured the nation's attention and, in the words of the Stanford University historian David Kennedy, "won a clear moral victory."

The Lincoln–Douglas debate competitions of today take more than their name from these historical confrontations. Although the formats of the debates are significantly different, the emphasis on intellect, strategy, and speaking ability remain crucial to the success of the debater. Furthermore, the competitors, like Lincoln before them, try to convince those people sitting in judgment that they have won clear moral victories.

Source: David Kennedy and Thomas Bailey, The American Pageant, D.C. Heath and Co., 1987.

Questions

1. Given Lincoln's unsightly appearance, do you think that the outcome of the debates would have changed had television coverage been possible at that time in history?

2. How important is it that a victory be moral?

Value propositions like "Is listening to the Beatles better than listening to Elvis?" form the basis for Lincoln–Douglas debate.

ical dilemmas. Such ethical dilemmas occur when choices have to be made between alternatives that are equally desirable or undesirable.

The process you will follow in doing these things is **Lincoln–Douglas debate** (or L–D for short). L–D is a competitive type of formal debate practiced at high schools across the nation. Even if you never compete in a tournament, though, understanding the process of Lincoln–Douglas debate is of great value. It teaches you to argue logically and persuasively about ethical issues: Is honesty more important than loyalty? Ought we be allowed to burn the American flag? Should high school administrators be able to search student lockers?

In Chapter 15 you learned about propositions in debate. The next section in this chapter will discuss the specific kind of proposition used in L–D competition.

Have I Got a Proposition for You!

At the end of the Beatles' song "Strawberry Fields Forever," does John Lennon say, "I buried Paul," or does he say "cranberry sauce"? This question is an example of a factual proposition. **Factual propositions** are either true or false. To determine whether John says "I buried Paul" or not, you need only play back a tape of this song until you arrive at a conclusion.

Contrast the "I buried Paul" versus "cranberry sauce" question with the following proposition: "Should the United States government conduct scientific studies to determine whether Elvis is alive?" This type of proposition, a **policy proposition,** focuses on the desirability of a particular course of action. To evaluate the action, we could create a plan to find Elvis and then debate the advantages and disadvantages of the proposed plan. (Chapter 17, on policy debate, explores this kind of proposition more fully.) By weighing the advantages and disadvantages as well as the workability of our plan, we are able to answer the question.

The **value proposition,** however, cannot be answered by knowing the facts or by predicting the effects of a plan. Value propositions—such as "Is listening to the Beatles better than listening to Elvis?"— are the basis for Lincoln–Douglas debate. The value proposition debated is generally called the resolution. (Recall from Chapter 15 that in formal debate, propositions are stated as resolutions.) Typically, these resolutions involve philosophical judgments and thus are more difficult to answer than questions of fact or policy. Why? Because there is no right or wrong answer. For example, to answer the Beatles–Elvis question, you must somehow compare the worth of listening to the Liverpool lads versus the worth of kicking back with the King. How do you decide which has greater "worth"? The answer is by applying values.

What is a value? A **value** is simply a standard we apply to judge something right or wrong, good or bad. You have a set of values. You may value the loyalty of a friend or the privacy of being left alone in your room. As the novelist James Michener explains, "Values are the emotional rules by which a nation governs itself. Values summarize the accumulated folk wisdom by which a society organizes and disciplines itself. And values are the precious reminders that individuals obey to bring order and meaning into their lives."

These standards can be of different types. They may be moral values: Is

something just or unjust, fair or unfair? They may be aesthetic values: Is something beautiful or ugly, artistic or inartistic? They may be political values: Is something democratic or tyrannical, helpful to freedom or harmful to it? To resolve the Beatles–Elvis question, you might apply the value of musical importance. In that case, you would make a choice based on the standard of who played a more important role in the history of rock 'n' roll. If you applied a different value—say, an aesthetic one based on the quality of lyrics—you might come to another conclusion.

The choices we make as a society reflect the values that we as individuals hold most dear. Consider the question of whether the death penalty ought to be legal. If you believe the *sanctity* of human life is the highest value, then, by that standard, you would oppose the death penalty. Suppose you are debating the question of whether the government ought to place restrictions on certain types of handguns. If you wished to uphold the value of public safety, you might answer yes, handguns should be restricted to protect the general public. If, on the other hand, you wished to uphold the value of personal freedom, you might answer no, handguns should not be restricted because any limitation would make people less free.

The Rules of the Game: Value Analysis

So you now know what values are, and you know that Lincoln–Douglas debate is concerned with questions of value. The responsibility of the L–D debater is to find the values within a resolution, to apply those values, and then to prove or disprove the resolution. Consider, for example, the following resolution: "Resolved: that the United States ought to value global concerns above its own national concerns." In order to learn how to "find" values in such statements, you must first understand more about the nature of values. Furthermore, analyzing and applying values involves certain rules. You need to know some of those rules.

Perhaps the best way to understand how value analysis works is to imagine that you wake up one morning and you rule the world. You may do virtually anything you want (within the laws of nature—in your fantasy, you still can't fly, nor can you leap tall buildings in a single bound). Given your great power, you may decide to allow abortion on demand, or you may decide to make it illegal. You may choose to force students to perform community service. Maybe not. It's your choice. Whatever you think is right. But before you make your decisions, you have much thinking to do: Why should you prefer one action over another? What is important to you? In short, the ultimate question you must ask yourself is "How *ought* things be?"

Ought refers to your idea of the ideal. When you are discussing what "ought" to be, you are describing how you think things should be, regardless of how they actually are now. Although some debaters use the terms *should* and *ought* interchangeably, there is a difference. *Should* simply suggests doing what is appropriate or fitting. *Ought*, on the other hand, refers to a moral obligation based on a sense of duty. Furthermore, how things ought to be and how things actually exist are two

different issues. Many people make the mistake of assuming that things are supposed to be the way they are.

As you learned in Chapter 9, on logic and reasoning, it is an error in reasoning to state that just because something is, it also ought to be. To understand why, consider the following examples: There is homelessness. Does that mean that there ought to be homelessness? People are suffering. Does that mean people ought to suffer? People ought not starve to death in the wealthiest nation in the world, but they do. People ought not steal, but they do. Lincoln–Douglas debate explores the world of *ought*, not the world of *is*. L–D leaves the world of *is* to economists, scientists, and historians.

Facts and Values: Establishing Valid Arguments

Our explanation of what ought to be may seem to imply that facts have no place in Lincoln–Douglas debate. Not true. Facts and other forms of evidence are a crucial part of debate, just as they are crucial in any discussion. For example, if you were debating whether or not limitations on firearms sales are justified, you would want to provide statistics indicating the number of deaths caused by handguns each year.

Facts alone cannot establish the validity of a value statement, but facts combined with the right values can. If your best friend is drowning, for example, the fact that you can swim does not necessarily mean you ought to save her. If you agree, though, that all people who can help others in trouble ought to do so (a value judgment), and then point out that you can swim, and that your friend is drown-

INSTANT IMPACT

Low Marx for Progress

On a Moscow statue of Karl Marx, graffiti have altered the original engraving "Workers of the world unite" to "Workers of the world, excuse me." Clearly, societies change as values change. Marx was convinced that capitalism contained the seeds of its own destruction and would be replaced by communism through revolution. His followers, according to the British historian Paul Johnson, "seized control of one of the world's largest countries and held it for three-quarters of a century."

Philosophers are now debating the survivability of Marxism. Supporters of Marx credit his criticism of capitalism for the durability of his theories. Johnson, though, believes, "Without the Soviet state to sustain it, Marxism will be dead in twenty years." Perhaps the end of Marxism has been inevitable for some time. Marx, himself, horrified by some interpretations of his theories, declared shortly before his death: "As for me, I am not a Marxist."

ing, then you have proven that you ought to help your friend. Of course, if it can be shown that both of you would drown in the attempt, then that value judgment can be challenged.

Now suppose that you are arguing that the government ought not legalize drugs. You may list various harmful effects of drugs: antisocial behavior, increased crime rates, cost to society, and so on. These harmful effects, by themselves, do not prove that drugs should be illegal. You must also make the value judgment that allowing people to harm themselves and those around them is wrong. When you make this judgment, the argument is complete: (1) harming oneself and others is wrong, (2) drugs harm people in numerous ways, (3) therefore, the government ought not legalize drugs.

Some Values Commonly Used in Lincoln–Douglas Debate

Some of the values most commonly used in Lincoln–Douglas debate include the following.

1. Liberty. People and governments ought to act so that each individual has the greatest possible freedom (without harming others). *Possible applications:* arguing for free speech, against compulsory national service, for legalizing drugs.
2. Equality of opportunity. Government policies should give all citizens fair access to jobs and services. *Possible applications:* arguing for affirmative action programs to remedy past discrimination, against dividing high schools into vocational and college preparatory programs.
3. Democracy. The people ought to have the maximum possible role in determining questions of right and wrong. Major policy decisions should be put to public debate or vote. *Possible applications:* arguing in favor of making sensitive government information available to the

public, against allowing the government to take *covert* actions.

4. Justice. This is usually seen as a value that protects other values, such as liberty and fairness. Plato's classic definition of *justice* is "giving equal amounts to equals and unequal amounts to unequals." Examples of what may be given include wealth, political privilege, and punishment. *Possible applications:* arguing that the *affluent* nations of the world ought to feed the poorer nations, or that the right to a fair trial justifies limiting press coverage.

Knowledge of these values—liberty, equality of opportunity, democracy, and justice—will help you to analyze most L–D debate resolutions. Many other values are argued in L–D debate, however.

Remember: A value is a concept, not a particular document or a court ruling. Some debaters, for example, try to use the United States Constitution as a value. The Constitution as a document is not, in itself, a value. There are, however, values embodied within the Constitution. These values include freedom of speech, the right to a fair trial, and individual liberty.

TAKING CHARGE

The purpose of this chapter is not just to teach you about values as they are applied in Lincoln–Douglas debate. A broader purpose is to help you to speak and reason intelligently about ethical issues in general. These issues are discussed and debated by people in all walks of life. Interview someone and report on the moral complexities that arise for that person in the workplace. Possible interviewees include the following:

1. A local judge or politician. Judges sometimes must make decisions that conform to the law but are in conflict with their personal beliefs; politicians often pass laws that sacrifice some people's interests. How do they justify these compromises?
2. A reporter. Journalists often have their "journalistic integrity" challenged in cases where they have to decide what to print and what to withhold. What are some of the guidelines that they use in making those judgments?
3. A scientist. Scientists, too, must confront moral issues—building the atomic bomb, genetic engineering, the disposal of nuclear waste, and so on. How do they weigh risks and benefits in their work?
4. A teacher. Should a teacher reward a student with a passing grade for exceptional effort even though the student's test scores earn a failing mark? How can a teacher fairly measure and reward subjective areas like class participation?

Values Commonly Used in Lincoln-Douglas Debate	
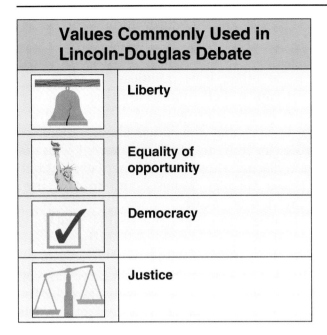	Liberty
	Equality of opportunity
	Democracy
	Justice

II Preparing for Battle: Writing Cases

Armed with your knowledge of values, you are ready to learn how to write cases. Remember from Chapter 15 that your case is your total group of arguments—your basic position on the resolution. It is made up of all the arguments that you choose to present. Most L–D debaters use a format that includes four steps: (1) introduction, (2) definitions and analysis of the resolution, (3) establishing of values, and (4) arguments.

A general rule about writing cases: You should always tell the judge and your opponent when you are moving from section to section in your case: "First, we should examine the key terms in the resolution (give your definitions). Now, I will present my value for the round (give your value). With these definitions and my value in mind, let's turn to my first argu-

ment (state the argument)." This technique of telling people when you are moving from section to section of your case is called **signposting.**

The Introduction

In the introduction, you always state your position in the debate—whether you are arguing the negative or the affirmative. In addition, you would like to start with a compelling statement to support your position. Many debaters choose to begin their speeches with a quotation. The quotation should lead smoothly into the specific resolution and should support your side. For example, suppose that you're on the affirmative side and the resolution is "Resolved: that paid *surrogacy* ought to be legal." You are arguing that the government should allow contracts for surrogate mothers. You might begin like this:

> In *Maher v. Roe,* the Supreme Court ruled, "the right of *procreation* without state interference has long been recognized as one of the basic civil rights of man . . . fundamental to the very existence and survival of the race." Because I agree with the court's ruling that couples must be allowed to establish families without government interference, I affirm the resolution: that paid surrogacy ought to be legal.

If you represent the negative side, on the other hand, you might begin this way:

> The journalist Ellen Goodman recently wrote in the *Boston Globe:* "It is fair to ask about the moral limits of *commerce.* . . . We impose limits on our medical commerce. We cannot sell a kidney. We should not be able to sell a pregnancy." Because I agree with Ms. Goodman that it is morally unacceptable to place pregnancy on the market, I negate the resolution and stand resolved that paid surrogacy ought not be legal.

Of course, picking an appropriate quotation is not the only way to begin your debate case. Try experimenting with the different methods of introducing speeches that were discussed earlier in this book.

Definitions and Analysis of the Resolution

You will need to offer definitions for the key terms in the resolution; otherwise, there is no common ground for debate. Take, for example, the resolution: "Resolved: that honesty is more important than loyalty." What do *honesty* and *loyalty* mean? Since different people have different meanings for these terms, it's important to agree on meanings. In defining such terms, you should try to be reasonable—not too broad ("loyalty is being faithful") nor too restrictive ("honesty is telling the truth when your mother asks where you were last Saturday night").

Some debaters may try to "define you out of the round" by presenting completely unreasonable interpretations—for example, honesty is telling the truth specifically to hurt someone's feelings and loyalty is performing noble acts to demonstrate faithfulness. These unreasonable definitions make fair debate impossible. Skilled debaters point out these unfair interpretations to the judge.

If you are observant, you noticed that the sample resolution just given does not contain the word *ought*. The resolution says *is*. Does this particular wording mean that the resolution is one of fact, not values? No. All Lincoln–Douglas debate resolutions are propositions of value. What the resolution really asks is, "Ought loyalty be valued above honesty?"

Furthermore, in order for the debate to be meaningful, there must be a conflict. That is, you must come down on one side or the other. It is pointless to argue that you can be both honest and loyal—so neither loyalty nor honesty is more important—and that the judge should therefore vote for the negative speaker. If you do not discuss those times when you had to choose between honesty and loyalty, then why debate at all?

Consider this conflict scenario: You are in a grocery store with your best friend. Your friend shoplifts a candy bar but is seen by the store manager. Your friend flees as you are detained by the security guard. The guard knows you are innocent but insists that you name the shoplifter. Honesty or loyalty—which is more important?

Clearly, conflict is necessary for debate. If, however, you can watch *60 Minutes* on Sunday and also go to a movie on Saturday, you do not have to decide which entertainment choice should be more highly valued. But if the movie and the TV show are at the same time on the same day, you have a conflict.

Establishing Values

An important step in developing your case is to establish a **value premise.** The value premise provides a standard of judgment to evaluate whether the resolution is true. A value premise also provides a starting point for an argument by summarizing the value you are using as the basis for the argument. In giving the value premise, you are asking the judge to accept it as the standard for deciding the debate. In other words, you are telling the judge that whichever speaker better upholds your value premise should win the debate.

Consider the following example. You are debating the resolution: "Resolved: that limitations on the right to bear arms in the United States are justified." If you are on the affirmative side, you want to choose a value that will support the resolution, so you select the value "public safety." By using this as your value premise, you are saying to the judge, in effect, that the decision in the debate should be based on which position better protects or preserves public safety—yours or your opponent's. You will argue that limiting handguns (the affirmative position) would better uphold public safety and that you should therefore win.

Suppose that you are on the negative side of the resolution: "Resolved: that searching through student property in an effort to maintain discipline in school is justified." As the negative speaker, you are arguing that random searches through students' property by teachers and other school officials are not justified. Therefore, you might want to choose the value of privacy as your value premise and assert that the side whose arguments allow for greater privacy should win. You will argue that the affirmative speaker favors violating privacy by permitting searches through student property. You, the negative speaker, support a position that better upholds privacy and, by that standard, should win.

Both the negative and affirmative speakers may state value criteria. Value criteria provide further standards of judgment for evaluating the resolution. If a student upholds the value premise of justice, the student may argue that the value criterion should be based on which speaker better preserves and protects justice. Preservation and protection of justice becomes, then, the value criterion (standard of judgment) for deciding who wins.

Argumentation

After offering definitions, a value premise, and value criteria, you're ready to present your arguments—the reasons for favoring your side of the resolution. Here are two important points to remember.

1. Always Make Your Arguments Refer Back to Your Value Premise

Your value premise is the core of your case. Consider the handgun resolution—"Resolved: that limitations on the right to bear arms in the United States are justified." You are the affirmative speaker and have presented the value premise of public safety. Each of your arguments, then, must mention public safety. For example, in your first argument, you might give statistics indicating that unlimited handgun sales present a high risk to human life. Then you would state that the risk to human life also risks public safety. Therefore, you would conclude, limitations are justified. (We could represent this reasoning as follows: 1. Public safety is the most important value. 2. Guns threaten public safety. 3. Limitations on guns are justified to protect public safety.)

Suppose, though, that you are debating, "Resolved: that burning the American flag is morally acceptable." As the affirmative speaker, you present the value premise of free speech and state that all political speech is morally acceptable. Your first argument asserts that flag burning is a type of political speech. Because political speech must be protected, flag burning is morally acceptable. (1. Free speech is the most important value, so all political speech should be protected. 2. Flag burning is a type of political speech. 3. Flag burning is morally acceptable, since it upholds free speech.)

2. Always Relate Your Evidence to Your Value Premise

Remember that evidence only supports your case if you relate it to your value premise. Suppose you're debating the resolution: "Resolved: that protection of the environment ought to be valued above the development of natural resources." The affirmative speaker may present evidence that proves the environment is being destroyed in various ways. This evidence, however, does not help the affirmative case unless the affirmative speaker has also presented a value premise that suggests that the environment ought to be protected.

One type of evidence that L-D debaters commonly use is quotations from famous philosophers. Make certain when you use such quotations that they actually apply to your arguments and aren't just thrown in to impress the judge. Consider the "Flag burning is morally acceptable" resolution. It would be appropriate to use the following quotation from former Supreme Court Justice William Brennan: "We do not venerate the flag by prohibiting its desecration, for in so doing, we dilute the freedom that this cherished emblem represents."

If, on the other hand, you quote the French philosopher Descartes's saying, "I think, therefore, I am," you are not thinking, nor are you debating the specific resolution.

Debate Skills

A good round of debate will include two features: clash and crystallization.

Clash

Clashing means making your arguments directly conflict with your opponent's. While clashing may be something you try to avoid in your day-to-day communication, it is a desirable goal in L–D debate. Debate rounds without clash are sometimes described as being like two ships passing in the night.

You clash with your opponent's arguments by refuting them—by showing how they are flawed. To refute is not merely to repeat what you have said in earlier speeches.

In refuting your opponent's arguments, you should address them in order. You might, for example, say: "In John's first argument, he claims that all political speech should be protected. I have two responses. First, some types of political speeches clearly ought not receive protection. John, you cannot express your dissatisfaction with the president by bombing the White House. Second . . ."

Note that in giving your refutation, you follow a pattern:

1. You briefly state your opponent's argument.
2. You say how many responses you have.
3. You make the responses, numbering each one as you go.

This pattern will help keep your speeches organized and clear.

Let's look at some common techniques of refutation: counterexamples, analogies, and contradictions.

Counterexamples Suppose that your opponent offers an example in an attempt to support a general principle. For instance, suppose you are debating whether or not

COMMUNICATION WORKS

Arthur Chu, College Student

"L–D was, by far, the most beneficial of all my high school extracurricular activities," says Arthur Chu. Chu graduated from high school in 1990 and is now considering a career in law because of his experience in debate. Chu started in L–D in November of his junior year. By the time he was a senior, he placed second in the Tournament of Champions held at the University of Kentucky.

Chu explains that L–D taught him to argue more logically and persuasively, although he adds, "It's still impossible to win any argument with my parents." Moreover, he says, debating improved his other schoolwork. "When you're taking a test, and you find yourself with only twelve minutes to write the long essay, you don't panic as much because you know that last weekend at the debate tournament you prepared a six-minute rebuttal in less than a minute."

The political theory that Chu learned in high school L–D has paid off in college classes. For example, he says, he took a class called "Political Ethics and Public Policy" that covered several topics that he had already studied in preparing for debate tournaments. L–D can, according to Chu, be profitable in other ways. He placed third in the 1990 American Legion Oratorical Contest and won a $15,000 scholarship. "After competing in L–D, I realized that you have to adapt to different audiences when discussing controversial issues based on ethical choices," he explains. "Without that knowledge, I probably wouldn't have been able to afford college today."

it is an invasion of a pedestrian's privacy for homeless people to beg. Your opponent points out that some beggars are alcoholics just trying to support their addiction. You could respond with the counterexample of families forced to beg in order to survive on the streets.

Analogies Analogies can be useful in refuting arguments that are not supported by evidence. Suppose you're the negative speaker debating the resolution: "Resolved: that the United States ought to value global concerns above its own national concerns." Your opponent makes the following points: (1) The United States

is a world leader with the capability of helping other nations. (2) All leaders capable of helping others in need ought to. (3) Therefore, the United States should value global concerns above its own national concerns. You can attempt to refute this argument with an analogy: Just because you are the best student in your biology class does not mean that you have a study session at your house every night to bring up the grades of the other students. This analogy exposes the fallacious assumption in the argument of the affirmative speaker.

As another example, suppose you are the affirmative speaker and you're defending global concerns. The negative speaker states: 1) The United states must first take care of national concerns before addressing global concerns. As the philosopher Hans Morganthau once wrote, "A foreign policy guided by universal moral principles . . . relegating the national interest to the background is . . . a policy of national suicide." (2) Therefore, national concerns ought to be valued above global concerns. The negative speaker's reasoning is flawed because valuing something "before" something else is not the same as valuing it "above" that other thing. You can illustrate the flaw to the judge by analogy. Cocoa beans may come before chocolate, but that doesn't make them more valuable than chocolate; algebra comes before calculus, but that doesn't make algebra more valuable than calculus; you may ride the bus before you go to school, but that doesn't mean you value the bus more than school. Analogies can be a concise and compelling strategy in debate—as long as they apply to the argument.

Contradictions Sometimes speakers present values that contradict their arguments. Suppose that you are debating the resolution: "Resolved: that communities in the United States ought to have the right to suppress pornography." If the affirmative speaker defends free speech, you should point out to the judge that suppressing pornography will make speech less free—a contradictory position taken by the affirmative.

Crystallization

Crystallizing means choosing the most important arguments and linking them back to the values presented in the round. Numerous issues will be introduced in any debate. It is your responsibility to focus on the key issues that the judge should weigh in reaching a decision. When you crystallize, you tell the judge the major issues that have been presented, and why your value is superior. Finally, you give impact to the process of crystallization by explaining to the judge why you are winning each of the key issues.

TAKING CHARGE

Read the following sample Lincoln–Douglas debate topics.

- ✦ Resolved: That no war is ever morally justified.
- ✦ Resolved: That speech training is more beneficial than participation in sports.
- ✦ Resolved: That domestic assistance programs should be valued more than international assistance programs.

Now it's your turn. List some of the major issues involved in one of these topics. After creating your list, find at least one piece of evidence to support both the affirmative and negative sides of what you consider to be the most important issue.

III Structuring Your Speeches

Because Lincoln–Douglas debate is practiced nationwide, the National Forensic League has endorsed a special format for all L–D debaters to use:

1. First affirmative constructive (1AC): six minutes

2. Negative cross-examines affirmative: three minutes

3. First negative constructive (1NC): seven minutes

4. Affirmative cross-examines negative: three minutes

5. First affirmative rebuttal (1AR): four minutes

6. Negative rebuttal (NR): six minutes

7. Second affirmative rebuttal (2AR): three minutes

All of these speeches taken together make up one round of Lincoln–Douglas debate. Note that the total speaking time for the affirmative and the negative is the same, thirteen minutes (with three minutes apiece for cross-examination). Each debater is usually given three minutes of total preparation time to be used throughout the debate.

Let's look at each part of this format in detail to see how each is structured.

The Constructives

Recall from Chapter 15 that constructives are the speeches that put forward your arguments. In L–D debate, the affirmative and the negative speakers have one chance each to present constructives.

First Affirmative Constructive (1AC)—Six Minutes

The **first affirmative constructive (1AC)** is the one speech that is prepared entirely before the round. If you are taking the affirmative position, you begin the debate by reading your affirmative case, and then you wait to be cross-examined by your opponent.

The elements of the 1AC were described earlier, when we discussed writing cases: the introduction, definitions, value premise, value criteria, and arguments. In addition you should include a brief conclusion that summarizes your position. In terms of time allocation, your introduction should be about one-half minute long; your definitions, value premise, and value criteria, about one minute; your arguments, about four minutes; and your conclusion, about one-half minute.

A cross-examination period follows each of the constructives. The same strategies apply to both, so we will consider them together later.

First Negative Constructive (1NC)—Seven Minutes

In the **first negative constructive (1NC)**, most speakers also begin with their prepared constructive presentation (lasting three to four minutes). The remainder of the speech is devoted to refuting the affirmative constructive. The negative constructive speech, then, should do two sets of things: First, it should include an introduction, possibly value criteria; a value premise; counterdefinitions, if necessary; and the negative arguments. Second, it should clash with and refute the affirmative value and arguments.

The National Forensic League endorses a format for Lincoln–Douglas debate that consists of seven speeches, totalling 13 minutes. These speeches, taken together, make up one round of Lincoln–Douglas debate.

When you are taking the negative position, make certain that you respond to all of the affirmative arguments. If you fail to discuss any (referred to as "dropping" an argument), that error can come back to haunt you in rebuttals. Most judges will not allow you to pick up a dropped argument in rebuttals, so once you forget it in constructives, you've lost that point and any significance that might be attached to that argument by your opponent. Remember to link all arguments to the values that are being debated in the round and always demonstrate why your value position is superior.

The Cross-Examination Periods

As we have mentioned, a **cross-examination** follows each constructive. Here, the opponent questions the one who has just spoken. Your purpose in cross-examining your opponent is threefold: (1) to clarify points that you didn't understand, (2) to establish the credibility of your arguments, and (3) to undermine the credibility of your opponent's positions. We will look at each of these areas and then discuss responding to cross-examination.

Clarifying Arguments

Clarification is relatively simple. You should ask your opponent to explain anything that confused you. Many beginning debaters are reluctant to admit their confusion because they are afraid that the judge will think less of them. Such foolish pride can cost you the decision—debating the unknown is difficult at best. Don't let another debater intimidate you with big words or unfamiliar jargon. Always ask for clear explanations.

Establishing Credibility

Establishing the credibility of your own arguments is a wise use of cross-examination time. Try to get your opponent to admit that the important arguments in your case are true. If an opponent grants the assumptions in these arguments, then the conclusions that you are asserting seem inescapable. For example, suppose your opponent grants your assertion that freedom is the highest value. All the arguments that show that your position better guarantees freedom have additional weight because of your opponent's admission.

Undermining Positions

Undermining your opponent's positions can be a difficult task. Sometimes opponents won't answer questions. Sometimes you can't think of any good questions to ask. In general, you are less likely to be caught off guard here if you have thought through those arguments that are probably going to be relevant on a given topic and have prepared potential questions in advance. In particular, you might try to construct traps. Sometimes, though, you may simply want to ask why.

Setting Traps   Traps begin with reasonable questions that call for obvious yes or no responses. Your goal is to force an admission that is damaging to your opponent's case. Suppose that you were debating a resolution that we mentioned earlier, "that the United States ought to value global concerns above its own national concerns." You are the affirmative, cross-examining the negative. The negative has made the following argument: (1) The United States has enough problems of its own, such as homelessness, drugs, and crime. It ought to take care of these concerns and then consider global matters. (2) Because the United States ought to solve national concerns first, it ought to value national concerns above global concerns.

You might trap your opponent as follows. You begin with a seemingly harmless question:

> **You:** Bob, is it true that you state in your case that because the United States ought to value national concerns before global concerns, it ought to value national concerns above global concerns?
> **Bob:** That's right.
> **You:** OK, Bob, let's consider an analogous situation. You might ride the bus before you go to school, but does that mean that you actually value riding the bus above going to school?

Unless Bob has anticipated this ploy, he is in trouble. Bob may, at this point, become uncooperative. Do not waste time pursuing answers that you know your opponent will not give, but raise your opponent's unwillingness to provide a damaging admission later, in your rebuttal argumentation. For any statements made or not made in cross-examination to count in the round, they must be mentioned in the constructives or the rebuttals.

Asking Why   Generally (except to clarify arguments) you do not want to ask any questions unless you are fairly certain what your opponent's answer will be. A notable exception to this principle is the question, "Why?" Debaters often make assertions that they don't fully understand— the rhetoric is eloquent, but they haven't examined the underlying assumptions. In such cases, asking why may help you undermine your opponent's position.

Suppose that you and Karen are debating the resolution "that communities in the United States ought to be able to decide whether or not flag burning will be legal." Karen is on the affirmative side, and she chooses to defend the value of democracy. In the following exchange, you gamble with a why question.

> **You:** Karen, you offer us the value of democracy.
> **Karen:** Right.
> **You:** What is the justification for democracy—why is democracy better than tyranny?
> **Karen:** Er . . . because we ought to always allow the majority to decide what is right and wrong.
> **You:** Hmmm . . . the majority, eh? Aren't there certain issues that the majority ought not be able to decide?
> **Karen:** Er . . . no, I don't think so.
> **You:** What if the majority in this country decided that all people born in 1970 will be executed tomorrow? Would that be OK?
> **Karen:** No, I don't think so . . . (Karen has just contradicted herself).

In this exchange, you have established that some things ought to be outside the influence of majority opinion. All you have to do now is to show that flag burning is one of those things.

Responding to Questions

Finally, let's consider some guidelines for responding to questions during cross-examination.

- ◆ Never let them see you sweat.
- ◆ Respond to each question thoughtfully and confidently. If you appear *evasive*, then the judge may wonder what else you are trying to hide.
- ◆ Know your case thoroughly and plan responses to anticipated questions.

- ◆ Avoid making speeches (stick to the question asked; don't offer long, rambling explanations).
- ◆ Prepare carefully. Preparation will help you avoid falling into cross-examination traps.

The Rebuttals

As you learned in Chapter 15, rebuttal is the act of countering your opponent's attacks on your arguments so that you can rebuild your arguments. The rebuttal speeches come after the constructives. Before learning about the specific strategies for each rebuttal, you should know some of the general principles.

1. The purpose of a rebuttal speech is to bring the round into focus in such a way that you are able to defeat your opponent's arguments. You "sign the ballot for the judge" by giving the judge clear and specific reasons to vote for you.

2. You may extend (provide new responses to) arguments introduced in the constructives, but you should not initiate whole new arguments. Bringing up new arguments in rebuttals is described by some as "sliming." Sliming is a term that is also used to describe other debate tactics considered questionable or unethical—for example, distorting your opponent's position or asserting that an argument was dropped when, in fact, that is not the case.

3. When you run short on time and still have several arguments to answer, then you must attempt to

| COMMUNICATION | | BREAKDOWN |

Know Thyself

The style of cross-examination that you are now learning was practiced in ancient Greece by the philosopher Socrates. Socrates wandered the streets of Athens asking citizens questions in an effort to find the truth. Often, however, in his *relentless* pursuit of the truth, Socrates found himself uncovering unpleasant faults of those he questioned. Socrates described himself as a stinging *gadfly* that would bite and provoke the giant, lazy beast of Athens to prevent the "beast" from becoming too passive.

Unfortunately, many people in Athens could not endure the sting of Socrates' *incisive* questioning. They charged Socrates with corrupting the youth of Athens after he tried to teach them his method of inquiry.

The jury in the trial found Socrates guilty and sentenced him to die by drinking hemlock. Yet Socrates' lessons in philosophical questioning live on. As Myles Burnyeat, a professor of ancient philosophy at the University of Cambridge, states, "[Socrates] had

a lot of devoted followers and some of them, amongst them Plato, began writing Socratic dialogues: philosophical conversations in which Socrates takes the lead. It must have been like a chorus of voices saying to the Athenians, 'Look, he's not gone after all. He's still here, still asking those awkward questions, still tripping you up with his arguments.' And of course these Socratic dialogues were also defending his reputation and showing that he had been unjustly condemned: he was the great educator of the young, not the great corrupter."

Adapted from: Bryan Magee, The Great Philosophers, *Oxford University Press* (Oxford, England): 1987, p. 15.

Questions
1. Socrates was sentenced to die for asking questions. Can you give examples of some questions that should never be asked?
2. Are there any questions that you would not want to answer? Why?

find a common fault in the arguments. This technique of attacking the common flaw is known as grouping. For example, you and Farzana are debating the resolution "that communities in the United States ought to have the right to suppress pornography." You are the affirmative speaker, and in the first rebuttal you find yourself with only thirty seconds to respond to two more arguments. The arguments are that pornography is a le-

gitimate form of political speech and that communities ought not have the right to censor political speech. All is not lost, because you can refute both these arguments by proving that pornography is not a form of political speech (much evidence exists to support this position). Here's how you might structure the few remaining seconds of your time:

Farzana has two more arguments. First, she says that pornography is a form of political speech. Second, she says that communities ought to have the right to censor political speech. Realize, however, that both of these arguments assume that pornography is political speech. This assumption is incorrect because. . . .

4. Point out dropped arguments to the judge. The significance of any argument dropped by your opponent should be explained and weighed in the context of the resolution.

5. Fallacious assumptions and glaring contradictions should be highlighted at the beginning of the rebuttal to provide a showcase for these potentially devastating attacks.

6. Most debaters begin their rebuttals by refuting their opponent's analysis, and then they return to their own case. If you end the speech with your own arguments, then, you focus the judge's attention on the resolution from your perspective. In short, you place the round in your ballpark—a technique known as ballparking

7. You should always crystallize, as described earlier. Tell the judge why the arguments that you are winning matter in the round. Explain to the judge what is important and what isn't. You may be winning some arguments and losing some arguments—clarify why the ones you are winning outweigh the others. Finally, link the crucial arguments back to your value. After all, the value is the standard you provided for deciding the round.

First Affirmative Rebuttal (1AR)—Four Minutes

The **first affirmative rebuttal (1AR)** is generally considered to be the most challenging speech in L–D. You have only four minutes to answer the seven minutes of negative constructive. Beginning debaters, victimized by poor time allocation, often lose rounds because they unwisely drop arguments. To avoid such *dire* consequences, consider this approach:

1. Spend from thirty to forty-five seconds highlighting the value clash. Emphasize why your value position is superior.

2. Use approximately one and a half minutes refuting the negative argumentation. Group arguments when necessary, but at least mention each position advanced by your opponent. Clash with any unreasonable counterdefinitions that might undermine your entire case.

3. Use the remaining time to reestablish the strength of your case. Give impact to any arguments dropped by your opponent. Incorporate damaging admissions from cross-examination. Extend your original positions with evidence when appropriate (to respond to challenges for additional support). Link all of your arguments back to your value, and sign the ballot for the judge.

Negative Rebuttal (NR)—Six Minutes

The **negative rebuttal (NR)** is the negative speaker's last chance to speak. You will have no opportunity to respond to the final affirmative rebuttal, so you must "shut down" those arguments that you anticipate will be raised in that rebuttal. Shutting down arguments means preempting responses that the affirmative debater could offer that could sway the judge to vote for the resolution. You should emphasize the arguments that you think can win the round for you and minimize the arguments that you believe have the potential to defeat you.

The first part of the NR (about four to four and a half minutes) is structured like the 1AR—you begin with the value clash, refute the affirmative case, and return to defending your own case. The last one and a half to two minutes, though, should be spent crystallizing your arguments: Pick the two or three most important issues in the round from your perspective and state why you are winning them. This crystallization will force the affirmative speaker to address the issues of your choosing and to appear to be somewhat on the defensive. Do not get sidetracked by trivial technicalities or dropped arguments that have no significance. Select, instead, the issues that stake out fundamental disagreements.

Second Affirmative Rebuttal (2AR)—Three Minutes

Although your time is limited for the **second affirmative rebuttal (2AR),** you no longer need to be so concerned with coverage. You can focus on three or four issues of crucial importance (one should always be the value clash). You can avoid getting "ballparked" by the negative if you emphasize the value clash first and then examine the negative crystallization from the perspective of the affirmative case. Link all arguments to the value clash, and conclude by signing the ballot for the judge.

INSTANT IMPACT

Something of Value

"I fell off the stage, ripped my skirt, and cut my hand," remembers Mary Ambrose, the first national champion in high school Lincoln–Douglas debate competition. Ambrose took her tumble in June of 1980 immediately following the final round of the National Forensic League tournament in Huntsville, Alabama.

The topic in that first national competition focused on whether social security financing mechanisms should be preserved. Ambrose believes she won the final round because her argumentation was more "values-centered." She offered "self-sufficiency of the system" as her value position. Her opponent presented no competing value, Ambrose recalls.

Today, Ambrose is a trial lawyer and teaches law at Loyola University in Chicago. She credits her Lincoln–Douglas debate experience for giving her the ability to argue in front of a jury. "I learned that there has to be a theme and persuasiveness, not just the presenting of evidence," Ambrose says. "Lincoln–Douglas gave me added sophistication and it taught me that you need a kernel value."

Using Prep Time

In most rounds, you will be given three minutes of preparation time, or **prep time.** Affirmative speakers try to allocate two minutes before the 1AR and one minute before the 2AR. More time is needed before the 1AR because of the difficulty of organizing responses to the negative constructive. Most negative speakers split their prep time, using half before the 1NC and half before the NR. You should try to avoid using prep time before cross-examination—instead, prepare some questions ahead, and generate additional ones during your opponent's constructive.

REVIEW AND ENRICHMENT

LOOKING BACK

Listed below are the major ideas discussed in this chapter.

+ Debate propositions are of three kinds: factual, policy, and value.
+ A value is a standard we apply to judge something right or wrong, good or bad.
+ Standards of judgment may be moral, aesthetic, or political, among others.
+ The responsibility of the L–D debater is to find the values within a resolution, to apply those values, and to then prove or disprove the resolution.
+ "Ought" refers to your idea of the ideal.
+ Commonly used values in L–D debate include liberty, equality of opportunity, democracy, and justice.
+ All evidence and arguments used in L–D debate should refer back to the value premises.
+ L–D debate should include clash—arguments that directly conflict—and crystallization—selection by the debaters of the most important issues.
+ Common techniques of refutation are counterexamples, analogies, and contradictions.
+ Most L–D debaters write first affirmative constructive speeches that have four parts: (1) introduction, (2) definitions and analysis of the resolution, (3) establishing of values, and (4) arguments.
+ The negative constructive should (1) present a value premise, counterdefinitions (if necessary), and the negative arguments and (2) clash with and refute the affirmative value and arguments.
+ The purpose of cross-examination is threefold: (1) to clarify points that you didn't understand, (2) to establish the credibility of your arguments, and (3) to undermine the credibility of your opponent's positions.
+ The purpose of the rebuttal speeches is to place the round into focus by crystallizing the most important issues and by providing a comparison of the two value positions.

SPEECH VOCABULARY

Match the speech term on the left with the definition on the right.

1. ought
2. 2AR
3. NR
4. value
5. value premise
6. policy proposition
7. 1NC
8. 1AC
9. cross-examination
10. factual proposition

a. the first speech in a debate round
b. the period for asking and answering questions
c. final affirmative speech
d. refers to your idea of the ideal
e. a standard we apply to judge something right or wrong
f. a statement that is either true or false
g. focuses on the desirability of a particular course of action
h. a standard of judgement to evaluate whether the resolution is true
i. the first time the affirmative constructive is refuted
j. final negative speech

GENERAL VOCABULARY

Define the following terms and use each in a sentence.

renowned
sanctity
covert
affluent
surrogacy
procreation

commerce
evasive
relentless
gadfly
incisive
dire

THINGS TO REMEMBER

1. The _____ is considered to be the most difficult speech in Lincoln–Douglas debate.
2. "Resolved: that the United States government should conduct scientific research to determine whether Elvis still lives" is an example of a _____ proposition.
3. Bringing up new arguments in a rebuttal is commonly referred to as _____.
4. In the original Lincoln–Douglas debates, _____ represented the side of states' rights.

5. If you are running out of time in a speech, you can _____ your opponent's arguments and answer them all at once.
6. Your _____ is the value that you will be defending in the round.
7. Lincoln–Douglas debates consider propositions of _____.
8. The side that supports the resolution is called the _____, while the side that opposes it is called the _____.

THINGS TO DO

1. Research the original Lincoln–Douglas debates in the library. Examine the arguments and strategies used by both sides. Do you think Lincoln or Douglas was more persuasive?
2. Contact local government officials and ask them about the role of values in fulfilling their duties.
3. If you are not on a debate team, find a nearby tournament to attend as an observer. Assess the Lincoln–Douglas debaters' performances based on your knowledge of the process.

THINGS TO TALK ABOUT

1. Discuss how debating values might be applicable in our everyday lives.
2. Four values were mentioned in this chapter: liberty, equality of opportunity, democracy, and justice. What are some other values that you could defend in a Lincoln-Douglas debate?
3. Which should be the most important factor in a judge's decision: evidence, analysis, or speaking skill?
4. You are cross-examining someone who won't answer any of your questions. What should you do?

THINGS TO WRITE ABOUT

1. Some people advocate a "two-track" system for education in which some students would receive preparation for college and some students would receive vocational training. Those who support the two-track system argue that it will increase the quality of American education. Opponents object that a two-track system is unfair and would deprive many qualified students of the chance for a college education. Write either an affirmative

or a negative case for the resolution: "Resolved: that a two-track system of education is justified."
2. Although we know today that slavery is morally wrong, there was a time in this country when slavery was acceptable to most people. Write a brief essay about another value that has changed over time.
3. The AIDS epidemic threatens our

nation in many ways. Some people have proposed that schools ought to distribute contraceptives, especially condoms, to prevent the spread of AIDS among teenagers. Others, however, worry that distributing birth control devices will encourage students to become sexually active. Outline the arguments you would use to defend either side of this issue.

CRITICAL THINKING

1. Create three L–D topics that would be suitable for forcing a clash of values.
2. The American philosopher Henry David Thoreau wrote, "What is most important is not what law requires but what justice demands." Do you think that citizens ought to break the law when they think that the law is unjust?
3. The Australian philosopher Peter Singer has argued that the wealthier nations of the world ought to do everything that they can to help the poorer nations, including making significant sacrifices of luxuries, food consumption, and so on. He uses this analogy: If you are walking by a small pond and see a young girl drowning, you ought to save her even if you will ruin your beautiful new Nike Pumps in the process. Is Singer's analogy appropriate? Does it strengthen his argument?
4. Is morality a value?

RELATED SPEECH TOPICS

Competition versus cooperation: Which ought we value more?
Ought we allow mandatory prayer in schools?
The values of Martin Luther King
Flag burning: Is it morally acceptable?
Should the protection of the environment be valued above the development of natural resources?

Ought the rights of the fetus be valued above the rights of the mother?
National security versus the people's right to know: Ought the government keep sensitive information away from the public?
Should schools teach values, or is that the role of the parents?

CHAPTER 17

Policy Debate

"It is better to debate a question without settling it, than to settle a question without debating it."

— Joseph Joubert

The famous "Mr. Ed. vs. Francis the Talking Mule" debates

Learning Objectives

After completing this chapter, you will be able to do the following.

- ✦ Define *policy debate*.
- ✦ Identify the stock issues or voting issues in a debate.
- ✦ Research and prepare an affirmative case.
- ✦ Prepare negative arguments.
- ✦ Defeat negative arguments.
- ✦ Describe the format for a debate.
- ✦ Select speaker positions.
- ✦ Describe the proper functions for each speaker.
- ✦ Conduct a cross-examination period.
- ✦ Take a good flowsheet.

Chapter Outline

Following are the main sections in this chapter.

New Speech Terms

In this chapter, you will learn the meanings of the speech terms listed below.

policy debate
plan
rationale
prima facie
stock issues
harm
inherency
solvency
topicality
a priori
extension
block

alternate causality attacks
circumvention attacks
workability attacks
solvency turns
counterplan
competitive
mutual exclusivity
net benefits
flowsheet

General Vocabulary

Expanding your general vocabulary will help you become a more effective communicator. Listed below are some words appearing in this chapter that you should make part of your everyday vocabulary.

reassess
advocacy
quantitative
qualitative
viability
indictments
innuendo

intimidation
tangible
empirical
invalid
preempt
adhere

LOOKING AHEAD

In his early working life, Lyndon Johnson was a policy debate coach at Sam Houston High School in Houston, Texas. Johnson often said that no occupation could have given him better preparation and finer training for his future. This chapter introduces you to policy debate. You will learn how to prepare to defend both the affirmative and negative sides of a policy resolution. You will also learn the skills necessary to participate successfully in a policy debate round.

I What Is Policy Debate?

If you've never heard of or learned about policy debate, this chapter is going to look very difficult. At first you may think that policy debaters seem to speak some strange language. The jargon—the words and expressions used by these particular speakers—is sometimes hard for someone new to the activity to understand. Fortunately, though, learning how to debate policy is similar to learning any new activity. Admittedly, when you begin, the unfamiliar vocabulary and the many new concepts do appear overwhelming. If you are persistent, however, you will master the rules of this game.

In the debate world, a policy is nothing more than a plan of action. Many policies that affect your life were at some point debated. Should teenagers be allowed to see R-rated movies? Should schools have dress codes? Should we raise the legal age for drinking alcohol? Even when your parents decided what rules should be followed around your house, the advantages and disadvantages of different policies were probably debated. How should the family chores be divided? What is a reasonable hour for your curfew?

Perhaps you feel frustrated when you fail to get policies changed that you don't like. You may have strong opinions about these policies, but to convince others that they should agree with you often requires a great deal of skill and preparation. Participating in policy debate trains you to present your ideas in a clear and meaningful way. It helps you fight for what you want. Furthermore, it prepares you to participate in a democracy because the language of debate is the language of democracy.

In fact, the founding fathers of our country were highly skilled debaters. By the 1650s, most colonial colleges required debate as a means of training young scholars. For example, when Thomas Jefferson was a student at William and Mary, he participated in debates. Jefferson was taught by George Wythe, the same "debate coach" who tutored such famous speakers as Henry Clay and John Marshall. At the time, debate was considered to be the best way to develop the charac-

George Wythe, pictured here, tutored Thomas Jefferson, Henry Clay, and John Marshall in debate. Colonial colleges taught debate in the training of young scholars.

ter and skills required of citizens in our young nation.

The challenge of learning to debate policy awaits you in this chapter. True, hard work lies ahead, but the rewards are significant. You will improve your ability to research and develop arguments, to organize your thoughts, and to speak extemporaneously—and you will soon discover that policy debate can be a lot of fun.

Let's begin our examination of policy debate by defining what a policy debate is. In a **policy debate,** a team of two de-

baters affirm and a team of two debaters negate a question of social policy. Remember that *affirm* is simply a more formal way of saying yes to the question, and *negate* a more formal way of saying no.

The question of social policy is the resolution. In any given year, high school students throughout the country debate the same resolution. During the 1991–1992 school year, for example, most policy debate students researched and debated the following resolution: That the federal government should significantly increase social services to homeless individuals in the United States.

All policy resolutions follow certain guidelines:

1. The resolution should focus on a current, controversial issue.

2. The resolution is stated in a way that forces the affirmative to change a policy. "Resolved: That foreign aid should be increased" is a topic that requires the affirmative to come up with a plan to carry

COMMUNICATION WORKS

Aileen Gatterman, State Chairperson of "Take Back the System"

"This was a blast," concluded one of the nine candidates for mayor of Albuquerque, New Mexico. Chuckling as she recalls the debater's closing statement, Aileen Gatterman explains that this particular candidate favored a policy of growing and selling marijuana as a way to raise money for the city.

Organizing local debates is just one of Gatterman's many duties as state chairperson of "Take Back the System," a national program sponsored by the League of Women Voters. This program, which attempts to register and educate voters, is a response to the league's concern over voter apathy.

Gatterman points out that the League of Women Voters has a history of focusing election campaigns on issues and helping voters get clear answers to their questions. As early as 1928, the league used radio broadcasts to present a weekly ten-month series of debates on important issues. More recently, they sponsored the presidential debates from 1976 to 1984. They ended their participation in the presidential debates with the election of 1988 but continue to organize debates at the state and local levels.

These debates, Gatterman says, increase the chances for a true democracy: "When individuals can ask questions from the audience, they have the opportunity to get the candidates to listen to them instead of listening to Political Action Committees."

out that increase. In contrast, the topic "Resolved: That foreign aid should remain at current levels" would require the affirmative to defend the status quo—the way things already are—so it is not an appropriate resolution.

3. The resolution should contain only one topic. The topic "Resolved: That the United States should have a program of national health care and a job for everyone" would involve two debates.

4. The resolution should avoid ambiguous language. The topic "Re-

solved: That the federal government should *reassess* tax reforms" is not clear in its intent. The vague wording leaves the debaters wondering such things as: "Which tax reforms?" "Should taxes be increased or decreased?" "Is thinking about the reforms enough? Does the affirmative have to actually change anything or merely reassess?"

As a debater, you gather evidence and organize it so that you can both affirm and negate the resolution. Just as in Lincoln–Douglas debate, you are required to debate both as the affirmative and the negative in alternating rounds, so you must be prepared to debate either side of the question. In debate, you may find you have to defend a side of the resolution with which you disagree. This situation is not unlike that of the lawyer who defends a client who is guilty because the lawyer believes that the client deserves the best possible defense.

Affirmative debaters can defend any policy that falls under the resolution. To meet the homeless resolution, for example, an affirmative team can argue for any of the following policies:

◆ Improved homeless shelters.

◆ Better medical care for the homeless.

◆ Free legal services for the homeless.

◆ More emergency relief for those left homeless after a natural disaster.

◆ Rental assistance for the homeless.

The policy that the affirmative team supports is explained in its plan. The **plan,** or the affirmative's proposal to put the resolution into effect, plus the **ratio-** **nale,** or the reasons for adopting the resolution, make up the affirmative case.

Typically, students, limited by time, prepare only one or two affirmative cases. As potential negatives, however, they prepare against many affirmative strategies.

As a debater, you will analyze the policies you debate much as a judge or a congressperson analyzes a real policy. You will ask the same questions that our elected or appointed officials ask:

1. Without this policy, will something bad happen (a *harm*)?
2. Without this policy change, will the harm go away?
3. Will this policy eliminate or solve for this harm?
4. Will adoption of this policy create more disadvantages than advantages?

Debate is not exactly like the real world, since it must provide all participants a fair chance to prepare. Thus, debaters ask one more question:

5. Does this policy—the affirmative plan—fairly reflect what the resolution asks us to debate?

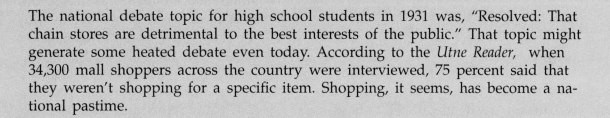

TAKING CHARGE

The national debate topic for high school students in 1931 was, "Resolved: That chain stores are detrimental to the best interests of the public." That topic might generate some heated debate even today. According to the *Utne Reader,* when 34,300 mall shoppers across the country were interviewed, 75 percent said that they weren't shopping for a specific item. Shopping, it seems, has become a national pastime.

TAKING CHARGE (CONTINUED)

■

Now it's your turn. After reviewing the guidelines for wording a debate resolution, write your own. Try to choose a topic area in which you are interested, such as minimum educational standards, required community service, or student rights.

Note that the wording of the debate resolution from 1931 is more suited to Lincoln–Douglas competition than to policy debate today. The question of what is "detrimental" calls for a value judgment rather than a change in policy.

II Preparing the Affirmative

The affirmative team bears the burden of proof in a debate. As mentioned, it must prove that a policy should be changed. If you are on the affirmative team, it is your job to advocate a policy change just as your representative might do for a bill he or she has proposed in Congress.

You are more familiar with this process of *advocacy* than you might think. The lawyers that you have seen prosecute or defend someone in a trial are advocates. In the same way that you must be an advocate for the affirmative policy, a lawyer is an advocate during a trial. In the world of high school debate, therefore, you must prove beyond a reasonable doubt that your policy is a good one—a needed one.

Stock Issues

You must present a prima facie affirmative case. **Prima facie** means "at first view." In law, it describes a case that is legally sufficient. To be prima facie, your case must meet several traditional requirements. These requirements form the **stock issues,** or voting issues, in policy debate:

◆ **Harm:** This word may seem strange to you used as it is here, but it's really just a way of describing the problem presented by the affirmative team. As the affirmative, you try to show a significant problem, or harm. This harm might be *quantitative*—it might focus on the number of people hurt, the amount of money lost, or the like. It might instead be *qualitative*—focusing on a situation that is not fair, not just. The harm should be greater than the disadvantages of adopting the policy you propose.

◆ **Inherency:** Inherency is a very important word in policy debate. To the affirmative team, inherency means that the policies that now exist will not eliminate the harm you are presenting in the affirmative plan. Something about our current efforts to solve the problem—such as a law or an attitude—creates an inherent barrier that prevents the present system from working as well as the affirmative plan would. In establishing inherency, you should provide evidence that, without your policy, the harm would not be solved.

◆ **Solvency:** Solvency means the ability of your plan to work and to achieve the advantages you are claiming. In other words, you must solve for the harm that you have presented.

◆ **Topicality:** The topicality requirement means that the affirmative case must deal with the topic precisely as it is stated, with each word taken into consideration. In other words, your policy must fall under the terms in the resolution rather than outside the resolution.

Since debate must be fair, topicality is an especially important question in policy debate. In fact, it is called an **a priori** issue. That means the judge will decide whether or not the affirmative plan is topical before considering any other arguments in the round (*a priori* means "before").

You may have to defend against negative topicality attacks. To do so, you will define the terms of the resolution and show how your policy meets those definitions. A smart affirmative team will question each of its potential policies by asking if each policy is topical—and if it is not, discarding it.

Let's look at an example. During the 1991–1992 season, a team at one high school—Vikki and Mark—read some articles about homeless people suffering from hypertension (high blood pressure). Since hypertension carries with it an increased risk of heart attack and stroke, they want-

During any given school year, most policy debate students throughout the United States debate the same resolution. During the 1991–1992 school year, for instance, students debated the following resolution: That the federal government should significantly increase social services to homeless individuals in the United States.

ed to advocate a policy that would reduce hypertension.

Some studies suggested a possible policy: testing blood pressure in homeless shelters and then dispensing arm patches containing antihypertension drugs to those who needed them. Before Vikki and Mark settled on this policy, however, they asked: Does it meet every term in the resolution? The resolution, if you recall, was "That the federal government should significantly increase social services to homeless individuals in the United States."

They determined that their policy met the terms of the resolution in the following ways:

✦ The *federal government* could implement this policy with *homeless individuals in the United States* through federal homeless shelters.

✦ Medical services are generally considered *social services*.

✦ The policy provided an important new medical service and therefore met the term *significantly increase*.

After analyzing their policy, they felt reasonably confident that the policy would be topical, but they did not stop there. They went to a library and found definitions that supported their interpretation of the resolution.

After determining that they could defend the topicality of their plan, Vikki and Mark were ready to document the other stock issues—those concerned with the *viability* of the policy itself. They cut evidence from the articles and books they found on hypertension. They bracketed important quotations supporting the stock issues of harm, inherency, and solvency. They also bracketed evidence that sup-

ported their topicality claims and answered potential negative attacks on their policy.

Evidence

Let's look more closely at evidence—at what it's used for, how to find it, how to evaluate it, and how to organize it.

Debate is an activity that depends on persuasion, and finding the right evidence increases your ability to persuade other people to agree with your arguments. Evidence is the raw material with which you prove or support your case.

Debaters use evidence for many reasons. First, evidence itself (and your reading of it) guides your analysis of the resolution and confirms that your thinking is realistic and reasonable. Second, through evidence, you seek the advice of experts, those who know more than you and who have carefully considered the implications of the topic. Third, the use of evidence improves your own ethos as you present arguments, making you more credible because of your display of knowledge.

Finding Evidence

Debaters spend many hours reading newspapers, magazines, scholarly journals, and books, seeking the most convincing evidence to support their arguments. As you learned in Chapter 7, the library is the place where most of their research takes place. An ambitious debate team will visit a nearby college library to examine government documents and specialized reference material such as the *Social Sciences Index* and the *Index to Legal Periodicals*. After spending hours researching in the library, tournament debaters can be spotted in airports and on vans, easily identifiable because of their file boxes crammed with evidence.

Evaluating Evidence

How do you know when to believe evidence? If you can answer yes to the following questions, then the evidence is believable, or credible.

1. Is the Authority Qualified? An authority is a person with specialized knowledge, an expert in a particular field. The authority is qualified to give evidence in that field. What talk show hosts, such as Phil Donahue, and their guests say on television does not often count as evidence from qualified authorities. Even the statements of a university professor are suspect, if that person is speaking about a field other than his or her own. Just being a university professor does not make a person an expert about everything. How reliable, for example, is the evidence of a math professor giving opinions about the need for hypertension patches for the homeless?

2. Is the Authority Cited? That is, do you know exactly whom the evidence came from? For example, do you know the name of the person who made a certain statement, and not just the name of the magazine in which the statement appeared? *Time, Forensic Quarterly,* and the *Congressional Record,* among others, are not always the best sources, because they simply report the work of others. Sources that obtain information from other sources rather than creating that information are called secondary sources.

3. Is the Person a Reluctant Witness? If so, his or her evidence is more credible. If a cigarette manufacturer admits that smoking causes cancer, for example, the statement has greater weight than the same words from a cancer victim. Reluctant sources are preferable because sources, when they freely offer information, often make statements biased by self-interest. Are you surprised when a Pentagon source says that we need more funding for national defense?

4. Is the Evidence Independently Verifiable? In other words, is it possible to check the truth or correctness of the evidence? Can you find similar conclusions elsewhere? If so, you have greater reason to believe that evidence.

5. In Statistical Studies, are Supporting Reasons Given for the Conclusions? Unfortunately, statistics are sometimes used to inflate, confuse, or oversimplify. We cannot outline all of the many shortcomings of statistical research here, but some of the common concerns include the following:

◆ Is the sample large enough to generalize? The sample is simply the people used in the study. These people are selected because they are believed to represent the whole. Nielsen television ratings, for example, are based on the viewing habits of a handful of Americans known as the Nielsen families. A sample that is too small may not accurately reflect the whole. (See Chapter 9 for more information.)

◆ Is the sample population relevant to the policy being discussed? For example, many studies use samples made up of college students because they are readily available to

Debaters do most of their research in the library, where they spend hours reading books, magazines, newspapers, and scholarly journals in search of evidence to support their arguments.

researchers in psychology classes. Do you think the beliefs of college sophomores on the subject of premarital sex reflect the beliefs of the nation as a whole?

◆ What are the limitations on this study? Consider, for example, a computer program that allows researchers to project the future of health care needs in this country. The reliability of the results will depend on the information that is entered into the program. Similarly, the quality of any study can be limited by unknown or uncontrolled factors.

◆ Has the study used consistent definitions? For example, is there a difference between "low income" and "poverty"?

The secret language of statistics can be misleading. As a debater, you must be careful when you use a statistical study to support your case.

6. Is the Evidence Recent Enough to Support the Claims Made? Some issues change over time. Does it matter if, in analyzing America's energy needs, you refer to a study conducted during the Arab oil embargo of 1973?

Although these standards are important, you must be careful not to reject evidence simply because it seems to violate one of them. For example, consider the following exceptions:

1. Biased Sources Can Be Excellent. Ralph Nader, for example, is pro-consumer, but he has written carefully documented *indictments* of big business. His perceived bias against big business has not kept him from providing objective reports on abuses by those businesses.

| COMMUNICATION | | BREAKDOWN |

Painful Policies

School administrators and parents in the Conejo Valley Unified School District in California found themselves debating policy when an eleven-year-old Westlake Elementary School student dressed as the Nazi dictator Adolf Hitler delivered a speech that failed to mention the deaths of 6 million Jews in Nazi concentration camps. The speech was given at a districtwide fifth-grade oratorical contest, and the student was awarded second place by a panel of three teachers.

Superintendent William Seaver, responding to parental concern, ruled that during future oratorical presentations, students would only be allowed to portray "positive figures" in American history. Seaver, who originally opposed the idea of prohibiting students from choosing controversial fig-

ures, changed his mind after meeting with a school board official.

Some parents had argued that their children were upset by the presentation and that the issue was a humanitarian one in which people's feelings were at stake. One parent, though, observed that "perhaps attention should be paid not to who is portrayed, but how." Seaver, granting that freedom of speech is an important issue, stated that "we also have to be aware of the impact it has on other people."

Questions
1. Do you think it will be difficult to define who are "positive figures"?
2. What role should parental concerns play in determining school policy?

---

2. Evidence Needs to Be Recent Only When Time Is a Factor. For example, you can quote Thomas Jefferson discussing the rights of individuals and know that his credibility is timeless. You can't use the Arab oil embargo study cited earlier, however, if more recent studies have been done.

3. Don't Automatically Dismiss Evidence If It's from a Secondary Source. A recent article on inflation in *Time* may include valid statistics that you can use in developing an argument.

Organizing Evidence

Any debate team must not only evaluate evidence but must also organize it. The task of organizing so much evidence can seem overwhelming.

Let's return to Vikki and Mark, the affirmative team mentioned earlier in this chapter. Recall that they collected a great deal of evidence to support their claims. In fact, they bracketed numerous quotations from ten articles and two books. They needed a system for organizing the evidence—and you will, too, when you

INSTANT IMPACT

See It Again

In March, 1954, Edward R. Murrow, a prominent news commentator, used the medium of television to debate Joseph McCarthy, the Wisconsin senator and Communist hunter. Murrow devoted an entire half-hour program in his series "See It Now" to attacking statements made by McCarthy. Pointing out contradictions in McCarthy's statements and challenging his "facts," Murrow invited McCarthy to respond.

On April 6, McCarthy responded on the program "See It Now" that Murrow was "the leader and the cleverest of the jackal pack which is always found at the throat of anyone who dares to expose individual Communists and traitors." Throughout the broadcast, McCarthy used the very tactics—*innuendo, intimidation,* falsehood—that Murrow had accused him of using. This second broadcast defined the characters of the two debaters. Wanting to be precise, Murrow read from a prepared text, while McCarthy made personal attacks on Murrow. McCarthy resorted to exaggeration; Murrow documented claims carefully.

In discussing the importance of the debate format, Kathleen Hall Jamieson and David S. Birdsell, in their book *Presidential Debates,* conclude that: "Had McCarthy not engaged Murrow in debate before a common audience, and in the process confirmed the charges he was attempting to dispatch, the damage to McCarthy's credibility would have been less severe."

By the end of 1954, McCarthy was condemned by other members of the Senate. His public support eroded, and McCarthy died in 1957 from health problems brought on by alcoholism.

reach this point in your preparation. Do not despair. Just follow "the system":

Step 1: Make a numbered list of all the sources you have read. For each, include the author's name, the author's qualifications, the title of the source, and the date.

Step 2: Photocopy the pages of the source that contain evidence you want. With scissors, cut each bracketed quote from the photocopied pages.

Step 3: On the back of each of these pieces of evidence, write the number of the source, the page number of the quote, and a sentence describing what the evidence proves. (This sentence is commonly called the tag. Vikki and Mark, for example, might have tagged one piece of evidence "Hypertension causes heart disease" and another "Arm patches produce few side effects.")

Step 4: Group evidence into envelopes labeled by argument or by stock issue. For example, all of the solvency evidence could go in one envelope, all of the harm evidence in another, and so on. Then subdivide the evidence into more envelopes. Each of these envelopes contains evidence on a specific issue (for example, one could contain evidence on the number of deaths caused by hypertension). The number of envelopes you will have depends on the amount of research you have done and the complexity of the policy.

Writing the Case

After you have organized your evidence, you are ready to write the affirmative case. As noted earlier, the affirmative case includes the plan, which tells what policy the affirmative is supporting, and the rationale, which tells why the resolution should be adopted. The case has two parts: the original statement of the policy and the defense of the policy, which is made in later speeches. The original statement of the policy is called the first affirmative constructive, or the 1AC. The later defenses are called the extensions.

The 1AC

In general, the first affirmative speech follows this structure:

I. Present an observation on inherency.

(Remember that inherency refers to those problems that will not go away unless the affirmative plan is adopted. Use evidence to show that laws, attitudes, or procedures prevent the status quo—the present system—from dealing with these problems. These laws, attitudes, or procedures are the inherent barriers that must be overcome.)

II. Present the resolution and define any key terms that are not clear or self-evident.

III. Present your plan. Each plan should have the following:
A. Mandates—These tell what your plan does.
B. Enabling provisions—These tell how you are going to carry out the mandates. The mandates may be carried out through the following means:
1. Administration
2. Funding
3. Enforcement

IV. Present an advantage. An advantage is a benefit that will result from the adoption of the resolution.
A. Show the harm of the status quo.
B. Show that your plan solves for the harm.

V. Present additional advantages, using the same format.

Extension Blocks

In debate, the term **extension** refers to arguments used after the first affirmative speech to defend the affirmative proposal. A **block** is simply a group of arguments prepared to answer an opponent's attack.

If you have researched well, you will have more good evidence than you can use in the first affirmative speech. You will want to use the best of your remaining evidence as extension blocks to answer the arguments that your opponents will make. The "name of the game" is anticipation—figuring out what your opponent is going to say. In preparing your case, anticipate your opponent's arguments and prepare to defeat them by writing extension blocks that include answers to potential attacks.

Some debaters like to put their best evidence in the first affirmative speech. In this way, they can be sure that they give their best evidence in every debate. Others, however, prefer to save the best cards for extension. They hope to draw their opponents into weak arguments easily defeated by the extensions. If you have evidence claiming that most experts or the best studies support the affirmative position, you may want to put that evidence in extension blocks rather than in the first affirmative speech. If the evidence answers a disadvantage to the policy, explains how a solvency problem might not apply, weighs the advantages versus the disadvantages, or provides a topicality defense from an expert, it probably belongs in an extension block.

Remember, one of the most exciting activities an affirmative team undertakes each year is to choose a case to research and then use in competition. If you meet your burden of research and advocacy, your case should be virtually unbeatable. A well-prepared team knows its case better than anyone else and has considered all of the best objections against it.

TAKING CHARGE

Now it's your turn. Write an outline for a case on the resolution you created earlier in this chapter (or you might want to prepare your outline on this year's debate resolution). Be sure you organize it according to the sample outline.

Let's say the topic deals with improving the environment, and you want to write a case on reducing global warming by limiting the burning of fossil fuels such as gas and oil. In your observation on inherency, you would outline how present laws and attitudes are ineffective in reducing fossil fuel use. Therefore, you might advocate passing stricter laws requiring mass transit systems in cities. State how you would enforce and fund your plan. Then write at least one advantage. As a first step in creating an advantage, you would list the harms of global warming and how fossil fuels contribute to it. Finally, outline how the use of mass transit would limit emissions of fossil fuels, thus reducing warming.

III Preparing the Negative

In general, while the affirmative must win all of the stock issues to win the debate, the negative need only disprove one to win. Though this may seem unfair at first, it is just common sense. Why, for example, adopt a hypertension policy if no one has hypertension or if hypertension carries no ill effects? Why dispense patches if they do not reduce hypertension or if they produce side effects worse than hypertension itself? Why adopt a federal policy if states already have programs in place?

The challenge for the negative team is to anticipate possible affirmative positions. You don't know what the affirmative plan will be, so you have to be prepared for a variety of different cases. Most negative teams prepare the following arguments (also called *blocks*) in advance: disadvantages, topicality violations, solvency attacks, harm attacks, inherency attacks, and counterplans.

Disadvantages

The disadvantages are the problems created by the affirmative plan. A disadvantage against Vikki and Mark's hypertension case, for example, might claim that the drugs in antihypertension patches cause severe side effects.

A disadvantage must first of all have a thesis—a label or central idea, along with a brief explanation of the logical connections to the affirmative plan that you will develop in the debate. The explanation will include the following features:

1. Link—Here, you show that the affirmative plan has a direct link to your disadvantage—that you are really describing a disadvantage of the plan. If the plan clearly states the link, you will not need evidence for this. In some cases, you will need evidence to show that the affirmative's plan and the disadvantage are linked.

2. Uniqueness—Here, you demonstrate that the disadvantage will not occur under the present system—that it is unique to the affirmative plan.

3. Internal links (if necessary)—This is not the same as the link to the affirmative plan. Here, you document the events that the affirmative will set in motion. These events are linked by cause and effect (for example, a deficit spending disadvantage would state that deficit spending leads to inflation, which makes investors less confident, which causes stock market collapse and world recession).

4. Impact—Here, you show that the final effects are bad (for example, world recession increases the risk of war).

Topicality Violations

Remember that topicality involves dealing precisely with the terms of the resolution. Topicality arguments contend that the affirmative violates a specific term. For example, a topicality violation against the hypertension case might claim that a *tangible* patch is not a social service because social services are intangible services—counseling, for example.

A well-structured topicality violation has three parts:

1. A definition of the term in the resolution that the affirmative violates.

2. An explanation of how the affirmative violates the definition.

3. Standards for evaluating conflicting definitions or interpretations of the resolution.

Solvency Attacks

Solvency is the ability of the affirmative plan to solve the harm. Thus, solvency at-

The two people who form a policy debate team divide the responsibilities for preparation and presentation.

tacks demonstrate that the affirmative plan does not eliminate the harm. Solvency attacks fall into several distinct categories:

- ◆ **Alternate causality attacks** argue that the affirmative has not identified the true cause of the problem and therefore cannot solve it. Negatives against the hypertension case, for example, might argue that stress causes hypertension and that patches cannot reduce stress-related hypertension.

- ◆ **Circumvention attacks** argue that key people will circumvent, or avoid, the affirmative plan, thus preventing it from working. An excellent circumvention attack against the hypertension case maintains that the homeless themselves will avoid the shelters because they fear authority, because they are worried about food more than about medical services, and because many are drug addicts or alcoholics. A good circumvention attack describes both why and how the plan will be circumvented.

- ◆ **Workability attacks** point to a flaw in the plan that prevents its solvency. For example, patches may not regulate the flow of drugs to meet individual needs of homeless people with different levels of high blood pressure or different physical responses to the drug. If the patches don't work, the affirmative plan doesn't work.

- ◆ **Solvency turns** argue that the plan not only does not solve the harm but actually worsens the problem. For example, if a homeless person returns for patches only once in awhile, the changing dosages of the drug might actually heighten the risk of heart attack. (*Turn,* short for *turnaround,* is a general term that refers to reversing the impact of an argument so that it favors the opposite position. A turn is sometimes called a *flip.*) Solvency turns may also be argued as disadvantages.

Harm Attacks

Harm attacks address the harm the affirmative claims. Some harm attacks minimize the harm presented by the affirmative team. A negative might claim, for example, that hypertension rarely leads to serious heart disease and even more rarely to death. Others actually "turn" the harm—that is, demonstrate that the alleged harm is actually beneficial. Though it is unlikely, a study might show that hypertension reduces heart disease.

Inherency Attacks

Inherency, remember, says that the harm will not be solved unless the affirmative's policy is carried out. Inherency attacks by the negative contend that there already are laws, attitudes, or procedures for dealing with the harm. These attacks are becoming very rare because (1) it is difficult to prove that any procedure can completely solve the harm and (2) inherency attacks often contradict claims of uniqueness made in the disadvantages. Let's look at an example. As the negative in the hypertension case, you could claim that federally funded medical clinics already distribute hypertension patches to

poor people. However, you probably wouldn't win the debate on this issue. It would be impossible to prove that every homeless person has access to such a clinic or to the patches. Furthermore, suppose that you were claiming that side effects would be a unique disadvantage of the plan. The inherency argument would prove that this claim is untrue—if it were true, side effects would be occurring with the status quo program.

Counterplans

A **counterplan** is a negative proposal to solve all or most of the harm but avoid one or more of the disadvantages. A counterplan has two requirements.

First, it should be nontopical—that is, outside of the resolution. If the counterplan is topical, then that means both the affirmative team and the negative team are supporting the resolution, and there is no reason to debate. In recent years, topical counterplans have become more acceptable; but since defending a topical counterplan takes a great deal of skill, you probably should not attempt it as a beginning debater. A typical nontopical counterplan against the hypertension case would merely have the states (which are not part of the federal government), rather than the federal government, distribute the patches.

Second, the counterplan must be **competitive**—that is, it must offer a reason to reject the affirmative plan. Defending against the counterplan just described, a sharp affirmative might claim that if both state and federal shelters distributed patches, the patches would reach more people, thus improving the plan's solvency. In other words, both the plan and the counterplan could be used—the counterplan would simply add to the plan, not replace it. The negative must show why this is not so—why the states and the federal government either *cannot* or *should not* act together.

Let's look at these two alternatives more closely. If the negative shows that the federal government *cannot* act together with the states, it can claim that the two plans compete because they are mutually exclusive—one cannot exist if the other does. What sort of counterplan against the hypertension case would have this **mutual exclusivity?** Such a counterplan might argue for reducing hypertension treatment rather than increasing it. Since it is impossible to reduce and to increase treatment simultaneously, this counterplan is com-petitive. Alternatively, if the negative proves that the federal government *should not* act with the state government, it can claim that the two plans compete because the counterplan has more **net benefits.** Net benefits weigh a plan's benefits against its disadvantages. To prove that the counterplan has more net benefits, the negative needs to show that the counterplan solves most of the harm claimed by the affirmative while avoiding at least one of the disadvantages that apply to the affirmative. For example, state action might avoid harmful deficit spending, which would occur if the federal government paid for hypertension patches. Since it does not matter how the homeless get the patch, a state program would solve the case harm while avoiding a disadvantage.

TAKING CHARGE

Whether you are preparing your affirmative or your negative arguments, it is crucial to analyze the supporting evidence. The credibility of your arguments will in large part be determined by the quality of evidence you use.

Now it's your turn. Find five quotations from five different sources citing statistics or opinions on the state of the United States economy. Evaluate the strengths and weaknesses of each quotation and each source with your teacher or your classmates.

IV How to Defend against Negative Attacks

Remember, as the affirmative, you will need to write extension blocks to answer potential negative arguments against your case. You can use the arguments below to deliver deadly blows to most negative attacks.

Defeating the Disadvantage

Your goal in answering a disadvantage is to make it less damaging, to eliminate it altogether, or to turn it into an affirmative advantage. Your answers should fall into these categories:

1. **No link.** The policy advocated by the affirmative team does nothing to cause the disadvantage. Vikki and Mark responded to a disadvantage on the harmful effects of deficit spending by arguing that their plan used money already allocated to homeless medical services.

2. **Link turn.** The affirmative plan does not cause the disadvantage; it prevents the disadvantage. Vikki and Mark's plan was linked by the negative team to the disadvantage of increased deficit spending. Vikki and Mark turned the link by arguing that their plan would save the money the federal government would otherwise spend on future heart disease in homeless persons with hypertension. In other words, not only did the plan not increase spending; it saved money in the long run.

3. **Not unique.** The disadvantage is "nonunique" to the affirmative; it will occur anyway, with or without the affirmative. This is essentially an alternative causality argument. Recall that alternative causality arguments say that other policies are equally linked to the disadvantage. Vikki and Mark claimed that the deficit disadvantage was nonunique because the federal government planned to increase deficit spending on homeless programs within the month.

4. **Empirically disproven.** *Empirical* means based on observation. Other observable events that have taken place ought to have triggered the disadvantage but did not. Therefore, the disadvantage must be *invalid*. Vikki and Mark pointed out that the government had increased deficit spending by 5 percent the preceding year without triggering these events.

   The "empirically disproven" argument sometimes takes the form of a threshold challenge. A threshold argument asks the negative team to prove at what point the disadvantage will begin. Here, the affirmative team would say that the negative evidence never stated how much deficit spending has to increase for the disadvantage to take place.

5. **No internal link.** A key link in the chain of events that starts with the first link to the affirmative plan and extends to the final impact is missing or suspect. Remember that the deficit disadvantage involved the claim that spending leads to inflation, which leads to a lessening of investor confidence, a stock market collapse, world recession, and finally war. Vikki and Mark read evidence that inflation does not shake investors' confidence, thus beating the disadvantage at the internal link level.

6. **Impact does not outweigh.** The harm caused by the disadvantage is not as great as the affirmative case's advantage—that is, it does not outweigh the advantage. Vikki and Mark responded to the side-

effects disadvantage by arguing that the side effects were not as severe as heart disease, which often results in death.

7. Impact turn. The impacts of the disadvantage are not bad; they are good. Against the deficit disadvantage, Vikki and Mark argued that a world recession would prevent rather than cause war because in times of recession, nations cannot build arms and cannot afford to engage in expensive military activities.

Experienced debaters know that they should not argue link turns and impact turns on the same disadvantage. This mistake, often called the *double-turn*, can cost you the debate because you have essentially admitted that your plan would prevent something good from happening.

8. No threshold. The affirmative does not do enough to trigger the impact. Vikki and Mark sometimes admitted that their plan involved spending some federal money on hypertension, but they argued that the minimal spending could not possibly shake investor confidence enough to cause a stock market collapse.

9. Time frame. The affirmative advantages occur long before the impacts of the disadvantage, and these impacts can be solved later. They may even become irrelevant if the affirmative advantage is huge. Vikki and Mark asserted that the benefits of hypertension patches are immediate, while the chain

events from deficit spending would take years to occur. If the judge decided for the negative, homeless people would die needlessly to prevent a war that might never occur.

Defeating Harm, Solvency, or Inherency Attacks

Disadvantages are not the only negative strategy for which you must be prepared. Most negative teams also offer harm, solvency, or inherency attacks. In most instances, you should point out that these attacks are not absolute. That is, they do not eliminate the advantage; they merely reduce it.

Turns on the harm or on solvency attacks are more damaging and should be handled like disadvantages. (In fact, they really *are* disadvantages.) Citing studies, the consensus of opinion, or sources that are more qualified can also effectively refute the more damaging harm and solvency attacks.

Defeating Topicality Attacks

Topicality attacks contend that the affirmative violates a specific term of the resolution. You can respond to topicality attacks with three types of answers:

1. You can show how your definition is consistent with the definition offered by the negative.

2. You can counterdefine—that is, you can provide your own definition of the term in question. Explain how your definition is a better definition and how your plan meets it.

3. Many judges will not vote on topicality unless the negative team can prove that the affirmative team's position makes debate unfair somehow or abuses the debate process. Therefore, you can argue that your interpretation of the resolution is a fair one that does not abuse the debate process.

Defeating Counterplans

You can defeat a counterplan on two levels. First, you can prove that the counterplan is topical, thus justifying a decision for the affirmative. In asserting that its counterplan is not topical, the negative will identify the words of the resolution that the counterplan does not meet. You will need to read your own definitions, explaining how the counterplan does meet these definitions. For example, if the negative argued a counterplan in which the states, rather than the federal government, gave out anti-hypertension patches, the affirmative could try to define *federal government* as "the government in Washington, D.C., acting together with the states."

Under this definition, state action would be topical.

Second, you can show that the counterplan is not competitive because it does not offer a net benefit. Thus, it would be better to adopt the affirmative without the counterplan. You can show that the counterplan offers no net benefit by (1) showing that all the negative's disadvantages apply to the counterplan as well, (2) arguing your own disadvantages to the counterplan, or (3) proving that the counterplan does not solve the problem as well as the affirmative plan.

You can also prove that the counterplan is not competitive by arguing permutations to the counterplan. Permutations simply claim that some portion of the affirmative plan together with the counterplan would be advantageous. Permutations show that the judge need not reject the affirmative to get the benefits of the counterplan—that, in fact, implementing both together would create the most net benefits.

TAKING CHARGE

Now it's your turn. After pairing up with a classmate, exchange the affirmative case outlines you constructed earlier in this chapter. Next, prepare negative arguments against the affirmative case outline of your classmate. Finally, after exchanging the negative arguments, write out the responses that you would use to defend your affirmative case against the negative attacks offered by your classmate. Try to incorporate some of the strategies you have learned in this chapter.

Ⅴ The First Debate

So you've done your groundwork. You've written an affirmative case, and you're prepared to debate on the negative. Now you're facing your first real debate—in class, after school, or at a tournament. What else do you need to know?

The Format for a Debate

Debates are divided into three parts: constructive speeches, rebuttal speeches, and cross-examination questions. Each of the four speakers gives a constructive and a rebuttal speech as well as participating in two cross-examination periods.

- ✦ Constructive. This speech allows you to construct your major arguments either for or against the resolution, depending on which side of the resolution you are taking.

- ✦ Rebuttal. This second speech given by each speaker in the round gives you the opportunity to explain and extend the arguments introduced in the constructive speeches.

- ✦ Cross-examination. This time period allows you to question your opponents regarding flaws in arguments or to clarify points you do not understand.

Which Partner Should Do Which Speech?

In any policy debate, each team of two persons establishes a "division of labor" in order to meet its burdens in the debate round. The format given indicates the major responsibilities of each speaker. Let's look more closely at these responsibilities and at the personality of each speaker.

Format of a Debate

Speech	Description	Time
First affirmative constructive (1AC)	Presents the prepared case and plan	8 minutes
Cross-examination by 2nd Neg.	Questions the 1AC	3 minutes
First negative constructive (1NC)	Presents the negative attacks	8 minutes
Cross-examination by 1st Aff.	Questions the 1NC	3 minutes
Second affirmative constructive (2AC)	Responds to the negative attacks and develops the advantages further	8 minutes
Cross-examination by 1st Neg.	Questions the 2AC	3 minutes
Second negative constructive (2NC)	Extends approximately two-thirds of the winning negative arguments, answering each affirmative response	8 minutes
Cross-examination by 2nd Aff.	Questions the 2NC	3 minutes
First negative rebuttal (1NR)	Answers affirmative responses to winning negative arguments not covered by 2NC	5 minutes
First affirmative rebuttal (1AR)	Extends key affirmative answers to issues remaining in the debate	5 minutes
Second negative rebuttal (2NR)	Chooses winning issues, explaining why the negative wins the debate	5 minutes
Second affirmative rebuttal (2AR)	Chooses winning issues, explaining why the affirmative wins the debate	5 minutes

The first affirmative speaker presents the only speech in the debate that is prepared entirely before the round. A good first affirmative speaker will be thoroughly knowledgeable about the contents of the speech, its research history, and the likely negative approaches. First affirmative speakers must be capable of clear delivery so that they can impart a great deal of information to the judge while they instill a sense of calm and confidence about the team.

Many people feel that the first affirmative speaker is the "person in the bow of the canoe." That means she just paddles along while the smart partner handles the tough attacks in the debate. This myth is dispelled by the first affirmative rebuttal, which is arguably the most difficult and critical speech in the round. Why? Because it must answer twelve minutes of negative analysis from the second negative constructive and the first negative rebuttal (consecutive speeches known as the negative block) in only four minutes. In this rebuttal, the first affirmative speaker groups arguments based on like assumptions, extends the arguments that the second affirmative rebuttal will need to win the debate, and makes sure that no deadly negative argument is left untouched. The first affirmative speaker must be clear and efficient—no job for a slouch.

The first negative speaker presents the negative position in the debate in the first negative constructive, establishing the ethos of the team. Typically, this speaker will present a topicality violation (if applicable), straight case refutation diminishing harm and solvency, and disadvantages. Thus, the speaker must be familiar with the negative positions and must have the ability to respond clearly to the first affir-

mative constructive and to raise doubts in the judge's mind about the logical adequacy of the affirmative case. This speaker must also have a freewheeling mind and an ability to make arguments that undermine the affirmative without cluttering the negative approach.

In the first negative rebuttal, the first negative speaker picks up one or two negative arguments not covered by the second negative constructive and develops them by answering affirmative responses and extending the arguments further. The speaker has more preparation time for this speech than any other in the debate, because he or she can prepare during the second negative constructive and the cross-examination that follows it.

The second affirmative speaker must command the debate by the end of the second affirmative constructive. If the first affirmative rebuttal is to succeed, the second affirmative constructive will have to lay the groundwork for that speech by defeating some of the negative arguments so that the negative team will drop them. The second affirmative rebuttal must be a convincing speech, a clear presentation explaining why the major issues in the debate have gone affirmative and how the negative lost the debate as much through its own arguments as through the affirmative's. The best second affirmative rebuttal "writes the ballot" for the judge.

The second negative speaker gives impact to most of the winning negative arguments by answering all affirmative responses to those issues. This speaker will show that the affirmative speakers' position locks them into accepting the impact of these arguments and then weighs those impacts against the affirmative case. The goal is to show that even if the affirmative wins some of its case and solvency, the negative positions are still a clear reason for rejecting the resolution. The second negative rebuttal is the speech in which the negative crystallizes the debate by explaining why the negative wins and attempts to *preempt* the second affirmative rebuttal so that the judge will write a negative ballot. You preempt affirmative arguments by anticipating them and providing the necessary responses in advance.

Cross-examination

"The issue of a cause rarely depends upon a speech and is but seldom even affected by it. But there is never a cause contested, the result of which is not mainly dependent upon the skill with which the advocate conducts his cross-examination" (Francis L. Wellman, *The Art of Cross-examination*).

One of the most exciting features of contemporary policy debate is cross-examination. It often provides the greatest drama and clash in the debate, and it guarantees that vital arguments will be addressed. Cross-examination was introduced into academic debate in 1924 by Professor J. Stanley Gray of the University of Oregon and was adopted by the National Forensic League in 1952. Because of its origins, cross-examination debate is often referred to as "Oregon debate."

Cross-examination is designed to heighten the clash in the debate by clarifying points in the opponent's case, weakening evidence or exposing lack of evidence, gaining admission from your opponent of weakness in analysis, obtaining data for later use, and pointing out fallacies in reasoning. Cross-examination provides a more stimulating debate for the audience and judge. It also provides a better test of the strength of the case, thus promoting the search for truth in the debate.

You must learn to think of cross-examination as "time to be won" in the debate. Whether examining or being examined, you should attempt to capture the time by asking and answering questions in a way that reveals preparation, depth of understanding, solid analysis of the topic, familiarity with evidence, and intelligence. A self-confident debater can set the agenda for the debate by skillfully emphasizing the points developed in cross-examination.

Flowing the Debate

Probably the most important basic debate skill involves learning to take an accurate flowsheet. Taking a **flowsheet,** or flowing the debate, simply means recording the "flow" of words or arguments from both you and your opponent. You will use the flowsheet to remember what to say in your speech. If you do not keep track of all the arguments, you may forget important points, and that may cost you the debate.

Here are the basic rules of flowing:

1. Write down your opponents' major arguments.
2. Write down your own arguments and those of your partner.
3. Write arguments in columns, using lines to connect your argument to your opponents' response.
4. Keep track of arguments to which your opponents do not respond by using a large X.

5. Flow in two colors to separate your arguments from your opponents'.

6. Use abbreviations of frequently used terms. (T for topicality, I for impact, HL for homeless, and so on.)

7. Write very small so that you have room for all the speeches in the debate.

8. Leave space between arguments in case you or your opponents want to make multiple responses.

9. Keep columns straight. (You may want to draw columns for each speech before the debate begins.)

10. Flow all of your arguments before your speech. If you do not have time, either flow your arguments after the speech or have your partner flow your arguments for you during cross-examination. This is called *back-flowing*.

11. As you are flowing, circle key arguments you don't want to forget to answer.

12. The first negative speaker does not need to flow the second negative speaker's constructive. During the second negative constructive, the first negative speaker prepares the first negative rebuttal. All other speakers should flow the entire debate.

13. Flow each major constructive issue on a separate sheet of paper. (That is, each disadvantage, each counterplan, each advantage, and each topicality violation occupy a separate sheet.)

Who Wins the Debate?

In the final analysis, most debates come down to the issue of net benefits, which simply means that the judge is likely to vote for the team with the most benefits (or advantages).

First, the judge must decide if the affirmative is topical. Remember, topicality is an a priori issue, the issue the judge decides first. If she finds the affirmative topical, she begins to look at the policy implications of the affirmative proposal to decide if adopting it would be beneficial or advantageous. In this role, she acts much like a real policy maker, looking at the policy to see if it is a good idea.

Many inexperienced negative speakers think that if they win one solvency attack, one harm attack, or one disadvantage, they win the round. Nothing could be further from the truth. If you were arguing the negative position against the hypertension case, would you win if you proved that death from heart disease is not as frequent as the affirmative claims? Of course not—because you have only minimized the harm; you have not completely eliminated it. Would you win if you proved that 5 percent of patches do not *adhere* to the skin? No again—because you have admitted that patches adhere properly 95 percent of the time. Would you win if you proved that patches caused side effects like dizziness and nausea occasionally? Probably not, because the death and disease from hypertension are far worse than nausea or dizziness. These are all valuable arguments because they reduce the affirmative advantage, but you would not win the debate on any of these attacks. Even in combination, these three arguments would probably still

COMMUNICATION   BREAKTHROUGH

International Debate

Tim Averill's original idea for the London trip was for the Manchester, Massachusetts, High School debate team to celebrate its twentieth anniversary by traveling to Europe. The trip would include exhibitions of American debating, allowing all thirteen members of the team to participate. Averill, who has headed the program at Manchester since 1971, coached the National Forensic League and Tournament of Champions winning policy debate teams in 1987.

As Averill organized the trip, his London contacts kept suggesting that Manchester represent the U.S. in the World School Debating Championships. Manchester accepted the invitation and joined twelve other countries—Australia, Bangladesh, Bermuda, Canada, England, Ireland, Israel, The Netherlands, New Zealand, Pakistan, Scotland, and Wales—for the London event. Conducted in English, all debates followed a parliamentary format: resolutions were value or policy.

Some topics were sent to the debaters several months before the competition, and the remainder of the topics were announced at one-and-a-half hours' notice and prepared by the teams with no assistance from their coaches. For the 1992 debates, the U.S. team from Manchester was assigned the following topics:

✦ This House believes that Nuclear Energy is worth the Risk.

✦ This House believes that Today's Heroes are Hollow.

✦ This House would abolish all Monarchies.

Manchester was also assigned the following topics, for which they had ninety minutes' preparation time:

✦ Resolved: that this House welcomes the fall of Communism.

✦ Resolved: that this House would close down Hollywood.

✦ Resolved: that this House believes that the war against discrimination has been fought badly.

"The emphasis is upon 'public persuasion'" said Averill, "and the careful use of a relatively small amount of evidence." Averill went on to explain that each team is encouraged to have an advocacy position but that it is the ethos of the individual speakers that determines the outcome—humor and wit are required and rewarded. Unlike policy debates in America, the international debates focus more on the speaker's own knowledge than on documentation.

Members of the Manchester debate team were impressed by the quality of argument and delivery of the international champions (New Zealand, 1992). They agreed that they learned much about style and technique from this memorable competition. Averill adds, "More importantly, we had the opportunity to get to know students from all over the world, to share ideas and opinions, and to assess our educational system by comparison."

Questions
1. Do you think the ethos of individual debaters should determine the outcome of debates? Why or why not?
2. One of the topics debated was "Resolved: that this House would close down Hollywood." What arguments might you have presented on this topic?

leave the affirmative a substantial advantage.

You would only win the debate if you proved that the affirmative case had *no* harm, *no* solvency, or *no* inherency—or perhaps that it created a disadvantage far worse than the harm it corrected. Since it is difficult to prove that there is *no* harm or *no* solvency or *no* inherency, the usual strategy is to minimize these as much as possible while winning enough of a disadvantage to outweigh the remaining advantage. Another popular strategy has negatives solving all or most of the case with a counterplan but avoiding a disadvantage.

At the end of the round, though, the judge should always weigh the consequences of voting affirmative against the consequences of voting negative. The team with the most advantages (or net benefits) should win.

TAKING CHARGE

1. Read a one- or two-minute debate argument to the class. After a classmate cross-examines you, your teacher and your classmates can critique both your performance and that of your questioner.
2. Try to flow some of the sample arguments in this chapter as your teacher or a classmate reads them out loud. Keep trying even if at first you do not succeed.

REVIEW AND ENRICHMENT

LOOKING BACK

Listed below are the major ideas discussed in this chapter.

- ✦ Policy debaters examine policies much as a real policy maker would.
- ✦ The affirmative team has the burden to present harms that outweigh the disadvantages, prove inherency, solve the harm, and prove topicality.
- ✦ Topicality is an a priori issue for reasons of fairness.
- ✦ You should prepare answers to arguments you anticipate hearing in the debate. These arguments are called *extensions*.
- ✦ On the negative, you should prepare disadvantages, topicality violations, solvency attacks, harm attacks, inherency attacks, and counterplans.
- ✦ Solvency attacks fall into four categories: alternate causality attacks, circumvention attacks, workability attacks, and solvency turns.
- ✦ Counterplans must be nontopical and competitive.
- ✦ Counterplans can compete through mutual exclusivity or net benefits.
- ✦ Taking thorough notes during the debate is called *flowing*.
- ✦ If the affirmative is topical, the team with the most net benefits will win the debate.

SPEECH VOCABULARY

Match the speech term on the left with the appropriate phrase on the right.

1. prima facie
2. solvency
3. topicality
4. plan
5. alternate causality attack
6. circumvention attack
7. workability attack
8. rationale
9. harm
10. a priori

a. proof that the plan solves the harm

b. reasons for adopting the resolution

c. a flaw in the plan prevents solvency

d. a way of describing the problem

e. "at first view," the policy meets the stock issues

f. the plan meets the terms of the resolution

g. means "before"

h. a cause other than the one the affirmative has identified would prevent solvency

i. key people will avoid the plan, preventing its solvency

j. the affirmative proposal

GENERAL VOCABULARY

Look up the words in the following list. Write down a definition for each and use it in a sentence.

reassess
advocacy
quantitative
qualitative
viability
indictments
innuendo

intimidation
tangible
empirical
invalid
preempt
adhere

THINGS TO REMEMBER

1. The affirmative bears the _____ in a debate.
2. The affirmative's _____ should outweigh the negative's _____.
3. _____ requires that the affirmative prove that without the resolution, the problem will not be solved.
4. _____ is an a priori issue.
5. Organize answers to potential negative attacks on _____.
6. _____ requires that a counterplan offer a reason to reject the affirmative.
7. If the plan cannot coexist with the counterplan, it is _____; if it should not, it is _____.
8. If a disadvantage will occur without the affirmative plan, it is not _____.
9. An argument that only minimizes the advantage rather than eliminating it is not _____.
10. Some combination of the plan and the counterplan is a _____.

THINGS TO DO

1. Browsing in the current periodical section of the library, find five magazine articles relevant to the resolution you're debating. Find five more relevant articles by using the *Reader's Guide to Periodical Literature.*
2. Organize files for the blocks you've prepared, using file folders for each

block. You will probably have several file folders for your affirmative. In general, you can put the negative on each case in a different folder.
3. Using the subject guide to *Books in Print*, find five books published in the last two years relevant to your debate resolution. Talk to your librarian about obtaining one or two of them on interlibrary loan if your library does not own the books, or try to find them in a university library.

THINGS TO TALK ABOUT

1. What benefits derive from studying and debating both sides of an issue even when you may strongly disagree with one side? Does it compromise your sense of personal ethics to uphold a point of view with which you disagree?
2. Attend a local debate tournament. Discuss how what you observed differs from the fundamentals you have learned in this chapter.
3. How do the formats for presidential debates on television differ from the format for policy debate? Do you think that voters would benefit from seeing the candidates use a format similar to the one described in this chapter? Why or why not?

THINGS TO WRITE ABOUT

1. Describe in an essay why the stock issues exist. What is the logical purpose of each?
2. Write an essay describing the benefits you might receive from debate. Can it help you in real life? In other classes? Will it help you in the future? How?

CRITICAL THINKING

1. In a debate, the affirmative upholds First Amendment rights. The negative presents a disadvantage claiming that too much stress on individual rights threatens a general safety. Is the negative correct? If you were the affirmative, how would you convince the judge that First Amendment rights outweigh safety concerns? If you were the negative, how would you argue that safety concerns outweigh First Amendment rights?

2. As the affirmative, you are upholding a plan that advocates building low-income housing for the homeless. The negative argues that the federal government is already building enough low-income housing. The negative also presents a disadvantage that claims that cutting trees for housing will lead to global deforestation and environmental collapse. How would you respond as the affirmative?

3. As noted in this chapter, Lyndon Johnson once coached high school debate. Johnson gave this advice to students: "As debaters, you must search for the truth and you must speak the truth and you must surrender yourself to the truth. For the genius of our democracy is that it admits variety and permits criticism, knowing always that in the long run truth will prevail." Do you agree with Johnson that truth always prevails? Why?

RELATED SPEECH TOPICS

Political debates
Congressional debate
Study methodology
Note taking
Preparation for law school

Evaluating consequences of policy
  decisions
Cost–benefit analysis
Organizing files

CHAPTER 18

Parliamentary Procedure

"The job of a citizen is to keep his mouth open."

— Günter Grass, novelist

AS THE PRESIDENT OF STUDENT COUNCIL, I THINK WE SHOULD START A RECYCLING PROGRAM FOR THE SCHOOL! WOULD ANYONE CARE TO MAKE A MOTION?

SOMETIMES I THINK I PREFER PLAIN OLD, RUN-OF-THE-MILL APATHY!

LEARNING OBJECTIVES

After completing this chapter, you will be able to do the following.

◆ Explain how parliamentary procedure supports the democratic process.
◆ Organize the first meeting of a new club.
◆ Lead a meeting in the role of the presiding officer.
◆ Participate in a group meeting by making, seconding, and amending motions.
◆ List the most commonly used motions in ranked order.

CHAPTER OUTLINE

Following are the main sections in this chapter.

I Learning the Rules
II Getting Down to Business
III A Member's Responsibilities
IV The Order of Precedence
V Making Decisions by Voting

Chapter Review

NEW SPEECH TERMS

In this chapter, you will learn the meanings of the speech terms listed below.

parliamentary procedure
chair
house
orders of the day
old business
new business
adjourn
minutes
main motion
reconsider
quorum

executive session
order of precedence
subsidiary motion
privileged motion
incidental motion
table a motion
call the question
amend

GENERAL VOCABULARY

Expanding your general vocabulary will help you become a more effective communicator. Listed below are some words appearing in this chapter that you should make part of your everyday vocabulary.

Parliament
innumerable
etiquette
cliques
railroad
painstakingly

agenda
restate
germane
preamble
suspend
plurality

LOOKING AHEAD

The best meetings are often noisy, exciting affairs with people bouncing ideas off one another. But beneath the noise and commotion is an orderly system, a system of rules that ensures the right of each person to be heard.

This system, called parliamentary procedure, empowers the members of the meeting to take action through a majority vote. By learning the system and especially by frequent practice, you will become a more effective participant in meetings and hence, a better citizen.

1   Learning the Rules

Each player takes the colored token nearest to him on the board, and uses it throughout the game. The player having the red token, Miss Scarlet, rolls the die and moves first.

The description above, in case you haven't guessed, is taken from the rules of the popular board game Clue. In that game, players try to discover the identity of a murderer. To do so, however, they must follow a strict set of rules. A player could cheat, of course, by ignoring one of the rules (for instance, sneaking a peek at another player's clue cards), but by so doing that player would defeat the purpose of the rules: namely, to give each player an even chance to win.

We play many games throughout our lives. Some are more serious than others, but in each we agree to play by the rules. Our ability to play well often depends on whether we understand the rules and how well we can use them to our advantage.

Democracy is much more than a game, of course, but it, too, has its rules. Our ability to act as effective citizens in a democracy depends to a great extent on our knowing the rules and learning how to play by them. Let's look more closely at why we need rules in a democracy. Then we'll begin to examine the rules themselves.

Democracy in Action

We use several different sets of rules in our democracy. The Constitution, for example, is the basis of our legal system, and the Bill of Rights defines our individual freedoms. When we meet in groups, however, we follow a system of rules called **parliamentary procedure.** We use these rules whether we are meeting with the student council, a school club, or any other organization. These rules also apply to the meetings of all our governing bodies from the town council to the U.S. Congress.

The rules of parliamentary procedure provide the fair and balanced system we need to work together. The rules are called parliamentary because they follow ideas originally developed by the British

The rules of parliamentary procedure follow ideas originally developed by the British Parliament. Pictured here is the British House of Commons circa 1840.

Parliament. In fact, these rules represent more than five hundred years of human history. Over the past centuries, people have written and rewritten the rules as they learned how to make them better. As a result, the rules have come to reflect the experience and wisdom of hundreds of organizations and *innumerable* individuals.

The British rules of government were brought to North America by the early colonists and introduced at the first New England town meetings. When Thomas Jefferson became president of the United States in 1801, he published the first American book on parliamentary procedure. "I have begun a sketch," Jefferson wrote, "which those who come after will successfully correct and fill up, till a code of rules shall be formed." Jefferson's book became the basis for the rules adopted by Congress and was the fore-

most authority on parliamentary procedure for many years.

Robert and His Rules

As time passed, it became necessary to adapt Jefferson's rules to meet the needs of day-to-day life. General Henry Robert, an Army engineer, took on the task after a frustrating personal experience. Robert belonged to many church and civic

> "I would never attend another meeting until I knew something of parliamentary law."
>
> **Henry Robert**

groups and was asked once, quite without warning, to lead a meeting. "My embarrassment was supreme," Robert later recalled. "I plunged in, trusting to Providence that the assembly would behave itself, but with the plunge went the determination that I would never attend another meeting until I knew something of parliamentary law."

Robert studied the rules of the British Parliament and the American Congress. Eventually he blended the best of both into *Robert's Rules of Order,* a handbook which he published in 1876. Robert hoped to create a system of *etiquette* that could guide people through their meetings. He wanted to show group members how to resist overbearing leaders and ruthless *cliques.* He also wanted to give group members the know-how they needed to combat those seeking to railroad their way to power. (*Railroad* means to push something through in great haste.)

Robert's book was an instant hit and has remained popular ever since. In 1970, a team of experts brought out a modern, updated version, *Robert's Rules of Order Newly Revised,* which serves today as the parliamentary handbook for most organizations. Thus, Robert's famous book has become our foremost guide to democratic action. Thoughtful study and a few days of practice will help you master the democratic procedures he so *painstakingly* described.

"The careful reading and use of *Robert's Rules* can help guarantee orderliness and fair play in the conduct of a variety of our everyday activities," said Floyd Riddick, parliamentarian of the U.S. Senate.

As you begin to learn parliamentary procedure, you may feel intimidated by

INSTANT IMPACT

No Place to Go, Nothing to Do

The life of General Henry M. Robert reminds us of the saying that "what a man amounts to is what he does with his time when he has nothing to do." Robert, a U.S. Army engineer, had helped build the defenses of Washington, D.C., and Philadelphia during the Civil War. After the war, he found himself stationed at a lonely fort during a harsh winter. With nothing to do and no place to go, Robert decided to make the most of his leisure time—by writing a handbook to help people run meetings.

At the end of the winter, Robert had a fifteen-page manuscript ready for printing. Surprisingly, publishing houses turned it down, saying there was little demand for such a book. Robert decided to pay for its publication himself, a decision that would turn out to be a blessing in disguise. Since Robert was paying the bills, he could revise and add to the book as he pleased.

When sales of Robert's book reached a half-million copies, he published an enlarged edition called *Rules of Order Revised.* He also wrote two other books on the subject—one for those who wanted an advanced version (*Parliamentary Law*) and one for beginners (*Parliamentary Practice*).

the complexity of the system. These feelings will soon disappear, though, with a little patience and perhaps a handy reference or crib sheet nearby. Learning parliamentary procedure is important because it gives us a chance to put democracy into practice.

Failure to learn these rules will lead to the frustration of attending meetings where you don't understand what is going on. Worse, it may lead to your suffering defeat because your opponents know more than you about parliamentary procedure.

Fundamental Principles of Parliamentary Procedure

A good place to start learning the rules of parliamentary procedure is with a few basic principles. These principles will enable you to reason out the answers to most parliamentary questions. The principles may seem simple and familiar, but you should be careful not to underestimate their importance. The basic principles of parliamentary procedure are as follows.

1. Do One Thing at a Time

The principle "one thing at a time" emphasizes the importance of order. Group members may consider, for example, only one motion at a time. By keeping everyone's attention focused on just one thing, the group leader can keep a meeting on track. This makes it more likely that difficult issues will be resolved in a reasonable amount of time.

2. The Majority Decides

A primary purpose of parliamentary procedure is to see that the wishes of the majority are carried out. Majority simply means more than half of the votes cast. (This is also called a *simple* majority.)

When you join a group, you voluntarily agree to accept what the majority decides. Until the vote on a question is taken, every member has the right to speak for or against a proposal and to persuade others to share that opinion. Once the votes are in, however, the decision of the majority becomes everyone's decision.

3. The Rights of the Minority Are Protected

Truly democratic organizations make arrangements to protect those who are in the minority—that is, on the side with less than half the votes. These members are entitled to the same consideration and respect as those who are in the majority. The fact that you may be in the majority today but in the minority tomorrow means that everyone has a stake in protecting these rights.

One specific way that parliamentary procedure protects minority rights is the two-thirds vote. Several motions, including any that limit the right to speak or debate, require a two-thirds vote to pass. Thus, a simple majority of members cannot close off discussion if others still wish to be heard.

4. Conduct a Full and Free Discussion

All members of the group have the right to express their opinion fully and freely without interruption or interference, provided they stay within the rules. Members also have the right to know the meaning of the question under discussion and what its effect will be. A member can always request information on any motion that he does not understand so that he can vote intelligently.

5. Act With Fairness and Good Faith

Trickery, delaying tactics, and railroading can destroy the fairness of any meeting. Members can ethically use parliamentary principles to support or defeat a

COMMUNICATION BREAKTHROUGH

"I . . . Looked Down into My Open Grave."

In a lonely grave lies the man who saved a president, the man who performed what one historian has called "the most heroic act in American history." Yet he is a man whose name few if any of us remember: Edmund G. Ross.

In 1866, when Ross was elected to the U.S. Senate from Kansas, President Andrew Johnson and the Congress were locked in a ferocious battle over how the South should be treated after the Civil War. The president vetoed bill after bill because he thought that Congress wanted to treat the former Confederate states too harshly. Johnson himself was a Southerner. Finally, in complete frustration, the senators decided to get the president out of office. If two-thirds of the senators would vote to impeach Johnson, he would be forced to leave.

Those in the Senate who opposed the president were hopeful that Ross would join their side because he had a long history of opposing slavery. At the age of twenty-eight, Ross had helped rescue a fugitive slave. Later, he had given up his job at a newspaper to enlist in the Union Army.

On March 5, 1868, the impeachment trial began; and before long, observers realized that matters of law were not important to the senators. They wanted Johnson out, and any reason would do.

As the trial neared its conclusion, it became clear that only one more vote was needed to impeach Johnson. The one senator who had not yet announced how he would vote was Edmund Ross. Most people were sure Ross would vote to impeach. "I

did not think," said Senator Sumner of Massachusetts, "that a Kansas man could quibble against his country." Yet Ross remained silent, vowing that Johnson should have a fair trial.

As a result of his silence, Ross was pestered, spied upon, and subjected to every kind of pressure, including threats of violence. He was the target of every eye, his name was on every tongue, and his intentions were discussed in every newspaper.

At last the fateful day arrived. Ross described it this way: "The galleries were packed. Tickets of admission were at an enormous premium." Every senator was in his seat, including one who was desperately ill and had to be carried in. When it came time for Ross to vote, the Senate chamber fell silent.

"How say you?" said the Chief Justice. "Is Andrew Johnson guilty or not?"

"I almost literally looked down into my open grave," Ross said later. "Friendships, position, fortune, everything that makes life desirable to an ambitious man were about to be swept away by the breath of my mouth, perhaps forever."

Ross spoke so quietly that he was asked to repeat his answer. And then in a voice that everyone could hear, he said, "Not guilty." The president was saved.

Question
Why does the impeachment rule require a two-thirds vote and not a majority vote?

proposal; but when they use these principles to intimidate their opponents or deny the rights of others, their tactics are destructive and contrary to the spirit of fair play.

These five principles show that parliamentary procedure is founded on common sense, which makes them easy to learn and remember. After a little practice,

you will feel at home with the vocabulary, patterns, and rhythm of parliamentary procedure. Before long, you will feel confident in presenting and defending your ideas in a group. As you gain knowledge of parliamentary procedure, you will help the groups you belong to become more effective, and you will also take a big step toward assuming a leadership position yourself.

TAKING CHARGE

1. Discuss some of the rules that govern our lives. Examples might include the rules your parents set at home, school rules, local and state laws, and perhaps some unstated rules, like the ones that define what is socially acceptable. Consider how these rules have come into being, how they can be changed, and how they are enforced.
2. Make a complete list of school and community groups, then find out whether they conduct their meetings according to parliamentary procedure. If you find some that don't, try to discover why they don't.
3. Invite a representative of a local governing body—the town council, the state legislature, or a county board—to visit your class and talk about how parliamentary procedure works. Ask the speaker how the meetings of the governing body to which he or she belongs would be different if they weren't conducted according to parliamentary procedure.

II Getting Down to Business

Let us suppose that you and a group of friends have decided to start a new school club. It seems that all of you are

upset about having to dissect a fetal pig in biology class, and you wish to start an animal rights group. As far as you know, the school has never had such a club before. For the purpose of our discussion here, we won't worry about how to get the school to officially recognize your club. We'll focus our attention on how you organize a new club and hold a meeting.

Your first step is to arrange a time and place for the meeting. Let's say that several people who share your interest in animal rights agree to meet after school on Tuesday in a science classroom. On that Tuesday, you call the meeting to order (acting as the unofficial group leader). This is a signal to the people present that from this moment forward, they should conduct themselves according to the rules of parliamentary procedure.

You next announce the first order of business—in other words, the first item on the meeting's *agenda*. This task is to elect a temporary president and secretary. The temporary president will act as the meeting's chairperson, often simply called the **chair.** Later, permanent officers can be elected after the group has adopted a set of rules to govern its meetings. In our case, your three best friends—the only people attending this meeting—elect you chair.

Now that you are legitimately the chair, and hence the person in charge of the meeting, the group can really get down to business. The group, by the way, is referred to as the **house** during its meetings. You will probably start by discussing the purpose and goals of your group, but you will also want to agree on a few special rules called bylaws. A rule that sets a time and place for regular meetings is a bylaw. Years ago, groups usually had both a constitution and bylaws. They would put their most important rules in the constitution because the constitution was harder to change. Today, however, most experts recommend that an organization's basic rules be placed in a single document called the bylaws.

What Officers Do

An important part of any group's bylaws is a description of the officers the group needs. Let's take a look at these positions and their responsibilities.

The President

Now that the Animal Rights Club has named you president, what are you supposed to do? In the simplest sense, you conduct the meetings. Your responsibility is to see that the group handles its business in a fair and efficient manner. Specifically, you must balance two competing claims: the right of the majority to prevail and the right of the minority to be heard. As Thomas Jefferson, the author of the Declaration of Independence, once said, "Let us hear both sides of the question."

Your first task is to call the meeting to order, which basically means that members stop talking among themselves and give you their full attention. Tap the gavel (no chair should be without one) to signal that the meeting is going to begin, and then state in your firmest voice: "The regular meeting of the Animal Rights Club is now open." Having accomplished that, you work your way, step by step, through an agenda that has been prepared ahead of time—a list of topics and items of business that are to be discussed.

The correct parliamentary name for the agenda is **orders of the day.** In most organizations, the orders of the day begin with the reading and approval of the minutes of the preceding meeting, followed by officer reports, committee reports, unfinished business (sometimes called **old business**), **new business** (subjects brought up for the first time), and

announcements. The final action of the group is to **adjourn**—in other words, close the meeting.

One of your most difficult jobs as chair will be to keep the members' minds on the business before them. Discussions have a tendency to get out of hand—one stray comment can lead to another, and soon the group is talking about last night's party instead of a committee report. As chair, you must make sure the discussion stays focused.

One way you can keep discussion focused is to ban any discussion unless there is a motion before the group. Members can't actually take any action as a group until a motion has been made. Therefore, discussion without a motion before the house is pointless. After a member has made a motion, another member must second the motion (in other words, endorse what the first member said). To assist the maker of the motion, the chair should *restate* it before debate is allowed. Restating the motion helps clarify it for the members and it

also transfers ownership: The motion now belongs to the group, not to the maker.

At this point, the chair can open the floor for discussion. A member who obtains the floor has the right to speak. As chair, you, and only you, decide who "gets the floor." Normally, you call on the person who made the motion to speak first, although it is not necessary to do so. After that person has spoken (and under the rules, no one may speak for more than ten minutes), you call on others who wish to speak. If possible, choose a speaker in favor of the motion, then one opposed, then one in favor, and so on. You should let everyone who wishes to speak do so before you allow anyone to speak a second time. Ordinarily, no one may speak more than twice on any particular motion.

After you feel the discussion is over, say, "Are you ready for the question?" This asks the members if they are ready to vote. If no one objects, you put the question to a vote. If someone does object, discussion continues unless two-thirds of the members vote to close debate. To conduct a vote, you say, "The question is on the adoption of the motion to donate $25 to the animal shelter. All those in favor of the motion say 'aye.'" Those members who are in favor will now say "aye." After you have heard the response, you say, "Those opposed say 'no.'" Next, you announce the result with the words, "The ayes have it; the motion is carried," or "The motion is defeated."

If anyone doubts whether you have correctly interpreted the voice vote, that person may call for a "division of the house." In that case, another vote will be taken. The second time a vote is taken, the chair normally asks members to raise their hands to vote and counts their hands. Then, if a division of the house is called again, the chair may call for a standing vote. Those in favor stand up—the better to be counted—and then those opposed stand up. If the majority wishes, a secret, written ballot may be used.

As chair, you have a number of other, more technical duties. You are required, for example, to determine whether something is *germane*, or pertinent, to the discussion. For example, on a motion to meet with the school's science teachers to discuss their dissection policies, one member begins to speak about how her little brother once put his pet hamster in the microwave. Another member objects, saying that the fate of the hamster is not germane to the motion at hand. You rule that the hamster is indeed out of order and ask the hamster owner's big sister to confine her remarks to the subject before the group. Anyone bringing up a topic that is not germane may be ruled "out of order" by the presiding officer.

The Vice President

Ideally, the vice president (and all the officers) should have poise; a clear, strong voice; and a thorough understanding of parliamentary rules. The vice president's most important responsibility is to take the place of the president when he or she must be absent. Occasionally, the vice president may be assigned additional special duties.

The Treasurer

The treasurer acts as the group's banker. He collects and spends money on the group's behalf. Normally, the treasurer gives a report on the group's financial status at each meeting, as well as an annual written report.

The Secretary

The secretary keeps written records of the organization's activities. These records are called **minutes** and become the official history of the organization. Members can refer to the minutes of past meetings to find out what they have said about a particular issue before. The secretary reads the minutes of the previous meeting at the beginning of each meeting to check their accuracy and to remind the group of what it did at the last meeting.

The secretary's minutes should include the following:

1. The name of the organization and the type of meeting (regular or special) that was held.
2. The date, place, and time of the meeting.
3. The names of the officers and guests present and, if the group is small, of the members too.

4. Whether the minutes of the previous meeting were read and approved.

5. A summary of the treasurer's report.

6. A summary of officer and committee reports.

7. All main motions, including the name of the member who made the motion.

8. Major points of discussion and whether main motions were passed or defeated.

9. Any requests for information, appeals, or other minor motions.

10. Announcements and the time of adjournment.

The secretary is also responsible for keeping a roll of all members and for calling the roll when requested. From time to time, the president may ask the secretary to read a motion back to the group, especially when the motion has been changed or reworded.

Additional Officers in Large Organizations

Large organizations may need additional officers. These positions might include a corresponding secretary, who has the job of writing letters on the organization's behalf; a sergeant-at-arms, who helps maintain order and acts as a doorkeeper; and a parliamentarian. The parliamentarian usually sits next to the chair so that she can easily offer advice when needed. The parliamentarian assists the chair by referring to the relevant section of the bylaws or *Robert's Rules* to settle an argument. The chair may ask the parliamentarian for her opinion, but only the chair can actually make a ruling on what the group should do.

Quorum and Executive Session

You can play video games by yourself, but you can't hold a meeting alone. No meeting can officially take place without a **quorum** (pronounced kwor' um), which is the minimum number of members who must be present for the group's decisions to take effect. Normally, a quorum means a majority of the members. Congress, for example, can make no law unless a majority of its members are present. Although a majority works well as a quorum for most groups, some very large organizations have set their quorum at one-fourth of the membership, one-tenth, or even less if low attendance is common.

Quorum refers only to the number of members present, not the number who are voting. Suppose, for example, that an organization has fifty members and its bylaws state that 50 percent of the members must be present to constitute a quorum. If thirty members show up for a meeting, a quorum has been reached. Suppose, however, that only twenty of those attending actually vote. The results will still be official. Thus, if twelve votes are cast in favor and eight votes against, the motion carries because it has a majority of those voting, even though it has the support of only 24 percent of the total membership (twelve of fifty).

If there are not enough members present to make a quorum, the group can do nothing more than adjourn. If, during the course of a meeting, the chair notices that a quorum has been lost (members have begun leaving, say, to watch the Super Bowl on television), the chair should stop the meeting.

Sometimes, the discussion of an organization can attract the attention of media and other interested parties. When a matter of a very personal nature comes up, a group may wish to close a meeting to outsiders and go into executive session.

On some occasions, a group may wish to close its meeting to outsiders. Imagine, for example, that a reporter from the school paper is attending an Animal Rights Club meeting when a matter of an extremely personal nature comes up. At this point, a member can request that the group go into **executive session.** An executive session is a special kind of meeting or a special portion of a meeting that is open only to members.

Such sessions are called to discuss the conduct and possible discipline of group members. In our case, for example, the group has learned that one of its members recently shot a deer on a hunting

"Whatever you do, participate. That is the only way to get a genuine feel for parliamentary procedure."

Thomas Jefferson

trip. Members are honor-bound not to divulge to outsiders what has been discussed during executive session.

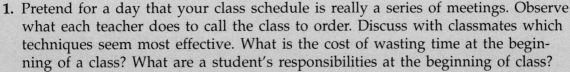

TAKING CHARGE

1. Pretend for a day that your class schedule is really a series of meetings. Observe what each teacher does to call the class to order. Discuss with classmates which techniques seem most effective. What is the cost of wasting time at the beginning of a class? What are a student's responsibilities at the beginning of class?

2. Have a class discussion on the qualities of a good leader. Who do you feel are the best leaders on the local, state, national, or international level, and why? What leadership qualities does each possess? What are some of the mistakes a leader can make to alienate his or her followers?

3. Practice analyzing a set of minutes. Obtain the minutes of a recent meeting from some organization and analyze what happened during the meeting. Can you determine what decisions the group made? Discuss with classmates which of the group's actions was the most significant and why.

III A Member's Responsibilities

Members, too, have their duties and responsibilities. Even if you are not an officer, you should, for example, attend the meetings with reasonable regularity. During a meeting, you should pay attention to the business at hand and to the speaker who holds the floor. You should not talk, move about, or stand unless you want to be recognized by the chair. Feel free to express your opinion while a subject is being discussed.

Once the question is settled, support the outcome and withhold any criticism you might have of either the action or those who supported it. This is one of the most important principles of parliamentary procedure, one that allows us to live in an atmosphere of mutual respect and regard no matter how much we may disagree with one another.

We can summarize the responsibilities of a member like this:

1. Arrive promptly at meetings.
2. Address the chair as Miss President, Madame President, or Mr. President.
3. Await recognition from the chair before speaking.
4. When you are recognized, stand, speak clearly, and then sit down.
5. Use these words when making a motion: "I move that . . ." Do not say, "I make a motion."
6. Address all remarks to the chair. Make no personal comments toward another member.

7. Ask questions if you do not understand the question on the floor.

8. Call out "Division" if you doubt the result of the vote as announced by the chair.

9. Call for a vote if you feel debate has gone far enough.

10. Respect the right of the majority to decide.

One of the most important things a member can do is to make a motion. Most games begin with a throw of the dice, a flick of the spinner, or a card drawn from the deck. In parliamentary procedure, the real action begins when someone makes a motion. Any member has the right to present a motion. To do so, he or she rises, addresses the chair, and waits for recognition. The chair recognizes a member by calling the member's name, at which time the member has the floor and is thus entitled to speak. In the next section we will discuss main motions and how they are discussed.

The Main Motion

Motions that ask the group to take action are called **main motions.** (Several other kinds of motions will be discussed later.) Main motions should be stated in a positive form if possible. That is because most of us find positive statements ("let's do this") easier to grasp than negative ones ("let's don't do that"). If a member happens to offer a motion in the negative, the chair can suggest changing it. Suppose a member of the Animal Rights Club says, "I move that we don't eat meat at school." Club members may be confused about exactly what the motion means. The

chair might ask the person who made the motion to rephrase it like this: "I move that we boycott meals in the cafeteria until the school agrees to provide a vegetarian alternative."

Anyone who proposes a long or complicated motion should prepare a written copy ahead of time and give it to the secretary. (By the way, the chair can request that all motions be submitted in writing.) After a motion has been made, it must be seconded by another member. Members may simply call out, "Second the motion" or "Second" without waiting to be recognized. Once that happens, the chair restates the motion and opens the issue to debate. If no one seconds the motion, the motion is dead.

Members of the Animal Rights Club might, for example, make the following main motions:

◆ "I move that we ask the school board to ban fur; leather belts, shoes, and watchbands; and any other types of clothing made from animals from the school building."

◆ "I move that the Student Council make an annual donation to the local Humane Society."

◆ "I move that we change our school mascot from the Bunnies to the Silicon Chips."

Generally, four things can happen to a main motion. It can be passed, postponed, sent to a committee for study, or defeated. We should note that if a motion is defeated, it cannot be brought up again at the same meeting. Parliamentary procedure stresses the principle that a motion may have only one hearing per meeting, but it does allow one exception. A member may move to **reconsider** a main motion that has already been passed or defeated. This exception, as Robert puts it, "permits correction of hasty, ill-advised, or erroneous action." Only a member who voted on the winning side may move to reconsider.

Resolutions

Special occasions sometimes call for a special kind of main motion called a resolution. A resolution traditionally begins with an explanation of why the motion should be passed. This *preamble* includes a list of reasons, each in a paragraph beginning with "Whereas." Following the preamble, the main motion is stated, usually with this formula: "Now therefore be it resolved" or simply "Resolved, that . . ." A complete resolution might look something like this:

> WHEREAS Mr. Bob Olson has served our school well as a sensitive counselor, and
> WHEREAS his concern for animals has led to his decision to turn his own home into a shelter for stray cats and dogs, and
> WHEREAS Mr. Olson has worked as a volunteer for a week at the Humane Society,
> NOW THEREFORE BE IT RESOLVED that the Animal Rights Club does hereby congratulate Mr. Olson on his contributions to a better life for small animals and in recognition thereof, awards Mr. Olson the club's Good Citizen of the Year Award.

Seconding a Motion

As mentioned earlier, after someone has made a motion, another member must second the motion without waiting to be recognized. A motion is seconded to show that more than one person favors the proposal, although you can second a motion simply because you want to hear it discussed. The major purpose of requiring a

---

INSTANT IMPACT

Curfew in Paradise

A curfew bill created by a group of Honolulu high school students was signed into state law recently by Governor John Waihee of Hawaii. Although the original bill, drafted by students at Kaimuki High School, was altered by state legislators, its goal of keeping teenagers off the city's streets late at night remained intact. The curfew prohibits anyone under age sixteen from being in public areas between 10 P.M. and 4 A.M. unless accompanied by an adult.

The new law recommends that violators of the curfew and their parents or guardians participate in family counseling or community service.

"As far as we know," said a spokesman for the Hawaii Department of Education, "this is the first time Hawaiian students have submitted and lobbied [for] a bill in the state government."

Adapted from: Education Week, *Dec. 17, 1991.*

---

second is to prevent groups from wasting time on something that only one person wants to talk about.

If a motion is not seconded immediately, the chair should not ask anyone in particular to second it because that might show support for the motion. Instead, the chair says, "Is the motion seconded?" or "Is there a second?" Some routine motions, such as approving the minutes, are frequently put to a vote without a second. (If any member objects to the lack of a second, however, the chair must call for one.) In addition, a few special kinds of motions do not need a second. We will discuss these motions later.

COMMUNICATION WORKS

George Paul, Parish Council Treasurer

When passions run high and tempers flare, parliamentary procedure is sometimes the only thing keeping members of an organization from each other's throats. That's the lesson George Paul, treasurer of the parish council at St. Sophia's Greek Orthodox Cathedral in Washington, D.C., has learned after nearly ten years of church work.

"We have a saying that indicates how diverse our opinions can get," Paul says. "Whenever you have two Greeks together, you can be sure of having at least three opinions."

Paul served for eight years as president of the parish council at a church in Charlottesville, Virginia, before moving to Washington, D.C., an experience that has given him insights into how parliamentary procedure can work in both small and large groups.

"It's fundamental," he says, "because it enables you to conduct business in some orderly manner. Even in the most informal setting, parliamentary procedure defines the structure of the meeting."

Paul says that following parliamentary procedure can produce unexpected results. He recalled a time when the church decided to commission twenty paintings to decorate the sanctuary. The decorations committee recommended that the church hire the artist who had submitted the lowest bid. But a member of the church council argued that another artist, one who had worked for the church before, should be hired, even though his bid was higher.

"We thought the low bid would win for sure," said Paul.

A surprise was in store, however. During the meeting a motion was made to hire the artist with the low bid. Then a member moved to amend the motion by substituting the name of the other artist. That amendment passed, and, a few minutes later, so did the main motion.

Paul says he suspects the amendment process may have confused one member and caused him to cast his vote for the wrong artist. Once this member realized his mistake, he could have moved to reconsider. The member decided to let things stand, however, angering several others on the losing side.

Fortunately, parliamentary procedure also creates some breathing room between opponents.

"Parliamentary procedure does not prevent animosities," says Paul. "They come out, but if nothing else, it's controlled them." He adds jokingly, "It's saved a few murders."

Debate and Discussion

"Democracy is that form of government," wrote James Dale Davidson, executive director of the National Taxpayers Union, "where everybody gets what the majority deserves." Finding out what the majority deserves—or at least what it wants—is why we have debate. But no matter how freewheeling the debate may be, it must follow certain rules: Speakers are limited to ten minutes at a time, their comments must be germane, they must address their remarks to the chair, and they must at all times keep their remarks courteous.

If you wish to be successful in debate, you must be well informed, sure of your convictions, and fearless in the face of opposition. At the same time, successful debate depends to some extent on good manners. In debating a motion, you should avoid making comments about someone else's personality and should never question another person's motives. If you feel another speaker is mistaken, do not call him a liar. Instead, simply say, "I think the last speaker was misinformed." A member's name should not be mentioned, either, although a speaker can refer to "the last person who spoke."

A parliamentary discussion should help members reach a better understanding of the proposal before them. If the discussion is carried on in the proper spirit, members will leave their differences at the meeting and not let grudges keep them from remaining friends.

TAKING CHARGE

1. Write motions that could be presented at meetings for each of the following groups: an athletic booster club, a snow skiing club, an international club, and a student council. Try to create three motions for each group.

2. Write short arguments for and against each of the following motions:

   ◆ "I move that we oppose the city's new curfew law, which requires all teenagers to be off the street by 10 P.M. each night."

   ◆ "I move that we support the school board's decision to ban any clothing, like bandanas or pro football jackets, that might show membership in a gang."

3. Find out what constitutes a quorum for each of the governing bodies in your community. Do your school clubs have official quorums? Why or why not?

IV The Order of Precedence

Parliamentary procedure becomes complicated at times because people are complicated. Our thinking process is not as simple as yes, no, and maybe. We may feel, for example, that we don't have enough information to make a sound decision, that the room is too hot or too cold, or that the meeting has been going on too long and we need a break. Parliamentary procedure makes room for these concerns and many others through a system of minor motions, all of which are governed by the order of precedence.

Some Motions Have Higher Rank than Others

In a large, formal meeting where people are experienced in parliamentary procedure, the action can seem furious. "Motions seem to dart in and out like bees around a beehive," as one expert puts it. Before one motion can be settled, another takes its place before the house, and then another and another.

All this commotion may be confusing at first, but once the chair sorts things out, this much is clear: Parliamentary procedure requires that some kinds of motions be considered before others.

The concept that underlies the relationship of motions to each other is called the **order of precedence.** You might think of it as a ranking system, with the most important motion at the top (where it has priority over all the others) and the least important at the bottom. (See the chart on page 515 for a detailed description.) When a motion of greater priority is raised, it moves any other business to the back burner. This motion may then be resolved or may itself be pushed out of the way by another, higher-ranking motion.

The order of precedence enables the chair to determine with precision what issue should be discussed. It also tells the chair when a particular motion is out of order (and must, therefore, be ignored for the time being) and in what order votes should be taken on pending motions. Any motion before the house that has not been settled is said to be "pending."

Let's see how the order of precedence actually works. The two most basic rules in the order of precedence are these: (1) Motions of higher precedence are acted on first. (2) Motions are acted on in reverse order of introduction—in other words, the last motion made is the first one discussed and voted on.

Suppose someone says, "I move that we stage a demonstration in front of Pets R Us to protest the sale of parrots, an endangered species." The motion is seconded and debate begins. Before long, someone makes a motion to amend the main motion. "I move that we amend the motion by striking 'Pets R Us' and inserting 'all three pet stores in town.'" The motion to amend is in order at this point because it ranks higher than the main motion. Before the motion to amend is seconded, however, someone else gains the floor and says, "I move that we refer this question to a committee. I don't know if parrots are really endangered or not." The motion to refer ranks higher than the motion to amend. Thus, this motion is now in order and must be considered before the other two.

Handling parliamentary motions is a little like making a stack of blocks. As you work your way up (by making motions), you place one block on top of another. As you work your way down (by voting), the top block is taken off first. When a group does not observe the order of precedence and tries to pull the bottom block out first, the whole structure collapses.

Three Kinds of Minor Motions

Motions other than main motions can be divided into three categories: subsidiary, privileged, and incidental. Each type of motion has its own role to play in bringing problems to a reasonable, democratic solution. **Subsidiary motions** help to settle the main motion. Sometimes called a parliamentary "tool kit," they give members the means to tinker with main motions until they are in just the right form. **Privileged motions** deal with problems aside from the main motion that need urgent attention. You might move, for example, to take a short recess until "the fire goes out and the smoke has cleared." This motion has higher status than a subsidiary motion because what it calls for is of immediate importance. Finally, **incidental motions** deal more with the process than with the actual content of any motion. An example of an incidental motion is a request for a roll call vote. Each type of minor motion includes several specific subtypes, as described in the following sections.

Subsidiary Motions

While a main motion is pending, members may wish to change it, postpone it, or set it aside for a while. The motion to amend the main motion is a subsidiary motion. Other subsidiary motions include limiting, extending, or cutting off debate.

The seven subsidiary motions are, in their order of rank (with the highest at the top):

1. To lay a question on the table.
2. To call for the question.
3. To modify debate.
4. To postpone definitely.
5. To refer to a committee.
6. To amend.
7. To postpone indefinitely.

Let's take a closer look at each motion.

To Table a Question. The purpose of the motion to table a question is to set the topic aside temporarily so that the house can turn to something else. (The term "lay on the table" grew out of an old parliamentary custom of laying a written motion on the clerk's table.) Suppose a particular subject is being discussed. You want to speak on the subject but must leave the meeting for a few minutes. In such situations, you may say, "I move to lay the question on the table," or simply, "I move to **table the motion.**" If you are successful, the issue will be set aside. The idea is not to kill a motion but to delay its discussion. Whenever you are ready to get back to the motion, you can move to "take the motion off the table."

To Call for the Question. When people continue to discuss a subject beyond your patience or endurance, you may **"call the question."** That simply means to stop talking and vote. The chair then calls for a second and, upon receiving it, takes a vote on whether or not to close the discussion. Note that members vote on the motion to call for the question before voting on the main motion. In more informal groups, members may call out "Question!" and the chair, if it seems there is no objection, may simply go to a vote on the motion itself.

To Modify Debate. If time is short, you may wish to limit debate on a particular subject. Although normal procedure permits each person to speak twice for ten minutes, you may decide it would be better to limit each person to one five-minute comment. If so, you "move that debate be limited." If, on the other hand, the issue needs more discussion than usual, you may move to extend debate.

To Postpone Definitely. When it seems best to delay the discussion of a question (perhaps because a member who has vital information on the subject is not present), you should use the motion to postpone definitely. In doing so, you must specify the particular date or time the motion will be reconsidered. If, for example, you believe a motion should receive further study, you might say, "I move to postpone until the next meeting." If you think another issue should be decided first, you might say, "I move we postpone considering dues until we have first taken action on our budget."

To Refer to a Committee. Sometimes it may be necessary to send a motion to a committee for fine-tuning. A committee is a small, representative group of members, usually no more than twelve, who give careful attention to a particular topic.

Parliamentary law provides for two kinds of committees. Standing committees have duties that must be carried out every year. These are permanent committees named in the group's bylaws—a nominations committee, for instance. Special committees are temporary committees created for a specific task. When they finish their work, they cease to exist.

To Amend. A main motion sometimes needs a few changes before it will be acceptable to a majority of the members. In such cases, you may wish to **amend** the main motion. An amendment to a motion can be made in one of three ways:

1. By inserting, or adding, words.
2. By striking words (in other words, removing them).
3. By striking some words and inserting others.

In simplest terms, the amending process is chiefly a way of editing the original motion.

Sometimes the person who made the original motion agrees to accept a change someone else has suggested. In that case, no vote on the amendment is needed. Such a change is called a friendly amendment. Friendly amendments can often save time, particularly when they reflect only small changes.

Amendments themselves can be amended. During debate on an amendment, you may discover that no one is completely happy with the wording even though everyone seems to favor its basic idea. If so, you may make a motion to amend the amendment, a procedure called a secondary amendment. Fortunately, there is no such thing as a third-degree amendment or meetings might never end.

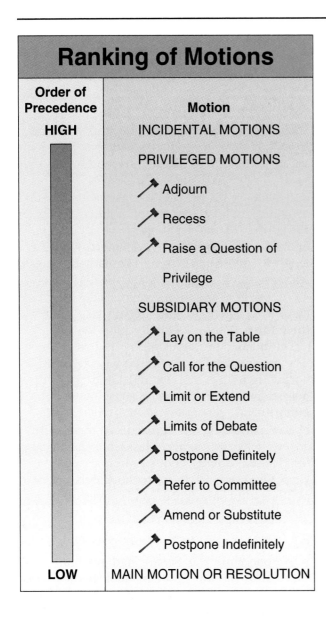

the school board to ban junk food from school premises. After some discussion, the board members come to realize that banning junk food might hurt the speech team. (The team sells candy bars to help pay for trips to tournaments.) Still, the board does not want to vote in favor of junk food. So the members decide to postpone the motion indefinitely. In this way, they can kill the motion without ever actually voting on it.

Privileged Motions

Privileged motions have no direct connection with current business but instead have to do with mistakes or problems that must be corrected immediately. Because of their urgency, they are given high priority. Privileged motions include requests to stop the meeting or to set a meeting time for another day. Let us take a closer look at some of the most commonly used privileged motions.

Adjourn. *Adjourn* is the term to use for ending a meeting. A member may move that the meeting be adjourned. More often, the chair just announces that, if there are no objections, the meeting is adjourned. When all the business before the house has been completed, the chair typically says, "Since there is no further business, the meeting is adjourned."

Recess. A recess is just a short intermission. Most organizations use a recess to give members a break, usually lasting no more than a few minutes. Following a recess, members take up the business of the house at the point where they left off.

Raise a Question of Privilege. A motion to raise a question of privilege

To Postpone Indefinitely. Despite how it sounds, the motion to postpone indefinitely is designed to kill and not postpone. Normally, opponents of a motion try to defeat it by a vote; but once in a while, they prefer to avoid voting entirely. For example, suppose a motion comes before

COMMUNICATION | BREAKDOWN

A Filibuster Stalls the Civil Rights Act

Your parents may think you talk a long time on the phone, but no matter how long-winded you are, you probably can't hold a candle to a United States Senator in the middle of a filibuster.

The filibuster has been used as a parliamentary tactic since Roman times, but it is most often associated with the U.S. Senate. Filibusters are simply an attempt to delay a meeting so long that those in the majority will give up whatever motion it is that they wish to pass. Sometimes a tiny minority of members may try a filibuster to block the passage of some motion they have no hope of defeating in a vote. The tactic is especially effective at the end of a congressional session when senators are pressed for time to pass other major bills.

At times filibusters are quite comical. Some senators have been known to read from the telephone directory just to waste time. Others have resorted to reading the *World Almanac,* baseball statistics, and Aesop's fables.

Senator Strom Thurmond of South Carolina established the one-man endurance record of 24 hours and 18 minutes when filibustering against the 1957 Civil Rights Act, but he had the benefit of friendly interruptions, such as frequent quorum calls. Senator Wayne Morse of Oregon spoke alone and without interruption for 22 hours and 26 minutes, fighting an oil bill in 1953.

Filibusters can be used to stop a group from taking action, even when the majority view is clear. The most notorious filibuster was organized by Russell Long of Louisiana, who led 18 southern senators in a battle against the Civil Rights Act of 1964. Each of the senators spoke about four hours at a time and was interrupted by lengthy questions from sympathetic colleagues. Only after 74 days of this delay were enough senators willing to vote for cloture (a move to end debate requiring a three-fifths vote) and finally pass the bill.

The major argument for the filibuster centers around the protection it offers for minority rights. Senator Everett Dirksen of Illinois called it "the only weapon which the minority has to protect itself." On the other hand, parliamentary procedure must also ensure majority rights. Massachusetts Senator Henry Cabot Lodge summarized this view by saying to "vote without debating is perilous, but to debate and never vote is imbecilic."

Questions

1. At one time the Senate had no limit on debate. Should governmental bodies set limits on debate and, if so, what should those limits be?
2. Can you find any information on filibusters in your state legislature?

makes an urgent request touching the welfare of the group as a whole. You may ask, for example, that "the group help catch the gerbil I let loose by mistake." Or you could request, through the same procedure, that the house go into executive session to discuss a sensitive personal matter.

Motion	Requires Second	Debatable	Amendable	Vote Required
INCIDENTAL MOTIONS				
Appeal Decision of the Chair	Yes	Yes	No	Majority
Point of Information	No	No	No	None
Point of Order	No	No	No	None
Suspend the Rules	Yes	No	No	Two-thirds
PRIVILEGED MOTIONS				
Adjourn	Yes	No	No	Majority
Recess	Yes	No	Yes	Majority
Raise a Question of Privilege	Yes	No	No	Majority
SUBSIDIARY MOTIONS				
Lay on the Table	Yes	No	No	Majority
Call for the Question	Yes	No	No	Two-thirds
Limit or Extend Debate	Yes	No	Yes	Two-thirds
Postpone Definitely	Yes	Yes	Yes	Majority
Refer to Committee	Yes	Yes	Yes	Majority
Amend the Amendment	Yes	Yes	No	Majority
Amend	Yes	Yes	Yes	Majority
Postpone Indefinitely	Yes	Yes	No	Majority
MAIN MOTIONS				
Main Motion or Resolution	Yes	Yes	Yes	Majority
Reconsider	Yes	Yes	No	Majority
Take from Table	Yes	No	No	Majority

Incidental Motions

The final category of minor motions is a broad group called incidental motions. Like privileged motions, these motions usually apply to something other than the business at hand. Since they arise only incidentally—that is, from time to time—and must be decided as soon as they are raised, they have the highest priority of any motion.

The chair must deal with each incidental motion immediately, so there is never more than one incidental motion pending. Consequently, the incidental motions have no order of precedence among themselves. Incidental motions give members the ability to appeal a ruling by the chair, to *suspend* the rules, and to raise a point of order, among a variety of other possibilities. Again, let us take a closer look at several.

Appeal the Decision of the Chair. If you disagree with the chair's decision, you may appeal and ask that the house decide the question instead. The purpose of this appeal is to protect members against unjust rulings or technical errors. You should not hesitate to appeal if you disagree with the chair's ruling, but you should use good judgment, too. Unjustified or excessive appeals may damage the chair's credibility and thereby weaken the whole organization.

Point of Information. A point of information is usually a request for a simple explanation. For example, you might rise and say: "Point of information. Is there enough money in our account to cover the cost of the dance?"

Point of Order. The purpose of a point of order is to enforce the rules. A member can even interrupt another speaker to make a point of order. The chair, for example, may have given the floor to the wrong person. You could rise and say: "Point of order. This speaker has already been given two opportunities to speak." Once a point of order has been raised, the chair must make an immediate ruling.

Suspend the Rules. A group can suspend any of its rules if they get in the way of the group's progress. The Animal Rights Club may have a rule, for example, that says all meetings must adjourn by 4:30. If a discussion is still going strong at 4:25, you may move to suspend the rule about adjournment to allow the discussion to continue past 4:30.

TAKING CHARGE

1. Discuss the ranking of motions. What are some reasons why one motion might be ranked above another? Why is the main motion the lowest-ranking motion? Why is a motion to adjourn ranked so high?

V Making Decisions by Voting

"The right to be heard does not automatically include the right to be taken seriously," said Hubert Humphrey, a master of parliamentary procedure as a U.S. Senator from Minnesota. Indeed, being heard is one thing, but convincing other people to agree with you is quite another. The proof of your ability to persuade others comes through voting, the process in a democracy where the "rubber hits the road." In this section we will discuss the rules for voting and the process for electing officers.

Voting Procedures

When no one has anything else to say or the question has been called, the time has come to vote. The chair calls for the vote by saying: "Those in favor, say 'aye.' Those opposed, say 'no.'" Sometimes a chair is tempted to take a shortcut by abbreviating to this: "Those in favor, say 'aye.' Opposed?" Doing so is a mistake, however. The chair must remember to always give each side the same cues. This may seem like a small point, but when acted out in a meeting, it conveys a sense of fair play and balance to group members.

In announcing the result of the vote, the chair should be sure to give the affirmative vote first. Many people think that the larger number should always be reported first, but according to parliamentary procedure, the vote should be announced in the same order in which it was taken. Thus, when the vote is two in favor and twelve opposed, the chair should say, "By a vote of two to twelve, the motion is rejected." Following the announcement of the vote, the chair should explain any effect that the vote might have and then introduce the next item of business. The chair's announcement of a vote might sound like this:

By a vote of twenty-five to thirty-seven, the motion to protest the athletic director's annual quail hunt is rejected. We will, however, send him a letter encouraging him to sponsor a conservation habitat project thanks to a previous motion that did pass.

We turn now to the new business.

Nothing ever ends in a tie in parliamentary procedure. A motion either passes or fails. Since a majority vote is defined as one more than half, a tie vote simply means that the motion has lost. In such an event, the chair states, "By a vote of ten in favor and ten opposed, the motion is rejected." Ties can be broken by the chair, if he or she has not voted yet. In the U.S. Senate, for example, the vice president (the presiding officer) votes in case of a tie, although unlike most chair persons, the vice president can only vote when a tie occurs.

A majority vote is required to carry a motion and normally, to elect officers. Some clubs, however, have adopted a rule that allows officers to be elected by a plurality. A candidate has a *plurality* if he or she receives more votes than any other nominee, regardless of whether that number is more than half of the votes cast. Thus, if Carlos receives twenty-five votes, Angelina sixteen, and Shawn thirteen, Carlos wins the election with a plurality, even though he does not have a majority of the votes.

Some actions require a two-thirds vote. A two-thirds vote means two-thirds of the votes cast, not two-thirds of those present. Any motion that affects a member's right to speak (to call the question, for example) requires a two-thirds vote. A two-thirds vote is also required to suspend the rules, to close nominations, and to change the bylaws.

INSTANT IMPACT

The Closest Race

Throughout the long night of Tuesday, November 8, 1960, Americans waited to find out who their next president would be. As the hours wore on, neither candidate could gain an edge. Finally, shortly before dawn, the Democrat eased ahead, ever so slightly. The nation now knew that John F. Kennedy had become its thirty-fifth president.

It was—as the losing candidate, Richard Nixon, had predicted—the closest election in modern times. Out of 67 million votes cast, Kennedy had about 100,000 more than Nixon—a difference of less than one half of a percentage point. In fact, Nixon won a majority of states (twenty-six to Kennedy's twenty-three), but Kennedy won the larger states. Their electoral votes gave him the victory.

If just one voter in each precinct in three states—Texas, California, and Illinois—had chosen Nixon instead of Kennedy, the result of the election would have been different. As it was, Kennedy narrowly avoided joining a group of twelve American presidents who gained office with less than a majority of the popular vote.

Nominating and Electing Officers

In most clubs, a nominations committee develops a list of candidates for the elective positions in the organization. Nominations may also be made from the floor during a meeting. Making a *nomination* is approximately the same thing as making an ordinary motion, except that it does not require a second. Members should be sure that their nominees are willing and able to serve if elected.

The preferred method of voting for officers is by ballot. If the ballots are prepared ahead of time, space should be left on them for the names of additional nominees from the floor. The chair should appoint several trustworthy members to tally the ballots. When they are finished, they give a tally sheet to the chair, who then announces the results. For example, the chair might say, "For president, Sally Nickson received a majority vote. The chair declares Sally Nickson elected president," and so on.

The election of officers should be held early in a meeting in case the balloting must be repeated. If two candidates receive an equal number of votes, the house may need another ballot to break the deadlock, or the two candidates may draw straws to determine a winner. If a person is elected to more than one office, he or she may choose the one to accept. Groups should avoid having anyone serve in more than one office at a time. "Although, strictly speaking, there is no prohibition against a person's holding more than one office," notes *Robert's Rules*, "it is understood in most societies that a member can serve in only one such capacity at a time."

Learn by Doing

With amazing regularity, group decisions have direct consequences on our lives. Graduation requirements change, seat belt laws pass, and taxes go up and down as the result of decisions made by various groups. Indeed, many groups actually act in your name—the student council, for example. You need to make sure they act on your behalf.

As a citizen concerned for your own survival, then, you have an obligation to pay attention to what groups are doing. That gives you a powerful incentive to learn *how* they do what they do. Most of us learn the fundamentals of parliamentary procedure by watching people operate in meetings. Before long, though, you need to jump in and try it yourself. It's a bit like learning to use roller blades. You can read about it all you want, but there comes a time when you've just got to do it.

So snap on a helmet and give yourself a little push. Play a more active role in the groups you belong to, and attend other group meetings when their decisions affect or interest you. If a group you belong to doesn't use parliamentary procedure, persuade the members to adopt *Robert's Rules*. It will help the group make better decisions.

TAKING CHARGE

1. Invite the local election commissioner to visit your class. Ask that person to discuss how he or she predicts the voter turnout, how voting machines work, and what a normal voter turnout in your area would be.

TAKING CHARGE (CONTINUED)

2. Stage a mock campaign and election in your class. You might choose among competing school board candidates, for instance. You could also put several local issues (requiring returnable bottles or lowering the driving age, for example) on your ballot.
3. Create a list naming every elected official in your town and his or her position. You may be surprised to see just how many there are.

REVIEW AND ENRICHMENT

LOOKING BACK

Listed below are the major ideas discussed in this chapter.

◆ The rules we use to make group decisions are called parliamentary procedure. They are essentially the same whether the group is the local Weed Board or the United States Senate.

◆ The goal of parliamentary procedure is to help people conduct their business in an orderly and effective way. The rules are designed to make sure that the will of the majority prevails but also that the minority has an opportunity to speak and be heard.

◆ The system we call parliamentary procedure evolved from the rules of the British Parliament. An American, Henry Robert, developed a version that ordinary groups could use in their meetings. This version is contained in a guidebook called *Robert's Rules of Order Newly Revised*.

◆ The basic principles of parliamentary procedure are based on common sense. They include: do one thing at a time, the majority decides, the minority must be protected, conduct a full and free discussion, and act with fairness and good faith.

◆ In addition to using *Robert's Rules*, organizations may draft specialized sets of rules called bylaws to cover their own individual circumstances.

◆ The chair, or presiding officer, runs each meeting. He or she decides who gets to speak and keeps the group on task. The chair also makes rulings from time to time on whether something someone says is appropriate at that point in the meeting.

◆ Typically, small organizations have a vice president, a treasurer, and a secretary in addition to a president. Large organizations may have several other officers.

◆ Groups must have a quorum present at a meeting to conduct business. If a group wishes to close its meeting to outsiders, it may go into executive session.

◆ Members ask their groups to take action or make decisions through main motions. A main motion must be seconded by another member. It can be passed, postponed, sent to committee for study, or defeated.

◆ Other, minor motions may also be used. Each motion is given a position of rank according to the order of precedence.

◆ Members use subsidiary motions to fine tune main motions. They use privileged motions to interrupt current business for something of great urgency, and they use incidental motions to make requests concerning the way the meeting is being run.

◆ Members vote to decide whether a motion passes or not. Depending on the motion, a majority vote or a two-thirds vote may be necessary. Candidates for office may sometimes be elected by a plurality rather than a majority.

SPEECH VOCABULARY

Match the speech term on the left with the definition on the right.

1. parliamentary procedure
2. chair
3. house
4. orders of the day
5. old business
6. new business
7. adjourn
8. amend
9. minutes
10. main motion
11. reconsider
12. quorum
13. executive session
14. order of precedence
15. subsidiary motion
16. privileged motion
17. incidental motion
18. table the motion
19. call the question

a. the person in charge of a meeting
b. business being discussed for the first time
c. motion to close a meeting
d. system for ranking motions
e. minor motion to correct an urgent problem
f. motion to request a roll call vote
g. motion for the group to take an important action
h. official written record of a meeting
i. kind of meeting closed to outsiders
j. motion to take a vote
k. the agenda for a meeting
l. business carried over from a previous meeting
m. minimum number of members needed for an official meeting
n. the group assembled for a meeting
o. to change or modify a motion
p. motion to set aside discussion for the time being
q. set of rules based on British example
r. motion to fine-tune the main motion
s. motion to look again at a motion

GENERAL VOCABULARY

Use each of the general vocabulary terms in a sentence that helps explain its meaning.

Parliament   agenda
innumerable   restate
etiquette   germane
cliques   preamble
railroad   suspend
painstakingly   plurality

THINGS TO REMEMBER

1. Parliamentary procedure protects two vital democratic rights: the right of the majority to _____ and the right of the minority to _____.
2. The rules of parliamentary procedure are based on the rules of what governing body?
3. The most important guidebook for parliamentary procedure is called _____.
4. The first principle of parliamentary procedure, _____, helps groups stay on task.
5. Issues left over from a previous meeting are called _____. Issues that come up for the first time during a meeting are called _____.
6. One of the most important jobs the chair has during a meeting is to decide who _____ the floor.
7. The secretary keeps records of each meeting. These records are called _____.
8. How many members must be present at a meeting for there to be a quorum?
9. A special kind of main motion, usually written with a preamble, is called a _____.
10. Why must a motion be seconded?
11. Why does the chair restate the motion?
12. The highest-ranking privileged motion is _____.
13. The lowest-ranking motion is _____.
14. When members want a short intermission, they make a motion to _____.
15. What is the difference between a majority vote and a plurality vote?

THINGS TO DO

1. Contact your state legislature and inquire about its own specialized rules—its bylaws. What are some of these rules and what is their purpose?
2. Watch newspapers and magazines for stories about people who have broken the rules. Examples include Pete Rose, a famous baseball player who was accused of betting on his own team, Wall Street stockbrokers who used inside information illegally, and government officials who told racist or sexist jokes. Clip these articles out, bring them to class, and discuss them with your classmates.
3. Find out what it takes to start a new club at your school.

THINGS TO TALK ABOUT

1. Discuss whether the rules of parliamentary procedure work for everyday use or are better suited for large, formal gatherings like those of state legislatures and the U.S. Congress.
2. What danger exists if one person in a meeting knows the rules of parliamentary procedure better than everyone else?
3. What power does knowledge of the rules of parliamentary procedure give a person?

THINGS TO WRITE ABOUT

1. Write an essay about other rules that apply in a democratic society. Consider the legal system, the unwritten "social system" that tells us how we should treat each other in public, codes of ethics, and value systems. To what extent do these systems protect us from our own worst instincts?
2. Obtain a copy of the minutes of a recent meeting of any organization. Reconstruct the meeting in the form of a dramatic play.

CRITICAL THINKING

1. Can small, informal groups modify the rules of parliamentary procedure to keep their meetings from becoming too technical? What shortcuts could they take? What rules should never be altered, no matter how small the group?
2. Consider this statement: "Americans spend more time at meetings than they do working, eating, or sleeping, unless of course they sleep at meetings." Do we spend too much time in meetings? What is lost by meeting too often? What is lost by not meeting often enough?
3. What are some of the ways groups become bogged down in meetings? How can a good presiding officer rescue the meeting from total collapse at those points?

RELATED SPEECH TOPICS

British Parliament
Thomas Jefferson and the Declaration of Independence
Qualities of a good leader
Qualities of a good follower
U.S. Congress—How well is it working?

Henry Robert, author of *Robert's Rules*
Voter turnout: Rising or falling?
The presidential nominating process
Election campaigns
Election reform

CHAPTER 19

Oral Interpretation

"Above all, the art of reading aloud should be cultivated."

— Alfred Lord Whitehead, discussing
the aims of education.

Cartoon readings

LEARNING OBJECTIVES

After completing this chapter, you will be able to do the following.

- ◆ Define oral interpretation.
- ◆ Choose material to use for reading.
- ◆ Analyze the meaning and feeling of a selection.
- ◆ Practice the delivery of a selection.
- ◆ Discuss the elements of Reader's Theater.

CHAPTER OUTLINE

Following are the main sections in this chapter.

I What Is Oral Interpretation?

II Choosing Your Material

III Interpreting Your Material

IV Presenting Your Material

V Reader's Theater

Student Speech

Chapter Review

NEW SPEECH TERMS

In this chapter, you will learn the meanings of the speech terms listed below.

oral
  interpretation
rhapsodes
anthologies
themes
mood
persona
first person
second person
third person
dramatic
  monologue

interior
  monologue
omniscient
meter
rhythm
rhyme
auditory
scene setting
offstage focus
aural

GENERAL VOCABULARY

Expanding your general vocabulary will help you become a more effective communicator. Listed below are some words appearing in this chapter that you should make part of your everyday vocabulary.

enhanced
mimic
minstrels
recitation
spellbound
paraphernalia

faltering
compelling
tedium
introspective
nectar
motif

LOOKING AHEAD

When Dr. Seuss died, an entire nation mourned. Appearing on the television program "Saturday Night Live," the Reverend Jesse Jackson read from Dr. Seuss's beloved story *Green Eggs and Ham*. It was a fitting tribute: Millions of children, after all, have grown up in a world peopled by Hunches in Bunches and Brown Bar-ba-Loots. In fact, your first experience with oral interpretation might have been when one of your parents interpreted Dr. Seuss for you: "I do not like green eggs and ham. I do not like them, Sam-I-am."

Whether you realize it or not, oral interpretation is still an important part of your life. When you read aloud in class from an essay you've written, you're interpreting your words for your classmates. When you listen to the news on radio or television, the reporters are practicing the art of oral interpretation for you. Moreover, oral interpretation can be great fun. In a memorable episode of the television show "The Simpsons," Marge (the

mother) flashes back to her high school days and her participation on the speech team. In one scene, Marge, an academic standout, performs her interpretation of the play *Butterflies Are Free* and wins the heart of the classic bad boy Homer (the father).

In this chapter, you will learn about the remarkable history of oral interpretation and how the long tradition of sharing literature orally continues today. You will discover that this experience of sharing can benefit you and others. As you become a better oral interpreter, your understanding of literature will be *enhanced* because you will become a more careful reader. Careful reading will lead you to new insights about the meaning of the literature as well as make you more sensitive to the beauty of language. The audience, too, will share in this intellectual and emotional experience, for you will not only entertain audience members with your performance, you will bring literature alive for them.

I What Is Oral Interpretation?

If you can accurately *mimic* the voice of your favorite celebrity or cartoon character, you are gifted in the skill of impres-

sion. You should not, however, confuse this ability with the art of oral interpretation. In oral interpretation, you do not impersonate a familiar voice—be it Eddie Murphy or Bugs Bunny. Rather, you try to create an appropriate and original voice to give life to words on a page. After analyzing the meaning and feeling behind those words, you use your voice and body to share the words with others. **Oral interpretation,** then, is the art of communicating works of literature by reading aloud well.

The history of oral interpretation as a distinct art—apart from public speaking and theater—is difficult to define. The formal study of oral interpretation as a separate activity didn't begin until early in the nineteenth century. In 1806, Harvard offered courses that included "the interpretive approach to literary materials."

However, oral interpretation is one of the oldest of human social activities. Until paper replaced memory, people needed to communicate ideas orally. Literature was passed down from generation to generation in oral form. Professional storytellers made their livings by traveling through the countryside and entertaining people.

Even though the oral tradition has been with us as long as human interaction, historians point to ancient Greece as the birthplace for the art of interpretation. Wandering *minstrels* known as **rhapsodes** would assemble to read their works in public competition. The recitations were often accompanied by music from a lyre or other primitive instrument.

Poetry reading was popular during the Augustan Age (27 B.C. – 14 A.D.) in Rome. It is said that the Emperor Nero would allow no one to leave a reading in which he was competing until he himself had finished reading. Dr. Paul Hunsinger, a professor of speech, characterized Nero as a "ruthless contestant" who paid five thousand young men to applaud him at one competition. After losing to the poet Lucan, Nero ordered him never to read

INSTANT IMPACT

The Power of Oral Interpretation

In December 1960, John F. Kennedy, who had just been elected president of the United States, invited the distinguished poet Robert Frost to participate in the inaugural ceremonies to be held that January. Frost's answer by wire read: "If you can bear at your age the honor of being made president of the United States, I ought to be able at my age to bear the honor of taking some part in your inauguration. I may not be equal to it but I can accept it for my cause—the arts, poetry, now for the first time taken into the affairs of statesman."

Frost's oral interpretation at the inaugural ceremony was not without difficulty. His failing eyesight and the bright sunlight made reading from a script troublesome. Frost had planned to read a poem of dedication that he had written for this occasion. After much *faltering,* Frost admitted to his unfamiliarity with the new poem and recited from memory his poem "The Gift Outright."

An article in the *Washington Post* the next morning reported that Frost "in his natural way had stolen the hearts of the inaugural crowd."

again. Nero went so far as to destroy the statues and busts of other poetry readers.

Recitation contests continued throughout the Middle Ages among minstrels, who competed for prizes provided by the nobility. In Margaret Bahn's book *A History of Oral Interpretation,* you can learn about

COMMUNICATION   BREAKDOWN

Public Clutterance . . .

Peggy Noonan, a speechwriter for former President Ronald Reagan, explains the importance of oral interpretation in delivering any public speech:

The irony of modern speeches is that as our ability to disseminate them has exploded (an American president can speak live not only to America but to Europe, to most of the world), their quality has declined.

Why? Lots of reasons, including that we as a nation no longer learn the rhythms of public utterance from Shakespeare and the Bible. When young Lincoln was sprawled in front of the fireplace reading *Julius Caesar*—"Th' abuse of greatness is, when it disjoins remorse

from power"—he was, unconsciously, learning to be a poet. You say, "That was Lincoln, not the common man." But the common man was flocking to the docks to get the latest installment of Dickens off the ship from England.

Source: Peggy Noonan, What I Saw at the Revolution, *copyright © 1990, Random House (New York).*

Questions
1. Do you agree with Peggy Noonan that the quality of "public utterance" has declined in this country?
2. Should students be required to read aloud from Shakespeare, the Bible, and Dickens to learn the rhythms of language?

Anglo-Saxon, Celtic, and Norse oral literatures. Any study of the oral tradition should also include a review of the literary works in India, China, Africa, and the Middle East.

Reading aloud has played an important role in the cultural history of our country as well. Before radio and television, many families would read aloud in the evenings. Young children, *spellbound* by the great works of literature, would spend hours in shared adventure. Much as musicians give concerts today, oral interpreters around the turn of the century would go on tour. These tours brought entertainment and culture to even the most remote regions of our country.

Today, as writers attempt to reach a wider audience, "performance poetry" is gaining popularity. Larry Goodell, a poet and practitioner of the art, explores the creative possibilities of oral interpretation. Costumed in an old robe and makeup, Goodell dances and chants. He has been known to read poem fragments written on cardboard dog biscuits as a musician accompanies him on an electronic saxophone. Although few poets perform oral interpretation with such *paraphernalia*, most writers now recognize the need for students to hear the range and diversity of contemporary works—works that enrich and expand our enjoyment of literature and each other.

IS IT TOTALLY AWESOME OR WHAT, THAT MTV'S BEEN ON TEN YEARS?... TEN YEARS! I'LL BET NOTHIN' GOOD'S EVER BEEN AROUND THAT LONG BEFORE...

JEFF KOTERBA
Courtesy Omaha World-Herald

TAKING CHARGE

Performance poets like Larry Goodell are dedicated to "oral poetry." These artists use things other than the words—such as costumes, props, and music—to help the audience appreciate the power and magic of language. Goodell explains: "Things I make extend from the words, sometimes cradle them like a mouth cradles the words you say, before they are said."

Now it's your turn. Choose a short poem to read. As you interpret the poem for the class, incorporate things that will "extend" the meaning of the words. You could, for example, perform dribbling tricks with a basketball as you interpret John Updike's poem "Ex–Basketball Player."

II Choosing Your Material

When you are assigned to give an oral interpretation in class, you have a problem: where to look for material to perform. Although you have a seemingly unlimited range of material available to you, how do you find it? Many interpreters have found anthologies to be useful, because they include a wide selection of materials in a single volume. **Anthologies** are books that include literary works by subject matter, such as love, war, or nature. Other anthologies collect poetry or different types of prose, such as short stories, essays, or humorous pieces. If you are interested in contemporary music, for example, you could turn to the anthology *The Poetry of Rock*, edited by Richard Goldstein. If you are interested, on the other hand, in interpreting poems on the subject of loneliness, several excellent selections appear in the anthology *Pictures That Storm Inside My Head*, edited by Richard Peck.

Another way to find material for oral interpretation is to ask your parents to provide suggestions based on the books they have read. Your teachers have a wealth of reading experience that they can share. Your school librarians can recommend literature that they believe might be suitable for reading aloud.

Perhaps your most important consideration, though, should be your own personal tastes in literature. You are more likely to devote time and energy to the performance of material that you care about. When forced to read material that you find boring or confusing, your performance will suffer.

The key, then, is to choose a work that you enjoy reading. Think back over the poems and stories you have read. Which ones moved you the most? Which ones made you stop and think? Chances are that the selections you remember as favorites will be good choices for your first oral interpretation.

As you select material to read aloud, you will also want to consider the quality of the literature. Why? Because literature that has worth or merit gives you, the reader, something to interpret. True, a grocery list is writing that matters—eating is essential for life—but how many different interpretations can you give to a gallon of milk and a loaf of bread? If, however, you read Henry David Thoreau's observation that "the mass of men lead lives of quiet desperation," then you have layers of meaning to interpret. What did Thoreau mean by "quiet desperation?" How does that desperation affect people's lives? For you as an interpreter, Thoreau provides much food for thought.

> **"The mass of men lead lives of quiet desperation."**
>
> **Henry David Thoreau**

Literature you should look for, then, consists of writings that are valued both for their beauty of form or expression and for their permanence or universal interest. You should value these writings not only because they give you material for oral interpretation but also because you can learn so much from them. Literature of high quality offers insights into life, inner truths that teach lasting lessons. When T. S. Eliot, in his poem "The Love Song of J. Alfred Prufrock," has the speaker admit that he has measured out his life "in coffee spoons," you are introduced to a *compelling* symbol. The spoons represent the *tedium* of a life lived from one cup of coffee to the next. Your challenge as a reader is to present the speaker's struggle against

Choosing Material for Oral Interpretation

When selecting material for an oral interpretation, you should consider your personal tastes in literature and the occasion for the interpretation. The writers below will appeal to different speakers and be appropriate for different occasions.

T. S. Eliot

Alex Haley

William Shakespeare

Ernest Hemingway

Emily Dickinson

F. Scott Fitzgerald

this tedium so that the listeners share in his frustration.

In choosing material, you should also consider the occasion and the desires of your audience. If you are given three minutes to share a work of literature in class, you may want to avoid choices like Tolstoy's very long novel *War and Peace.*

You should always meet the audience's expectations about time limits. Material should also be suitable. If asked to read at a wedding, you might choose a poem that celebrates love. If performing at a graduation ceremony, however, you would probably not want to read a work about the prospects for future unemployment.

TAKING CHARGE

Make a list of five selections that you might use for an oral interpretation in class. Remember to consider these four factors: your personal tastes, the quality of the literature, the occasion, and the desires of the audience.

III Interpreting Your Material

To interpret a selection well, you must first understand it. You reach this understanding by considering both the meaning and the feeling of the selection. Once you have determined the meaning and feeling of a particular work, you must adapt your interpretation to the requirements of the form: prose, poetry, or drama.

Meaning

The meaning of any selection includes all the ideas that are communicated by the work. You analyze those ideas as a means to an end—the performance. An important part of the process of analysis is to know what each word means (and how each word relates to every other word) so that you can share that understanding with the audience. For example, if you are reading from Harper Lee's novel *To Kill a Mockingbird* and you don't know that *apoplectic* can describe a person in a fit of rage, then you may not correctly understand how to interpret that passage.

You must, of course, determine the denotation of words like *apoplectic*—that is, the dictionary definition or explicit meaning. You should also determine the connotations—the implied meanings. The connotations are especially important to an interpreter because they suggest associations that go beyond the dictionary definition. If you were to ask your classmates to define *love*, you would have as many different definitions as you have classmates. The same is true for poets writing of love; some will say love is affection, some, an affliction.

To make sure you understand the meaning of a selection, try paraphrasing it. If you can put the ideas of the work into your own words, then you are off to a good start in understanding what the author is trying to say to you. These "author messages" or central ideas in a literary work are the **themes** that you must make clear in your interpretation. In *To Kill a Mockingbird*, for example, an important theme is that to understand a person you must climb in that person's skin and walk around in it. Knowing this theme helps you to make choices in interpreting the denotative and the connotative meanings of all the words.

Feeling

After you have analyzed the connotative meanings of the words in your selection, you will begin to understand not only the themes of the work but also the feelings the author is trying to arouse. A particular feeling in a work is often described as the **mood.** The mood is the emotional tone created by the work.

Just as your moods change throughout the day, however, so does the emotional tone of any work of literature. Consider the Dylan Thomas poem "Do not go gentle into that good night:"

Do not go gentle into that good night,
Old age should burn and rave at close of
    day;
Rage, rage against the dying of the light.

Though wise men at their end know dark
    is right,
Because their words had forked no light-
    ning they
Do not go gentle into that good night.

Good men, the last wave by, crying how
    bright
Their frail deeds might have danced in a
    green bay,
Rage, rage against the dying of the light.

Wild men who caught and sang the sun in
    flight,
And learn, too late, they grieved it on its
    way,
Do not go gentle into that good night.

Grave men, near death, who see the blind-
    ing sight
Blind eyes could blaze like meteors and be
    gay,
Rage, rage against the dying of the light.

And you, my father, there on the sad
    height,
Curse, bless, me now with your fierce tears,
    I pray.

Do not go gentle into that good night.
Rage, rage against the dying of the light.

What is the general mood of the Thomas poem? If you know that Thomas was angry that his father had given up the will to live, do you think it would make a difference in your interpretation? Do you think Thomas admires the "wild men" who are described in the poem? If you do, then you must use your voice to show the mood changing from anger to admiration and back to anger again.

Interpreting Prose

When you tell a personal story, you are the narrator of the events that you relate. In interpreting a work of prose, however, you need to analyze the form of the written narration to determine who is the narrator. The form of the narration tells you who is telling the story, whom that person is telling the story to, what relationship that person has to the events described, and how much knowledge that person has of those events.

Once you have determined who is the fictional speaker (the **persona**), you use your imagination to fill in the details—such as vocal characteristics and facial expressions—necessary to re-create that speaker, that "voice," in the minds of the listeners.

The outlook from which the events in a novel or short story are related, called the point of view, varies from story to story and within stories. Many authors write in the **first person,** using *I* to identify the narrator. Others prefer the **third person,** describing characters as *he* or *she.* Occasionally, you will find a work written in the **second person,** in which the author addresses *you* (for example, this sentence and this textbook). Let's look at each of these more closely.

First-Person Narrations

In a first-person narration—a story whose narrator is *I*—the author may be using a variety of approaches. One popular form of first-person narration is the **dramatic monologue.** A dramatic monologue presents a single character speaking. Although you may associate this approach with the theater, authors of prose use the technique when they want you to overhear somebody speaking aloud to another person. Another form of first-person narration is the **interior monologue.** Here, the author has the narrator speaking to himself or herself. We hear the narrator's thoughts. Consider this passage from Tom McAfee's short story "This Is My Living Room."

> My Living Room
> It ain't big but big enough for me and my family—my wife Rosie setting over there reading recipes in the *Birmingham News* and my two girls Ellen Jean and Martha Kay watching the TV. I am sitting here holding *Life* magazine in my lap. I get *Life,* the *News,* and *Christian Living.* I read a lots, the newspaper everyday from cover to cover. I don't just look at the pictures in *Life.* I read what's under them and the stories.

Read the McAfee selection again, and ask yourself these questions: What does the narrator look like? How is he dressed? Where does he live? What kind of accent might he have? How old is he? How does the narrator feel about his wife and children? Is he "happy" with his life? Answering these kinds of questions will help you decide how to portray this narrator in your interpretation.

Third-Person Narrations

In a third-person narration, the narrator is not *I*—the person to whom the story is happening—but an observer of the action. Third person can allow the narrator to tell the story through the eyes of more than one character. Typically, the narrator is all-knowing—or **omniscient**—and moves free-ly into and out of the minds of various characters. As an example, consider this passage from Flannery O'Connor's short story "A Good Man Is Hard to Find":

> The grandmother didn't want to go to Florida. She wanted to visit some of her connections in east Tennessee and she was seizing at every chance to change Bailey's mind. "Now look here, Bailey," she said, "see here, read this . . . Here this fellow that calls himself The Misfit is aloose from the Federal Pen and headed toward Florida and you read here what it says he did to these people. Just you read it."

Read this selection again, asking your-self the same kinds of questions that you answered for the McAfee passage. Note that a significant difference exists between the McAfee and O'Connor stories. As you interpret the McAfee story, you must por-tray one character: the "I." In the O'Con-nor story, however, you have two charac-ters: the author's omniscient narrator's "voice" and the grandmother's "voice." The challenge for you as an interpreter is to create two unique voices for these characters. The grandmother must talk like this specific grandmother would talk. Furthermore, the narrator must sound dif-ferent from the grandmother.

Interpreting Poetry

As you interpret prose or poetry, you need to be especially sensitive to the au-thor's intent. Determining the author's intent is crucial, because you must al-ways respect the integrity of the words in the work. Understanding some technical terms—*meter, rhythm, rhyme, imagery*—will help you determine the author's intent in poetry.

Meter

When you hear the word **meter,** you probably think of a unit of measurement. Meter, in poetry, is also a way of mea-suring. Instead of measuring distance, though, meter measures the rhythm in a line of poetry. The pattern of this rhythm is determined by what syllables you stress in the words that make up the line.

You place stress on particular syllables based on your knowledge of proper pro-nunciation and on your interpretation of the poem. You can look up proper pro-nunciation in any dictionary, but your un-derstanding of the poem is up to you. You should never sacrifice meaning as you vocalize the meter, but you should also never lose sight of the pattern pro-vided by the poet. As an interpreter, you must balance these two factors, meaning and pattern.

Remember that the choices you make about meter do make a difference. For ex-ample, rapid, regular recurrence of stress often suggests increased tension, and a slower repetition of stress suggests a more *introspective* mood.

Rhythm

Rhythm is defined as the flow of stressed and unstressed syllables in a poem. The effect of rhythm on meaning should be your primary concern as a reader. Listeners can only concentrate on a given idea for a brief period of time.

At the inauguration ceremony of President Bill Clinton, Maya Angelou, pictured here, delivered an oral interpretation of a poem she wrote specifically for the occasion.

Therefore, you must pace your reading to allow the listener to relax occasionally and reflect on what has been said.

The poet may use pauses within a line to establish a rhythm that is like a melody. Note the breaks created by Shakespeare's use of commas in the lines that follow. Shakespeare was a master of pauses, those "sounds of silence."

> It was a lover and his lass,
> With a hey, and a ho, and a hey nonino,
> That o'er the green corn-field did pass
> In the spring time, the only pretty ring
>   time,
> When birds do sing, hey ding a ding,
>   ding;
> Sweet lovers love the spring.

Read the poem again as if there were no commas in the middles of lines 2, 4, and 5. Do not pause at all as you read these lines. Do you hear how the poem's rhythm has been lost? As an oral interpreter, you must always be aware of the rhythm of any literature that you perform.

Rhyme

Rhyme is a repetition of sounds between words or syllables or the endings of lines of verse. This repetition pleases the ear; author M. H. Abrams described the effect as the "delight given by the expected but variable end chime." You, as an oral interpreter, must be careful not to change this "delight" into a sing-song pattern of delivery that distracts from the effectiveness of your reading. To ensure that the rhyme scheme doesn't overwhelm the listeners, experienced interpreters often pause in unexpected places and emphasize words that are not at the ends of lines. In analyzing different poems, you have to decide in each case how to maintain control over the rhyme of the work, as well as the rhythm and meter, to avoid a mechanical or predictable pattern that takes away from the audience's enjoyment of your performance.

Let's consider how to do this by examining the poem "Success Is Counted

Sweetest," by Emily Dickinson. The poem describes how those who lose at something understand better what it means to win than those who are the victors. Perhaps you know this truth already.

Success is counted sweetest
By those who ne'er succeed.
To comprehend a *nectar*
Requires sorest need.

Not one of all the purple host
Who took the flag today
Can tell the definition,
So clear of victory.

As he, defeated—dying—
On whose forbidden ear
The distant strains of triumph
Burst agonized and clear!

Note how Dickinson rhymes the second and fourth lines in each stanza—for example, *succeed* and *need* in the first stanza. One way that you might avoid a too-strong, sing-song pattern in your delivery of the first stanza would be to give special emphasis to the words *ne'er* and *comprehend*. You might also briefly pause before delivering each of these words. In addition, you might try pausing after *requires* rather than *nectar*. A final suggestion: When you read the word *need*, lower your pitch slightly and say the word quietly. By doing so, you will deemphasize the rhyme and also suggest the mood of the poem.

If you study the second stanza, you will find an imperfect rhyme in the second and fourth lines: *today* and *victory*. We think of Dickinson as a "modern" poet, and one of the reasons is her willingness to subordinate rhyme to meaning. As an oral inter-

INSTANT IMPACT

Poetry with a Punch

In Taos, New Mexico, Peter Rabbit and Anne MacNaughton have taken the possibility of boredom out of poetry readings. Together, they founded the Society of the Muse of the Southwest (SOMOS), which, until 1992, sponsored the annual Taos Poetry Circus and Heavyweight Championship Bout. The event presented poetry reading in a mock-boxing-match format, complete with round-by-round scoring and an audience of nearly five hundred screaming fans.

The idea behind this popular festival was to revitalize poetry, to get it off the printed page and into a real-world setting. Rabbit explains that he was "fishing for a way to develop an audience. I met some European poets who were telling me about poetry readings in football stadiums with 20,000 people. In Russia, poets were killed—or used to be. Here, we're just ignored."

The first heavyweight bout was staged in 1982. Self-proclaimed "Captain Poetry" Gregory Corso withdrew in the fifth round, leaving Terry Jacobus of Chicago as the winner. Some of the past heavyweight poetry champions include Ntozake Shange, Lewis MacAdams, Andrei Codrescu, and Victor Hernandez-Cruz.

In a telephone interview with the *Albuquerque Journal*, Shange, author of *For Colored Girls Who Have Considered Suicide When the Rainbow Is Enuf*, said, "We have to get American poetry into the hearts and minds of the people and out of the books that they never read anyway."

preter, you have to be willing to make those same artistic choices.

Imagery

As you may recall from Chapter 10, the word *imagery* refers to language that creates mental pictures. These pictures differ in the minds of the reader and the listener. An image creates in each person an association with some real-life experience that is unique to that person. For example, the image of a bicycle in a poem may remind you of your first trip to the grocery store alone. The person sitting next to you may think, instead, of crashing into the neighbor's new car. This recalling of what we have previously experienced gives the poetry (or prose) its emotional power.

As an oral interpreter, you should pay special attention to a writer's use of imagery. In Grace Butcher's poem "On Driving Behind a School Bus for Mentally Retarded Children," the poet compares the children to flowers. This metaphor is used throughout the poem to illustrate the unique challenges faced by the children. In reading this work aloud, you must use your voice creatively to suggest the meaning and feeling of the poet's metaphor.

> Full deep green
> bloom-fallen spring
> here outside,
> for us.
>
> They,
> like winter-covered crocuses:
> strange bright beauty
> peeping through snow that never melts—
>
> (How quietly,
> how quietly,
> the bus.)
>
> These flowers have no fragrance.
> They move to an eerie wind

> I cannot feel.
> They rise, with petals fully opened,
> from a twisted seed
> and neither grow
> nor wither.
>
> They will be taught
> the colors of their names.

Interpreting Drama

When you see a play performed on stage, the actors attempt to "become" the characters portrayed. The goal of the actor is to make the performance as close to real life as possible. In contrast, the reader in traditional oral interpretation of drama tries to "suggest" those characters. For example, a reader, at a dramatic moment in the script, might have tears welling up in his eyes. The actor, to go beyond the mere suggestion of an emotional climax, might have tears streaming down his face.

In contemporary speech competition, "Humorous Interpretation" and "Dramatic Interpretation" are memorized events often described as "acting from the waist up." This description arises from the practice by many competitors of pretending to be the characters in their selections. Some of these performances include extensive use of gestures and actual movement around the room. By taking on the techniques of acting, these speech competitors may no longer be presenting a traditional oral interpretation, but they are creating a powerful union of the two arts.

Regardless of your approach, as an interpreter of drama, you need to help your listeners create a mental image of the characters you are suggesting. You must provide the visual and **auditory** (of hearing) clues that will stimulate the imagination of each audience member.

TAKING CHARGE

Many interpreters read two or more selections built around a theme. This "program" of reading provides an opportunity to show how different authors approach similar themes. You will find an example of a programmed reading at the end of this chapter. The student chose selections that celebrated the many sounds of poetry that cause the listener to want to "speak like rain" (her theme).

Now it's your turn. After deciding on a subject—death, friendship, patriotism, or the like—find two to five short poems and formulate a theme that shows the relationships among them.

IV Presenting Your Material

Choosing and analyzing material for oral interpretation is only part of your preparation. Next, you have to prepare and practice for the actual performance. Some of the keys to unlocking the mystery of effective presentation involve introducing material, cutting material, developing material, and practicing material.

Introducing Your Material

You will need to prepare an introduction for your interpretation. The principles you learned in earlier chapters about writing a good speech introduction still apply here. Some distinctions, though, should be noted.

First, you are responsible for giving your listeners the information they need to understand the selection. Characters need to be identified, relationships explained, and important plot points outlined. You don't want to spoil the story by "giving away the ending," but you don't want your listeners confused either.

A second requirement for an effective introduction is to establish a mood that is consistent with the mood of the selection itself. For example, if you were reading from *Romeo and Juliet,* a Shakespearean tragedy, you probably wouldn't begin by cracking jokes. A humorous introduction, however, might be appropriate for *Romeo and Juliet* if you were going to perform only the scenes with speeches by Juliet's nosy nurse, who provides comic relief in the play.

Finally, keep your introductions brief. If you are allowed five minutes for your entire performance, you shouldn't spend most of that time explaining what you're going to do. Most introductions can be kept to around a minute (or less). Remember, you need only include the information necessary for the audience to share the meaning and feeling of your selection. (For an example, see the student speech at the end of the chapter.)

Oral interpretation requires delivery skills such as eye contact, character placement, characterization, word color, and showmanship.

Cutting Your Material

You may need to cut, or condense, your selection. This may be necessary for several reasons: You may have too much material for the time allowed, certain parts of your selection may be inappropriate, or a particular episode may lessen the overall effect you are seeking. If you are working with a longer short story or a novel, you will usually choose a climactic scene and present only that scene. In that case, when writing the introduction, you will tell the audience what they need to know to understand the scene. Other guidelines that may prove useful include the following:

1. Always cut *in*, not *out*. In other words, build your cutting around your favorite lines and those lines that you feel are the most important to understanding the selection. If you tried to cut *Gone with the Wind* down to a five-minute presentation by taking out—one by one—the lines you didn't need, you would quickly lose your interest in the project (and your youth). What you should do is pick your favorite scene and highlight those lines you most want to keep (in priority order), as well as those needed to make the story make sense. As soon as you've highlighted a total of four minutes worth of lines—stop! Save the extra minute for your introduction.

2. Eliminate dialogue tags, the parts of written dialogue that tell us who is speaking. Consider the following example:

   "May I have another chocolate bar?" Jane asked.

   "But you have already had three this morning," Elizabeth replied.

"Jane asked" and "Elizabeth replied" are dialogue tags. Such tags can usually be cut. However, if it might not be clear who is speaking or if this is the first time a character has spoken in the material you are using, the tags should not be cut.

3. In drama, eliminate stage directions (*Elena rises, crosses left*) as well as lines that suggest physical action. For example, suppose in your selection Larry asks Melvin why he is tap-dancing. You have to eliminate that line so that your listeners don't expect you to tap-dance. (Alternatively, you could suggest the movements in some limited way or start taking tap-dancing lessons.)

4. Eliminate minor characters who might confuse your listeners.

5. Cut references to events that you do not have time to fully explain.

Developing Your Material

In developing your selection for performance, you need to work on certain skills that will improve your effectiveness as a reader. These delivery skills include eye contact, character placement, characterization, word color, and showmanship.

Eye Contact

You have already learned about the importance of eye contact. In oral interpretation, how much eye contact is enough? How often should you look up from the script, and when? These questions are a source of great controversy among the teachers of interpretation. Some say that a fifty-fifty balance is appropriate. Others argue for maintaining eye contact with the audience as much as 90 percent of the time. Regardless of your position on this issue, you need to remember two factors: (1) You must look at the script often enough to remind the audience that you are sharing a work of literature. (2) You must not be tied to the script, or the audience will soon tire of staring at the top of your head.

Effective interpreters often use a technique known as **scene setting.** They use their eyes to focus the scene that they are describing on an imaginary stage in front of them. This helps the audience members to see that same scene in their imaginations. When not scene setting, these speakers look in the eyes of individual audience members or at the script.

Character Placement

If you are portraying various characters, then you must "place" them by looking at a different location for each one. By directing your focus to different locations, you can create the illusion that a number of characters are speaking to each other. Readings of drama require this skill; but prose, too, can necessitate character placement. In prose readings, most interpreters place the narrator directly in front of them with the rest of the "voices" distributed to the left and to the right. In drama, the most important characters are placed closest to the center, with the minor characters farther to the sides.

Take care not to place characters too far apart. If the characters are widely separated, the time it will take for you to rotate your head to the proper position will cause you to pause too long between speakers. The effect of these long pauses is similar to what happens in plays when actors do not pick up their lines: The performance drags. It is also important to be consistent in your character placement, or the audience may become confused as to who is speaking.

Characterization

Look around your classroom. No two of your classmates sound or act the same. Similarly, each character you portray in a selection must be distinct. Each should be characterized by a unique voice, facial expression, and body position.

To create distinctions in voice, some interpreters experiment with a variety of pitch patterns. Some vary the pacing, making the characters speak at different rates of speed. Others try to re-create dialects, the pronunciation that is used in a particular area. Whether or not you use a dialect should depend on your ability to make it convincing. An annoying or distracting characterization damages the integrity of the selection and makes for a disappointing performance.

You should also avoid using a stereotypical voice that lessens the believability of a character. Stereotypical voices usually turn into nothing more than caricatures, comic exaggerations that lack uniqueness. Not everyone from the South talks with a drawl, and not every football lineman plays without a helmet.

Along with vocal distinctions, you should respond with your face and the rest of your body to each word spoken by a character. If a character is happy, the audience should not only hear that happiness in the warmth of your voice but see it in a smiling face and relaxed body as well. Each character and each moment in the script require subtle changes in facial

expressiveness and posture. The audience must see you suggest the individual characteristics of each person in the selection in order to get caught up in the magic of the illusion that these people are real.

Word Color

You must give each word in your selection its due. Your responsibility is to change written symbols into sound symbols by "coloring" them with your voice. You would not, for example, say "I want to kiss you" and "Please pass the butter" in the same way. You must suggest the denotative and connotative meanings with vocal variety. But how? Experienced interpreters use, in combination or alone, some of the following techniques: pauses of varying lengths before key words, changes in pitch, holding vowels, hitting consonants, manipulating tempo, and unusual or unexpected emphasis.

To see how these techniques can make a significant difference in an interpretation, experiment with them on any literary work included in this chapter. You can change the entire meaning of a particular work by varying your voice in these ways.

Showmanship

Showmanship refers to the sense of professionalism that you must have when performing. From the moment you leave your seat until you have returned to your place, you should make it clear that you enjoy the act of sharing literature with an audience. If you mumble misgivings under your breath or seem hesitant at any point, the experience of your listeners is lessened. Care about your material. Care about the people in your audience. Show them.

COMMUNICATION   BREAKTHROUGH

Accenting the Positive

Tracy Ullman phones car dealers in Baltimore and comparison shops. Gary Oldman plays tapes on the freeway and ponders the uncanny congruities between Lee Harvey Oswald and Yogi Bear. Barbara Hershey tools through the Louisiana swamps and climbs ashore now and then for a chat.

All these slightly undignified enterprises are dramatic research, simply the lengths to which some actors will go to find and perfect an acceptable accent.

Almost every big-name American actor has entered the office of a dialect coach at one time or another, seeking advice for problems as small as a nasal New Jersey accent or as pressing as a director's mandate to master South African in a day or two.

Recreating an accent can take anywhere from a one-hour session to several months; it may need no more than a pointer or two, or it may demand a steady regimen of voice and breathing exercises, phonetic analysis, and a tape review.

For Tom Hulce's role as Stalin's projectionist in "The Inner Circle" (1991)—a part that required the actor to deliver flawless English in a wholly unlikely Russian accent—he met with his coach every morning for two months rehearsing his lines, analyzing Russian intonation, and listening to Russian folk music.

Learning dialect can exact more of an actor than mere diligence and stretching of vocal cords. He or she may have to learn to hold the mouth differently or shift what the dialogue coach Carla Meyer calls "vocal placement" up or down an octave.

"One of the dangers of any accent is that if you're not careful, it will start to make acting choices for you," said Meyer. "You hop on board the melody of it, and all of the sudden you're talking like this with a funny lilt and saying, 'Top o' the morning to ya.'"

Not every script can live up to the stringent demands of conscientious actors . . . or to the dialogue coach's skeptical ear. That's when the job of coaching can become surprisingly creative.

"Once I was working with Robert Wagner on his show when he had to pretend to be his own Swiss uncle," dialect coach Robert Easton recalled. "There was this line of dialogue where someone asked him, 'Are you really Swiss?' And in the script he said, 'Yah.' Well, you can be sure that we changed that. I offered him this line: 'Eef I was any more Svees, I vood be a cuckoo clock.'

"That sounds a bit better, don't you think?"

Source: Judith Shulevitz, New York Times, "Speech Coaches Accent the Positive" (*reprinted in the* San Francisco Chronicle Datebook, *February 23, 1992.*)

Questions

1. As a performer, do you think it is better not to do an accent at all rather than to do one poorly?
2. If you were trying to interpret the speech pattern of, say, a coal miner from Wales, what would you do to prepare?

COMMUNICATION WORKS

Sue Ann Gunn, Children's Theater Director

"I put more thought into choosing my clothes for oral interpretation than I did into choosing my wedding dress," recalls Sue Ann Gunn, director of the Albuquerque Children's Theatre. Gunn, the 1963 Texas state champion in prose reading, explains that she always wore neutral colors. Her favorite was a cream two-piece suit with shoes to match. She laughs as she remembers her sprayed-down, sixties-style hair.

Gunn says that the most difficult challenge she faced in competition arose the year she entered poetry reading: "At the regional contest, there were eleven contestants, and nine of us, including myself, performed the same selection, 'Renascence' by Edna St. Vincent Millay."

In looking back at her experience in high school speech, Gunn is thankful for the self-confidence she gained and for the skills she acquired. Gunn says, "What it taught me, I think, was some of the techniques of oral interp which I'm only now beginning to recognize and use. What it does is give you a way to approach a part so that you don't have to rely on your intuition or method-inside stuff because it won't always be there."

Gunn explains that during those performances where you are not there emotionally, you must rely on technique. "In fact, in my senior year in college," Gunn remembers, "I played Eleanor in *The Lion in Winter*, and I knew that I was not doing great acting, and everyone gave me raves except for one reviewer. He pointed out that it was the carefully modulated reading of the lines and the gestures that made the performance succeed. I was oral interpreting the part."

The ability to audition well is another advantage for the experienced oral interpreter. An oral interpreter can pick up a script that she has never seen before and have eye contact with another actor or the audience. Gunn says, "A cold reading is so easy for me now. I not only can have a lot of eye contact but I can switch from one character to another much more effectively."

She adds that oral interpretation has also paid off in other ways. While she was teaching at the Hampstead International School in London, Gunn gave the graduation address to the eighth grade class each year. Most of the students attending this school did not speak English as their first language. Gunn says, "We had everything from 'I just arrived here yesterday; I've never spoken a word of English' to sixth graders speaking English at the tenth grade level. It became very important that the way you said things spoke to the people who didn't understand what you were saying."

Asked what it's like when her oral interpretation skills work for her, Gunn replies, "It's what somebody recently described as flow. It's beautiful, the knowledge that you are doing something well and moving other people and bringing something wonderful into the world."

Practicing Your Material

You need to practice your material by reading it aloud. Silent rehearsal does not allow you to experiment with a variety of vocal approaches. Furthermore, you should try to practice the material exactly as you plan to present it. In the early stages, however, you might want to break the performance down by practicing a few lines at a time. By polishing shorter sections, you won't fall into the trap of simply running through the material to get the practice session over. Memorized material should never sound as if you are merely reciting the words off of your brain cells. You must make the material seem fresh, as if you were performing it for the first time. You must seem to be "thinking" as the character you are portraying. This quality is necessary for a believable reading.

Try tape-recording your practice to check word color, articulation, pronunciation, pacing, and use of pauses and emphasis. It is important that you have absolutely crisp, clear vocalization. Some interpreters find it helpful to mark manuscripts as a reminder of when to pause and which words to emphasize. Whether you mark your manuscript or not, you should spend the time necessary to become completely familiar with your material. In other words, you should look down at your manuscript because you choose to, not because you have to. Avoid looking down on words: The up-and-down movement of your head should come between words so as not to create motion that will distract from giving each word its full worth.

In using a manuscript, be careful not to wave it around as you gesture. The manuscript should remain still at all times. Furthermore, do not hold it too low. If you hold it too low, you will have the tendency to drop your head too far as you struggle to see the words on the page. A final suggestion: Rather than reading from a book, most interpreters photocopy or type up their material. They then cut and paste the sections they are going to read onto sheets of paper and place them in a binder.

TAKING CHARGE

A successful oral interpreter creates an environment for understanding the selection shared. This introduction to the reading should not only be appropriate but should also demonstrate the imagination of the performer. Consider the following example from a student performance.

". . . though some say the world is Numbers, and some say the world is a mouth, how can science explain the fact that if, at this moment, I approach the mirror on my wall, and raise my right hand, it is really my left hand I am raising in the mirror?"

Taking Charge (Continued)

Joyce Carol Oates poses this question in her poem "Love Letter, with Static Interference from Einstein's Brain." Perhaps Oates borrowed this mirror *motif* from a story about Lewis Carroll reported in the London *Times* on January 22, 1932. According to this story, Carroll asked his cousin Alice Raikes in which hand she held an orange. Alice replied, "The right." So Carroll asked the young girl to stand before a mirror and tell him in which hand she now held the orange. And Alice replied, "The left." For you see, in a mirror all asymmetrical objects go the other way. So let us go the other way . . . through the looking glass . . . that is poetry. We begin our journey with Ishmael Reed's "beware: do not read this poem."

tonite, thriller was
abt an ol woman, so vain she
surrounded herself w/
   many mirrors

it got so bad that finally she
locked herself indoors & her
whole life became the
   mirrors
one day the villagers broke
into her house, but she was too
swift for them, she disappeared
   into a mirror
each tenant who bought the house
after that, lost a loved one to
   the ol woman in the mirror:
   first a little girl
   then a young woman
   then the young woman/s husband

the hunger of this poem is legendary
it has taken in many victims
back off from this poem
it has drawn in yr feet
back off from this poem
it has drawn in yr legs
back off from this poem

it is a greedy mirror
you are into this poem . from
   the waist down
nobody can hear you can they?
this poem has had you up to here
   belch
this poem ain't got no manners
you cant call out from this poem
relax now & go w/this poem
move & roll on to this poem
do not resist this poem
this poem has yr eyes
this poem has his head
this poem has his arms
this poem has his fingers
this poem has his fingertips

this poem is the reader & the
reader this poem

statistic: the us bureau of missing persons
   reports
that in 1968 over 100,000 people disappeared
leaving no solid clues
nor trace only
a space in the lives of their friends

Now it's your turn. Choose a short poem and write an imaginative introduction for it. Share both your introduction and the poem in a performance for the class.

V Reader's Theater

Group reading of literature offers the participants the opportunity to create what has been described as "theater of the mind." The reason for this description is that in group reading, most of the action does not occur onstage with the interpreters, as it does in drama, but rather takes place in the imaginations of audience members. Typically, the readers "suggest" movement rather than actually moving as actors do. Group reading sometimes takes the form of Reader's Theater. Although definitions vary, Reader's Theater generally involves two or more interpreters sharing an oral reading with an audience.

The sharing process in Reader's Theater includes not only vocal and physical suggestion but quite often the elements of staging. Staging is usually minimal, but scenery, lighting, costuming, and makeup have been successfully used in some productions. The emphasis in staging choices should be determined by whether the meaning of the literature is made clearer or not. Elements of play production should always enhance the literature.

Other common characteristics of Reader's Theater include the following:

◆ A narrator who introduces the different portions of the program and provides transitions between them.

◆ **Offstage focus**—a technique by which the readers use scripts and envision the scene out in the audience.

Remember, the primary concern in Reader's Theater is intensifying the **aural** appeal of the performance—that is, its appeal to the sense of hearing.

TAKING CHARGE

A Reader's Theater performance differs from a conventional play because of its emphasis on the aural elements of the material. This "theater of the mind" approach works best when the literature strongly appeals to the imagination. One of the most popular and acclaimed works for Reader's Theater is Edgar Lee Masters's *Spoon River Anthology*. In this work of poetry, the men and women in Spoon River narrate their own biographies from the cemetery. The realistic quality of their monologues makes their speeches unusually compelling. *The World of Carl Sandburg* and Dylan Thomas's *Under Milkwood* are two Reader's Theater scripts developed with great success at the professional level.

Now it's your turn. Divide your class into groups of three to five students. Each group should stage a Reader's Theater presentation. One student should serve as the narrator, and another should plan the limited movement to be used. A third student can decide what costuming, if any, is appropriate. Your group—with guidance from your teacher—should choose material that is suitable for Reader's Theater.

STUDENT SPEECH

Sharahn McClung was the 1991 Catholic Forensic League high school national champion in oral interpretation of prose and poetry. Her poetry program consisted of five poems unified by the theme "speak like rain."

Speak Like Rain

Good morning, daddy!
Ain't you heard
The boogie-woogie rumble
Of a dream deferred?

Listen closely:
You'll hear their feet
Beating out and beating out a—

You think
It's a happy beat?

Listen to it closely:
Ain't you heard
something underneath
like a—

What did I say?

Sure,
I'm happy!
Take it away!

Hey, pop!
Re-bop!
Mop!

Y-e-a-h!

For Langston Hughes, the "yeah" in his poem "Dream Boogie" is an affirmation of life. The knowing that no matter how many dreams may be deferred, there is still the possibility, the hope for a happy beat. And we hear this happy beat from the playgrounds in Harlem to the plantations of East Africa.

Isak Dinesen, who spent part of her life on a plantation in Kenya, once observed how Kikuyu tribesmen reacted to their first hearing of rhymed verse. Although the tribesmen had a strong sense of rhythm, they knew nothing of verse. That is, until they were sent to missionary schools. "On Reading Poems to a Senior Class at South High," by D. C. Berry:

Before
I opened my mouth
I noticed them sitting there
as orderly as frozen fish
in a package.

Slowly water began to fill the room
though I did not notice it
till it reached my ears

and then I heard the sounds
of fish in an aquarium

and I knew that though I had
tried to drown them
with my words
that they had only opened up
like gills for them
and let me in.

Together we swam around the room
like thirty tails whacking words
till the bell rang
puncturing
a hole in the door

where we all leaked out

They went to another class
I suppose and I home

where Queen Elizabeth
my cat met me
and licked my fins
till they were hands again.

To amuse herself one evening, Isak Dinesen spoke to the tribesmen in Swahili verse. "Ngumbe na-pende chumbe, Malayambaya. Wakamba na-kula mamba." Nonsense rhymes that meant "the oxen like salt—whores are bad—the Wakamba do eat snakes." The meaning of the poetry was of no consequence to the tribesman . . . only the sounds. "Jabberwocky" by Lewis Carroll:

'Twas brillig, and the slithy toves
    Did gyre and gimble in the wabe;
All mimsy were the borogoves,
    And the mome raths outgrabe.

"Beware the Jabberwock, my son!
    The jaws that bite, the claws that
    catch!
Beware the Jubjub bird, and shun
    The frumious Bandersnatch!"

He took his vorpal sword in hand;
    Long time the manxome foe he
    sought—
So rested he by the Tumtum tree,
    And stood awhile in thought.

And, as in uffish thought he stood,
    The Jabberwock, with eyes of flame,
Came whiffling through the tulgey
    wood,
    And burbled as it came!

One, two! One, two! And through and
    through
    The vorpal blade went snicker-snack!
He left it dead, and with its head
    He went galumphing back.

"And hast thou slain the Jabberwock?
    Come to my arms, my beamish
    boy!
O frabjous day! Callooh! Callay!"
    He chortled in his joy.

'Twas brillig, and the slithy toves
    Did gyre and gimble in the wabe;
All mimsy were the barogoves,
    And the mome raths outgrabe.

Isak Dinesen discovered that the tribesmen would wait for the rhyme and laugh at it when it came. When she tried to get them to finish a poem she had begun, they would not. They turned their heads away. "Cracked Record Blues" by Kenneth Fearing:

If you watch it long enough you can
    see the clock move,
If you try hard enough you can hold a
    little water in the palm of your hand,
If you listen once or twice you know
    it's not the needle, or the tune, but
    a crack in the record when some-
    times a phonograph falters and re-
    peats, and repeats, and repeats, and
    repeats—

And if you think about it long
    enough, long enough, long enough,
    long enough then everything is sim-
    ple and you can understand the
    times,
You can see for yourself that the
    Hudson still flows, that the
    seasons change as ever, that love is
    always love,
Words still have a meaning, still clear
    and still the same;
You can count upon your fingers
    that two plus two still equals, still
    equals, still equals, still equals—

There is nothing in this world that should bother the mind.

Because the mind is a common sense affair filled with common sense answers to common sense facts,
It can add up, can add up, can add up, can add up earthquakes and subtract them from fires,
It can bisect an atom or analyze the planets—
All it has to do is to, do is to, do is to, do is to start at the beginning and continue to the end.

Dinesen recalled that as the tribesmen became used to the idea of poetry, they begged: "Speak again. Speak like rain." Although Dinesen did not know why they thought verse to be like rain, she believed it to be an expression of applause. For, in Africa, rain was always longed for and welcomed. "Jazz Fantasia" by Carl Sandburg:

Drum on your drums, batter on your banjoes, sob on the long cool winding saxophones.
Go to it, O jazzmen.

Sling your knuckles on the bottoms of the happy tin pans, let your trombones ooze, and go husha-husha-hush with the slippery sand-paper.

Moan like an autumn wind high in the lonesome treetops, moan soft like you wanted somebody terrible, cry like a racing car slipping away from a motorcycle cop, bang-bang! you jazzmen, bang altogether drums, traps, banjoes, horns, tin cans—make two people fight on the top of a stairway and scratch each other's eyes in a clinch tumbling down the stairs.

Can the rough stuff . . . now a Mississippi steamboat pushes up the night river with a hoo-hoo-hoo-oo . . . and the green lanterns calling to the high soft stars . . . a red moon rides on the humps of the low river hills . . . go to it, O jazzmen.

So let us always give this gift to each other, to speak like rain.

REVIEW AND ENRICHMENT

LOOKING BACK

Listed below are the major ideas discussed in this chapter.

✦ The oral tradition is as old as human interaction.

✦ Ancient Greece is the birthplace of the art of interpretation.

✦ When selecting material to read, you should consider the quality of the literature.

✦ In addition to the literary worth of material, you should consider the occasion and the desires of the audience.

✦ In order to interpret a selection, you must analyze the meaning and feeling of the material.

✦ As an interpreter of prose, you must analyze the narration to determine the point of view.

✦ In interpreting poetry, you must control the meter, rhythm, rhyme, and imagery in the work.

✦ When interpreting drama, you must help the listeners create a mental image of the characters you are suggesting.

✦ Your introduction should give the listeners the information they need to understand the selection.

✦ You may need to cut your selection when you have too much material for the time allowed, when certain sections are inappropriate, or when a particular episode lessens the overall effect.

✦ Effective presentation requires mastery of these techniques: eye contact, character placement, characterization, word color, and showmanship.

✦ Tape-recording your practice sessions can help you evaluate your progress as you prepare for a performance.

✦ Reader's Theater offers the participants the opportunity to create what has been described as "theater of the mind."

SPEECH VOCABULARY

Match the speech term on the left with the appropriate description on the right.

1. rhapsodes
2. persona
3. anthologies
4. mood
5. rhythm
6. meter

a. narrator
b. measures rhythm
c. wandering minstrel
d. all-knowing
e. figurative language
f. using an imaginary stage

7. imagery   g. books that include literary works by subject matter
8. aural   h. related to sense of hearing
9. scene setting   i. flow of stressed and unstressed syllables
10. omniscient   j. emotional tone

GENERAL VOCABULARY

Define the following terms and use each in a sentence.

enhanced	spellbound	tedium
mimic	paraphernalia	introspective
minstrels	faltering	nectar
recitation	compelling	motif

THINGS TO REMEMBER

1. Impersonating a familiar voice is not interpretation but _____.
2. Poetry reading was popular during the _____ Age in Rome.
3. Name three things you should consider in selecting material for oral interpretation.
4. The _____ is the emotional tone that predominates in a selection.
5. A story in which the narrator uses "I" is written in _____ person.
6. When an author moves freely into and out of the minds of the characters, the story is probably written in _____ person.
7. Rhyme is a repetition of _____.
8. When readers use their eyes to place what they are describing on an imaginary stage, they are using a technique known as _____.
9. _____ refers to the sense of professionalism you have when performing.
10. Name three guidelines that you should use in cutting, or condensing, material.

THINGS TO DO

1. Young children are a responsive audience; their feedback is immediate and honest. Arrange to visit a nearby elementary school so that you can try out the skills you have learned in this chapter. After reading an appropriate selection—such as a work by Dr. Seuss or Shel Silverstein—to the children, ask them to critique your effort.
2. Record yourself reading a brief poem on audio tape. Evaluate your interpretation for word color, pacing, articulation, pronunciation, and use of pauses and emphasis.
3. Following the example of the Taos Poetry Circus and Heavyweight

Championship Bout, stage your own boxing/poetry reading matches. Divide the class into groups of two, and create an elimination tournament. In an individual match, two students take turns reading poems of their own choosing (each student reads one poem). The referees/audience members announce a decision, and the winning fighter/reader advances to the next round.

THINGS TO TALK ABOUT

1. When an announcer on the evening news reads a story about the damage caused by an earthquake, is that an example of oral interpretation? Why or why not?
2. What is "suitable" material for oral interpretation? The list of ingredients on a cereal box? The telephone book? The instruction manual for assembling a VCR? Explain.
3. If you were to pay tribute to Dr. Seuss by interpreting one of his books, which one would you choose? Why?

THINGS TO WRITE ABOUT

1. Write a poem consisting of nonsense words that suggest meaning by the sounds they create. For inspiration, you might refer to "Jabberwocky" by Lewis Carroll (this poem is included in the poetry program at the end of the chapter).
2. Write a one-page essay in which you discuss why it is important for all parents to be skilled at oral interpretation.
3. Choose a country in which you are interested. Research and write a brief description of the oral tradition in that nation.

CRITICAL THINKING

1. Peggy Noonan argues that the quality of modern speeches has declined because we no longer learn the rhythm of public utterances from Shakespeare and the Bible. If Noonan's assessment is accurate, then what should be done to improve oratory today?
2. Suppose that you are invited to give a reading at a retirement home. The material you select is of a humorous nature until the end of the story. At that point, the central character, a lovable senior citizen, dies unexpectedly. Will you (a) change the ending to a happy one, (b) edit out the death, or (c) leave the story as originally written? Should an oral interpreter ever violate the author's intent?

RELATED SPEECH TOPICS

Professional storytellers
Learning dialects
Norse oral literature
Celtic oral literature

Pageant declamations
The history of reader's theater
Your favorite poet

CHAPTER 20

Drama

"'Acting,' Ralph Richardson of the Old Vic pronounced last week, 'is merely the art of keeping a large group of people from coughing.'"

— New York *Herald Tribune*,
May 19, 1946

LEARNING OBJECTIVES

After completing this chapter, you will be able to do the following.

◆ Explain the elements of drama.
◆ Identify significant moments in the history of theater.
◆ Describe the tools an actor uses to develop a character.
◆ Develop an understanding of a character through script analysis and background research.
◆ Know the elements of theatrical production.

CHAPTER OUTLINE

Following are the main sections in this chapter.

I The Theatrical Experience
II Elements of Theatrical Production
III The Actor's Craft

      Chapter Review
      Student Speech

NEW SPEECH TERMS

In this chapter, you will learn the meanings of the speech terms listed below.

drama
Greek chorus
Thespian
dialogue
mask
Passion play
Noh theater
Kabuki
commedia
  dell'arte
improvisation
pantomime

Restoration
  theater
romanticism
epic theater
theatre of the
  absurd
proscenium
  stage
thrust stage
arena stage
set design
director
blocking

GENERAL VOCABULARY

Expanding your general vocabulary will help you become a more effective communicator. Listed below are some words appearing in this chapter that you should make part of your everyday vocabulary.

unison
remnant
incomprehensible
pretense
hypocrisy
monarchy

frivolity
alienation
calamitous
nuances
autism

LOOKING AHEAD

A theatrical event can be simple or elaborate, mildly amusing or profoundly moving, but must consist of both actor and audience. As the legendary actor John Barrymore once quipped, "My only regret in the theater is that I could never sit out front and watch me." The television and movie stars of today, on the other hand, can not only watch themselves, but can applaud their own performances.

In this chapter, you will learn what all of the applause is about. You will explore the actor's craft and elements of theatrical production. Before you begin making those entrances and exits, though, you need to understand the theatrical experience.

I The Theatrical Experience

Have you ever wanted to star in a blockbuster movie? Play a character in a popular television series? See your name up in lights on Broadway? Such are the dreams of many drama students. The truth is, however, that for each actor at an audition who gets a part, hundreds do not. Fortunately, other careers are available for students who have fallen in love with the art form of drama. Some career possibilities include drama teacher, children's theater director, scenic designer, costume designer, lighting designer, sound person, and makeup artist, to mention just a few.

Just what is drama? The terms *drama* and *theater* are often used interchangeably (in this text, for example), but it is useful to draw a distinction. **Drama** is a literary form that uses language and actions to relate a story of human conflict. *Theater,* strictly speaking, refers to the structure in which a play is performed. By extension, *theater* is often used to refer to the dramatic presentations that are performed live in theaters.

Of course, you may see the performance of a drama on television or at the movies. Indeed, if you are like most people, you probably have been exposed to many more hours of television and film than live theater. Yet live theater has been around centuries longer than either film or television. The earliest records of human activities suggest rituals that include all of the elements of theater today: a performance space, performers, masks or makeup, music, dance, and an audience.

The Greek philosopher Aristotle wrote in his *Poetics* that drama is a representation of human beings in action. Indeed, the word *drama* comes from the Greek word for action. We might think of this as suggesting not only the action that takes place on the stage between the actors but

COMMUNICATION   BREAKDOWN

Learning from Failure

August Wilson, a Pulitzer Prize–winning playwright, was born and raised on The Hill, a slum in Pittsburgh. Although he dropped out of school in the ninth grade, Wilson spent much time in the public library studying the works of African American writers. He then turned to writing as a way of fighting for social change. In an interview in 1987, Wilson was asked what he thought of American theater today. Wilson replied:

"For the most part, I've been disappointed in the work, even from some very talented playwrights. First, it's the influence of television. A whole generation of playwrights has been raised on television. I think it's a bad influence on theater, which in many ways is almost an archaic art form. I'm fearful it may go the way of opera, which is an elitist art, one that doesn't engage the larger society.

"Theater engages very few people. I don't think it has to be that way. I think it should be a part of everyone's life, the way television is. But it's not. It's moving the other way. As it costs more and more to produce plays, you see fewer and fewer. Fewer playwrights are given the opportunity to fail. You can learn immeasurably from a failure. You should at least be given the opportunity to bat—if you strike out, you strike out. The costs of production, the price of tickets, all of these things further remove theater from the people and make it an elitist art form, which I think is wrong."

Reprinted by permission from David Savran, In Their Own Words: Interviews with Contemporary Playwrights, *Theatre Communications Group (New York).*

Questions
1. Has television influenced your writing? How?
2. Do you agree with August Wilson that you "can learn immeasurably from failure"? In what ways?

also the *inter*action that takes place between the actors and the audience.

Theater, unlike film and television, involves a simultaneous relationship between live actors and audience members in the same room. When you attend the theater, you experience a sense of immediacy, a quality of lifelikeness. No camera directs your eye to what the director wants seen. Instead, you choose how you want to interact.

To fully appreciate the theatrical experience, though, you need to know some-

thing about the remarkable history of this art form. Understanding the history of theater consists of more than just knowing who William Shakespeare is. Theater's history is not separate from the rest of history; political, cultural, and religious histories are all interconnected and must be woven together to give us a sense of the past. In the past, theatrical events may have reflected a way of life or may have been the first signs of change in an old way of life. Many kings and queens felt threatened by the ideas contained in the

Strictly speaking, the term *theater* refers to the structure in which a play is performed.

plays. More than once, theater was banned, sometimes for centuries at a time. As you read the brief highlights of the history of theater that follow, remember that a relationship exists between the stories told by the playwrights, actors, and directors and the world in which they lived.

The history of formal theater begins in ancient Greece with festivals held three weeks out of every year to honor Dionysus, the Greek god of wine and fertile crops. These festivals were eagerly awaited. The audience was intensely involved and learned parts of the plays by heart.

The plays were written in verse, like poetry, but the verse was close to the patterns of normal speech. The lines were spoken in *unison* by a chorus of people. The **Greek chorus** consisted of members of the local population, and participation was considered a civic duty, much as voting is today. In fact, the plays became a forum for public discussion of social issues.

The plays were performed outdoors, and the audience sat on hillsides, which formed a bowl-shaped theater. If audience members became bored with the play they sometimes threw pebbles or fruit at the actors. The costumes were paid for by a tax on a rich citizen. The stage was bare, leaving the audience to imagine the scenes as painted by the spoken words.

There were no real "actors" in Greek theater until 534 B.C., when a man named Thespis stepped out of the chorus and spoke lines of his own. (Many schools have **Thespian** societies, groups of actors who take their name from Thespis, the first actor.) A second actor was added by the playwright Aeschylus, and a third by the playwright Sophocles. These additions provided the first opportunity for **dialogue,** or conversations between the actors. Playwrights could not write parts for too many actors because there was not enough money to pay them.

As it was, the actors had to play several parts during the performance. The actors, as well as the members of the chorus, wore **masks** on their faces, which helped the audience identify the various characters an actor portrayed. The masks were also built to help an actor project his voice.

Whereas the Greek theater was a forum for social discussion, the theater of the Middle Ages (roughly from A.D. 975 to A.D. 1453) was devoted to conserving tradition. Christian leaders used theater to teach the worship of Christianity's Holy Trinity and to stop the worship of pagan gods. The actors were clerics, such as priests, and their costumes were church vestments. The plays were performed inside the churches, with the altar as the focal point. The churches were not like the churches of today. Instead, they had wide open spaces where the actors and audience could move about freely.

One *remnant* of the theater of the Middle Ages can be found today in the Bavarian Alps in the small town of Oberammergau. To fulfill a pledge for having been spared during a period of widespread illness, the community performs the Passion play every ten years. The **Passion play** is a dramatic representation of the suffering, crucifixion, and resurrection of Christ. The play has become a part of family traditions and the same roles are handed down from generation to generation.

During the Middle Ages, theater was evolving in non-Western countries as well. In Japan, the **Noh theater** was similar to Greek theater in the use of a chorus and only a few actors. A typical Noh drama is

INSTANT IMPACT

All Croaked Up

If you were an actor in the Middle Ages with a throat ailment, the "cure" might have caused more discomfort than the disease. According to one author, Christine Ammer: "In the Middle Ages, throat infections, such as thrush, were treated by putting a live frog head first into the patient's mouth; by inhaling, the frog was believed to draw out the patient's infection into its own body. The treatment happily is obsolete, but its memory survives in the 19th Century term Frog in One's Throat, still used for a hoarseness due to phlegm or mucous."

Source: Christine Ammer, It's Raining Cats & Dogs . . . & Other Beastly Expressions, *Dell (New York): 1989, p. 210*

written as the journey of the main actor to a shrine or historic spot, where a lesson is learned. The plays taught Buddhist traditions. The Noh theater still exists in Japan today in much the same form. The actors' gestures and movements, which are highly symbolic, would have been easily understood by Japanese audiences of earlier times, but they are *incomprehensible* to the unschooled today.

Kabuki, another type of Japanese theater, first appeared in the seventeenth century. Similar in form to Noh theater, the Kabuki plays were different in content. Kabuki plays consisted of several acts made up of highly emotional incidents strung together in loosely connected scenes. Kabuki incorporated song, stylized speaking, and dance. Some plays include a chorus. According to Oscar G. Brockett, in his

Japanese Kabuki plays use song, dance, and stylized speaking to portray emotionally charged incidents.

book *The Essential Theater:* "The most popular of all Kabuki plays is Takedo Izumo's *Chushingura,* the eleven acts of which require a full day to perform. A play of honor and revenge, it tells how forty-seven faithful samurai [warriors] avenge the wrongs done to their master."

The European Renaissance, or rebirth, was the next major phase of theater history. It began in the fifteenth century and lasted into the seventeenth. During this period, theater evolved differently in each of the European nations. In Italy, a type of comedic theater called **commedia dell'arte** flourished. The plays were performed without a prewritten script. Instead, the actors played stock characters—that is, characters who represented specific types of people—and the play unfolded according to their unwritten but predictable attitudes and behaviors. The stock characters were of three types: lovers, masters, and servants. Interestingly, the servants, who figured prominently in the merry mix-ups, were called the *zanni* (the origin of the English word *zany*).

This approach to performing, in which the actors made up speeches, songs, dances, and pantomimes as they went along, is similar to the improvisations that you might see today. **Improvisation** is theater that relies on the inspiration of the moment and the response of the audience. **Pantomime,** a dramatic form of communication without words, may or may not be part of an improvisation.

Spain made an important contribution to theater during the Renaissance. It employed the first women to act in female roles. Prior to this innovation, female parts had been played by men.

French theater, quite literally, was shaped by its surroundings. As a reaction to unfair laws regulating the number of theaters, theater companies decided to transform unused tennis courts into performance areas. The stage was placed at one end of the court. Plays were written with the limitation of the long, narrow theatrical space in mind.

The leading French playwright of the time, Molière, wrote comedies poking fun at the *pretense* of the upper class. Often called the father of French comedy, he attacked the *hypocrisy* and vice in seventeenth-century French society.

Perhaps the most impressive legacy of the Renaissance came out of England.

William Shakespeare, the best-known playwright in history, wrote thirty-eight plays during the late sixteenth and early seventeenth centuries. He wrote comedies, tragedies, and historical plays. In reading Shakespeare today, you might believe the words must sound better when spoken by an Englishman. Yet the dialect of Shakespeare's England sounded remarkably like the dialect of the American South today.

As the Renaissance was ending, England was experiencing a significant political change. In 1649, King Charles I was beheaded, and from 1649 until 1660 the Commonwealth government, led by the Puritans, ruled the country. One of its actions was to close England's theaters. Soon after the death of Oliver Cromwell, leader of the Puritan government, the *monarchy* was restored in England, and a period known as the Restoration began.

As a reaction against the simplicity and restraint for which Puritanism stood, **Restoration theater** was marked by glittering displays of excessive behavior. Audiences attended plays not only to show support for the new government but to show themselves off. This period of *frivolity* ended in 1737. It was already drawing to a close when a play written by Henry Fielding so angered the government of the day that a licensing act was imposed. This act meant that plays would be censored and the number of theaters in operation restricted.

At the end of the eighteenth century, around the time of the American and French revolutions and England's Industrial Revolution, a revolution began to take shape in the theater as well. During this period—the period of **romanticism**—playwrights were no longer bound by rules and conventions of how plays should be written. They did not want to pattern

INSTANT IMPACT

Not Prince Hamlet

In her book *No Turn Unstoned*, Diana Rigg gathers together a treasure trove of awful theatrical reviews. What follows is some of the worst the critics have had to say about actors taking on the challenge of Shakespeare's Hamlet.

◆ Richard Briers, while at the Royal Academy of Dramatic Arts, reviewed by W. A. Darlington in the *Daily Telegraph*:

Richard Briers last night played Hamlet like a demented typewriter. Richard comments, "I may not have been a great Hamlet but I was about the fastest."

◆ Esme Percy, Royal Court, February, 1930, reviewed by James Agate:

When Hamlet debates the question of being or not being, we ought to feel that the matter has been vexing his bosom ever since his father died. . . . Percy did not take up arms against his sea of troubles so much as bob up and down upon them like a cork.

◆ Albert Finney, Old Vic, 1975, reviewed by Jason Hillgate in *Theatre*:

Finney's roughneck Hamlet is no prince at all, let alone a sweet prince. More of a "Spamlet" really.

their plays after works of the past whose concerns and subject matter were not relevant for their day. Thus, romanticism emphasized the imagination and emotions over intellect and reason. Perhaps the best

William Shakespeare wrote 38 plays, consisting of histories like Richard II, pictured here, as well as comedies and tragedies.

known romantic play is Edmond Rostand's *Cyrano de Bergerac*, written in 1897, near the end of this time period.

Next came a shift toward realism (first recognized during the 1850s), in which the subject matter for the plays came from real life. Realist playwrights believed theater should reflect life, not only in subject matter but also in the approach to acting and the stage settings and costumes. Furthermore, the concept of realism did not apply only to new productions. Performances of Shakespeare were being staged that, for the first time, attempted to accurately recreate the historical time period in which the plays were set.

In the twentieth century, Bertolt Brecht, a German playwright, viewed theater as a way to reveal important social and political messages. Brecht's views developed in Germany during the 1920s into what is known as **epic theater.** Brecht believed an audience should not passively soak up social messages from a play and assume the messages are true. He wanted audiences to think critically about the messages and then work to bring about the needed changes in society. Consequently, he preferred his audiences to keep in mind that they were watching a play, so they would be less likely to believe whatever was put before them. For this reason, he believed plays should be staged not in a way that imitated real life but in a way that revealed the "realness" of the stage area. The actors acted on a bare platform, and the light sources were visible to the audience.

A somewhat later twentieth-century development was the theater of the absurd. This movement reflected attempts to come to some understanding of the terrible devastation that occurred during World War II. In the **theatre of the absurd,** human existence is viewed as meaningless, and

COMMUNICATION   BREAKTHROUGH

The Show Must Go On

In 1937, John Houseman and Orson Welles produced Marc Blitztein's "play with music," *The Cradle Will Rock*. The rehearsals of this production took place in the midst of much protest: riots in Akron and Pontiac and strikes halting work in the Chrysler and Hudson auto plants. The arts projects of the WPA, including Blitztein's play, were affected by these national disturbances. As the play went into final rehearsals, Houseman and Welles were notified that the New York opening of their new play would be prohibited because of the social unrest.

After the doors of their theater were locked, Houseman and Welles promised the opening night audience that the play would go on even if Blitztein had to perform it alone. Next, they managed to persuade a friend to let them into the Venice Theater. It cost them a $100 bribe, which was paid with money borrowed from members of the press. As they led the parade from 39th Street to the Venice, the size of the audience tripled. The actors, in doubt as to whether they would be performing or watching, sat with the audience members. By curtain time, there was standing room only.

After Houseman and Welles described to the audience what they would not be seeing that night, Blitztein began to set the scene—"A Street Corner, Steeltown USA"— as he played an untuned upright piano. In his memoir *Unfinished Business*, Houseman recalls what happened next:

> Within a few seconds Marc became aware that he was not singing alone. To his strained tenor another voice, a faint, wavering soprano, had been added. It took [a] hand-held spotlight a few seconds to locate the source of that second voice: it came to rest on the lower stage-right box in which a frail girl in a green dress with red-dyed hair was standing glassy-eyed, stiff with fear, only half-audible at first in that huge theatre but gathering strength with every note. It is almost impossible, at this distance in time, to convey the throat-catching, sickeningly exciting quality of that moment or to describe the emotions of gratitude and love with which we saw and heard that slim green figure. Her name was Olive Stanton; she had been cast as "the Moll" almost by default and I knew that she was entirely dependent on the weekly cheque she was receiving from the WPA.

> One by one, the actors stood up from their chairs and said their lines—although a few declined, not wishing to risk their livelihood in such difficult times. Replacements for the missing actors were found spontaneously, and scenes were improvised at various locations in the audience. The audience members found themselves turning their heads as if at a tennis match. By the final, triumphal climax of the play, "they were all on their feet, singing and shouting from all over the theatre . . . *The Cradle Will Rock*."

Source: John Houseman, Unfinished Business, *Chatto & Windus (London): 1986, pp. 128–138.*

Questions

1. If you had been an actor in the 1937 production of *The Cradle Will Rock*, would you have risked your livelihood to make sure that the show went on?

2. How much responsibility do playwrights have to address social problems in their works for the stage?

language loses its ability to communicate. The meaninglessness of life is demonstrated by the meaninglessness of the play. The major dramatists—Samuel Beckett, Jean Genet, and Eugène Ionesco—attempt to explore people's helplessness in a senseless universe. Because they portray this helplessness in a detached and critical way, the theater of the absurd has been described as the theater of *alienation.*

TAKING CHARGE

Contemporary writers often borrow the successful plots of their predecessors. The award-winning musical *West Side Story,* for example, takes Shakespeare's *Romeo and Juliet* to the streets of New York City. A few years ago, the comedian Steve Martin updated Rostand's *Cyrano de Bergerac* in the film *Roxanne.* Martin lifted some of Cyrano's most eloquent lines and revised them for his leading man, C. D. Bales.

After studying the famous speech in which Cyrano, as a response to an insult, satirizes the size of his own nose, try—as Martin did—to use humor to your advantage. Write three of your own responses as if someone had said to you, "Your nose is . . . um . . . very big."

A sample excerpt from *Cyrano de Bergerac:*

Descriptive: 'It's a rock, a peak, a cape! No, more than a cape: a peninsula!'
Gracious: 'What a kind man you are! You love birds so much that you've given them a perch to roost on.'
Military: 'The enemy is charging! Aim your cannon!'
Admiring: 'What a sign for a perfume shop!'
Rustic: 'That don't look like no nose to me. It's either a big cucumber or a little watermelon.'

A sample excerpt from *Roxanne:*

Polite: 'Would you mind not bobbing your head? The orchestra keeps changing tempo.'
Inquiring: 'When you stop and smell the flowers, are they afraid?'
Punctual: 'All right, Delman, your nose was on time but you were fifteen minutes late!'
Complimentary: 'You must love the little birdies to give them this to perch on.'
Meteorological: 'Everybody take cover; she's going to blow!'

Ⅱ Elements of Theatrical Production

As you have seen, the theatrical experience has varied widely from one period to another and from one society to another. Now we'll turn our attention to what is involved in the creation of a play. If you and your friends were to put on a play, you would need to know and understand the different elements of production, such as setting, lighting, sound, and costumes.

Throughout history, different elements of production were stressed at different times. For example, in the United States during the late 1800s, elaborate stage settings were common, while in contemporary drama it is not uncommon to have the stage left bare. Regardless of how the elements are used, they all work together to tell us something. These elements reinforce the intent of the play: to make us laugh or cry or think. The setting, lighting, sound, and costumes communicate specific details about the play, and they can tell us as much about the plot of the play as the dialogue.

The Script

The elements of any given production are based on the script of the play. A play is very different from most other kinds of literature. Most novels, for example, provide a complete picture of what is happening at any particular time. The playwright, however, will often leave important details out. The reason for these omissions is that most plays are complete experiences only when they appear on the stage. The script, while it is the basis for all decisions related to the production, is really nothing more than a series of clues from which to begin work on the elements of production. A script tells us the time period in which the play is set, the time of day it is, how many people are on stage, and so on. With this information, the elements of production are shaped.

The Stage

The size and shape of the house (where the audience sits) and the stage often contribute to the experience of the theater, even though they are not necessarily formal elements of production. The house's size can range from a Greek hillside theater's capacity for thousands of spectators to some small, intimate houses of today that seat only twenty.

The audience's relation to the stage will also shape the theatrical experience. A **proscenium stage** is the traditional type of stage. It has essentially two rooms, one for the audience and one for the performers, with a large hole in the common wall through which the audience views the play. This type of stage is also known as a *picture-frame stage*, since the audience has the feeling of observing the action as if looking at a picture.

A **thrust stage** has a back wall and places the audience on the other three sides of the stage, instead of just in front. Because the stage juts out into the audience, the audience feels much more a part of the action. In an **arena stage,** an even more intimate relationship is established by placing the actors in the midst of the audience. Typically, the seating is a

The costumes worn by actors onstage reveal a great deal about the characters being portrayed, including age, occupation, and social status.

bleacherlike arrangement on four sides of the acting area. Therefore, all elements of theatrical production are viewed from every angle.

The Set Design

The **set design** is a plan for the organization and appearance of the acting space. It is used to establish the location where the action takes place. Without even knowing what a play is about, we expect much different events to take place in the big halls of a mansion than in the close quarters of a poor man's shack. Often, the set design reveals aspects of the characters: What kind of books are on the bookshelves? Do the characters surround themselves with modern furniture or antiques? The physical details of the set can suggest the emotional mind-set of the characters who interact within the space.

The Lighting Design

The lighting designer uses light or the absence of it to further create mood. A brighter, more intensely lighted set might be used to illuminate a festive, outdoor picnic, whereas a much more somber, gloomy atmosphere could be created by the darker, more shadowy lighting of a cobweb-filled cellar. Gels, or pieces of acetate, of varying colors can be placed in the lighting instrument to assist in the creation of atmosphere. For example, an orange gel would give the light a warmness, suggesting perhaps a summer day. Blue gels cast a cooler light and are often used to create the illusion of moonlight. In addition to creating mood, lights are used to draw the audience's attention from one part of the stage to another. You must not forget, however, that at the very least, the lighting design should assist the audience in seeing both the set and the actor's movements within it.

The Costumes

The clothing, or costumes, worn onstage, as in life, tell us a great deal about the people wearing them. Costumes may tell us the jobs the wearers have, their ages, and their social status, among many other things. There are differences between what a bag lady and a queen might wear; these stylistic differences are shown to the audience through the costumes. Often, costumes may not reveal the "truth" about the character but may instead show what the character wants us to believe about himself or herself.

The Sound Effects

Like the costumes, set, and lighting designs, the sound effects become important in communicating the meaning of a play. The sounds—a heavy rainstorm, a door slamming shut, a telephone ringing—all add to the action onstage and are usually suggested by the script. Imagine the different responses an audience might have to a scene portraying children camping in the wilderness if the sound accompanying the scene were wolves howling instead of crickets chirping.

The Director

The **director** is responsible for putting all of the elements of a theatrical production together. The director accomplishes this task by:

1. Interpreting the chosen script.
2. Casting the actors.
3. Working with the designers.

4. Rehearsing the actors.

In casting the actors, the director tries to match the demands of a particular role to the potential of a particular actor. Once the play is cast, rehearsals begin. The director's goal is to help the actors explore and develop their characters. A good director listens to suggestions and adapts to the needs of her cast as she brings the script to life on stage.

You are probably familiar with the need to rehearse the actors, but an equally important function of the director is to hold production meetings with the set designer, costume designer, and lighting designer. These people meet to discuss their interpretation of the script and to make sure each of them is moving toward a common goal. In these meetings, director and designers work to solve whatever technical problems might have arisen.

During production meetings, the set designer will show a floor plan of the set to the director. Once potential problems with the plan have been addressed, a miniature model is constructed to give the director an even clearer sense of what the stage will look like. In the beginning, any changes that might have to be made can be made quickly and inexpensively. After the real set is constructed, changes become more difficult to make.

Next, the lighting designer draws up a diagram that shows how the stage will be lit. At this time, specific lighting effects will be discussed—perhaps, for example, how to light the set so that, to the audience, the light appears to come from a single candle on a table.

The costume designer will prepare detailed drawings of each costume to be worn in the play. Swatches of the actual material to be used will be shown to the director as well.

Many plays take place during time periods about which we know little. Those involved in the production have an implied responsibility to accurately depict life during the era being portrayed. As a result, much library research is needed to ensure that the costumes and set design do reflect the way people lived and dressed.

TAKING CHARGE

John Guare is a contemporary playwright whose scripts have received much critical acclaim, including the New York Drama Critics Circle Award. His play *Six Degrees of Separation* was described by Frank Rich of the *New York Times* as "magical . . . a masterwork." The following excerpt, which explains the title of the play, also demonstrates Guare's gift as a scriptwriter.

I read somewhere that everybody on this planet is separated by only six other people. Six degrees of separation. Between us and everybody else on this planet. The president of the United States. A gondolier in Venice. Fill in the names. I find that (A) tremendously comforting that we're so close and (B) like Chinese water torture that we're so close. Because you have to find the right six people to make the connection. It's not just big names. It's anyone. A native in a rain forest. A Tierra del Fuegan. An Eskimo. I am bound to everyone on this planet by a trail of six people. It's a profound thought . . . How every person is a new door, opening up into other worlds. Six degrees of separation between me and everyone else on this planet. But to find the right six people.

Now it's your turn. Write and deliver a brief monologue—a speech by one performer—in which you describe "the right six people" and how you found them. This exercise in scriptwriting challenges you to create six imaginary characters that have a connection to you and to each other.

III The Actor's Craft

Although the experience of theater is made up of all of the elements of production, the actor's role on the stage is perhaps the most crucial. The lights, costumes, and set design enhance the experience, but it is through the actor that the action, or drama, takes place. To understand the process through which the actor prepares for a role, we must examine the tools with which an actor works—the actor's body, voice, and imagination—and then look at how the actor uses them to develop a character.

Body and voice are the instruments through which the actor reaches the audience. When you see actors who seem to play themselves over and over again, often it is because their "tools" are not sharp enough. Audience members see physical behavior and hear voice patterns that remind them of the individual actor and not the character in the play. Spencer Tracy once quipped that acting was easy, you just have to know your lines and avoid bumping into the furniture. In truth, though, professional actors who have reached a high level of achievement often have spent years training their instruments so that they may be able to respond to the demands of their characters. Actors must practice the use of their voices and bodies just as an opera singer must practice singing scales so that when the music requires her to sing a high note, she can reach it without difficulty.

The Actor's Body

An actor's body needs to be in shape. This is not to say that if you want to be an actor you will have to work out in a gym. The characters in plays come in all shapes and sizes, so it would not be useful if all of the men looked like bodybuilders or all of the women like supermodels. Instead, your body is in shape when it is free from excess muscular tension. This does not mean that it is like a wet noodle. What it does mean is that you eliminate your own physical habits so that you can begin to create the physical habits of a new character. In effect, you lose your own tensions to better take on the tensions of another character.

In general, the methods actors use to train their bodies are grouped together and called movement classes. Dance and acrobatic classes help you learn to become

Drama ultimately takes place through the actor, who reaches the audience through body, voice, and imagination.

more expressive with your body. Martial arts classes teach you the connection between mind and body. Many formal training programs take place in rooms with mirrors, where you would use a white expressionless mask, or neutral mask, to cover your face so that your body would become more noticeable. After you had become aware of your physical habits by observing yourself, you would put on various character masks. These masks have many expressions, such as happy, sad, and angry. You would look in the mirror and create the physical body appropriate for the expression on the mask.

There are many other kinds of movement classes, but their goals are the same: to help you, the actor, better create the physical character required by the script.

The Actor's Voice

Voice is as important as body in the communication of a character to an audience. As an actor, you must be concerned with several aspects of vocal production, including volume, flexibility, and energy.

When deciding on volume level, remember that your voice must be heard without difficulty to the very last row of the audience. The goal is more than just being loud, though. With the proper breath support behind it, a whispering sound will be easily heard.

In addition, you must form each sound of a word completely. Good diction—the manner of uttering or pronouncing words—will aid an audience in understanding the dialogue.

Your voice must also have flexibility—the ability to alter pitch (high and low tones) and rate of delivery. Along with volume, flexibility helps in communicating the emotions of a character.

Your energy level is related to volume in that your breath support must be sufficient to prevent you from running out of breath at the ends of words or sentences. If you appear to be pushing or straining to get all of the words out, the audience quickly forgets about the character in the play and instead worries that you may be hurting your throat.

An actor must also work to eliminate regionalisms, sounds common to particular parts of the country, such as the southern drawl. These could prevent you from creating a voice appropriate to the character. As with the body, the idea is to avoid forcing your physical and vocal mannerisms on the character.

The Actor's Imagination

The third tool you have as an actor is your imagination. Acting is behaving as if you were the character in the specific circumstances of the play. Acting is not lying; it is believing that you are, on one level, telling the truth. Of course, everyone involved in the production knows that it is not real but joins with the audience in the suspension of disbelief. That is, with the actor's help, audience members are willing to believe in the people and places created on the stage.

In creating a new reality, you always begin with the script. Through the script, the playwright provides the answers to the basic questions of who, what, where, and when. You must always create a character in the way in which the playwright intended, following the clues from the script. If you find yourself asking, "What would I do in this situation?" you are only partly correct. A better question would be, "What would I do if I were the character in this situation?"

For each line spoken onstage, an actor must understand what the character hopes to accomplish as a result of speaking. This is called the intention, or objective, behind the line. What your character wants drives you into action throughout the play. You must be careful not just to say, "I am angry" or "I want to be angry." Instead, you must say, "I want to slam my fists down on the table." An audience might not be able to understand an actor who tries to be angry, but if you slam your fists down on the table, the audience has little doubt about how to interpret that action.

The actions that you use to establish or identify a given character are called business. You should look at a script in terms of what business the character must do to fulfill his objective. Does he, for example, pick up the telephone, stare out the window, sip from a cup of tea? Additionally, most play scripts indicate through stage directions some general suggestions for movement—for example, exits and entrances. The director of the play gives the actor other directions for movement. These directions are referred to as **blocking.**

The interest in a play comes from a character struggling to accomplish his goals in spite of the physical or psychological obstacles that stand in his way. Understanding this fundamental principle—that all drama is conflict—is a necessary prerequisite for preparing any role.

The process of building a character takes time. One way to add depth to your character is to supply your character with an imaginary background. The events suggested in the script become only one part of the life of your character. What did the character like to do as a small child? What kinds of relationships did the character have with her grandparents, parents, and teachers? What does the character like to eat? And so on.

Using your imagination, you can add to the believability of the character by creating that character's history. Your job is to continually ask questions about the character and the character's life. You might not even be able to answer some of the questions you ask, but you give the character depth by having asked them.

The idea of creating an imaginary history is also important when you exit or enter a scene. Where are you going? Where have you been? By creating vivid pictures of these places in your mind, you create for your character an imaginary world, and the audience is left with the impression that that imaginary world never ends.

The Actor's Relationships

An actor rarely acts onstage alone. By examining the script, you learn about your relationships with other characters. Again, asking questions about past histories can help create the illusion that the relationships with the other characters did not just begin when the characters met onstage in performance. During rehearsals, you should explore the relationships with the other characters through the dialogue. Furthermore, it is especially important that you remember to talk with the other characters, not at them. You need to be more concerned with reacting to their lines than with acting your own lines. In this way, your attempts to achieve your own goals become more convincing to the audience.

The Actor's Preparation

Often, actors are asked how they memorize all of their lines. Many of them learn the lines by going through the process of understanding what the character wants, or what the character's intentions are. The dialogue becomes a way for the character to obtain this goal, and with the goal in mind, the lines follow naturally. The actor Jason Robards, Jr., describes the process: "You only do a little section, then you put it together with the other parts. Then it falls apart. But the next time it

COMMUNICATION WORKS

Devon Raymond, Professional Actor

"You have to go beyond the script," says professional actor Devon Raymond. "You shouldn't invent something that's not consistent with what the playwright intended, so you use the script as a blueprint and fill in the rest of the colors. You build a character from the blueprint."

Raymond received her theatrical training from the Juilliard School of Drama in New York City and has spent the years since her graduation working in theater and film.

Raymond recognizes the importance of library research in helping to create a character. She uses it not only to learn the facts surrounding the setting of the play but also to gain a "sense of the daily existence of people in that time period." Certain books, such as biographies, are particularly useful to Raymond. She uses the personal experiences found in the biographies, the small details of someone's life, to add depth and believability to her characters.

Another way Raymond adds depth to her characters is by determining "what it is that they do every day." She thinks about how their activities might affect them physically. For example, one character she recently portrayed worked in a laundry. As a result of her work in a laundry, her character's hands might be chapped and not bend easily. Her back might have a hunch to it from bending over all day, and so on. This information helps Raymond get the "feel" of her character.

Real-life observation also plays a large part in building a character. "What you understand about people in real life is taken onto the stage with you," says Raymond. She will watch other people to capture the small *nuances* of their lives. For example, she might try to recreate on stage the patterns of conversation she has observed. She has noticed that individuals who are in a conversation do not always talk out loud to each other. There may be periods of silence as one person thinks about what to say next. When she is onstage, she tries to remember what she has learned and not be afraid to let there be silences in the dialogue when they are appropriate. "I store away my observations in my mind," states Raymond, "for use in developing characters in the future."

doesn't fall apart so much. Acting is like playing the piano . . . finally a note falls into place."

Often, the real significance of the dialogue is not in the information obtained from the lines but in the meaning behind the lines, which is called the subtext. The subtext helps you create an inner monologue. You, the actor, should work to have an inner monologue always running through your mind while onstage. This monologue consists of the character's

INSTANT IMPACT

Those Icy Fingers . . .

Sir Laurence Olivier, a legend of the theater, often felt the icy fingers that choke off an actor's voice—stage fright. In describing one *calamitous* attack during his opening as Solness in Ibsen's *The Master Builder*, Olivier admitted, "My courage sank and with each succeeding minute it became less possible to resist this horror."

Although his voice faded and his throat constricted, Olivier managed to struggle through the remainder of the performance. How did he keep going? Olivier was more afraid of a career-ending scandal than his torment of the moment. Surprisingly, this episode of stage fright occurred in 1965 at the height of Olivier's fame.

thoughts. It helps you concentrate on a scene even when you might not have many lines to say. It also works to keep an audience involved in the play; the audience will find interesting whatever you find interesting. Remember, however, that an inner monologue is the thoughts running through the character's mind, not the actor's. You should be concerned only about carrying out your character's stage tasks.

Through the action of your character, you help the audience understand the basic meaning of the play. Even if you do not realize it, everything you do communicates a message. In a theatrical performance, the task is to put all of the various elements of production together in such a way as to communicate the message intended.

TAKING CHARGE

When Dustin Hoffman was preparing for the role of Ray in *Rain Man*, he spent much time studying people with *autism*. Meryl Streep confides that she "copies specific people in specific circumstances." Successful actors do their homework.

Now it's your turn. While not in school, observe strangers going about their daily activities. Take notes. Shopping malls provide a number of opportunities to see people from various walks of life, from sales clerks to security guards. Write an imaginary background for one of these persons that is consistent with the actions you observe and that you could use to develop a character.

STUDENT SPEECH

While still a high school student at Milton Academy in Milton, Massachusetts, David Abaire began his career as a playwright by using his classmates to stage his works. This monologue was taken from his play *A Show of Hands*. The character, Dana, is twenty-two. He recalls an event during his childhood that changed his life.

My father had a . . . had a birthmark shaped like the Statue of Liberty on his left shoulder. This made him extraordinary. There was a magazine called *Epiderm Quarterly*, which actually only came out twice a year, and I thought that that was a little strange since it was called a quarterly. . . . But . . . they were doing this story on America's most intriguing skin blemishes. They decided to go into the heartland of America to look for these fascinating facial warts and . . . and . . . fissures, and things. So, somehow they got ahold of my father, flew him to New York City, and took pictures of him up in the torch, exposing his birthmark and waving an American flag. On his way back to the hotel, crossing Lexington Avenue, he was struck and killed by a checkered taxi cab. The summer issue of *Epiderm Quarterly* came out in August, my father on page thirty-four, next to a woman from Tuscaloosa whose freckles formed an exact map of three star constellations on her back. Big Bear, Little Dipper, and Orion. It was my father's one shining moment in life. I was twelve years old.

REVIEW AND ENRICHMENT

LOOKING BACK

Listed below are the major ideas discussed in this chapter.

✦ The earliest records of human activity suggest rituals that include all of the elements of theater today: a performance space, performers, masks or makeup, music, dance, and an audience.

✦ Drama, the Greek word for action, suggests not only the action that takes place on the stage between the actors but also the interaction that takes place between the actors and the audience.

✦ The history of formal theater begins in ancient Greece.

✦ The first real actor was Thespis. A second actor was added by Aeschylus, and a third by Sophocles, which provided the opportunity for dialogue.

✦ Whereas the Greek theater was a forum for social discussion, theater of the Middle Ages was devoted to conserving tradition.

✦ Noh and Kabuki were two forms of theater that developed in Japan.

✦ During the European Renaissance, a type of comedic theater called commedia dell'arte flourished in Italy.

✦ Spain employed the first women to act female roles.

✦ The most important legacy of the Renaissance came out of England. William Shakespeare, the best-known playwright in history, wrote thirty-eight plays during this time.

✦ From 1649 until 1660, the Commonwealth government, led by the Puritans, closed theaters in England. After the death of Oliver Cromwell, the Puritan leader, a period known as the Restoration began.

✦ During the period of romanticism, playwrights were no longer bound by the rules and conventions of how plays should be written.

✦ In the twentieth century, some playwrights viewed theater as a way to reveal important social and political messages.

✦ The theater of the absurd reflected attempts to come to some understanding of the terrible devastation that occurred during World War II.

✦ The setting, lighting, sound, and costumes communicate specific details about the play, and they can tell us as much about the plot of the play as the dialogue.

✦ The elements of any production are based on the script of the play.

✦ Three types of stages are proscenium, thrust, and arena stages.

✦ The set design is used to establish the location where the action takes place.

✦ The lighting designer uses light or the absence of it to create mood.

✦ The clothing, or costumes, worn onstage may tell us the jobs the wearers have, their ages, and their social status, among other things.

◆ Like the costumes, set, and lighting designs, the sound effects become important in communicating the meaning of a play.
◆ The director is responsible for putting all of the elements of a theatrical production together.
◆ Although the experience of theater is made up of all the elements of production, the actor's role on the stage is perhaps the most crucial.
◆ The actor's body, voice, and imagination are the tools used to develop a character.
◆ Effective vocal production requires volume, flexibility, and energy.
◆ An actor must have imagination. Acting is not lying; it is believing that you are, on one level, telling the truth.
◆ Through the action of the characters, the audience comes to understand the basic meaning of the play.

SPEECH VOCABULARY

Match the speech term on the left with the definition on the right.

1. dialogue
2. romanticism
3. theatre of the absurd
4. drama
5. thrust stage
6. proscenium stage
7. set design
8. Noh theatre
9. blocking
10. director

a. picture-frame stage
b. conversations between the actors
c. plan for organization of the acting space
d. emphasized imagination and emotions
e. responsible for putting all of the elements together
f. viewed human existence as meaningless
g. arranging the actors' movements
h. Greek word for action
i. Japanese drama
j. places the audience on three sides

GENERAL VOCABULARY

Look up the words in the following list. Write down a definition for each and use it in a sentence.

unison
remnant
incomprehensible
pretense

hypocrisy
monarchy
frivolity
alienation

calamitous
nuances
autism

| REVIEW AND ENRICHMENT |
| Continued |

THINGS TO REMEMBER

1. The history of formal theater begins in ancient Greece with festivals held to honor _____, the Greek god of wine and fertile crops.
2. There were no real "actors" in Greek theater until 534 B.C. when a man named _____ stepped out of the chorus and spoke lines of his own.
3. _____ was the first country to employ women to act in female roles.
4. The best-known romantic play is Edmond Rostand's _____.
5. Bertolt Brecht's ideas developed in Germany during the 1920s into what is known as _____ theater.
6. In the theater of the absurd, human existence is viewed as _____.
7. Name three types of staging.
8. *Six Degrees of Separation* was written by _____.
9. The _____ is responsible for putting all of the elements of a theatrical production together.
10. The actor's _____ and _____ are the instruments through which he or she reaches the audience.

THINGS TO DO

1. Choose a play. Study the play and determine what technical elements would be necessary to stage a production. For example, what time of day, what setting, what pieces of furniture might be appropriate? What costumes might the various characters wear?
2. Divide the class into pairs. Find a monologue in a play and have one student be the director and the other be the actor. Rehearse and then present the scenes to the rest of the class for their critiques.
3. Have two students improvise the interaction of two people who are waiting for the bus. Add another classmate to the scene, and then another. Students should feel free to go in and out of the scene as they wish. Other possibilities for scenes include a supermarket, a park, and a pet store.

THINGS TO TALK ABOUT

1. Should the drama teacher at a high school choose weaker plays with more roles for students over better plays with fewer parts?
2. It has been said that "there are no small parts, only small actors." Do you agree? Disagree? Why?
3. Many students never audition for a play because they believe they can't act. What would you say to these students to encourage their involvement in theater?

THINGS TO WRITE ABOUT

1. Pick an important period in theater history and write an essay on a specific topic of your choosing. For example, you might research the role of improvisation in commedia dell'arte.
2. Michael Kinsley, in an essay in *Time* magazine, speculated on what would happen if Shakespeare could have written television commercials. Lady MacBeth might have washed the blood from her hands as she turned to the camera and said, "And out it came, thanks to pure Ivory soap!" After selecting a popular product, write a commercial in the style of Shakespeare.
3. Create a monologue for a character who has just transferred to your school from a rival school. Explore the inevitable conflicts that this new student would face on the first day.

CRITICAL THINKING

1. The playwright August Wilson warns that theater might become an elitist art form. He blames many factors, including the influence of television, high production costs, and ticket prices. What do you think can be done to engage more people in supporting theater as an art form for everyone?
2. Many actors are reluctant to do nude scenes. Others find it difficult to portray characters whose values conflict with their own. If you are only "acting," how do you decide where to draw the line?

3. If a play teaches the audience about a moment in history, then do those presenting the play have the responsibility to stage the play as it was originally intended? For example, would it be wrong to change *My Fair Lady* into a vehicle for the promotion of rap music?

RELATED SPEECH TOPICS

Regional theater: the future of drama
How to audition
The history of theater in your high
  school
Careers in theater
Method acting

American musicals
Off-off Broadway
Technical theater
Mimes
Masks
Kabuki theater

CHAPTER 21

Radio

"It has been said that of all the peoples in the world, Americans, with their millions of television and radio sets, stand in great fear of a moment of silence."

— **Anonymous**

"You were supposed to use the sound effects record for the fireworks."

LEARNING OBJECTIVES

After completing this chapter, you will be able to do the following.

◆ Describe how radio has functioned as a social force in our nation's history.

◆ Explain the various jobs needed to run a radio station.

◆ Demonstrate effective delivery techniques for reading scripts over the air.

◆ Write a thirty-second commercial or public service announcement.

CHAPTER OUTLINE

Following are the main sections in this chapter.

I The World of Radio

II Running a Radio Station

III Performing and Writing Techniques

Student Speech

Chapter Review

NEW SPEECH TERMS

In this chapter, you will learn the meanings of the speech terms listed below.

mass media	audio console
wireless	inputs
air	outputs
networks	VU meters
narrowcast	pots
deejay	announcer
playlists	general manager
AM	program director
FM	traffic director
music radio	copywriter
news/talk radio	continuity
full-service radio	sales manager
cart	chief engineer
format	music bed

GENERAL VOCABULARY

Expanding your general vocabulary will help you become a more effective communicator. Listed below are some words appearing in this chapter that you should make part of your everyday vocabulary.

aptly	landmark
fledgling	parity
bedlam	fidelity
niches	phonetic
superseded	

LOOKING AHEAD

Radio is probably as much a part of your daily life as waking up (to a clock radio, of course) or riding to school (with your radio's volume cranked up and the rear speakers blaring). An electronic companion that goes where you go, radio keeps you up-to-date on news, sports, weather, and a host of other information, not to mention your favorite music.

Today, there are more radio stations and listeners than ever. In this chapter, we examine the history of radio, how radio stations operate, and some production and writing techniques you can master.

1 The World of Radio

Teenagers are perhaps the most important group of radio listeners in America. Arbitron (the company that compiles radio ratings) says its surveys show that about 97 percent of teens aged twelve through seventeen listen to the radio at least once a week. "Radio is simply a part of their daily lives," concluded one study.

Some business leaders have learned that radio may be the best way to talk to teens. "The film *New Jack City* is a great example of a successful marketing campaign," says Warrington Hudlin, president of the Black Filmmakers Foundation. "The marketers used heavy radio, which makes the most sense with teens." Teens heard about the movie on the radio and helped make it a hit.

Not only is radio immensely popular with teens, but it is the most universal of all the **mass media**—the means of communication that can reach large audiences. Nowhere is there a patch of land or stretch of ocean so remote that it cannot be reached by radio signals beamed from more than 26,000 stations worldwide. Over a third of those stations are located in the United States, where nearly every home has at least one radio. In fact, with 500 million radios nationwide, we have twice as many radios as people.

Radio can swiftly take you to the outer reaches of your imagination. It can put a circus, the Super Bowl, or a rock concert between your ears. Radio provides the sounds, and you provide the rest. Consider this: A team of experts would need months to create the following commercial for television. Two people in a radio studio could do it in minutes:

> "Fred, we're here today on the shores of Lake Michigan to witness an incredible demonstration."
>
> "Yes, that's right, Frank. A team of scientists is about to create the world's largest cup of hot chocolate."
>
> "It looks like they have just begun. Let's listen."
>
> (Sounds of Lake Michigan being emptied— water sucked down the drain.)
>
> "Amazing, isn't it? Look at that mud!"
>
> (Sounds of someone stepping into and out of mud.)

"Look at this, Frank. Hundreds of tankers are pulling up to the shore."

"If I don't miss my guess, Fred, they're loaded with hot chocolate."

(Sounds of tankers rolling to a stop, then pumping liquid.)

"Look at the steam rise. And hey, what's that?"

"We're scheduled to have a fleet of crop dusting planes fly over next and they're loaded with whipped topping. Here they come."

(Sounds of planes flying over and then sound of whipped cream can shooting out cream.)

"That's quite a sight. A mountain of cream on top of a lake of steaming hot chocolate. What's next?"

(Sound of helicopter overhead.)

"This is the best of all, Fred. That whirlybird is towing an enormous cherry. It must weigh five hundred pounds. I think he's going to drop it any minute. There it goes . . ."

(Sound of giant cherry plummeting from high altitude; sound of enormous cherry landing on whipped topping.)

"Well, there you have it. Another world first for radio."

Radio's special effects—simple and yet completely convincing—give listeners a feeling of being right where the action is.

Radio is probably a vital part of your life, bringing you the latest in music and keeping you up-to-date on local and national news. Radio is also a constant companion, staying with you while you wash your car, do the laundry, or struggle with your homework. What you may not realize is that radio also offers some of the best opportunities to enter a broadcasting career. Many young people have found that a part-time job at a radio station eventually led to full-time work as a deejay or to a position in television. In this section, we will discuss how radio devel-

oped and why it has become such an important and popular medium.

What Radio Does Best

Radio has a number of significant advantages over other forms of communication.

◆ Radios are portable, cheap, and handy. You can take them wherever you go. In times of extreme danger, such as blizzards, tornadoes, and floods, they can save lives.

◆ In emergencies, radio keeps people in touch with what's happening.

◆ Radio news coverage is fast and adaptable. When a major news event occurs, radio can get the story first. Reporters armed only with cellular phones can be on the air instantly. Television reports require heavier, bulkier equipment, and most TV stations have limited resources for remote broadcasts. Radio, on the other hand, can go just about anywhere quickly.

◆ You can listen to your radio while you are busy with other activities: driving, working, cleaning house, sunbathing, even trying half-heartedly to wake up. It's harder to be quite so free while watching television or talking on the telephone.

Marconi's Magic

Radio is a relatively recent invention. In fact, you probably know someone who can remember a time before radio was in widespread use. The idea of radio was born in the 1860s, when James Maxwell, a Scottish physicist, discovered that electric

In 1895, young Italian inventor Guglielmo Marconi, pictured here, sent and received the first radio signals. Early radios were bulky boxes listened to through earphones.

impulses could travel through space at the speed of light. The real hero of the development of radio, however, was Guglielmo Marconi, a young Italian inventor who sent and received the first radio signals in 1895. Marconi's signals—limited to the dots and dashes of Morse code—were called "wireless" because they didn't need to be sent along telegraph wires.

The most important early use of the **wireless,** as early radios came to be known, was at sea, where they were a huge benefit to sailors. During the first decade of this century, Marconi's invention was used to link ships with the rest of the world. Until that time, ships could not communicate once they left port. The U.S. Navy was especially interested in Marconi's invention and equipped each of its warships with the new device. By 1919, however, radio was still no more than a hobby for the few hundred civilians who owned one.

The First Radio Station

The first breakthrough for what we might call home radio came in 1920, when an engineer for the Westinghouse Corporation, Dr. Frank Conrad, built a tiny radio station in his garage in Pittsburgh, Pennsylvania. As an experiment, Conrad went on the air three times a week and asked anyone who was listening to send him a postcard. If he ran out of things to talk about, he would place the speaker of his hand-cranked record player next to the microphone and play music. You might say that this made Conrad the first disc jockey.

Conrad eventually received enough mail to attract the attention of a local department store. The store manager persuaded Conrad to use his broadcasts to advertise the store's radio receivers. Thus, the commercial was born. The receivers quickly sold out, and broadcasting as we know it had arrived. Conrad's station later became KDKA, which is still operating in Pittsburgh today.

Radio Catches On

"The radio craze . . . will die out in time," said Thomas Edison. Edison was rarely mistaken, but on this point he was

INSTANT   IMPACT

Saving Titanic Survivors

In 1912, a young wireless operator named David Sarnoff gave the world a dramatic demonstration of what radio could do. One lonely night on Nantucket Island, Sarnoff picked up a distress signal from a sinking ship—the supposedly unsinkable *Titanic*. He relayed the message to other ships in the vicinity, which then came to the *Titanic's* rescue.

Sarnoff stayed at the job for seventy-two consecutive hours, and all other wireless stations shut down to avoid interfering with his work. Perhaps as many as seven hundred survivors owed their lives to Sarnoff's quick thinking. Sarnoff would later become president of RCA, one of America's most important electronics companies.

dead wrong. By the early 1920s, Americans were going crazy over their wonderful new toy. Whoever was lucky enough to own one, was probably the most popular person on the block. Sooner or later, the neighbors were sure to drop by to hear this amazing gadget that somehow pulled voices and music out of thin air.

> "The radio craze ... will die out in time."
>
> **Thomas Edison**

Of course, those early radio sets didn't look much like our modern chrome and plastic versions. They were basically crystal sets in bulky boxes. In one respect, however, they resembled the radio headsets joggers use today: They had no loudspeakers. To hear them, you wore a set of earphones. Yet those radios really worked, and just about everyone wanted one.

Radio suited the Roaring Twenties perfectly. That decade has been *aptly* called "the age of wonderful nonsense." Female dancers wore their skirts just above the knees, young couples entered marathon dance contests, and men competed to see who could sit the longest on top of a flagpole. For people longing for fun, radio was the perfect plaything. You didn't have to go out of the house to enjoy it, the entertainment was light, and you could dance to music all night (or at least until the station went off the air).

Radio Goes Commercial

One of the first problems faced by the new radio stations was how to support themselves. A few stations were owned by radio manufacturers who simply wanted a way to sell radios. Others looked to private contributors or public donations, but that was a losing battle. By 1925, it was clear that radio stations could endure only by selling time for commercial messages. One ingenious salesman capitalized handsomely on the trend. He bought an hour's worth of time from one station and then peddled it by the minute (at a profit) to companies eager to advertise their products. By the mid-twenties, "commercials" had become a fact of life in radio.

Federal Regulation

Soon, about seven hundred stations were transmitting signals to millions of listeners nationwide. Confusion ruled the air waves. So many stations were broadcasting, almost at will, on the same frequencies, that no one got good reception. (Different frequencies are similar to different television channels and are represented by the numbers on a radio dial.) Interference was widespread. Frustration grew among both the listening public and the broadcasters, who feared their *fledgling* industry might soon strangle itself.

Concerned about the situation, delegates to the National Radio Conference in 1925 appealed to the U.S. secretary of commerce to place limits on station operating hours and power. The *bedlam* continued, however, because the secretary lacked the power needed to make effective changes. Eventually, President Coolidge and the Congress addressed the issue. Together, they created the Federal Radio Commission (FRC) in 1927. This five-member group was given authority to issue licenses, assign frequencies, and dictate station power and hours of operation.

Networking

Station operators began to learn that they could join forces to produce more appealing programs. By sending their signals over telephone lines to other stations, operators could beam broadcasts to different areas at the same time. Sports events were among the first programs to be broadcast in this way. Stations WJZ in New York City and WGY in Schenectady, New York, for example, joined together to **air** (or broadcast) the 1922 World Series.

Through radio networking, Groucho Marx was able to reach American households from coast to coast.

Later the same year, President Coolidge's message to Congress was aired over six different stations at the same time. Eventually, these chains of stations became the first broadcast **networks.**

By the late 1920s, four major broadcasting networks had been formed, linking stations from coast to coast. This meant that vast audiences could now listen to the same show at the same time. "Wasn't *Fibber McGee* a howl last night?" might be heard on a farm in Kansas, in an office in Chicago, or on a ranch in Texas. Comedian Groucho Marx's famous punch line "You wanna buy a duck?" became a household expression in weeks. New personalities became nationally famous, and so did many sponsors' products.

End of the Golden Age

The "golden age" of radio came to an end in 1950, when large numbers of Americans began to buy televisions. One by one, the major radio shows shifted over to the new medium, and shows that could not make the move to the small black-and-white screen died. Radio groped desperately for a way to survive. It finally found one by converting its stations from their drama, comedy, and variety formats to music, news, and talk.

The key to radio's revival was flexibility. Radio people came to understand that they could not keep their audience by offering the same kinds of programs they had offered in the past. No longer could radio play general-interest programs that might reach a large audience. Instead, stations began to specialize, or **narrowcast,** gearing their programs to specific segments of the audience. Individual stations survived and profited by serving small *niches* of the population. Eventually, radio stations offered listeners hundreds of choices, from classical to country and from rock to all-talk, hoping to build a loyal core of listeners.

Rock 'n' Roll Is Here to Stay

The mid-fifties saw the birth of rock 'n' roll, a new form of music derived from rhythm and blues. The term *rock 'n' roll* was invented by a **deejay,** a term itself

George Burns and Gracie Allen, pictured here, were popular radio comics of the 1930s.

COMMUNICATION   BREAKTHROUGH

War News or the Gospel?

When the networks broke into the Sunday afternoon radio programs on December 7, 1941, to announce that the Japanese had bombed Pearl Harbor, switchboards across the country lit up with complaints about the interruption. Football broadcasts, in particular, fell victim to the announcement, but people had other complaints too. Denver's KFEL, which broadcast a religious program that hour, logged one particularly irate call from a man who asked, "Which is more important: war news or gospel?"

But less than twenty-four hours later, when President Franklin Roosevelt asked Congress to declare war, 80 million Americans (almost two-thirds of the population) were listening. "Yesterday," Roosevelt began, "December 7, 1941—a day which will live in infamy—the United States of America was suddenly and deliberately attacked by naval and air forces of the Empire of Japan." What followed was one of the most forceful speeches ever given on the floor of Congress.

The six-and-a-half-minute speech, interrupted frequently by applause, set the nation on a course toward global conflict. Within five days, Congress had declared war on the allied powers of Japan, Italy, and Germany. Roosevelt rallied the people, aroused a feeling of international responsibility, and demonstrated anew his mastery of the young medium.

"The whole issue of electronic journalism came alive at this time," recalls John Charles Daly, a CBS correspondent. "We felt he'd make a good speech," said Daly. "[It] fulfilled all of our hopes and then some."

Questions
1. Are presidential speeches on radio and television effective in persuading people to give their support?
2. Can you think of any occasions when you've heard a radio program interrupted for a special news announcement? How important should such an announcement be for the program director to interrupt a regular program so that it can be heard?

coming into popularity to replace the more old-fashioned *disc jockey*. The new sound took hold of the nation's youth and helped radio return to a position of prominence.

In 1955, Bill Haley's recording of "Rock Around the Clock" struck paydirt, selling over a million copies to become rock music's first great hit. The following year, Elvis Presley took the nation by storm.

Dozens of stations around the country began to build their **playlists** (the lists of music they put on the air) around the new music. The Top Forty radio format, which was conceived about the time rock made its debut, began to attract many young listeners.

In its original form, Top Forty appealed to a large cross-section of the public because it included many musical styles. Artists such as Perry Como and Doris Day were as common as Elvis. Before long, though, the Top Forty program had become synonymous with rock and teens.

FM Ascends to the Throne

The popularity of rock music eventually triggered the wider acceptance of FM, a static-free alternative to the older standard, AM. In an amplitude-modulated **(AM)** wave, the station changes the size of the sound wave. In a frequency-modulated **(FM)** wave, the station changes how rapidly the wave vibrates. Although stations began broadcasting on FM channels as early as 1940, the signal was slow to catch on.

FM remained the poor cousin to AM until new technology gave its stations a boost. In 1961, the Federal Communications Commission or FCC (which *superseded* the old FRC in 1934) authorized stereo broadcasting on FM. This would prove to be a *landmark* decision because it allowed stations to give their audiences a much-

improved sound. FM stations, already heavy on music, were also ideal for automation. These stations could now program computers to play a steady stream of music and commercials and dispense for the most part with human hosts. This meant that staff size and production expenses could be kept to a minimum. The more-music, less-talk stereo operations began to attract larger and larger audiences.

After three decades of living in the shadow of AM, FM finally achieved *parity* in 1979, when it equaled AM's listenership. The following year, it moved ahead; and since that time, FM has pulled away, now attracting as much as 70 percent of the radio audience. The older medium, AM, still has a thousand more stations (4,726) than FM (3,490), but only a third of the audience. Faced with their own challenge to survive, many AM stations have dropped music altogether in favor of news and talk. Popular question-and-answer shows like "The Rush Limbaugh Show" have helped AM stations remain profitable and viable for the future.

TAKING CHARGE

1. Take a survey to find out which station is the most popular among your classmates. Give the same survey to everyone's parents. How can you account for whatever differences you find?
2. Obtain a tape or record of an old radio show from your school or city library and play it in class. What observations can you make about why the show was popular? Will today's programs seem as odd twenty-five years from now?
3. Make a complete list of the stations that listeners in your area can receive with an ordinary radio. How many are FM and how many are AM? Are there stations you can pick up at night that you can't get during the day?

II Running a Radio Station

Radio stations come in all shapes and sizes, but they can usually be classified according to the type of program they offer. Generally speaking, you can group stations into one of three broad categories: **music radio** (stations that play almost nothing but music), **news/talk radio** (stations that play only news and talk shows), and **full-service radio** (stations that play a little bit of everything—music, news, talk, and perhaps some sports events).

Stations can also be grouped by the kind of audience they try to serve. All-music stations usually hope to appeal to people from fifteen to thirty years old; news/talk stations shoot for the thirty-to-fifty age range; and full-service stations aim for people aged forty-five and over. Music stations develop a playlist each week, a list of all the songs that station plans to play. These songs are kept easily available—probably on a **cart** (a tape cartridge) or a CD—and arranged according to when they will be played and how often. An oldies station might have a playlist of three hundred songs, while a full-service station might have only sixty songs on its playlist.

In this section, we take a closer look at the different kinds of radio stations and the people needed to run them.

A Wide Variety of Formats

In today's competitive market, radio stations have learned to specialize to a greater and greater degree. You can now find, for example, more than a hundred **formats,** or programming styles, in the radio marketplace, compared with just a handful ten or twenty years ago. New formats are constantly evolving—including an all-Elvis station. A station's format gives it an identity. Among the most popular formats are these: all-Beatles, country, light rock, rap, all-comedy, big band, easy listening, Motown, religious, children's radio, bluegrass, folk rock, oldies, rhythm and blues, all-sports, classical, jazz, punk rock, Top Forty, and all-weather.

Believe it or not, listeners in Adel, Georgia, can even tune in an all-commercial station. At one time, the FCC limited stations to no more than eighteen minutes of commercials per hour, but that rule was dropped in the early eighties when radio was deregulated. Now "Exit 10 Listener Information Radio" (WDDQ) plays commercials round-the-clock. The station hopes to attract the many travelers passing by on a nearby interstate highway, but it has also managed to irritate many of its local listeners.

Call Letters

Every radio station has its own set of call letters. Stations located west of the Mississippi use four-letter call signs beginning with the letter K, and those east of the Mississippi use signs that begin with the letter W. (A few pioneer stations that existed before these rules were adopted have call letters that don't fit this pattern.) The FCC approves the selection of each station's call letters in order to prevent duplication. A station's call letters may reflect its area (KLIN in Lincoln, for example) or may simply be a catchy group of letters that is easy to remember (KFRX). Clever call letters have sometimes been traded or sold to another station.

Operating the Studio

Most of the broadcast work in a radio station takes place in an on-air studio or a production studio. The on-air studio is used by the deejay for live music and talk programs, while production studios are used to develop commercials and other material that will air at a later time. Both share the same basic design features and have similar equipment. For ease of use, equipment in the studio is usually set up in a U-shape, with the operator sitting in the center.

The standard equipment found in most studios includes reel-to-reel tape machines, cartridge machines, cassette decks, turntables, compact disc players, and a patch panel. A patch panel is essentially a blending device that allows the operator to mix audio from several sources (remote locations or network lines, for example) with the regular programming. At the heart of the studio is the audio console.

The Audio Console

The **audio console** is an apparatus that looks like something out of *Star Wars* but it can be mastered by nearly anyone with a little training. It puts a combination of recording and playback machines, volume controls, and other audio equipment at the operator's fingertips. All consoles contain the following:

+ **Inputs** that bring audio into the console.
+ **Outputs** that send audio to other locations.
+ **VU meters** that measure the volume of the sound.
+ **Pots** that can fade sound in or out.

Learning to operate the console is one of the first tasks to accomplish if you want to work in radio.

The Console Operator

An effective console operator is part artist and part engineer. All the sounds that attract and keep listeners—the blend of voices and music—must come through

Reel-to-reel tape machines, cassette decks, turntables, compact disc players, and a patch panel used to blend audio from several sources are standard equipment found in most radio stations.

the audio console. The console operator must be agile enough to rapidly adjust dials, flip switches, and push buttons. The operator must also develop a sensitive ear in order to judge the proper sound balance.

As the human connection between the studio and the station's transmitter (the equipment that sends the radio signal out to listeners), the console operator plays a variety of roles. The operator must set up tapes and records in advance, prepare microphone setups and levels for live studio material, and play everything at the exact time scheduled. The operator must also know FCC rules and regulations concerning accurate record keeping and when and how to give station breaks (when the station identifies itself for listeners).

In the small or automated station, the console operator may be the only person on duty. In such circumstances, the operator must also answer the phone, greet visitors, conduct interviews, and talk on the air.

Using Microphones

Knowing what microphones (frequently called "mikes"), can and cannot do will help when your turn comes to go on the air. Microphones have come a long way from the days when they were wrapped in asbestos or cooled with water so as not to burn the lips of performers who got too close. Today, microphones contain diaphragms (thin metal disks) that vibrate when sound waves strike them. Those vibrations are converted into electrical impulses which can then be amplified and transmitted or recorded on tape. The impulses can be converted back into sound by similar vibrating diaphragms in radio loudspeakers.

Experienced radio announcers offer these tips for using a mike:

◆ Avoid touching the mike when it's on. Make all adjustments before you begin. Once you start, never move the mike.

◆ Don't breathe into the mike.

◆ Always keep your head in front of the mike. The sides of some mikes are "dead" and won't pick up your voice.

◆ The proper distance from the mike can vary. Most radio people work eight to twelve inches from the mike.

◆ Hold the script up (and behind the mike) so that your voice goes out, not down.

◆ Never, if humanly possible, cough into a live mike. Turn the mike off before getting that frog out of your throat.

Working in Radio

Your high school diploma or even a college degree in communications will probably not lead you straight to a job in a Hollywood movie studio or a television station. But if you're willing to start at the bottom, work hard, and learn the business inside and out, you have an excellent chance to break into radio, perhaps even before you finish high school. Among the many famous people who started out in radio are Ronald Reagan, Dan Rather, and George Carlin.

The radio industry currently employs over 100,000 people, a number that is likely to grow as more stations go on the air. An average-size station employs between twenty and twenty-five people. About a third of those will have on-air responsibilities.

Entry-level positions in radio seldom pay well. In fact, many small stations may start you at little better than minimum wage, but the experience gained at these low-budget operations more than makes up for the small salaries. During the first year or two in radio, you pay your dues by learning the ropes. The small radio station provides inexperienced people with a chance to become involved in all facets of the business.

On-Air Positions

People who speak on the air often become familiar companions as they pass the days with us on the radio in our homes and cars. On-air positions include announcers, deejays, newscasters and sportscasters, talk show hosts, and the people who lend their voices to the hundreds of commercials we hear every day.

An **announcer** is simply anyone who reads news, weather, public service announcements, or station breaks. The duties of an announcer vary depending on the size of a station. In a small station, announcers work as writers, too. A midday announcer who is on the air from 10 A.M. until 3 P.M., for example, may also be responsible for writing the 4 and 5 P.M. newscasts, plus any commercials that are needed.

Deejay is the name for the host of a music program. The deejay has the most sought-after job in radio. Deejays must be announcers and entertainers, especially during radio's prime time (from 7 to 9 A.M. and from 5 to 7 P.M.), when people are listening in their cars driving to and from work.

Many deejays got their start in radio while in their teens. They might have shown an early interest in music by playing an instrument or perhaps simply by being a big music fan. Teenagers who hope to be deejays can gain experience by hosting high school parties or dance clubs. There, they can develop a "patter" or rapport with the public.

Deejays are actually on the air less than you might think. Music and commercials

COMMUNICATION WORKS

Scott Young, Deejay and Program Director

"Put a smile in your voice," advises Scott Young, deejay and host of KFOR's top-rated morning show in Lincoln, Nebraska. What he means is that a physical action, like smiling, can help stimulate your speaking ability. "By smiling, you can force more energy and enthusiasm into your voice."

Young needs that enthusiasm because he works the early morning shift. He arrives at the office well before he goes on the air at 6 A.M. Young stays on the air until 10 A.M., holding down one of radio's prime time slots (prime because so many people like to listen while they drive to work).

After he leaves the air, Young lines up guests for future shows, writes and tapes commercials, and attends to other responsibilities around the station.

He says that very few people on radio have had formal voice training. "Most have learned by doing." He has plenty of advice for young people interested in radio careers.

"Stick to short sentences on the air," he says. "The longer the sentence, the more you may have to take a breath." Radio speaking is designed to be conversational, with a faster pace than television.

"Try to tell a story instead of read it," he suggests. "Picture your listeners in your mind and speak to them."

Young says he likes the immediacy of radio, which can put the listener on the scene with sounds of taps played at a funeral, chants shouted at a rally, or a band marching at a parade. On the other hand, he notes, radio provides only superficial coverage of most events. A typical radio news report lasts no longer than ninety seconds.

"Time yourself reading," Young suggests, "and read aloud a lot. You'll learn pacing and poise. Eventually, of course, you will realize that you've got to be yourself when you go on the air."

usually take up at least fifty minutes of every hour. A typical hour on the morning show of a full-service station may consist of fifteen minutes of news, fourteen minutes of commercials, six minutes of sports, twelve to fifteen minutes of music, and five minutes of network news. That leaves just six minutes or so for the host to speak. Many of today's most popular deejays have sidekicks, and most specialize in comedy.

Off-Air Positions

Every radio station needs a number of off-air staff positions to keep things running smoothly. These positions may include an office manager, a bookkeeper, an accountant, and various clerical assistants, such as receptionists and typists. The higher-paying, managerial positions at a station usually include the following:

◆ A **general manager** who may also be the station's owner. The general manager must make sure that the station is profitable and keeps its license. On a day-to-day basis, the manager is also responsible for maintaining good public relations with the community.

◆ A **program director** who makes decisions about the amount of news to carry, the type of deejay to hire, and what music the playlist will include. This is a high-turnover job; if the ratings are low, the program director is usually the first to go.

◆ A **traffic director** who is responsible for planning the daily on-air schedule. The traffic director watches to see that competing businesses—say, two floral shops—do not have their commercials running next to each other.

◆ A **copywriter** who writes many of the commercials that go on the air. The copywriter also selects the music and chooses the people who will supply the voices for the commercial. Copywriters may also write **continuity**—the material used between songs or to set up commercial breaks—for announcers and deejays.

◆ A **sales manager** who sells the station's air time by contacting and working with local businesses.

◆ A **chief engineer** who makes sure that the station's signal goes as far as possible and that it reaches every person in the signal area with the greatest quality and *fidelity.*

TAKING CHARGE

1. A station's format describes the type of music it plays or the kinds of programs it broadcasts. Find out what format each station in your area uses and report your findings to the class. What do these formats suggest about the audience each station is trying to reach?
2. How do radio stations decide which songs to play? Call the program director at several stations and ask. Share your findings with the rest of the class.
3. Obtain a copy of the diary the Arbitron company asks people to keep for a week. Have everyone in the class keep a similar diary for a week, and tabulate the results. What conclusions can you draw from the information?

Performing and Writing Techniques

To do their jobs well, radio broadcasters must speak well, of course, and they must be able to read well from a written script. Because they also write most of their own material, copywriting skills are important too.

A radio broadcaster must, first and foremost, possess the ability to read aloud effectively. Among other things, this involves proper articulation and inflection, which can be improved through practice. Furthermore, the broadcaster must understand what is on the page in order to make it meaningful for listeners. Announcing, in this sense, is similar to oral interpretation (discussed in Chapter 19).

Having a naturally resonant and pleasant-sounding voice is certainly an advantage if you want to be on radio. Listeners seem to prefer deeper voices; this is true for female announcers as well as male. Most voices possess considerable range, and with training, even a person with a high-pitched voice can develop an appealing on-air sound. Don't force your voice into a lower range to achieve a deeper sound, though. This can result in injury to your vocal chords.

Often, a positive personality can overcome a variety of vocal handicaps. One announcer says "Making the most of what you already have is a lot better than trying to be something you're not. Perfect yourself and be natural." The qualities that make a good radio voice, according to one talk-show host, are "clarity, animation, enthusiasm, and credibility." He suggests that radio newcomers develop a "full-bodied voice," one that has plenty of support from the diaphragm.

INSTANT IMPACT

The Voice That Caused a Seizure

Whether you have a pleasant voice or not, you probably have never driven anyone up the wall simply by speaking. That is not the case with television personality Mary Hart, whose voice once caused an epileptic seizure.

According to Dr. Venkat Ramani, who reported the case in the *New England Journal of Medicine*, Hart's voice has caused one of his patients to have seizures. Ramani said that when he played a tape of Hart's voice in a laboratory test, his patient would rub her stomach and hold her head. "Then she would look confused and . . . act like she was far away and out of it." He added that the woman has not had any seizures since she stopped watching Hart on television.

Swamped with hundreds of requests for a response, Hart could only say, "My heart goes out to anyone with this problem."

Unless you sound like a piece of chalk squeaking on the blackboard, you can probably take some comfort from this strange story. At one time, nearly all the voices on radio were a rich masculine baritone. Now, however, radio has made room for a wide variety of voices, and perhaps yours will be one of them.

Many beginners don't believe the sounds of their own voices played back on a recorder. "That's not me," they say; but, of course, it is. Try to get over the discomfort of hearing yourself on tape as quickly as possible, and get used to simply being yourself on the air.

Learn to Relax

At first, speaking into a radio mike can be an intimidating experience. You may feel fear or extreme nervousness, either of which can put a strain on your body and your voice. You've already learned a great deal about building confidence and overcoming stage fright throughout this book. Something else you can try is learning to relax.

Proper breathing, for instance, is a crucial element in good speaking, and it is only possible when your body is free of stress. Good posture is also important, as is poise. You need to be able to keep your cool when you make a mistake or something goes wrong.

Here are some things that you might do to relax:

1. Read your material aloud before going on the air. Get the feel of it. This will automatically increase your confidence, a key to complete relaxation. Mark places where you know you want to pause.

2. Before you start speaking, take several deep breaths and slowly exhale while keeping your eyes closed.

3. Sit still for a couple of moments with your arms at your sides. Tune out. Allow yourself to drift a bit, and then slowly return to the job at hand.

4. Stand and flex your shoulders and arms. Stretch.

5. When seated again, check your posture. Do not slump over as you announce. A curved diaphragm impedes breathing.

6. Hum a few bars of your favorite song. The vibration helps relax your throat muscles and vocal chords.

7. Give yourself ample time to settle in before going on. Dashing to the console at the last second will ruin your composure.

8. When speaking, imagine yourself talking to a good friend. Adopt a friendly, conversational tone.

Posture

Don't let the rest of your body go on vacation while you're talking on the air. Getting every muscle involved in your performance will improve your delivery. Sit up straight, preferably on the front half of your chair. Use facial expressions. Forcing yourself to smile, as strange as it may sound, actually makes you put more energy and enthusiasm into your voice.

Poise

Occasionally, you will make a mistake when you read something over the air. The important thing is not to let errors cause you even more anxiety. No matter how serious your mistake, keep going. It's the only way to learn to overcome your slips. Everyone makes them sooner or later. Veteran announcers frequently say "check that" when they have made an error. Another useful phrase is "Correction, that should be . . . "

Practice sessions can help you get used to dealing with all sorts of errors. Whatever you do, don't call more attention to the error by saying something like "O dadgum it, I blew it" (or something much worse). Shrug your shoulders, but otherwise keep your frustration to yourself.

COMMUNICATION BREAKDOWN

Radio's Invasion from Mars

The power of radio to influence the imagination was never so vividly demonstrated as on the evening of October 30, 1938, when the Mercury Theatre of the Air presented *The War of the Worlds.* Perhaps no other broadcast has ever had as strange and powerful an effect on a listening audience.

On that Sunday, in a studio littered with coffee cups and sandwich wrappers, a young Orson Welles put on his earphones, raised his long fingers, and threw the cue for the Mercury theme to begin. After the music dropped, there were routine introductions, and then an announcer broke in to say that the earth had been invaded by Martians. Over the next half hour, Welles and his staff described how the Martians advanced across the countryside, causing death and destruction.

Within minutes, people all over the country were praying, crying, or frantically trying to escape death from space invaders. Some raced to inform neighbors, others summoned ambulances, and still others flagged down police cars.

The reaction was strongest at points nearest the supposed location of the Martian landing: Grovers Mill, New Jersey. In Newark, New Jersey, more than twenty families in a single block rushed out with wet handkerchiefs and towels over their faces as protection from poison gas. Some began moving household furniture. In Minneapolis, a woman ran into church screaming, "New York destroyed, this is the end of the world. You might as well go home to die. I heard it on the radio."

By the next day, the general public began to realize it had been had. Newspaper columnists and public figures chastised Welles and his cast for putting one over on everyone. They expressed amazement at the "incredible stupidity" and "gullibility" of the American public. Yet the show has become an enduring testament to the power of radio; no other medium could have pulled it off.

Questions
1. Why do you think so many people panicked when they heard the news of a Martian invasion?
2. How important is a radio station's credibility today? Would any station risk such a daring hoax?

Writing for Radio

"A good word is worth a thousand pictures," said Eric Sevareid, a radio correspondent who eventually became a well-known television commentator. Sevareid's observation points out how effective well-chosen words can be. To some degree, everything on the air must have a script.

An experienced radio performer can probably ad-lib brilliantly on occasion, but speaking without a plan is like walking on a tightrope. Sooner or later, you're bound to fall. Written scripts supply a safety net for high-flying performers; they provide a place to land when the imagination freezes up and the ego begins to wobble. The best radio scripts are short, conversational, and dramatic.

Don't Ask for Trouble

When you write material for radio, you must be aware of some restrictions on what may be said over the air. When substantial parts of the program are to be ad-libbed, it is even more important that the deejay be well acquainted with the laws of broadcasting. Here are just a few points to keep in mind when preparing material for broadcast.

1. Material which is profane or obscene and therefore likely to offend most people is forbidden.

2. False or misleading claims are illegal.

3. Statements that harm a person's or group's reputation or expose that person or group to humiliation or ridicule, are illegal if the statements are not true. Such statements may result in lawsuits.

4. You may not invade a person's privacy, nor can you use a person's name in a commercial without written consent.

5. People who are interviewed over the phone must be warned that their comments are intended for broadcast use.

Write with Your Ear

You must learn to write with your ear as well as with your eye. For example, a radio news announcer once mentioned that a rally would be held to protest "a tax on skateboarders." At least, that was what it sounded like. Only after some time had passed did it become clear that what the announcer had said was "attacks on skateboarders." As far as the eye is concerned, there is no reason to confuse "a tax" with "attacks." To the ear, though, the two sound the same. The announcer could perhaps have distinguished the two phrases by speaking more carefully, but the writer should have anticipated the problem in the first place and rephrased the statement.

Certain word combinations can cause confusion because of our natural tendency to let words run together when we speak. For example, problems may arise when a word ending in a consonant is followed by one beginning with a vowel. If you say, "his solution was costly and effective," some of the audience may hear "costly and defective."

When you prepare a written radio script, put a wavy line under any tricky words that you might have trouble pronouncing. You might also type a *phonetic* spelling of a difficult word in parentheses after the word. You can make it easier for yourself if you underline the word *not* or set it off like this: "The senator says he has . . . <u>not</u> . . . decided if he will run again." The word *not* gets special emphasis because it changes the meaning of the entire sentence.

Finally, avoid sentences filled with numbers. They slow you down and tend to confuse the listener.

Radio Commercials

Some of the most creative work in radio is done by the people who produce commercials. Advertisers like radio for the

"We just figured out some more things the FCC says we can't say. You'd better change that lead to 'The darn has busted.'"

opportunity it gives them to target specific audiences. They also appreciate radio for its flexibility. Last-minute changes can be made more easily there than on television. Most of all, advertisers like radio for its low rates—it is one of the cheapest ways to advertise.

The first question a radio copywriter working on a commercial must face is how to get a message across without pictures. The answer is that you paint a picture with words and sounds. You have great freedom in choosing the locale of your commercial and relatively few costs to worry about. If you want to set your commercial beside the Blarney Stone in Ireland or on the planet Saturn, you can do so simply by pressing the right keys on your word processor and adding a few sound effects. The mind is a far better stage than any movie lot.

Radio commercials should be pitched to some basic human need. Will your product make the listener feel more secure? More loved? Better respected? Highlight what the product can do for the listener,

but don't be too obvious. Don't tell the listener, "Eat Whatsit cereal, and you won't feel hungry." People eat because they are hungry, of course, but any food can meet that need. Your job is to stress what Whatsit alone can do—for example, make you healthier, stronger, smarter, thinner, or whatever. You must convince the listener that Whatsit will do the job better than competing products in its general price range.

If the price of the product being advertised is low, make the potential buyer feel smarter by getting good quality at less than the regular price. If, on the other hand, the price is rather high, tell the listener that there is prestige involved in buying something that is not cheap. This can be reinforced by stressing the brand name of the product.

Tools of the Trade

Over the years, radio broadcasters have learned that nothing improves a commercial message more than appropriate music and occasionally, a special sound effect.

Music

Music is frequently used to enhance an advertiser's message—to make it more appealing or attention-grabbing. The music used in a radio commercial is called a **music bed** because it supports the speaker's voice. A station may bed thousands of commercials over the course of a year.

Stations find bed music in a variety of places. Recording companies send hundreds of demonstration albums to radio stations each year. Since few of these albums actually make it onto playlists, they are good sources for music beds, especially because the music is unfamiliar to the

In the early days, sound effects for radio shows and commercials were produced using methods like those pictured here.

listening audience. Familiar melodies or songs with words generally are avoided for commercials because they distract the listener from the message. Occasionally, though, a station will use a familiar tune—usually for comic effect.

Sound Effects

In the early days of radio, sound effects were improvised show by show, commercial by commercial. In some cases, the effects were produced by shattering glass, firing guns, and overturning furniture.

Creating sound effects can sometimes be as much fun as throwing a pizza party. When Sound Records, Inc., was asked to supply the sound of an elegant banquet as background noise for a recording of an Edgar Allen Poe story, they invited thirty-five people over for a pizza party. The di-

rector of the commercial said he hoped that the party, when blended with narration and harpsichord music, would sound just like a fantastic banquet.

For another effect, the same director wanted to simulate the sound of snow falling from a tree onto a fire. "We heated some pennies and dropped them in water," he said. "It made this hissing noise that sounded just right." No matter how creative the staff at a station might be, however, they usually turn to large libraries of special effects that can be purchased on vinyl disc, tape, or CD.

The following commercial illustrates how the use of music and sound effects can help keep listeners interested:

Announcer: And now the perfect recipe for a successful wedding . . . wedding music, please . . .

(Sound Effects: Wedding Song.)
Announcer: First we need a bride . . .
Bride: I do.
Announcer: And a groom . . .
Groom: (timidly) I do.
Announcer: And here's the minister . . .
Minister: I now pronounce you man and wife.
Announcer: OK, perfect so far . . . next the reception . . . ahh, better go to Russ's IGA Bakery for that perfect wedding cake . . . *(sound effects: running)* and don't forget the rolls, cookies, and the party trays. OK, well, what's next . . . you can't expect the guests to just eat cake . . . no, not at this wedding, so back to Russ's IGA *(sound effects: running)* for trays and trays of meats, cheeses, relishes, and fresh salads. Better yet, let Russ's come to you *(sound effects: car horn)* with their catering service . . . they can create anything!

Commercial produced by KFOR, Lincoln, Nebraska.

Public Service Announcements

All stations run a variety of special commercials called public service announcements (PSAs). They do so as a courtesy to good causes and charities and to satisfy FCC requirements. You may have heard, for example, PSAs promoting safe driving habits, literacy programs, or community clean-up projects. In some cases, these announcements are prepared by advertising agencies; at other times, the station itself produces them.

As a copywriter, you need to prepare to write a PSA in the same way you would prepare any other radio commercial. Determine what audience you want to reach. Decide what message you want to get across and what appeal will work best.

TAKING CHARGE

1. Try imitating a popular radio voice. You might use Paul Harvey, Tom Snyder, Rush Limbaugh, or someone in your own area. Practice with your classmates to see if you can capture that well-known voice through pace, intonation, and emphasis.

2. Imagine yourself as a deejay for an evening radio program. Choose a group of five songs to play. Then write a short script to provide continuity between the songs. Add a station break and a brief commercial for added realism.

3. Invent your own radio station. What would your format be? What kind of listeners would you try to attract?

4. Make a list of the products advertised during one hour of radio on one station. Assign different students to monitor different stations. Examine your lists and discuss what relationships you can find between the products being advertised and the programs and music being played. Listen to the radio during different hours of the day to see if that makes a difference in what products are advertised.

You might have fun experimenting with radio drama—the kind of program that entertained millions of Americans before television. Here is a brief sample of a radio drama, one that recalls the golden age of radio, when each episode ended in a cliffhanger. The hero of this episode, Biff Chambers, is a stunt pilot during the 1920s who hopes to build his own aircraft factory. He has an assistant, Scottie McCloud, and a girlfriend, Betty Purehead. In this episode, Biff is trying to line up some financial support.

Biff Chambers, Pilot of the Plains

Announcer: Let's refresh our memories, boys and girls. Biff Chambers and Scottie McCloud have decided to stage an aerial circus to help raise money for their dream of building an airplane factory. Worthington Hathaway, the scheming owner of Hathaway Aeroplanes, and his henchman Bubba O'Boy are onto the boys and will stop at nothing to see that the pageant and the dream are crushed like so many eggshells. Betty Purehead (who, shall we say, is more than a little attracted to Biff) suggested the pageant to Biff and Scottie.

We now return to the small and humble chicken farm that Biff calls home, just on the outskirts of town.

Biff: Betty, can I get you some more oatmeal cookies?

Betty: Oh no, Biff, I like to watch my girlish figure.

Biff: Boy, so do I, Betty.

Betty: Biff!

Biff: Sorry, Betty, I just meant that I need to watch your waistline, too.

Betty: Biff!

Biff: My waistline. My waistline.

Betty: That's all right, Biff. Actually, I'm flattered. But I can't be staying anyway. I've started a little knitting project at home.

Biff: My poor widowed grandmother used to love knitting.

Betty: Biff, I was going to keep it a secret, but I'm just so excited, I have to tell you. Biff, I'm knitting you one of those dashing scarves to wear for the aerial pageant.

Biff: Jumpin' Jupiter, Betty, nobody ever did anything like that for me.

Betty: Oh Biff, I do so want it to be special, but I'm afraid I'm not very good at knitting.

Biff: Aw gosh, Betty, if it's from you, I reckon it would have to be perfect. Everything about you is.

Betty: Oh Biff.

Biff: Oh Betty!

Announcer: Oh brother.

Biff: Betty, there's something I think I've worked up the courage to ask you.

Betty: Yes, Biff.

Biff: Well I . . . I . . . er . . .

Betty: Go on, Biff, what is it?

Biff: Could you loan Scottie and me twenty-five dollars?

Announcer: Well. Seems some guys really know how to take advantage of a romantic moment. Will Betty lend the boys the money? Will Biff ever be able to have a meaningful relationship with a woman? Find out tomorrow on "Biff Chambers, Pilot of the Plains," and until then, boys and girls, this is Jerry Krueger saying so long and happy landings.

REVIEW AND ENRICHMENT

LOOKING BACK

Listed below are the major ideas discussed in this chapter.

✦ Radio stations blanket the entire planet, delivering music, news, and entertainment to people everywhere.

✦ Radio has several important advantages over other media. Radios are cheap and portable, and they free listeners to do other things while still hearing the message.

✦ In 1920, a young engineer named Frank Conrad built the first broadcast station in his own garage.

✦ The federal government became a player in the radio business in 1927 when it formed the Federal Radio Commission to regulate radio stations. In 1934, the FRC became the Federal Communications Commission.

✦ Television nearly killed radio in the 1950s, but radio stations rebounded by aiming their programs at very narrowly defined portions of the listening audience.

✦ FM stations, which can produce a clearer signal, have now become more popular than the older AM stations.

✦ Radio stations today generally use one of three basic formats: music, news/talk, or full-service, which is essentially a combination of music and talk.

✦ The heart of a radio studio is the audio console—a combination of recording and playback machines, volume controls, and other audio equipment.

✦ On-air positions, such as announcers and deejays, are among the most popular jobs in radio. Off-air positions, such as program director and copywriter, are equally important even though less well known.

✦ Having a great natural voice might be an advantage in radio, but almost anyone can become an effective radio speaker with a little effort and training.

✦ Radio scripts must be short, conversational, and dramatic. They must also avoid any material which is false, misleading, or obscene.

✦ By blending music, copy, and sound effects, a radio commercial writer can take listeners anywhere in the world at any time in history.

✦ Public service announcements promote good causes and charities.

SPEECH VOCABULARY

Write a summary of this chapter in which you accurately use and underline all the new speech terms listed here.

mass media	news/talk radio	general manager
wireless	full-service radio	program director
air	carts	traffic director
networks	formats	copywriter
narrowcast	audio console	continuity
deejay	inputs	sales manager
playlists	outputs	chief engineer
AM	VU meters	music bed
FM	pots	
music radio	announcer	

GENERAL VOCABULARY

Use each of the general vocabulary words in a sentence that illustrates its meaning.

aptly	niche	parity
fledgling	superseded	fidelity
bedlam	landmark	phonetic

THINGS TO REMEMBER

1. What makes radio the most readily available source of entertainment, information, and companionship?
2. How did chain broadcasting systems grow into national networks?
3. Name two factors that enabled FM stations to surpass AM stations in popularity.
4. Explain how narrowcasting helped save radio during the early years of television.
5. What are the major differences in format and target audience among music radio, news/talk radio, and full-service radio stations?
6. How would knowing the call letters of a radio station tell you something about where the station is located?
7. What kind of equipment might you find in a typical radio studio?
8. Name three tips to keep in mind when speaking into a microphone.
9. In writing broadcast material, what are some guidelines you should follow to avoid problems with the FCC?

10. Nearly every radio commercial is designed around some basic human need. Give three examples of such needs.
11. What is a public service announcement?

THINGS TO DO

1. Arrange for your class to tour a local radio station, or invite a station manager, program director, or deejay to visit your class as a guest speaker.
2. Interview a station's general manager. Ask about what qualities the manager looks for when hiring young people to work at the station.
3. Create a sixty-second commercial for several voices. If possible, tape the commercial and play it back for the class. Include music and sound effects.
4. Use a tape recorder and practice reading items from *Time, Newsweek,* or *U.S. News & World Report.* Listen to the playback at least twice. Make notes on the following: (a) Is the meaning of what I said clear? (b) Did I go too fast or too slow? (c) Was my delivery smooth or choppy? (d) What vocal characteristics do I need to work on?
5. Compare a newscast on an all-rock station with one on a full-service or news/talk station. Consider both content and style. Report what you find to the class.
6. The rates advertisers pay for time on the air depend on the size of the audience and the time of day. Find out what rates your local stations charge for commercials at various times of the day.

THINGS TO TALK ABOUT

1. Compare radio with television, newspapers, and news magazines. What are radio's advantages and its drawbacks?
2. Consider your own listening habits. What is it that attracts you to a particular station? Is it the personalities of the deejays, the kinds of music played, the contests and promotions, or the news and information programs? How would a program director design a station's format to be sure you were a regular listener?
3. Do the decisions radio stations make about what songs to play have a major impact on the kinds of music you like? On the kinds you buy? Are there regional bands or songs that are favorites in your area but that are not heard on radio?
4. What school activities or local clubs might help you get experience that would be useful in a radio career?

THINGS TO WRITE ABOUT

1. Do some research on the payola scandal in the mid-1970s. Some deejays accepted money from record companies to play records that the companies wanted to push. Check with a local station to find out what arrangements the station now has with the record companies that supply new music.
2. Work with your classmates in small groups to write a brief radio drama. Do some research on popular radio shows of the thirties and forties to use as models for your drama. (Check the student speech at the end of the chapter for an example.) Practice your script and then present it to the class, either live or recorded on tape.
3. Tape-record a five-minute newscast based on events at your school. Include short clips of interviews with key school personnel.
4. Create a public service announcement for something you feel strongly about. Possible topics include smoking, drugs, seat belts, and alcohol.
5. Create three commercials for the same product—one ten seconds long, one twenty seconds long, and one thirty seconds long. Create the longest commercial first and then selectively cut out material to reach the ten and twenty second limits.

CRITICAL THINKING

1. At the present time, the federal government requires stations to serve the public interest, primarily by alerting listeners to weather emergencies and by playing public service announcements. If the government didn't regulate radio, would content be better or worse?
2. Evaluate the effectiveness of radio commercials. Reach an agreement with your classmates about three commercials that are successful and three that fail. Then determine why it might be that some commercials succeed and others fail.
3. Analyze a "classic" radio program from the twenties or thirties such as "Fibber McGee" or "Amos 'n' Andy." What stereotypes of its day does it reflect? Would audiences today find any parts objectionable? Why?

RELATED SPEECH TOPICS

Here are some topics for classroom speeches on radio.

The emergency broadcast system
Payola
"Underground" stations
National Public Radio

Fred Allen
Citizens-band radio
Stan Freberg
Talk radio

CHAPTER 22

Television

"Reading maketh a well-rounded person. So doth watching TV with a bowl of potato chips."

— **Bob Orben, comedy writer**

"They must have the new TelePrompTer on upside down."

LEARNING OBJECTIVES

After completing this chapter, you will be able to do the following.

◆ Discuss the impact of the television industry on American society.

◆ Make production decisions based on camera movements and angles.

◆ Demonstrate the techniques necessary to deliver effective on-air performances.

◆ Write a broadcast script with instructions for both video and audio material.

◆ Evaluate the ethical values presented by television in its programming and news coverage.

CHAPTER OUTLINE

Following are the main sections in this chapter.

I The World of Television

II Broadcasting Know-how

III Production Techniques

IV Delivery Techniques

Chapter Review

NEW SPEECH TERMS

In this chapter, you will learn the meanings of the speech terms listed below.

ratings system
commercial
  stations
public stations
talent
video
audio
panning
tilting
trucking
dollying
zooming
field of view

TelePrompTer
headroom
noseroom
omnidirectional
  microphones
lavaliere
  microphones
wireless
  microphones
shotgun
  microphones
storyboard
anchor

GENERAL VOCABULARY

Expanding your general vocabulary will help you become a more effective communicator. Listed below are some words appearing in this chapter that you should make part of your everyday vocabulary.

malicious
spontaneity
panoramic
framing
maneuverability

makeshift
judicious
colloquial
charisma
censorship

I The World of Television

"Cowabunga, dudes." "Don't have a cow, man." "Happy, happy, joy, joy." If these distinctive phrases sound familiar to you, welcome to the club. America has become a nation of TV-aholics. Whether you are rich, poor, snowbound, bedridden, or just passing the time, television has probably become one of your favorite companions. It takes you to movies and plays, concerts and operas, prizefights and ball games. It brings you face-to-face with floods, earthquakes, and fires; introduces you to presidents, kings, and sultans; and teaches you French, home building, and first aid. Alas, it is also, as many critics have observed, "chewing gum for the eyes."

The word *television* comes from the Greek word *tele*, meaning "far," and the Latin word *videre*, meaning "to see." In other words, television means "to see far." And when it comes to seeing far, nothing approaches television, either in the sheer abundance of its programs or the vast size of its audience. It offers a mammoth handout of news, fun, art, and sport, all just for turning a dial or punching a button. It is the next best thing to curling up in front of a national fireplace. In this section, we will consider the history of television and its impact on American society.

The Tuned-in Generation

Unless you're very unusual, you're part of a tuned-in generation. Recent studies indicate that American students watch an average of twenty-three hours of television a week. If you keep up that pace, you will have spent a full year of your life in front of the "boob tube" by age seventy. The A. C. Nielsen Company, whose powerful **ratings system** determines the fate of your favorite show, reports that a television set is on at least six hours a day in the average American home. To measure the ratings, Nielsen recruits about two thousand families a week. These families agree to have "people meters" installed on their sets. The people meter allows family members to log in what they are watching by pushing a few buttons.

At its best, television can touch your heart and mind. It delivers generous amounts of information and entertainment on command. It can bring an entire nation together to celebrate, as Americans did with the return of the troops from the Persian Gulf, or to mourn, as we did over the deaths of the seven *Challenger* astronauts. At its worst, television can be a *malicious* influence. Critics charge that it halts conversation, teaches children the power of violence, and may be one of the reasons children don't read much. "Because of television," said the radio comedian Fred Allen thirty years ago, "the next generation will have eyes as big as cantaloupes—and no brains at all."

Television can rob public events of their *spontaneity*—we stay home now to watch parades on TV—and it has changed our political process beyond recognition. Could Abraham Lincoln, for example, be elected president today with his lanky physique and unsightly mole? Last but not least, we must not forget the sales talk. Experts say we watch more than twenty thousand commercials each year. If you find yourself humming a jingle from one of those thirty-second ads, small wonder. They are written by many of our best musicians. The amount of money businesses spend to peddle their products on television (about $18.5 billion annually) staggers the imagination.

Television is popular with big business because it can reach an enormous audience. Consumer guides tell us that there are televisions in about 98 percent of all American homes, more than have bathtubs. In fact, we are rapidly nearing the day when there will be a television set for every man, woman, and child in the United States. In 1969, about 125 million Americans watched Neil Armstrong as he took humanity's first step on the moon. In 1985, a worldwide audience estimated at 1.5 billion people, probably the largest single audience in history, watched the Live Aid concert, a benefit for famine victims in Africa. More than any other medium of communication, television has the power to make all of us residents of a single global village.

Cable Channels Offer More Choice

Approximately three-fourths of the 1,300 television stations in the United States are **commercial stations.** That means that they depend on advertising to provide their income. Most of these stations are affiliated with one of the three major networks—ABC, NBC, and CBS—which provides the great majority of their programs. These stations produce some of their own shows, but they must run network programming during "prime time" (the hours between 8 and 11 P.M., EST). The rest of the stations are **public stations;** they rely on grants and contributions to pay their operating costs.

The signal provided by both commercial and public stations is free, assuming that you have a receiver and an antenna. Yet millions of Americans choose to pay for their television. Cable television is probably the fastest-growing area of the television industry. Originally, its only purpose was to bring programs to places that could not receive clear signals otherwise. People who lived in towns great distances from the nearest transmitter, for instance, needed cable, as did those who lived in places that the signals could not reach, like mountain valleys or homes beneath the skyscrapers of Manhattan.

INSTANT IMPACT

Chances Are . . .

The chances that an American has appeared on television are 1 in 4. Here are a few other intriguing facts about television:

◆ *Annual* budget of the Miami vice squad: $1.2 million. Budget *per episode* of "Miami Vice": $1.5 million.

◆ Percentage decrease in a household's television viewing after the acquisition of a personal computer: 40 percent.

◆ Most Americans depend on television for their news (about 64 percent in a recent Gallup poll).

Vladimir Zworykin, pictured here, emigrated to the United States from Russia in 1919. He is credited by historians as having made the major advances necessary for the invention of television in the 1920s.

Today, however, many people enjoy cable for other reasons. They like it for the improved reception it provides for regular television programs. They also like it for the great variety it offers. A basic cable system can carry as many as sixty different signals. Thus, a cable system can transmit regular network programs as well as special shows like continuous news, weather, and sports; programming from independent stations; first-run movies; and special events like the Olympic games or political conventions.

The Invention of Television

Television had no single inventor. Many scientists and engineers contributed to the technology that now enables us to beam a signal from one corner of the globe to another. Nevertheless, most historians credit an American immigrant from Russia named Vladimir Zworykin with developing the major advances needed to create a successful video camera and receiver. Zworykin learned engineering as a radio officer with the Russian armed forces during World War I. In 1919, at the age of thirty, he came to the United States to work for the Westinghouse Electric Company.

His most important work there was the development of the first practical television camera in 1923, a device he called the iconoscope. The iconoscope was essentially an electronic tube that converted light rays into electric signals. The signals could then be changed into radio waves. Zworykin also invented the kinescope, a device that could receive the signals and reassemble them into a picture. In 1929, Zworykin demonstrated the practicality of his electronic television system and became director of electronics research for the Radio Corporation of America (RCA).

By 1936, RCA had installed television receivers in 150 homes in the New York City area and had begun experimental telecasts. The first program was a cartoon featuring Felix the Cat. The National Broadcasting Company (NBC), owned by RCA, began the first regular television broadcasts in 1939, but all television broadcasting was suspended during World War II. After the war, NBC, now joined by two other networks—CBS and ABC—resumed regular broadcasts. By 1951, it had extended its telecasts from coast to coast. Television stations were springing up everywhere.

In television's early days, most screens were only seven or ten inches across (measured diagonally), a far cry from today's robust twenty-one, thirty-two, or even sixty-four inch screens. Most telecasts were either shown live or recorded on film. Unfortunately, film must be developed before it can be broadcast, a tedious and time-consuming process that slowed down production. During the mid-1950s, television producers switched to a new invention—videotape—as a way of recording programs. Videotape can produce high-quality pictures and sound. More importantly, it can be replayed immediately after taping. Color broadcasting began in 1954 and has now almost completely replaced black-and-white production.

Roll the Highlights, Please

"The impact of television on our culture is just indescribable," wrote the poet Carl Sandburg. "There's a certain sense in which it is nearly as important as the invention of printing." Some of the highlights of the early history of television include the following:

◆ The first politician to appear on television was Herbert Hoover. Hoover's rather grim face was transmitted from Washington to New York on April 7, 1927, over a pair of telephone wires.

◆ A television camera and a portable transmitter were flown over New York City in 1940 to give viewers a bird's-eye look at the city. That same year, NBC covered a national political convention for the first time, reaching an audience estimated at fifty thousand.

◆ In 1941, television broadcast its first commercial. It would not be the last.

◆ The number of viewers virtually exploded over a brief fifteen-year period. In 1945, there were fewer than ten thousand sets in the country; by 1950, there were about 6 million, and just ten years later, in 1960, there were more than 60 million.

"The impact of television on our culture is just indescribable."

Carl Sandburg

TAKING CHARGE

1. Keep a television viewing log for a week. Ask your parents and siblings to do the same. Compare the viewing habits of teenagers with those of young children and older adults.
2. Find the family on television that most resembles your own and explain both similarities and differences.
3. Contact your local cable television company and find out what kind of local access programming is available. Could you get a home video of your own on the air?
4. Watching television certainly takes time. Do your parents set any rules in your home about how much you can watch? Are certain programs off-limits? Why?
5. Andy Warhol once said, "The day will come when everyone will be famous for fifteen minutes." What do you think he meant? What role has television played in creating celebrities?

II Broadcasting Know-how

Although many of the things you have already learned about speech will serve you well in television broadcasting, there are a number of other skills that are specific to this particular medium. You will communicate much more successfully if you have a working knowledge of what goes on behind the scenes. In this section, we explore what a television speaker needs to know about what the other people in a television studio are doing.

Careers in Television

Television offers an exciting and rewarding field for ambitious young people. Because television is still so young, it has not become set in its ways. Thus, it offers attractive challenges for those who enjoy a competitive atmosphere. More importantly, broadcasting provides a way to get in-

volved in your community. Television stations play a major role in the daily lives of the people they serve.

The best place for beginners to find employment is usually at a small commercial station, at an educational station, or with the local cable company. Because small stations have fewer employees and jobs often overlap, working at a small station will probably give you a chance to learn several different phases of the station's operation. Beginners, however, must be prepared to work odd hours, weekends, and holidays. Seniority brings better working conditions and, eventually, a chance to work at a larger station.

The variety of jobs available at a typical television station provides room for a wide range of skills. Most stations divide their jobs into four major areas: programming, engineering, sales, and administration. The smaller the station, the more likely that each staff member will have to wear several "hats." The larger the sta-

COMMUNICATION BREAKTHROUGH

Television Covers the War in the Gulf

It was the most-watched event in television history, and Cable News Network (CNN), not NBC, CBS, or ABC, dominated our attention. Within minutes of the first bomb-burst over Baghdad in January 1991, CNN had achieved total air superiority over the other television networks. It held that position until Iraq temporarily shut down the news operation some sixteen hours later.

Formed in 1981, CNN is a news organization that was once dismissed as the "Chicken Noodle Network." It ordinarily received ratings less than one-tenth as high as those of its competitors. But on January 16, the first day of the Persian Gulf War, nearly 11 million households tuned in to CNN.

Perhaps even more than Vietnam, the Persian Gulf conflict was a television war. Americans watched in shock and alarm as the bombs went off over Baghdad. They marched forward with the troops across the Saudi desert, and they joined the victorious caravans streaming into liberated Kuwait. It was a moment of triumph for the Allied Forces and a moment of triumph for television.

Questions
1. World leaders, including Iraqi president Saddam Hussein, said that they watch CNN regularly. Does CNN seem to be more objective in its coverage of international news than the other American networks?
2. How does television coverage of a war affect how viewers think about the war?

tion, the more specialized each job becomes. Although the glamour of being a "star" makes television work seem very attractive, most jobs are *behind* the cameras. This is especially true of the entry-level positions where you have the best opportunities for finding a job.

Programming

A programming department selects, plans, and produces the programs that the station broadcasts. Nearly every station produces some of its own shows, including news and sports events. The program director not only plans the daily schedule but also develops the station's policies together with the general manager and the sales manager. Others who work in the program-

ming department include producers, directors, writers, staff announcers, and a public affairs director. Most stations also have a news staff, which includes a news director, reporters, writers, and assignment editors.

Depending on the size of the station, more technical positions in programming can include art directors, set designers, makeup artists, graphic artists, wardrobe designers, music librarians, camera operators, film and tape editors, lighting directors, floor directors, and sound effects technicians.

Engineering

People who work in engineering operate, maintain, and monitor the equipment that sends programs to home television sets. They are also responsible for keeping

COMMUNICATION WORKS

Steve Gaines, Community Access Coordinator

"When it's done well, it looks so easy," explains Steve Gaines, a community access coordinator who works for the Nebraska Educational Television Network. "But making television programs is a complex business."

"You can't let the fact that it's a technical medium dictate what you end up with," Gaines says. "You can't let it get in the way of creativity."

Gaines himself is a good example of what creativity can do. In 1968, after several years of teaching elementary school, Gaines found a job at Nebraska Educational Television (NETV) as a set designer. Since that time, he has also had numerous opportunities to act, appearing in the television miniseries "Amerika" and in a nationally known series on poetry called "Anyone for Tennyson?"

In 1987, Gaines became the government educational access coordinator for NETV. As the access coordinator, Gaines teaches people what they need to know to get a program on the air. He has worked with many groups, including a center for senior citizens, a home for orphans, and a class of high school students.

Television "has certainly reduced the size of the world," Gaines says, but the power of television is not always a good thing. Gaines said the emphasis placed on good looks is television's "biggest shortcoming." The emphasis on good looks is "part of the whole problem of anorexia and bulimia." Many are led to believe that the television image "is what you have to look like."

But on a positive note, television can also be used to benefit its viewers. "You can learn things," Gaines says. "TV can be educational." Channels such as the Public Broadcasting System (PBS), the Arts and Entertainment network, and the Discovery Channel allow people to learn things "quickly and succinctly." Community access programs like the one Steve Gaines directs will certainly play a major role in determining what television can teach all of us.

---

the station transmitter operating within the technical limits set by the FCC. Electronic training is usually required of engineering applicants, but some technical work does not require a high degree of training—the operation of cameras, lights, microphone booms, and tape machines, for example.

Sales and General Administration

A sales department sells air time to sponsors, advertising agencies, and other buyers. Their work also includes developing sales plans that can tie in with certain seasons of the year or special programs the station plans to broadcast. In addition to the sales manager, other positions include salespeople (who call on advertisers and advertising agencies), copywriters, and the traffic manager (who schedules the commercials).

The general administration department runs the business side of the station. The station manager is responsible for day-to-day operations and, in particular, for promotional activities. Entry-level jobs here include secretaries, typists, bookkeepers, clerks, and messengers.

Crew Positions for a Typical Production

The production of a television program requires teamwork. It takes total cooperation from both the people in front of the camera (called **talent**) and those behind (the production staff). The following is a list of basic crew positions for a typical television studio production.

◆ *Producer.* Oversees entire program. Works with director to select talent and coordinate technical details, such as sets and lights.

◆ *Director.* Transforms a written script into a visual experience. Directs the cast and crew. Once taping starts, the director runs the show.

◆ *Talent.* Speak and perform before a camera. These positions may include anchors (hosts for news or information programs), announcers, talk show hosts, actors, and reporters.

◆ *Technical director.* Usually acts as crew chief and does the video switching—the process of choosing

By manipulating the audio control board, the audio engineer raises and lowers microphone levels during the production of a television program.

which of several camera signals to send to viewers.

- ◆ *Camera operator.* Operates a camera and often takes care of lighting.
- ◆ *Floor director.* In charge of all studio activities. Relays director's instructions to all studio personnel.
- ◆ *Graphic artist.* Prepares titles, slides, and other visual materials.
- ◆ *Character generator.* Prepares and operates a device used to put words on the screen.
- ◆ *Audio engineer.* In charge of all audio operations. Runs the audio control board, which raises and lowers microphone levels, during the production.
- ◆ *Set designer.* Designs and constructs the sets. Provides necessary props.

The Camera

The camera is the single most important piece of television equipment. Even if you spend all your time in front of the camera, you should understand how it works and what it can do. Simply speaking, a television camera—whether a $50,000 studio model or a much cheaper hand-held portable—changes the light reflected from a scene into electronic signals. At the same time, a microphone picks up the sounds from the scene and changes them, too, into electronic signals.

Television engineers refer to the signals from a camera as **video** and the signals from a microphone as **audio.** In this section we will discuss how a camera moves, what kinds of pictures it can produce, and how camera operators can achieve certain effects by the way they frame their subjects.

Camera Movements

Managing the movement and positioning of a video camera is an art in itself. All camera movements must be done as smoothly as possible. To accomplish this, you—as a video operator—should learn the five basic camera movements: panning, tilting, trucking, dollying, and zooming.

Panning occurs when you swing the camera from side to side. In other words, you rotate the camera left or right while the base of the camera remains in the same position. You use a pan to show viewers the size of an area, to follow action, or to indicate the distance between two subjects in a scene. You might, for example, use a panning shot to show people in a courtroom.

Tilting is similar to panning, but it is a vertical movement instead of a horizontal one. You tip the camera either up or down while the camera base again remains stationary. A tilt can be used to show the height of a large building or to keep a subject's face centered during a zoom (discussed below).

Trucking takes place when you move the entire camera to the left or right. This differs from panning, where the camera does not move from its spot on the floor. Trucking can best be accomplished if the camera is mounted on a movable pedestal. A truck shot is more difficult to execute smoothly than a pan shot because you have to move a heavy camera over an uneven studio floor littered with obstacles like other camera cables. A trucking movement can be the right shot, however, when you wish to follow a moving subject.

Moving the camera forward or back is known as **dollying.** When you dolly-in,

Field of View

Extreme Long Shot (XLS)

Long Shot (LS)

Medium Shot (MS)

Medium Close-up (MCU)

Close-up (CU)

Extreme Close-up (ECU)

you move forward. This movement gives the viewer the impression that he or she is entering the scene as the camera moves in for a closer shot. The dolly-in is very useful at the beginning of a program following a wide shot that shows the entire scene. Similarly, a dolly-back (a move backward) can be used to signal the end of a program.

Zooming is one of the camera operator's most important options. To zoom, you enlarge or reduce the size of the subject in the picture (by turning the handle of a studio camera or pressing a button on a hand-held camera). You can either zoom in on a subject (filling the screen with the subject's face) or zoom back (showing the subject in his or her surroundings). Zooming in, for example, is very effective when you want the viewer to concentrate on what someone is saying or feeling.

Field of View

Field of view refers to how much of the scene the camera shows. The terms related to field of view are particularly important because they are used by television writers, directors, and other crew members in their shot descriptions:

✦ *Extreme long shot (XLS)*. The extreme long shot gives the audience a panoramic view of the scene. The viewer may not be able to see all the important details in this shot, but it is valuable for establishing a relationship between the parts and the whole. An XLS of a baseball game, for example, might be taken from a blimp and would show the entire stadium.

✦ *Long shot (LS)*. The long shot is not as wide as the extreme long shot, but it is still large enough to show viewers the relationship between the actors and their setting. A long shot at the baseball game might show the field of play and the scoreboard. Extreme long shots and long shots are often referred to as *establishing shots* because they establish the setting and the relationships between the individual parts of the shot.

✦ *Medium shot (MS)*. The medium shot is tighter (that is, closer to the subject) than the long shot but not as tight as a close-up. A medium shot at a baseball game might let you look in toward home plate from center field, revealing the pitcher, batter, catcher, and umpire.

✦ *Medium close-up (MCU)*. The medium close-up is one of the most frequently used shots in television. It usually consists of a head-and-shoulders shot of the subject. In the baseball game, for example, you might see the batter taking a practice swing in an MCU.

✦ *Close-up (CU)*. The close-up is an extremely powerful image conveyed by a tight shot of the subject's head. A close-up of an object should fill the screen. The close-up is one of the most effective shots for providing a view of the details of a face or an object. A close-up at the ball game might show the pitcher's face as he looks toward the catcher for a sign.

✦ *Extreme close-up (ECU)*. The extreme close-up is the tightest shot possible. The extreme close-up will show a portion of a subject's face—just the eyes and nose, for instance. At the baseball game, the operator might use an extreme close-up to show the pitcher's hand gripping the ball to throw a curve.

Framing a Subject

Framing refers to the placement of a person within the picture. When a person is the subject of a shot, you should consider both headroom and noseroom. **Headroom** refers to the distance between the top of the person's head and the top edge of the picture. With too little headroom, the person appears to stick to the top of the frame. Similarly, if the subject is placed too low in the frame, the person appears to be sinking. More headroom is appropriate on longer shots, and less headroom works better on close-ups.

You should pay particular attention to headroom whenever you zoom in or out. Typically, as you zoom out and the subject becomes smaller, headroom will increase. Therefore, you will need to tilt the camera down to compensate. On the other

TelePrompTer Helps Eye Contact

The **TelePrompTer** is an important piece of equipment that enables people reading scripts (on a news program, for example) to look directly into the camera. Speakers, after all, are supposed to look at the audience. A speaker whose head is down in the script is merely reading, not communicating.

The TelePrompTer, which is usually attached to the front of one of the studio cameras, contains a set of mirrors that reflect the words of the script toward the speaker. To the speaker, it looks as if the words are written on a screen at the front of the camera. To the people in the audience, it looks as if the speaker is looking directly at them.

hand, as you zoom in and the subject becomes larger, the amount of headroom will decrease. In this case, you may need to tilt up to correct the framing.

The concept of **noseroom** is similar. Noseroom refers to the distance between the nose of the person in a shot and the edge of the television screen. If the subject looks to one side of the frame, you should pan the camera slightly to maintain enough noseroom ahead of the person so that she doesn't appear glued to the side of the frame. (If, however, a subject is supposedly being chased, framing him with little noseroom reinforces the idea that he is trapped. This technique is commonly used in horror films.)

You should also pay close attention to the background of a video picture. Objects in the background can distract the viewer from what is really important. Consider a shot of someone sitting in a chair with a painting on the wall in the background. Frame the shot so that the outline of the person's head doesn't touch the bottom of the painting—the viewer may think the painting is balanced on the subject's head. Also, avoid shots in which trees and poles in the background appear to grow out of the head of a person in the foreground.

Using Microphones

As a television speaker, you should also be familiar with television microphones, which are somewhat different from radio mikes. Engineers typically use four kinds of microphones as basic equipment: the hand-held omnidirectional mike, the tiny lavaliere mike, the transmitter (wireless) mike, and the shotgun mike. Each has its own particular characteristics.

Omnidirectional Microphones

Omni means "all," and hand-held **omni-directional microphones** pick up the sound from all directions. They come in many different shapes and sizes and are useful in situations where the background noise is fairly low. They work best when pointed directly at the sound source. Where the background sound is very loud, an omnidirectional microphone may not work well.

Lavaliere Microphones

Lavaliere microphones are very small mikes attached to the speaker's clothing with clips or worn around the neck on a cord. They provide very good sound quality, especially where the background sound is high. Because they are quite directional, however, they must be aimed carefully at the sound source they are expected to pick up.

Wireless Microphones

Wireless microphones contain a tiny transmitter that can send the audio signal to a remote receiver. These mikes are very handy for close-in situations and are also useful when the speaker doesn't want to be (or can't be) attached to the tape recorder by a cable. The range of a wireless mike varies according to the power of its transmitter. A disadvantage of wireless mikes is that they use common radio frequencies, so their receivers often pick up such distracting things as phone calls or other wireless mikes being used in the same area.

Shotgun Microphones

Shotgun microphones are designed to pick up sound at a considerable distance. They are very directional and must be aimed right at the sound source. When that is done, however, they can obtain good sound quality from many feet away. They are excellent for getting the questions from the floor at a public meeting, for instance, or the words of a speaker who is surrounded by a crowd.

Shotgun mikes should be used only for getting specific sound from some distance away. They can look very awkward when they are hand-held because they bear a resemblance to the barrel of a gun. Network crews working with a newly developed shotgun mike in El Salvador found this out the hard way. A sound crewman cautiously pointed the mike over a wall, drawing rifle fire from somewhere nearby within a few seconds.

TAKING CHARGE

1. Arrange a tour of a local television station. If possible, sit in on a live news program.
2. Challenge each other to bring your funniest home videos to class. Watch for technical mistakes you can spot, such as too much panning or uneven camera movement.
3. Use a camcorder to test your ability to pan, zoom, and tilt.
4. Find out what goes on behind the scenes. Many local cable television companies offer free instructional courses on television production. Sign up for one.
5. Make a list of how different camera movements are used on your favorite television show.

III Production Techniques

Television production is a fascinating, demanding, and exciting enterprise. Some productions are staged in mammoth studios with millions of dollars' worth of equipment and large crews. Other, more modest productions take place in tiny, *makeshift* quarters with a few hundred dollars' worth of equipment and a crew of two or three. In either case, the success of the production begins with the producer, a person who is responsible for pulling the whole project together.

The producer is in charge of hiring writers and performers, setting up a budget, developing a lighting plan, designing a set, and arranging for costumes. These and a hundred other details must be dealt with successfully if the whole production is to come together. In this section, we focus on two of the tools a producer has to work with: a written script and a storyboard.

Broadcast Scriptwriting

Broadcast words lack permanence. Viewers have no chance to go back over parts of a story that they haven't understood. Consequently, simplicity and ease of understanding are the primary requirements for writing broadcast scripts. Television writers strive for a style that closely resembles ordinary conversation.

Conversational Style

As much as possible, script writers try to write like people talk. A *judicious* mixture of sentences of varying lengths, with shorter sentences predominating, seems to work best. Compound sentences and unusually long sentences are less suitable.

INSTANT IMPACT

Testing a Story Out Loud

As you practice reading your story, you will also be "testing" it because you will find places that are difficult to read, or sound funny, or both. Read the following sentence silently. Then try reading it aloud.

> She said small-size businesses are especially susceptible to idiosyncrasies in business cycles.

How about this one:

> Poor planning precipitated a basically perpendicular plummet in popular-priced products.

Tongue-tied? Think how you might feel reading these for the first time on television. Granted, these are extreme examples, but be sure to listen to how your copy sounds when it is read aloud—before the audience does.

Short words are usually better than long words, and short, familiar words are the best of all.

Contractions are usually acceptable in broadcast writing because they give a story a sense of informality, but use them with caution. Too many contractions can make you sound sloppy.

Broadcast scriptwriting is informal and often *colloquial*, but never slangy. Compare the words in the following lists:

Formal (*official writing*)	Conversational (*good for broadcast*)	Slang (*inappropriate*)
male, female	man, woman	dude, chick
physician	doctor	doc
reside	live	hang out
vehicle	car, truck	wheels
dismissed	fired	axed

COMMUNICATION BREAKDOWN

Television Commercials Insult Women

According to a study by the New York Chapter of the National Organization for Women, watching commercials is like being blasted by a propaganda machine dedicated to the humiliation of women. Less than 1 percent of the commercials the organization studied showed women as independent people, leading lives of their own. In 43 percent, women were involved in household tasks; in 38 percent, they were domestic assistants to men; and in 17 percent, they were simply sex objects.

In most commercials, the woman is there to serve. Her life alternates between the kitchen and the bedroom, persecuting germs, scrubbing dirt off floors, and coloring her hair to make it look more natural. A fabric softener commercial offered this definition of a wife: "Honey, here's your laundry," the new bride gushes. "Did I wash it right?" Her husband indicates his approval, and she is fulfilled. "He noticed," she says happily. "I'm a wife."

In other ads, women frolic on the beach, in the gym, or at a party; but almost without exception, their single-minded goal appears to be attracting the attention of men. Even in these ads, women rarely have the satisfaction of endorsing a product. The female character's voice is almost always followed by a male voice-over (a narration by a speaker whose face is not seen)—the voice of authority, which confers the stamp of approval on the product. Nearly 90 percent of the voice-overs in American commercials are done by men, even though the vast majority of characters in those commercials are women.

Questions
1. Are men also stereotyped by television commercials? If so, how?
2. What positive role models for young women are there in television commercials?

Try to hit a happy medium in your writing between formal language and street slang.

Pauses

Pauses are helpful because they make written scripts sound more like spoken language. Pauses can also add a twist of irony or humor at the end of a story. To indicate that a speaker should pause, the writer may use either a dash (—) or a series of dots (. . .) in the script. The length of the dash or series of dots indicates how long the pause should last. The longer the dash or series of dots, the longer the pause.

Pronunciation

When the writer must use a word that may be difficult to pronounce, the best thing to do is to find the correct pronunciation and then type a phonetic version into the script. This should be done each time that word occurs in the text. For example:

> A teenager seeking to learn the fate of Lebanon's lost Shiite (SHEE'-EYET) Moslem leader hijacked a Lebanese jetliner today.

Check pronunciations by asking. This is no place for guesswork.

Timing

You must know how long a story is going to run on air before you can turn it over to the person who will do the reading. The only way to find out is to time yourself as you read it aloud. Silent reading will not work. We all read faster silently than aloud.

Here is a rule of thumb: If you read aloud at a normal rate, you will cover about fifteen lines of typed material in one minute. You can use this to estimate the length of your story. But check the timing by reading the story aloud yourself.

How Television Copy Looks

A television script is usually prepared in the *split-page* format. The video and audio directions are on the left half of each page; the words to be read are on the right. (In the drawing on the next page music *under* means soft music can be heard under the announcer's voice and music *out* means no music can be heard.)

Storyboards

A **storyboard** is the visual plan for a potential television production. In developing a storyboard, the planners draw pictures of what the camera will show and arrange them in sequence with a written script. Storyboards have long been used in the production of commercials, where the visual parts of the program can be drawn in detail. Often, directors make preliminary decisions about camera shots and angles on the basis of the pictures in the storyboards.

TAKING CHARGE

1. Write and tape-record a five-minute newscast about the activities of a single day in your school. Compare your decisions on the order and time allocated to each story with the work of other students in the class.
2. Create a storyboard for a public service announcement on education.
3. Prepare a documentary on videotape about your school. Direct it to a special audience—for instance, students new to the school. Focus on one segment of the school, perhaps the activities program, athletics, or the science curriculum.

Sample Television Script

VIDEO	AUDIO	TEXT
WIDE SHOT	MUSIC: ESTABLISH FIVE SECONDS AND UNDER	
CAMERA 2		ANNCR: A 2-YEAR GOVERNMENT STUDY SHOWS THERE MAY BE NEW HOPE FOR AIDS PATIENTS.
MCU	MUSIC: OUT.	
CAMERA 1		ANNCR: HEALTH SECRETARY LOUIS SULLIVAN SAYS WE'RE ENTERING A PERIOD WHEN AIDS MAY BECOME A TREATABLE DISEASE.
CU, CAMERA 2		ANNCR: NO CURE HAS BEEN FOUND, . . . , BUT THE TESTS SHOW THAT THE DRUG AZT SIGNIFICANTLY SLOWS THE PROGRESS OF AIDS IN SOME PATIENTS WHO ARE IN THE EARLIEST STAGES OF THE DISEASE.

IV Delivery Techniques

All of the planning and rehearsal work that goes into a television program comes to a climax when it goes on the air. At that moment, television performers are, in a sense, invited into the homes of the audience. They may be looking into a camera, but they should constantly remind themselves that they are speaking to real viewers somewhere out there.

One of the most familiar kinds of speakers on television is the news **anchor,** a person who holds an entire program together, at times by speaking directly to the audience, and at times by introducing other speakers or prepared segments. We will use television news anchors in this section as examples of television speakers to enable us to dramatize the skills a good television speaker needs.

The Anchors

Although most of us could probably do a competent job of reading the news, not everyone can learn to be an anchor. Succeeding on television requires skill, luck, and a great deal of determination. Clearly, you have to want to be an anchor to be good at it. Russell Tornabene, a long-time NBC news executive, said, "The best anchor is a person who feels the best they've felt all day when the red light on the camera goes on, and who feels depressed when the news goes off the air."

> "The best anchor is a person who feels the best they've felt all day when the red light on the camera goes on, and who feels depressed when the news goes off the air."
>
> **Russell Tornabene**

Let's assume you are reasonably skillful, more than a little lucky, and get a kick out of being on the air. What else do you need to succeed? Here are several attributes, in no particular order, collected from a variety of news directors and consultants.

1. Pleasant on-air personality.
2. Charisma.
3. Good appearance.
4. Effective speaking voice.
5. Poise.
6. Authoritativeness.
7. Concentration.
8. Desire to practice.
9. Writing ability.

Let's take a quick look at each of these qualities in detail.

Pleasant On-air Personality

Obviously, it's hard to define what makes a personality pleasant. Let's say that having a pleasant on-air personality means you show that you like being on the air talking to people. You make it clear by your body language and enthusiasm that this time is important to you. You have valuable information to deliver; you are comfortable and ready to go. You project the image of a take-charge person who is businesslike but friendly.

Charisma

Charisma is even harder to define than personality. Some have it and some don't. Murphy Brown, for example, has it; Arsenio Hall has it; Pat Sajak doesn't. Charisma has something to do with the ability to connect. In the case of television personalities, it means the ability to touch or move an audience. *Charisma* comes from a Greek word meaning "gift of God," a good definition for an elusive quality that inspires allegiance and devotion. If you have charisma, you belong in front of a television camera.

Bernard Shaw, pictured here, is a CNN anchor. A television news anchor must possess a pleasant on-air personality, an effective speaking voice, poise, authoritativeness, and writing ability, among other attributes and skills.

Good Appearance

Some critics charge that anchors are always chosen for their looks and not their brains. An anchor in Kansas City sued her station not long ago when she was fired; she said the station decided she looked too old for the job. Certainly a good appearance will enhance your chances, but there are a few things you can do to improve the odds.

The rule at most stations seems to be "take the middle of the road." Don't look too young. Don't look too old. Don't look too handsome or too pretty. If you do, nobody will believe you. Conservative clothing and a no-nonsense manner will go far in making a television performer seem more mature and credible, whatever his or her looks may be.

Effective Speaking Voice

An anchor needs a strong, clear voice that people will enjoy hearing. Remember, you have been invited into the viewer's living room for polite but lively conversation. Review Chapter 11 for tips on developing an effective speaking voice.

Poise

Many things can happen when you are on the air, some of them bad and nearly all of them unexpected. Tom Brokaw, anchor for "NBC Nightly News," said after a particularly bumpy show, "When I went in there I was thirty-five, now I am seventy." Actually, those who watched the program never knew anything was wrong. Brokaw and hundreds of others like him have developed the knack of remaining calm when it seems the world is coming to an end.

Authoritativeness

The authority that anchors convey comes in large part from speaking with an authoritative tone. To develop this tone, you must learn to speak firmly, crisply, and decisively. Hesitations, "ums," "ers," mispronunciations, and slurring all detract from your message and distract viewers from what you have to say. You should learn to read with as few errors as possible. If you make an error, you must correct it quickly and precisely. As one producer said, "Attack it, don't wrestle it."

Concentration

The ability to concentrate on the complex activity that makes up a television news program is the key to calmness and authority. When you are on the air, every nerve and fiber of your body must concentrate on the task at hand—telling the audience what happened today. Like a good actor, you must learn to stay in your role as newscaster no matter what happens.

Practice

On-air work, like any other skill that requires precision and concentration, takes practice. You can simply get a script and read into a mirror, but you should also take advantage of every opportunity to practice your verbal skills before an audience. Practice maintaining eye contact in interpersonal situations. Practice, too, remaining calm and objective while reading stories that arouse your emotions.

Writing Ability

Ordinarily, anchors are expected to write their own material. This means that they must have all the skills the station would expect of its full-time writers. Most television anchors come to work around noon and spend the afternoon writing for the early evening news (at 6 or 7 P.M.). Then they spend the next few hours updating the show for the late news (at 10 or 11 P.M.).

Dress by the Book

Clothing styles that would not be objectionable in "real life" can be very distracting on the television screen. Anyone who wishes to be successful as on-air television talent must conform to the requirements of the medium as defined by employers. If you have a serious interest in making it in television, and if you want to reduce the obstacles to being accepted, consider these suggestions:

1. Television producers like a conservative, tailored look. Men's shirt collars should not gap, and ties should be pulled up tight. Solid colors are usually best. "Busy" patterns should be avoided.

   Women's clothing should also be well fitted. Open-neck dresses or blouses often look too informal for an authoritative image. Shiny fabrics may look too bright on television. Avoid anything with a horizontal pattern unless you are very thin. The television camera adds weight, and horizontal patterns enhance the effect.

2. Keep your hair cut fairly short. Women on television usually have hair that is shoulder length or slightly shorter. Men usually have a regular cut—no buzz cuts, punk styles, or pony tails. Invest in a few cans of industrial-strength hair spray if you're serious about being a professional.

3. Clean-shaven men have fewer problems being accepted than do those with beards. Facial hair is more acceptable now than twenty years ago, but the prejudice against beards remains at most stations.

4. Glasses are not seen as a positive accessory for television talent. If you need glasses to read the TelePrompTer, you would be wise to get contact lenses. You may be

able to use glasses while on camera once you have proven yourself to the boss, but you must get hired first.

5. Women should wear dresses or skirts that fall over the knee when they cross their legs. Men should be sure to wear dark socks that are long enough to cover their ankles when they cross their legs. Wear dress shoes to match your other clothing.

6. Men should wear long-sleeved shirts, even under sport coats. A long expanse of hairy arm that shows when you reach for something will not win the director's approval. Most young women will look older—and therefore more credible—with long sleeves. Short sleeves are for parties and informal gatherings; long sleeves are for formal, serious business.

Posture Pointers

Television anchors also need to pay special attention to their body language. Consider these suggestions for conveying a positive appearance:

1. Hold your head still when you appear on camera. People with a normal amount of enthusiasm tend to move their heads when they talk. Television exaggerates any movement. On camera, normal head movement makes you look like your head is attached to your body by a spring. Work on locking your head in place and holding your gaze steady. You'll feel uncomfortable, but you will look better.

2. Sit up straight. Scoot back in the chair and keep your spine touching the back of the chair all the way up. No slumping allowed.

3. Keep your elbows close to your sides. If you're seated in a chair with arms, avoid using the arms as supports. If you are sitting at an anchor desk or a table, don't use it to support your weight—your clothes will bunch at the shoulders.

4. Keep your feet and knees close together when on camera. Most men plant their feet as wide apart as possible and sprawl, an unbecoming habit that has no place on television.

5. Move very slowly, even if you are just turning your head to look at a guest. Pretend you are under water; move in slow motion.

Broadcast Ethics

Explicit sex! Full frontal nudity! Blood and gore! Well, not yet. Since the television industry began, however, those who produce its programs have been accused of presenting material that shocks and offends. To what degree are broadcasters guilty of these charges? Are they simply giving the public what it wants? Are there guidelines, rules, or restrictions that govern what can and can't be shown on television?

The Federal Communications Commission

Television depends on a limited resource, the air waves, to deliver messages to its viewers. The air waves are considered a natural resource like water or air and cannot be bought or sold. Because so

In the 1950s, censors prohibited the use of the word *pregnant* to describe Lucille Ball when she performed in that condition on the television show "I Love Lucy."

many people would like to use the air waves, though, some government regulation is necessary. Without the assignment of space (what we frequently call channels) by a central authority, television without signal interference would be impossible.

For this reason, Congress established the Federal Communications Commission (FCC) in 1934. The FCC is an independent federal agency composed of five commissioners appointed by the president and confirmed by the Senate. It licenses radio and television stations and assigns frequencies for their use. It determines the call letters a station will use and regulates the amount of power a station can have.

More to the point, the FCC also sets standards that must be met if a station

hopes to have its license renewed. The number of commercials a station may carry, for example, is strictly limited by the FCC. (Fortunately, there is no rule yet to prevent all of us from switching channels during those commercials.) What about the content of the programs themselves, though?

Network Censors

The FCC is rarely involved with specific cases of *censorship,* that is, removing objectionable material from a program. When performers and directors complain that their ideas have been rejected, they are usually complaining about the major television networks, which set their own standards for what is acceptable and in good taste. In the 1950s, for instance, Lucy Ricardo was never allowed to refer to herself as being "pregnant" on the "I Love Lucy" show, even though there was little doubt she would soon be a mother. Times change. In 1990, the cast of "Saturday Night Live" went out of its way to show off a new attitude toward censorship. In a skit set at a nudist club, the cast stood at a bar and discussed the human anatomy in graphic terms.

Not everything goes, however. MTV, the all-music channel, rejected a Madonna video that was too explicit. The networks all observe some rules of thumb about what should be shown during "prime time" and "family time" (8 and 9 P.M., EST). Advertisers occasionally pull their ads if they find something objectionable in a program. Parent groups have brought considerable pressure on the networks to monitor the level of violence in children's cartoons.

TAKING CHARGE

1. Select four or five class members and set up a camera demonstration to see how their school clothes look on television. Select those who are wearing clothing and accessories that may present specific problems. (Examples include clothing with wide stripes, small patterns, or high contrast, as well as jewelry.) Make a videotape of each student talking for a few moments and then critique the tape strictly from the point of view of the impression the student's clothing creates.

2. Ask a local station for a copy of one of its anchor scripts. Practice reading the script with as few errors as possible.

3. Make a videotape demonstrating some dos and don'ts for on-air talent.

4. Find out how much advertising time costs on the local television stations.

5. Determine how much time in each television hour is given to commercials. The percentage of time devoted to advertising will vary according to the time of day—daytime, prime time, and late night. Keep track of these differences.

REVIEW AND ENRICHMENT

LOOKING BACK

Listed below are the major ideas discussed in this chapter.

✦ Television is the most popular of all the mass media. Its greatest advantage is its ability to reach so many people at the same time.

✦ About a thousand television stations in the United States are commercial operations; another three hundred are public stations.

✦ The first experimental television broadcasts to a mass audience were made in 1936. By 1939, television was providing regular coverage of news and sports.

✦ A television production typically consists of many people working behind the scenes and just a few who appear on the screen.

✦ Camera operators must be familiar with the five major camera options: panning, tilting, trucking, dollying, and zooming.

✦ Field of view refers to how much of the scene the camera shows. Shots include the extreme long shot, long shot, medium shot, medium close-up, close-up, and extreme close-up.

✦ Anchors need to remain calm in the midst of swirling activity and a wide variety of distractions.

✦ A conservative look in both clothing and personal grooming is the norm for most television work.

✦ When appearing on television, speakers should try to keep their heads still and move slowly.

✦ Since 1934, the Federal Communications Commission has regulated television stations in the United States.

SPEECH VOCABULARY

Use the terms listed below in the sentences that follow. Use each word only once. Not every word will be used.

ratings system	tilting	noseroom
commercial stations	trucking	omnidirectional microphones
public stations	dollying	lavaliere microphones
talent	zooming	wireless microphones
video	field of view	shotgun microphones
audio	TelePrompTer	storyboard
panning	headroom	anchor

1. _____ is swinging the camera to the left or right. The movement is called _____ when the camera is moved up or down.
2. _____ in on a subject with a television camera creates a tight close-up.
3. A _____, the visual plan for a television commercial, also includes directions for long, medium, and close-up shots, which are varieties of something called _____.
4. Two other important camera movements include _____, which occurs when the camera operator moves the camera and its base forward or back, and _____, where the operator moves the camera and its base from side to side.
5. _____ refers to the amount of space above a subject's head in the television screen; _____ refers to the amount of room in front of the subject's face.
6. _____ must be very concerned with the work of the A. C. Nielsen Company, which places specially equipped television sets in the homes of a few thousand Americans to establish a _____.
7. Educational programs are mainstays of _____, which depend on donations and government support for its existence.
8. An _____, or host, of a television news program is also referred to as an on-camera person, or _____. This person reads from written material that appears at the front of the camera on a _____.
9. A portable television camera is capable of recording both visual signals, called _____, and sound signals, called _____.
10. The four major kinds of television microphones include those worn on the clothing (_____), those that can pick up sound from all directions (_____), those that can send a signal to a remote receiver (_____), and those that can pick up a speaker in a large crowd (_____).

GENERAL VOCABULARY

Define the following terms and use each in a sentence.

malicious	maneuverability	colloquial
spontaneity	makeshift	charisma
panoramic	judicious	censorship
framing		

THINGS TO REMEMBER

1. About how much time do American students spend watching television per week?
2. What is the most important difference between commercial and public television stations?
3. What program drew the largest television viewing audience in history?
4. Name the most important figure in the development of television technology.
5. What are the producer's responsibilities for a television program?
6. What is the main reason to use a panning shot?
7. How can a television speaker create the impression of being authoritative?
8. Should a television speaker try to be more enthusiastic than usual? Why or why not?
9. What is the split-page format for scriptwriting?
10. Name the governmental authority responsible for licensing and supervising radio and television stations.

THINGS TO DO

1. Contact the local television stations in your area. Which station is affiliated with which network? Who owns the stations? Are any of them independent (not affiliated with a network)?
2. Take a class survey to find out the number of television sets in each student's home. Compare this number with the number of telephones or bathtubs in each home.
3. Interview someone who remembers the days before television. Ask this person how he or she thinks television has changed family life and the way people spend their time.
4. Evaluate the reality level of a popular television program. Use a checklist with one category on the left ("Realistic") and one on the right ("Unrealistic") to record your comments. Discuss your findings in class.

THINGS TO TALK ABOUT

1. Some people claim that television inspires people to imitate what they see on the screen. This has even been used as a defense in several murder cases. Does television influence how people behave?
2. Studies have shown that there are an average of eight incidents per hour on television of "physical force intended to hurt or kill." Is television too violent?

3. Discuss how television has influenced sports in the United States. Consider (a) how television has helped sports, (b) whether television encourages or discourages people from participating in sports, (c) whether watching sports on television might replace watching them in person, and (d) which sports are most and least successful on television.
4. Discuss why soap operas are so popular.
5. Recall the last time the family television set broke down. How long was the set out of order, and what happened to everyone's habits? Agree not to watch television for forty-eight hours. What will you do with your time instead?
6. Take a survey of the class to find out which program is watched by the most class members. Discuss why that program is popular and what ideas, attitudes, or behaviors it teaches.
7. Have a class discussion to select the three worst programs on television. Explain and defend your choices.

THINGS TO WRITE ABOUT

1. Write a short fictional story describing what happens "The Day Television Disappeared." Base your story on an incredibly large sunspot or some other catastrophe that knocks out television reception all over the world. What impact would that have on your life and the lives of those around you?
2. Design a television schedule for one day of programming for your own experimental television station. Your schedule should run for one twenty-four-hour day. It can include past or present programs from other networks, brand-new programs of your own devising, or some combination.
3. Write a critical review of a television program you have watched recently. Point out both the weak points and the strong points of the show.
4. The Whittle Corporation has created a special ten-minute news program for students called "Channel One." (If a school in your area is using the program, you may be able to get a videotape sample.) Although the program has been praised for its emphasis on current events and geography, it has also been condemned for including two commercials. Write a letter to your local school board in which you either propose that your school begin using the program or argue that it should not be used.

```
┌─────────────────────────────┐
│   REVIEW AND ENRICHMENT      │
│   ────────────────────       │
│        Continued             │
└─────────────────────────────┘
```

CRITICAL THINKING

1. Why do you think newspapers are not licensed by the government when radio and television stations are?
2. Does television do more harm than good? Consider both what television programming could do and what it actually does do.
3. Why do television producers favor a conservative look for hosts, anchors, and other on-air speakers? What exceptions are there to this standard?
4. A famous test of television viewers concluded that the more hours people watch television, the less accurate an idea they have about the real world. Researchers found, for instance, that those who watch a lot of television are much more likely to fear they will be the victims of a crime than those who watch little television. Imagine you are an alien on another planet who is somehow able to get television reception from Earth. What conclusions would you draw about American life from watching our television programs?

RELATED SPEECH TOPICS

Television is too much with us.

We have everything (or nothing) to learn from television.

The day the television broke

What television teaches us (about life, about school, about being a teenager)

What if Abraham Lincoln were running for president today?

Television can bring us together (or pull us apart).

Televised sports are turning us into a nation of couch potatoes.

Television censors have ruined (or saved) television programming.

Television shows should carry a rating system just as movies do.

Parents should exercise more control over what their children are watching.

How to talk back to your television (through citizen action groups against violence, etc.)

Television commercials insult women (or men).

Television encourages (or discourages) the stereotyping of women and minorities.

Television violence and American culture: an explosive combination

What music videos have done to build (or destroy) certain musicians

CHAPTER 23

Leadership and You

"A platoon leader doesn't get his platoon to go by getting up and shouting and saying, 'I am smarter, I am stronger, I am bigger. I am the leader.' He gets men to go along with him because they want to do it for him and they believe in him."

— Dwight David Eisenhower,
thirty-fourth president of the
United States (1953–1961)

LEARNING OBJECTIVES

After completing this chapter, you will be able to do the following.

♦ Define the terms *leadership* and *leader* and then effectively apply these terms to intrapersonal and interpersonal communication.
♦ List the specific components of leadership.
♦ Understand the correlation between leadership skills and self-confidence.
♦ Realize the importance of effective speaking in leadership.
♦ Implement leadership skills in your daily life.

CHAPTER OUTLINE

Following are the main sections in this chapter.

I What Does Leadership Mean?
II The Planks of Leadership

      Student Speech

      Chapter Review

NEW SPEECH TERMS

In this chapter, you will learn the meanings of the speech terms listed below.

leadership
leader
vision

learning styles
conflict
management

GENERAL VOCABULARY

Expanding your general vocabulary will help you become a more effective communicator. Listed below are some words appearing in this chapter that you should make part of your everyday vocabulary.

magnate
culmination
empowerment
facilitate

harmoniously
forfeiting
simulated

LOOKING AHEAD

In this chapter, you will, first of all, find out what the word *leadership* means. Next, you will think back to some of the oral communication skills presented in earlier chapters to see how leadership is often a consequence of many of those skills. Third, you will read about the planks of leadership (along with specific speaking strategies for each plank) that form the framework of effective leadership skills. Finally, you will be reminded that being a good speaker and a good leader means being a good person— a person who uses the spoken word to build, inspire, teach, and motivate others.

1 What Does Leadership Mean?

What does the word *leadership* mean to you? Is a leader the person who is the "boss"? Is it simply the person who is an authority figure? The biggest? The loudest? The smartest?

If you look for a clear-cut definition, you will find that opinions vary. The hotel *magnate* Conrad Hilton once stated that he saw real signs of leadership in any person smart enough to keep the shower curtain *in* while taking a shower! A popular entertainer said that while he was growing up, he thought *leadership* referred to anyone, male or female, who had the physical prowess to beat him up. The effective speaker and conscientious communicator knows, however, that **leadership** goes beyond shower curtains and brute strength. It deals with (1) how you effectively motivate yourself, and (2) how you effectively motivate and unite others to work together to accomplish a specific task.

Speech and leadership work hand in hand. Keep in mind that when we say this and when we discuss leadership skills, we are talking about not just corporate executives, high-ranking politicians, and military generals. Robert Kelly, a noted educator, speech coach, and communication consultant, says that at some point in your life, by choice or otherwise, you will find yourself in a position of leadership—perhaps as a parent, a professional, or a friend. When that moment arises, he adds, effective communication skills are necessary. Your spoken words and the way you use them become your credibility.

In 1992, a high school student attended the nationally recognized Hugh O'Brien Leadership Conference. She said that the main point the speakers made was that leadership is not some magical quality that you can quickly purchase the way you would purchase fast food, a new car, or a pair of name-brand shoes. On the contrary, leadership is a consequence of a number of qualities and components that must be individually considered. In other words, leadership, said the student, is hard work, and it takes real effort to "know the parts."

Several chapters in this text have presented you with some essential "parts" of leadership. For example, a **leader**—someone who actually puts leadership skills to good use—needs to be able to do the following things:

- ◆ Know how to listen (Chapter 3).
- ◆ Know how to work with a group (Chapter 6).
- ◆ Know how to organize (Chapter 8).
- ◆ Know how to use logic and reasoning (Chapter 9).
- ◆ Know how to persuade others (Chapter 13).

Leadership, then, is the *culmination* of a number of skills. Since many of the preceding chapters have dealt with essential leadership characteristics, it makes sense that the final chapter should put leadership into a realistic perspective and, in a sense, revisit you—the person—to see what you have learned and what you can apply to your oral communication.

Some earlier chapters compared the building of a good speaker to the building of a well-made house, stressing the importance of a strong value foundation. Just as a house must have a solid internal skeletal structure, so must a speaker. In a house, this skeletal structure is supplied by planks. Chapter 2 ended by presenting the planks of confidence. Let's conclude this final chapter by applying the same principle and looking at the planks of leadership that make up the framework of your leadership abilities.

INSTANT IMPACT

Nolan Ryan Speaks Out on Leadership

Known as the greatest strikeout pitcher in the history of baseball and the pitcher of seven no-hit games, Nolan Ryan of the Texas Rangers is certainly an amazing athlete. Although over forty-five years of age, Nolan Ryan is still pitching and is in top condition. He has won more than 300 games and struck out more than 5,500 batters during his career. What is his secret? He claims that there really is no secret. You should watch what you eat, exercise, and live a good, healthy life.

Nolan Ryan has written his biography, *Miracle Man*. In it, he speaks on the value of "mental well-being." He states that although he follows a vigorous exercise program during the off-season (weight lifting, sit-ups, sprints, swimming, ball tossing, and exercise bicycling), he also places a high value on some nonphysical factors—namely self-respect and a solid sense of family. He makes the point that before he can lead anyone else, he must have the self-discipline and value structure to lead himself. What is his advice? Regardless of your problems or your past history, you can improve and make a significant change in your life. However, you must lead and motivate yourself.

How's that for some leadership advice that is, like a Nolan Ryan fastball, "right down the middle"?

Source: Parade Magazine. *Reprinted with permission from Parade, copyright © 1992.*

Leadership

What qualities make these people leaders?

Colin Powell

Ann Richards

Cesar Chavez

Daniel Inouye

Bill Clinton

Henry Cisneros

TAKING CHARGE

1. What does the term *leadership* mean to you? Without using a dictionary, construct your own personal definition. When you think of the term, what person or persons come to mind? Why? Does student leadership differ from adult leadership? How are they the same? How are they different? Can you cite specific examples? Be prepared to explain your answers to the class.

TAKING CHARGE (CONTINUED)

---

2. It has been said that before you can lead others, you must lead yourself (read the Instant Impact on Nolan Ryan in this chapter). In groups of two or three, list at least three reasons why this is true. Be prepared to offer examples to prove your points.

3. In 1992, California took legal action against Sears, Roebuck & Company because the company's automotive department was caught systematically cheating the customers. The State Consumer Affairs Director placed the blame on the company's leadership, saying that there was intense corporate pressure on mechanics to sell certain automotive parts. What are some of the ways that leadership can abuse its authority and go wrong? Who are the victims? Either write your response or conduct a class panel discussion.

II The Planks of Leadership

Dr. Dirk E. Baer, a longtime high school principal and a graduate of his state's Principal's Leadership Academy, states that leadership is "the *empowerment* of people—through colleagueship, goal-setting, and role modeling—to create effective change." In other words, leaders are people who aren't afraid to give power and authority to others and who, in addition, have the power and the drive to "make things happen." There are, as we have said, several important leadership traits. Dr. Baer and a number of other noted educators in the leadership field agree on the importance of the seven characteristics that make up the planks of leadership that follow.

As you read the following discussion, pay attention to the specific speaking strategy at the end of each plank. The strategies will show you how leadership characteristics can be applied through your speaking.

Plank 1: A Leader Has a Sense of Vision

Simply put, **vision,** as it applies to leadership, means the ability to see more than just the obvious. A leader can often see a need that should be met, an idea or program that has tremendous possibilities, or how the pieces of the "big picture" fit together. Leaders can often "solve the puzzle" because they have the ability to see the scope of a situation in its entirety and then focus on what really matters.

The late Bruno E. Jacob was a person who saw a need and then had the vision to turn his dream into a reality. He wished to build an educational organization for students that would promote leadership through speaking—specifically, through competitive speech and debate. His idea was an organization called the National Forensic League; and at the time, 1925, it had only a handful of backers. However, because of his vision and persistence, the organization survived. Today, the NFL (not the National Football League) has grown to include over 2,500 secondary schools around the United States. Many of the speeches that appear at the ends of the chapters were presented in NFL competition. Bruno E. Jacob was a leader with a sense of vision. Appropriately, the motto of the National Forensic League is "Building Youth through Leadership."

Specific Speaking Strategy: As a leader, share your plans with other people. Sometimes sharing your ideas with others will result in the creation of an even more effective long-range objective. So don't keep your friends in the dark. Followers are more effective and enthusiastic if they know what is going on and where you are going with your ideas. Allow your oral communication to keep others accurately informed.

Plank 2: A Leader Is Willing to Act

Leaders are doers. Leaders believe in action and in taking charge. Not only do they have the vision to perceive a problem, but they also act in order to solve that problem. After all the talking, analyzing, and pondering, it is the leader who says to the rest of the group, "OK, let's get started. Let's do something *now*!"

While speaking to more than two hundred students from twenty high schools at a leadership seminar, a university profes-

sor said that it was time for students to quit thinking and talking about success and time for them to start acting! He suggested that the students map out a specific plan of action and then start working to actualize their goals. The seminar, which was titled "Now Is the Time to Start Thinking and Growing Rich," dealt with both personal and material success. It stressed that personal leadership begins with a philosophy of action. Here's an example of what happens when a leader combines vision with a willingness to act.

L. Strauss was the last of his brothers to leave Bavaria (now part of Germany) for the United States. The year was 1847, and he was only eighteen years old. Quick to learn English and an excellent salesman, L. Strauss reached California during the gold rush. His brothers, who owned a dry goods business, quickly put him to work. On one specific venture, he was told to fill his backpack with goods and not to return until everything in the pack had been sold. Soon everything was sold except for a few rolls of canvas. He approached an old miner and offered him the canvas for his tent. The miner responded that he didn't need material for a tent; instead, he needed pants that wouldn't wear out.

L. Strauss took the canvas to a tailor, who stitched together a pair of sturdy, waist-high overalls. The miner bought the jeans, and soon the word spread. What was the man's name? Levi Strauss. His pants were known simply as Levi's. Soon after, Levi started to make shirts, jackets, and other clothing. Why? He saw a need, he saw a market, he saw an opportunity. *Levi* is a household name today because Levi Strauss had the nerve to act back in 1847. Levi Strauss was a leader! You can learn a valuable lesson from this story. Allow your vision to work for you, and then "get in there and get your hands dirty." While luck may *facilitate* positive results, it is leadership that will make those results happen.

Specific Speaking Strategy: When leadership is needed, take charge. Make statements to the group such as these: "Here is what we now need to do." "Let's now make a specific list of who is responsible for what. We'll report back tomorrow on our progress." "It's time that we quit talking and start doing!" Let your spoken words show that you are not afraid of a challenge and that you will act on getting the task completed.

Plank 3: A Leader Knows That People Learn Differently

It would be nice if everyone learned the same way; however, this is not the case. A good leader knows that before there can be effective motivation, there must be effective communication. Obviously, if you know how people learn best, you have a better chance of getting and keeping their attention.

Perhaps when you read the sentence "A leader knows that people learn differently," you think it is referring only to classroom teachers. Not so. All leaders are teachers in some way. They teach specific strategies and lessons. They teach and promote certain attitudes. They teach about people and life.

The best speakers, teachers, and leaders are those people who can use their words to communicate with the greatest number of people. To do that, you need to be familiar with people's **learning styles**—the ways that they learn most effectively. We

examine four learning styles here: discussion, logic, design, and emotion.

Learning Style 1: Discussion

Some people learn best through meaningful discussion. They want to be actively involved in the oral communication process, with lots of dialogue and feedback. They appreciate face-to-face communication. Getting everyone's opinion is important to them, and they love to brainstorm, or throw many ideas out onto the table. They enjoy discussing each item before making a decision. They are alert and involved when they have the opportunity for verbal interaction.

Learning Style 2: Logic

Others learn best when things are presented logically, with a "just the facts" approach. Discussed in Chapter 9, logic stresses analysis, organization, and an approach focusing on "good sense." Some members of this group, not impressed by a lot of talk, are genuinely interested when they hear a direct, logical, to-the-point plan of action.

Learning Style 3: Design

Some people learn best when they can see and hear how the "big picture" fits together. People in this category might include engineers and other builders and designers. They are encouraged when the leader presents a clear picture of relationships and shows how the different parts are all going to work together as a smooth-running unit.

Learning Style 4: Emotion

For many people, the best communication is a hands-on approach, one in which the leader is energetic and fired up. As you have probably heard before, enthusiasm is contagious. Often, a leader who will show the group that he or she is emotionally involved with a specific project or idea will quickly have highly involved and committed followers.

Do any of these methods sound familiar? Which would work best for you? Knowing about learning styles can help a leader communicate with others. There are other ways of categorizing learning styles, but keeping these four types in mind should help when you are thinking about using your words to reach everyone. If you know how people learn—what approach "turns them on"—you have a much better chance of communicating effectively with them.

Specific Speaking Strategy: As an effective leader, take the time to get to know the people in your group. They will probably represent a number of learning styles. Use the spoken word as a directed instrument of discussion, analysis, design, and emotional involvement in order to target the various learning styles of all the group members.

Plank 4: A Leader Makes Good Decisions

As mentioned, there comes a time when the discussion stops and a decision must be reached. Nothing will kill the credibility of a leader more quickly than to be perceived by others as indecisive when the time comes for decision making. However, there is a world of difference between simply making a decision and making the right decision. Let's look at three

specific questions that a good leader might answer before making a final decision.

Question 1: Am I knowledgeable about the issues and the people involved?

A good leader does homework and is informed about facts that might affect his or her decision on a particular issue. Are important statistics about the issue needed? What about past history? What does the current literature say about this concern? Knowing all you can about the issues involved can provide you with the scope necessary to make a good decision and can give real teeth to your position as a solid decision maker.

In addition to being knowledgeable about issues, you need to know about people. How will the group react to this decision? Do you have the group's best interest in mind? Are you considering their hearts as well as their heads? What will be the long-range effect on everyone involved? A good leader knows that *people* are the most important part of any decision made!

Question 2: Am I making decisions in the correct order?

A good leader has to know how to prioritize and to put what is most important first. A school committee that spends hours on getting a big-name band to entertain the hundreds of people who will be attending an end-of-the-year dance—before it decides on a location large enough to accommodate all of those people—might run into problems later. A good leader decides on the larger issues first and then moves down the list, realistically considering needs versus wants be-

COMMUNICATION WORKS

Dorothy L. Alabach, Homemaker and Political Activist

If you want to talk to Dorothy L. Alabach, you had better be fast, because this "whirlwind" whose life is in "compulsive disorder" is constantly on the move. The mother of two grown children and the wife of a businessman, Alabach has devoted over thirty years of her life to raising her family while staying in the midst of the political arena. When her children were growing up, she was active in their 4-H club and their high school speech and debate and music programs. She always taught her children one primary lesson: Be able to think and to evaluate what is happening around you.

She certainly puts this lesson to good use. By taking over a hundred trips per year and writing scores and scores of letters to lawyers, corporations, politicians, and key public officials (all at her own expense), Alabach keeps abreast of what is happening regarding the rights of citizens. Serving as a self-proclaimed watchdog for the public and working to safeguard the foundation and principles of the Constitution and the Bill of Rights is a calling that she takes seriously. To her, the word *leadership* means having both "initiative and a sense of responsible awareness—not just brains!" Alabach also follows what is happening to the environment and has been active in environmental efforts to clean up the land. Her efforts have resulted in specific state legislation aimed at strictly monitoring the dumping of hazardous waste.

"Some people hate to see me coming," she states, "because they know that I've 'got the goods' on them!" This is because Alabach does her homework. She spends hours reading, listening, and researching to find out what is happening in her community, the state, the nation, and even the world. She says simply, "Citizenship is the most important thing that education can teach and that our society can protect. I hope that what I have been doing will cause some others to 'take the ball and run with it.' I don't want any awards, free trips, or fancy balls to attend. I just want to make people aware that leaders, real leaders, must have an ethical approach to how the people are governed and that our checks-and-balances system must really be for the people." She adds, "I do what I do not for myself or even for the adults. I do it for the kids—for their future."

When asked what she saw for her own future, she answered with a laugh, "A nice long rest!" For all that she has done, for the example that she has set, and for the unselfish leadership that she has shown, Alabach certainly deserves one.

fore prioritizing. Are you working with something that is essential or something that would be a luxury? How will one decision affect another? Making a correct decision is a big job; making the decision *when* it should be made is equally important.

Question 3: Am I aware of the risks involved?

While a good leader should be informed and able to prioritize, he or she must also be willing to consider taking a chance sometimes if the situation is right. You can't always act according to what has been done before. Sometimes risk taking shows creativity, insight, and progress.

In taking risks, however, a good leader is never caught off-guard. You must know ahead of time the potential consequences of your decision. Is the risk a smart one? Might the risk be too costly? It would be silly for the pilot of a commercial aircraft to suddenly disregard the instructions of the air-traffic controller and strike out on his own. He would be putting the lives of everyone on the plane in jeopardy. As an effective leader and decision maker, you must sometimes use your instincts, but you must also use your common sense and sound judgment when the well-being of others is at stake.

The fourth plank of leadership—making a decision—can make or break you as a leader. You can't lead others unless you convince them that you know where you are going. Consequently, be direct in your decision making, and don't wander in indecision. If you consider each of the three questions in this section when making important decisions in your personal, school, community, and family life, then you may find stepping to the front and leading others less fearful and more productive.

Specific Speaking Strategy: As an effective leader, keep others informed as to what your decisions are and why you have made them. Also, tell the members of the group that you appreciate their input and that you have considered everyone's opinion. Decisions are most often met with approval when people understand what went into the decision-making process and why the decision maker decided the way that he or she did. Allow the spoken word to keep everyone informed.

Plank 5: A Leader Can Handle Conflict

Of all the qualities of a leader, none ranks higher than being able to work *harmoniously* with people and make them feel good about themselves and about the group's objectives. A fact of life for anyone in charge of a group, however, is that everything does not always run smoothly. Problems arise and personalities clash.

How should a problem situation be handled? First of all, good leaders know that intense arguing and emotional outbursts won't help. All that happens when emotions are allowed to run wild is that communication takes a back seat to confrontation, which gets in the way of what both the leader and the group are after. Cool heads must prevail. An awareness of the principles of conflict management can help. **Conflict management** is the ability to turn a potentially negative situation into a positive one.

A speech consultant who was working with a group of business supervisors and

COMMUNICATION   BREAKTHROUGH

The Special Olympics

Eunice Kennedy Shriver, the sister of John F. Kennedy, had a sister, Rosemary, who was mentally retarded. After visiting many hospitals for the retarded, Eunice Shriver was appalled at the crowding and understaffing she saw. She was also appalled that the patients never had to engage in any type of exercise and, thus, were in poor physical condition. Told that running, jumping, and playing could injure the children, Shriver took matters into her own hands. She started an exercise class and playing field for the mentally handicapped in her own back yard! Her involvement grew until, in 1968, what is known as the Special Olympics was officially started.

The Special Olympics trains mentally retarded children and adults for athletic competition. Events include basketball, bowling, diving, floor hockey, gymnastics, ice skating, soccer, track and field, volleyball, wheelchair events, and several others. Currently, over 10,000 communities around the world offer Special Olympics programs, with over a million athlete–participants in the United States alone.

The Special Olympics has two major objectives: to promote physical and emotional growth through friendship and family support and to offer opportunities for achievement and courage through athletics. Eunice Kennedy Shriver is a leader because she saw a need and then acted. What is the result? The Special Olympics has become a symbol that communicates to the entire world that people really do care about each other.

All of the work for the Special Olympics is done by volunteers. Over 100,000 volunteers worldwide are involved. One of the most rewarding jobs as a volunteer is to be one of the "huggers." It is their job to grab and hug the competitors as they cross the finish line. Every contestant has a "hugger."

Says one volunteer mother, "Everyone involved with the Special Olympics is a leader because when all of the voices are heard laughing and cheering together, we all feel inspired and understand that each of us is depending on the other person. That makes me feel good inside!"

Questions
1. What does the volunteer mother mean by this last statement? Why could it be true that "everyone involved with the Special Olympics is a leader"?
2. Why is it noteworthy that all of the work done in the Special Olympics is done by volunteers?

---

executives on "Improved Communication and Better Public Speaking" offered the following plan for conflict management. The plan, which had worked for him and countless others, includes four steps: Shut up! Look up! Hook up! Chill down!

1. *Shut up!* A good leader doesn't always have to be the one doing the talking. If you are having a problem with a person, keep quiet and listen to what that person is saying. Don't interrupt! Allow the

Since 1968, the Special Olympics has trained mentally retarded children and adults for athletic competition. The program began in the backyard of Eunice Kennedy Shriver, who recognized a need and acted to fulfill it.

other person to finish speaking before you talk.

2. *Look up!* Establish eye contact with the person. Don't look off to the side or down at the floor. Let the person know that you are genuinely involved with what he or she is saying by looking at him or her, showing an understanding, responsive attitude.

3. *Hook up!* It is important to "hook up" emotionally with the other person to try to understand his or her point of view. You may need to see the situation from another perspective and understand why someone else might not feel as you do.

4. *Chill down!* When you do verbally respond to the other person, make your comments rational, sensitive, and constructive. Don't permit your temper or the heat of the moment to control a situation and allow it to escalate into an even larger problem.

Try this four-point plan in your dealings with other people. Your conflict management skills may not only improve the situation but also increase your confidence in how you communicate with others on a daily basis. It's worth a try!

Closely associated with conflict management is a leader's willingness to get along with others. Even though getting along often takes hard work, it's worth the effort. After all, you can't make it all alone—but a leader who won't make an effort to create a harmonious working environment might find that he or she is having to do all of the work alone.

INSTANT IMPACT

A Voice Speaks Out for Walden Woods

Don Henley, the musician who brought "The End of the Innocence," "All She Wants to Do Is Dance," and "The Boys of Summer" to the music charts, is now leading the way to preserve Walden Woods in Concord, Massachusetts. Walden Woods is a famous landmark because it was the birthplace for the ideas of Henry David Thoreau, the great mid-nineteenth-century American thinker, writer, and philosopher.

When Henley learned that developers were planning to construct condos and office buildings on the land, he founded the Walden Woods Project, aimed at purchasing a part of Walden Woods, saving it from builders, and preserving it for history. Henley estimates that the entire project will cost 8 to 10 million dollars.

In an interview, Henley urged students to get involved and start fund-raisers. Leadership, he says, means that you don't wait for somebody else to "get the ball rolling"—you take the initiative yourself. He believes that the efforts to save Walden Woods can work because "people—the media stars, the politicians, the average citizen, the young people of the country—working together can make a difference. We all need to realize that the earth belongs to everybody."

One of Don Henley's favorite quotes by Henry David Thoreau is this: "I went to the woods because I wished to live deliberately . . . to see if I could learn what it had to teach, and not, when I came to die, discover that I had not lived." Thanks to Don Henley's speaking out, future generations might still be able to study the woods that inspired these words.

Source: Scholastic Scope.

One way to create a harmonious working environment is to praise people's efforts. Studies have shown that people like to be told when they are doing things right. It establishes a group rapport and also increases productivity. In complimenting people, vary the words that you use. Words lose their impact if they are repeated over and over. For instance, here are some words you could use to compliment and encourage others: *perfect, marvelous, great, tremendous, fantastic, sensational, outstanding, conscientious, excellent, awesome, considerate.* Can you add to the list?

It is said that the age of "memo management," or communicating with others only in writing, is virtually over. Certainly, "paper communication" is sometimes important, but it can become cold and impersonal. To the leader, it will never be as important as "people communication."

Specific Speaking Strategy: In a tactful manner, summarize for others what they have said to you so that they know that you were paying attention to them. Also, pay attention to *how* you say something. You can add to your effectiveness as a good leader if you will pay close attention to the nonverbal signals that you are giving. Body language speaks just as loudly as words, so convey through body language a message that shows people, "I take seriously what you have to say and I am really listening!"

Plank 6: A Leader Works to Avoid Pitfalls

You have probably heard the saying "Forewarned is forearmed." It means that being conscious of a potential problem ahead of time might help you "cut it off at the pass"—stop it before it gets started. With this in mind, be alert to the following three pitfalls of leadership and work to avoid them.

Pitfall 1: Being Afraid to Fail

Leaders don't like to make mistakes. A good leader tries to be conscientious and show the group that he or she can be counted on to do things correctly. However, a leader should not always play it safe. If, as a leader, your attitude is "I'd like to try that but I'm afraid that I'll fail," then you might be *forfeiting* some of the creativity and personal vision that the group counts on you to provide.

Don't be afraid of what your instincts and personal intuition might be telling you to do. Of course, you have to make sure that you are not being reckless in your judgment, but you should also keep in mind that many great leaders failed at one time or another. The baseball great Babe Ruth was a home-run king, but he also led the major leagues in strikeouts. The explorer Christopher Columbus left Europe to find the East Indies; he failed to find the East Indies, but he found America. The inventor and genius Thomas Edison had an interesting philosophy about failure. He said that when his work produced ninety-nine failures in a row, he then knew ninety-nine ways that *didn't* work and was closing in on finding the solution. Abraham Lincoln lost five political elections before he eventually became president.

As a good leader, don't live with a fear of failure. If your group knows that you have its best interests at heart, it will most likely support your efforts. Go for it!

Pitfall 2: Not Paying Attention to Details

Of course, a good leader should focus on the big picture, but a good leader should also pay attention to the small things. A good leader is aware that paying attention to details early will help make the big picture much clearer and better defined.

Details matter! If handled correctly, they can make you appear organized and competent to your group. If handled incorrectly, they can make you appear foolish and inept. In 1987, for example, the Nobel Prize Committee for Science and Economics notified Donald O. Cram that he had won the Nobel Prize in chemistry. The problem was that Donald O. Cram is a California rug-shampooer. The award was really meant for Donald J. Cram.

Ignoring details or dismissing them as being "too trivial" often results in projects that don't work or organizations that fall apart. It was a detail—the seemingly insignificant O-ring—on the space shuttle *Challenger* that ultimately caused the loss of seven lives.

Pitfall 3: Forgetting People and the Original Objectives

A major pitfall for any leader is to forget the human factor in the decision-making process or to lose sight of what it was that the group was originally after. As a conscientious leader, you need to ask yourself these questions: "What exactly is it that we were trying to accomplish?" "Who were the people who played key roles and worked hard right from the start?" It is often easy for those in charge to get side-tracked or detoured. Stay on track. Furthermore, reward group mem-

COMMUNICATION BREAKDOWN

The Call That Wasn't Made

It was a day like any other day in the spring of 1992 on the campus of Valparaiso University, a small educational institution in the heart of the Midwest. Then it happened—an explosion. Suddenly the usually serene campus setting turned into mass hysteria. The explosion had occurred in an advanced chemistry class, and nearly forty students and a professor had been seriously injured. Some of the victims wandered around in shock, while others simply stared ahead, numb and disbelieving.

Within a matter of minutes, calls had been made to police, fire fighters, hazardous material specialists, and medical personnel. Almost immediately, all were on the scene. However, in the midst of the confusion and rush, one phone call was *not* immediately made: a phone call to the hospital emergency room alerting its staff that a large number of people injured by a chemical explosion would be on their way.

Don't be alarmed. The situation just described is a *simulated* disaster, the fourth to take place in as many years as part of the community's Disaster Drill Alert. In a newspaper article, the drill coordinator, Gregory L. Eckhardt, said of the failure to call the Emergency Room: "It's communication. We've got to get everyone on the same frequency." He noted that everything else in the drill worked well that day and the cooperation was tremendous.

A hospital spokesperson said it best. She said that the bad news was that people in a leadership position forgot to take care of the call. However, the good news was that it happened when everything was pretend. "When lives are on the line," she said, "the job will get done because now everyone has learned."

Exerpted from the Gary Post-Tribune.

Questions
1. Why are details important to leaders?
2. Why is it important for leaders to have followers that they can count on to get jobs done?
3. The Valparaiso University example is a type of directed practice experience. Why is a trial run-through often a good idea for those in charge?

---

bers who deserve special consideration for being there when times were tough.

Specific Speaking Strategy: This is a good time to make use of your intrapersonal communication skills and remind yourself of some important points. Give yourself a good talking-to and consider all of your options. What are the risks? Have you thought through all of the details? What was the primary issue and who were the people there from the start? Answer these questions to yourself. Hopefully this activity will eliminate a few of the pitfalls that signal "Beware: Danger Ahead!"

Plank 7: A Leader Knows How to Motivate

This plank is last for a reason. Motivation is the consequence of all that this

```
┌─────────────────────────────────────┐
│                                     │
│         WANTED: LEADER              │
│                                     │
│  Must be able to see the "big       │
│  picture;" solve problems through   │
│  analysis and discussion, followed  │
│  by action; teach people according  │
│  to different learning styles       │
│  (discussion, logic, design, and    │
│  emotion); make good decisions      │
│  based on knowledge, priorities,    │
│  and awareness of risks; handle     │
│  conflict; avoid pitfalls like      │
│  being afraid to fail, not paying   │
│  attention to details, and          │
│  forgetting original objectives;    │
│  and motivate self and others.      │
│                                     │
└─────────────────────────────────────┘
```

Motivation is a very personal thing. What motivates some won't motivate others. Thus, the job of a good leader is to know his or her group well enough to know what will work with whom. There is no textbook that can specifically prescribe how every leader can motivate every group member. The truth of the matter is that in the end, motivation occurs as a result of the people in your group trusting you enough to follow your advice.

Specific Speaking Strategy: Read the advice given for Planks 1–6. Work on making both your verbal and your nonverbal communication clear and meaningful. At the same time, leave room for the creativity and spontaneity that often comes when the leader and the group are functioning cooperatively as a productive unit.

So there you have the seven planks of leadership. To be a good speaker and a good leader, you must work from the inside out and establish a strong value system that will anchor your words and give them substance.

chapter has discussed. Recall from Chapter 1 that to *motivate* means to inspire either yourself or others (or both) to act. Motivation may be created by any number of factors:

- ◆ The honesty and integrity that you show.
- ◆ The strong work ethic that you exhibit.
- ◆ The discussion that you promote.
- ◆ The logic and intelligence that you put forward.
- ◆ The "master plan" that you offer.
- ◆ The emotion that you share.
- ◆ The creativity that you lend.
- ◆ The confidence and decisiveness that you exhibit.

In this book, you have learned about various types of oral expression, about the parts of a speech, and about the ways to become an effective speaker. However, the real test of a good speaker is what he or she uses words to do. If you will use your words to tell the truth, to make people feel better about themselves, and to teach and inspire others, then you will prove that the phrase *communication matters* is more than simply the title of this book. You will prove that the power of the spoken word can help you understand your world, other people, and yourself just a little bit better.

TAKING CHARGE

1. How do you learn best? Go back to the four learning styles and rank them from first to fourth. What is the reasoning behind your first pick? Find someone in your class who selected one of the other three and interview that person to find out why. Be prepared to write down your answers.

2. Go to the library and research a person from history who exhibited a noteworthy sense of vision. What about our world today? Who currently in the news is a leader because he or she will act on a problem? Bring your findings to class and discuss them with other students. Be ready to explain your choices.

3. Several leadership pitfalls are listed in the chapter. What are your leadership problems? List two pitfalls that you find difficult to overcome when attempting to lead. (Don't use the ones given in the chapter.) Can you think of solutions for each? Write them down and then be prepared to discuss your observations.

STUDENT SPEECH

The author Gertrude Stein wrote the famous line, "Rose is a rose is a rose." In the spirit of this line, we might also say, "A good speech is a good speech is a good speech." In other words, regardless of when it was written, a good speech presents truths that can apply to our lives. The following speech, which was briefly referred to in Chapter 1, is offered here in its entirety. The speech, by Diane Matesic, was not only an Indiana state runner-up oration in 1977 but also an extremely popular presentation among various community groups. Its message still rings true today. Keep leadership in mind as you read.

The Last American Hero

I'm going to give you three pairs of men. For each category, choose the one best personifying the quality of leadership. In the area of sports, Babe Ruth or Hank Aaron; national leaders, Winston Churchill or Gerald Ford; and as statesmen, Patrick Henry or Henry Kissinger. If you picked the first man in each category, congratulations, for you are part of the 82 percent of Americans who felt likewise, as indicated by a recent Stanford University poll. But why? What seems to separate the heroic figures of the past from the leaders of today, who seek a parallel admiration?

The hero of the past was the primal "man of action"—the man of adventure whose courage or sense of duty led to his great achievements. Looking back, we can see a long line of legendary heroes. We stand in awe at the determination of Caesar and Napoleon's absolute power of conquest. And Joan of Arc, Daniel Boone, Abraham Lincoln, and Thomas Edison all show off heroic stature. In more recent times, we have seen Charles Lindbergh become "The Legend of the Lone Eagle," while other figures such as Oliver Hazard Perry, Sergeant York, and General MacArthur capture the popular imagination of Americans. But where are the heroes of today? A nation hungry for heroes who ignite people's imaginations is finding no successors to "Lucky Lindy" or "Honest Abe."

Joan Valdez, in her book *The Media Works,* has stated that the last traditional American heroes were the television cowboys of the 1950s. And so, as Roy Rogers and the Lone Ranger rode off into the sunset, unfortunately, so did an American myth! Today, we can no longer tell tales of noble men because we don't believe that noble men exist. And we really can't be blamed, can we? In the last twenty years, we have seen President Kennedy assassinated; 50,000 needless deaths in Vietnam; and a president and a vice president denounce, defend, deny, diminish, and then die before our very eyes. We have seen politicians unwilling to stand

for anything, sports become big business, and technology perfect the "three-year car." In short, one of the reasons why the hero has become an endangered species is that no one trusts anyone anymore. Naturally, the more self-conscious we become, the more intolerant. We don't believe in solutions or solution makers.

For much of this, we can blame the media. It has done such a masterful job of "telling it like it is" that almost everyone knows everything about everybody. And any figure threatening to rise above the masses is systematically dissected with surgeon-like precision. The media no longer builds heroes, it unmasks them. Gone are the days where we read of Babe Ruth pointing to center field before clouting a home run. Today the media zooms in on Johnny Bench crying after his divorce, Gerald Ford falling on the ski slopes, and Jimmy Carter lusting after women in *Playboy* magazine. More and more, the average citizen knows that the men in the spotlight, just like everyone else, put on and take off their trousers one leg at a time—often in places where they shouldn't!

However, it's not as if we aren't trying. Mick Jagger, Farrah Fawcett, and Robert Redford are all idolized by many. Unfortunately, though, we're getting to the point where, as Andy Warhol predicted, soon everyone will be the hero of his or her choice for fifteen minutes. Now, instead of seeing John Wayne struggling in the sands of Iwo Jima, we see something very different.

The van went down the road in Woodstock, Illinois, at about 60 miles per hour. Seeing the lights from an oncoming car, it was time for the game to begin. The boys, holding ten- to fifteen-pound rocks in their hands, waited for the right instant. Then they threw! David Claus was the driver coming the other way. The first rock merely shattered the windshield. The second tore off the top of his head. Three days later, five young men were arrested and taken to the police station. When they arrived, admirers yelled and cheered. For what?

You see, the harm of losing our authentic heroes goes much, much deeper and is far more significant than merely voiding our bubble-gum card fantasies. One harm is that we have allowed ourselves to pay homage to those certainly less than virtuous. Isn't Alice Cooper a hero to the thousands who go wild when, at the end of his performance, he tears off the limbs of a baby doll? And in the film version of *Bonnie and Clyde*, who were you eventually rooting for?

Still reeling from the leaders who have let us down and bored with the present, we see ourselves moving toward a condition of stoicism, which is symptomatic of our problem. We no longer strive for excellence or originality. Thus, harm number two ushers in the Age of Mediocrity, for if there is no one to inspire us to do great and noble things—quite frankly, we don't! At Cornell University, an Arts and Science student can now receive a Bachelor of Arts degree without ever having to read a single line of Plato, the Bible, Shakespeare, or Einstein. A prominent attitude is that if Johnny isn't "turned on" to Plato, or if Shakespeare isn't "his thing," then, well, to each his own. And what about the pride we have in our language? A newspaper recently came out with an interesting article. In it, companies handling health insurance reported some revealing word concoctions.

Among them were people with "falls teeth," "very coarse veins," "high pretention," and one woman who had had a "misconception."

This may seem humorous or surprising to some, but others won't believe it; and that wouldn't be surprising either—for our third harm, although less obvious, is perhaps the most damaging. It involves our attitude. We've become a nation of ready-made cynics, skeptics, and critics, where mockery is fashionable and "to score" on someone is "the thing."

Solving these problems isn't easy. It's hard to find the man or woman who can lead us out of controversy and into the light when controversy is all that we see. In 1977, there are no more black or white issues. The answer, I think, is one of perspective. In classical times, heroes were God–men. In the Middle Ages, they were God's men. In the Renaissance, they were universal men. In the nineteenth century, they were self-made men. Now, we must look to the common man, for it is with the common man that the future of heroism and national spirit lies.

I feel that we have two obligations. One is to recognize an act of nobility as being heroic in itself. The second is to realize that the common man actually does have heroic potential. Your mission (should you decide to accept it) is to make a stand for democracy by voting in elections at all levels, for the family by turning off the television set, and for people by telling someone that not all Polish jokes are funny.

Contemporary theologian Paul Tillich stated in his book *The Courage to Be* that religion is anything that you take seriously. Acts of nobility needn't be based solely on issues of earth-shattering proportion, but more on quiet, personal ones which we take very, very seriously.

Earlier, you were given some choices. You now have another. You can take seriously what I've mentioned, or you can forget me and all that I've said. If you again choose the former, you can help actualize the idea that the only person who can ever be termed "The Last American Hero"—will be the last American! Then, with a Walter Mitty smile playing about our lips, a cloud of dust, and a mighty "high-oo Silver," each of us can walk off triumphantly . . . into the sunset.

REVIEW AND ENRICHMENT

LOOKING BACK

Listed below are the major ideas discussed in this chapter.

- ◆ Leadership involves your ability to motivate yourself and others to accomplish a specific task.
- ◆ The leader is the person who puts leadership skills into action.
- ◆ Just as the planks of confidence support your speaking, the planks of leadership provide a framework for leadership.
- ◆ A good leader has a sense of vision and sees how the "big picture" fits together.
- ◆ A good leader is a doer who will take charge of a situation and get things done.
- ◆ A good leader is aware that people learn differently and therefore adjusts his or her leadership style to meet the demands of the group.
- ◆ A good leader knows not only how to make decisions but also the order in which decisions should be made.
- ◆ A good leader knows conflict management skills and how to turn a potentially negative situation into a positive one.

┌─────────────────────────────┐
│   REVIEW AND ENRICHMENT   │
│   ───────────────────────   │
│   Continued   │
└─────────────────────────────┘

- ✦ A good leader is always aware of body language and the tremendous impact of nonverbal communication.
- ✦ A good leader is aware of pitfalls to avoid, such as being afraid to fail, ignoring details, and losing sight of the original objectives.
- ✦ A good leader can effectively do whatever it takes to motivate others.
- ✦ The spoken word should always be used constructively to make people and situations better.

SPEECH VOCABULARY

leadership   learning styles
leader   conflict management
vision

1. For each new speech term, write the definition as given in the chapter. Be sure to list the page number for each word. Now write an original sentence showing the speech term "in action."
2. Prepare a quiz. On the left-hand side of your paper, list the new speech terms, leaving out some of the letters of each word. (Example: —e—der—hi— for leadership.) Next, on the right-hand side of your paper, list the definitions of the terms in a different order. Have a classmate take your quiz by matching each term with the correct definition. Be sure to have an answer key ready.

GENERAL VOCABULARY

magnate   harmoniously
culmination   forfeiting
empowerment   simulated
facilitate

1. Define each general vocabulary term and use it in an original sentence.
2. Write a story titled "The Day I Had to Take Over the Class and Become the Leader." Select at least three words from the new speech terms and at least three from the general vocabulary and use them effectively in the story. Be sure that your story is at least one page long, and make your story coherent! Both the story and the vocabulary words should make sense when read aloud.

REVIEW AND ENRICHMENT
Continued

THINGS TO REMEMBER

1. A leader who has a sense of _____ can see a situation in its entirety and keep both details and the big picture in perspective.
2. A leader must be willing to _____ if he or she is ever going to accomplish anything.
3. List the four learning styles that every leader should know.
4. If you are able to handle a stressful situation and turn a potentially negative situation into a positive one, then you have excellent _____ skills.
5. Often, your nonverbal communication, or your _____ language, will convey more to people than the words that you speak.
6. List the three leadership pitfalls.
7. People who _____—that is, who do something on their own for no pay—often show a great leadership example for others to follow.
8. The planks of leadership illustrate seven characteristics of a good leader. List at least five of the planks.
9. Who is the founder of the Special Olympics?
10. What specific woods is Don Henley taking a leadership role to protect?

THINGS TO DO

1. Construct a chart on a large sheet of paper. On one side of the chart (or on the top half), make a heading that says, "What a Leader Does." On the other side of the chart (or on the bottom half), make a heading that says, "What a Leader Doesn't Do." Now fill in the chart. Be sure to make your work colorful and attractive, and be sure that you include some original ideas on leadership in addition to what the chapter taught.
2. Interview a leader. The person can be in your school, your community, or your family. Find out that person's views on (a) why leadership is important, (b) where leadership is most needed in our society, (c) why some people are afraid to lead, and (d) how best to motivate others. Be ready to present your findings to the class. Also, note why you selected the person and why you consider him or her a noteworthy leader.
3. Make a collage—"an artistic composition of materials pasted over a surface, often with a unifying theme." The theme is "Leadership Around the World." Cut out pictures, words, and phrases that you can use to portray

> REVIEW AND ENRICHMENT
> ─────────────────────
> Continued

this theme. Your collage should have many words and pictures if you are going to create the impact that you want. With your teacher's permission, you might be able to work in teams of two. Be neat and complete in your work.

THINGS TO TALK ABOUT

1. Why in today's world are people often skeptical about many of their leaders? Why don't they trust some of them? Use newspapers, magazines, radio, and television to give some specific examples of what you mean. What lessons can you learn about your own leadership from what you see some other leaders doing?
2. A leader often sees a need and then takes the initiative to fill that need. In Japan, productivity and efficiency are primary concerns. This has created grueling work schedules, reducing the time workers have to spend with their families. Now, a company called Japan Efficiency has made it possible for busy workers to "rent" people to take their places in family visits. It sounds silly, but it's true. Sons and daughters who don't have the time to visit the family anymore can hire professional actors or actresses (at $1,150 for three hours) as substitutes. Says one Japanese reporter, "The parents are aware of what's going on, but they just want to hold a child or give advice to the younger generation." What is your reaction to this whole situation? What do you think of this company, Japan Efficiency? What do you think of what the children are doing? What about the elderly?
3. When should you take a risk? What specific things should you consider before you decide to do something?
4. If you had to select the most important quality that a leader can possess, what would it be and why?
5. The quality of leadership is often dependent on the quality of "followership." Why are followers important? What are some important responsibilities that followers should have, and why is "followership" a vital element in a democracy?

THINGS TO WRITE ABOUT

1. Write a one-page essay on the topic "What the Average Person Can Do to Be a Leader." Suggest at least two things the average person can do and try to offer examples of what you mean. Think of what can be done in

school, at home, in the workplace, or in the community.
2. An Illinois girl wishes to be on the all-male wrestling team. Does she have the right? What problems might she encounter? What might be something positive that could come out of her wrestling? Write your responses to these questions in complete sentences.

Be sure to make your reasoning clear.
3. Why is it important to get along with others? In an essay at least one page long, give your own three- or four-point plan for conflict management, the steps that you would take to handle a stressful situation. Give examples, if possible, and explain your reasoning.

CRITICAL THINKING

1. How's this for leadership? A company in Rochester, New York, called Cards from the Beyond will send greeting cards to your loved ones after you die. Of course, you pay for the cards in advance. One company spokesperson said, "Being dead is no excuse for not sending birthday and anniversary cards." What is wrong with this? What is right with it? Should we merely laugh at the idea?
2. If you were going to be in charge of the American Leadership Academy, and you were given the opportunity to select five staff members from anywhere in the world, whom would you select, and why? Who would be the head of the academy?

RELATED SPEECH TOPICS

How I can be a leader in the classroom and the Community
Why getting along with people matters in leadership
The person in the news that I most admire as a leader
Why parents must be leaders at home
Why a leader must sometimes be a follower
How nonverbal communication can make or break a leader

Why self-discipline is important to a leader
The elements of leadership that most people forget
Why everyone is a leader at one time or another
Media stars as leaders: do they shine or not?

GLOSSARY

A

AM An amplitude-modulated wave. Stations operating on this system change the size of the wave to vary their signals from each other.

abstract words Words that name intangibles, such as qualities, attributes, and concepts.

active listening A listening role in which the listener participates and shares in the communication process by guiding the speaker toward common interests.

adjourn The final action of the group—to close the meeting.

advance organizer Introductory statements that forecast what the audience may expect.

advantage A benefit which will result from the adoption of the resolution.

aesthetic value A value that involves standards of beauty and artistic merit.

affirmative Yes or true.

after-dinner speech An entertaining speech that follows a banquet or meal.

air To broadcast any program on radio or television.

alliteration The repetition of the sounds at the beginnings of two or more words that are close together.

allusion A reference to a well-known person, place, thing, or idea.

alternate causality attack An argument that the affirmative has not identified the true cause of the problem and therefore cannot solve it.

amend A proposal to change a motion.

analogy An illustration in which the characteristics of a familiar object or event are used to explain or describe the characteristics of an unfamiliar object or event. The extended use of a metaphor or simile, often in the form of a story.

anchor Host of a television news program.

anecdote A short story used by a speaker to illustrate a point.

announcer A person who reads commercials, public service announcements, promotions, or station breaks.

anthology A collection of passages from literature.

antithesis A contrasting of ideas by means of parallel arrangement of words, phrases, etc.; the opposite.

appreciative listening A listening style used to enjoy and savor pleasurable sounds such as music or nature.

arena stage A stage that is surrounded on four sides by the audience.

argument A reason for favoring one side of a proposition and the facts that support that reason.

articulation The crispness and distinctness of a speaker.

articulators The parts of the mouth (tongue, lips, teeth, lower jaw) used to form sounds into recognizable words.

assonance The repetition of vowel sounds.

audience analysis The process by which a speaker considers the needs and expectations of the audience that will be listening to the speech.

audio The signals from a microphone.

audio console An apparatus that is a combination of recording and playback machines, volume controls and other audio equipment.

auditory Relating to or experienced through hearing.

aural Relating to the sense of hearing.

author cards Cards cataloguing books that are organized by authors' last names.

a priori "Before." An issue that is decided upon before other arguments may be considered.

B

back-flowing Flowing one's arguments after a speech or a teammate's flowing his or her partner's arguments during cross-examination.

ballparking Ending a rebuttal speech with one's own case. This brings the focus back to the speaker's purpose.

begging the question An argument that assumes whatever is trying to be proven is already true.

blocking Directions for movement given to actors by a director.

block A group of arguments prepared to answer an opponent's attack.

body The part of the speech that provides the content and analysis that prove the thesis statements.

body language The way one uses his or her body to send messages.

brainstorming A process in which group members offer their ideas—as many as possible, as quickly as possible—as a way to encourage creative thought and solutions.

bridge A transition from one answer to another.

briefing A speech informing members of a group of changes in policy or procedure.

brief An outline that summarizes specific case arguments.

burden of proof A term used in formal debate and in law to refer to the duty or responsibility to prove something.

business The actions used to establish or identify a character.

bylaws A set of special rules agreed upon by the members of a group.

C

cable television Programming paid for by viewer subscriptions.

call the meeting to order A request that the members stop talking among themselves and give their undivided attention to the chair.

call the question A proposal to take an immediate vote on a motion.

captive audience An audience that has been forced to be in attendance.

card catalog A catalog that tells what books a library has and where they can be found.

cart A tape cartridge.

case The debater's ideas and evidence organized and arranged into a position supporting one side of a resolution.

case study The analysis of a "typical" example in great detail, in order to draw general conclusions.

causality A claim that one event is the result of another event.

cause-effect pattern A pattern of organization that arranges elements of an argument in a "because this happened, this resulted" sequence.

chair The meeting's chairperson.

chalk talk A speech in which the speaker uses a visual aid—a chalkboard—to convey information.

chief engineer The person who is responsible for insuring that the station's radio signal reaches as far as possible and has the highest quality of sound possible.

chronological pattern A pattern of organization that arranges the elements in time sequence, or in the order in which they happened.

circumstantial evidence The evidence at hand. It may suggest a conclusion, but it does not prove it.

circumvention attack An argument that key people will get around the affirmative plan and therefore prevent it from working.

clashing Making one's argument directly conflict with an opponent's argument.

climatic pattern A pattern of organization that arranges the elements in order of importance.

cohesion A quality of group discussion in which members have respect for each other, share similar values and rely on one another for support.

commedia dell'arte Italian comedic theater that developed during the Renaissance. The plays were performed without prewritten script and featured stock characters.

commemorative speech An inspiring speech recalling heroic events or persons.

commencement address A speech given during a graduation ceremony.

commercial station A station whose income is provided by paid advertising.

common ground A sense of a shared goal or interest.

communication The process of sending and receiving messages.

competency An ability to get something done.

competitive (1) An atmosphere that can foster divisiveness among members because they contend with each other as rivals. (2) The burden of a negative counterplan to show that both the affirmative and negative proposals should not be adopted.

completion point The moment at which the speaker in a conversation has completed his thought and the listener is given an opportunity to respond.

composure A calm, controlled manner.

comprehensive listening A listening style used to decipher and understand.

compromise A settlement of differences based on mutual concessions.

concrete words Words that name things that are perceived through the senses.

confidence A feeling of belief in oneself and one's ability to control a specific situation.

conflict management The ability to turn a potentially negative situation into a positive one.

connotation The meanings and feelings associated with a word by an individual, based on personal experience.

consensus A nearly unanimous agreement among the group's members about a particular solution.

consonance The repetition of consonant sounds.

constructive A speech in which arguments are initially advanced and defended.

constructive conflict A situation in which group members use their differences to discover the best ideas.

content A "solid" message made up of relevant facts, evidence, and valid arguments; the subject or topic of one's speech.

continuity Material that is used between songs or as an introduction to commercial breaks.

conversation An exchange of thoughts and feelings between two or more people.

conviction A strong belief in one's message and a determination to convey that message to the audience.

cooperative An atmosphere that encourages members to work together toward a common end or goal.

copywriter The person who writes commercials and other material for broadcast.

correlation A claim that two or more events are related in some way.

counterplan A negative proposal to solve all or most of the affirmative harm but avoid one or more of the disadvantages.

credentials Qualifications.

credibility A person's ability to inspire belief.

criteria A set of standards that a solution must meet.

critical listening A listening style used to evaluate and analyze a message for logic and value.

cross-examination A period following each speaker's constructive during which the speaker who has just spoken is questioned.

crystallizing Choosing the most important arguments and linking them to the values presented in the round of debate.

cultural literacy The information that an average American citizen can be expected to know.

cutaway A model that shows the inner workings of an object.

D

database A collection of related information.

debate A method to solve problems; a formal contest of skill in reasoned argument.

decode To interpret a message.

dedication A willing desire to practice and be committed to one's speech.

deduction A form of reasoning in which one argues from generalizations to a specific instance.

deejay The host of a radio music program.

definition An explanation of a term; it reflects the speaker's intended meaning or specialized use in the context of a speech.

delivery The mode or manner that a speaker uses to transmit words to an audience.

demonstration A show or display illustrating how something works.

denotation The basic and generally understood meaning of a word found in the dictionary.

detail Specific pieces of information, such as dates and statistics, that provide evidence in support of the main headings of a speech.

diagram A visual aid used by a speaker to explain a process.

dialogue Conversations between actors, two persons, or groups.

diction The manner of uttering or pronouncing words.

director The person responsible for putting all of the elements of a theatrical production together.

disadvantages The problems created by an affirmative plan.

disclaimer A speaker's attempt to explain what is not to be inferred by the speech or an acknowledgment of incomplete expertise on the subject.

discriminative listening A listening style used to single out one particular sound from a noisy environment.

discussion A cooperative exchange of information, opinions, and ideas.

disruptive conflict A conflict that divides members into competing sides, which refuse to compromise to the point that no group decision can be achieved.

dollying Moving the entire camera (mounted on a movable pedestal) forward or backward.

door openers Phrases used by the listener to invite and encourage the speaker to continue.

dramatic interpretation A speech contest event in which a speaker memorizes and performs a work of literature of a more serious nature.

dramatic monologue A first-person narration in which a single character speaks.

drama A literary form that uses language and actions to relate a story of human conflict.

dropped argument An argument that the speaker neglects to discuss or refute.

E

emotional appeal A persuasive technique that involves "striking an emotional chord"; the speaker uses issues and values such as patriotism, family, and honor to win the audience's favor.

empathy A sincere understanding of the feelings, thoughts and motives of others.

emphasis The stress that a speaker uses to draw attention to specific words.

enabling provisions Provisions that describe how the plan will be carried out and that usually include administration, funding, and enforcement.

encode To assign meaning to a message.

enthusiasm The energy, both intellectual and physical, a speaker transmits to inspire an audience.

epic theater A form of theater developed in Germany during the 1920s and used to present important political and social messages.

establishing shot A shot that establishes the setting and the relationships between the individual parts of the shot.

ethical (personal) appeal A persuasive quality based on the speaker's natural honesty, sincerity, and commitment to what is right and good.

ethics A person's sense of right and wrong.

ethos The Greek word for character; the term is associated with Aristotle's personal (ethical) appeal.

eulogy A speech praising or honoring someone who has died.

euphemism A word or group of words substituted for a word that is offensive or distasteful.

evidence Anything that establishes a fact or gives cause to believe something.

executive session A special meeting or portion of a meeting that is only open to members; outsiders are not allowed to observe.

extemporaneous method A delivery method in which the speaker refers only to notes or a brief outline.

extemporaneous speaking A speech contest event in which a speaker writes and delivers a speech on a topic of current interest. These speeches are usually prepared within thirty minutes and delivered with few or no notes.

extension The progression or development of an argument or issue.

eye contact A device speakers use whereby they look directly into their listener's eyes in order to emphasize a point or to show how strongly they feel about something.

F

FM A frequency-modulated wave. Stations operating on this system change how rapidly (frequently) the wave vibrates to vary their signals from each other.

factual proposition A proposition that is either true or false.

fallacy An error in reasoning or a mistaken belief.

false analogy A comparison of two things that are not really the same.

false comparison A comparison of unlike things.

false premise An erroneous assertion; a premise that is faulty and will lead to an error in deduction.

feedback A reaction that the receiver gives to a message offered by the sender.

field of view The portion of the scene the camera shows.

filibustering Making a long continuous speech for the purpose of delaying or preventing action.

fireside chat A speech in which a leader informally addresses the concerns, worries, and issues of the group.

first affirmative constructive (1AC) A speech that is prepared before the round in which the affirmative speaker presents the affirmative case.

first affirmative rebuttal (1AR) In L-D, the speech made

by the affirmative speaker that responds to the negative case and rebuilds the affirmative case. (1) In policy debate, this speech responds to the negative block and extends the argument that the second affirmative rebuttal will need to win the debate.

first negative constructive (1NC) In L-D, the speech in which the negative speaker presents the negative case and refutes the affirmative constructive. (1) In policy debate the first negative speaker presents the negative position in the debate.

first negative rebuttal (1NR) In policy debates, the first negative speaker picks up one or two negative arguments not covered by the second negative constructive and develops them by answering affirmative responses and extending the arguments further.

first person Referring to the person speaking (I, me, we, us).

flowsheet A record of the words or arguments written down during the debate.

follow-up question A question that helps the interviewer pursue topics that come up unexpectedly in the course of the interview.

formal debate A highly structured debate that proceeds according to specific rules.

format (1) A programming style or specialization. (2) The general organization established for the conduct of the debate. It specifies the amount of time and the order in which each debater is allowed to speak.

forum A post-panel discussion in which panel members invite questions and comments from the audience.

friendliness A warm, congenial attitude.

full-service radio A station that plays a variety of things—music, news, talk, and sporting events.

G

gels Pieces of acetate, of varying colors that are placed in a stage-lighting instrument in order to help create atmosphere.

general manager The person who is responsible for a station's profitability, licensing, and public relations concerns.

gestures Actions in which the body or parts of the body move to express an idea or emotion.

gesture The use of hands, limbs, or the body to send a message.

ghostwriter A person who writes for, and in the name of, another person.

good will A genuine interest or concern.

graph A visual aid used by a speaker to demonstrate a statistical relationship.

Greek chorus A group of Greek citizens who read verse in unison.

grouping A rebuttal technique in which the speaker attempts to save time by establishing a common flaw in several of the opponent's arguments.

groupthink A desire to go along with the group even at the possible cost of abandoning one's personal beliefs.

H

handout Written material (fliers, brochures, or information sheets) prepared and duplicated before a speech and supplied to the audience as reference material.

harm The problem presented by the affirmative team.

hasty generalization A faulty argument based on incomplete or unrepresentative information.

headroom The distance between the top of a person's head and the top edge of the picture.

hearing An automatic reaction of the senses and nervous system.

hidden meanings Subtle, unstated meanings that must be guessed at or inferred from the tone or body language.

house (1) A term used to refer to the group during its meetings. (2) The area in which the audience sits.

humorous interpretation A speech contest in which a speaker memorizes and performs a work of literature of a lighter nature.

hyperbole A method of saying more than what is true, or exaggerating, for the sake of emphasis.

I

ignoring the question A speaker's attempt to divert the attention of the audience from the matter at hand.

imagery Language that creates pictures in the mind and excites the senses.

impact An explanation by the negative team demonstrating that the final effects of the affirmative plan are negative and harmful.

impact turn A response to negative attacks that attempts to prove that the impacts of the disadvantages are not bad, but rather they are good.

impression How the audience perceives the speaker based on the way he presents himself and his ideas.

impromptu method A delivery method that is completely unrehearsed; the speaker uses no notes and relies on his or her ability to offer an immediate verbal response.

impromptu speaking Talking on a subject with little or no preparation.

improvisation Theater in which the actors make up speeches, songs, dances, and pantomimes spontaneously as the play progresses. It relies on the inspiration of the moment and the response of the audience.

incidental motion Any proposal to change how the meeting is being run.

index An alphabetical list found in the back of the book that tells the reader the exact page on which one can find particular information.

indifferent audience An audience that is apathetic or disinterested in the speaker and his topic. This audience does not find the topic relevant to their personal situation.

induction A form of reasoning in which specific cases are used to prove a general truth.

inflection The altering of a speaker's tone or pitch to create emphasis.

informal debate Any debate conducted without specific rules.

inherency The fact that existing policies do not address and will not eliminate the harm presented by the affirmative team.

input A device that brings audio into the console.

integrity A person's strong sense of right and wrong.

intention What an actor hopes to accomplish as a result of speaking. The actor's objective.

interior monologue A first-person narration in which the narrator is speaking to himself or herself.

interlibrary loan A cooperative system by which libraries lend specific books to one another.

internal link The negative team's documentation of the events that the affirmative plan will set in motion.

interpersonal communication Communication that takes place any time messages are transmitted between two or more people.

interviewer The person who asks the questions in an interview.

interview A conversation controlled by one person who asks questions of another person.

intimate distance The distance used primarily for confidential exchanges, almost always reserved for close friends (within eighteen inches).

intrapersonal communication An inner dialogue conducted with oneself to assess one's thoughts, feelings, and reactions.

introduction The beginning of a speech; it contains the attention-getter, the link statement, the thesis statement, and frequently a preview statement.

irony A figure of speech using words that imply the opposite of what they seem to say on the surface.

J

jargon The specialized vocabulary of people in the same profession or similar group.

jump on the bandwagon Persuasive technique based on the need to conform.

K

Kabuki Japanese theater, first appearing in the seventeenth century, which incorporated song, stylized speaking, and dance.

kinesics The science of body movements.

L

lavaliere microphone A small microphone attached to the speaker's clothing with clips or worn around the neck on a cord.

leadership An ability to motivate and unite others to work together to accomplish a specific task.

leader A person who effectively uses leadership skills.

leading question A question that "puts words" in the subject's mouth.

learning styles The different ways in which people learn most effectively.

lectern A stand used to support a speaker's notes.

Lincoln-Douglas debate A competitive type of formal debate practiced at high schools across the nation. This type of debate addresses propositions of value.

link (1) An explanation by the negative team demonstrating that the affirmative plan has a direct link to its disadvantage. (2) The statement in an introduction that comes between the attention-getter and the thesis statement and logically connects the two.

link turn A response to negative attacks that attempts to prove that the affirmative plan prevents, rather than causes a disadvantage.

listening spare time Thinking time created by the ability to listen faster than people can speak.

logical appeal The use of sequence, analysis, organization, and evidence to prove a point and persuade.

logic The science of reasoning which uses a system of rules to help one think correctly.

logos A Greek word for logic and reason; the term is associated with Aristotle's logical appeal.

M

main headings The major divisions, areas, or arguments of the speaker's purpose statement.

main motion A proposal that asks the group to take action.

majority A principle which provides that the votes of 50 percent of a group, plus one vote, shall have the power to make decisions for the whole group.

mandate Provisions that describe what the plan does.

manuscript method A delivery method in which the speaker writes out and subsequently reads the speech, word for word.

map A visual aid used by a speaker to demonstrate a geographical relationship.

mask A mask worn on the face representing one of several characters an actor would portray.

mass media The various channels of communication that can reach large audiences.

memorized method A delivery method in which the speaker memorizes and then gives the speech word for word without the use of notes.

message That which is sent or said.

metaphor A figure of speech that compares two unlike things without using the words like or as.

meter A measure of the rhythm in a line of poetry.

minority Group members who have less than the number of votes needed for control.

minutes The written records of an organization's meetings.

model A miniature representation of something.

moderator The person in the group who leads the discussion. He or she gets the discussion started, keeps the discussion on track, and brings the discussion to a close.

monotone A tone in which words are delivered at the same rate and pitch without variation.

mood The emotional tone created or expressed in a work.

moral value A value that involves standards of fairness.

motivation An inner drive, need, or impulse that causes a person to act.

music bed Background music used in a radio commercial or entertainment program.

music radio A station that plays only music.

mutual exclusivity A state in which the affirmative plan cannot exist if the negative counterplan does.

N

name calling To give someone a negative label without any evidence.

narrative The telling of a story.

narrowcast To specialize programming in order to appeal to specific segments of the audience.

narrowing To limit and more closely define a topic.

negative block The second negative constructive followed by the first negative rebuttal.

negative No or false.

negative rebuttal (NR) In L-D, the final speech made by the negative speaker that summarizes the debate and attempts to "shut down" the arguments that can be anticipated in the affirmative speaker's rebuttal.

network A group of radio or television stations that can broadcast the same program at the same time.

net benefits An evaluation of a plan's benefits compared to its disadvantages.

newness An original or unique approach to a topic.

news/talk radio A station that plays only news and talk shows.

new business Subjects brought up for the first time in a meeting.

Noh theater Theater in Japan that developed during the Middle Ages and was similar to Greek theater in its use of a chorus and only a few actors playing several roles.

noise Sounds that interfere with the listening process.

nonverbal communication Facial expressions or body

movements used to express attitudes or moods about a person, situation, or idea.

nonverbal message Facial expressions and body language used to convey messages not spoken.

noseroom The distance between the nose of a person and the edge of the television screen.

notes A listing of ideas in brief, outlined form.

O

obtain the floor Gaining the right to speak with the permission of the chair.

offstage focus A technique used in Reader's Theater in which readers use scripts and envision the scene out in the audience.

old business Business not completed in a previous meeting.

omnidirectional microphone A microphone that picks up sound from all directions.

omniscient A type of narration (third-person) in which the narrator is all-knowing and moves freely in and out of the minds of the various characters.

on-line A service that provides rapid access to many computer databases.

open-ended question A question that allows the subject to decide how best to answer. It encourages a comprehensive, in-depth response and discourages a yes-no or true-false response.

opposed audience An audience that is hostile to the speaker or the speaker's topic.

oral cavity The mouth.

oral interpretation The art of communicating works of literature by reading aloud well.

oral (or verbal) communication Communication that is primarily spoken.

oratory (or rhetoric) The art or study of public speaking.

orator A person who delivers oratory and uses words effectively.

orders of the day An agenda or list of topics to be discussed during a meeting.

order of precedence The relationship of motions to each other.

organization A system of structure and form that enables the audience to follow along easily in a speech.

original oratory A speech contest in which contestants write on a topic of their choice.

ought A person's idea or concept of the ideal. Ought refers to a moral obligation based on a sense of duty.

outline A logical, organized framework for a speech; it shows how the speech will progress.

output A device that sends audio from the console to other locations.

overhead projector A visual aid used by a speaker to project transparencies (often charts and graphs) onto a blank wall or screen.

oxymoron A literary device that places words that are in opposition directly beside one another, such as cruel kindness.

P

panel An informal discussion that takes place before an audience.

panning Rotating a camera left or right while the base of the camera remains in the same position.

pantomime A dramatic form of communication without words.

parallel structure (or parallelism) The use of the same grammatical form to express ideas that should, logically, be treated equally. This often involves the repeating of words or phrases.

paraphrasing Rewording an original passage.

parliamentary procedure A system of rules followed in group meetings based on ideas developed in the British Parliament.

Passion play A dramatic representation of the suffering, crucifixion, and resurrection of Christ. This play is performed every ten years in the small town of Oberammergau, Germany.

passive listening A listening role in which the listener does not share in the responsibility, nor involve himself in the communication process.

pathos The Greek word for feelings and emotions; the term is associated with Aristotle's emotional appeal.

pause A lull in the conversation. It often provides a good opportunity for the interviewer (unprompted) to convey more information.

perception How one sees things.

performance anxiety A specific stage fright, often associated with musicians, actors and other entertainers.

permutation A claim that some portion of the affirmative plan together with the counterplan would be advantageous.

personal distance The distance comfortable for conversation between friends (a foot and a half to four feet).

personal space A comfort zone each person maintains around himself or herself where intrusions would be unwelcome.

persona The fictional speaker of the work to be interpreted.

personification Giving human characteristics to nonhuman things.

persuasive speaking Speaking that influences others to believe or think something, or to take action.

phobia A persistent, irrational fear that causes a person to avoid specific situations.

phonation Voice production.

phonophobia A fear of speaking aloud. Many who suffer from this fear are afraid of hearing their own voices or of having poor voice quality.

pitch The vocal notes (highs and lows) that a speaker reaches while speaking.

plagiarism Copying or imitating the language, ideas, or thoughts of another and passing them off as one's original work.

plan An affirmative team's proposal to put a resolution into effect.

platform movement Walking or stepping in a directed manner from one spot to another while speaking.

playlist The list of music a radio station puts on the air.

plurality The number of votes cast for a candidate in a contest of more than two people that is greater than the number cast for any other candidate but not greater than half the total votes cast.

policy debate A debate in which a team of two debaters affirms and a team of two debaters negates a question of social policy.

policy proposition A proposition that focuses on the desirability of a particular course of action.

political value A value that involves standards of governing.

posture The position of the body when it is still.

pot A device that causes a sound to fade in or out.

power source The origin of the energy needed to make things go.

premise An assertion that serves as the basis for argument.

prep time The preparation time allotted during rounds for organizing responses and preparing questions.

preview statement The statement at the end of the introduction that presents an overview of the major areas that will be discussed in the body of the speech.

prima facie "At first view." A case that is sufficient based on meeting the requirements which make up the stock issues.

privileged motion A proposal to resolve an urgent problem other than the main motion.

problem-solution pattern A pattern of organization that presents a problem and then provides possible solutions.

program director The person who makes the decisions about what a station will air and what type of deejay will represent the station.

pronunciation The production of correct sound and syllable stresses when speaking.

proof Specific evidence that established the truth of something.

proposition A statement of the point to be debated.

proscenium stage A stage made up of two rooms, one for the audience and one for the performers, separated by a wall that has a large hole in it through which the audience views the play.

proxemics The study of spatial communication; in oral communication, refers specifically to the distance between the speaker and the audience.

public distance The distance maintained between strangers. At this distance people barely acknowledge each other's presence (twelve feet and beyond).

public lecture A lecture delivered to a community or school group.

public station A station whose operating costs are paid by grants and corporate and individual contributions.

puff ball An easy, open-ended question.

purpose statement A statement that presents the selected speech topic and the speaker's specific purpose in speaking.

Q

question of evaluation A question that asks group members to agree or disagree on possible solutions and to make a value judgment.

question of fact A question that asks group members to recall information that pertains to the question at hand.

question of interpretation A question that asks group members to give their opinions on what the information means.

quorum The minimum number of members that must be present in order for the group's decisions to take effect.

quotation A statement which repeats the exact words that someone else has said.

R

rate The speed at which a person speaks.

ratings system A means of measuring how many people are watching a particular program. A random group of viewers keep a diary of what they watch—the results are summarized in published results.

rationale An affirmative team's reasons for adopting a resolution.

reasoning The process of thinking, understanding, and drawing conclusions about some evidence.

rebuttal The act of countering an opponent's attacks to one's argument and thereby rebuilding the argument.

receiver A person who intercepts a message and then decodes it.

recess A short intermission during a meeting.

reconsider A move to reexamine a main motion that has already been passed or defeated.

refute To prove that something is wrong or false (using evidence).

regionalisms Sounds common to particular parts of the country. These include accents and unique ways of pronouncing words.

repetition The act or process of repeating.

reputation The way that a person is known to others.

resolution (1) A formal statement of opinion. (2) A special type of main motion that begins with an explanation of why the motion should be passed.

resonant Having a full, rich voice that is pleasing to the ear.

Restoration theater A form of theater marked by glittering displays of excessive behavior. Restoration theater began as a reaction to Puritanism.

rhapsodes Wandering minstrels in ancient Greece that would assemble to read their works in public competition.

rhetorical question Questions that don't demand a verbal response. They elicit a silent response and often answer themselves.

rhyme The repetition of sound between words or syllables or the endings of lines of verse.

rhythm The flow of stressed and unstressed syllables in a poem.

romanticism A movement that emphasized the imagination and emotions over intellect and reason.

round table A special panel discussion in which a small group of participants talk about a topic of common concern while sitting around a table, or in an open circle.

S

sales manager The person who sells the station's advertising air time to local businesses.

scene or setting Focusing the scene described on an imaginary stage in front of the reader.

script The text of a play which outlines the components of a production—the setting, characters, etc.; it provides a basis for all decisions related to the performance.

second affirmative constructive (2AC) In policy debate, this speech extends the initial affirmative analysis and responds to the first negative constructive arguments.

second affirmative rebuttal (2AR) In policy debate, this speech summarizes the affirmative position and gives a clear presentation explaining why the major issues in the debate have gone affirmative.

second a motion To endorse a motion made by another member.

second negative constructive (2NC) In policy debate, this speech gives impact to most of the winning negative arguments by answering all affirmative responses to these issues.

second negative rebuttal (2NR) In policy debate, this speech crystalizes the debate from the negative perspective and attempts to pre-empt the second affirmative rebuttal.

second person Referring to the person spoken to (you).

self-esteem The person value that one feels for oneself, often realized through self-discovery.

sender A person who transmits a message.

serendipity Making a pleasant discovery by accident.

set design A plan for the organization and appearance of the acting space.

shotgun microphone A microphone designed to pick up sound at a considerable distance.

signposting A preview of arguments to be made later in a speech.

sign A type of inductive reasoning in which one draws conclusions about a situation based on physical evidence.

simile A figure of speech that compares two unlike things using the words like or as.

sincerity The quality of being honest or genuine.

slang Nonstandard words associated with certain groups.

sliming A questionable or unethical debate tactic.

social distance The distance generally maintained between people in most social and business exchanges (four to twelve feet).

social phobias Phobias that involve the fear of being evaluated by others.

solvency The ability of the affirmative team's plan to work and to achieve the advantages claimed by the team.

solvency turn An argument that the plan does not solve the harm, but actually worsens the problem.

sparkler Information given in the course of a response that makes the point come alive. Analogies, stories, anecdotes, and quotes all make great sparklers.

spatial pattern A pattern of organization that arranges the elements on the basis of space or situational relationships.

speech of acceptance A brief speech given by a person who receives a gift or an award.

speech of presentation A brief speech presenting a person with an award or gift.

stack the deck Unbalanced evidence that only presents one side.

stage fright The nervousness felt by a speaker or performer in front of an audience.

status quo The existing conditions or the way things are at the present moment.

status report A report summarizing a group's past achievements and future goals.

stereotyping Labeling every person in a group based on a preconceived idea as to what that group represents.

stock issues The voting issues in policy debate.

storyboard A visual plan for a potential television production made up of a series of pictures organized in sequence together with a written script.

subject The person who answers the questions in an interview.

subject cards Cards cataloguing books that are organized by subject.

subordination Ranking in terms of importance.

subsidiary motion A proposal to adjust or fine-tune a main motion.

supporting material Information that supports and reinforces the main headings of a speech. Supporting material is not to be confused with details, which are more specific.

supportive audience An audience that likes the speaker and what the speaker has to say. This audience is willing to support and promote a speaker's ideas.

sustained eye contact Maintaining direct eye contact with a person for a comfortable amount of time.

syllogism A form of deductive reasoning made up of two premises and a conclusion.

symbol Anything that stands for an idea and is used for communication.

symposium A formal discussion in which several experts present a variety of points of view in the form of short speeches. Open discussion between the experts and the audience may follow the speeches.

T

table a motion A proposal to set aside a motion for the time being.

table of contents An outline of the general plan or organization of a book. Generally found at the beginning of the book, it is a list of the book's main sections and chapters.

tag A sentence describing what the evidence proves.

talent Anyone who appears on camera.

telegraphing A speaker's attempt to convey and transmit an emotion to an audience by experiencing (feeling) it personally.

teleprompter A device attached to the front of one of the studio cameras that reflects words of a script toward a speaker.

testimonials Celebrity or expert endorsements of a message.

testimonial speech A speech of praise or celebration honoring a living person.

theatre of the absurd Theater in which human existence is portrayed as meaningless, and language loses its ability to communicate. This theater explores people's helplessness in a senseless universe.

theme The central idea of a literary work.

therapeutic listening A listening style used to encourage the speaker to speak freely without fear of embarrassment or judgment.

thesis A statement defining or expressing the purpose of a speech.

thesis statement The statement that presents the overall purpose of the speech.

Thespian An actor.

third person Referring to the person spoken of (he, him, her, she, it, they, them).

threshold An argument by the affirmative team that challenges the negative team to prove at what point the disadvantage will begin.

thrust stage A stage that has a back wall and places the audience on the other three sides.

tilting Tipping a camera up or down while the base of the camera remains in the same position.

time frame A response to negative attacks that attempts to prove that the affirmative advantages will occur before the impacts of the disadvantage, and that the impacts can be solved later.

timing The ability to sense when it is appropriate to initiate a conversation.

title cards Cards cataloguing books that are organized by title.

tone A combination of the pitch and timbre of a person's voice, one's pauses, rhythm, and unique pronunciation. It is often a reliable clue to a speaker's feelings.

topicality A requirement that the affirmative case must deal with the topic precisely as it is stated, with each word taken into consideration.

topophobia The scientific term often given for stage fright.

town hall meeting A discussion in which a group of citizens meets in a public place to discuss community problems and vote on possible solutions.

traffic director The person who is responsible for planning the daily on-air schedule.

transitions The words and phrases in a speech that connect one part of a speech to the next.

trucking Moving the entire camera (mounted on a movable pedestal) to the left or right.

U

unbiased Objective.

uncommitted audience An audience that is neutral (or has not made up its mind) about the speaker's topic.

understatement The use of "reverse exaggeration" to draw attention to an absurdity for the sake of emphasis.

uniqueness An explanation by the negative team to demonstrate that the disadvantage will not occur under the present system—that it is unique to the affirmative plan.

V

VU meter A device that measures the volume of a sound.

value A standard applied to judge whether something is right or wrong.

value criteria Provide further standards of judgment to evaluate a resolution.

value premise Provides a standard of judgment to evaluate whether or not a resolution is true.

value proposition A proposition for which there is no

right or wrong answer. This type of proposition involves philosophical judgments.

verbatim Word for word account of an interview.

video The signals from a camera.

vision The ability to see more than the obvious; to look beyond and ahead for answers and possibilities.

vocalized pauses Meaningless sayings such as "you know," "uh," "and a," used to fill moments when the speaker is not sure what to say next.

vocal process The system that produces sound.

volume The loudness or softness of a speaker's voice.

W

wireless The name used for early radios.

wireless microphone A microphone that contains a tiny transmitter that sends an audio signal to a remote receiver.

workability attack An argument that points out a flaw in the plan that would prevent the plan's solvency.

written communication Any communication that must be read.

Y

yes-no question A question that may be answered with a simple yes or no and allows the subject to answer the question without elaborating.

Z

zooming Manipulating the lens to telescope in or out on a subject while the camera remains stationary. This enlarges or reduces the size of a subject in the picture.

INDEX

Text Acknowledgments

10 *Vital Speeches of the Day,* Vol. 56, No 5: December 15, 1989; **10** ''Stage parents create videos'' reprinted by permission of Associated Press, Copyright © 1990; **32** ''A Case of Deception'' reprinted by permission of Associated Press, Copyright © 1991; **49** Deborah Laverty, ''Despite loss, zest remains,'' excerpted by permission of the *Post-Tribune,* November 10, 1991, H-3; **69** Copyright © 1964/ copyright renewed Paul Simon. Used by permission of the publisher; **124** Hal Boedeker, ''90210 Star Luke Perry Plays 'Beat the Press' TV Critics Less Than Thrilled,'' the *Miami Herald,* January 11, 1992, 1E; **151** Reprinted by permission of *The New Republic,* March 6, 1989; **181** Copyright © 1987 by the New York Times Company. Reprinted by permission; **209** ''First Lady tells graduates the measures of success,'' reprinted by permission of Associated Press, Copyright © 1992; **270** From NEWSWEEK, January 13, 1992 and © 1992, Newsweek, Inc. All rights reserved. Reprinted by permission; **395** ''The Talk Circuit,'' Copyright 1983 Time Inc. Reprinted by permission; **401** Reprinted by permission of Kareem Abdul-Jabbar, Copyright © 1992; **535** Dylan Thomas, *Poems of Dylan Thomas.* Copyright 1952 by Dylan Thomas. Reprinted by permission of New Directions Publishing Corporation; **535** The MTV Ad ''The Medium Is The Message'' appears Courtesy of MTV Networks. MTV: Music Television is a registered trademark of MTV Networks, a division of Viacom International Inc. © 1993 MTV Networks. All Rights Reserved; **539** Reprinted by permission of the publishers and the Trustees of Amherst College from *THE POEMS OF EMILY DICKINSON,* Thomas H. Johnson, ed., Cambridge, Mass.: The Belknap Press of Harvard University Press, Copyright © 1951, 1955, 1979, 1983 by the President and Fellows of Harvard College; **450** Grace Butcher ''On Driving Behind a School Bus for Mentally Retarded Children,'' from *Rumors of Ecstasy. . . Rumors of Death* by Grace Butcher, Ashland Poetry Press 1971, Reprinted by Barnwood Press 1981; **548** Reprinted with permission of Atheneum Publishers, an implant of Macmillan Publishing Company, from *NEW AND COLLECTED POEMS* by Ishmael Reed, Copyright © 1972 by Ishmael Reed; **550** Langston Hughes, ''Dream Boogie'' from *MONTAGE OF A DREAM DEFERRED.* Reprinted by permission of Harold Ober Associates Incorporated. Copyright 1951 by Langston Hughes. Copyright renewed 1979 by George Houston Bass; **550** D. C. Berry, ''On Reading Poems to a Senior Class at South High,'' reprinted by permission of D. C. Berry; **551** ''Cracked Record Blues'' from *AFTERNOON OF A PAWNBROKER AND OTHER POEMS,* copyright 1943 by Kenneth Fearing and renewed 1971 by Bruce Fearing, reprinted by permission of Harcourt Brace & Company; **552** ''Jazz Fantasia'' from *SMOKE AND STEEL* by Carl Sandburg, copyright 1920 by Harcourt Brace & Company and renewed 1948 by Carl Sandburg, reprinted by permission of the publisher; **643** Michael Ryan, ''First, Respect Yourself,'' Reprinted with permission from *Parade,* copyright © 1992. Reprinted by permission of the author and the author's agents, Scott Meredith Literary agency, Inc., 845 Third Avenue, New York, New York 10022; **653** Copyright © 1991 by Scholastic SCOPE. Used by permission of Scholastic, Inc.; **655** Joseph N. DiStefano, ''A failure to communicate noted in yearly disaster drill,'' excerpted by permission of the *Post-Tribune,* May 31, 1992, B-1.